wq- Bug-998

"International Human Resource Management, 5e by Ibraiz Tarique, Dennis Briscoe and Randall Schuler has long been regarded as one of leading resources in the field. This new edition reinforces that reputation and brings the content up to date with contemporary trends in research and practice. Written by three of the leading scholars in the area, the volume is distinguished by its combination of insights from academic research and rich insights into IHRM in practice. It is comprehensive, accessible and authoritative, and should be required reading for any student or reflective practitioner of IHRM."

–David Collings, Dublin City University, Ireland, and
Senior Editor of the Journal of World Business

"This excellent book, a leader in the field, comprehensively covers the field of International Human Resource Management and focuses on the HRM issues and challenges facing firms as they internationalise their business operations. Each chapter provides a clear exposition and critique of the specialist literature, and case studies are used to provide rich insights into current practice. The combination of sound theory and examples from practice around the globe provides an important and up to date contribution to the field. The book is well geared to students interested in the international dimensions of HRM, and the excellent links between international strategy and HRM give students an in depth knowledge of the people management challenges faced by MNC managers in a globalised business world."

–Hugh Scullion, Established Professor of International Management,
Cairnes School of Business and Economics, NUI Galway, Ireland

"This edition of the book does a wonderful job of framing IHRM issues in the evolving, strategic context of running an international business. Pedagogically, the many practical applications and graphical presentations beautifully illustrate concepts and frameworks that will help readers grasp the rich content that the book provides."

–Wayne F. Cascio, Robert H. Reynolds Chair in Global Leadership, University of
Colorado Denver, USA, and Senior Editor of the Journal of World Business

International Human Resource Management
Fifth edition

Thoroughly updated and expanded, the fifth edition of *International Human Resource Management* focuses on international human resource management (IHRM) within multinational enterprises (MNEs). The book has been designed to lead readers through all of the key topics of IHRM in a highly engaging and approachable way. In addition to the key topics and rich pedagogy students have come to expect, chapters have been updated, including an expanded chapter on Comparative and National Culture. Uncovering precisely why IHRM is important for success in international business, and how IHRM policies and practices function within the multinational enterprise, this comprehensive textbook provides an outstanding foundation for understanding the theory and practice of IHRM. It is essential reading for all students, instructors, and IHRM professionals.

Ibraiz Tarique is an Associate Professor of Management and Director of Global HR programs at the Lubin School of Business, at Pace University in New York City, USA. He teaches at the executive, graduate, and undergraduate levels.

Dennis Briscoe is Professor Emeritus of International Human Resource Management at the University of San Diego, USA, and owner/consultant at International Management and Personnel Systems (IMAPS).

Randall Schuler is Distinguished Professor of Strategic International Human Resources at the School of Management and Labor Relations at Rutgers University, USA, and Research Professor at the Lancaster University School of Management, UK, as well as the University of Zurich, Switzerland.

Routledge Global Human Resource Management Series
Edited by Randall S. Schuler, Susan E. Jackson, Paul Sparrow and Michael Poole

Routledge Global Human Resource Management is an important new series that examines human resources in its global context. The series is organized into three strands: content and issues in global human resource management (HRM); specific HR functions in a global context; and comparative HRM. Authored by some of the world's leading authorities on HRM, each book in the series aims to give readers comprehensive, in-depth and accessible texts that combine essential theory and best practice. Topics covered include cross-border alliances, global leadership, global legal systems, HRM in Asia, Africa, and the Americas, industrial relations, and global staffing.

International Human Resource Management

Policies and Practices for Multinational Enterprises

Fifth edition

Ibraiz Tarique
Dennis R. Briscoe
Randall S. Schuler

NEW YORK AND LONDON

First published 1995
by Prentice Hall
Fifth edition published 2016
by Routledge
711 Third Avenue, New York, NY 10017

and by Routledge
2 Park Square, Milton Park, Abingdon, Oxon, OX14 4RN

Routledge is an imprint of the Taylor & Francis Group, an informa business

[First edition published by Prentice Hall 1995]

[Fourth edition published by Routledge 2011]

Library of Congress Cataloguing-in-Publication Data

Briscoe, Dennis R., 1945–
    International human resource management : policies and practices for
multinational enterprises / Ibraiz Tarique, Dennis R. Briscoe, Randall S.
Schuler. — 5th edition.
        pages cm
    Includes bibliographical references and index.
  1. International business enterprises—Personnel management.
I. Tarique, Ibraiz.   II. Schuler, Randall S.   III. Title.
    HF5549.5.E45B74 2012
    658.3—dc23
    2015001046

ISBN: 978-0-415-71052-7 (hbk)
ISBN: 978-0-415-71053-4 (pbk)
ISBN: 978-1-315-88500-1 (ebk)

Typeset in Berling Roman and Futura
by Apex CoVantage, LLC
Printed In Canada

Contents

Figures

Exhibits

Case Studies

IHRM in Actions

End-of-Book Integrative Cases

Acronyms

ADA	Americans with Disabilities Act
ADEA	Age Discrimination in Employment Act
APEC	Asia-Pacific Economic Cooperation
ASEAN	Association of South East Asian Nations
BOK	Body of Knowledge
BRIC	Brazil, Russia, India, China
BT	Business Traveler
C&B	Compensation and Benefits
CBT	Computer-Based Training
CEE	Central and Eastern Europe
CEO	Chief Executive Officer
CFO	Chief Financial Officer
CIPD	Chartered Institute of Personnel and Development
COLA	Cost of Living Allowance
CSR	Corporate Social Responsibility
EEA	European Economic Area
EFTA	European Free Trade Agreement
EPI	Efficient Purchaser Index
ESOP	Employee Stock Ownership Plan
ESPP	Employee Stock Purchase Plan
ETUC	European Trade Union Confederation
EU	European Union
FCN	Friendship, Commerce, and Navigation Treaty
FCPA	Foreign Corrupt Practices Act
FDI	Foreign Direct Investment
FTAA	Free Trade Area of the Americas
Fx	Exchange Rate
GATT	General Agreement on Trade and Tariffs

GEC	Global Employment Company
GHRIS	Global Human Resource Information System
GI	Global Integration
GLOBE	Global Leadership and Organizational Behavior Effectiveness
GPHR	Global Professional in Human Resources
GUFs	Global Union Federations
HCN	Host-Country National
HQ	Headquarters
HR	Human Resources
HRCI	Human Resource Certification Institute
HRIS	Human Resource Information System
HRM	Human Resource Management
IA	International Assignee or International Assignment
IB	International Business
ICC	International Chamber of Commerce
ICFTU	International Confederation of Free Trade Unions
IE	International Employee
IHR	International Human Resources
IHRM	International Human Resource Management
IJV	International Joint Venture
ILO	International Labor Organization
ILP	International Labor Organization
IMF	International Monetary Fund
INS	Immigration and Naturalization Service
IPM	International Performance Management
IPO	Intellectual Property Office
IT	Information Technology
ITUC	International Trade Union Confederation
JV	Joint Venture
LR	Local Responsiveness
M&A	Merger and Acquisition
MNE	Multinational Enterprise
NAALC	North American Agreement on Labor Cooperation
NAFTA	North American Free Trade Agreement
NGO	Non-Governmental Organization
OECD	Organization for Economic Cooperation and Development
OEEC	Office of European Economic Cooperation
PA	Performance Appraisal
PCN	Parent-Country National
PCT	Patent Cooperation Treaty
PM	Performance Management
PRC	People's Republic of China

R&D	Research and Development
SAR	Stock Appreciation Rights
SEC	Securities and Exchange Commission
SHRM	Society for Human Resource Management
SIHRM	Strategic International Human Resource Management
SME	Small- and Medium-sized Enterprises
SOX	Sarbanes-Oxley
TCN	Third-Country National
T&D	Training & Development
TI	Transparency International
TNC	Transnational Corporation
TUAC	Trade Union Advisory Committee
UN	United Nations
UNCTAD	United Nations Conference on Trade and Development
UK	United Kingdom
US	United States

Acknowledgments

We are grateful to many individuals who have provided valuable information, insights, cases, and assistance in completing this book. They include: Susan E. Jackson, Rutgers University; Paul Sparrow and Cary Cooper, Lancaster University Management School; Jyotsna Bhatnagar and Rakesh Sharma, Management Development Institute India; Chris Brewster, Reading University; Yadong Luo, University of Miami; Ingmar Björkman, the Swedish School of Economics; James Hayton, University of Warick; Shaun Tyson and Michael Dickmann, Cranfield School of Management; Gary Florkowski, University of Pittsburgh; Cal Reynolds, Calvin Reynolds & Associates; Hugh Scullion, National University of Ireland; Dave Collings, Dublin City University; Vlad Vaiman, California Lutheran University; Stu Youngblood, Texas Christian University; Bruno Staffelbach, University of Zurich; Bill Castellano, Rutgers University; Ed Schuler, The Schuler Group; Gerold Frick, Aalen University; Manfred Stania, Stania Management; Martin Hilb, University of St. Gallen; Christian Scholz, University of Saarlandes; Mark Saxer, Saxer Consulting; Nigel Shaw and Nadia Wicki de la Puente, Novartis; Michael Morley, University of Limerick; Charles Galunic and Isable Assureira, INSEAD; Simon Dolan, ESADE; Georges Bachtold, Blumer Machines Company; Darryl Weiss, Lockheed Martin Orincon, San Diego; Jerry Edge, RMC Consultants; Joann Stang, Solar Turbines (retired); Bernie Kulchin, Cubic Corporation; Ben Shaw, Bond University; Ed Watson, KPMG; Gardiner Hempel, Deloitte & Touche; Wayne Cascio and Manuel Serapio, University of Colorado-Denver; Bob Grove, San Diego Employers' Association (retired), Jason Exley, MSI, Denver, CO; Shaista Khilji, The George Washington University; Akram Al Ariss, Toulouse Business School; and Elaine Farndale, Pennsylvania State University.

A special thanks to Lisbeth Claus, Willamette University, for her permission to use her contributions to the fourth and fifth editions.

Dr. Schuler thanks many students at Rutgers University in the Department of Human Resource Management for their teaching and writing suggestions, and the department's webmaster, Renee Walker, for her work on the construction of his global website.

Dr. Briscoe thanks his graduate students at the University of San Diego and at the many other schools in the some 19 countries where he has taught IHRM, and particularly his most recent graduate assistant, Chanyu Miao, for her help in research into IHRM and country HR practices.

Dr. Ibraiz Tarique is indebted to his father, Dr. Asif Tarique, who passed away in January 2015, for teaching him the value of cultural diversity. Dr. Asif Tarique (an international marine biologist by profession) was a global citizen who had a true passion for cultural diversity developed from living in numerous countries and experiencing different cultures, people from all walks of life, poetry, and languages. Dr. Ibraiz Tarique is grateful to his father for an upbringing as a "third culture kid" (a child who grows up in a culture other than that of his or her parents).

Dr. Ibraiz Tarique gives thanks to his family for providing unwavering support to work on this book. He is thankful to both co-authors for providing the guidance, encouragement, and support to contribute to the fifth edition. For Dr. Ibraiz Tarique, working with Dr. Schuler and Dr. Briscoe has been one of the best experiences. Dr. Ibraiz Tarique is thankful to all the individuals who helped in the research for this book. He would like to thank the Lubin School of Business, Pace University, and his excellent colleagues for supporting his interests in international human resource management. Finally, he would like to thank his students (both current and past) who continuously inspire him and remind him every day that learning is a lifelong process.

And last, Dr. Briscoe acknowledges the support from his wife, Georgia, who provided inspiration and example during a particularly difficult time for her during the writing of this fifth edition as well as the example being set by his son, Forrest, who is now showing his father how the role of professor can be so fulfilling. He also acknowledges how great it has been to work with his co-authors, Ibraiz Tarique and Randall Schuler. They went above and beyond the call of duty to provide the support and effort necessary to complete the project within tight deadlines. Their contributions made the final product much better.

Finally the authors thank the many great people at Routledge for their wonderful assistance and support throughout this project, in particular, the Global HRM Series senior editor, Sharon Golan.

Thank you all!

Ibraiz Tarique
Dennis Briscoe
Randall Schuler
January 2016

Foreword

Global HRM is a series of books edited and authored by some of the best and most well-known researchers in the field of human resource management. This series is aimed at offering students and practitioners accessible, coordinated and comprehensive books in global HRM. To be used individually or together, these books cover the main areas in international and comparative HRM. Taking an expert look at an increasingly important and complex area of global business, it is a groundbreaking series that answers a real need for useful and affordable textbooks on global HRM.

Several books in the Global HRM series are devoted to human resource management policies and practices in multinational enterprises. Some books focus on specific areas of global HRM policies and practices, such as global leadership, global compensation, global talent management and global labor relations. Other books address special topics that arise in multinational enterprises, such as managing HR in cross-border alliances, managing global legal systems, and the structure of the global HR function. There is also a book of global human resource management cases. Several other books in the series adopt a comparative approach to understanding human resource management. These books on comparative human resource management describe HRM topics found at the country level in selected countries. The comparative books utilize a common framework that makes it easier for the reader to systematically understand the rationale for the similarities and differences in findings across countries.

The fifth edition of *International Human Resource Management*, written by Ibraiz Tarique, Dennis Briscoe and Randall Schuler, serves as the foundation book for all the other books that focus on specific areas of global HRM policies and practices, and for the books that address special topics such as alliances, strategies, and structures and legal systems. As such, its 15 chapters provide the broadest possible base for an overview of all the major areas in the field of international human resource management. As with all the books in the Global HRM series, the chapters are based upon the most recent and classic research, as well as numerous examples of what multinational enterprises are doing today. This latest edition of this foundation book contains numerous updates and revisions that make the book even more relevant and useful to the reader, whether university student or practitioner. More material has been put into tables and exhibits to help summarize a lot of information, thus making it more quickly accessible and more interesting for the reader.

This Routledge series, Global HRM, is intended to serve the growing market of global scholars and practitioners who are seeking a deeper and broader understanding of the role and importance of human resource management in companies that operate throughout the world. With this in mind, all books in the series provide a thorough review of existing research and numerous examples of companies around the world. Mini-company stories and examples are found throughout the chapters. In addition, many of the books in the series include at least one detailed case description that serves as convenient practical illustrations of topics discussed in the book. The companion website for this book contains additional cases and resources for students and faculty to use for greater discussions of the topics in all the chapters.

Because a significant number of scholars and practitioners throughout the world are involved in researching and practicing the topics examined in this series of books, the authorship of the books and the experiences of the companies cited in the books reflect a vast global representation. The authors in the series bring with them exceptional knowledge of the human resource management topics they address, and in many cases the authors are the pioneers for their topics. So we feel fortunate to have the involvement of such a distinguished group of academics in this series.

The publisher and editor have played a very major role in making this series possible. Routledge has provided its global production, marketing and reputation to make this series feasible and affordable to academics and practitioners throughout the world. In addition, Routledge has provided its own highly qualified professionals to make this series a reality. In particular, we want to indicate our deep appreciation for the work of our series editor, Sharon Golan. She has been very supportive of the Global HRM series and has been invaluable in providing the needed support and encouragement to us and the many authors and editors in the series. She, and the entire Routledge staff, has helped make the process of completing this series an enjoyable one. For everything they have done, we thank them all. Together we are all very excited about the Global HRM series and hope you find an opportunity to use *International Human Resource Management*, fifth edition, and all the other books in the series!

Randall S. Schuler, Rutgers University and the Lancaster
University School of Management
Susan E. Jackson, Rutgers University and the Lancaster
University School of Management
Paul Sparrow, Manchester University Management School
July 2015

Introduction

This book is about international human resource management (IHRM). That is, it is about human resource management in a global context. The conduct of business is increasingly global in scope, and managing human resources has become even more important in the successful conduct of global business. The motives for writing this book originally—to provide a professional and academic overview for an understanding of the design and implementation of IHRM policy and practice—continue in this edition. This fifth edition has also been written to update this most important but fast changing discipline. As with the previous editions, the majority of the book discusses the IHRM issues faced by multinational enterprises (MNEs) of all sizes, primarily—but not exclusively—from the perspective of the parent company or headquarters. But it also provides increasing attention to other forms of international organizations as well, such as governments, non-profits, and non-governmental organizations (NGOs). Since MNEs increasingly manage their workforces on a global basis, this edition not only examines global management of parent companies' workforces, with globalized policies, shared services, and global centers of HR excellence, but also provides increased focus on management of workforces in subsidiaries, international joint ventures, and global partnerships.

In the previous two editions, a major effort was made to obtain relevant examples from many different countries. This effort has continued in the fifth edition. So the examples in the chapters as well as the end-of-chapter cases (in the book and on the text website) draw from many small and medium-sized companies (many of which will be new to the reader) from many countries, as well as some traditional and well-known large firms, which come from both large and small countries.

SECTIONS AND CHAPTERS

This book is divided into four sections (see Figure I.1 to understand how the topics relate to each other) and 15 chapters. The first two sections set the scene for *International Human Resource Management: Policies and Practices for Multinational Enterprises*, fifth edition, and explain why IHRM is so important to the success of international business, describing the context of global business as it relates to IHRM. Section 1 "Strategic Context," describes the key strategic components of the context within which IHRM operates. Each of these components represents a critical part of the global environment that determines the nature of IHRM. Section 2, "National and Cultural Context," describes three important aspects of the country and/or national environments that determine the cultural and legal contexts within which IHRM operates. Then Section 3, "Global Talent Management," describes the IHRM policies and practices that are shaped by the context described in the first two sections. These seven chapters provide a comprehensive and thorough overview of the policies and practices of IHRM. These policies and practices are described both from a centralized, headquarters-focused perspective, as well as from the local perspective of subsidiaries, joint ventures, partnerships, and contractors. Finally Section 4, "Role and Future of IHRM," describes the nature of today's IHRM department, the professionalization of IHRM, and takes a look at future trends in the field. Now we describe the chapters briefly.

Chapter 1 introduces the globalization of business and describes how that has changed the nature of IHRM. It describes the evolving nature of IHRM as it meets the needs of changing multinational enterprises and explains how this has led to the development of strategic IHRM in helping MNEs attain sustainable competitive advantage in the global marketplace. This chapter also describes the basic nature and development of IHRM, differentiates IHRM from domestic HRM, and discusses some of the difficulties experienced in that development.

Chapter 2 describes the various responsibilities of IHRM and links them to the pursuit of international business strategies. The strategic decision to "go international" is one of the most important components of the IHRM environment. IHRM must understand these strategic choices and should contribute input to them in order to contribute to their successful achievement. This chapter also examines IHRM strategy and its relation to overall MNE business strategy, focusing on how varying approaches to MNE business strategy affect the nature of IHRM strategy. Finally this chapter explains how IHRM changes and contributes to the development of those various MNE strategies.

Chapter 3 discusses the growing complexities in designing the structure of multinational firms and the important role that IHRM plays in those design decisions. The conduct of international business is increasingly complex, involving the need to—at the same time—focus on central control and influence and local adaptation to customers and culture. Too often these efforts fail, at least partially because of inadequate attention to issues within the responsibility of IHRM. This chapter describes the contributions that IHRM can and should make to the success of these organizational choices.

Chapter 4 describes the role of IHRM in cross-border mergers and acquisitions, international joint ventures, and international alliances. Cross-border acquisitions, joint ventures, teams, and alliances of various sorts are increasingly the means by which firms choose to go international and thus they constitute one of the most important components of the context for IHRM. Much of the chapter describes the role of IHRM and the IHR professional in designing, facilitating, and implementing these four specific types of cross-border

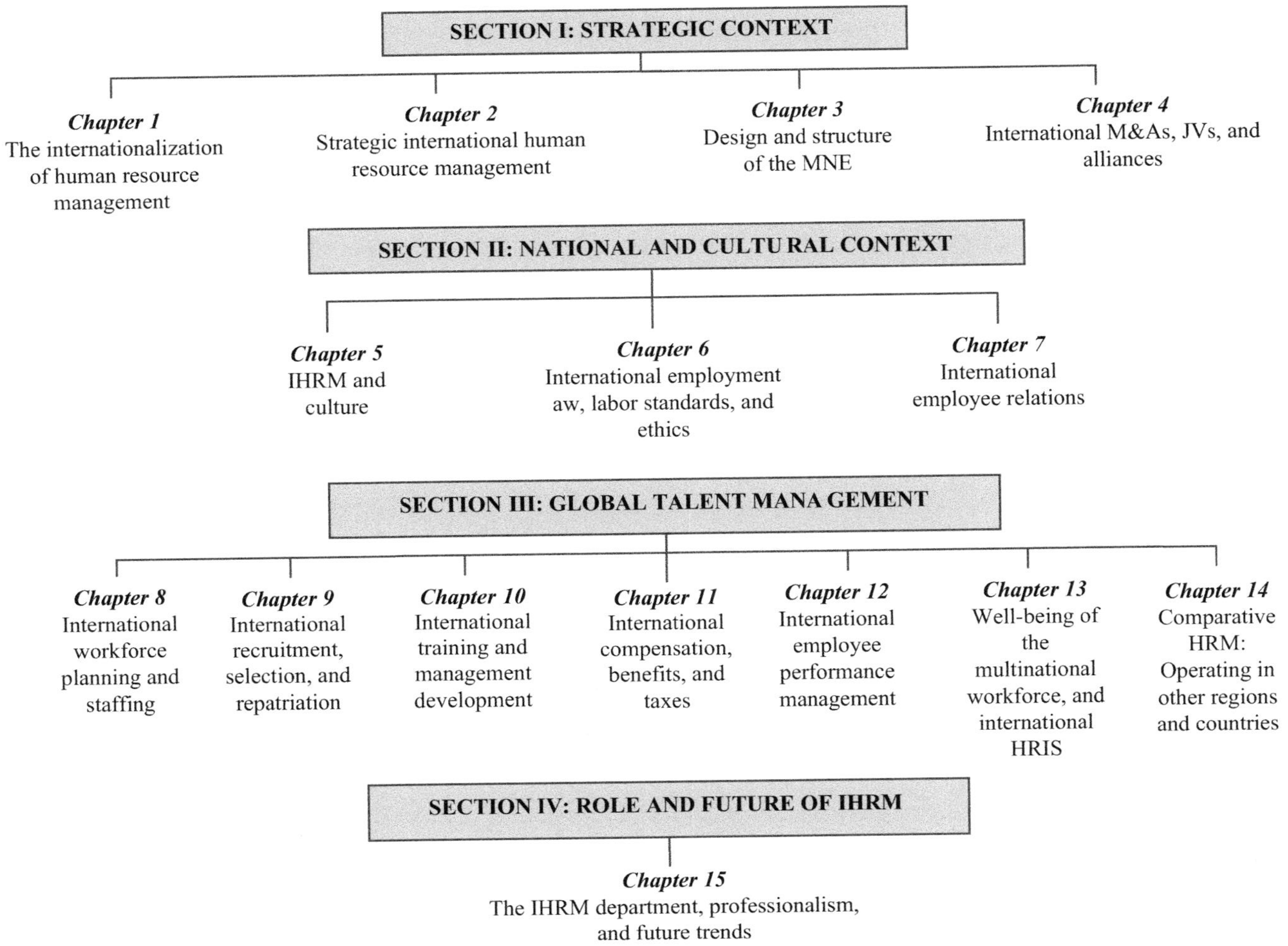
SECTION I: STRATEGIC CONTEXT
Chapter 1
The internationalization of human resource management
Chapter 2
Strategic international human resource management
Chapter 3
Design and structure of the MNE
Chapter 4
International M&As, JVs, and alliances
SECTION II: NATIONAL AND CULTU RAL CONTEXT
Chapter 5
IHRM and culture
Chapter 6
International employment aw, labor standards, and ethics
Chapter 7
International employee relations
SECTION III: GLOBAL TALENT MANA GEMENT
Chapter 8
International workforce planning and staffing
Chapter 9
International recruitment, selection, and repatriation
Chapter 10
International training and management development
Chapter 11
International compensation, benefits, and taxes
Chapter 12
International employee performance management
Chapter 13
Well-being of the multinational workforce, and international HRIS
Chapter 14
Comparative HRM: Operating in other regions and countries
SECTION IV: ROLE AND FUTURE OF IHRM
Chapter 15
The IHRM department, professionalism, and future trends

FIGURE I.1 Chapter Map

International Human Resource Management, 5th ed. Tarique, Briscoe, Schuler.

combinations. All four types of these combinations are increasingly used and IHRM can and should play a major role in helping ensure the success of their design and implementation.

Chapter 5, starting Section II, expands the theme that is revisited frequently throughout the text: the critical importance of country and corporate culture. Cultural differences impact everything that is done in international business and are, if possible, even more important to everything that IHR managers do. Success in international business requires a thorough understanding of cultural factors, and IHRM is involved both with helping provide that expertise to the firm as well as having to incorporate such understanding in its own global activities. Thus this introduction to IB and IHRM, by necessity, includes an introduction to the concepts of country and corporate culture. The chapter also discusses the importance of culture in both the conduct and the interpretation of IHRM research, explaining how culture affects both our understanding of IHRM and its impact. Like everything else, culture influences what we know and what we think we know about IHR.

Chapter 6 describes international aspects of the legal and regulatory environment, another of the key components in the context of IHRM. Just as is true for HRM in a domestic context, there are many aspects of law that impact the practice of human resource management when working in the global arena. This chapter discusses five of these aspects:

- international employment law and the institutions that develop and apply it;
- major legal systems and their key differences;
- goals of the various international trade agreements
- major issues international employment issues impacting HR;
- immigration/visas, personal, data protection, anti-discrimination, harassment, ethical standards, CSR, and corporate governance.

All of these areas of the legal and regulatory environment related to the conduct of IHRM are increasingly important to the successful contribution of IHR managers and all have a growing impact on IHR and firms operating in the global business environment.

Chapter 7 examines the broad nature of international labor standards, global employment law and regulations, and international ethics and social responsibility. First, this chapter looks at the institutional context of international business. International organizations have promulgated labor standards for MNEs. Next, this chapter looks at the global legal environment in which the MNE operates. It focuses on compliance with national and supranational laws. Further, a number of comparative regulatory issues are discussed that affect the MNE such as immigration controls, data protection, anti-discrimination and harassment, termination and reduction in force, and intellectual property. Finally, this chapter looks at international ethics, its relation to culture, and how ethical dilemmas must be solved

Chapter 8 provides an introduction to the overall concern with planning, forecasting, and staffing the global enterprise. Chapter 8 begins by providing a description of the constantly changing labor markets around the world and discusses how MNEs plan for creating their workforces from those labor markets. The nature of those markets in various countries, in terms of their demographic characteristics, the skills and abilities of their individuals, and their accessibility and cost varies dramatically from country to country and region to region and can be a major determinant in the success of international decisions such as where to locate operations. Chapter 8 also provides an overview of the many options that MNEs have available to them for that staffing.

Chapter 9 focuses on the IHRM responsibility for staffing, but primarily on the issue of expatriation and repatriation, the movement of employees of MNE from either the parent company to a foreign subsidiary or from a foreign subsidiary to another subsidiary or to the parent firm. This chapter examines the difficulties experienced in the selection and management of expatriates and repatriates and suggests some of the approaches successful MNEs use to ensure positive experiences with those expatriates and repatriates. In addition, the chapter discusses problems that MNEs are experiencing with women and other types of non-traditional expatriates.

Chapter 10 focuses on the training and development of the MNE's global workforce. This includes training of host-country workforces, training and preparation of international assignees, and global management development, including the nature and development of a global mindset, the competencies of global managers, and the nature of management development programs in a global context. This chapter has provided both many examples and research and writing of what firms from around the world are currently doing to offer successful global training and development programs. It is now up to IHR managers in other firms to use what was described here to develop successful global training and development programs in their own organizations.

Chapter 11 describes the complex area of compensation, benefits, and taxes for both international assignees as well as for local workforces. The chapter presents IHRM practices related to the development of compensation and benefit programs among MNEs and describes seven alternative approaches to compensation for expatriates. The chapter also discusses the many problems that MNEs confront as they try to design and implement global compensation and benefit programs throughout their global operations. Lastly, the chapter discusses many of the various approaches taken to compensation and benefits, such as vacation and pension practices, in a number of different countries.

Chapter 12 addresses the crucial issue of performance evaluation and performance management for international assignees and managers in foreign operations. It describes the many difficulties encountered in trying to implement an effective PM system in the international arena, not the least of which is figuring out how to accommodate in the evaluation process factors stemming from the nature of the local cultural environment. It is clear that it is inadequate to simply apply a PM process designed at the home-country level for domestic use to the international setting. The chapter ends with a discussion of a number of suggestions and guidelines for improving the process of implementing an effective IPM system.

Chapter 13 describes topics of importance to the IHR manager: employee health and safety in the context of the foreign subsidiary and joint venture, and health, safety, and security for global business travelers and employees on international assignments and their families. Often, because health and safety practices differ so much from country to country, responsibility for them is left in the hands of subsidiary (local) HR managers. Nevertheless, MNEs must understand and cope with local and international health and safety regulations, the widely variable practices faced in different countries, and strategic business decisions that may influence workforces and employee relations in multiple locations. This chapter also discusses the important topic of HRIS.

Chapter 14 provides an overview of the wide variances in HR practices from country to country and region to region. International enterprises have the necessity to understand local HR policies and practices so as to make intelligent decisions as to the practical fit of headquarters' policies with tradition and law in local jurisdictions. This chapter focuses on five specific regions: Europe, North America, Asia, Latin America, and Africa. Within each region, key HRM issues are examined with implications for HRM policies and practices. In addition, this chapter discusses various HRM issues that converge among regions and countries, including managing two generations of employees including older workers, discrimination and the glass ceiling, and gaps in talent supply and demand.

Chapter 15, the last chapter, provides a glimpse at the challenges that confront IHRM. These challenges include the organizational advancement and the professionalization of IHRM. International HR managers have to further develop their understanding of their global enterprises and, as a consequence, will become better integrated into the planning and strategic management of those enterprises. As these challenges are met and IHR managers further develop their global HR competencies, multinational firms will find themselves developing world-class IHR departments. What this chapter demonstrates is that only when such an integrated, responsive, and accepted IHRM is developed will IHRM reach its potential and take its rightful place in the management of today's successful global enterprises.

TERMINOLOGY

In the 15 chapters of this fifth edition of *International Human Resource Management*, a number of terms are used to refer to organizations that conduct international business. In general, the term MNE (multinational enterprise) is used to refer to all organizations that conduct business outside their countries of origin. Today, this can apply to bricks-and-mortar firms as well as virtual firms with primarily only a website. The term MNE is used rather than MNC (multinational corporation—which is often a more commonly used term) because in many countries there is no form of legal ownership equivalent to the American corporation, from whence derives the term MNC. So we chose a term that can be used with wider application without being tied technically to the legal structure of one particular country. Thus, in this text the generic term "enterprise" is used to refer to any type of organization involved with international business. For small- and medium-sized MNEs, the term SME is sometimes used. Generally, the term MNE is used throughout the book. When appropriate, SME will be used to highlight special characteristics of small- and medium-sized MNEs. We have also increased the discussion of non-business organizations, such as governments, NGOs, and non-profit organizations, many of which have more international exposure than do many business enterprises.

MNEs can be described as operating multi-domestically, internationally, globally, or transnationally. While these terms often seem to be used interchangeably, some distinctions can be made (for details about the differences as they relate to IHRM, refer to Chapter 3). For example, the term "global" refers to enterprises that operate all over the world and have consistent policies and practices throughout their operations. Such MNEs have a high percentage of international turnover or sales (over 50 percent outside their home countries) and a high percentage of employees outside their home countries, as well, with operations in a large number of countries, and a global perspective and attitude reflected in their business strategies and in their mission statements. These firms tend to have a highly centralized (or, at least, regionalized) policy, at least as it applies to financial issues and sharing of resources and innovations and world-class standards for their global products and services.

In contrast, transnational firms are global in scope but decentralized and localized in products, marketing strategies, and operations. That is, they take advantage of their global presence to gain access to resources (ideas, technology, capital, people, products, and services) and develop economies of scale, while at the same time maintaining a local presence that is seen as comparable to that of domestic competitors. The other terms, such as "multinational" or "international," generally refer to MNEs that have not yet developed their levels of international operations to this extent. Because more and more enterprises are moving in the direction of being more global, in thought at least, if not in action, the word "global" is used in the title of the series of which this book is a part. But the word "international" is used in the title and chapter headings of this text to reinforce the reality that IHRM policies and practices are often and mostly not standardized and centralized, as might be implied with the use of the term "global."

Thus most of the topics, policies, and practices discussed throughout this text are currently applicable to most enterprises, and are likely to soon apply to most others. In this text, if the terms global, multinational, or international enterprise make a difference to the particular topic, policy, or practice being discussed, then an attempt is made to make it clear through explanation or the use of the terminology as to which type of enterprise is being described.

PEDAGOGY

Each chapter begins with "Learning objectives." These are the main objectives that we would like to see you focus on as you consider the material in the chapter. Although key terms are defined in the chapter when they first appear, they are also defined on the website under "Glossary." Of course you will learn more than these particular objectives and terms.

Each chapter offers a case study at the end that illustrates the current experiences of a particular multinational enterprise.

Each chapter contains a case study at the end illustrating current experiences of multinational enterprises. In addition, at the end of each chapter there are "Discussion questions" that might be answered individually or in small teams. These are provided to allow the reader to apply many of the ideas in the chapter to other situations. To help instructors and readers identify cases and IHRM in Actions from specific regions or countries, there are two matrices that list countries down the left side and with IIA and cases vertically across top.

The end-of-book materials include the notes that are used in each of the chapters. These materials reflect the relevant classic and contemporary academic research worldwide and the experiences and stories of multinational enterprises. To add even more relevant information as it unfolds, the reader is encouraged to visit numerous websites that are available and suggested here. Additional websites and other materials are found on the website designed for this book: www.routledge.com/textbooks/globalhrm.

At the end of the book are two integrative cases. These cases illustrate the challenges in trying to become a successful MNE, the importance of international human resource policies and practices, and the impact of the local country environment on the effectiveness of those policies and practices.

Finally there are author and subject/company indexes. These are to provide the reader with further information about the various topics covered in this book as well as the many authors whose work has been used to compile this book.

There is an extensive website for this book, which includes:

- history of the development of IHRM;
- list of major websites for research on IHRM topics;
- instructor's manual, with slides for lectures, sample syllabi, exam questions, and discussion guides for end-of-chapter discussion questions and for the discussion questions that accompany the cases in the text.

END OF CHAPTER/BOOK CASES MATRIX

Region/ Country Focus	Case 1.1	Case 2.1	Case 3.1	Case 4.1	Case 5.1	Case 6.1	Case 7.1	Case 8.1	Case 9.1	Case 10.1	Case 11.1	Case 12.1	Case 13.1	Case 14.1	Case 15.1	End of Book Integrated Case 1	End of Book Integrated Case 2
Global		X	X	X	X	X	X	X	X		X		X	X	X		
EU																	
Australia																	
Bangladesh																	
Bolivia											X						
Brazil						X											
Canada				X													
Finland																	
France			X														
Ghana													X				
Germany					X												X
India																	
Indonesia																	X
Italy						X											
Japan											X					X	
Malawi										X							
Netherlands																	
Niger																	
Philippines											X						
Romania													X				
Spain																	
Switzerland												X					
Thailand											X	X					
Turkey	X																
United Kingdom												X	X				
United States		X			X	X	X				X					X	

"IHRM IN ACTION" MATRIX

Region/Country Focus	IIA 1.1	IIA 1.2	IIA 1.3	IIA 2.1	IIA 3.1	IIA 4.1	IIA 5.1	IIA 6.1	IIA 7.1	IIA 8.1	IIA 9.1	IIA 9.2	IIA 10.1	IIA 11.1	IIA 12.1	IIA 13.1	IIA 15.1
Global		X	X		X	X	X	X			X		X	X	X	X	X
EU									X								
Australia																	X
Bangladesh								X									
Bolivia																	
Brazil																	
Canada																	
Finland															X		
France																	
Germany																	
Global				X													
India	X																
Indonesia																	
Italy																	
Japan				X													
Malawi																	
Netherlands										X							
Niger																X	
Philippines																	
Spain																	X
Switzerland																	
Thailand																	
Turkey																	
United Kingdom			X						X							X	X
United States	X				X	X	X	X	X			X	X	X	X		

IHRM in Action = IIA

SECTION 1

Strategic Context

The first section of the book, "Strategic Context," has four chapters:

- Chapter 1: The Internationalization of Human Resource Management
- Chapter 2: Strategic International Human Resource Management
- Chapter 3: Design and Structure of the Multinational Enterprise
- Chapter 4: International Mergers and Acquisitions, Joint Ventures, and Alliances

These chapters set the scene for *International Human Resource Management: Policies and Practices for Multinational Enterprises*, fifth edition, and explain why international human resource management is important for the success of international business. Together they describe the important components of the strategic context within which international human resource management policies and practices are designed and implemented. Each of these components represents an important part of the strategic context that determines the nature of IHRM. Chapter 1 describes the content and importance of international human resource management practices and policies. Chapter 2 links these international human resource management practices and policies to a multinational enterprise's (MNE's) business strategy. Chapter 3 describes the various choices MNEs have in the ways they divide themselves across geographically dispersed units around the world and the implications for the design and implementation of international human resource management practices and policies. Chapter 3 also describes the various structure options available to the MNE in combining those geographically dispersed units and the implications for the design and implementation of international human resource policies and practices. Finally, Chapter 4 describes the role of international human resource management practices and policies in three unique international structures of MNEs: international mergers and acquisitions, international joint ventures, and international alliances.

Chapter 1

The Internationalization of Human Resource Management

In the future, there will be no markets left waiting to emerge.

HSBC Corporation[1]

A company's actions should be consequent to its beliefs. We believe that our ability to win is due in no small part to our people, whom we consider a competitive advantage.

Peter Brabeck-Letmathe
Chairman, Nestle[2]

Learning Objectives

This chapter enables the reader to:

- Describe the many drivers of the internationalization of business.
- Describe the growth and spread of internationalization.
- Describe the different settings of international human resource management.
- Explain the development of international human resource management.

Over the last 50 years, the economies of the world have become increasingly integrated.[3] This has been driven by many forces and led by what is now referred to as the *multinational enterprise* (MNE)—and more recently contributed to by internationalized *government agencies* (such as the United Nations and the World Trade Organization), *small- and medium-sized enterprises* (SMEs), countries through their *state- and family-owned enterprises, born-global organizations*, and *non-governmental organizations* (NGOs). As all forms of organization have increased their global activities, all of their management functions have required adaptation to the global environment, including human resource management (HRM).

This book is about the policies and practices of HRM in those organizations that operate in the global economy.

This first chapter introduces the concept of *internationalization* and how it has impacted HRM, how that led to the development of international human resource management (IHRM), and why IHRM has become so critical to the success of global organizations. In addition, this chapter explains why IHRM is so different from traditional and purely domestic HRM. Broadly defined, the field of *international human resource management* is the *study and application of all human resource management activities as they impact the process of managing human resources in enterprises in the global environment*. HRM in the MNE is playing an increasingly significant role in providing solutions to business problems at the global level. Consequently, there is a need to examine how HRM policies and practices can best support the rapid advance of globalization. That is, this chapter is about the internationalization of HRM (referred to in this text as *International HRM* or *IHRM*).[4]

> International human resource management is the study and application of all human resource management activities as they impact the process of managing human resources in enterprises in the global environment.

The following provides a short summary of what is driving the internationalization of business and its impact on HRM. Markets for most goods and services are global—with every firm or industry experiencing competitors from multiple countries; increasing cross-border investment; expanding number and value of cross-border joint ventures, partnerships, and alliances; increasing numbers of small, internet-based, multinationals (often referred to as micro-MNEs); and increasing numbers of people who cross borders (legally and illegally). Thousands of firms and millions of people work outside their countries of origin and millions of people work in their home countries for foreign-owned enterprises. Firms everywhere face foreign competition. And inputs to business activity (financial, labor, materials, technology, supplies, and consultancies) are now available everywhere at world-class quality, price, and speed, creating global standards and competition in virtually every industry and sector.

> *5.27 million Americans* worked for foreign-owned subsidiaries in 2010 in the United States (the most recent data published by the Bureau of Economic Analysis: http://www.bea.gov/scb). A similar number of foreigners worked for foreign subsidiaries of American firms overseas. This phenomenon can be found in many countries.

What this implies is that every business and every person confronts constant global pressure for competitive excellence. Business, as well as other activities such as politics, travel, environmental concerns, and sports, has become a truly international activity, with every aspect of every organization affected, including HRM. Thus the purpose of this introductory chapter is to provide a framework for understanding how this pervasive internationalization is affecting HRM—and to introduce how IHRM today is carrying out its new obligations and how it is changing to meet the demands of this interconnected world.

THE DRIVERS OF INTERNATIONALIZATION OF BUSINESS

Many enterprises, large and small, from all countries (developed economies and emerging) are already global—or are in the process of going global. There are many drivers of this *internationalization of business*, the most important of which include the items listed in Exhibit 1.1.

EXHIBIT 1.1: Drivers of Internationalization of Business

Driver	Impact on internationalization
Decreased trade barriers through trade agreements and treaties	Negotiated to facilitate and increase trade between member countries (e.g., WTO, EU, NAFTA, ASEAN, MERCUSOR)
Search for new markets and reduced costs	New markets and lower-cost operations found in other countries
Rapid and extensive global communication	Made possible with new technologies and facilitates international collaboration and easier communication and control among dispersed operations
Rapid development and transfer of new technology, including improved transportation	Technological advances are now global, created everywhere, and shared across borders, making global commerce possible
Increased travel and migration, exposure to new countries and cultures	Billions of people experience other countries and cultures every year and develop new attitudes and expectations
Knowledge sharing across borders	With global education, travel, trade, and the Internet, knowledge and ideas are spreading across borders rapidly
E-commerce	By its nature is international and is increasing rapidly

Continued overleaf

EXHIBIT 1.1 *Continued*

Driver	Impact on internationalization
Homogenization of culture and consumer demands	Increasingly, consumer demands are the same everywhere
Global Internet and social media, television, music, movies, sports, publications, news	All media are now shared everywhere and participated in by everyone, creating global expectations
Competitiveness of emerging market MNEs and SMEs	Internationalization largely came from developed countries; now there are innovative and competitive firms everywhere; much world economic growth is now located in emerging markets

Together these drivers are creating new global realities for all organizations—large and small, publicly traded, privately held, family-owned, government-owned, web-based, and NGOs. When businesses internationalize (for more about this process, refer to Chapters 2 through 4), HRM responsibilities, such as recruiting and hiring, management development, performance management, compensation, employee benefits, health and safety, and labor relations, take on international characteristics, requiring international HRM professionals to facilitate HRM practices with a global focus.

THE GROWTH AND SPREAD OF INTERNATIONALIZATION

Because of the rapid development of these drivers, internationalization is spreading faster than ever. It has led some observers to refer to it as *globalization* and to define it as:

> the inexorable integration of markets, nation-states, and technologies to a degree never witnessed before—in a way that is enabling individuals, corporations, and nation-states to reach around the world farther, faster, deeper, and cheaper than ever before and in a way that is enabling the world to reach into individuals, corporations, and nation-states farther, faster, deeper, and cheaper than ever before.[5]

Both terms—internationalization and globalization—refer to the ever-increasing interaction, interconnectedness, and integration of individuals, companies, cultures, and countries. The expanding connections between people, companies, countries, and cultures are real, powerful, all-encompassing, and increasing in importance. Because of this, *international business* continues to grow in terms of the numbers and types of enterprises conducting business across borders, the amount of foreign direct investment (FDI), and the value of trade between countries.

The United Nations estimates (2010) that there are more than 82,000 large multinational enterprises (referred to by the UN as transnationals) with more than 870,000 affiliates that employ more than 77 million people worldwide (not counting sub-contractors and outsourcing).[6] And these numbers grow every year. Even though the amount of new FDI dropped rather dramatically during the 2007–2009 global economic and financial crisis, it began to recover by 2010 and by 2012–2013 it had recovered to the pre-crisis level.[7] Even during the crisis, the economic and financial health of the major emerging markets, such as the BRIC(S) countries (Brazil, Russia, India, and China—to which South Africa has been added), remained fairly robust. Indeed, emerging markets are now providing the major growth in the world's economy.

Internationalization began with large firms from the major developed countries, primarily the US, the UK, Germany, France, and Japan. But international business is no longer only—or even primarily—the domain of well-known firms from the large or developed countries. Surveys show that enterprises from small, or developing and emerging markets are also contributing increasingly to global trade as are the tens of thousands of entrepreneurial but global micro-MNEs. For an example, refer to IHRM in Action 1.1, which illustrates how a small—200-employee—accounting business in Salem, Oregon, grew into a global business (now one of the top 100 accounting firms in the US, with branches in a number of other locations, including other countries. In addition, for another example, refer to the case at the end of the chapter, which profiles Yarn-Paradise, a small, entrepreneurial business—referred to as a micro-MNE—in Turkey, with Internet customers around the world.

IHRM in Action 1.1: Creating a Global Accounting Firm

A 200-employee accounting firm may not top your list of global businesses with IHRM issues, but it should. Aldrich Kilbride & Tatone (AKT), an Oregon, US, accounting firm, has operated since 1973 in the small town of Salem. Wanting to grow the business, it made a number of strategic decisions to add services and locations. It opened two offices in Mumbai and Coimbatore (India) and merged with Grice Lund & Tarkington, an accounting firm based in San Diego, California. Rather than outsourcing, a route commonly used by accounting firms, AKT decided to establish its Indian offices through direct investment and hire its own year-round staff. Yet, because of the cyclical nature of the tax business, it had to overcome major hurdles to increase efficiency and create sustainable careers for its employees, regardless of location. The biggest hurdles, initially, included computer security, file sharing, and time zones. But it soon realized that culture differences and maintaining a similar organizational culture in each of its locations was an additional challenge. While AKT encourages each office to form teams of experts who can focus on specific customer needs, it also early on faced the challenge of deploying its Indian tax professionals when the frantic US tax season was done. AKT decided to partner with one of England's top firms. Now, from May through December (the heavy time pressure for the US tax season ends in April), AKT's India staff work to prepare the tax returns of their English partner's clients. The global expansion of this small US accounting firm (now one of the top 100 accounting firms in the US with partnerships and offices all over the US and world) proved to be successful for employees and customers alike, because of the attention paid to people issues.

Fifty years ago the US economy accounted for 53 percent of global Gross Domestic Product (GDP), but today it accounts for less than 28 percent of global GDP (or less than 20 percent in terms of global purchasing power parity), albeit both of a much larger US GDP and of a very much larger global economy.[8]

Not only is the world economy much larger in absolute terms, but an ever-increasing number of countries are participating in a significant way. For many, the world is becoming flat (in the sense that no country has a commercial advantage in any particular industry), and we are entering an era of *globality*, with everyone competing with everyone from everywhere for everything.[9] For example, one measure of this is the ever-growing number of countries whose publicly held enterprises are represented among the world's largest MNEs (and, of course, there are also many thousands more SMEs and family-owned enterprises—from large and small and both developed and emerging economies—that don't show in the surveys or rankings but that also play a significant role in the conduct of international commerce). The next couple of paragraphs summarize a number of these rankings and illustrate how quickly globalization is expanding.

For example, the *Fortune* Global 500 (which is a ranking of the largest publicly traded and reported firms in the world, based on their revenues) now (2013) includes companies from 38 countries—obviously including firms from a number of emerging markets.[10] A dozen years ago there were only 25 countries represented. Today (2013), *Forbes'* Global 2000 list (a ranking of the largest public companies based on a composite of sales, profits, assets, and market value) includes firms from 63 countries.[11] All regions of the world are represented, indicating how global business has become: Asia-Pacific (715 companies), Europe/Middle East/Africa (606), United States (543), and the Americas (143). In 1999, the *Wall Street Journal* began a list of the largest firms as determined by their market capitalization. The largest 25 firms (based on this metric) were from five countries [US (19), Japan (3), Germany (1), UK (1), and Finland (1)].[12] But by 2013, there were seven (quite different) countries represented [US (14), China (4), UK (2), Switzerland (2), Australia (1), Brazil (1), and the Netherlands (1)].[13] In addition, the London *Financial Times* developed a list of the top Global 500 firms (based on market capitalization in all the major stock markets from around the world). In 2013, the FT list included firms from 35 countries.[14]

When business publications first started developing these lists, their primary focus was on ranking the largest global firms. But with the increasing integration of the global economy, these publications have become additionally interested in analyses of more specific characteristics. For example, *Fortune* magazine developed a list of the top global companies for leaders.[15] This analysis of approximately 10,000 companies worldwide was narrowed to 45 companies from 16 countries, with the top 20 companies found in eight different countries. *Fortune* magazine also developed a list of the most powerful women in the global economy, which profiled women from 21 different countries.[16] *Bloomberg Businessweek* has developed, among its many lists, the Global InfoTech 100, the world's most important information technology firms, based on a composite ranking of shareholder return, return on equity, total revenues, and revenue growth.[17] This list includes firms from 24 countries, large and small, developed and emerging. *Bloomberg Businessweek* has also developed a list of the 100 Best Global Brands, which includes firms from 13 countries, which is also based on a composite score—of marketing and financial data and expert evaluations.[18] In addition, *Bloomberg Businessweek* has developed a list of the 50 most innovative companies,[19] based on a global survey of executives plus stock returns and three-year revenue and margin growth. In the 2010 results, "fifteen of the top 50 are Asian—and for the first time since the rankings began in 2005, the majority in the top 25 are based outside the U.S." A final example demonstrating the internationalization of business includes a ranking of the 100 best-performing CEOs in the world by the *Harvard Business Review*.[20] In this ranking, 67 firms were from developed countries, six were from the Asian tigers, 22 were from the BRIC countries, and five were from new emerging market countries.

All of these surveys focus on large, publicly traded firms. The key reason, of course, is that data about these firms are readily available from their stock market and government filings. The surveys do not, however, include private and family-held businesses or government-owned enterprises (no matter how large), because they do not typically publish their financial results. Some privately held firms (such as superbrands in the UK and the Hangzhou Wahaha Group in China), family-owned firms (such as Ikea in Sweden and Gianni Versace in Italy), as well as government-owned enterprises (such as Japan Post and China National Pharmaceutical Group) are among the world's largest and most global firms. In many countries, large privately held, family-owned and -run, and government-owned businesses contribute a major component to the size of their economies. And then, of course, there are also hundreds and thousands of SMEs in most countries that sell and purchase in the global marketplace.

The United Nations Conference on Trade and Development (UNCTAD) tracks the world's transnational corporations (TNCs), analyzing how important these firms are to the global economy. As part of this effort, UNCTAD developed the TNI—Transnational Index, based on the composite of a firm's average percentage of its foreign assets, foreign sales, and

EXHIBIT 1.2: The World's Top 20 Non-financial TNCs (Ranked by Foreign Assets)

Rank	TNC	Home country	Industry	Assets ($ million)		Sales ($ million)		Employment		TNI
				Foreign	Total	Foreign	Total	Foreign	Total	
1	General Electric Co	United States	Electrical and electronic equipment	331 160	656 560	74 382	142 937	135 000	307 000	48.8
2	Royal Dutch Shell Plc	United Kingdom	Petroleum expl./ ref./distr.	301 898	357 512	275 651	451 235	67 000	92 000	72.8
3	Toyota Motor Corporation	Japan	Motor vehicles	274 380	403 088	171 231	256 381	137 000	333 498	58.6
4	Exxon Mobil Corporation	United States	Petroleum expl./ ref./distr.	231 033	346 808	237 438	390 247	45 216	75 000	62.6
5	Total SA	France	Petroleum expl./ ref./distr.	226 717	238 870	175 703	227 901	65 602	98 799	79.5
6	BP Plc	United Kingdom	Petroleum expl./ ref./distr.	202 899	305 690	250 372	379 136	64 300	83 900	69.7
7	Vodafone Group Plc	United Kingdom	Telecommunications	182 837	202 763	59 059	69 276	83 422	91 272	88.9
8	Volkswagen Group	Germany	Motor vehicles	176 656	446 555	211 488	261 560	317 800	572 800	58.6
9	Chevron Corporation	United States	Petroleum expl./ ref./distr.	175 736	253 753	122 982	211 664	32 600	64 600	59.3
10	Eni SpA	Italy	Petroleum expl./ ref./distr.	141 021	190 125	109 886	152 313	56 509	83 887	71.2

EXHIBIT 1.2 (Continued)

Rank	TNC	Home country	Industry	Assets ($ million)		Sales ($ million)		Employment		TNI
				Foreign	Total	Foreign	Total	Foreign	Total	
11	Enel SpA	Italy	Electricity, gas and water	140 396	226 006	61 867	106 924	37 125	71 394	57.3
12	Glencore Xstrata Plc	Switzerland	Mining and quarrying	135 080	154 932	153 912	232 694	180 527	190 000	82.8
13	Anheuser-Busch InBev NV	Belgium	Food, beverages and tobacco	134 549	141 666	39 414	43 195	144 887	154 587	93.3
14	EDF SA	France	Utilities (Electricity, gas and water)	130 161	353 574	46 978	100 364	28 975	158 467	34.0
15	Nestlé SA	Switzerland	Food, beverages and tobacco	124 730	129 969	98 034	99 669	322 996	333 000	97.1
16	E.ON AG	Germany	Utilities (Electricity, gas and water)	124 429	179 988	115 072	162 573	49 809	62 239	73.3
17	GDF Suez	France	Utilities (Electricity, gas and water)	121 402	219 759	72 133	118 561	73 000	147 199	55.2
18	Deutsche Telekom AG	Germany	Telecommunications	120 350	162 671	50 049	79 835	111 953	228 596	61.9
19	Apple Computer Inc	United States	Electrical and electronic equipment	119 918	207 000	104 713	170 910	50 322	84 400	59.6
20	Honda Motor Co Ltd	Japan	Motor vehicles	118 476	151 965	96 055	118 176	120 985	190 338	74.3

TNI refers to the Transnationality Index, which is computed as the average of three ratios: foreign assets to total assets, foreign sales to total sales, and foreign employment to total employment.

Source: *World Investment Report 2014: Investing in SDG An Action Plan*, UNCTAD (www.unctad.org/wir).

foreign employment to its total assets, sales, and employment, which identifies the relative importance of foreign business activity to the world's largest firms. Exhibit 1.2 shows the top 20 non-financial transnationals ranked by the value of their foreign assets. The table illustrates that the largest firms by foreign assets are not necessarily the largest by sales, number of employees, or as percentages-of-total figures. For example, this table shows that General Electric has the highest absolute value of foreign assets of all transnationals tracked by UNCTAD, yet their TNI places them quite a way down the overall rankings (TNI = 48.8).

These many surveys and rankings illustrate that the global economy increasingly involves all kinds of products and services from all kinds of organizations located in virtually every country in the world. This is radically different from the situation of even a few years ago, when only a few countries and a relatively few companies participated widely in the global economy. In addition, this internationalization is proceeding at an unanticipated and unprecedented rate. The opening of markets and the appearance of competitive foreign firms and their products in virtually every marketplace puts intense pressure on every enterprise to develop the capacity to operate at lower costs and with greater speed, quality, customer service, and innovation, both at home and abroad. As a consequence, HR is called upon to recruit, select, develop, and retain workforce talent that can achieve this global competitiveness in a world that is increasingly complex and challenging. IBM's chairman, Samuel Palmisano, indicates that IBM's survey of global CEOs shows that coping with this new world is seen as the most significant challenge they face (see IHRM in Action 1.2).[21] And one of the most difficult components of that challenge is finding the employees and management that are needed, which is directly the responsibility of IHRM.

IHRM in Action 1.2: CEOs' Perspectives on Globalization

Introductory letter from Samuel J. Palmisano, Chairman, President, and CEO of IBM

In a very short time, we've become aware of global climate change; of the geopolitical issues surrounding energy and water supplies; of the vulnerabilities of supply chains for food, medicine and even talent; and of sobering threats to global security.

The common denominator? The realities—and challenges—of global integration [these are all issues that connect across borders].

We occupy a world that is connected on multiple dimensions, and at a deep level—a global system of systems. That means, among other things, that it is subject to systems-level failures, which require systems-level thinking about the effectiveness of its physical and digital infrastructures.

It is this unprecedented level of interconnection and interdependency that underpins the most important findings contained in this report. Inside this revealing view into the agendas of global business and public sector leaders, three widely shared perspectives stand in relief:

- The world's private and public sector leaders believe that a rapid escalation of "complexity" is the biggest challenge confronting them. They expect it to continue—indeed, to accelerate—in the coming years.
- They are equally clear that their enterprises today are not equipped to cope effectively with this complexity in the global environment.
- Finally, they identify "creativity" as the single most important leadership competency for enterprises seeking a path through this complexity.

What we heard through the course of these in-depth discussions is that events, threats, and opportunities aren't just coming at us faster or with less predictability; they are converging and influencing each other to create entirely unique situations. These first-of-their-kind developments require unprecedented degrees of creativity—which has become a more important leadership quality than attributes like management discipline, rigor or operational acumen.

As always, our biennial examination of the priorities of CEOs around the world provides terrific insight into both the world as they see it, and ultimately, what sets the highest-performing enterprises apart. For me personally, I find one fact especially fascinating. Over the course of more than 1,500 face-to-face interviews with CEOs and other leaders, with not a single question containing the term "Smarter Planet"— and yet the conversations yielded primary findings that speak directly to exactly what IBM has been saying about the challenges and opportunities of this fundamental shift in the way the world works.

DIFFERENT SETTINGS OF INTERNATIONAL HUMAN RESOURCE MANAGEMENT

Internationalization of HRM occurs in many different settings. For practical purposes, HR managers in most types of organizations will confront at least some aspects of internationalization. That is to say, the internationalization and technology factors (refer to the list of drivers earlier in this chapter) that have led to there being "no place to hide" from the internationalization of business have also led to there being no place to hide for HRM professionals. HRM professionals find themselves having to deal with—and must therefore understand and become competent in—IHRM issues in almost every job setting (see Figure 1.1.). The following provides a short summary of the most significant of these settings.

FIGURE 1.1 Who Needs International Human Resource Management?

Headquarters of Multinationals

This setting involves working as an HRM professional in the central or regional headquarters of the traditional MNE. This setting receives most of the attention in research and literature about the internationalization of business and is, by far, the most common situation for HR managers who confront international responsibilities. The focus is from the center (headquarters) out to the subsidiaries and sub-contractors, developing and overseeing HRM practices in all foreign operations and administering the movement of employees between headquarters and foreign locations. Increasingly, the movement of employees is also between foreign subsidiaries and headquarters and between foreign locales—all often referred to generically as international assignees. It can also mean that HRM professionals are likely to find themselves working on international assignments. The case in at least some MNEs involves IHRM becoming a major strategic partner in the organization's global planning and in talent management of the global workforce, relegating many of the international assignee responsibilities to centralized shared service centers, or outsourcing them to specialized service providers. Typically, headquarters either applies its parent company HRM policies and practices directly to its foreign subsidiaries, or it tries to merge its HRM policies and practices with those that are common in the host countries of their subsidiaries. However, it is common that a local HR manager will handle HR in the subsidiary, even if he or she is primarily responsible for implementing centralized (from headquarters) HRM policies and practices.

Home-country Subsidiaries of Foreign-owned Firms

The second common setting for IHR involves the HR manager working in his or her home country but being employed by a local subsidiary or acquisition of a foreign MNE. Now the HR manager is likely be on the receiving end of policy and practice coming from the foreign headquarters, reversing the role as experienced by the HR manager in the first situation. This HR manager will typically have to integrate a local national culture plus the foreign organizational culture into his or her local operations. This role has received little attention (except when a major legal or culture clash occurs), but is by no means uncommon in many countries. Examples of such situations would involve local HR managers working in the local subsidiaries or acquisitions of MNEs in places like Central Europe (auto companies, pharmaceutical companies, tobacco companies, telecommunications firms), India (software developers, call centers), China (manufacturing facilities, services), Africa (energy and extraction firms), and Latin America (commodity and natural resource firms, retail companies, banks), or even, maybe especially, HR managers working in the local subsidiaries of the large multinationals in Asia, Latin America, the US, and Europe, such as for Siemens, Walmart, Novartis, Johnson & Johnson, or IBM.

The different communication styles, worker motivation philosophies, and organizational structures and frequent lack of understanding of the host country cultures, markets, employment laws and practices, even language itself, by the parent company can cause major problems for the local HR manager, and thus force the host country HR manager to confront aspects of internationalization that are just as difficult as those confronted by the home country HR manager working at headquarters having to deal with the "export" of policy and practices.

Domestic Firms

Although they may be overlooked, another important setting for IHRM is the purely domestic (local) firm, such as a hospital, farm, dry cleaners or laundry, ski or beachside resort, road or building construction contractor, or restaurant (or the purely domestic operation of an MNE, such as a local fast food or real estate franchise or a local petrol station). In many countries (particularly true in most locales in Europe and North America), these types of firms also confront many of the complexities of international business, particularly as they relate to IHRM. These complexities include:

- the hiring of employees who come from another country, culture, and language (recent immigrants) or their families (who may have been born in the new country, and may be, therefore, now citizens, but who may still be more familiar with the language and culture with which they grew up at home than with that of their new country); as well as
- having to deal with competition from foreign firms for customers and suppliers;
- or for capital which may well come from foreign-owned firms, or competition from these firms for resources, including employees.

The hiring—or recruiting—of immigrants (or even the first generation since immigration) in local, domestic firms can lead to many of the same internationalization concerns as those faced by traditional MNEs, such as how to merge the cultures, languages, and general work expectations of employees from multiple countries, and how to respond to employees who bring to their new work situations sometimes very different languages and very different attitudes toward supervision and have very different expectations related to the practice of management and IHRM (such as performance management and compensation). Thus, even in the domestic firm, HR managers must develop much of the knowledge and experience necessary to succeed in an international environment.

In addition, traditionally local, domestic firms can find themselves "going global," which can involve the establishing of small offices in other countries (e.g., a small accounting or architectural firm opening an office in a foreign locale, either to tap into talent for its home office operations or to provide an entrée into the foreign location). Or they might find themselves needing to recruit talent "overseas" in order to meet their needs for specialized skills that are in short supply in their home locales. In either case, the HRM challenges are not much different than those confronted by IHR managers in large MNEs.

Even though these domestic companies tend to be relatively small, increasingly they are what are referred to as "domestic multinationals." These are successful, initially small, domestic companies—frequently in emerging markets—that are going abroad and becoming MNEs themselves. Examples of such firms include Pliva (generic pharmaceuticals, Croatia), Mittal (steel, India), Tata Consulting Services, Infosys, and Wipro (IT services, India), Lukoil (oil, Russia), Gazprom (oil and gas, Russia), Haier (home appliances, China), Mahindra & Mahindra (tractors and cars, India), Sadia (food and beverages, Brazil), Harry Ramsden's Fish and Chips (UK), Embraer (aerospace, Brazil), Koc (diversified industries, Turkey), Cemex (building materials, Mexico), and Comex (paint manufacturer and retailer, Mexico) to name just a few. These companies have become global players in their respective industries and are demonstrating the potential of reaching the top ranks of global competitors.[22]

Government Agencies and Non-governmental Organizations

Even though this text primarily discusses IHRM from the perspective of MNEs, many other types of organizations are also global in scope and are concerned with many of the same international HRM issues. For example, government agencies such as the foreign ministries of countries and their embassies and the hundreds of non-governmental organizations (NGOs) that send hundreds of people from their parent countries to their overseas operations and often also employ many local and third-country people to staff their activities around the globe, such as religious organizations including the Catholic Church, LDS Church, Moon Church, Life Church; and humanitarian organizations such as World Vision, Care, Mercy Corps, Red Cross, Habitat for Humanity, and Doctors Without Borders.

In addition, there are an increasing number of agencies that are global by purpose and function—such as the United Nations and all of its agencies,[23] the World Bank, the World Trade Organization (WTO), the Organization for Economic Cooperation and Development (OECD), the Association of Southeast Asian Nations (ASEAN), and the EU with its large concentration of employees in Brussels, Strasbourg, and Luxembourg. Many IHRM responsibilities for these organizations are similar to those faced by their commercial counterparts. Indeed, many of them have experience with international operations over a longer period of time than is true for most firms and have accumulated much significant expertise on how to best handle international HRM challenges. Challenges associated with recruiting, compensating, and managing employees in multiple countries are not much different for the International Red Cross or the World Health Organization than they are for IBM. HR managers in these types of organizations must also be internationally savvy in order to effectively carry out their responsibilities, and they often have much experience from which they can teach their private sector counterparts.

THE DEVELOPMENT OF INTERNATIONAL HUMAN RESOURCE MANAGEMENT

The previous paragraphs point out that HR managers, no matter the type of organization for which they work, can and do confront aspects of IHRM. The extent of this involvement will vary according to a number of factors, such as the degree of development of the global strategy of the organization, and will invariably increase with time. But as the general internationalization of business increases in extent and intensity, HR managers are being called upon to contribute increasing expertise to that internationalization.

One aspect of internationalizing HRM that makes the task difficult and complex comes from the following: whether local HR managers are from headquarters, from the host country, or from a third country, they end up being sandwiched between their own national cultures and legal traditions—and experiences—and the cultures and practices of the firm, whether at headquarters or at the local affiliate. HR managers at the local, regional, and headquarters levels must learn to integrate and coordinate policies and practices taking place in diverse environments and with people of diverse backgrounds. Plus they are frequently also looked to for expertise in helping other managers be successful in their cross-border endeavors.

For example, some of the IHRM-related questions that need to be answered within an MNE as it establishes its international strategy include the items in Exhibit 1.3.

Since most organizations today experience one or more aspects of international HRM, the success or failure of those enterprises is often a function of how they handle their IHRM issues. As a consequence, a new set of competencies has developed within the HR function. The section below discusses some of the issues surrounding these new competencies.

Some of the differences between HRM and IHRM include the following, with IHRM being responsible for:

- *More HR functions and activities*, for example, the management of international assignees, including such things as foreign income and social taxes, foreign work visas, and assistance with international relocations.
- *A broader expertise and perspective*, including knowledge about foreign countries, their employment laws and practices, and cultural differences.
- *More involvement in employees' lives*, as the firm relocates employees and their families from country to country.

EXHIBIT 1.3: IHRM Questions for International Strategy

1   Do we have knowledgeable staffing for a global strategy?
2   Are the countries being considered for global expansion good from an IHRM point of view, such as will it be easy to operate within a different set of employment laws?
3   Does the firm have adequate personnel to implement foreign operations?
4   How many employees will need to be relocated? How many local employees will we need to hire and does the local labor force have the necessary skills?
5   Will we be able to find and recruit the talent necessary for international operations?
6   Should we pursue centralized or localized HRM policies?

- *Dealing with and managing a much wider mix of employees*, adding considerable complexity to the IHRM management job—with each of the various types of international employees requiring different training, staffing, compensation, and benefits programs.
- *More external factors and influences*, such as dealing with issues stemming from multiple governments, country laws, cultures, currencies, and languages.
- *A greater level of risk*, with greater exposure to problems and difficulties and, thus, exposure to much greater potential liabilities for making mistakes in HRM decisions (for example, political risk and uncertainties, legal compliance issues, and early return of employees from foreign assignments).

In addition to these factors, the geographic dispersion, multiculturalism, different legal and social systems, and the cross-border movement of capital, goods, services, and people that are faced by the international firm add a need for competency and sensitivity that is not found in the domestic firm. The personal and professional attitudes and perspectives of the IHR manager must be greatly expanded to handle the multiple countries and cultures confronted in the global arena—both to manage their IHRM responsibilities and to contribute to successful international business strategies by their firms—beyond those that their domestic HRM counterparts must develop. Typical domestic HR managers do not have the global contacts or networks that become necessary to learn about and to handle the new global responsibilities. They don't typically have any experience with the business and social protocols needed to interact successfully with foreign colleagues or with the forms of organizational structure used to pursue international strategies (such as international joint ventures or cross-border acquisitions). And the still relatively limited body of literature and publicly available seminars and training programs make it much more difficult to develop the competencies needed to successfully manage the IHRM function.

The example of Harry Ramsden's (see IHRM in Action 1.3) illustrates just how difficult it can be to make the move to being an international firm.[24]

IHRM in Action 1.3: Developing a Global Appetite for Fish and Chips

Deep-fried fish and chips have long been a popular snack in England. One of England's premium fish-and-chip shops, Harry Ramsden's, which was founded in Guiseley, West Yorkshire, in 1928, is one of the few that have opened shops at multiple locations. By 1994 the company had eight branches in Britain, with more scheduled for opening, one in Dublin, Ireland, and one in Hong Kong. Harry Ramsden's managers, however, dissatisfied with this success, wanted to turn Harry Ramsden's into a truly global enterprise.

As a start, the company had set up its first international operation in Hong Kong. According to finance director Richard Taylor, "We marketed the product as Britain's fast food, and it proved extremely successful." Within two years the Hong Kong venture was generating annual sales equivalent to its most-successful UK operations. Half of the initial clientele in Hong Kong were British expatriates, but within a couple of years, more than 80 percent of customers were ethnic Chinese, illustrating the relative ease with which at least some products and services, such as a country's favorite food, can transfer to another country and culture.

Emboldened by this success, Harry Ramsden's began to open additional overseas branches, in such places as Melbourne, Australia, as well as in other more exotic locales, such as Singapore, Dubai in the United Arab Emirates, Saudi Arabia, Walt Disney World in the US, and Japan. In the first experimental shop in Tokyo, Japan, for example, the Japanese took to this product, despite their traditional aversion to greasy food.

Richard Taylor stated their international strategy:

> We want Harry Ramsden's to become a global brand. In the short term the greatest returns will be in the UK. But it would be a mistake to saturate the UK and then turn to the rest of the world. We'd probably come a cropper when we internationalized. We need experience now.

As of 2006, Harry Ramsden's had 170 owned and franchised outlets in the UK and internationally, and had become both Britain's longest-established restaurant chain and the biggest fish-and-chips shop brand in the world. However, due to some poor location decisions and problems with staffing and management, some international locales have been closed, and over the last 10 years the chain has been sold a couple of times, including most recently—in 2010—to Boparan Ventures Limited, a British fish and food company, with ambitions to once again further expand Harry Ramsden's in the UK and overseas. Clearly global knowledge and human resources capability set limits on how far and how fast a firm can "go international."

EVOLUTION OF THE INTERNATIONAL HUMAN RESOURCE MANAGEMENT PROFESSIONAL

Some large MNEs, such as Royal Dutch Shell, Unilever, and Ford Motor Company, have long histories of conducting international business, going back 100 years or more. By necessity of having to manage operations in many countries, these firms developed—at least at the headquarters level—considerable international HRM expertise. Even so, the specific management function called "international human resource management" is relatively new as a professional and academic area of practice and interest.

The two largest national human resource management professional associations are the Chartered Institute for Personnel and Development (CIPD) in the UK and the Society for Human Resource Management (SHRM) in the US. Many other countries have their own professional HR associations and most, including the US and the UK, belong to the much larger umbrella organization called the World Federation of Personnel Management Associations (WFPMA), now with over 60 national HRM professional societies as members.

Yet, it has only been in the last 30 years or so that HRM service providers (such as training firms, relocation firms, accounting firms, employment law firms, and HRM consulting firms) have developed a special focus on IHRM. SHRM and CIPD and a number of universities are now providing conferences and training seminars and courses on topics related to IHRM, as do many IHRM service providers, consultant groups, and other IHRM-related organizations. For details about CIPD, for example, see Sparrow, Brewster, and De Cieri's *Globalizing Human Resource Management*, 2nd edition, in the series on global HRM of which this book is a member, a series that is itself a sign of the growing attention to IHRM, being the first major series of books covering many of the policies and practices of IHRM.

A turning point in the professionalization of IHRM occurred with the establishment of the *GPHR (Global Professional in Human Resources)* certification by the Human Resource Certification Institute (HRCI) in the US in 2003. The professionalization of IHRM is further discussed in Chapter 15. The body of knowledge for this exam is codified into six domains (all of which are covered—at least the international aspects—in this book or the additional books in the Global HRM series published by Routledge). The domains—for international HRM—include:

- Strategic HR Management;
- Global Talent Acquisition and Mobility;
- Global Compensation and Benefits;
- Organizational Effectiveness and Talent Development;
- Workforce Relations and Risk Management;
- Core Knowledge of IHRM.

HRM professionals can attain certification in these domains based on their experience and the passing of an examination, verifying their understanding of the body of knowledge in

IHRM. Increasingly, the GPHR exam is attracting HRM professionals from around the world.

As a business discipline and an academic field of study, IHRM may well still be in its youth; yet it is very real and firmly established. There are many reasons for its youth, some of which have to do with the generally limited role of HRM within many firms, including some of the large MNEs, and some of which have to do with the lack of international knowledge and experience of HR managers themselves. With the increasing globalization discussed in the first sections of this chapter, HRM professionals have been called upon to manage a number of new (global) activities for which they often have little or no preparation, to work alongside HRM professionals from other countries with whom they have had little prior interaction, and to adapt their HRM policies and practices to multicultural and cross-cultural environments, with which they have little experience.

Since the field of HRM focuses primarily on local staffing and employment issues, its professionals have often been the last ones in their firms to focus on the impact of increasing internationalization, the last ones to take on international assignments, and thus often the last ones on the management team to contribute as fully fledged strategic partners in the internationalization of their firms. Today this is changing. IHRM professionals are now much more proactive in dealing with many new challenges and issues, including:[25]

- *Attracting, engaging, and retaining thousands of MNE employees in many different countries* to achieve strategic global business objectives. This not only includes engaging employees and executives in many countries but also the role and importance of internationally mobile employees.
- *Aligning core HRM policies and practices* with the new requirements of competing internationally, while simultaneously responding to local issues and requirements in each country of operation.
- *Enhancing global competencies and capabilities* within the IHRM department, including developing global centers of excellence, shared service centers, global talent management, and mastering the necessary HR due diligence in cross-border mergers and acquisitions.[26]

These challenges, along with many others, are the focus of the next 14 chapters. The next three chapters in Section 1 discuss various aspects of the structure of MNEs and the role IHRM plays in their development. Section 2 discusses three important aspects of the cultural and legal context within which IHRM must operate. Section 3 includes six chapters on the many aspects of the policies and practices of IHRM—including staffing, compensation, health and safety, performance management, and a comparison of HR practices in differing countries and regions around the world—while Section 4 describes the nature of the IHRM department, further aspects of the developing professionalism of IHRM, and trends in the future development and challenges of IHRM.

CONCLUSION

This chapter introduced international human resource management in the context of the increasing importance of international business. It illustrated how economic activity around the world has become increasingly integrated and pervasive and thus how it has impacted the development and evolution of HRM in the MNE. One of the most difficult challenges to international operations is the management of their human resources. An effective and informed HR department is vital to the success of all organizations with international operations. As a result, as organizations have internationalized, so has HRM.

DISCUSSION QUESTIONS

1   What forces have been driving the increased internationalization of business?
2   What are the various organizational situations in which an HR manager might be involved with aspects of internationalization?
3   What are the major differences between domestic and international HR?

CASE STUDY 1.1: Yarn Paradise: World's Biggest Online Yarn Store (Turkey)

Yarn Paradise was created by Ferit Göksen, who was born and raised in Kaseri, Turkey. After attending college, he relocated to Istanbul to obtain his MBA from Marmara University, where he became interested in international trade and development. After he received his degree in 2001, he and his partner began selling different items on the eBay platform in Istanbul. In 2004, he combined his technology skills with his partner's traditional business skills and together they founded GSC Tesktil. "After a few years, we wanted to focus on a specific product. We noticed there was a market for yarn, and we decided to try selling it on eBay." Today, the business successfully utilizes the power and reach of the Internet marketplace to sell yarn products worldwide. Yarn Paradise has two websites—www.yarnparadise.com and www.iceyarns.com—and also sells on ebay.com.

The company employs between 15 and 20 people. "It's great to be able to give 20 different families in my community a job," explains Ferit, even though 98 percent of the company's sales are outside of Turkey. While that was not his original intention, the Internet allowed Ferit to reach customers all over the world. About 35–36 percent of sales are to the US and the rest are divided between European countries and Asia. "Yarn Paradise has sold to almost every country in the world including Norway, France, Germany, the UK, Denmark, Sweden, Canada, Australia, Malaysia, New Zealand, Thailand, Trinidad, Ecuador, Egypt, Haiti, and many more. Sometimes I have never even heard of the country, until I get ready to ship the product," says Ferit. Obviously, there is still much room for growth. Yarn Paradise uses companies like DHL and UPS to help with shipping and logistics. While most transactions are quick and seamless, there are some problems in countries where online commerce is still new, such as Eastern Europe. The biggest issue for Yarn Paradise is customs and customs duties. Buyers are often surprised by them and this creates a bad customer experience.

Source: eBay inc (2014). Micro-multinationals, global consumers, and the WTO, Report from a global conference at the 2013 WTO Public Forum on e-commerce and trade, downloaded at http://www.ebay mainstreet.com/sites/default/files/eBay-WTO-PF2013.pdf

Discussion Questions

1   Yarn Paradise is a micro-MNE. What is likely to be its next stage of growth? What will be its next human resource challenges stemming from further growth?

2   Based on the case study describe important HR issues facing the company.

NOTES

1   HSBC corporate website: http://www.hsbc.com/about-hsbc/advertising/in-the-future.
2   Source: http://www.nestle.com/asset-library/documents/investors/others/nestle_ar_2013_en_let

3 There have been many books written on internationalization and globalization. Here is a sampling of some of the recent better ones: Bhagwati, J. (2004, 2007), *In Defense of Globalization*, Oxford/New York: Oxford University Press; Friedman, T. L. (2005, 2006, 2007), *The World Is Flat: A Brief History of the Twenty-First Century (versions 1.0, 2.0, 3.0)*, New York: Farrar, Straus and Giroux; Friedman, T. L. (2008), *Hot, Flat, and Crowded*, New York: Farrar, Straus and Giroux; Sirkin, H. L., Hemerling, J. W., and Bhattacharya, A. K. (2008), *Globality: Competing with Everyone from Everywhere for Everything*, New York: Business Plus; Steger, M. B. (2003), *Globalization: A Very Short Introduction*, Oxford: Oxford University Press; Stiglitz, J. E. (2003), *Globalization and Its Discontents*, New York: W. W. Norton & Co.; and Wolf, M. (2004), *Why Globalization Works*, New Haven, CT and London: Yale University Press.

4 For a complete overview of the field of international human resource management, please see the full set of books on various IHRM policies and practices and varying regional and country approaches in the Routledge Global HRM series.

5 Friedman, T. L. (1999). *The Lexus and the Olive Tree*, New York: Farrar, Straus and Giroux.

6 United Nations Conference on Trade and Development, *World Investment Report 2010* (most recent report available), New York and Geneva: United Nations.

7 Ibid.

8 *CIA World Factbook* (2013). www.cia.gov.cia/publicationsfactbook; World Bank: www.world-bank .org/WEBSITE/EXTERNAL/DATASTATISTICS; Bureau of Economic Analysis, US Department of Commerce: www.bea.gov/national/xls/gdplev.xls.

9 Friedman (2005, 2006, 2007); Sirkin et al. (2008).

10 The *Fortune* Global 500 (2013). *Fortune*, July.

11 De Carlo, S. (Sr. Editor) (2013). The world's biggest public companies, *Forbes*, April 17. http://www .forbes.com/sites/scottdecarlo/2013/04/17/the-worlds-biggest-companies.

12 *Wall Street Journal*, 2013.

13 WSJ, 2013.

14 *Financial Times* Global 500 (2013), 17th Annual, as of 28 March, http://www.ft.com/intl/indepth/ft500.

15 Burke, D., Hajim, C., Elliott, J., and Tkaczyk, C. (2007). The top companies for leaders, *Fortune*, October 1, pp. 109–116.

16 *Fortune* 50 most powerful women, downloaded 03/07/2010 from: www.CNNMoney.com/Fortune/ rankings.

17 The InfoTech 100 (2013), *Bloomberg Businessweek*, June 1, pp. 41–42.

18 100 Best Global Brands (2013), *Bloomberg Businessweek*, September 28, pp. 50–56.

19 Arndt, M., and Einhorn, B. (2010), The 50 most innovative companies, *Bloomberg Business Week*, April 25, pp. 34–40.

20 Hansen, M. T., Ibarra, H., and Peyer, U. (2013), The best performing CEOs in the World, *Harvard Business Review*, 91: ½, Jan.–Feb., 81–95.

21 Excerpted from the introductory letter from John Palmisano, Chairman, President, and CEO of IBM, to the 2010 report *Capitalizing on Complexity: Insights from the IBM Global Chief Executive Officer Study*. Downloaded July 4, 2010, from: ftp://public.che.ibm.com/common/ssi/pm/xb/n/gbe03297usen/GBE 03297USEN.PDF.

22 *Business Week* (2006), Emerging giants, July 31, pp. 41–49; O'Neill, J. (2001), Building better global economic BRICs. *Research Report*, New York: Goldman Sachs; Sirkin et al, (2008); Stengel, R. (2010), The Global Forum, *Time*, February 8, p. 4.

23 Fernandez, F. (2005). *Globalization and Human Resource Management: Adapting Successful UN Practices for the Private and Public Sectors*, New York: HNB Publishing.

24 Abrahams, P. (1994). Getting hooked on fish and chips in Japan, *Financial Times*, May 17; updated in 2014 from websites: www.harryramsdens.co.uk; http://en.wikipedia.org/wiki/Harry_Ramsden's; www .market-reports.co.uk; www.telegraph.co.uk/HarryRamsdens-new-owner-mulls-Asian-expansion.html.

25 Based on Sparrow, P., Brewster, C., and De Cieri, H. (2012), *Globalizing Human Resource Management*, 2nd ed., London: Routledge; Brewster, C., and Sparrow, P. (2008), Les noveaux róles et les defies et la

GRHi (The new roles and challenges of the IHRM function), in Waxin, M.-F., and Barmeyer, C. (eds.), *Gestion des Ressources Humaines*, France: Editions Liaisons Rueil-Malmaison, pp. 507–547; Faugoo, Deepika (2009), Globalization and its impact on human resource management, competitive advantage and organizational success in modern day organizations, in Odrakiewicz, P. (ed.), *Innovation in Management: Cooperating Globally*, Poznan: Poznan University College of Business and Foreign Languages, Poznari: PWS BiJo Publications, pp. 529–535; Fernandez (2005); Schramm, J. (2008), Workplace trends: An overview of the findings of the latest *SHRM Workplace Forecast, SHRM Workplace Visions*, 3, 1–8; Scullion, H., Collings, D.G., and Gunnigle, P. (2007), International human resource management in the 21st century: Emerging themes and contemporary debates, *Human Resource Management Journal*, *17*(4), 309–319.

26 Sparrow et al. (2012); Briscoe, D.R. (2008). Talent management and the global learning organization, in Vaiman, V., and Vance, C.M. (eds.), *Smart Talent Management: Building Knowledge Assets for Competitove Advantage*, Cheltenham, UK, and Northampton, MA: Edward Elgar, pp. 195–216; Farndale, E., Scullion, H., and Sparrow, P. (2010), The role of the corporate HR function in global talent management, *Journal of World Business*, 45(2), 161–168; Fernandez (2005); Schuler, R.S., Jackson, S.E., and Tarique, I. (2010). Framework for global talent management: HR actions for dealing with global talent challenges, in Scullion, H., and Collings, D. (eds.), *Global Talent Management*, London: Routledge, pp. 17–36; and Tarique, I., and Schuler, R.S. (2010), Global talent management: Literature review, integrative framework, and suggestions for further research, *Journal of World Business*, 45(2), 122–133.

Chapter 2

Strategic International Human Resource Management

I think as a company, if you can get those two things right—having a clear direction on what you are trying to do and bringing in great people who can execute on the stuff—then you can do pretty well.

Mark Zuckerberg
CEO, Facebook[1]

Learning Objectives

This chapter will enable the reader to:

■ Describe the development of SIHRM and the process of international strategic management.
■ Describe the evolution of the MNE in terms of various stages of internationalization and the methods firms use to enter international markets.
■ Describe the process for developing MNE strategy and IHRM strategy and the relationship between the two.
■ Understand the extent and nature of research into the practice of strategic IHRM.

This chapter is about *Strategic International Human Resource Management* (SIHRM). While the first chapter described the new global business realities and introduced IHRM,[2] this chapter describes international business strategy and how IHRM supports and enhances the international business strategies of the firm.

MNEs, in order to be successful in the global marketplace, must develop strategies to conduct business that take advantage of global resources and markets. In order for IHRM managers to make an effective contribution to that success, they must contribute to and be a part of the global *strategic management* of the business. *Strategic management* refers to the approaches that managers employ in running a company and that are derived from the firm's vision and objectives.

Since firms differ in their levels of international development and in the extent of their international operations, IHRM managers must develop the capabilities to assist in that development and in those various levels of global operation. This chapter provides an introduction to how these variances in the strategic development of the international activities of firms influence IHRM and how SIHRM supports those varying strategies and activities.

As outlined in Chapter 1, the new realities for MNEs, including reduced transportation and information costs around the world and the removal of social and political barriers to trade, are making the globalization of business proceed at unexpected and unprecedented rates.[3] The opening of markets and the appearance of competitive foreign firms places pressures on virtually every major (and most minor) industries in virtually every country. These developments impact HRM on a number of fronts.[4] The increased intensity of competition places great pressure on firms to develop the capacity to operate at lower costs and with greater speed, quality, customer service, and innovation, both at home and abroad. IHRM is called upon to hire, develop, and retain the workforce that can achieve this global competitiveness, often in dozens of countries. Therefore, this chapter introduces the contribution of IHRM to the strategic management of the MNE and introduces the ways in which the global strategy impacts the management of IHRM.

The chapter starts with a general description of the process of international strategic management and then follows with an explanation of the evolution of international business strategy and describes how IHRM fits into the overall strategic management of the MNE. This includes describing the links of global business strategy to the performance of HR responsibilities in international business and discussing the outcomes that a strategically managed international business might expect from effectively tying together an international business strategy and SIHRM. The chapter then summarizes the findings of research studies on the nature and role of strategic IHRM.

STRATEGIC INTERNATIONAL HUMAN RESOURCE MANAGEMENT: AN INTRODUCTION

SIHRM is the part of IHRM that focuses on creating and implementing IHRM policies and practices that help achieve an MNE's international vision and objectives, that is, its international strategy. It also involves the strategic management of the IHR function and department itself.

In an *ideal* world, a firm conducting international business will be actively engaged in *strategic planning and strategic management process* on a global basis (see Figure 2.1). Based on an organization's vision, goal, and mission, the organization will regularly perform an environmental analysis or scan (of its external threats and opportunities and its organizational strengths and weaknesses) and from that analysis develop its global strategies, which are then implemented for global success. Finally, evaluation of success of implementation

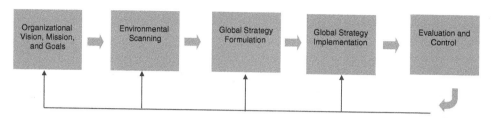

FIGURE 2.1 Basic Elements of the Strategic Management Process

of chosen strategy is needed to make any changes and re-evaluate the strategy, with whatever changes are called for by the results of the evaluation (this is the feedback loop of the model). Still in this *ideal* world, all components of the firm will be closely integrated into that planning and will be involved with similar strategic planning within their own areas of responsibility.

As mentioned earlier, strategic management, in general, is the array of competitive moves and business approaches that managers employ in running a company and that are derived from the firm's vision and objectives. In crafting a strategic course, management is saying that "among all the paths and actions we could choose, we have decided to go in this direction and rely on these particular ways of doing business."[5] A *strategy* signals an organization's commitment to specific markets, competitive approaches, and ways of operating. A company's strategy is thus the "game plan" its management has for positioning the firm in its chosen market arena, for investing money and people in the development of particular business capabilities, for developing sustainable competitive advantage, for pleasing its customers, and, thus, for achieving superior business performance. These strategies are developed in either or both of two ways: *pro-actively*, as a forward-looking plan to deal with anticipated market forces, or *reactively*, as a response to what the firm is experiencing in the marketplace. In most firms, strategies that are developed stem from a combination of these forces.

A *strategy* signals an organization's commitment to specific markets, competitive approaches, and ways of operating. A company's strategy is thus the "game plan" its management has for positioning the firm in its chosen market arena, for investing money and people in the development of particular business capabilities, for developing sustainable competitive advantage, for pleasing its customers, and, thus, for achieving superior business performance.

Senior executives devise specific strategies for their organizations because of two very compelling needs:

- the need to actively shape how their firm's business will be conducted;
- the need to mold the independent decisions and actions initiated by departments, managers, and employees across the company into a coordinated, company-wide game plan.

Both motives have become increasingly complex in today's global business environment. Yet . . .

> Among all the things managers do, nothing affects a company's ultimate success or failure more fundamentally than how well its management team charts the company's long-term direction, develops competitively effective strategic moves and business approaches, and implements what needs to be done internally to produce good day-in/day-out strategy execution. Indeed, good strategy and good strategy execution are the most trustworthy signs of good management.[6]

In terms of HR, many of the same issues arise—albeit in a much more complex way—when a firm's strategic planning "goes international" as when its strategic planning is concerned only with domestic issues. When management begins to develop and implement global strategic plans, they also begin to concern themselves with global human resource issues.[7] Indeed, HR issues are among the most critical issues for successfully competing in the international marketplace. And because of that, HR should be providing input to the international strategic decision making at every step, helping with mission and goal setting, the environmental scan, design of specific strategies, and, of course, helping to implement the chosen strategies.

Once the decision is made to go international (whether this is a pro-active or reactive choice), the task of all managers—including HR managers—is to implement that decision, to convert the strategic plan into action and get on with whatever needs to be done to achieve the international vision and targeted objectives.

The following IHRM in Action is a story of a Japanese pharma company, Takeda, tracing the decision to become more global and how that impacted all parts of the organization.[8] In order to effectively implement this decision, Takeda needed to change its internal culture, starting at the top, which included—among other things—many HR decisions and programs, from hiring key non-Japanese executives with outside experience, changing the core language to English, first at the top and increasingly throughout the organization, and recruiting Japanese employees who had studied abroad.

IHRM in Action 2.1: Implementing a Global Strategy at a Japanese Pharmaceutical

Takeda is one of Japan's oldest and largest pharmaceutical groups, a family business founded by the Takeda family seven generations ago. The last member of the Takeda family to chair the firm, Kunio Takeda, began the process of turning the strategic focus of the firm to the outside. The basic challenge that Mr. Takeda had to address was: How does a company change its corporate culture to adapt to a focus on new and different markets outside the home country?

The first major decision was to appoint someone as president from outside the Takeda family. Yasuchika Hasegawa was appointed as Takeda's president in 2003. He not only was not a member of the Takeda family, but he had also spent long periods working outside of the country, a major shift in traditional Japanese organizational practice.

As Mr. Hasegawa indicated: "The Japanese market has very slow growth. We were left behind. We had no choice but globalization," he says in excellent English, the legacy of more than a decade working for the company in Germany and then the US as Takeda began to sell off its non-medicine divisions and to diversify into foreign markets. For his first six years overseas, Kunio Takeda (chairman of Takeda Enterprises) was his direct boss and mentor. He undertook a drastic reorganization by refocusing on a much more diversified group. When Mr. Hasegawa was asked to take the presidency (the first non-Takeda to be so asked), he felt that Mr. Takeda had finished his role with the restructuring and the next phase was to globalize. And thus began many steps to implement this new strategy to "go international."

Mr. Hasegawa accelerated an ambitious program of overseas acquisitions, such as Nycomed of Switzerland, as well as the recruitment of high-level outsiders to the very top of the business at home. He created an international advisory board, bringing in Karen Katen of Pfizer and Sidney Taurel from Eli Lilly, as well as Tachi Yamada, a Japanese-born executive who had spent his adult life based in the US. He left non-Japanese leaders to run the group's international divisions, and recruited others to the headquarters in Tokyo and Osaka, including Paul Chapman, an American who now co-ordinates research and development.

Two years after Mr. Takeda stepped down, Mr. Hasegawa put Mr. Yamada on the main board. And a year later he added two other heads to Takeda divisions who have even fewer cultural connections to the country. In conjunction with these personnel decisions, he also switched the working language at senior levels to English, both for board meetings and his larger global leadership committee, aided by simultaneous translation. At more junior levels, he introduced a requirement for high levels of English proficiency among recruits, and aggressively recruited non-Japanese staff, who he encourages to work for extended periods in Japan. The reforms were not easy—resisted by members of the Takeda family as well as by other senior executives. But Mr. Hasegawa explained the needs to expand internationally: "There was strong resistance. There is a big cultural difference, but Japan is now only 35 percent of our business. Our challenge is to globalize more rapidly. To make changes, you need a core group of support." He has also taken a pragmatic approach, for example by boosting his English-speaking recruitment drive by hiring 300 Japanese who had been studying abroad.

His reforms are far from finished, and critics suggest the linguistic challenges are nothing compared with the efforts he must make to boost innovation and co-ordinate with Nycomed, whose main business is focused on emerging markets and has a heavy generic drug component. Takeda's international expansion began conservatively with a joint venture with Abbott of the US before expanding through acquisitions. And now with the efforts of Mr. Hasegawa—and his many global recruits, both Japanese and non-Japanese—this historic Japanese firm is now one of the truly global pharmaceutical giants.

It has all been made possible through the close involvement of the HR department in the strategic implementation of this new global strategy.

EVOLUTION OF THE MULTINATIONAL ENTERPRISE

In order to place IHRM in the strategic context of the MNE, it is necessary to have an appreciation for the development of the international firm. As a firm internationalizes, it moves through *stages* and in each stage it must make a choice of *methods for market entry* (see Figure 2.2).

These market entry choices will partially be dictated by the firm's own internationalization approach, the options it has in particular countries (due to legal requirements and opportunities), the timing of its entry into the market (early versus late entrant), and the

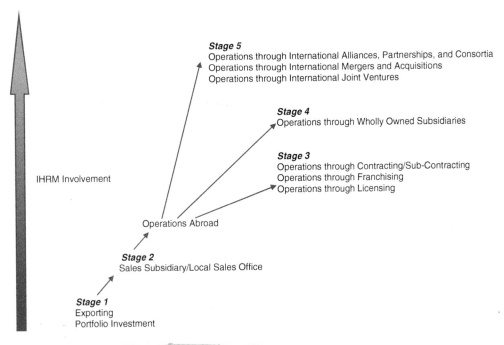

FIGURE 2.2 Evolution of the Multinational Enterprise

risks it wants to bear. All of these forms of international involvement create major coordination and integration challenges, and thus are aspects of international business that IHRM professionals must thoroughly understand in order to provide senior managers with the advice they need for designing effective global businesses. An important point here is that as firms pass through the various stages, they increase their degree of international activity, and as firms increase their levels of international activity, their IHRM responsibilities become increasingly complex.

Often, IHRM is expected to provide expertise in helping the executive team make the market entry choices and to evaluate which choices work best and under which circumstances, including assessing the particular strengths and weaknesses of the firm and its managers and evaluating labor force issues in various international options. The story of Takeda described above provides one example of how IHRM can help make the kinds of decisions required to make these transitions successful.

Stage 1 of the Internationalization Process

Portfolio Investment

At the simplest level of involvement, a firm may just decide to make financial investments in foreign firms, buying shares of stock, much as it could do within its own domestic equities markets. In general, HR is not likely to be very involved in this form of international business activity.

Exporting

Historically, this has been the initial step of internationalization for most firms and usually occurs while the firm is relatively small. Due to a foreign inquiry (often unsolicited) as to the possibility of buying or selling the firm's product(s) or the desire by the firm to expand beyond its domestic markets, many firms begin to export their products or services to foreign markets through the use of direct sales to foreign customers (via direct mail or Internet sales, for example), or they sell through import/export firms or through foreign distributors.

At this stage, there is relatively little impact on the organization and IHRM, other than possible training opportunities to ensure that employees have the knowledge necessary to carry on cross-border commerce (or staffing to recruit the few employees whose responsibilities under this scenario are international).

Stage 2 of the Internationalization Process

Sales Subsidiary/Local Sales Office

If foreign sales or purchasing increase in importance, the firm will assign a sales manager or purchasing agent responsibility for international sales. This individual may travel to foreign countries in which the firm has sales but is likely to be chosen purely for reasons of sales or purchasing experience or product or service knowledge. If direct export sales or imports are successful enough, the firm is likely to next establish its own sales or purchasing offices in those countries where sales or imports are large enough to warrant such efforts.

The next three stages in the evolution involve establishing operations abroad, that is, producing the products or services directly in foreign countries.

Stage 3 of the Internationalization Process

Operations through Licensing

Licensing the rights to manufacture or market one's product(s) or service(s) is an option for "going international" that does not involve the setting up of directly owned subsidiaries. In this stage, the firm usually locates foreign firms that have the experience to manufacture (and sometimes market) their products—with minimal technology transfer—in order to bypass import duties and to provide the simplest avenue to local sales.

Operations through Franchising

Franchising is another form of licensing. Here the organization puts together a package of the "successful" ingredients that made them a success in their home market and then franchises this package to overseas investors. The franchisor may help out by providing training and marketing the services or product. McDonald's is a popular example of a franchising option for expanding in international markets.

Because franchise businesses, such as McDonald's, are usually owned locally, the impact on IHRM, other than a role in training local franchisees in staffing and other HR practices and skill training of new employees, is pretty minimal.

Operations through Contracting/Sub-Contracting

A similar strategy for entrance into foreign markets is to contract the manufacture or assembly of a firm's products to an existing local firm. Increasingly, as firms manage their supply chains on a global basis, they sub-contract all or most of their manufacturing to firms abroad, in order to take advantage of lower labor and operating costs. Typically the firm will only have a few individuals who will travel to the foreign locales in order to transfer whatever technology is necessary and to monitor the quality of the manufacturing and final products.

The next two stages in the evolution process involve the assembly and then manufacture of products directly in the foreign country.

Stage 4 of the Internationalization Process

Wholly Owned Subsidiaries

Until quite recently, the most common way to enter international markets (beyond sub-contracting and exporting) was to conduct business through wholly owned foreign subsidiaries. Still, this is a popular form of entry into other countries. Subsidiaries can be developed in a number of ways, including through *greenfield* or *brownfield* projects or through acquisition of existing foreign-owned businesses. The development of a subsidiary through a greenfield project involves acquiring an open (green) "field" in order to build the subsidiary facilities from scratch. A brownfield project involves the purchase of existing facilities (buildings) and developing the subsidiary inside those facilities (sometimes referred to as a turnkey operation). The third alternative is often seen as providing the easiest access to new (foreign) markets and involves the acquisition of an existing enterprise that is already established in the target country.

From an IHRM standpoint, a start-up project (greenfield or brownfield) requires staffing (usually with a combination of personnel from headquarters and local nationals) and creating all IHRM policies and practices for a totally new workforce (there is a choice of transferring all policies and practices from the parent's headquarters or basically adopting the policies and practices that are common in the new country—or, possibly, a combination of these two options).[9] An acquisition, however, poses different challenges—either accepting the IHRM practices of the acquired firm or partially or totally changing them to those of the new parent firm. In both choices, however, the major challenge for the firm and for IHRM is to integrate the acquired firm's practices (and its workforce) with those of the parent. In all cases, the knowledge base and competencies required of the parent firm's IHRM department are clearly more complex and complicated than is the case prior to investment in any foreign subsidiaries. The effectiveness with which IHRM and the firm manages these issues goes a long way toward determining the success or failure of the venture.

Stage 5 of the Internationalization Process

Operations through International Joint Ventures (IJVs)

In recent years, the structure of choice for many businesses, including firms such as Kellogg[10] and Jaguar Land Rover,[11] as they go international, is the international joint venture, in which two or more firms (at least one from each of at least two countries) create a new business entity (the joint venture) with shared ownership and managerial responsibilities. IJVs have become extremely common and are covered in more detail in Chapter 4.

Operations through International Mergers and Acquisitions (IM&As)

For many MNEs and industries, IM&A is the preferred market entry method in both developed and emerging markets in order to most easily consolidate the scope of activities and the parent firms' positions in the global marketplace. Even so, foreign acquisitions often face national (local) economic protectionism sentiments and anti-trust laws. Similar to IJVs, IM&As are discussed in detail in Chapter 4.

Operations through International Alliances, Partnerships, and Consortia

These are defined as informal or formal partnerships or agreements that do not result in an independent legal entity. Firms using these methods do not necessarily replace their wholly owned subsidiaries. But rather they develop less formal structures, such as alliances, partnerships (e.g., in research and development projects), and other forms of linkages to operate internationally. Alliances are discussed more fully in Chapter 4.

Auxiliary Methods of Internationalization

In addition to the above methods, organizations can also use a variety of auxiliary methods to internationalize their operations. Auxiliary methods refer to approaches firms can use to further internationalize their operations at any stage. Figure 2.3 illustrates two of the most popular methods, *outsourcing*[12] and *off-shoring*.[13]

Outsourcing

This is a form of sub-contracting. Beginning in the 1990s, firms began to sub-contract on a major scale with foreign firms to do more than produce their products. With the development of computers and the Internet, making long-distance control easier, firms began to contract out other business processes, such as information technology and business processes including call centers, accounting, claims processing, customer service, and data analysis, to other firms in their home country and in other countries. Typically, the initial reason for outsourcing to a third party (whether a single function or an entire business process) was to reduce costs, but improving quality (because the service provider specializes in the outsourced function) and freeing company resources for greater focus on core competencies have also become reasons given for outsourcing. The term "outsourcing" was developed to describe this process of contracting with an external firm to provide products or services that would otherwise be completed internally.

In all cases, outsourcing success depends on three factors:

- Executive-level support in the client organization for the outsourcing mission;
- Ample communication to affected employees;

■ The client's ability to manage its service providers, ensuring delivery of quality service and support to the client and to customers.

The outsourcing professionals in charge of the work on both the client and provider sides (including HRM) need a combination of skills (all in a cross-cultural setting) in such areas as negotiation, communication, project management, human resource management (employee assignment and management, compensation and benefits, training, employee relations, performance management, etc.), and the ability to develop and understand the terms and conditions of the contracts and agreements.

Off-shoring

Often the terms off-shoring and outsourcing are used interchangeably. However, as originally conceived, the concepts have different meanings. As used here, off-shoring differs from outsourcing in that off-shoring involves the relocation of one or more aspects of a firm's business processes to a location in another country for the purpose, at least initially, of lowering costs. That is, the function is now performed by an entity owned by the firm but staffed with foreign personnel in an off-shore location (although sometimes at least some of the employees are relocated from the home locale). This can include any business process, such as operations, manufacturing, or services. So, the unit performing the process in a foreign country is still a part of the parent firm and the employees are employees of the parent. Thus the HR responsibilities of staffing, training, compensating, employee relations, and performance management are the same, albeit in another country's legal system and culture, as they are with the function being performed "at home."

Though off-shoring (and off-shore outsourcing) saves businesses labor costs as well as other expenses associated with personnel, it also contributes to an atmosphere of anxiety among workers who feel their jobs are being threatened.[1]

The primary issues that companies should consider when they think about relocating operations or services off-shore are:

■ organization's expertise in managing remote locations;
■ caliber and skill sets of the foreign labor force;
■ cost of labor, language skills on both sides;
■ level of technology use and capability;
■ cost and reliability at the foreign location;
■ country infrastructure;
■ political stability;
■ enforceability of intellectual property rights and business contracts;
■ general maturity of the business environment.[2]

Obviously, many of these issues are of primary focus for IHRM and thus must be understood by IHRM, and the IHRM department must develop the expertise to deal effectively with them.

1 Outsourcing—what is outsourcing? Retrieved from www.sourcingmag.com, 12/11/2006.
2 Definition retrieved (2014) from http://en.wikipedia.org and www.investordictionary.com. See also, Blinder, A.E. (2006). Offshoring: The next Industrial Revolution? *Foreign Affairs*, 85(2), 113–128; Erber, G., and Sayed-Ahmed, A. (2005). Offshore outsourcing—A global shift in the present IT industry. *Intereconomics*, 40(2), 100–112; and Friedman, T.L. (2005). *The World Is Flat: A Brief History of the Twenty-First Century*, New York: Farrar, Straus and Giroux.

FIGURE 2.3 Auxiliary Methods of Internationalization

Regus Professional Services and SBC International in Hong Kong are two examples of firms that provide service centers for international firms located or headquartered in Hong Kong, offering suites of services ranging from financial administration duties, such as accounting and payroll, to office space, photocopying, human resources, and trusted in-house advice on issues such as local employment law, company registration services, trademark registration, taxation, etc.[14] By helping foreign firms in Asia to outsource these types of services, firms like Regus and SBC help these firms make the transition to becoming culturally effective organizations.

The Born-global Firm

Although many existing firms internationalize through stages, some new enterprises, especially but not exclusively in the IT industry, are *born global* and almost immediately operate across the globe. The reasons they operate in key global markets from their inceptions essentially stem from the nature of their products (Internet products, IT applications, and other highly specialized products with global niches), the global networking and possible partnering on projects of the engineers and scientists involved, and the marketing by these firms through the Internet. In addition, the lowering of market entry barriers as a result of the democratization of the sources of competitive advantage (venture capital, IT resources, intellectual capital, etc.) in a flat world also provides global access. The IHRM activities of these firms are focused primarily on frequent international business travel of key individuals and legal protection of intellectual property rights (patents and trademarks) in the various countries in which they operate, the hiring of key local staff, and the management of international project teams for local client service. As mentioned in the first chapter, when any firm creates a website (announcing either a product or service)—it is global. Anyone, anywhere, can (and will) access that site and some will want to buy the site's products or services. A "classic" example of this involves the experiences of Amazon.com when they initially went "live" with their website. On the first day of operation, Amazon received inquiries and orders from dozens of countries, a situation they had not anticipated. In addition, as suggested earlier, many "born global" enterprises are created by people from multiple countries who have met each other online or at global professional or trade conferences who decide to work together in a new enterprise to use their joint skills and ideas.

IHRM and the Evolution of Internationalization

The point of the above discussion is to demonstrate that businesses typically pass through a number of stages as they increase their degree of internationalization, although this pattern is changing with the increase of service businesses and the development of internet-based and dot.com businesses that can follow different patterns and because of the increased use of cross-border partnerships and alliances. Not all businesses pass through all of these stages as they progress from being purely domestic firms to global ones. In general, though, most companies experience most of these stages. These stages are important to the discussion of IHRM because each stage makes unique demands on the HR department. The HRM function in a firm just beginning to internationalize faces very different responsibilities and challenges than does the IHRM department in a multinational firm with several worldwide subsidiaries.

As firms increase their levels of international activity, their organizational structures (discussed in the next chapter) and IHRM responsibilities become increasingly complex. Many older, large multinational (particularly manufacturing) firms that now have numerous subsidiaries all over the world began their foreign activities by exporting. As this stage became successful for them, they typically proceeded to establish sales offices overseas to market their exports. Where and when the sales offices were able to develop sufficiently large markets, plants to assemble imported parts were established, and, finally, the complete product was manufactured locally, sometimes for local sales and sometimes for export. These overseas operations typically mimicked the firm's domestic operations. Eventually, then, these firms have moved toward stages 4 and 5 of the evolution process.

In some ways this is a simplistic view of the development of international firms. In recent years, new patterns have developed. Some firms have used complete assembly or manufacturing plants as their means of initial entry to certain countries, normally to take advantage of cheap labor or sources of material, manufacturing products for export, such as is often the case for American and Asian firms in the maquiladora sector of the Mexican economy. Others have internationalized through sub-contracting or licensing their manufacturing. Still others have used franchising or joint ventures or partnerships to internationalize. And still others acquire their foreign operations directly. Of course, as soon as firms put up websites to offer (or even just to describe) their products or services, they become international immediately as they receive foreign inquiries and orders online. Many firms, of course, end up relying on some combination of these entry strategies.

The pattern of development experienced in different industries also varies widely. Businesses in extraction industries, such as oil and mining, set up foreign subsidiaries to manage their extraction (and sometimes processing) operations. Banks, such as Citibank, or insurance companies, such as Lloyd's, may initially locate in a foreign country in order to provide services to home-country clients who are active in the foreign country. Firms such as McDonald's typically sell franchises to local individuals, but often have to first prepare an infrastructure in foreign locations in order to provide their foreign businesses with the quality and types of inputs needed before they establish their local outlets. And department store or grocery store chains, such as Walmart, CarreFour, Toys "R" Us, Ikea, or Safeway, may acquire existing similar businesses or enter foreign markets by building new stores similar to those in their home countries.

MNE BUSINESS STRATEGY

As shown in Figure 2.2, firms in stage 4 and beyond become a complex system of linked units that includes at least a headquarters and several geographically dispersed subsidiaries. An MNE's business strategy provides a direction for managing the various subsidiaries. The nature of an MNE's business strategy is primarily guided by the extent of *integration* and/*or local responsiveness* required by the firm to manage its worldwide operations.[15] Integration versus local responsiveness refers to the varying degree of required interconnectedness of the MNE's various subsidiaries with each other and with headquarters. Integration is defined as the extent to which the subsidiaries and the headquarters develop a unified whole and can thus provide the MNE with a variety of competitive advantages such as economies of scale (being able to utilize all of the firm's global resources), improved quality, and standardization.[16] In contrast, local responsiveness is defined as the extent to which subsidiaries respond to local differences, which involves the modification of products or services in order to fully meet local customer needs, respond to local competition and culture, remain compliant with various government regulations, more readily attract local employees, and penetrate local business networks.[17]

Integration and local responsiveness form a framework (see Figure 2.4) that can be used to describe an MNE's business strategy.[18] The horizontal axis shows the degree of local responsiveness (from low to high). The vertical axis shows the degree of integration (from low to high). This framework highlights the conflicting demands on MNEs in terms of these two countervailing forces (integration versus local responsiveness) and can be used to categorize the strategy of an MNE into four types:[19] 1) *International*; 2) *Multi-domestic*; 3) *Global*; and 4) *Transnational*. The following provides a brief overview of these types of MNE business strategies:

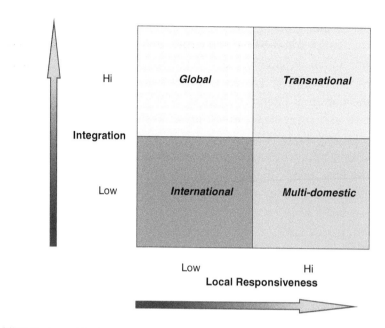

FIGURE 2.4 MNE Business Strategy

Adapted from: Bartlet, C., Ghoshal, S., and Beamish, P. (2010). *Transnational Management: Text, Cases and Readings in Cross-Border Management*, Boston: Irwin McGraw Hill; Bartlet, C., and Ghoshal, S. (2002). *Managing Across Borders. The Transnational Solution*, Boston, MA: Harvard Business School Press.

International Business Strategy

This is the simplest business strategy, requiring quite limited local responsiveness as well as quite limited integration. An organization with this strategy markets and sells the same product or service locally and internationally. This is the type of strategy that begins with export or import and may be limited to licensing or sub-contracting. It typically involves no overseas offices or operations, other than possibly small sales offices.

Multi-domestic Business Strategy

MNEs with this strategy use an approach that responds to the high needs, values, and demands of the local market. This strategy is mostly used by MNEs with a multi-domestic organizational structure (see Chapter 3). With subsidiaries in multiple countries, these subsidiaries typically operate independently within each country, independently of operations in other countries, and often fairly independently, even, of the parent company headquarters. In this strategy, MNEs generally view each national market as a specialized market for its particular subsidiaries' products and services. Examples of organizations using this type of strategy include Nestlé and Bridgestone.[20]

As independent as subsidiaries in this approach often become, the organization's operations in a number of countries may reach such size and importance that the firm begins to see a need for an increased level of integration with headquarters—on at least a *regional basis*. At this point, the MNE may coordinate its major country subsidiaries with *regional headquarters* in order to more effectively manage its international operations. The regional operations are normally created through an assumption that countries within a region share some common characteristics such as cultures, geographic proximity, or stage of economic development. See Case Study 2.1 (end of the chapter) which tells the internationalization story of one well-known automotive firm—Ford Motor Company. It built auto manufacturing plants in many countries early in its history and early in the history of the automobile industry, illustrating how many firms have developed into global firms over the last 100 years and how these firms created—largely through trial and error and response to ever-changing economic circumstances—the many approaches to the conduct of international business.

Global Business Strategy

MNEs with this strategy take a unified approach that is implemented for all countries regardless of their cultural and national differences. Thus there is a high degree of centralization or integration. Products and services will be increasingly designed for and marketed to customers all over the world. This strategy is mostly implemented by MNEs through a global organizational structure (see Chapter 3). The subsidiaries are tightly connected to the headquarters, and are heavily dependent on resources, brand identities, ideas, policies, and know-how from the headquarters. Examples of organizations using type of stragey include Lenova and Infosys.[21]

The experiences of global MNEs suggest that running a global company is an order of magnitude more complicated than managing a multinational or international firm. The global corporation looks at the whole world as one market. It manufactures, conducts research, raises capital, and buys supplies wherever it can do the job best. It keeps in touch with technology and market trends all around the world. National boundaries and regulations tend to be irrelevant, or at least a mere hindrance. Corporate headquarters might be anywhere.

Transnational Business Strategy

MNEs with this strategy use an approach that attempts to maximize both responsiveness and integration. They are both global and multi-domestic at the same time. In the sense that the transnational firm has a global focus, it is similar to the global firm, described in the previous section. But it differs from the global firm in that, rather than developing global products and services, the transnational works hard to localize, to be seen not as a global firm but as a local firm, albeit one that draws upon global expertise, technology, and resources. The transnational firm operates as a global network, with each subsidiary given responsibility related to its capabilities and strategic mission. This strategy is mostly implemented by firms through a transnational organizational structure (see Chapter 3). Examples of companies using this type of strategy include Procter & Gamble, and Bertelsmann.[22]

Headquarters' International Orientation and MNE Business Strategy

One aspect of MNE's business strategy that has been relatively well discussed and studied involves the orientation of senior executives, usually referred to with terms such as ethnocentrism, regio-centrism, poly-centrism, and geocentrism.[23] The key strategic issue in these orientations (or mindsets) is the degree of domination of the MNE headquarters over subsidiary management and HR practices as compared to the degree of localization of subsidiary practices. Normally these orientations are explained in the context of progressive development over time from one mindset to another, as a firm develops greater international experience and sophistication. There are three different types of orientations, as illustrated in Figure 2.5: Ethnocentrism,[24] poly-centrism or regio-centrism, and geocentrism.

Overall, it would be expected that IHRM policies and practices would be as centralized (similar to integration) or decentralized (similar to local responsiveness) as the overall strategic mindset of the firm. In firms with an ethnocentric orientation, IHRM practices for international operations tend to copy parent company practices and are very centralized. In firms with a poly-centric mindset, IHRM practices tend to be decentralized and local subsidiaries tend to be much more likely to be left alone to follow local HRM practice. As shown in Case 2.1 at the end of the chapter, Henry Ford had a very poly-centric mindset, although initially he merely reproduced his original operations from the US in his foreign operations. And in firms with a geocentric orientation, IHRM practices tend to be more

THE ORIENTATION OF SENIOR EXECUTIVES Degree of domination of the MNE headquarters over subsidiary management and HR practices as compared to the degree of localization of subsidiary practices		
ETHNOCENTRISM This is the initial orientation of many managers, especially those from a more homogeneous national population and culture or from a country with a strong patriotic culture. In this orientation, managers use a home-country standard as a reference in managing international activities. The outlook is one of centralized decision-making and high control over operations. Managers with such a mindset are likely to follow an international business strategy or a global business strategy of maintaining control from the home-country and parent-firm headquarters, and replicating home-country systems and procedures and structure abroad.	**POLY-CENTRISM OR REGIO-CENTRISM** Poly-centrism or regio-centrism is the next level of development or evolution of the managerial orientation. Here, as international investment and involvement increase, host-country cultures and practices assume increased salience. This poly-centric mindset may be expanded to include a number of similar countries in a region, with host-country standards increasingly used as a reference point in managing company operations. The strategies typically followed are likely to be multinational (or multi-domestic) strategies that emphasize decentralized and autonomous operations of wholly owned subsidiaries.	**GEOCENTRISM** When a firm reaches this level of orientation, a geocentric mindset will have developed and been adopted. Here the managerial outlook is one of creating a global network and a preference for following a transnational strategy that is integrative and interdependent among various elements of the global organization. With a geocentric orientation, IHRM practices tend to be more eclectic, borrowing best practices from around the world, rather than giving preference necessarily to either headquarters or local practices.

FIGURE 2.5 Headquarters' International Orientation (Senior Executives)

eclectic, borrowing best practices from around the world, rather than giving preference necessarily to either headquarters or local practices.

IHRM STRATEGY

As IHRM becomes more involved with helping organizations be successful in their international endeavors, it hopefully will develop a strategic focus itself. That is, it will develop its own strategies to hire, manage, and retain the best employees (employees who will help achieve the organization's global strategies) throughout the organization's international business activities, and it will thus contribute to the firm's overall international strategic planning.

   IHRM strategy is defined as the creation and implementation of IHR practices that help achieve an MNE's international vision and objectives, i.e., its business strategy. It also involves the strategic management of the HR function and department itself. Similar to the MNE's business strategy, a firm's IHRM strategy serves as a guiding principle that helps to shape and govern the firm's international activities, particularly as they relate to the firm's HR, worldwide. IHRM strategies are implemented through IHRM policies and practices—which are the subjects of the chapters of Section 3.

IHRM Strategy Formulation

Historically, basic trade-offs have come into play when managers have considered where in the organization certain decisions should be made. For IHRM, the central trade-off pits pressures for *centralization* against the need for *decentralization*. Centralization is very similar to the notion of integration and refers to the concentration of authority and decision making toward the top (HQs) of an organization. Decentralization is very similar to the notion of local responsiveness and is defined as the dispersion of authority and decision making to operating units throughout the organization. In the international context, this involves the degree of centralization or decentralization of corporate authority and decision making throughout a firm's global operations.

   This tension between integration (centralization) and differentiation (localization) is becoming a major dilemma for IHRM and large global firms. As mentioned previously firms must become simultaneously more highly differentiated and more integrated or coordinated. Local nationals may feel that they can run operations in their own countries, even though their firms now require a global perspective and global qualifications. Local laws and practices may dictate certain HR practices and yet an international perspective may require different approaches to routine HR responsibilities.

   MNEs are frequently both praised and criticized for being tools of global integration. There are many forces for *convergence*, or the use of parent-company policies and procedures throughout a firm's global operations. MNEs face strong incentives to maximize economies of scale in research and development, purchasing, production, and markets, and encounter relatively low barriers to the dissemination of technologies and best practices.

These incentives and low barriers encourage the continued use in foreign locales of practices and procedures found to work well "at home." Of course, all of this is supported by overall firm strategies to internationalize and country cultures that encourage the view that our (company and country) way is best.

On the other hand, many firms in the past evolved in such a way in their international operations that their local and regional offices became, in many ways, independent organizations (again, refer to the Ford Motor Company story in Case 2.1). Even in markets where adaptation to local circumstances is mandatory, MNEs work hard to bridge the gap between global and local and to identify ways of reconciling global integration, e.g., in production, with the required extent of local responsiveness, e.g., in marketing and product design and in management and HR practices. Thus MNEs function as motors of a process of international convergence that may ultimately make national differences rooted in institutional and cultural characteristics less relevant or even disappear.

In addition to convergence due to company-wide policies, though, there are also enduring sources of *divergence*, such as attempts by local subsidiaries to become centers of excellence. Furthermore, there is considerable evidence demonstrating that cultural and institutional differences play a role in the manner in which seemingly universal techniques and procedures (globally applied) are implemented (in varying ways) within differing countries. In the end, however, the critical strategic decision for the IHRM department (as well as for the business as a whole) is the resolution of the dilemma created by the conflict between centralization for control and international (internal) control of policies and practices and decentralization to meet local requirements (localization). As was expressed in the first chapter, there is no easy answer to this choice: should the MNE superimpose practices (e.g., HRM practices) on its international subsidiaries and other forms of operations (with the local HR office run by an HR manager from the parent firm), or should it allow subsidiaries to follow local customs, laws, and practices as much as possible (with the local HR office usually run by a local national HR manager)?

The experiences of long-term multinational firms suggest that the trend is to move toward more local control and management over time, which is consistent with the pattern described in the first part of this chapter. And yet, as is discussed in greater detail later in the book, successful multinational firms have found ways (such as cross-national management training, cross-national assignments for management development and promotions, and cross-national project teams) to develop a common set of values and culture to ensure worldwide pursuit of a common corporate vision and objectives. Indeed, some firms are seeking ways to develop globally consistent HR practices throughout all of their operations as a way to reinforce a common corporate culture.

IHRM Strategies and MNE Business Strategies

The overall effectiveness of an IHRM strategy is contingent on the context in which it is used. An IHRM strategy's effect on organizational effectiveness is always dependent on how well the IHRM strategy *fits* with and supports an MNE's business strategy.

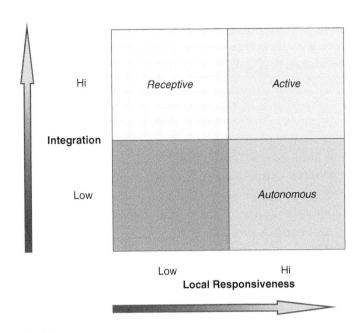

FIGURE 2.6 MNE IHRM Strategy

Adapted from Hannon, J., Huang, I., and Jaw, B. (1995). International human resource strategy and its determinants: The case of subsidiaries in Taiwan. *Journal of International Business Studies, 26*, 531–554.

Similar to an MNE's business strategy, IHRM strategy has to deal with the issue of whether to standardize IHRM policies and practices from headquarters, or to localize them to meet local conditions, or do both (e.g., combination of core policies established by HQs with localized practices to accommodate local culture and practices).

There are three types of IHRM strategies[25] that can be aligned with MNE business strategy and headquarters' international orientation (see Figure 2.6).

Autonomous IHRM Strategy[26]

As shown in Figure 2.6, this type of IHRM strategy has a low degree of global integration and a high degree of local responsiveness. Each subsidiary has the freedom to develop and implement its own IHRM policies and practices that support local rules and conditions. An MNE with this type of IHRM strategy most likely has a decentralized HR function with a small HR department at headquarters and the majority of key HR decisions made at the subsidiary level.[27] This IHRM strategy is most suitable when an MNE has a multi-domestic business strategy and a poly-centric or regio-centric IHR orientation.

Receptive IHRM Strategy[28]

As illustrated in Figure 2.6, this form of IHRM strategy has a high degree of global integration and a low degree of local responsiveness. Each subsidiary is tightly connected with headquarters with very little freedom to adapt to the local conditions. An MNE with this type of IHRM strategy is more likely to have a centralized HR function with a large HR department that exercises considerable control over key HR decisions.[29] This IHRM strategy is most suitable when an MNE has a global business strategy and an ethnocentric IHR orientation.

Active IHRM Strategy[30]

As Figure 2.6 shows, this type of IHRM strategy has a high degree of global integration and a high degree of local responsiveness. This strategy balances both, global integration and local responsiveness. An MNE with this type of IHRM strategy is more likely have a transition HR function with considerably more control over HR decision making than autonomous IHRM strategy but less than in a receptive IHRM strategy.[31] HR at corporate headquarters and HR at the subsidiary try to balance the control over HR decision making. This strategy is most suitable when an MNE has a transnational business strategy and a geocentric HR orientation.

RESEARCH ON STRATEGIC IHRM

Research on SIHRM has been growing in recent years.[32] This research has extended our understanding of SIHRM, yet there is still much that is not known about the factors that influence it. The existing research on SIHRM has found, as would be expected, that local culture and national managerial orientation influence the nature of HR practice; that the degree of global mindset influences the nature of an MNE's global strategy; and that global strategy influences the degree of global focus in the HR strategy.[33] In addition, it has been found that following appropriate global HR practices—rather than only using the parent firm's HR practices—was associated with the later stages of an organization's life cycle (as the MNE matures) and with better organizational performance.[34] Large global Japanese and European MNEs were found to be more likely to pursue global HR practices than was the case for similar American firms. Or, stated the other way around, American firms are more likely to pursue localization of IHR than are their Japanese or European counterparts.[35]

In general, this research has dealt with some form of linkage between headquarters' (corporate) international focus (for example, their degree of ethnocentrism or geocentrism) and HR policy and practice in foreign subsidiaries. If HR strategy must implement corporate strategy, then the extent to which HR practice in foreign subsidiaries reflects corporate international business strategy is an important consideration.[36] But as is typically observed by researchers, the examination of IHR strategy is in its infancy. Even though a number of models have been put forward to speculate on the possible linkages (with limited supporting data), there is still much more to examine to understand the complexities of SIHRM. Both the responses and the choices are more numerous and complex in practice than these models have yet demonstrated.

Models/Frameworks for Understanding SIHRM

In an effort to understand the role of IHRM in MNEs, scholars and researchers have suggested several SIHRM models or frameworks. Each of these has some very useful and interesting contributions to IHRM. Here we present one of the earliest models[37] for describing how IHRM is connected to the different strategic requirements of the MNE.

Figure 2.7 illustrates a model with five parts:

1 strategic MNE components;
2 exogenous factors;
3 endogenous factors;
4 IHRM issues, functions, and policies and practices; and
5 MNE concerns and goals.

Taken as a whole, the model enables researchers and consultants to discuss various components of SIHRM and their relationships.

Strategic MNE Components

This part of the model includes two components: the inter-unit linkages and internal operations. Inter-unit linkages focus on how MNEs manage the different geographically dispersed operating units and describe how they balance the competing pressures for differentiation

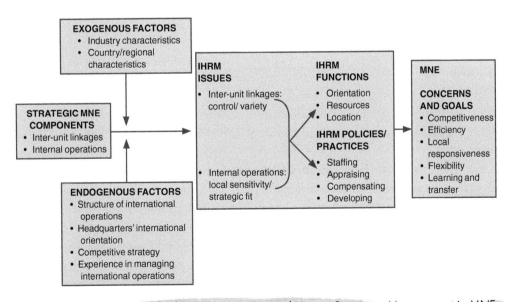

FIGURE 2.7 Integrative Framework of Strategic International Human Resources Management in MNEs

Source: Adapted from Schuler, R., Dowling, P., and DeCieri, H. (1993). An integrative framework of strategic international human resource management. *International Journal of Human Resource Management, 4,* 722–776

and integration. Internal operations, in contrast, describe how each unit operates within its local environment, laws, politics, culture, economy, and society. Section 1 of this book discusses issues related to this part of the model.

Exogenous Factors

These factors describe forces that are external to the firm that are largely beyond an MNE's control but can create challenges that affect an organization's IHRM issues, functions, policies and practices. These exogenous factors can include national culture, economic conditions, political system, legal environment, and workforce characteristics.

Section 2 of this book discusses issues related to this part of the model.

Endogenous Factors

These factors describe the issues and concerns that are internal to the firm and include structure of the organization, stage of internationalization, business strategy, and headquarters' international orientation.

The above three parts of the model affect IHRM function and associated issues, policies and practices. Indeed, the key strategic MNE objective is to balance the needs of variety (diversity), coordination, and control for purposes of global competitiveness, flexibility, and organizational learning while controlling and coordinating that variety. However, the nature of this balance is expected to vary depending on the exogenous and endogenous factors.

IHRM Issues

IHRM issues are HR issues that result from the inter-unit and intra-unit needs and challenges. As mentioned earlier the MNE has components spread across several nations, but it still remains a single enterprise and therefore must consider how to balance competing pressures for integration and local responsiveness. These issues of integration and local responsiveness are often facilitated by human resource management policies and practices, and therefore are important components in IHRM.

IHRM Functions

IHRM functions include the resources (time, energy, money) allocated to the human resource department or unit, and the location of those resources and HR decision making. The resources devoted to and the location of IHRM operations can be expected to vary considerably across MNEs and the IHRM function can take a variety of structural forms, including centralized, decentralized, and transition.

IHRM Policies and Practices

IHRM policies and practices involve the development of general guidelines on how individuals will be managed and specific HR initiatives or activities. This includes both formal policies of the organization and the actual daily practices that employees experience and include those related to planning, staffing, appraising, compensating, training and developing, and labor relations. Section 3 of this book focuses on this part of the model, discussing the core policies and practices of IHRM.

MNE Concerns and Goals

This part of the model can be defined in terms of utilizing and integrating appropriate IHRM practices and policies that enhance overall performance of the MNE on several criteria, both short term and long term. The five criteria include:

- Global competitiveness (How can IHRM policies and practices help provide competitive advantage?)
- Efficiency (How much can IHRM help make the MNE more efficient by delivering the most effective human resources that will deliver world-class products and services worldwide?)
- Local responsiveness (How much can IHRM help the MNE be locally responsive and globally competitive at the same time?)
- Flexibility (How much can IHRM help the MNE be more flexible in adapting to changing conditions—internal and external?)
- Organizational and transfer of learning (How much can IHRM facilitate learning and transfer of this learning across geographically dispersed units?)

The chapters of Section 3 focus on the answers to these questions, on how IHRM policies and practices help the firm achieve these critical outcomes.

CONCLUSION

This chapter presented the concept of strategic international human resource management. The chapter described the evolution of the MNE in terms of various stages of internationalization and the methods firms use to enter international markets. The integration-local responsiveness framework was used to describe how MNEs form business strategies and how the business strategies impact and are impacted by IHRM. The chapter then explained how IHRM strategy is formed and described the three types of IHRM strategies that are normally found in organizations. Finally, the chapter closed with a discussion of advanced topics in SIHRM.

DISCUSSION QUESTIONS

1 How has the multinational enterprise evolved? How have the changes in MNEs affected IHRM?

2 What are the various choices that MNEs have for entry into international business? How do the functions of HR vary with these various choices?

3 What is the link between SIHRM and IHRM? Why is it important for IHRM to be strategic?

4 How does IHRM strategy vary with an MNE's business strategy?

5 What are some of the IHRM challenges faced by an MNE with a transnational business strategy?

6 What are the pros and cons of centralization and decentralization of the IHRM function?

CASE STUDY 2.1: The Early Evolution of Manufacturing Firms: Ford Motor Company Goes International (USA)

Ford Motor Company has been in business for over 100 years and when it comes to a global mindset, Ford is ahead of most of its competitors, although this was not always the case.

Early in its history, Ford was like many large firms, which often sent people off to other major countries to set up companies just like the one back home. The first Henry Ford, the founder of the Ford Motor Company, was in many ways an internationalist, because within a few years of establishing his company in the US he was opening manufacturing and assembly plants all over the world—the first of which was a Model T assembly plant in Trafford Park, England, in 1911—that were essentially smaller versions of the original plant in Detroit. Over the years Ford evolved into a collection of local country and regional fiefdoms.

But by the mid-1920s (even earlier in some countries), a sense of local pride had developed in the Ford plants in many countries around the world. These countries all began to develop their own automotive companies. Suddenly there were local automotive companies in the UK, in France, Germany, Australia, all making their own vehicles. Nations wanted to assert their independence and saw the automotive industry as a means of investing in their own economies. Indeed, some early automotive pioneers in other countries even began to export their own cars to other countries as well as develop their own plants elsewhere. The Europeans exported, the Americans exported, the Japanese exported—that was the way the competitive game was being played. This was the beginnings of the "multi-domestic" structure for large multinational corporations, as described in this chapter.

In the 1960s, though, regionalism began to develop with the emergence of the European Common Market, NAFTA, ASEAN, and other regional trading groups. Countries kept their own political systems and social values but formed economic trading blocs. So . . . big companies established regional headquarters within the various major trading blocs. Ford Europe, Ford Asia-Pacific, and Ford South America were established in this period. This was when most of the regional and functional fiefdoms (with each region becoming very independent) became firmly entrenched at Ford. (This is what is referred to in the text as the "regional" corporate structure, an extension of the "multi-domestic" structure.) The fiefdoms were excellent at what they did: they squeezed every last ounce of efficiency out of the regional model. For example, back in the period of nationalism, Ford had multiple accounting activities around the world—there were 15 in Europe alone. The regional model got it down to four: one in Europe, one in the US, one in Asia-Pacific, and one in South America. But even with that efficiency, Ford felt that the model didn't work anymore.

Today Ford is moving to a fourth stage of economic evolution with the globalization of all aspects of its international operations: accounting, capital, communications, economic policy, trade policy, human resources, marketing, advertising, brands, etc. The auto industry around the world has become globalized. Germany and Japan produce cars in the US, Korea produces cars in Eastern Europe, the US produces cars in Mexico and China, and India, Malaysia, China, and Mexico export cars and parts throughout the world. And there is ongoing consolidation of auto companies throughout the world as firms such as Renault (France) acquired Nissan (Japan), Ford (US) acquired Volvo (Sweden), Tata (India) acquired Jaguar (UK/US), and Ford has just announced that Geely (China) is acquiring Volvo (Sweden). Ford now manufactures and distributes automobiles in at least 120 markets (some articles suggest 200 markets!) on six continents, with 176,000 employees (a major downsizing from over 350,000 in the last decade) in more than 80 plants worldwide (a downsizing from about 110 plants less than a decade ago). In addition, the automotive industry has become an electronics-driven industry. It is increasingly a business that requires huge investments in technology and intellectual capital, not only for constant innovations in development and manufacturing, but in automobiles themselves. And now it is technology and human capital that have globalized.

Sources: www.Ford.com (2014); www.NYTimes.com/FordMotorCompany (2014); Lapid, K. (2006). Outsourcing and offshoring under the general agreement on trade in services. *Journal of World Trade*, *40*(2), 341–364; Neff, J. (2006). Ford announces corporate realignment. *Autoblog*, December 14; Wetlaufer, S. (1999). Driving change: An interview with Ford Motor Company's Jacques Nasser. *Harvard Business Review*, March–April, 77–80; and Whitney, K. (2006). Ford: Driving learning and developing the "Way Forward." *Chief Learning Officer*, *5*(5), 44–47.

NOTES

1 Source: "10 Quotes on leadership from Mark Zuckerberg," see http://www.ceo.com/technology_and_innovation/10-quotes-on-leadership-from-mark-zuckerberg/. Accessed Nov. 2, 2014.
2 Sheehan, M., and Sparrow, P. (2012). Introduction: Global human resource management and economic change: A multiple level of analysis research agenda. *The International Journal of Human Resource Management*, *23*(12), 2393–2403; Björkman, I., Stahl, G., and Morris, S. (2012). *Handbook of Research in IHRM*. Edward Elgar Publishing, Cheltenham, UK; Edwards, P.K., Sánchez, R., Tregaskis, O., Levesque, C., McDonnell, A., and Quintanilla, J. (2013). Human resource management practices in the multinational company: A test of system, societal, and dominance effects. *Industry and Labour Relations Review*, *66*, 588–696; Zheng, C. (2013). Critiques and extension of strategic international human resource management framework for dragon multinationals. *Asia Pacific Business Review*, *19*(1), 1–15.
3 Evans, P., Pucik, V., and Bjorkman, I. (2010). *The Global Challenge: Frameworks for International Human Resource Management*, New York: McGraw-Hill/Irwin; Brockbank, W. (1997). HR's future on the way to a presence, *Human Resource Management*, Spring, *36*(1), 65–69.
4 Ibid.; Vance, C.M., and Paik, Y. (2011). *Managing a Global Workforce: Challenges and Opportunities in International Human Resource Management*, 2nd ed., London and New York: M.E. Sharpe; Albrecht, M.H. (ed.) (2001). *International HRM: Managing Diversity in the Workplace*, Oxford, UK: Blackwell Publishers; Marquardt, M.J. (1999). *The Global Advantage: How World-Class Organizations Improve Performance Through Globalization*, Houston: Gulf Publishing; Harttig, M.A., Strozik, M., and Mukherjee, A. (2010). Global workforce planning. *Benefits & Compensation International*, *40*(1), 19; Lertxundi, A., and Landeta, J. (2012). The dilemma facing multinational enterprises: Transfer or adaptation of their human resource management systems. *The International Journal of Human Resource Management*, *23*(9), 1788.
5 Thompson, A.A., Jr., and Strickland, A.J., III (1998). *Strategic Management: Concepts and Cases*, 10th ed., New York: McGraw-Hill.
6 Ibid.

7 Björkman, I., Stahl, G., and Morris, S. (2012). *Handbook of Research in IHRM*. Cheltenham, UK: Edward Elgar Publishing; Bremmer, I. (2014). The new rules of globalization. *Harvard Business Review, 92*(1/2), 103–107; Walker, J.W. (2001). Are we global yet? in Albrecht, M.H. (ed.), *International HRM*: Managing Diversity in Workplace, Oxford, UK: Blackwell Publishers, pp. 71–75; Bartlett, C. (1983). How multinational organizations evolve, *Journal of Business Strategy*, Summer, *1*, 10–32; Dowling, P.J., Welch, D.E., and Schuler, R.S. (1999). *International Human Resource Management*, 3rd ed., Cincinnati, OH: South-Western College Publishing; Fadel, J.J., and Petti, M. (2001). International HR policy basics, in Albrecht, M.H. (ed.), *International HRM*, Oxford, UK: Blackwell Publishers, pp. 76–78; Harzing, A.-H. (1995). Strategic planning in multinational corporations, in Harzing, A.-H., and Ruysseveldt, J.V. (eds.), *International Human Resource Management*, 2nd ed., London: Sage Publications, pp. 33–64.

8 Adapted from, A new corporate focus, *Financial Times*, Feb. 5, 2013, p. 14 (Business Life Section).

9 Lertxundi, A., and Landeta, J. (2012). The dilemma facing multinational enterprises: Transfer or adaptation of their human resource management systems. *The International Journal of Human Resource Management, 23*(9), 1788; Ando, N. (2011). Isomorphism and foreign subsidiary staffing policies. *Cross Cultural Management, 18*(2), 131–143; Colakoglu, S., Tarique, I., and Caligiuri, P. (2009). Towards a conceptual framework for the relationship between subsidiary staffing strategy and subsidiary performance. *The International Journal of Human Resource Management, 20*(6), 129; Collings, D.G., Scullion, H., and Morley, M.J. (2007). Changing patterns of global staffing in the multinational enterprise: Challenges to the conventional expatriate assignment and emerging alternatives. *Journal of World Business, 42*(2), 198; Peng, G.Z., and Beamish, P.W. (2014). MNC subsidiary size and expatriate control: Resource-dependence and learning perspectives. *Journal of World Business, 49*(1), 51–62.

10 Source: http://newsroom.kelloggcompany.com/2012–09–24-Kellogg-Company-And-Wilmar-International Limited-Announce-China-Joint-Venture.

11 Monaghan, A. (28 November 2014). Jaguar Land Rover seals Chinese joint venture, *The Telegraph, UK*. Retrieved from www.telegraph.co.uk.

12 See for example Ghauri, P.N., and Santangelo, G.D. (2012). Multinationals and the changing rules of competition: New challenges for IB research. *Management International Review*, (2), 145; Lapid, K. (2006). Outsourcing and offshoring under the General Agreement on Trade in Services, *Journal of World Trade, 40*(2), 431–364; Contractor, F.J. (2011). *Global Outsourcing and Offshoring: An Integrated Approach to Theory and Corporate Strategy*. Cambridge: Cambridge University Press; Robinson, M. and Kalakota, R. (2005). *Offshore Outsourcing: Business Models, ROI and Best Practices*, 2nd ed., Alpharetta, GA: Mivar Press; and Robinson, M., Kalakota, R. and Sharma, S. (2006). *Global Outsourcing: Executing an Onshore, Nearshore or Offshore Strategy*, Alpharetta, GA: Mivar Press.

13 See, for example, Linares-Navarro, E., Pedersen, T., and Pla-Barber, J. (2014). Fine slicing of the value chain and offshoring of essential activities: Empirical evidence from European multinationals. *Journal of Business Economics & Management, 15*(1), 111–134; Schwörer, T. (2013). Offshoring, domestic outsourcing and productivity: Evidence for a number of European countries. *Review of World Economics, 149*(1), 131–149; definition retrieved from http://en.wikipedia.org and www.investordictionary.com. See also, Blinder, A.E. (2006). Offshoring: The next industrial revolution?, *Foreign Affairs, 85*(2), 113–128; Erber, G., and Sayed-Ahmed, A. (2005). Offshore outsourcing—A global shift in the present IT industry, *Intereconomics, 40*(2), 100–112; and Friedman, T.L. (2007). *The World Is Flat: A Brief History of the Twenty-First Century*, New York: Farrar, Straus and Giroux.

14 Setting a trend for world to follow (2011), *South China Morning Post*, Feb. 7, downloaded from ProQuest at http://search.proquest.com/docview/849412056?accountid=13044.

15 See Bartlet, C., Ghoshal, S., and Beamish, P. (2010). *Transnational Management: Text, Cases and Readings in Cross-Border Management*, Boston: Irwin McGraw Hill; Bartlet, C., and Ghoshal, S. (2002). *Managing Across Borders. The Transnational Solution, Boston*, MA: Harvard Business School Press.

16 Bartlet, C., and Ghoshal, S. (2002). *Managing Across Borders. The Transnational Solution*, Boston, MA: Harvard Business School Press.

17 Ibid.

18 Harzing, A-W. (2000). An empirical analysis and extension of the Bartlett and Ghoshal typology of multinational companies, *Journal of International Business Studies*, *31*(1), 101–120; Harzing, A-H (2004). Strategy and structure of multinational companies, in Harzing, A-H, and Ruysseveldt, J. V. (eds.), *International Human Resource Management*, London, UK: Sage Publications, pp. 33–64; Bartlet, C., and Ghoshal, S. (2010). *Managing Across Borders. The Transnational Solution*, Boston, MA: Harvard Business School Press. Also see Drahokoupil, J. (2014). Decision-making in multinational corporations: Key issues in international business strategy. *Transfer: European Review of Labour & Research*, 20(2), 199–215.

19 Bartlet, C., and Ghoshal, S. (2002). *Managing Across Borders. The Transnational Solution*, Boston, MA: Harvard Business School Press; Harzing, A-W. (2000). An empirical analysis and extension of the Bartlett and Ghoshal typology of multinational companies, *Journal of International Business Studies*, *31*(1), 101–120; Harzing, A-H (2004). Strategy and structure of multinational companies, in Harzing, A-H and Ruysseveldt, J. V. (eds.), *International Human Resource Management*, London: Sage.

20 Rothaermel, F. (2013). *Strategic Management: Concepts and Cases*, New York: Irwin McGraw Hill.

21 Ibid.

22 Rothaermel, F. (2013).

23 Chakravarthy, B., and Perlmutter, H. V. (1985). Strategic planning for a global economy. *Columbia Journal of World Business*, Summer, 3–10; Kobrin, S.J. (1994). Is there a relationship between a geocentric mind-set and multinational strategy? *Journal of International Business Studies*, 25(3), 493–511; Perlmutter, H. V. (1969). The torturous evolution of the multinational corporation, *Columbia Journal of World Business*, January–February, 9–18.

24 See Story, J.P., Barbuto, J.E., Luthans, F., and Bovaird, J.A. (2014). Meeting the challenges of effective international HRM: Analysis of the antecedents of global mindset. *Human Resource Management*, 1, 31; Gupta, A.K., and Govindarajan, V. (2002). Cultivating a global mindset, *Academy of Management Executive*, 16, 116–125; Kedia, B.L., and Mukherji, A. (1999). Global managers: Developing a mindset for global competitiveness. *Journal of World Business*, 34, 230–251.

25 Hannon, J., Huang, I., and Jaw, B. (1995). International human resource strategy and its determinants: The case of subsidiaries in Tawian, *Journal of International Business Studies*, 26, 531–554.

26 Ibid.

27 See Scullion, H., and Paauwe, J. (2004). International human resource management: Recent developments in theory and empirical research, in Harzing, A. W. and Ruysseveldt, J. V., *International Human Resource Management*, London: Sage Publications, pp. 65–88.

28 Ibid.

29 Scullion, H., and Paauwe, J. (2004).

30 Ibid.

31 Ibid.

32 See, for example, Jackson, S.E., Schuler, R.S., and Jiang, K. (2014). An aspirational framework for strategic human resource management. *The Academy of Management Annals*, 8(1), 1–56; Caligiuri, P. (2014). Many moving parts: Factors influencing the effectiveness of HRM practices designed to improve knowledge transfer within MNCs. *Journal of International Business Studies*, 45(1), 63–72; Zheng, C. (2013). Critiques and extension of strategic international human resource management framework for dragon multinationals. *Asia Pacific Business Review*, 19(1), 1–15; Fan, D., Zhang, M., and Zhu, C. (2013). International human resource management strategies of Chinese multinationals operating abroad. *Asia Pacific Business Review*, 19(4), 526–541; Ananthram, S., and Chan, C. (2013). Challenges and strategies for global human resource executives: Perspectives from Canada and the United States. *European Management Journal*, 31(3), 22; Andersen, T.J., and Minbaeva, D. (2013). The role of human resource management in strategy making. *Human Resource Management*, 52(5), 809; An, D., Zhang, M.M., and Zhu, C.J. (2013). International human resource management strategies of Chinese multinationals operating abroad. *Asia Pacific Business Review*, 19(4), 526; Festing, M. (2012). Strategic human resource management in Germany: Evidence of convergence to the U.S. model, the European model, or a distinctive national

model? *The Academy of Management Perspectives*, 26(2), 37; Kramar, R., and Parry, E. (2014). Strategic human resource management in the Asia Pacific region: Similarities and differences? *Asia Pacific Journal of Human Resources*, 52(4), 400; Liang, X., Marler, J. H., and Cui, Z. (2012). Strategic human resource management in China: East meets West. *The Academy of Management Perspectives*, 26(2), 55; Sparrow, P. (2012). Globalising the international mobility function: The role of emerging markets, flexibility and strategic delivery models. *The International Journal of Human Resource Management*, 23(12), 2404; Clark, K., and Lengnick-Hall, M. L. (2012). MNC practice transfer: Institutional theory, strategic opportunities and subsidiary HR configuration. *International Journal of Human Resource Management*, 23(18), 3813–3837; De Cieri, H., and Dowling, P. J. (2012). Strategic human resource management in multinational enterprises: Developments and directions, in Stahl, G. K., Björkman, I., and Morris, S. S. (eds.), *Handbook of Research in International Human Resource Management*, 2nd ed., Northampton, MA: Edward Elgar Publishing, pp. 13–35; Chung, C., Bozkurt, Ö., and Sparrow, P. (2012). Managing the duality of IHRM: Unravelling the strategy and perceptions of key actors in South Korean MNCs. *International Journal of Human Resource Management*, 23(11), 2333–2353; Harvey, M., Fisher, R., McPhail, R., and Moeller, M. (2013). Aligning global organizations' human capital needs and global supply-chain strategies. *Asia Pacific Journal of Human Resources*, 51(1), 4; Perkins, S. J., and Shortland, S. M. (2006). *Strategic International Human Resource Management: Choices and Consequences in Multinational People Management*, 2nd ed., London: Kogan Page; Schuler, R. S., Budhwar, P. S., and Florkowski, G. W. (2002). International human resource management: Review and critique, *International Journal of Management Reviews*, 4 (1), 41–70; Schuler, R. S., Dowling, P. J., and De Cieri, H. (1993). An integrative framework of strategic international human resource management, *Journal of Management* 19(2), 419–459; Schuler, R. S., and Tarique, I. (2007). International HRM: A North American perspective, a thematic update and suggestions for future research, *International Journal of Human Resource Management*, 18(5), 717–744.

33 Beechler, S., Bird, A., and Raghuram, S. (1993). Linking business strategy and human resource management practices in multinational corporations: A theoretical framework, *Advances in International Comparative Management*, 8, 199–215; Hannon, J. M., Huang, I.-C., and Jaw, B.-S. (1995). International human resource strategy and its determinants: The case of subsidiaries in Taiwan, *Journal of International Business Studies*, third quarter, 531–554; Harris, H., and Holden, L. (2001). Between autonomy and control: Expatriate managers and strategic international human resource management in SMEs, Thunderbird, *International Business Review*, 43(1), 77–100; Kobrin, S. J. (1994). Is there a relationship between geocentric mindset and multinational strategy? *Journal of International Business Studies*, 25(3), 493–511; Lei, D., Slocum, J. W., Jr., and Slater, R. W. (1990). Global strategy and reward systems: The key roles of management development and corporate culture, *Organizational Dynamics*, 18, 63–77; Rosenzweig, P.M., and Nohria, N. (1994). Influences on human resource management practices in multinational corporations, *Journal of International Business Studies*, second quarter, 229–251; Sheridan, W. R. and Hansen, P. T. (1996). Linking international business and expatriate compensation strategies, *ACA Journal*, 5(2), 66–79.

34 Caligiuri, P.M., and Stroh, L. K. (1995). Multinational corporation management strategies and international human resource practices: Bringing international HR to the bottom line, *International Journal of Human Resource Management*, 6(3), 494–507; Milliman, J., Von Glinow, M. A., and Nathan, M. (1991). Organizational life cycles and strategic international human resource management in multinational companies. *Academy of Management Review*, 16, 318–339; Pucik, V., and Evans, P. (2004). *People Strategies for MNEs*, London: Routledge; Caligiuri, P.M., and Stroh, L. K. (1995). Multinational corporation management strategies and international human resources practices: Bringing HR to the bottom line. *International Journal of Human Resource Management*, 6, 494–507.

35 Yip, G. S., Johansson, J. K., and Ross, J. (1997). Effects of nationality on global strategy, *Management International Review*, 37 (4), 365–385.

36 See, e.g., Perkins and Shortland (2006).

37 Schuler, R. S., Dowling, P. J., and De Cieri, H. (1993). An integrative framework of strategic international human resource management. *Journal of Management*, 19(2), 419.

Chapter 3

Design and Structure of the Multinational Enterprise

The world has been going global for centuries, but that will mean very different things in the 21st century than it meant in the 19th or 20th. To be a leader in the future will mean thinking globally, and not only about geography.

Samuel J. Palmisano
Former CEO, IBM[1]

Learning Objectives

This chapter will enable the reader to:

- Explain the fundamentals of organizational design and structure and explain the process of designing an MNE.
- Describe the basic characteristics associated with different organizational structures.
- Explain the implications for IHRM from the different structures.
- Describe the importance of teams, networking, and the need for learning in MNEs.

One of the challenges for HR in international firms is to become an organizational architect. International organizations need appropriate structure in order to effectively conduct business in the chaotic and interconnected global economy. An important source of sustainable global competitive advantage is designing your organization for knowledge creation and sharing across borders and, thus, supporting learning and innovation on a global basis. The traditional needs for control and integration when applied across national borders in the highly complex global economy make the problems of organizational design especially difficult.

Accordingly, this chapter is about organizational design and structure for the successful conduct of international business. The development and complexity of international business is forcing firms to create new forms of organization and new applications of old forms, and these efforts are creating new challenges for management in general and IHRM in particular. Firms are having to cope with a greater number of countries (and their politics, governments, and cultures), protect a greater level of foreign investment, deal with greater overall political uncertainties, develop new mental mindsets, and manage an increasing number of sites and partnerships in order to learn faster and better than their competitors and, thus, to grapple effectively with today's global economy.[2]

This chapter starts with an introduction to organizational design and structure by focusing on the complexities involved in designing and structuring international organizations. Then the chapter describes how the pressures of integration and local responsiveness (introduced in Chapter 2) influence the design and structure of the organizations that international firms use to carry out their international activities. Then the chapter provides an overview of the various structures that international firms use as they evolve in their conduct of international business. Next the chapter describes the implications for IHRM from the different structures. And finally the chapter discusses the role of networks, global teams, and global learning organizations in maintaining complex organizational structures.

INTERNATIONAL ORGANIZATIONAL DESIGN AND STRUCTURE: AN INTRODUCTION

Organizational design refers to the process or style used by management to arrange these various components. In contrast, *organizational structure* refers to the formalized arrangement of organizational components such as the headquarters, subsidiaries, business units/ divisions within the headquarters and subsidiaries, product lines, jobs, positions, tasks, and reporting relationships in an organization. Organizational design is the process whereas organizational structure is the outcome.

The design process and the organizational structure that results from the process—from an internationalization perspective—is essentially based on four factors:[3]

> Organizational design is the process used by management to determine the formal arrangement of components such as the headquarters, subsidiaries, business units/ divisions within the headquarters and subsidiaries, product lines, jobs, positions, tasks, and reporting relationships in the organization.

1 the firm's forms and stages of international development (see Chapter 2, Figure 2.1);
2 the amount of cross-border coordination required by the firm's strategy (that is, the degree of desired integration versus the degree of acceptable and/or necessary localization) (Chapter 2);
3 the nature and extent of host governments' activities in the economic process; and
4 the diversity and complexity of the MNE's business operations.

To a large degree, this concerns the form of development and inter-connectedness of an MNE's various subsidiaries and alliances. Such subsidiaries and international alliances can range in structure from simple sales offices to complete, stand-alone operations (wholly or partially owned), formal joint ventures, and less formal partnerships of various kinds, as introduced in Chapters 2 and 4. More specifically they can take on one or more of the following three forms:[4]

1   The subsidiary or partnership can be a start-up (initially, probably a sales office), that can be used to establish the firm's international business; in such a case it usually will take the structural form of reporting directly to an executive in the domestic structure or to the head of an international and/or geographic division.

2   Once the firm has a well-established international business, it will extensively use its subsidiaries and alliances to support its business strategy. In such a case the firm is likely to develop a structure using a multidimensional network of business centers.

3   When the firm reaches the level of having a high proportion of assets/sales/employees outside of its home country, the subsidiaries become leaders in creating new market share and competitive advantages which are then transferred to the global network, and even back into the home country. In this case, the structure will be an even more complex network of multiple business centers with a strong focus on the integration of these many centers.

In all circumstances, the structure necessary to conduct international business is more complex than is the case for a purely domestic firm.

Convergence vs. Divergence

In the past, MNEs have dealt with the complexity of international business by trying to simplify their operations and organizations. This has often led to development of common policy and practice throughout their global operations and to simple forms of organization, typically copying their domestic organizational structures. This has minimized the problem of management and control in the global context, since the assumption was that if managers could handle domestic organizations, then they could also manage effectively the structures and systems duplicated to handle international commerce, transferring parent-company products, technology, and management style to foreign operations.

Major MNEs (ones with longer-term experience and with greater foreign investment and number of employees) have discovered that this doesn't work very well. The global economy is too complex and unpredictable. Other countries and cultures don't always accommodate the parent company products, styles, and culture. MNEs have often needed to develop more complex structures to deal with this complexity and to develop new managerial skills to deal with multiple cultures, languages, and ways of conducting business.

DESIGNING THE MULTINATIONAL ENTERPRISE

The basic problem that underlies the ability of firms to organize globally is the challenge of figuring out how to coordinate and balance the opposing forces of integrating their foreign operations with each other and with the parent firm while at the same time allowing the necessary autonomy and local control needed to meet unique national and cultural interests.[5] This is what has been referred to in earlier chapters as the integration-local responsiveness problem.

MNEs need integration and sharing of learning and experience, and they typically seek common policies in a number of areas related to overall performance, such as financial objectives, yet they need to allow localized adaptation to cultural differences. The emphasis on increased layers and size of formal structure and more sophisticated systems has in fact slowed down communication, learning, and decision making, and limited international firms' abilities to adapt effectively to local differences. Thus MNEs are turning increasingly to reduced size of business units, increased numbers of smaller business centers, and informal networks for improved communication, control, and coordination, as described later in the chapter.[6] As Jay Galbraith, one of the foremost researchers on issues related to the design of the global corporation, says, "Organizing a company to do business on a global scale remains one of the most complex organizational responsibilities."[7] And coping with the challenge of combining centralized control and integration with localized product and managerial adaptation creates one of the most significant of those complexities.

It should be obvious that no one type of international organization structure embodies the right system for all firms. Rather, the MNE needs to be a multidimensional network of businesses, countries, and functions. Global customers are demanding single points of business contact and global strategies seek simplified reporting structures. In response, firms are being forced into four- and five-dimensional networks, as discussed through the rest of this chapter. Thus global managers need to be trained and developed to operate effectively with multidimensional structures as well as multiple types of structures.

INTERNATIONAL ORGANIZATIONAL STRUCTURE CHOICES

Organizational structure refers to the formalized arrangement of organizational components such as the headquarters, subsidiaries, business units/divisions, and functional units within the headquarters and subsidiaries, product lines, jobs, positions, tasks, and reporting relationships in an organization. Two frameworks can be used to describe an MNE's organizational structure.

FRAMEWORK 1: ORGANIZATIONAL STRUCTURE IN TERMS OF INTEGRATION AND LOCAL RESPONSIVENESS

The *first framework* is based on the above discussion. Accordingly, the basic organizational challenge to MNEs has always been the integration of activities that take place in different countries and coordination of foreign subsidiaries with headquarters. The basic global structure, then, of every MNE can be described in terms of an integration and local responsiveness framework (see Figure 3.1). This framework highlights the conflicting demands on MNEs in terms of these two countervailing forces (integration versus local responsiveness) and can be used to describe an MNE's structure and strategy (basic strategy was described in Chapter 2).[8] The horizontal axis shows the extent of local responsiveness (high versus low). The vertical axis shows the degree of integration (high versus low).[9]

This approach (the integration-responsiveness grid) categorizes the internationalized structure of the firm—in terms of the HQ-subsidiaries relationship—into four types: 1) international; 2) multinational; 3) global; and 4) transnational.[10]

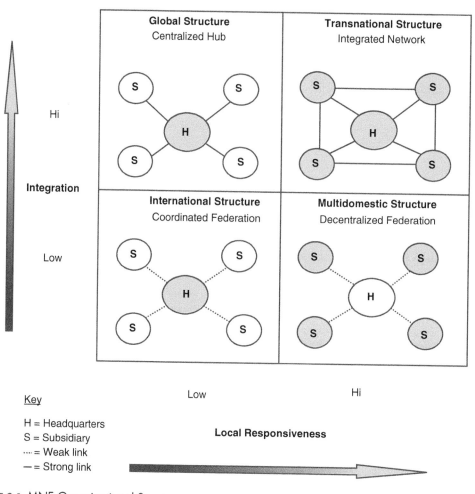

FIGURE 3.1 MNE Organizational Structure

Adapted from: Bartlet, C., Ghoshal, S., and Beamish, P. (2010). *Transnational Management: Text, Cases and Readings in Cross-Border Management*, Boston: Irwin McGraw Hill; Bartlet, C., and Ghoshal, S. (1998). *Managing Across Borders. The Transnational Solution*, Boston, MA: Harvard Business School Press; Harzing, A. (2004) *Strategy and Structure of Multinational Companies*, in Harzing, A.W.K., and Van Ryusseveldt, J. (eds.), *International Human Resource Management*, 2nd ed., London: Sage Publications, pp. 33–64.

These various structures are inter-related. Just as firms differ in their stages of internationalization, so too do they differ in terms of the structures they adopt in their international operations. The specific international structure chosen or developed influences the type of IHRM policies and practices necessary for effective international operation. Coping with the complexities of the structure turns out to be one of the most difficult areas in which IHRM can make a strategic contribution to a firm's international business strategy.

International Organizational Structure[11]

Organizations with an *international structure* face weak pressures for local responsiveness or differentiation and weak pressures for worldwide integration. As shown in Figure 3.1, this type of structure resembles a coordinated federation. Foreign subsidiaries may be dependent on headquarters for resources and limited direction but will still have major freedom to adapt to local conditions. Coordination and control by headquarters is likely to be even less important than in the multi-domestic structure and certainly less important than the global structure (we discuss this next). Since foreign operations in this condition are fairly limited, HRM decisions, policies, and practices will be of limited significance in the subsidiaries.

Multi-domestic Organizational Structure

Organizations with a multi-domestic structure face strong pressures for local responsiveness or differentiation and weak pressures for worldwide integration. As illustrated in Figure 3.1, a multi-domestic firm has subsidiaries in multiple countries, with these subsidiaries typically operating independently within each country, independently of operations in other countries, and often fairly independent, even, of the parent company headquarters. The MNE will have significant operations (assembly, manufacturing, service centers, R&D, branch offices) in many countries and may well reach the condition where half or more of its sales and employment is in foreign countries. Often these multi-domestic subsidiaries become almost independent fiefdoms, as described in the Ford Motor Company case at the end of Chapter 2.

Key personnel in the multi-domestic subsidiary offices—at least initially—are often from the company's home office with key decisions initially made at corporate headquarters. Thus, although the subsidiaries are largely staffed by people from the countries in which they are located, managers from the home office may retain authority in key areas (such as profitability and compensation bonuses), yet the subsidiary management increasingly focuses inward. The MNE at this level of development generally views each national market as a specialized market for its particular subsidiary's products. Each subsidiary concentrates its efforts on the nation in which it is located.

The HR department's role at this stage becomes more complex and difficult. Now HQ's HRM may initially provide a number of services—such as relocation, compensation, and benefits for employees (international assignees) working in these foreign (to them) locations—but they must also coordinate the HRM activities and practices of the many subsidiaries, seeking both consistency with the culture and policies of the parent company and accommodation of local values and practices. But, over time, these subsidiaries are likely to become increasingly independent of HQ. In addition, training for international assignees (from the parent company or from foreign locales), local nationals, and parent-company employees to handle foreign assignments and interaction with foreign counterparts will also increase from that experience under the international structure.

As independent as subsidiaries often become, in this structure the organization's operations in a number of countries may reach such size and importance that there is increased need for integration with corporate headquarters. The MNE may organize country subsidiaries from a close geographic region into a regional division with regional headquarters in order to coordinate operations on a regional basis, again as described in the Ford Motor Company case in Chapter 2. This will probably involve first organizing to conduct business in only one or two regions, such as Europe or Latin America (for an American firm) or maybe North America (for a European or Asian firm) or Asia (for an Asian or European firm). The HRM impacts in this regional structure are similar to those in the multi-domestic structure, although they will be managed from a regional headquarters. An assumption made is that countries within a region share some common characteristics such as country culture, geographical proximity, or stage of economic development.

Global Organizational Structure

Organizations with a *global organizational structure* face strong pressures for worldwide integration but face weak pressures for differentiation or local responsiveness. As illustrated in Figure 3.1, this type of structure resembles a centralized hub. These organizations structure their foreign subsidiaries into worldwide lines of business that are heavily managed and controlled by headquarters. Assets and resources are centralized. Foreign subsidiaries are heavily dependent on these assets and resources from the headquarters. Relative to subsidiaries in multi-domestic and international structures, "global" subsidiaries have much less freedom.

In recent years, many MNEs with this type of organizational structure have worked to develop a corporate culture or mindset with the intention to become blind to the importance of national borders. That is, the desire is to operate in such a way as to not have to be concerned with national cultural and legal differences. Even though most businesses still organize on a regional basis and adaptation to local customer preferences may still be necessary, products and services are increasingly designed for and marketed to customers all over the world. This is particularly true for industrial products, that is, for products sold from business to business, such as computer chips or machine tools or construction equipment. The best technology and innovative ideas are sought everywhere and applied to markets throughout the world. Products and services are created where costs are the lowest, quality is the highest, and time to delivery is the shortest, and delivered wherever demand is sufficient. And resources (money, material and parts, insurance, even people) are sought from wherever the best quality for cost can be found. Reaching this organizational structure is not merely a matter of company size or experience in internationalization. Sometimes it is a reflection of the nature of the pressures of the particular industry; often, it reflects a purposeful, strategic decision to "go global."

At this structural level, the role of the HR department must again shift. Key HR decisions are made at the headquarters and implemented worldwide. Employees are hired everywhere in the world, wherever the necessary skills, training, and experience can be found. Worldwide policies are developed and implemented for many aspects of HR responsibility, possibly based on practices followed in numerous places around the world. Management promotions will require international experience and managers and executives will be developed from all major countries or regions of operation. At the same time, increased sophistication in locating certain HRM practices will become even more important, as the firm tries to become a global enterprise.

This usually means fewer expatriates in local subsidiaries, an increased use of third-country nationals, and broader-based multinational composition of corporate boards and top-management and technical teams. And in most firms this means trying to develop or maintain an international corporate culture that transcends national boundaries and national cultures. Key employees need to be multilingual, experienced in a number of countries, and culturally sensitive, and their countries of origin make little difference.

Transnational Organizational Structure

Organizations with a *transnational organizational structure* face strong pressures for worldwide integration *and* for differentiation or local responsiveness. As shown in Figure 3.1, these organizations resemble an integrated and interdependent global network of subsidiaries that have the ability to manage across national boundaries, retaining local flexibility while achieving global integration. This form of organization has a truly global focus, making resource decisions without reference to national origins, sharing its ideas and technology with all of its units on a global scale, while cultivating a local character in all of its individual businesses. It is characterized by an interdependence of resources and responsibilities across all business units regardless of national boundaries. Subsidiaries are integral parts of a complete transnational system with both global and local objectives. IHRM policies and practices are based on a collaborative process between headquarters and subsidiaries.

Bartlett and Ghoshal suggested that many firms were evolving into this new form of international business that they termed "transnational."[12] In the sense that the transnational firm has a global focus, it is similar to the global firm, described in the previous section. But it differs from the global firm in that, rather than developing global products, services, brands, and standardized processes and policies and procedures, the transnational organization works hard to localize, to be seen not only as a global firm, but as a local firm as well, albeit one that draws upon global expertise, technology, and resources.[13] In a transnational firm, the focus is simultaneously on global integration, local responsiveness, and knowledge sharing among the different parts of the organization.

The transnational firm is often put forth as the direction in which all international firms are headed. The salient management and HR question may be how to manage the complex, national (cultural) diversity that this level of global business activity experiences. When integration is needed (as in joint ventures and in the development of global workforces), cultural diversity needs to be valued and utilized while minimizing its negative impacts; but when cultural diversity is needed to differentiate products and services to meet the needs of local markets, new corporate practices and organizational designs are required.

The Globally Integrated Structure

In addition to the four structural types just discussed (multi-domestic, international, global, and transnational), a popular model is a globally integrated enterprise that is very different in structure and operations.[14] Samuel Palmisano, the former chairman and CEO of IBM, described the difference between a 20th-century multinational and a 21st-century globally integrated enterprise as follows. In a multinational model, companies build local production capacity within key markets, while performing other tasks on a global basis. In contrast, in the globally integrated enterprise, strategy, management, and operations—which take place in many different locations—are integrated into production of goods and services to deliver value to clients worldwide. This integrated model is made possible because of shared technologies, global IT systems, and global communications infrastructure. In a globally integrated structure, different operations, expertise, and capabilities (especially as is the case for service organizations, as IBM now describes itself)—again, located around the world—allow the enterprise to connect with its customers, using all the resources of the firm, and engage in collaborative innovation to solve the customers' problems and challenges. HR activities in the globally integrated firm internally reflect the same laws of global integration as those provided to the external clients. Talent and expertise within the MNE flow to where they create the most value.

However, the differences between multi-domestic, global/transnational, and globally integrated firms are significant. In the traditional multi-domestic enterprise, freestanding subsidiaries or stand-alone foreign operations may be so loosely affiliated that valuable opportunities for economies of scale, joint marketing efforts, or shared technology and innovations may be lost. Country or regional operations and functional experts can develop attitudes of strong independence that can result in the loss of benefits that arise from sharing product ideas and technologies across national boundaries (refer to the Ford Motor Company case in the previous chapter). The transnational firm creates a structure and management system that takes advantage of global capabilities while allowing local subsidiaries to operate as independent businesses. The globally integrated enterprise tends to be more network-based. Whichever structure is developed, the global HR roles and activities must shift to meet the needs of the organization.

IHRM in Action 3.1: Moving HR from International to Global

The Ferro Corporation, a $1 billion manufacturer of coatings, plastics, specialty chemicals, and ceramics, has been a successful international enterprise for almost three quarters of a century and is now becoming a model for being a global company. Several of its foreign operations, particularly those in Europe and Latin America, have existed for as much as 70 years. About two thirds of its employees are non-US nationals, and over 60 percent of its revenues and profits are derived from foreign operations.

Despite its impressive international record, only recently has Ferro begun to see itself as a global company. According to David B. Woodburg Ferro's vice-president of human resources at that time, "There was quite a bit of sharing of information and technology among our operations in various countries, but each foreign division or subsidiary operated highly independently, formulating much of its own strategy for manufacturing, marketing, finance, and human resources."

Since then Ferro has reorganized its corporate structure to focus on products and business lines across international borders. "Each business thinks of the world as its marketplace now," says Woodbury. "We're developing broad-based global strategies, with increased communications and a greater sharing of assets throughout the world."

High on that list of "shared assets" is human resources. "We realize there is a strong need for global managers," says Woodburg. "We have to identify, train and develop people with an international outlook, skills, and experience. Like all other facets of the corporation, human resources has to evolve into a global operation."

Reaching this stage of development is not merely a matter of company size or experience in internationalization. Sometimes it is a reflection of the nature of the pressures of the particular industry, but often it reflects a purposeful, strategic decision to "go global." IHRM in Action 3.1 describes a moderately sized firm, the Ferro Corporation, which made a powerful shift to being a global MNE.[15]

FRAMEWORK 2: ORGANIZATIONAL STRUCTURE IN TERMS OF BUSINESS UNITS/DIVISIONS

The *second framework*[16] for describing organizational structure is relatively more detailed and describes the organizational structure in terms of the business units/divisions within the headquarters and subsidiaries (refer to Figure 3.2). The traditional choices include 1) functional division structure; 2) product division structure; 3) geographic division structure; and 4) global matrix division structure.

Functional Division Structure[17]

Departments in a functional structure are organized according to *functions*, e.g., operations, marketing, finance, accounting (see Figure 3.2). Subsidiaries either report directly to the CEO or the VP of operations or to marketing or manufacturing. Organizations that are in the early stages of internationalization usually have this divisional structure. In addition, this divisional structure is most likely found in firms with an international organizational structure.

Product Division Structure[18]

Departments in this structure are organized according to their product divisions (see Figure 3.3). Each of the product lines contains all of the business functions such as finance,

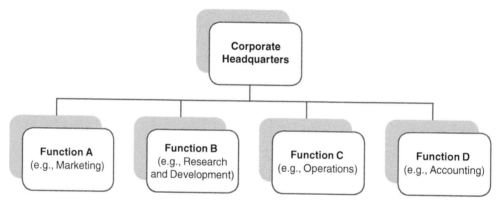

FIGURE 3.2 Functional Structure

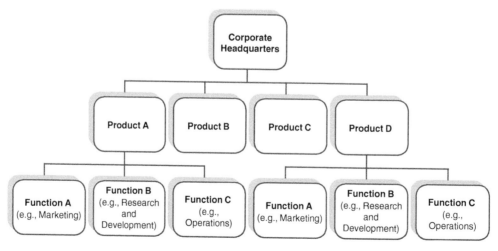

FIGURE 3.3 Product Structure

marketing, and accounting. That is, all functional activities are controlled by a product group. This divisional structure is most likely to be found in firms with a global organizational structure. Managers at the headquarters make most of the product decisions and input from subsidiaries is very limited.

Geographic Division Structure[19]

In this structure, the product division typically gives way to a *geographic divisional structure* with each region becoming an independent division reporting directly to the CEO. Each region has its own set of specialized functions (see Figure 3.4). Country or regional managers in each area are provided with substantial autonomy to adapt the strategies of the parent country product divisions to fit the specificity of the local conditions. Firms with a multi-domestic organizational structure are more likely to use this type of divisional structure.

As the need for more business centers increases, for example to accommodate additional countries and for additional research and development centers to adapt products to local customers, the simple hierarchical functional, product, and geographic divisional structures turn out to be inadequate to handle the complexities of the needs of today's MNEs, which often have multiple organizational forms and networks. The organizational needs of the modern MNE must be a mix of functional, product, and geographic divisional structures.

Global Matrix Structure[20]

As concerns for cost control compete with concerns for integration and cross-fertilization across national borders, firms tend to look for ways to coordinate all the many critical components of the firm: country subsidiaries, product lines, local and global customers,

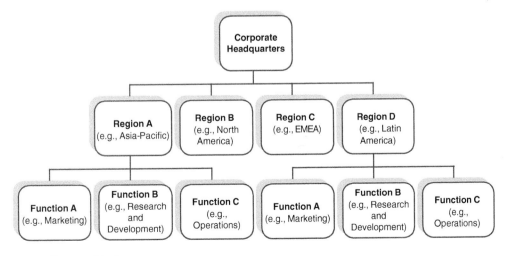

FIGURE 3.4 Geographic Structure

business functions, research and development, regional and central headquarters, etc. Thus, other combinations of the critical variables are developed to include structures to integrate the traditional business functions with country and product (see Figure 3.5). Often these organizational designs have evolved as the firm has increased its global presence and tried to cope more effectively with the complexities it encounters.

These matrix structures involve two or more lines of reporting. Typically there will be a country "leg" to the matrix with managers reporting to a local national boss plus reporting to a product group or regional or headquarters functional office, as well. Sometimes there are three or more legs and they may be given equal importance (solid-line reporting) or may have different levels of priority, with a solid line for direct reporting and dotted line for more indirect reporting relationships.

These structures cause a new set of dilemmas and require a new set of skills. The many diverse demands of global business require the global firm to give management focus to both the local and the corporate levels. The matrix doesn't resolve this dilemma, it just makes it a permanent part of the management environment. At best, the matrix structure allows local and global realities to be reconciled; at its worst, it allows individual managers to pursue narrow objectives without regard to their impact on the other legs of the matrix, that is, on the other parts of the organization. Problems with divided loyalties and multiple

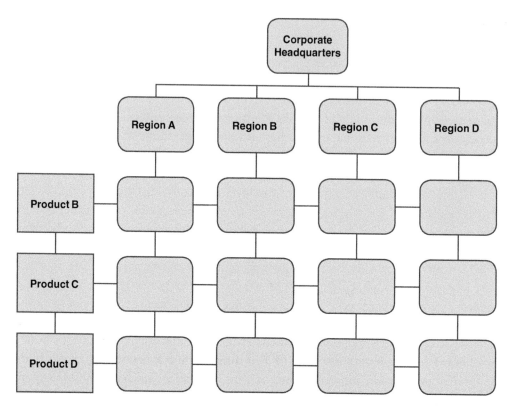

FIGURE 3.5 Matrix Structure

bosses have to be resolved. Ultimately, managers working in a global matrix organization must learn to think more broadly and, as stated earlier, to develop network skills to negotiate resources, resolve trade-offs, and to manage through influence and persuasion, not necessarily through direct authority.

At the level of the individual, the central dilemma that many managers face in this organizational need for integration is that of divided loyalties. Loyalty is local, that is, people are more loyal to the colleagues they socialize with, see daily, and spend time with. If the formal organizational structure requires interaction with strangers (particularly strangers in another country—even if that other country is headquarters), it is only to be expected that priority attention will flow to the local colleagues, unless significant effort is put into developing the relationships across borders. Interestingly, attitudes about loyalty vary according to country culture and to functional specialty. For example, managers in Spain and France prefer loyalty to the remote (normally central) part of the organization while managers in the UK, Ireland, and China prefer loyalty to local colleagues. HRM was one of the functions that most preferred loyalty to local colleagues. But, clearly, HR must get involved with training managers in the need to foster both local and central relationships and must foster such relationships themselves.

IHRM AND INTERNATIONAL ORGANIZATIONAL DESIGN AND STRUCTURE

As mentioned earlier *organizational design* refers to the process or style used by leaders and managers to arrange the various components of organizational structure. This process is increasingly complex and to a large degree presents mostly new and complex organizational and people issues, such as cross-border negotiations, cultural sensitivities, coordination and control across national boundaries and time zones, cross-border and cross-cultural teamwork, and global learning and integration. As the number of countries and cultures and variety of international business activities, as well as the use of cross-border teams and task forces, continue to increase, the more important IHRM has become in helping firms make sure that their globalization works. When designing organizations, IHRM is guided by the extent of desired integration versus the degree of acceptable and/or necessary differentiation.

IHRM needs to not only be able to support the organizational structure of the MNE and deliver the glue technology that these different groupings need to integrate, but it must also organize itself to effectively deliver HR transactional services for all locations of the MNE. The traditional IHRM view of how to best organize itself, in the early stages of internationalization, was focused on either servicing the subsidiary's HR needs (with outsourced help) at arms-length from the HQ, or hiring local HR country managers to deliver these services on location. However, both options had major drawbacks. HQ HR managers are often simply incapable (and dangerously unknowledgeable) in managing HR practices outside of their own countries (due to both their lack of international exposure and to the legal and cultural complexity of host countries) and locals, although knowledgeable to deliver transactional HR services in their local countries, may not be cost-effective and often lack the strategic HR components in their jobs that are used by HQs to implement corporate programs in the local environment.

To remedy some of these shortcomings and as a result of the capabilities provided through modern IT and communication technologies, a new organizational form has been emerging to deliver HR transactional services in the MNE. This new structure for the delivery of HR services throughout an MNE's global operations is referred to as "shared services" and "centers of excellence." In a shared service model, individual country operations can specialize in varying aspects of international HR services and then, given the power of intranets, countries can access these centers of excellence without having to develop them all themselves. In this way, all of the MNE's foreign operations can have available world-class IHRM capabilities.

FORMAL STRUCTURE AND BEYOND

The challenge for the management of MNEs and their IHR departments is to learn how to manage all of these networks and linkages. Here is a short introduction to networks, one of the most important forms of linkage.

Networks

One of the most important competencies that holds together these complex global businesses are the informal networks that individual managers develop throughout the many centers of the firm. These networks work only if the managers who interact with each other to get their planning and implementation done know and trust each other well enough to work out their different purposes. It requires constant attention to the skills of integration and to management development programs that have as one of their major foci the building of such networks and the competencies of integration.

Firms have tried a number of strategies to hold these complex global businesses together with increasingly complex formal structures—including multiple dimension matrixes, with formal reporting structures that include product lines, functional responsibilities, country business units, regional and parent-country headquarters, multiple specialty centers such as R&D and product development and global training and development, and cross-border acquisitions, IJVs, partnerships, and virtual teams, described in the next chapter.

Because of these multiple and complex layers, informal networks of relationships develop in order to handle the practical components of day-to-day business activity, such as business planning. Such informal networks only work if the people that need to interact and coordinate have a shared super-ordinate vision of the direction of the overall firm and their parts in it, high capacity for self-control and willingness to collaborate, and capacity to negotiate their differences. This requires constant attention to the application of what Evans calls "glue technology," or the management development technology of integration, that is, management development practices that have as a primary purpose the integration of the management and executive workforce of the firm and the building of the necessary competencies to use the resulting networks in an effective way.[21] Such global management development programs are discussed more fully in Chapter 10 on International Training and Management Development.

Use and Management of Cross-border Teams

Given the increasing complexity of organizations, much of the work that needs to get done in a global enterprise requires a high degree of interaction and interdependence between globally dispersed organizations and between people in various, globally dispersed sections of those organizations. This interaction is often relegated to a work group, or team.[22] And, increasingly, these teams are made up of people from multiple and varying organizations (or parts of the same organization), geographic locations, countries, cultures, languages, ways of thinking and working, and time zones. Often they have the characteristics of "virtual" teams, that is, they don't meet face-to-face and are not co-located; they are widely geographically dispersed.

Types of Cross-border Teams

These cross-border teams come with many different names: global teams, multinational, multicultural, transnational, transcultural, geographically distributed or geographically dispersed, non-co-located or out-of-sight teams. All of these terms refer to the phenomenon of people working together in teams, with common goals, but who are not physically located in the same place and often do not meet but rather conduct their "business" via electronic means. In this book, such teams will generally be referred to by the term cross-border teams, since this is the primary structure of interest in this chapter and the phrasing that seems to be most commonly used.

Challenges of Cross-border Teams

These cross-border teams represent a dramatic change in the ways managers function and they present two major new challenges.[23] Both of these challenges stem from issues related to the physical separation of workers and managers made necessary by globalization[24] and made possible by modern technology.[25]

The first challenge has to do with managing people you can't see. Managers must make the transition from managing activities to managing projects and their results. The second managerial challenge is to redefine the role of management itself, since the "virtual" nature of cross-border teams creates much uncertainty as to whether managers still have a role to play in managing employees who are no longer present in the same locale. As a consequence, these teams tend to be largely self-managing, with the members working very interdependently and coordinating via the internet.

Popularity of Virtual Teams

The goal in this discussion of cross-border teams is to provide enough understanding of the problems and their solutions so that IHRM managers can provide the necessary advice, training, and facilitation to ensure their global firms can gain the intended and possible benefits. (More detail is available in the Schuler, Jackson, and Luo book, *Managing Human Resources in Cross-Border Alliances*, in this series.[26]) Learning to manage these teams will become increasingly more important as such virtual teams become more prevalent for several reasons:

- The complexity of global business requires the interaction and networking of people with multiple competencies from many different locations.
- Virtual teams save firms the money involved in travel for teams to meet or to relocate team members so they can be together.
- Technology such as the internet, video teleconferencing, and Skype makes it much easier for cross-border teams to meet in a virtual fashion. These teams can function in one or both of two different modes:[27]

    1 They can do everything (or most things) face-to-face, which requires extensive travel to get team members together (and which eliminates one of the reasons for using such teams in the first place, that is, their ability to meet electronically); or
    2 They can do most of their work in virtual mode, relying on electronic technology to facilitate their interaction.

Best Practices in the Management of Virtual Teams

Many problems arise with over-reliance on virtual teams and on teams meeting in virtual mode, although one unanswered question is whether younger people who "grow up" using the computer and are much more used to interaction with others via a computer monitor or cell phone might be better able to interact effectively without the need for face-to-face time and be able to trust out-of-sight team members well enough to overcome these problems. The use of e-mail may increase the quantity of interaction, but some studies suggest the quality decreases.[28]

Most studies, in fact, suggest that the critical variable in the successful functioning of virtual teams is the level of trust between team members. This seems to be a function of the amount of time the team has spent in "face-to-face" time, particularly at the beginnings of the life of the team.[29] Some experience with virtual teams also suggests that the "half-life" of trust in virtual teams, i.e., the time it takes before the level of trust falls below some dangerous threshold, is less than three months.[30] What this indicates is that virtual teams, in order to maintain healthy working relationships, probably need to meet face-to-face every three months or so.

Managers supervising the physically remote legs of the global firm now have the additional challenge of managing these "virtual" teams. As already indicated, these teams operate across barriers of distance, and differing cultures, time zones, and technologies. Most management training still assumes that management skills are applied face-to-face and in the manager's own culture, which is no longer the reality for many of these managers. Using the old skills to manage these new remote operations results

---

EXHIBIT 3.1: Best Practices for the Effective Management of Cross-border and Virtual Teams[31]

- Develop an e-mail protocol, to include appropriate topics, frequency and time of use, definition of urgency, who should participate and when, the importance of respect in use of titles, definition and use of deadlines, etc.
- Select the appropriate people for virtual team membership, including people who are self-starters, have strong communication skills, and have good virtual-team skills (can use e-mail well, etc.).
- Identify from the beginning the team member who will have the team leadership role.
- Keep virtual team projects focused on the task, with clear goals, targets, and deadlines.
- Provide adequate face-to-face social time to build the trust necessary to work well in a virtual format.
- Celebrate the reaching of targets and completion of projects.
- Identify the barriers to collaboration that you want to overcome and work together to resolve them.
- Provide cultural mentors to the team to deal with cross-cultural problems and misunderstandings and IT technicians to help with technology problems.
- Identify what people should do when a crisis occurs, including whom to contact and the decision-making hierarchy within the group.
- Identify the ground rules for virtual teamwork, including establishing regular times for group interaction, setting up firm rules for communication, using visual forms of communication whenever possible, establishing rules for sharing project information outside the team, etc.

in too much travel, inappropriate attempts to micro-manage (since trust and relationships have not been developed), and concerns about personal visibility with remote staffs. Managers in these new organizations need to gain the skills of relationship building and teamwork from long distance. Exhibit 3.1 illustrates some of the lessons learned about the effective management of cross-border and virtual teams.

The Global Learning Organization

Ultimately, the "tie" that binds the global firm together is the intellectual and social capital it has in the experience, knowledge, and skills held by its employees around the world and its abilities to share, and use that knowledge on a global basis. In today's world, where the only sustainable competitive advantage any firm has is its ability to learn and innovate faster than its competitors and react more quickly to continual volatility and change, creating a culture of learning and nurturing, and facilitating that learning across borders may be the only avenue to success.[32] In today's global economy, "change is complex and messy, [so] many stick with the known for fear of the unknown. . . . It is much more reassuring to stay as you are . . . than to try to make a fundamental change when you cannot be certain that the effort will succeed."[33] Yet a firm has to do it, in order to survive and thrive in today's environment. It has to take the risk to find ways to facilitate learning so that change is possible. As John Browne, former CEO of BP Amoco, put it, "learning is at the heart of a company's ability to adapt to a rapidly changing environment."[34] From a global perspective, this means a firm must facilitate learning on a global basis—across borders, across parts of the organization in different country locales, within global and virtual teams, with people on foreign assignments and after they return from those assignments, and in international joint ventures and cross-border partnerships and alliances.

As Peter Senge says, "perhaps for the first time in history, humankind has the capacity to create far more information than anyone can absorb, to foster far greater interdependency than anyone can manage, and to accelerate change far faster than anyone's ability to keep pace."[35] Thus the challenge to firms is that learning on a global basis must become a central managerial focus. Technology alone (such as creating IT databases and repositories of knowledge and experience) will not solve the challenge. Nor will merely stating principles and values of collaboration. People must want to use such knowledge sources and must be willing to contribute their own "learnings" to them. In the end, people must be committed to:

1   the importance of learning;
2   the need to share and use information.

In turn, the MNE (and IHRM) needs to create the organizational culture and structure and the HR policies and practices that encourage and facilitate such attitudes and behaviors. This is the essence of learning in organizations and knowledge management.[36]

In terms of the conduct of international business, the global firm must use its people who have international experience and knowledge and who have been posted to international assignments, spreading them throughout the organization. It must ensure that individuals coming back from overseas assignments are provided new jobs that use the knowledge and skills learned overseas and are given opportunities to share that learning. In order for a firm to reap the benefits of global learning, it is imperative that its valuable expatriate employees remain with the organization long enough to share their experiences—and presumably even longer, to contribute to the firm's ongoing globalization. Since learning is so important, and learning across borders (taking advantage of the global experiences and multinational learning of a global firm's global workforce) is so necessary, then carefully managing employees on foreign assignments to ensure successful expatriation and repatriation would seem essential. (These issues are discussed in detail in Section 3, Global Talent Management.)

Special efforts also need to be made to expose employees and managers "at home" to the products and processes of foreign subsidiaries and foreign acquisitions and partners, and vice versa, including visits to each other's operations to observe and learn through direct interaction. The firm must spread employees and managers from the countries of its operations throughout its organization, including at the very highest levels of the executive team and the board of directors itself. Only in these ways can the global firm make effective use of any processes or technologies that have been adopted to facilitate learning on a global scale, such as talent directories, intranets for sharing information, etc.

CONCLUSION

This chapter has focused on the difficult task of designing organizational structure for the complexities of the modern international enterprise. First, it described how the conflicting demands on MNEs in terms of two countervailing forces (integration versus local responsiveness) influences the design and structure of the organizations that international firms use to carry out their international activities. Then the chapter provided an overview of the various structures that international firms have utilized as they have evolved in their conduct of international business. Next the chapter described the implications for IHRM of the different structures. And finally the chapter discussed the role of networks, global teams, and global learning organizations in maintaining complex organizational structures.

DISCUSSION QUESTIONS

1 Using materials from Chapter 3, explain how market entry methods are related to organizational structure.

2 What are the various choices that MNEs have for designing organizational structure? How do they differ from an HR point of view?

3 How can IHRM help to ensure the success of firms with a global organizational structure and a transnational organizational structure?

4 How do networks and learning organizations help to ensure an MNE's competitive advantage?

CASE STUDY 3.1: Capgemini: A Transnational Organization (France)

Capgemini, founded in 1967 and headquartered in Paris, France, is Europe's largest IT software and services group. The firm has taken all available means (organic growth, acquisitions, and alliances) to become Europe's number 1 in computer services and consulting and, as of 2014, among the top five of the world's IT management and services consultancies. Its almost 140,000 people work in over 40 countries. For example, in 2000 Capgemini acquired Ernst & Young Consulting and in 2002 they spun off their Sogeti Group as a wholly owned subsidiary specializing in IT consulting and outsourcing, which now has over 20,000 employees working in 7 countries.

The original merger of Cap, a computer services group, and Sogeti, a business management and information processing company, brought together operations in the UK, the Netherlands, Switzerland, and Germany, with a head office in France. Further acquisitions brought in a large number of small groups throughout Europe and the US. This expanded its coverage to IT consulting, customized software, outsourcing services, and education and training. In recent years, this strategy has expanded Capgemini's work to countries such as India, the Czech Republic, and Sweden, with major partnerships with major software firms such as SAP and Microsoft. Moreover, they now have operations in Asia-Pacific (including Australia and China) and Latin America. In 2013, sales increased by 12 percent in Asia-Pacific and Latin America. Similarly, revenue increased by 16 percent in Australia. Global expansion is important to Capgemini.

Capgemini has always been highly decentralized, but its internal strategy has been that when any of its branches reached 150 personnel, the branch is split in two. This gives the firm greater flexibility in responding to variations in local demand. Decision making and direct customer service are facilitated with smaller teams.

Capgemini has developed information pooling systems to ensure that innovative solutions developed in one country or business will be rapidly disseminated to other countries and businesses. These include electronic bulletin boards and extensive electronic and voicemail facilities, plus the organizational culture of informal networks of professionals who work frequently together in project teams.

The challenges for this fast-growing transnational have major HR components, e.g., integrating its wide variety of organizations into a group with a common culture capable of working within a complex web of ownership relationships, while benefiting from the strengths of the relationships that exist among its "family" of committed, semi-autonomous professionals. Internally, Capgemini and its IHR team work to clarify and coordinate roles, objectives, systems, and resources, particularly its skilled professional staff, across countries and markets. For example, its Genesis project took two years to achieve this integration, but now Capgemini sees itself as coming much closer to achieving its aim to be a modern transnational enterprise.

Sources: Capgemini website (2014), http://www.capgemini.com; also http://en.wikipedia.org/wiki/Capgemini; Segal-Horn, S., and Faulkner, D. (1999). *The Dynamics of International Strategy*, London:

International Thomson; and Segal-Horn, S., and Faulkner, D. (2010). *Understanding Global Strategy*, Andover, Hampshire, UK: South-Western Cengage Learning EMEA.

Discussion Questions

1 What makes a firm a "transnational enterprise"?

2 Does Capgemini meet the criteria for being a transnational? Why or why not?

3 What are the HR implications of being a transnational? What makes HRM in a transnational different from HRM in, for instance, a multi-domestic firm?

4 What kinds of problems do you see in Capgemini's strategy for structuring its business?

NOTES

1 Source: Change is the only constant, *The Business Times*, Feb. 14, 2014. Also mentioned in IBM Centennial Lecture, March 31, 2011 (www. http://www.ibm.com/ibm/files/Y856416N01277W70/centennial_lecture_erich_clementi_austria_preparedremarks.pdf).

2 Galbraith, J.A. (2014). *Designing Organizations: Strategy, Structure, and Process at the Business Unit and Enterprise Levels*, 3rd ed., San Francisco: Jossey-Bass Evans; Pucik, V., and Bjorkman, I. (2010). *The Global Challenge: Frameworks for International Human Resource Management*, New York: McGraw-Hill; Bartlett, C.A., and Ghoshal, S. (1989). *Managing Across Borders: The Transnational Solution*, Boston: Harvard Business School Press; Galbraith, J.R. (1998). Structuring Global Organizations, in Mohaman, S.A., Galbraith, J.A., and Lawler, E.E., III (eds.), *Tomorrow's Organization: Crafting Winning Capabilities in a Dynamic World*, San Francisco: Jossey-Bass, pp. 103–129.

3 Galbraith, J.R. (1998), Structuring global organizations, in Mohrman, S.A., Galbraith, J.R., and Lawler, E.E., III, (eds.), *Tomorrow's Organizations: Crafting Winning Capabilities in a Dynamic World*, San Francisco: Jossey-Bass, pp.103–129. Also see Galbraith, J.R. (2014). *Designing Organizations: Strategy, Structure, and Process at the Business Unit and Enterprise Levels*, San Francisco: Jossey-Bass & Pfeiffer Imprints, Wiley; Galbraith, J.R. (2010). The multi-dimensional and reconfigurable organization. *Organizational Dynamics*, 39(2), 115–125.

4 Based on ibid.

5 Evans, P.A.L. (1992). Human resource management and globalization. Keynote address delivered to the 2nd International Conference of the Western Academy of Management, June 24–26, Leuven, Belgium; Evans, P., Pucik, V., and Barsoux, J.-L. (2002). *The Global Challenge: Frameworks for International Human Resource Management*, Boston: McGraw-Hill Irwin; and Galbraith, J.R. (2000). *Designing the Global Corporation*, San Francisco: Jossey-Bass.

6 Evans, P.A.L. (1992).

7 Galbraith, J.R. (2000), p. 1.

8 Based on Bartlet, C., Ghoshal, S., and Beamish, P. (2010). *Transnational Management: Text, Cases and Readings in Cross-Border Management*, Boston: Irwin McGraw Hill; Bartlet, C., and Ghoshal, S. (1998). *Managing Across Borders. The Transnational Solution*, Boston, MA: Harvard Business School Press; Harzing, A. (2004) *Strategy and Structure of Multinational Companies*, in Harzing, A.W.K., and Van Ruysseveldt, J. (eds.), *International Human Resource Management*, 2nd ed., London: Sage Publications, pp. 33–64.

9 Based on Bartlet, C., Ghoshal, S., and Beamish, P. (2010). *Transnational Management: Text, Cases and Readings in Cross-Border Management*, Boston: Irwin McGraw Hill.

10 Ibid.

11 Ibid.

12 Pucik, V., and Evans, P. (2004). The human factor in mergers and acquisitions, chapter 8, in Morosini, P. and Steger, U. (eds.), *Managing Complex Mergers, Real World Lessons in Implementing Successful Cross-cultural Mergers and Acquisitions*, London: Prentice Hall, pp.161–187; Bartlett and Ghoshal (2010).

13 Segal-Horn, S., and Faulkner, D. (1999). *The Dynamics of International Strategy*, London: International Thomson Business Press.

14 Palmisano, S.J. (2006). Multinationals have to be superseded, *Financial Times*, June 12: 19.

15 Source: http://www.ferro.com/About/History/(2014). Adapted from E. Brandt, Global HR. *Personnel Journal*, March 1991. Also see Bartlett, C.A., and Ghoshal, S. (2010). *Managing Across Borders: The Transnational Solution*, Boston: Harvard Business School Press; Segal-Horn and Faulkner (1999).

16 This has been the traditional perspective to describe organizational structure. For early work on this topic see Rumelt, R. (1986). *Strategy, Structure, and Economic Performance* (Rev. ed.), Boston, MA: Harvard Business School Press; Chandler, A.D., Jr. (1962). *Strategy and Structure: Chapters in the History of the American Industrial Enterprise*. Cambridge, MA: MIT Press; Miles, R., and Charles S. (2003). *Organizational, Strategy, Structure and Process*, Stanford: Stanford University Press. For more current work see Galbraith, J.A. (2014). *Designing Organizations: Strategy, Structure, and Process at the Business Unit and Enterprise Levels*, 3rd ed., San Francisco: Jossey-Bass Evans.

17 Palmisano (2006).

18 Ibid.

19 Ibid.

20 For more information on the Global Matrix Structure see Galbraith, J.R. (2013). Matrix management: structure is the easy part. *People & Strategy*, (1), 6; Galbraith (2014).

21 Evans, P.A.L. (1992), *op. cit.*, p. 4.

22 See Rabotin, M. (2014). Connecting virtual teams: global, virtual teams must learn how to align behaviors and collaborate across cultures and around the world. *T+D*, (4), 32; Magnusson, P., Schuster, A., and Taras, V. (2014). A process-based explanation of the psychic distance paradox: Evidence from global virtual teams. *Management International Review*, (3), 283; Zander, L., Zettinig, P., and Makela, K. (2013). Leading global virtual teams to success. *Organizational Dynamics*, (3)., 228; Hoch, J.E., and Kozlowski, S.J. (2014). Leading virtual teams: Hierarchical leadership, structural supports, and shared team leadership. *Journal of Applied Psychology*, (3), 390; Erez, M., Lisak, A., Harush, R., Glikson, E., Nouri, R., and Shokef, E. (2013). Going global: Developing management students' cultural intelligence and global identity in culturally diverse virtual teams. *Academy of Management Learning & Education*, 12(3), 330–355; Klitmøller, A., and Lauring, J. (2013). When global virtual teams share knowledge: Media richness, cultural difference and language commonality. *Journal of World Business*, 48(3), 398–406; Armstrong, D.J., and Cole, P. (1995). Managing distances and differences in geographically distributed work groups, in Jackson, S.E., and Ruderman, M.N. (eds.), *Diversity in Work Teams*, Washington, DC: American Psychological Association, pp. 187–215; Cascio, W.F. (2000). Managing a virtual workplace, *Academy of Management Executive*, 14(3), 81–90.

23 This section borrows heavily from Cascio, W.F. (2000). Managing a virtual workplace, *Academy of Management Executive*, 14(3), 81–90.

24 Marquardt, M.J., and Horvath, L. (2001). *Global Teams: How Top Multinationals Span Boundaries and Cultures with High-Speed Teamwork*, Palo Alto, CA: Davies-Black; Moran, R.T., Harris, P.R., and Stripp, W.G. (1993). *Developing the Global Organization*, Houston, TX: Gulf Publishing; Odenwald, S.B. (1996). *op cit.;* and O'Hara-Devereaux, M., and Johansen, R. (1994). *Globalwork: Bridging Distance, Culture, and Time*, San Francisco: Jossey-Bass. Also see Cramton, C.D., and Hinds, P.J. (2014). An embedded model of cultural adaptation in global teams. *Organization Science*, 25(4), 1056–1108; Zander, L., Mockaitis, A.I., and Butler, C.L. (2012). Leading global teams. *Journal of World Business*, 47(4), 592; Sullivan, B. (2013, Jul 04), International teams must also be local. *Financial Times*.

25 Duarte, D.L., and Snyder, N.T. (2006). *Mastering Virtual Teams*, San Francisco: Jossey-Bass; and O'Hara-Devereaux and Johansen (1994).

26 Schuler, R.S., Jackson, S.E., and Luo, Y. (2004). *Managing Human Resources in Cross-border Alliances*, London: Routledge.

27 Duarte and Snyder (2006).

28 Evans, Pucik, and Barsoux (2002).

29 Ibid., 314–315.

30 Armstrong, D.J., and Cole, P. (1995). Managing distances and differences in geographically distributed work groups, in Jackson, S.E., and Ruderman, M.N. (eds.), *Diversity in Work Teams*, Washington, DC: American Psychological Association, pp. 187–215; Cramton, C.D. (2002). Finding common ground in dispersed collaboration. *Organizational Dynamics*, 30(4), 356–367; De Meyer, A. (1991). Tech talk: How managers are stimulating global R&D communication, *Sloan Management Review*, 32(3), 49–66.

31 This list is adapted from Solomon, C.M. (1998). Building teams across borders. *Workforce*, 3(6), 12–17; Solomon, C.M. (2001). Managing virtual teams. *Workforce*, 80, 60–64; and Johnson, C. (2002). Managing virtual teams. *HR Magazine*, 47(6), 68–73. Also see Goodman, N., and Bray, S.M. (2014). Preparing global virtual teams for success. *Training*, 51(5), 64–65; Klitmøller, A., and Lauring, J. (2013). When global virtual teams share knowledge: Media richness, cultural difference and language commonality. *Journal of World Business*, 48(3), 398; Purvanova, R.K. (2014). Face-to-face versus virtual teams: What have we really learned? *The Psychologist Manager Journal*, 17(1), 2.

32 See, for example, Berry, H. (2014). Global integration and innovation: Multicountry knowledge generation within MNCs. *Strategic Management Journal*, 35(6), 869–890; Shieh, C., Wang, I., and Wang, F. (2009). The relationships among cross-cultural management, learning organization, and organizational performance in multinationals. *Social Behavior and Personality*, 37(1), 15–30.; Blomkvist, K. (2012). Knowledge management in MNCs: The importance of subsidiary transfer performance. *Journal of Knowledge Management*, 16(6), 904–918; Najafi-Tavani, Z., Giroud, A., and Andersson, U. (2014). The interplay of networking activities and internal knowledge actions for subsidiary influence within MNCs. *Journal of World Business*, 49(1), 122–131; Hocking, J., Brown, M., and Harzing, A. (2007), Balancing global and local strategic contexts: Expatriate knowledge transfer, applications, and learning within a transnational organization, *Human Resource Management*, 46(4), 513; Klitmøller, A., and Lauring, J. (2013). When global virtual teams share knowledge: Media richness, cultural difference, and language commonality. *Journal of World Business*, 48(3), 398–406; McGuinness, M., Demirbag, M., and Bandara, S. (2013). Towards a multi-perspective model of reverse knowledge transfer in multinational enterprises: A case study of Coats plc. *European Management Journal*, 31(2), 179–195.; Fang, Y., Wade, M., Delios, A., and Beamish, P.W. (2013), An exploration of multinational enterprise knowledge resources and foreign subsidiary performance. *Journal of World Business*, 48(1), 30–38.; Kotter, J. (2012), Accelerate! *Harvard Business Review*, November, 2–13.

33 Daft, R. (2002). *The Leadership Experience*, 2nd ed., Orlando, FL: Harcourt College, 582.

34 Prokesch, S.E. (1997). Unleashing the power of learning: An interview with British Petroleum's John Browne. *Harvard Business Review*. Sept.–Oct., 148.

35 Senge, P. (2006). *The Fifth Discipline* (updated and revised). New York: Doubleday/Currency, 69.

36 Jackson, S.E., and Schuler, R.S. (2001). Turning Knowledge into Business Advantage, *Financial Times*, January 15: Special Section, Part 14.

Chapter 4

International Mergers and Acquisitions, International Joint Ventures, and Alliances

We form partnerships to help us make our products and services more sustainable and help us improve the communities in which we operate. . . . Together we can help solve the world's greatest challenges.

DuPont Corporation[1]

Learning Objectives

This chapter will enable the reader to:

- Describe the basic nature of international mergers and acquisitions, international joint ventures, and international alliances.
- Explain the major IHRM implications from international mergers and acquisitions, international joint ventures, and international alliances.
- Define the IHRM professional's role in implementing effective international mergers and acquisitions, international joint ventures, and international alliances.

This chapter examines the most common approaches to "going international," in addition to the options of starting a foreign operation "from scratch" as described in the previous chapters. These approaches involve forming one or more types of international combination. In this chapter we discuss the three most common types of combination.

International mergers and acquisitions (e.g., one firm from one country acquires a firm in another country), *international joint ventures* (e.g., two or more firms from two or more countries create a new and separate—legal—business entity), and *international alliances* (e.g., two or more firms enter into formal or informal partnerships that do not involve the creation of a new and separate legal entity). The chapter starts with a general discussion of some basic concepts in international combinations. Then the chapter discusses IHRM issues in international mergers and acquisitions and international joint ventures. And finally the chapter closes with a general discussion of IHRM issues in international alliances.

INTERNATIONAL COMBINATIONS: AN INTRODUCTION

All of these forms of international combination can be viewed as forms of partnership and thus create major coordination and integration challenges, as is true of all forms of partnership.[2] All of these involve areas of international business that IHRM professionals must thoroughly understand in order to provide senior managers with the advice they need for designing effective global businesses.

International mergers and acquisitions, joint ventures, and alliances of various types are increasingly used by firms to gain access to new global markets and global resources, such as technology and skilled people.[3] The number and value of such cross-border deals continues to increase dramatically. Recent examples of significant cross-border mergers and acquisitions include:[4]

- Microsoft *(USA)* and Nokia *(Finland)*;
- Pfizer *(USA)* and Polocard *(Poland)*;
- Google *(USA)* and Schaft *(Japan)*;
- Samsung *(South Korea)* and Nanoradio *(Sweden)*;
- Takeda Pharmaceutical *(Japan)* and Nycomed *(Norway)*.

Older cross-border deals include:

- British Petroleum (BP) *(United Kingdom)* and Amoco *(USA)*;
- Daimler Benz *(Germany)* and Chrysler *(USA)*;
- BMW *(Germany)* and The Rover Group *(United Kingdom)*.

Firms of every size and type from many different countries are using mergers or acquisitions to access or expand their global businesses.[5]

There are a number of pressures causing this wave of international acquisitions, including both a felt need to constantly grow the business—by acquiring a foreign competitor—to compete more successfully with other global firms and to achieve world-class market entry and industry leadership or to acquire assets and resources (usually technological and knowledge-based) needed to compete and that would otherwise be too expensive, take too long, or would just be impossible to develop internally.[6] When acquisition is the choice for entry into a new market, it is usually seen as a quicker and more effective way to develop a presence in a local market than to build such capability from scratch.

Other Types of International Combinations

There are a number of other forms of international combinations.[7] In some cultures or countries, partnerships are, if not the only way to enter the marketplace, at least the "smartest" way, either because foreigners can, for practical purposes, only do business in the country through local partnerships—joint ventures or other forms of combinations—either because relationships (established through the partnerships) are of primary importance to doing business in that culture or because the government requires such local partnering. International combinations, in general, refer to partnerships between firms that have their headquarters in different countries.

Two broad categories of international combinations include equity combinations and those that involve no shared equity investment.[8] *Equity-based international combinations* involve long-term relationships—with one partner buying all or most of the equity in the other partner—and that requires active day-to-day management by the controlling partner of a wide variety of business issues in the combined firm. *International mergers and acquisition* (IM&A) and *international joint ventures* (IJV) are two major types of equity-based international combinations. IJVs are defined as legally and economically new and separate organizational entities created by two or more parent firms that collectively invest financial as well as other resources in the new entity in order to pursue certain objectives. In an international joint venture, the new entity will have a new headquarters that will include participation from both partners and will likely be located in the country of the joint venture. In an international M&A, one firm buys controlling or full interest in another firm with the understanding that the buyer will determine how the combined operations will be managed.

Non-equity international combinations share profits, responsibilities, and resources according to specific contractual relationships—but do not involve one party buying equity in the other party. Each company cooperates as a separate legal entity, bears its own liabilities, and has the freedom to organize its own resources, production processes, and operations. Non-equity international combinations include joint exploration projects (e.g., in the energy sector), research and development consortia (e.g., in the pharmaceutical sector), co-production agreements (e.g., in the manufacturing sector), co-marketing arrangements (e.g., in consumer durable sectors), and long-term supply agreements (e.g., the retail sector).

Record of Success and Failure

Some surveys suggest that a large percentage (often reported to be over 50 percent) of international acquisitions, joint ventures, and partnerships fall short of their objectives and at least one-third are dissolved within a few months or years.[9] "Most organizations do not have the knowledge, experience, or capability to manage alliances to maximize returns on all sides."[10] As with mergers and acquisitions, international alliances can also be set up for the long-term and need to be governed throughout as relationships. Indeed, many top executives of multinational firms have not changed their "mental models" from the command-and-control approach often used in the past for mergers or acquisitions to the necessarily participatory, relation-building nature of a successful international acquisition, joint venture, or alliance.

Typically the reasons for pursuing an acquisition or international alliance are financial or strategic in nature due to perceived compatibility of or synergism in operations, products, services, markets, or technologies. Firms usually decide that an international merger or acquisition or joint venture (or, for that matter, a divestiture—creating an acquisition opportunity for someone else) will yield increased value and profits or improved market position for any one of five different reasons:[11]

1 It enhances industry consolidation (thus helping to eliminate expensive overcapacity), which is typically the situation when the overall market is mature and where market opportunities are flat or shrinking.
2 It enables geographic expansion into neighboring regions for a newly internationalizing, heretofore local, firm.
3 It enhances expansion into new markets for revenue growth, in which the opportunities will not wait for internal development.
4 It involves acquisition of new technology or products or knowledge when the firm doesn't have the resources to develop the product or technology internally.
5 It involves combining with one or more other firms in order to realize a synergy that will form a preeminent firm with superior market advantages or economies of scale, often when new industry configurations are being created by new technologies.

Due Diligence

In order to achieve these objectives (which, as pointed out above, happens all too rarely) firms need to conduct thorough preliminary *due diligence* to assess carefully the "real" values to be gained by acquisition of or partnering with potential target firms. However, in the typical situation,

> People often just jump into the deal and then [later] come the realization that you have to work at it. . . . There are no easy mergers or acquisitions. Mergers [and acquisitions] need to be more thoughtful, more precise with regard to their objectives, more deliberate with regard to their people and processes and yet be done in a rapid time.[12]

Effective due diligence prior to the eventual "marriage of the firms" tends to be highly underrated. Many global ventures fall prey to failure or reduced levels of success because this crucial research effort doesn't reveal the weaknesses or incompatibilities of a prospective foreign business partner.

Often the only due diligence that is performed involves a detailed audit of financial and legal issues and possibly product and market compatibilities or synergies. This normally includes a review of things like annual reports, financial statements, product brochures, corporate legal documents, and other documents relating to the prospective partner's business practices. General information consisting of credentials and certifications (such as ISO certifications) concerning principals, activities, and other requirements significant to the potential venture is also usually audited.

As a result, the typical due diligence review of the target firm during the pre-combination phase of partnering rarely considers the critical people, organizational, and HR issues that may well provide the eventual reasons for the success or failure of the combination. The HR complications often include issues such as overestimation of the abilities of the partner firm; an exaggerated assumption of the synergies available from the combination; inadequate attention to the incompatibilities of the firms' programs, ways of conducting business, and cultures; and unwillingness to prepare for the frequently experienced loss of productivity and staff after the merger or acquisition is completed. Add to these problems the typical differences experienced between legal and cultural systems in different countries, and it becomes easier to understand the necessity of HR due diligence (in addition to the normal financial and operations due diligence) prior to any international acquisition or international alliance and of paying attention to the necessary post-merger people integration issues. And yet, "globalization mandates alliances [and cross-border acquisitions], makes them absolutely essential to strategy. . . . Like it or not, the simultaneous developments that go under the name of globalization make alliances—entente—necessary."[13]

INTERNATIONAL MERGERS AND ACQUISITIONS AND THE ROLE OF IHRM

This section outlines the typical process followed by firms as they proceed through acquisition planning and implementation. In the best of circumstances, HR plays a significant role in the successful planning for and implementation of IM&As.

Process of Combination

The actual process of combination usually proceeds through three stages, as illustrated in Figure 4.1.[14] Every stage has its special problems and considerations. These stages are pretty much the same for the establishment of IM&As as for IJVs and international alliances, although there are enough unique characteristics for both IJVs and international alliances that those differences will be addressed in separate sections of the chapter.

The stages of combination include the following:

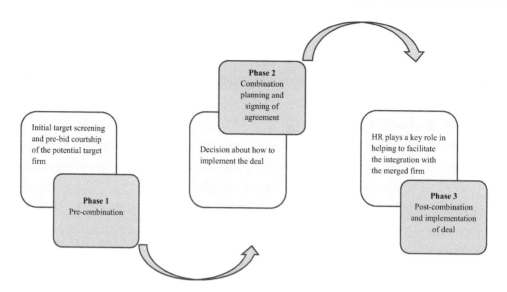

FIGURE 4.1 International Mergers and Acquisitions Process of Combination

Phase 1: Pre-combination

This first phase involves the initial target screening and pre-bid courtship of the potential target firm, the "due diligence" review of the target company, the price-setting and negotiation of the approach the partners will take to the combination, and the agreement on the contract wording of the deal. HR should be closely involved with each of these steps, particularly the due diligence process, since many aspects of the integration will involve issues of primary concern to HR and the workforce. This process of due diligence is discussed in more detail in the next section.

Phase 2: Combination Planning and Signing of the Agreement

Once the deal has been negotiated, this second phase involves deciding how to implement the deal, discovering and working through differences and different ideas about the deal, and actually signing the agreement. Here, too, HR should play a major role in providing advice on how to implement the deal and anticipating problems that will occur during the implementation.

Phase 3: Post-combination and Implementation of the Deal

Once the deal has been consummated, the hard work of implementation must be executed. In this third phase, HR has a key role in helping to facilitate the integration with the merged firm. One critical aspect of HR's role will be in creating and providing employee communication about the nature of the merger and about the vision for the business that will result after the merger has been consummated. In addition, HR will perform a critical role in training employees to accept and to fit into the new situation, in developing new assignments and staffing, in designing the new compensation and benefits systems, etc.

Problems that will be encountered in Phase 3 implementation should be addressed during the thorough due diligence in Phase 1 and implementation planning in Phase 2. Since this is often not done, it is little wonder that many combinations across national boundaries come unwound in a relatively short period of time.

Figure 4.2 summarizes the HR issues in the three stages of IM&As.

Due Diligence and the Role of HRM

One of the primary reasons for the high failure rate in cross-border acquisitions and joint ventures involves the lack of attention prior to "signing the agreement" as well as during the implementation phase to issues related to HRM. Increasingly, the lack of people and organization fit is coming to be seen as the main factor explaining why businesses fail to reap the benefits.[15]

Stage 1: Pre-combination	■ Identifying reasons for the IM&A ■ Forming IM&A team/leader ■ Searching for potential partners ■ Selecting a partner ■ Planning for managing the process of the IM and/or A ■ Planning to learn from the process
Stage 2: Combination and integration	■ Selecting the integration manager ■ Designing/implementing teams ■ Creating the new structure/strategies/leadership ■ Retaining key employees ■ Motivating the employees ■ Managing the change process ■ Communicating to and involving stakeholders ■ Deciding on the HR policies and practice
Stage 3: Solidification and assessment	■ Solidifying leadership and staffing ■ Assessing the new strategies and structures ■ Assessing the new culture ■ Assessing the new HRM policies and practices ■ Assessing the concerns of stakeholders ■ Revising as needed ■ Learning from the process

FIGURE 4.2 HR Issues in the Three Stages of IM&As

Source: R. S. Schuler, S. E. Jackson, and Y. Luo, *Managing Human Resources in Cross-Border Alliances* (Routledge Publishing, 2004). Used by permission.

Regrettably, many aspects of the potential partner that often determine success or failure are ignored or minimized during the due diligence process. Many of these relate to HRM, such as the compatibilities or differences in the corporate cultures and likely employee losses and the effect on later executive succession. The reasons for failure usually have more to do with the incompatibility of people, cultures, and/or HR systems than with problems with the originally perceived financial or strategic benefits. These issues are discussed in the next section, showing their importance to the likelihood of success. The actual due diligence process as it involves HRM can be quite complex. Thus the following describes both the process itself and suggested content for any IHRM-related due diligence.

Preparation

■ The primary point of due diligence from an HRM perspective is that HRM professionals should be involved. The development of a checklist of critical issues and the identification of task force membership should be prepared ahead of time. HRM professionals should take the initiative to ensure that critical HRM issues are considered before the combination becomes a "done deal."[16]
■ Pre-determine an action plan and checklist of HR items to evaluate.
■ Create a SWAT team of the key people that would be called into action as soon as executives begin to consider a foreign combination. Characteristics of such a team should include personal traits such as being inquisitive, having non-directive interviewing skills, the ability to "read" people, and the ability to recognize when they are not getting the full story, as well as, of course, the necessary cross-cultural, language, and HR business expertise. Planning should include when and how the SWAT team would operate.
■ These individuals should have the technical and professional ability to know what to look for and how to find it, familiarity with HR issues such as compensation and benefits financial data, differing accounting systems, differing employment law requirements, sensitivity to cultural and language differences, awareness of possible union and labor differences, and objectivity.
■ Forming and communicating the new organizational culture to all employees.

Content (Specific Issues to Assess During HR's Due Diligence)

■ General "people" issues. These are issues that impact the whole organization and all employees.

  ❑ The national and corporate cultures of both the acquiring and the acquired firms.[17]
  ❑ Comparison of key executive approaches to strategy, management, and decision making.

❏ Hidden "skeletons in the closet," such as pending lawsuits, executive scandals, secret executive compensation promises, labor problems, etc.
❏ Managerial succession plans and identification of key people in both firms.
❏ Management capabilities.
❏ Quality and depth of employee skills.

■ Language skills/concerns.
■ Specific IHR issues, particularly incompatibilities between acquiring and acquired firms.

❏ Adequate funding of obligations, such as pension and health care plans.
❏ Foreign employment regulations, both legal requirements and enforcement practices.
❏ HR department status, practices, policies, and organization.
❏ Merger of corporate cultures.

Once these issues are assessed, the HR team must focus on the many specific areas of HR policy and practice that typically vary significantly from country to country, as described below.

Staffing

Staffing practices—such as recruiting, hiring decisions, legal requirements, work contracts, job placement, job descriptions, etc.—can vary in significant ways between firms, particularly when the firms come from different countries and cultures.

Compensation

Compensation practices—such as pay levels, pay comparisons, valuation of differing jobs, form and delivery of pay, extra month's pay, bonuses—can vary dramatically and can cause major problems when integrated across firms.

Benefits

Government mandated and/or provided benefits, voluntary benefits, benefits considered as part of income or not, cost of benefits—such as health care, holidays, vacations, medical and family leave, pensions—can all cause major problems when merged across borders.

Training and Management/Career Development Programs

The importance and frequency and methods of delivery of training, and the presence of management development and career development programs are likely to vary from total absence to extensive inclusion. Making such diversity compatible can be quite complex and can lead to major differences of satisfaction between firms.

HR Information Systems

Merging HR information systems (workforce and employee data) will be difficult because of technical incompatibilities, legal differences between countries, and varying values related to maintenance of such information.

Unionization/Nature of Labor Relations/Labor Contracts

Parties to cross-border acquisitions and joint ventures cannot ignore consideration of country union and labor relations regulations and practices. Every country has its own legalities and traditions and most firms also have their own histories and practices.

Employee Involvement/Works Councils

Many countries require formal employee involvement in the management of their firms. Such works councils and co-determination practices need to be assessed and integrated into any cross-border planning.

Process of Integration

Once the due diligence has been completed, and the formal merger/acquisition process of combination has been completed, the firms must plan and implement the integration of the firms. Yet, organizational integration in the aftermath of mergers or acquisitions is often reported as being problematic.[18]

One frequently mentioned cause of integration problems is a general resistance to change. It is assumed that people seek stability and that any major change to one's employer such as an acquisition is anxiety provoking. Employees in both the acquired and the acquiring firms feel frustration, shock and apathy, and insecurity. This can hamper the day-to-day operations of both firms, among other things because teamwork can break down and people may start behaving destructively. Stress can become a common feature. Often employees lose faith in their organization's willingness to live up to expectations, promises, and legitimate demands. A lack of commitment, loyalty, and loss of enthusiasm can often result. Employees may lose their sense of identity and membership while the acquiring firm is viewed as being obsessed with controlling the acquired firm. Indeed, the most mobile of employees (in both firms, but for sure in the acquired firm) are likely to leave, making later recovery and integration even more difficult.

One of the sources of this resistance to change involves employees' sense of (or worry about) loss of their corporate (and, in this international context, national) culture and values. The process of acculturation (individuals and organizations adapting and reacting to each other's cultures) can take place in a number of different ways, not all of them healthy.[19] As much as both parties typically state the merger or acquisition is a combination of equals, in practice one group always dominates in the acculturation process. Thus, the process of acculturation can result in any of the following (see Figure 4.3):

- ■ *Portfolio*: Maintain separate cultures;
- ■ *Blending*: Choose the best element from each culture;
- ■ *New Creation*: Develop a new culture that fits the new organization;
- ■ *Assimilation*: Assign legitimacy to one culture and expect assimilation by members of the other culture.

The point is that assimilation is not always the result of the merger or acquisition of one firm by another. When there is a lack of agreement on the preferred adaptation process by the acquired and acquiring firms (due to things like the attractiveness of the acquirer to the acquired or the degree of similarity of the firms or the degree of existing multiculturalism of the acquiring firm, or whether or not the acquisition was hostile), problems will occur and integration may not happen.

How organizational combinations are handled affects the bottom line. Specifically, profits and revenues are impacted by the sharing of synergies and best practices from both companies. If the combination is not handled properly, the costs can be high such as lower

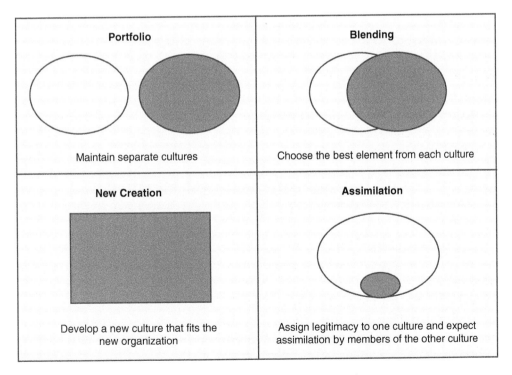

FIGURE 4.3 Four Approaches to Integration in International Mergers and Acquisitions

Source: Schuler, R.S., Jackson, S.E., and Luo, Y. (2004). *Managing Human Resources in Cross-Border Alliances*, London/New York: Routledge, p. 90.

productivity, loss of key talent, and an emergence of organizational cynicism and negative cultural effects. In some notable cases, such as the merger between Renault and Volvo and the merger between Chrysler and Mercedes-Benz, the resulting combinations suffered from cultural difficulties. Perhaps the most difficult aspect to manage is cultural integration.[20]

Since cultural integration is often so problematic, how can it be managed effectively? In general, in order to assess the possibilities, HRM professionals might want to ask the following questions:

- Have cultural gaps and differences been identified and addressed?
- Is there an executive leadership group, including participants from the acquired partner's senior leadership team, visibly leading the change process?
- Has the shared vision of the new organization been created and communicated to all employees with clearly defined goals, roles, and responsibilities? (See the BCE case at the end of this chapter.)
- Has a link been made between the business strategy and the quality, skills, and number of people to achieve the business plan?
- Has a decision to consolidate the processes and procedures around compensation, incentives, and recognition programs been made?
- Is there a plan to consolidate or maintain existing retirement benefits and health and welfare benefits?
- Are measures and rewards established, communicated, and aligned with the organization's desired state?

An example (see the IHRM in Action) of the "lessons learned" from many acquisitions in the integration process in a major MNE can be seen in the experiences of GE Capital (one of the world's largest providers of credit).[21]

IHRM in Action 4.1: Lessons Learned by GE in Cross-Border Acquisitions

Over the years and as the result of experience with many, many acquisitions, GE Capital Services' acquisition-integration process has been discussed, debated, tested, changed, and refined. It is now well established and codified. The following are some of the lessons they have learned about how to ensure the success of an acquisition.

Lesson 1: Acquisition integration is not a discrete phase of a deal and does not begin when the documents are signed. Rather, it is a process that begins with the early due diligence and runs through the ongoing management of the new enterprise.

Lesson 2: Integration management is a full-time job and needs to be recognized as a distinct business function, just like operations, marketing, or finance.

Lesson 3: Decisions about management structure, key roles, reporting relationships, layoffs, restructuring, and other career-affecting aspects of the integration should be made, announced, and implemented as soon as possible after the deal is signed—within days, if possible. Creeping changes, uncertainty, and anxiety that last for months are debilitating and immediately start to drain value from an acquisition.

Lesson 4: A successful integration melds not only various technical aspects of the businesses involved but also the different cultures. The best way to integrate cultures is to get people working together quickly to solve business problems and accomplish results that could not have been achieved before.

Even with the 10 and more years spent on refining the acquisition integration process and making "best practices" available via the intranet, including things like communication plans, 100-day plans, functional integration checklists, workshop agendas, consulting resources, and human resource department support, the process remains an ongoing challenge. Every acquisition is unique, with its own business strategy, personality, and culture. Thus, GE Capital continues to strive to make every new acquisition integration better than the last. Maybe the most important lesson that GE Capital has learned is that the competence to make the integration process work must always be worked on—it is never fully attained.

The Separation Process

Interestingly, the separation process (divestiture) is very similar to the acquisition process. Most of the issues of concern to IHR during a divestiture can be viewed as being similar to those examined during the acquisition process, except they are from the other side of the transaction, whenever the firm being purchased is a part of another, larger firm. The parent of the firm being sold needs to also be careful to do thorough due diligence to assess issues such as the impact on union contracts and pension liabilities (as well as other promises and liabilities) and the impact on the parent firm, which is trying to improve its own financial and operational situation. Dissolution, or divestiture, or de-merging, or spinning off, or selling off parts of an existing enterprise is often the result of a merger or acquisition that didn't work out well because the original planning was inadequate.[22]

Summary

In the process of international M&A, IHR professionals, in order to ensure they provide the critical business advice expected of them, need to make sure they are prepared to provide procedural and content advice to their executives in all three phases of planning, signing, and implementing, especially for issues related to due diligence, impact of culture, and specific IHR post-merger, program-integration issues. The degree to which all of these items need to be assessed and addressed and the nature of the solutions that will be required will depend on:[23]

- the firm's strategic purpose and desired results;
- the degree of planned operational integration of the resulting firm;
- management's orientation and intention for the resulting firm; and
- cultural environment factors.

Ultimately, the success of the acquisition may well depend on the abilities that the IHR team bring to the discussion, preparation, and implementation.

IHRM AND INTERNATIONAL JOINT VENTURES

The above discussion of IHR in IM&A was based on relatively extensive experience and literature. Similar literature is not as extensive, however, for the last subjects in this chapter: IJVs and international alliances. Nevertheless, as indicated early in the chapter, these forms of international combination are increasingly important and need to be understood by IHRM students and practitioners. The Schuler, Jackson, Luo book, *Managing Human Resources in Cross-Border Alliances*, in this series, was written in part to help address this very reality.[24]

When a firm acquires an existing entity in another country, the central problem is to integrate an existing firm and its culture and practices into the parent firm. In an international joint venture (IJV), a new legal entity is created. Although there are a number of definitions of an IJV, a typical definition is:

> A separate legal organizational entity representing the partial holdings of two or more parent firms, in which the headquarters of at least one is located outside the country of operation of the joint venture. This entity is subject to the joint control of its parent firms, each of which is economically and legally independent of the other.[25]

Examples of international joint ventures include:

- **Verizon Wireless**: Parent firms include Vodafone Group *(United Kingdom)* and Verizon Communications *(USA)*;
- **Transatlantic Joint Venture**: Parent firms include Air France *(France)*, KLM *(Netherlands)*, Alitalia *(Italy)*, and Delta *(USA)*;
- **Starbuck Coffee Japan, Ltd**: Parent firms include Sazaby League *(Japan)* and Starbucks Coffee International *(USA)*.

Thus the central challenge in an IJV is to create a new firm, with all its dimensions, culture, and practices. This new entity can emulate one or more of the partners; that is, it can be some form of integrated entity, drawing on the culture and practices of the partners. Or it can be designed to be an entirely new organization, separate from the cultures or practices of the partners.[26] One of the keys to success of an IJV is for the partners to be clear about and to agree on which one of these choices is being pursued. Lack of clarity on this issue can lead to conflicting expectations for the performance of the resulting organization and will typically lead to unmet expectations and eventual dissolution of the venture.

This section describes HR responsibilities related to international joint ventures. The aim is to describe the HR practices and policies that influence the success of IJVs, drawing on the studies that have focused on HR and IJVs.[27] As far back as the mid-1970s, IJVs replaced wholly owned subsidiaries as the most widespread form of US multinational investment[28] and has also become a favored form of foreign entry for firms from many other countries, as well. In general, IJVs have become a major (if not, the major) form of entry into most new global markets.[29]

Schuler et al. (2004) developed a model to help understand the complexities in the process of creation and implementation of IJVs (refer to Figure 4.4). The four stages of the IJV process include:

1 Formation: the partnership stage;
2 Development: the IJV itself;

Stage 1: Formation: the partnership	■ Identifying the reasons for forming the IJV ■ Planning for the utilization of its potential benefits ■ Selecting a manager for new business development ■ Finding potential partners ■ Selecting the partner(s) ■ Understanding control, building trust, managing conflict ■ Negotiating the arrangement
Stage 2: Development: the IJV itself	■ Locating the IJV and dealing with the local community ■ Establishing the appropriate structure ■ Getting the IJV management team
Stage 3: Implementation: the IJV itself	■ Establishing the vision, mission, values, culture, and strategy ■ Developing the HRM policies and practices ■ Dealing with unfolding issues ■ Staffing the IJV
Stage 4: Advancement: the IJV and beyond	■ Learning between partners ■ Transferring the new knowledge to the parents ■ Transferring the new knowledge to other locations

FIGURE 4.4 Four-stage Model of HR Issues in International Joint Ventures

Source: Schuler, R.S., Jackson, S.E., and Luo, Y. (2004). *Managing Human Resources in Cross-Border Alliances*, London/New York: Routledge, p. 37.

3 Implementation: the IJV itself; and
4 Advancement: the IJV and beyond.

The rest of this section on IJVs will expand on and explain these stages.

Stages 1 and 2: Formation and Development of the IJV

Reasons for IJVs

Reasons for entering into IJV agreements (not so different from the reasons for international acquisitions, except for the reduced risk, since it is shared in a new, separate entity) include the following:[30]

■ to gain knowledge about local markets, culture, and local ways of doing business in order to transfer that knowledge back to the parent firm, i.e., to learn from the joint venture partner;

■ to gain access to the partner's product technology, product knowledge, or methods of manufacturing;

■ to satisfy host government requirements and insistence;

■ to gain increased economies of scale without more direct investment;

■ to gain local market image and channel access;

■ to obtain vital raw materials or technology;

■ to spread the risks with the foreign partners;

■ to improve competitive advantage in the face of increasing global competition; and

■ to become more cost-effective and efficient in the face of increased globalization of markets.

The overriding motive in most joint ventures seems to be the desire by one or all parties to gain knowledge and learn from their partner(s). Obviously for a firm to learn from a partner, the partner must have some level of willingness to share what they know. If all partners wish to learn from the others, then to be successful, all the partners must be willing to share. This is often a source of conflict, in itself, particularly where there is not a sufficient level of trust among the partners. In this case, sharing will tend to be minimized and the original objective will be stymied. Often, the central strategy for learning from the IJV has to do with the choices for staffing. "Transfer of staff between the JV and the parent firms can provide a mechanism for sharing information, for learning from each other's abilities and expertise, and for the creation of synergies related to product development."[31] But if the wrong people are chosen to staff the IJV, that is people with poor interpersonal or cross-cultural skills or limited technical ability, this objective of the partners may be difficult to achieve.

Track Record

The prior section of this chapter spent considerable space on the importance of HRM due diligence to the eventual success of IM&As. Everything said there also applies to the development of international joint ventures. The compatibilities of the partners' cultures (both corporate and country), styles of management and decision making, HR practices, etc., are critical to the development of a successful IJV, as well.[32]

As with M&As, the high failure rate and managerial complexity of IJVs also suggests that particular examination of the human resource issues is required here, as well.[33] As far back as 1987, Shenkar and Zeira pointed out that even though IJVs had become the "most widespread form of . . . multi-national involvement, the substantial failure rate and managerial complexity suggest that a closer examination of human resource issues is required."[34] The reasons for failure are many and complex, but for any particular situation will include one or more of the following, many of which are directly or indirectly within the responsibility of HR:[35]

- There is a poor selection of partner(s).
- Partners don't clarify each others' goals and objectives or have differing goals.
- The negotiating teams lack JV experience.
- The parties do not conduct adequate or realistic feasibility studies.
- The parties lack clarity about the real capabilities of their partners.
- The partners fail to do adequate due diligence and thus don't learn enough about each other, which can be particularly true for cultural issues.
- The parties fail to judge realistically the impact of the venture on the parent organizations, particularly the loss of control and possibly profits, at least in the short run.
- There is too little thought during the design phase of the new venture to organizational and managerial issues.
- The partners fail to adequately integrate their activities.
- There is unequal commitment to the partnership or unequal contribution (real or perceived) to the joint venture.
- The partners do not trust each other.
- The parties to the venture make a poor selection of personnel to staff the JV.
- The managers from the parent firms do not get along.
- The established local partner does not assign its best people to the JV.
- One of the partners is a government, so that there is a built-in variance in objectives (profit versus possible political goals, for example).
- There are divergent national interests.
- There is "bad faith" on the part of one or more of the partners, that is, one or more of the partners has always planned on only extracting something of value from the partnership without giving anything in return, even though they claim otherwise during negotiations.

- The loyalty and commitment of the assigned managers is unclear (or is only to their assigning firm).
- The local employees resent the privileged position of assigned expatriate managers, particularly if they are only assigned to the JV on a temporary basis.
- The new entity cannot decide which parents' rules to follow (or which ones to establish, if there are to be new rules).
- There is a failure to adapt the business practices of the new venture to the local culture.

If the partners to an IJV can't cope with the demands of managing a joint venture (that is, dealing effectively with a partner), then it may be better for the partners to use non-equity forms of cooperation, such as partnerships or international alliances (as addressed in the next section), which can take the form of agreements for cross-marketing, cross-production, licensing, or research-and-development consortia and can be terminated with relative ease if insurmountable problems arise.[36]

Those who have studied IJVs find that some of the keys to creating a successful joint venture require the partners to seek complementary strategies and technical skills and resources among prospective partners, accept their mutual dependency, resolve issues related to differences in size of the partners, ensure the compatibility of the partners' operating policies and practices, work to eliminate communication barriers between the partners and between the new IJV management team and the IJV employees, and take strong steps to develop trust and commitment among the partners.[37]

Stage 3: Implementation of the IJV

Role of HRM in IJVs

From a human resource management point-of-view, the lessons learned from successful joint ventures include:[38]

- When national and corporate cultures are blended, the partners need to spend time building trust; understanding and accommodating each others' interests.[39]
- Job design can be enhanced when the partners are willing to learn from one another.
- Recruitment and staffing policies should be well-defined in the early stages of the venture.[40]
- Orientation and training of employees should focus on preparing employees to deal with the social context of their jobs, as well as the development of technical skills, for the new organization.[41]
- Performance appraisals need clear objectives and clearly assigned accountabilities, liberal time frames in which to achieve results, and built-in flexibility related to changing market and environmental demands of the new venture.[42]
- Compensation and benefit policies should be uniform to avoid employee feelings of inequity.

- Career opportunities must be ensured for local managers relative to managers assigned to the JV from the parents.
- In the early stages of the venture, the partners must agree on suitable terms for relations with any unions.
- The partners must establish the specific role of HR within the new venture (since the partners' HR policies and practices are likely to differ).
- HR managers in the JV must become process experts, managing issues like communication with employees about the new organization, expected nature of the integration of the partners in the JV.
- HR must implement the necessary training (e.g., cultural—both corporate and national, and technical), integrated and consistent compensation and benefit systems, and performance management systems that will give the IJV its own identity.

Stage 4: Advancement of the IJV

Since one of the main reasons for creating IJVs involves the desire of the partners to learn from each other, this becomes one of the central foci for determining the success or failure of an IJV. And if learning is taking place, the partners must ensure the transfer of the new knowledge to the partners, both within the IJV itself as well to the parent firms outside the IJV.

IHRM AND INTERNATIONAL ALLIANCES

As mentioned previously, international alliances are defined as informal or formal partnerships or agreements that do not result in an independent legal entity. These have become much more common and popular in recent years.[43] They provide ways to increase capabilities and to enter new markets in relatively low-risk and low-cost ways. As important as international acquisitions have become, the use of international alliances and partnerships may have become even more important.[44] They take many forms, for example, outsourcing, information sharing, web consortia, joint marketing, and research projects. The most radical take the form of corporate partnerships like Coca Cola's and Proctor and Gamble's alliance to market their non-fizzy beverages and snacks. Technology companies like IBM, pharmaceutical firms like Pfizer, and diversified manufacturers like Siemens and General Electric have partnering built into their operating plans, both for joint research partnerships and for joint marketing efforts.[45]

In most modern partnerships, the three most important reasons their members form international alliances are growth, access to competencies like technology and research capability, and expansion into new markets. E-mail, file-sharing, and web-based conferencing and collaboration tools make international alliances across corporate and national boundaries workable. In the past, the route to growth was paved with mergers and acquisitions. What firms lacked they could acquire. This is still a popular approach. But as indicated in the previous section, trying to create a competency your firm lacks is costly, time consuming, and often fails.[46] Too often, the best of the acquired assets (the acquired firm's people) leave for other firms (often the competition). M&As are often ruinously expensive (with the inflated stock market) in terms of debt accrued, cash depleted, equity diluted, and key employees lost through subsequent downsizings and voluntary turnover. International alliances have become the solution to the problem. International alliances, relative to IJVs and IM&As are the cheapest and least-risky way to grow and build—or acquire—technology and resources: no dilution of stock, no dangerous leveraging of the balance sheet, and if managed well, no loss of talent. If the deal doesn't work, it can be dissolved.[47]

Options for Managing International Alliances

As with IM&As and IJVs, there are a number of choices for the design of an international alliance. These include the following:[48]

- the operator model, where there is one dominant partner;
- the shared model, where the organization draws on culture and practices from both partners; and
- the autonomous model, where a new organizational culture and management structure is purposely developed.

The partners need to discuss and agree on which model for the international alliance they wish to pursue in order to forestall subsequent misunderstandings and conflict.

General HR Issues

There are a number of concerns that might be referred to as simply "people and general management issues" in international alliances for which HR might be expected to be the source of expertise and advice. If they are not addressed by HR, they are likely to not be addressed at all.[49] Most of these issues are similar to those faced by IM&As and IJVs, as well:

- **Organizational structure and reporting relationships:** a clear managerial structure is often non-existent in a partnership, and staff members—including HR professionals—tend to report to many people.[50] Partnerships tend to not have the traditional pyramidal management structure of the partner firms. They are usually established as projects, with typical project structure and with project members assigned temporarily from other areas of the partner firms, with employees having multiple responsibilities, some in the partnership and some in the parent firms.
- **Culture:** as with all other forms of international organization, both national and corporate cultures need to be assessed for incompatibilities. This is important for all interactions within the partnership and between the partnership and the parent firms.

- **Pre-alliance due diligence**: This requires that the parties be aware of any "skeletons in the closet" of their potential partners, e.g., scandals involving senior executives, recent negative media stories, nepotism (employment of family members), etc.
- **Global workforce**: Since the international alliance will involve employees and managers from more than one culture, the cross-cultural skills of involved executives also need to be assessed, both of those executives that will be assigned to the international alliance and those who must work with the international alliance.
- **Management capabilities**: Will the international alliance get high priority for assignment of top talent by all partners? If the latter is the case, assessing the quality of the talent to be assigned becomes particularly important, if the partners are truly committed to the success of the partnership.

Role of IHRM in International Alliances

Depending on the size of the international alliance itself, there may well be IHR professionals assigned to it.[51] Typically, the IHR professional assigned to an international partnership or international alliance has not only to deal with many more decision makers (from all of the partners), thus having to exercise much greater negotiation skills, but also tends to have to take on more extensive responsibilities, combining those of a local nature and those of an international nature.

Different Rules Often Apply

For example, people who work in partnerships are still employees of the separate partners, thus may not only be difficult to "supervise" but in terms of legal status may also not fall under employment protection statutes of the locale of the alliance. This may give the partnership greater flexibility with respect to compensation and job assignments, but may also create significant liability when "employees" are covered by the laws of their parent employer, such as under sexual harassment claims. Under tax laws, employees—from various partner parents—assigned to a partnership may not be entitled to the same benefit plans, thus causing problems of perceived unfairness and inequity.

CONCLUSION

International combinations or some forms of partnerships have become very popular in recent years. Yet a high percentage of these combinations fail to achieve financial or strategic objectives. This is often due to inadequate attention to issues of concern to the human resource function. This chapter examined the process of combination and provided a framework and content for performing a thorough due-diligence review of the IHRM policies and practices of firms being considered for cross-border alliances. Such a review is explained as critical to the success of such international combinations. These combinations include IM&As, IJVs, and international alliances. Much of the chapter describes the role of IHRM and the IHR professional in designing, facilitating, and implementing these three specific types of international combinations. All three types of these combinations are increasingly used and IHRM can and should play a major role in helping ensure the success of their design and implementation.

DISCUSSION QUESTIONS

1 Some managers argue that IJVs are fraught with problems and all but doomed to failure. Do you agree with this statement? Why or why not?

2 Name three well-known MNEs that have formed international mergers or acquisitions during the last few years. Are they successful? What role does HRM play in facilitating success in international mergers or acquisitions?

3 What are the advantages and disadvantages of working for an IJV? An international alliance?

4 What are some of the reasons that an MNE would choose international expansion through an acquisition? An IJV? An alliance? What are the variables that would influence the decision? Which choice do you think is best for the likely benefit of the firm?

CASE STUDY 4.1: BCE's Acquisition of Teleglobe International (Canada)

Lance Richards, former international director of HR at Teleglobe, has been through a number of major cross-border acquisitions and alliances. These included British Telecom with MCI and GTE with Bell Atlantic and then with Teleglobe and BCE. These experiences have taught Lance that in any cross-border acquisition or alliance, making sure that employees know what is going on, who is in charge, and where the combined organization is heading needs to be in the very front of any HR initiatives. Some of the specific lessons for guaranteeing success in an acquisition that Lance has learned include:

■ The CEOs (of both the acquiring and the acquired firms) must be visible to the employees and must continuously interact with them.
■ Both companies must communicate—clearly, constantly, and quickly.
■ The dialogue with employees must be two-way. Employees must have a way to feed questions and concerns back to the business and people in charge, and then to get answers.

As Lance puts it, in many acquisitions and alliances the corporate heads roll out a well-crafted vision of the new entity, how it will lead the market, and how it will now be able to leap ahead of its competitors. But for the average employee, all they want to hear is what is going to happen to their particular jobs. In M&A activity, where the intellectual capital that resides in the employees is often (or should be) the overriding concern, it is important, at the end of the day, to remember that employees are concerned about things like making their next car payments or paying the next term's tuition for their child.

The BCE acquisition of Teleglobe (completed in November 1, 2000) provided a great example of how to handle employee expectations and concerns with professionalism and candor. BCE Inc., is the largest communications company in Canada and provides a variety of services such as broadband communications and content services to private and public customers. Simultaneously with the after-market-hours announcement to the public, all employees received an e-mail with a link to a pre-recorded streaming video, with messages from the chairmen of both firms. They clearly outlined the reasons for the acquisition, as well as the benefits, and then committed to maintain clear communications throughout the process of merging the two firms.

A Q&A board was established on the companies' intranets, accessible in all 43 countries where the firms had employees, with a promise to answer most questions within five business days. Within a month, BCE had appointed a new CEO. Within a week of his arrival he held the first of several meetings with employees. Initially, he made presentations in person in all of the firms' primary employment cities, then changed to a live, multi-country broadcast format, followed by conference calls for outlying countries. Simultaneously, he launched a series of breakfast and lunch meetings with 15 to 20 employees, which continued for months, wherever his travels took him. In consequence, the new CEO won much favor with employees for his candor and style. The key was that Teleglobe International (and BCE) immediately opened a variety of one- and two-way communications venues for all employees, and ensured that there was a steady flow of information to everyone. Even though major financial problems with the acquisition led to divestiture of Teleglobe after about two years, the strong employee communications did result in quite limited voluntary employee turnover and led to strong engagement from employees, leading to a continuing healthy BCE.

Sources: www.bce.ca (2014); Richards, L.J. (2001). Joining forces. *Global HR*, April, 31–33.

Discussion Questions

1   Why were these various forms of communication so successful? Which do you think were most important? Why? Which barriers stand in the way of using these forms of communication?
2   What content is necessary for this form of communication? What do employees need (want) to hear? What difference does it make?
3   Does this sort of communication need to come from the top? Can someone else, such as the head of HR, provide the information with equal success?

NOTES

1   Source: Dupont Corporate Website (2014), Dupont Collaborations http://www.dupont.com/corporate-functions/our-approach/sustainability/collaboration.html. Accessed Dec. 10, 2014.
2   See, for example, *World Investment Report* 2014, United Nations Conference on Trade and Development, UNCTAD; Schuler, R.S., Jackson, S.E., and Luo, Y. (2004). *Managing Human Resources in Cross-Border Alliances*, London: Routledge; Reuer, J., and Ragozzino, R. (2014). Signals and international alliance formation: The roles of affiliations and international activities. *Journal of International Business Studies*, 45(3), 321–337; *World Investment Report* 2000: Cross-Border Mergers and Acquisitions and Development, New York and Geneva: United Nations Conference on Trade and Development.
3   Ibid.
4   We used a variety of sources to identify recent and old mergers and acquisitions. Sources include: *World Investment Report* 2014, United Nations Conference on Trade and Development, UNCTAD; *Mergent* online database; *Bloomberg Businessweek; Fortune* magazine.
5   See Summers, N. (2104). The 2014 M&A boom: Almost $ trillion and growing, *Bloomberg Businessweek*, April 24, 2014; Baigorri, M., Campbell, M., and Kirchfeld, A. (2014). Mergers are back in fashion—for now. *Bloomberg Businessweek*, (4373), 50–51; Mergers and Acquisitions review, *Financial Advisors*, 2013. Thomson Reuters; Brakman, S., Garretsen, H., Charles Van, M., and Arjen Van, W. (2013). Cross-border merger and acquisition activity and revealed comparative advantage in manufacturing industries. *Journal of Economics and Management Strategy*, (1), 28; Wyss, S. (2012). Growth strategy: Mergers and acquisitions. *Chain Store Age*, 88(2), 30–32; Lester T. (2001). Merger most torrid, *Global HR*, June, 10–12, 15–16.
6   Based on an interview with Heinrich von Pierer, CEO of Siemens, by Javidan, M. (2002), reported in, Siemens CEO Heinrich von Pierer on cross-border acquisitions, *Academy of Management Executive*, 126 (1), 13–15; and Karnitschnig, M. (2003). For Siemens, move into U.S. causes waves back home, *The Wall Street Journal*, Sept. 8, pp. A1, A8.

7 Schuler, Jackson, and Luo (2004).

8 Ibid.

9 See McLetchie, J., and West, A. (2010). *Beyond Risk Avoidance: A McKinsey Perspective on Creating Transformational Value from Mergers.* McKinsey & Company; McKinsey & Company, Coopers & Lybrand, and American Management Association, reported in Marks, M.L. (1997), *From Turmoil to Triumph: New Life After Mergers, Acquisitions, and Alliances,* New York: Lexington Books.

10 Reported in Bates, S. (2002). Few business alliances succeed, report reveals, in Executive Briefing, *HR Magazine,* May, 12.

11 Bower, J.L. (2001). Not all M&As are alike—and that matters, *Harvard Business Review,* March, 93–101. Also see Kullman, E. (2012). DuPont's CEO on executing a complex cross-border acquisition. *Harvard Business Review,* 90(7/8), 43–46.

12 Beard, M. (1996). quoted in Bourrie, S.R., Merger misery, *Colorado Business,* October, 82.

13 Ohmae, K. (1989). The global logic of strategic alliances, *Harvard Business Review,* March–April, 143.

14 In the last few years a number of references have been published dealing with the management of mergers and acquisitions. These include: Krug, J., Wright, O., and Kroll, M. (2014). Top management turnover following mergers and acquisitions: Solid research to date but still much to be learned. *Academy of Management Perspectives,* 28(2), 143–163; Adomako, S., Gasor, G., and Danso, A. (2013). Examining human resource managers' involvement in mergers and acquisitions (M&As) process in Ghana. *Journal of Management Policy & Practice,* 14(6), 25–36.; Buiter, J.M., and Harris, C.M. (2013). Post-merger influences of human resource practices and organizational leadership on employee perceptions and extra-role behaviors. *SAM Advanced Management Journal,* (4), 14; Castro-Casal, C., Neira-Fontela, E., and Alvarez-Perez, M. (2013). Human resources retention and knowledge transfer in mergers and acquisitions. *Journal of Management and Organization,* (2), 188; Lee, D., Kim, K., Kim, T., Kwon, S., and Cho, B. (2013). How and when organizational integration efforts matter in South Korea: A psychological process perspective on the post-merger integration. *International Journal of Human Resource Management,* 24(5), 944–965; Lupina-Wegener, A.A. (2013). Human resource integration in subsidiary mergers and acquisitions: Evidence from Poland. *Journal of Organizational Change Management,* 26(2), 286–304; Gill, C. (2012). The role of leadership in successful international mergers and acquisitions: Why Renault-Nissan succeeded and DaimlerChrysler-Mitsubishi failed. *Human Resource Management,* 51(3), 433–456; Marks, M., and Mirvis, P.H. (2011). A framework for the human resources role in managing culture in mergers and acquisitions. *Human Resource Management,* 50(6), 859–877.

15 Coffey, J., Garrow, V., and Holbeche, L. (2002). *Reaping the Benefits of Mergers and Acquisitions: In Search of the Golden Fleece,* Oxford, UK: Butterworth-Heinemann, 9. All of the major references in this chapter that involve mergers and acquisitions, joint ventures, and alliances expand on this point. In addition, some of this section is adapted from McClintock, F.W. (1996). Due diligence and global expansion, *World Trade Center San Diego Newsletter,* p. 6; and Greengard, S. (1999). Due diligence: The devil in the details. *Workforce,* October: 68–72.

16 Adapted from Richard, L.J. (2001). Joining forces, *Global HR,* June, 20.

17 Reported in Hopkins, M. (2002). HR going global . . ., *Global HR,* April, 31–33.

18 Adapted from Kleppestø, S. (1998). A quest for social identity—The pragmatics of communication in mergers and acquisitions, in Gertsen, M.C., et al. (eds.), op cit., pp. 147–166.

19 Berry, J.W. (1980). Acculturation as varieties of adaptation, in Padilla, A.M. (ed.), *Acculturation Theory, Models and Some New Findings,* Boulder, CO: Westview Press, pp. 9–25; Gertsen, M.C., Sıderberg, A-M, and Torp, J.E. (1998), Different Approaches to the Understanding of Culture in Mergers and Acquisitions, in Gertsen, M.C., et al. (eds.), op cit., pp. 17–38.

20 Ibid.

21 See website http://www.ge.com/news/company-information/ge-capital (2014). Adapted from Ashkenas, R.N., DeMonaco, L.J., and Francis, S.C. (1998). Making the deal real: How GE Capital integrates acquisitions, *Harvard Business Review,* January–February, 165–178.

22 See, for example, Owen, G., and Harrison, T. (1995). Why ICI chose to demerge, *Harvard Business Review*, March–April, 133–142.

23 M&A cultural considerations (2001). Reported in *International Mobility Management Newsletter*, 2nd quarter, 7.

24 Schuler, Jackson, and Luo (2004); Schuler, R., Tarique, I., and Jackson, S. (2004). *Managing Human Resources in Cross-Border Alliances*, in Cooper, C., and Finkelstein, S. (eds.), *Advances in Mergers and Acquisitions*, Volume 4. New York: JAI Press, pp. 103–129.

25 Schenkar, O., and Zeira, Y. (1987). Human resources management in international joint ventures: Directions for research, *Academy of Management Review*, 12(3), 547.

26 Schuler, Jackson, and Luo (2004); Cyr, D.J. (1995). *The Human Resource Challenge of International Joint Ventures*, Westport, CN: Quorum Books.

27 See, for example, Schuler, R., and Tarique, I. (2012). International joint venture system complexity and human resource management, in Björkman, I., and Stahl, G. (eds.), *Handbook of Research in IHRM*, Cheltenham: Edward Elgar Publishing, pp. 393–414; Baughn, C., Neupert, K.E., Phan Thi Thuc, A., and Ngo Thi Minh, H. (2011). Social capital and human resource management in international joint ventures in Vietnam: A perspective from a transitional economy. *International Journal of Human Resource Management*, (5), 1017; Goodman, N. (2012). T&D for global JVs and M&As: Training and development can play a significant role in making international joint ventures and mergers and acquisitions more rewarding and less risky. *Training*, (1), 126; Wong, Y. (2012). Job security and justice: Predicting employees' trust in Chinese international joint ventures. *International Journal of Human Resource Management*, 23(19), 4129–4144; Choi, C., and Beamish, P.W. (2013). Resource complementarity and international joint venture performance in Korea. *Asia Pacific Journal of Management*, 30(2), 561–576; Huang, M., and Chiu, Y. (2014). The antecedents and outcome of control in IJVs: A control gap framework. *Asia Pacific Journal of Management*, 31(1), 245–269; Welei, S., Sunny Li, S., Pinkham, B.C., and Peng, M.W. (2014). Domestic alliance network to attract foreign partners: Evidence from international joint ventures in China. *Journal of International Business Studies*, (3), 338; Cyr, D.J. (1995); Frayne, C.A. and Geringer, J.M. (2000). Challenges facing general managers of international joint ventures, in Mendenhall, M., and Oddou, G. (eds.), *Readings and Cases in International Human Resource Management*, 3rd ed., Cincinnati: South-Western College Publishing; Schuler, R.S. (2001). Human resource issues and activities in international joint ventures, *The International Journal of Human Resource Management*, 12, 1–5; Schuler, R., Dowling, P., and De Cieri, H. (1992), The formation of an international joint venture: Marley Automotive Components, *European Management Journal*, 10(3), 304–309; Schuler, R.S., Jackson, S.E., Dowling, P.J. and Welch, D.E. and DeCieri, H. (1991). Formation of an international joint venture: Davidson Instrument Panel. *Human Resource Planning*, 14, 51–60; Schuler, Jackson, and Luo (2004); and Shenkar and Zeira (1987), 546–557.

28 Hladik, K.J. (1985). *International Joint Ventures: An Economic Analysis of U.S.-Foreign Business Partnerships*, Lexington, MA: Heath; and Liebman, H.M. (1975). *U.S. and Foreign Taxation of Joint Ventures*, Washington, DC: Office of Tax Analysis, US Treasury Department.

29 Barkema, H.G., Shenkar, O., Vermeulen, F., and Bell, J.H.J. (1997). Working abroad, working with others: How firms learn to operate international joint ventures, *Academy of Management Journal*, 40(2), 426–442.

30 This list draws heavily on Schuler (2001). See also: Vaidya, S. (2012). Trust and commitment: Indicators of successful learning in international joint ventures (IJVs). *Journal of Comparative International Management*, 15(1), 29–49; Ghauri, P.N., Cave, A.H., and Park, B. (2013). The impact of foreign parent control mechanisms upon measurements of performance in IJVs in South Korea. *Critical Perspectives on International Business*, 9(3), 251; Tjemkes, B.V., Furrer, O., Adolfs, K., and Aydinlik, A. (2012). Response strategies in an international strategic alliance experimental context: Cross-country differences. *Journal of International Management*, (1), 66; Zoogah, D.B., Vora, D., Richard, O., and Peng, M.W. (2011). Strategic alliance team diversity, coordination, and effectiveness. *International Journal of Human Resource Management*, (3),

510; Estrada, I., Martín-Cruz, N., and Pérez-Santana, P. (2013). Multi-partner alliance teams for product innovation: The role of human resource management fit. *Innovation: Management, Policy & Practice*, 15(2), 161–169; Pangarkar, N., and Wu, J. (2013). Alliance formation, partner diversity, and performance of Singapore startups. *Asia Pacific Journal of Management*, 30(3), 791–807; Gudergan, S.P., Devinney, T., Richter, N., and Ellis, R. (2012). Strategic implications for (non-equity) alliance performance. Long range planning. *International Journal of Strategic Management*, 45(5–6), 451–476; Child, J., and Faulkner, D. (1998). *Strategies of Cooperation*, Oxford: Oxford University Press; Pucik, V. (1988). Strategic alliances, organizational learning and competitive advantage: The HRM agenda, *Human Resource Management*, 27(1): 77–93; Shenkar, O. and Zeira, Y. (1987). Human resource management in international joint ventures: Direction for research, *Academy of Management Review*, 12(3): 546–557.

31 Cyr, D.J., *op. cit.*, p. 116.
32 Petrovic, J., and Kakabadse, N. K. (2003). Strategic staffing of international joint ventures (IJVS): An integrative perspective for future research. *Management Decision*, 41, 4; Cyr, D.J., *op. cit.*; Geringer, J.M., *op. cit.*; Geringer, J.M. (1988). Partner selection criteria for developed country joint ventures, *Business Quarterly*, 53, 1; Schuler, Jackson, and Luo (2004).
33 Beamish, P.W. (1985). The characteristics of joint ventures in developed and developing countries, *Columbia Journal of World Business*, 20(3), 13–19; Harbison, J.R. (1996). *Strategic Alliances: Gaining a Competitive Advantage*, New York: The Conference Board; Harrigan, K.R. (1986). *Managing for Joint Venture Success*, Boston: Lexington; Schenkar, O., and Zeira, Y., *op. cit.*; Sparks, D. (1999). Partners, *Business Week*, October 5, 106.
34 Shenkar, O., and Zeira, Y., *op. cit.*, 546.[1987]
35 Adapted from Barkema, H., and Vermeulan, F. (1997). What differences in the cultural backgrounds of partners are detrimental for international joint ventures? *Journal of International Business Studies*, 28(4), 845–864; Harrigan, K.R. (1988). Strategic alliances and partner asymmetries, in Contractor, F. and Lorange, P. (eds.), *Cooperative Strategies in International Business*, Lexington, MA: Lexington Books; Park, S.H., and Russo, M.V. (1996). When competition eclipses cooperation: An event history analysis of joint venture failure, *Management Science*, 42(6), 875–890; Schuler, R.S. (2001), *op. cit.*; and Goodman, N.R. (2001). International joint ventures and overseas subsidiaries, presented at the Society for Human Resource Management Global Forum Audio Conference, December; and Cyr, D. (1995), *op. cit.*; and Yan, A., and Zeng, M. (1999), International joint venture instability: A critique of previous research, a reconceptualization, and directions for future research, *Journal of International Business Studies*, 30(2), 397–414. Also see Ertug, G., Cuypers, I., Noorderhaven, N., and Bensaou, B. (2013). Trust between international joint venture partners: Effects of home countries. *Journal of International Business Studies*, 44(3), 263–282.
36 Harrigan (1986).
37 Cyr (1995); Geringer, J.M. (1988), *Joint Venture Partner Selection: Strategies for Developed Countries*, Westport, CT: Quorum Books; Schuler, Jackson, and Luo (2004).
38 Cascio, W.F., and Serapio, M.G. (1991). Human resource systems in an international alliance: The undoing of a done deal? *Organizational Dynamics*, Winter, 63–74; Cyr (1995); Schuler, Jackson, and Luo (2004).
39 Bruton, G.D., and Samiee, S. (1998). Anatomy of a failed high technology strategic alliance, *Organizational Dynamics*, Summer, 51–63; Cascio, W.F., and Serapio, M.G., Jr. (1991), *Organizational Dynamics*, Winter, 63–74; Culpan, R. (2002). *Global Business Alliances: Theory and Practice*, Westport, CT: Quorum Books; Evans, P., Pucik, V., and Barsoux, J-L. (2002). *The Global Challenges: Frameworks for international Human Resource Management*. New York: McGraw-Hill Irwin; Fedor, K.J., and Werther, W.B., Jr. (1996). The fourth dimension: Creating culturally responsive international alliances, *Organizational Dynamics*, Autumn, 39–53; Inkpen, A.C. (1998). Learning and knowledge acquisition through international strategic alliances, *Academy of Management Executive*, 12(4), 69–80; Isabella, L.A. (2002). Managing an alliance is nothing like business as usual, *Organizational Dynamics*, 31(1), 47–59.
40 Schifrin, M. (2001). Best of the web: Partner or perish, *Forbes*, May 21, 26–28.
41 Ibid.

42 Schifrin, M. (2001).

43 Reported in You are not alone, *Fortune*, special advertising section, May, 2001, S2–S3.

44 Schifrin, M. (2001).

45 Fang, E., and Zou, S. (2009), Antecedents and consequences of marketing dynamic capabilities in international joint ventures, *Journal of International Business Studies*, 40, 742–761.

46 Michaels, J. W. (2001), Best of the web: Don't buy, bond instead, *Forbes*, May 21, 20.

47 Adapted from Applegate, J. (1996), Alliances quick way to grow: Links to Bombay firm open doors for architect, *The Denver Business Journal*, October 4–10, 3B.

48 Galbraith, J. R. (1995), *Designing Organizations: An Executive Briefing on Strategy, Structure and Process*, San Francisco: Jossey-Bass.

49 See, e.g., Schuler, R., and Tarique, I. (2012). International joint venture system complexity and human resource management, in I. Björkman and G. Stahl (eds.), *Handbook of Research in IHRM*, Cheltenham: Edward Elgar Publishing, pp. 393–414; Cascio and Serapio (1991); Fedor, K. J., and Werther, W. B., Jr. (1996). The fourth dimension: Creating culturally responsive international alliances, *Organizational Dynamics*, Autumn, 39–53; Isabella, L. A. (2002). Managing an alliance is nothing like business as usual, *Organizational Dynamics*, August, 47–59; Schuler et al. (2000); and Sunoo (1995): 28–30, 32–34.

50 Demby, E. R. (2002). Keeping partnerships on course, *HR Magazine*, December, 49–53.

51 Quoted in Demby (2002).

SECTION 2

National and Cultural Context

The second section of the book, "National and Cultural Context," has three chapters:

■ Chapter 5: Country and Company Culture and International Human Resource Management
■ Chapter 6: International Employment Law, Labor Standards, and Ethics
■ Chapter 7: International Employee Relations

The chapters in this section expand the theme that is revisited frequently throughout the text: the importance of external factors that influence the MNE and IHRM in a variety of ways. Together these factors represent the national and cultural context. Chapter 5 introduces the concepts of country and corporate culture and how these impact everything that is done in IHRM. The chapter also discusses the importance of culture in both the conduct and the interpretation of IHRM research, explaining how culture affects both our understanding of IHRM and its impact. Chapter 6 describes international aspects of the legal, regulatory environments, ethical behavior, and labor standards in the international arena. Finally, Chapter 7 examines the nature of employee relations and how each country's own, unique, union and employee representation institutions make the environment for employee relations quite complex for MNEs. All of these factors of the national and cultural context constitute the environment within which IHRM policies and practices are designed and implemented.

Chapter 5

Country and Company Culture and International Human Resource Management

At United Airlines: The word "foreign" is losing its meaning.

United Airlines Corporation[1]

Learning Objectives

This chapter will enable the reader to:

- Define and explain the concept of culture.
- Explain the importance of culture in international business (IB).
- Describe the basic research findings of G. Hofstede and F. Trompenaars.
- Explain the importance of culture to IHRM.
- Describe the importance of culture and the difficulties encountered in IHRM research.

This chapter provides a look at one of the most important aspects of the external context for IHRM.[2] Many of the most important and difficult challenges to the conduct of international human resource management stem from the differences encountered in various countries' and MNEs' cultures. Often these differences clash when firms conduct business in more than one country and with enterprises located in many countries. This can become a particularly salient challenge when businesspeople lack knowledge of or sensitivity to these differences, resulting in their making mistakes in both their business policies and practices and their personal interactions. Even when they know the differences, they can mistakenly assume that their own country's or company's ways of doing things provide the best way to conduct business. Thus they can make decisions and behave in ways that alienate their foreign counterparts, the people with whom they interact from other countries or companies, such as foreign customers, suppliers, and employees, or they make mistakes that lead to business and/or personal problems. Giving preference to one's own country and company culture can also result in the overlooking or dismissing of better ways of doing things that can be found in other countries and their enterprises.

As two long-time participants in the IB environment put it:

> More than any other aspect of the business experience, our knowledge and under-standing of culture affects the outcome of business ventures. Without insight into the ways of others, we can't expect to develop credibility, nurture goodwill, inspire a workforce, or develop marketable products. And that directly trans-lates to bottom-line results. Culture affects the way we develop and maintain relationships. It plays a significant role in determining success with colleagues and partners, and helps us grasp how to evolve into respected leaders around the world. Understanding culture fundamentally affects how we run our business, what characteristics to look for in selecting people, how to develop global talent, how to conduct meetings, and how to manage employees and work with teams.[3]

Knowledge about and competency in working with varying countries and organizational cultures is one of the most important issues impacting the success of IB activity and of IHRM. Therefore, this chapter provides a definition and an overview of the nature and importance of national and company cultures and their impacts on IHRM as well as pro-viding guidance as to how IHRM can perform its role within MNEs as the advisor and trainer on how to learn from cultural differences and how to use those differences in ways to help build global competitive advantage. This chapter examines the results of major research on culture as well as the findings of major research in IHRM (since it is so closely impacted by culture) and its role in understanding the impact of culture on the global organization and on IHRM.

THE NATURE AND IMPORTANCE OF CULTURE

Every country has at least some variances from all others, e.g., its history, government, and laws. Because of all of these differences, the more countries with which an MNE interacts, the more complex and difficult conducting business becomes. Today, it is common for MNEs to interact with customers and firms in dozens of other countries. So, one of the cen-tral causes of these difficulties has to do with the critical nature of the differences between the national cultures of these various countries.

Variances in people's values, beliefs, and behavior patterns (for example, what they con-sider to be right and wrong, normal and not normal) are critically important to such IB activities as cross-national negotiations, sales interactions between people from different countries, management of the performance of employees from different countries, the understanding and treatment of contracts between firms from different countries, and all HR responsibilities, such as recruiting and hiring, compensation, training, labor relations, and performance management.

People working for organizations that operate in the international arena (whether in business, government, or the non-profit sector), including HR practitioners, need a context into which they can place the culture(s) they know and the new ones they encounter, so they can modify their own and their firms' behaviors in order to be more effective in both business and social situations. They need a way to cope with the significant constraints imposed by cultural differences between countries. Indeed, dealing with these cultural differences may provide the most important factor in determining whether or not their international ventures succeed or fail.

The following paragraphs illustrate one example of a well-known firm (McDonald's hamburger restaurants) going international and some of the issues it confronted in coping with the cultures of the countries into which it expanded.[4]

IHRM in Action 5.1: Turning McDonalds into a Global Brand

An example of how even mass-market suppliers are heeding cultural diversity is illustrated by McDonald's. The Big Mac is so quintessentially American that "McWorld" has become an epithet for the homogenization of world tastes by the US. McDonald's discovered that the global popularity of the McDonald's product was increasingly qualified by exceptions.

The international division sustained McDonald's throughout much of the 1990s and 2000s. Domestic sales were in trouble and it was the company's local adaptations, introduced by franchisees and national coordinators, which showed the most sales success, registering 15 years of sustained revenue growth. More importantly, the autonomy first ceded to foreign operators now has become the policy of the whole corporation.

When the Indonesian currency collapsed in 1998, potato imports became too expensive. Rice was substituted and later maintained. In Korea, roast pork was substituted for beef, while soy sauce and garlic were added to the bun in much of south-east Asia. Austria introduced "McCafes" offering a variety of local coffee blends, which is now a mainstay at McDonald's restaurants throughout much of the world. And there are many other adaptations as well, such as beer in Germany and soy- and lamb-based burgers in India.

Yet in key values of quality, cleanliness, speed, and branding, McDonald's remains uniform. "Decentralisation does not mean anarchy," says McDonald's. "Those things aren't negotiable."

More recently, McDonald's opened its first restaurant in Ho Chi Minh City, Vietnam.[5] The establishment of McDonald's was good for the company and the country, according to the businessman who brought McDonald's to Vietnam.[6] He further said, "McDonald's is a very careful organization," and "If you show up in a market you've got to do things right."

The next few pages present a model for developing this awareness and understanding so as to enable IHR managers to more effectively cope with their international responsibilities, to interact more effectively with their international colleagues, and to enhance their learning from their exposure to and experience with HR practices in other countries.

A Definition and Description of Culture

There have been many definitions of "culture" offered over the years. For the purposes of this text the following definition is used: culture is the characteristic way of behaving and believing that a group of people have developed over time and share in common. In the context of this book, the "groups" whose cultures will be discussed are the people from a particular country or region and the members of a particular company. Of course, the concept is also used to describe the values and behaviors of other groups, such as members of particular professions, certain industries, age groups, and racial groups.

Definition of Culture

Culture is the characteristic way of behaving and believing that a group of people have developed over time and share in common.

■ Gives them a sense of who they are, of belonging, of how they should behave
■ Provides them with the capacity to adapt to circumstances (because the culture defines what is the appropriate behavior in that circumstance) and to transmit this knowledge to succeeding generations (in the case of countries) or to new employees (in the case of organizations).
■ Affects every aspect of the management process—how people think, solve problems, and make decisions (for a country or firm)

As Schell and Solomon phrase it:

Learned and absorbed during the earliest stages of childhood, reinforced by literature, history, and religion, embodied by . . . heroes, and expressed in . . . instinctive values and views, culture is a powerful force that shapes our thoughts and perceptions. It affects the way we perceive and judge events [and other people], how we respond to and interpret them, and how we communicate to one another in both spoken and unspoken language. Culture, with all of its implications [and forms], differs in every society. These differences might be profound or subtle; they might be obvious or invisible. Ever present yet constantly changing, culture permeates the world we know and molds the way we construct or define reality.[7]

When a firm enters a new country and performs activities such as creating job definitions and classifications and hiring, using only its home-country practices, it can cause significant alienation and lack of trust, which can have further ramifications, for example, in making it difficult to obtain a quality workforce.

Understanding Culture as Layers of Meaning

One of the complexities that makes "culture" so difficult to deal with is its multiple layers of meaning. There are many readily observable things about the culture of a country, a region, or a firm that differ quite obviously from those of other countries, regions, and firms. These characteristics, including such things as food, art, clothing, greetings, and historical landmarks, are clearly visible. Sometimes these are referred to as artifacts, or manifestations, of underlying values and assumptions.[8] But those underlying values and assumptions are much less obvious.

One way to understand this concept is illustrated in Figure 5.1, which represents culture as a series of concentric circles, or multiple layers, as in an onion.[9] The layers of culture

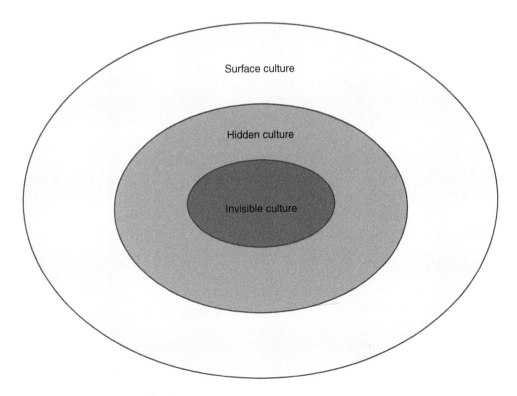

FIGURE 5.1 The Three Layers of Culture

model presents a way to understand culture, with each layer moving from the outside to the inside, representing less and less visible, or less explicit, values and assumptions, but correspondingly more and more important values and beliefs for determining attitudes and behaviors. These layers include:

- *Surface or explicit culture* (the outside layer): Things that are readily observable, such as dress, food, and ways of eating, architecture, customs (such as how to greet other people and the importance of relationships), body language, gestures, etiquette, and gift giving.
- *Hidden culture* (the middle layer): Values, religions, and philosophies about things like child rearing, views of what is right and wrong.
- *Invisible or implicit culture* (the core): The culture's universal truths, the bases for all of a culture's values and beliefs.

This approach to an understanding of culture is used throughout this book as various business and IHR practices, such as preparing employees for international assignments or developing compensation and motivation practices for application in foreign operations, are described and evaluated.

As people develop an ability to work successfully with differing cultures, they typically go through a process such as that illustrated in Figure 5.2, "Development of cross-cultural competence." This approach to building knowledge about another person or group's behavior and values and eventually adapting to or being able to integrate with that other person's or group's behaviors and attitudes assumes that people must first understand their own cultural values and beliefs before they can develop an appreciation and respect for other people's cultural differences, which then precedes the eventual ability to move toward reconciliation and integration with different national and organizational cultures.

All three stages are challenging. All three stages require progressing from basic education and training about one's own and others' cultures through gaining experience with other cultures to reflecting on and then developing an openness about and finally a willingness to seek feedback about one's own values and behaviors in relation to the foreign culture(s). Ultimately, as was found in an extensive study of the development of global executives, people learned best to deal with the complexities of "foreign" cultures by living in those cultures.[10] But the other steps illustrated in Figure 5.2 are also important in developing what is referred to here as "cultural competency."

The recent experiences of ConAgra Foods in China illustrate this process.[11]

When ConAgra came to China five years ago, the firm had high hopes and big worries. Prior to this, the company entered the Japanese market and repeatedly ran into obstacles like communication breakdowns, cultural missteps, and missed deadlines. While those problems were eventually straightened out, ConAgra knew it could not afford to make the same mistakes in China. Intent on finding someone who could help their managers shorten the cultural distance, the company's manager of human resources who was responsible for international organization, hired Carla Kearns, founder of TLI-The Mandarin School, based in Toronto, to provide its executives with intercultural business training and coaching.

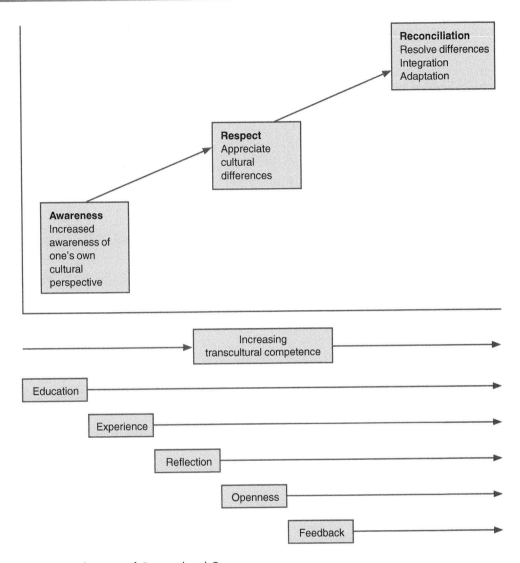

FIGURE 5.2 Development of Cross-cultural Competence

Ms. Kearns teaches companies to understand the fundamental values that Western and Chinese cultures see differently and that, if ignored, can wreak havoc on their bottom line. They include concepts of time, hierarchy, individualism, personal relationships, and saving face. Most novice foreign business professionals in China probably know to exchange business cards with both hands and the correct seating arrangements at banquets, but to gain agreement and to seal the deal, executives need to learn a more nuanced approach. TLI and Ms. Kearns were successful in these efforts for ConAgra, allowing them to become quite successful in their move into China.

For more information about preparation and training for learning to accept and adapt to one or more "foreign" cultures, refer to Chapter 10, on global training and management development.

COUNTRY AND REGIONAL CULTURES

An increasing number of researchers are assessing whether or not the wide variety of cultures around the world can be reduced to a more limited set of cultures with similar characteristics. If so, it would greatly reduce the number of problems associated with determining management and HR practices in various countries.

The Research of Geert Hofstede

The best known of the studies of national culture (and the first major study of cultural values in a large sample of countries) was performed by Dr. Geert Hofstede in the subsidiaries (initially in 53 countries) of one of the major multinational corporations, now known to have been IBM.[12] In particular, this study focused on identifying country differences and regional similarities on the basis of a series of work-related factors. Exhibit 5.1 provides a short summary of the factors identified in this research.[13]

EXHIBIT 5.1: Geert Hofstede's Cultural Dimensions

Cultural dimension	Description
Power distance	Degree of *acceptance of power distance* between bosses and subordinates. Degree to which the less powerful members of a society accept and expect that power is distributed unequally, i.e., that hierarchy is legitimate. In cultures with low power distance, people expect that power is distributed rather equally, and are furthermore also likely to accept that power is distributed to less powerful individuals. The emphasis is on challenging authority, expecting autonomy and independence. As opposed to this, people in high power distance cultures will likely both expect and accept inequality and steep hierarchies. There is high respect for authority, resulting in centralized power, acceptance of autocratic authority and direct supervision. Countries ranked high on power distance include Malaysia, Guatemala, Panama, Philippines, and Mexico. Countries ranked low on power distance include Austria, Israel, Denmark, New Zealand, and Ireland.
Individualism or collectivism	Degree of *individualism or collectivism*. This dimension focuses on relationships between the individual and the group. Highly individualistic cultures believe that the individual is the most important. Decisions are based on individual needs and interests.

Cultural dimension	Description
	In individualist cultures, people speak out, question, can be confrontational and direct. Highly collectivist cultures on the other hand believe the group is the most important and exhibit primary loyalty to the group (family, caste, tribe, region, organization). Decisions are based on what is best for the group. In collectivist cultures, people blend in, avoid conflict, use intermediaries. Greater emphasis is placed on the welfare of the group to which the individual belongs, where individual wants, needs, and dreams are set aside for the common good. Countries ranked high on individualism and thus low on collectivism include USA, Australia, Great Britain, Canada, and the Netherlands. Countries ranked high on collectivism and low on individualism include Guatemala, Ecuador, Panama, Venezuela, and Colombia.
Uncertainty avoidance	Degree of *uncertainty avoidance* or *tolerance for ambiguity*. This dimension refers to the need for formal rules and policies and the extent to which people feel threatened by uncertain or ambiguous situations. It focuses on how people adapt to changes and cope with uncertainty. The majority of people who live in cultures with a high degree of uncertainty avoidance are likely to feel uncomfortable in uncertain and ambiguous situations and will welcome rules for guiding their behaviors and attitudes. They tend to believe in absolute truth and to trust people with high perceived expertise. People who live in cultures with a low degree of uncertainty avoidance are likely to thrive in more uncertain and ambiguous situations and environments and will tend to resist having too many rules and policies. They are more likely to accept relativity in beliefs and values. Countries ranked high in uncertainty avoidance and low in tolerance for ambiguity include Greece, Portugal, Guatemala, Uruguay, and Belgium. Countries ranked low in uncertainty avoidance and high in tolerance for ambiguity include Singapore, Jamaica, Denmark, Sweden, and Hong Kong.
Masculinity versus femininity	Degree of *masculinity or femininity* in social values. This dimension focuses on the extent to which a society stresses achievement versus nurture. The masculinity side of this dimension represents a preference in society for achievement, heroism, assertiveness, and material rewards for success. Masculinity is seen to be the trait that emphasizes ambition, acquisition of wealth, and differentiated gender roles. Society at large is more competitive.

Continued overleaf

EXHIBIT 5.1 *Continued*

Cultural dimension	Description

Cultural dimension	Description
	Its opposite, femininity, stands for a preference for cooperation, modesty, caring for the weak, and for quality of life. Femininity is seen to be the trait that stresses caring and nurturing behaviors, sexual equality, environmental awareness, and more fluid gender roles. Society at large is more consensus oriented. Countries ranked high on masculinity include Japan, Austria, Venezuela, Italy, and Switzerland. Countries ranked high on femininity include Sweden, Norway, Netherlands, Denmark, and Costa Rica.
Longterm versus short-term orientation	Degree *of long-versus short-term orientation*. This dimension was added after the original four dimensions. The consequences for work-related values behavior springing from this dimension are rather hard to describe, but some characteristics include: ■ Long-term orientation—acceptance that business results may take time to achieve; employees valuing a long-term relationship with their employers ■ Short-term orientation—results and achievements are set, and can be reached within a specific time-frame; employees will potentially change employers quite often Countries ranked high on long-term orientation include China, Hong Kong, Taiwan, Japan, and South Korea. Countries ranked high on short-term orientation include Pakistan, Nigeria, Philippines, Canada, Zimbabwe, Great Britain, and United States.
Pragmatic versus normative orientation	Degree of *pragmatic versus normative orientation*. This dimension describes how people in the past, as well as today, relate to the fact that so much that happens around us cannot be explained. In societies with a normative orientation most people have a strong desire to explain as much as possible. People in such societies have a strong concern with establishing the absolute truth and a need for personal stability. They exhibit great respect for social conventions and traditions, a relatively small propensity to save for the future, and a focus on achieving quick results. In societies with a pragmatic orientation, most people don't have a need to explain everything, as they believe that it is impossible to understand fully the complexity of life. The challenge is not to know the truth but to live a virtuous life. In societies with a

Cultural dimension	Description
	pragmatic orientation, people believe that truth depends very much on the situation, context, and time. They show an ability to accept contradictions, to adapt according to circumstances; they show a strong propensity to save and invest; and they show thriftiness and perseverance in achieving results. Countries ranked high on pragmatic orientation include South Korea, Taiwan, Japan, China, and Germany. Countries ranked high on normative orientation include Egypt, Mozambique, Malta, Nigeria, Dominican Republic, and Colombia.
Indulgence versus restraint	Degree of *allowed individual indulgence* of basic human drives *versus social restraint* of such behavior. Indulgence stands for a society that allows relatively free gratification of basic and natural human drives related to enjoying life and having fun. Restraint stands for a society that suppresses gratification of needs and regulates it by means of strict social norms. Countries ranked high on indulgence include Venezuela, Mexico, El Salvador, Nigeria, Angola, and Colombia. Countries ranked high on restraint include Pakistan, Egypt, Latvia, Albania, Bulgaria, and Estonia.

Sources: www.geert-hofstede.com (the Hofstede Center); Hofstede, G. (2001). *Culture's Consequences*, 2nd ed., Thousand Oaks, CA/London: Sage Publications; Hofstede, G., Hofstede, G.J., and Minkov, M. (2010). *Cultures and Organizations: Software of the Mind*, 3rd ed., New York: McGraw-Hill.

Hofstede found not only that certain countries consistently show similarities based on the presence of these characteristics but also that there are clearly differences between the various groupings of countries on these value dimensions. The significant conclusion for MNEs was that the idea was wrong that managerial and organizational systems as developed and practiced in the parent country and parent company of an MNE should be—or could be—imposed upon all of the MNE's foreign subsidiaries.[14] As is discussed in more detail toward the end of this chapter, such large-scale research is difficult and expensive. And, not surprisingly, such research has been very difficult to replicate, although ongoing research in the original firm of Hofstede's research (IBM) as well as by new researchers in different organizations is generally confirming both the cultural characteristics and the country profiles.[15]

The Research of Fons Trompenaars and Charles Hampden-Turner

Dr. Fons Trompenaars and Dr. Charles Hampden-Turner published results of a similar large-scale study (over 15,000 employees from over 50 countries, again from one firm with long-term global experience, Royal Dutch Shell).[16] Even though they focused on different aspects of culture—such as how different cultures accord status to members of their cultures, the varying attitudes toward time and nature, and differing attitudes toward individuals and groups and resulting relationships between members of society—their overall conclusions are quite similar to those of Hofstede. Trompenaars and Hampden-Turner concluded that what distinguishes people from one culture compared with another is where these preferences fall in one of the following seven dimensions. Exhibit 5.2 illustrates these dimensions.

EXHIBIT 5.2: Trompenaar's and Hampden-Turner's Cultural Dimensions

Cultural dimension	Description
Universalism versus particularism (emphasis on rules versus relationships)	*Universalism* places a high importance on laws, rules, values, and obligations. Universalists try to deal fairly with people based on these rules, but rules come before relationships. In contrast, *particularism* suggests that each circumstance, and each relationship, dictates the rules to live by. Particularists' responses to a situation may change, based on what's happening in the moment, and who's involved. Typical universalist cultures include the US, Canada, the UK, the Netherlands, Germany, Scandinavia, New Zealand, Australia, and Switzerland. Typical particularistic cultures include Russia, Latin America, and China.
Individualism versus communitarianism (the individual versus the group)	*Individualism* emphasizes personal freedom and achievement. Individualists believe that you make your own decisions, and that you must take care of yourself. In contrast, *communitarianism* suggests that the group is more important than the individual. The group provides help and safety, in exchange for loyalty. The group always comes before the individual. Typical individualist cultures include the US, Canada, the UK, Scandinavia,

Cultural dimension	Description
	New Zealand, Australia, and Switzerland. Typical communitarian cultures include countries in Latin America, Africa, and Japan.
Neutral versus emotional (range of emotions expressed)	In *neutral* cultures people make a great effort to control their emotions. Reason influences their actions far more than their feelings. People don't reveal what they're thinking or how they're feeling. In contrast, in *emotional* cultures people want to find ways to express their emotions, even spontaneously, at work and in social situations. In emotional cultures, it's welcome and accepted to show emotion. Typical neutral cultures include the UK, Sweden, the Netherlands, Finland, and Germany. Typical emotional cultures include Poland, Italy, France, Spain, and countries in Latin America.
Specific versus diffuse (range of involvement with other people)	In *specific* cultures people keep work and personal lives separate. As a result, they believe that relationships don't have much of an impact on work objectives, and, although good relationships are important, they believe that people can work together without having good relationships. In *diffuse* cultures people see an overlap between their work and personal lives. They believe that good relationships are vital to meeting business objectives, and that their relationships with others will be important, whether they are at work or meeting socially. People spend time outside work hours with colleagues and clients. Typical specific cultures include the US, the UK, Switzerland, Germany, Scandinavia, and the Netherlands. Typical diffuse cultures include Argentina, Spain, Russia, India, and China.
Achievement versus ascription (basis for according status to other people)	In *achievement* cultures people believe that you are what you do, and they base your worth accordingly. These cultures value performance, no matter who you are. In *ascription* cultures, people believe that you should be valued for who you are. Power, title, and position matter in these cultures, and these roles define behavior. Typical achievement cultures include the US, Canada, Australia, and Scandinavia. Typical ascription cultures include France, Italy, Japan, and Saudi Arabia.

Continued overleaf

EXHIBIT 5.2 *Continued*

Cultural dimension	Description
Sequential time versus synchronous time (how people manage time)	In *sequential time* cultures people like events to happen in order. They place a high value on punctuality, planning (and sticking to your plans), and staying on schedule. In these cultures, "time is money," and people don't appreciate it when their schedules are thrown off. In *synchronous time* cultures people see the past, present, and future as interwoven periods. They often work on several projects at once, and view plans and commitments as flexible. Typical sequential-time cultures include Germany, the UK, and the US. Typical synchronous-time cultures include Japan, Argentina, and Mexico.
Internal direction versus outer direction (how people relate to their environment)	In *internal direction* cultures people believe that they can control nature or their environment to achieve goals. This includes how they work with teams and within organizations. In *outer direction* cultures people believe that nature, or their environment, controls them; they must work with their environment to achieve goals. At work or in relationships, they focus their actions on others, and they avoid conflict where possible. People often need reassurance that they're doing a good job. Typical internal-direction cultures include Israel, the US, Australia, New Zealand, and the UK. Typical outer-direction cultures include China, Russia, and Saudi Arabia.

Sources: Trompenaars, F. (1992/1993). *Riding the Waves of Culture: Understanding Diversity in Global Business*, Burr Ridge, IL: Irwin; Trompenaars, F., and Hampden-Turner, C. (2004). *Managing People across Cultures*, West Sussex: Capstone; http://www.mindtools.com/pages/article/seven-dimensions.htm.

Since the reporting of these studies by Hofstede and Trompenaars and Charles Hampden-Turner, other researchers and consultants have reported similar findings or developed alternative ways to categorize cultural values. For example, the Global Leadership and Organizational Behavior Effectiveness (GLOBE) research project (one of the most comprehensive studies yet, performed by a large multinational team of professors) categorized countries on nine cultural dimensions including assertiveness, future orientation, gender differentiation, uncertainty avoidance, power distance, institutional collectivism, in-group collectivism, performance orientation, and humane orientation,[17] which exhibit much overlap, even synthesizing of, the factors reported by Hofstede and Trompenaars. Exhibit 5.3 summarizes the GLOBE findings.

EXHIBIT 5.3: Global Leadership and Organizational Behavior Effectiveness (GLOBE): Cultural Dimensions

Cultural dimension	Description
Assertiveness	The degree to which individuals are assertive, confrontational, and aggressive in their relationships with others
Future orientation	The extent to which individuals engage in future-oriented behaviors such as delaying gratification, planning, and investing in the future
Gender differentiation	The degree to which a collective minimizes gender inequality
Uncertainty avoidance	The extent to which a society, organization, or group relies on social norms, rules, and procedures to alleviate unpredictability of future events
Power distance	The degree to which members of a collective expect power to be distributed equally
Institutional collectivism	The degree to which organizational and societal institutional practices encourage and reward collective distribution of resources and collective action
In-group collectivism	The degree to which individuals express pride, loyalty, and cohesiveness in their organizations or families
Performance orientation	The degree to which a collective encourages and rewards group members for performance improvement and excellence
Humane orientation	The degree to which a collective encourages and rewards individuals for being fair, altruistic, generous, caring, and kind to others

Sources: http://www.inspireimagineinnovate.com/PDF/GLOBEsummary-by-Michael-H-Hoppe.pdf; House R.J., Hanges, P.J., Javidan, M., Dorfman, P.W., and Gupta V. (2004). *Culture, Leadership, and Organizations. The GLOBE Study of 62 Societies*. Thousand Oaks, CA: Sage; Chhokar, J.S., et al. (eds.) (2007). *Culture and Leadership across the World: The GLOBE Book of In-Depth Studies of 25 Societies*, Mahwah, NJ: Lawrence Erlbaum.

Country Cultural Clusters

Because the number of different national and ethnic cultures is so great, the efforts by Hofstede, Trompenaars, and others, to cluster countries with similar cultural profiles and to identify a limited set of variables with which one can understand cultural differences have been welcomed by firms working in the international arena. The hope for these efforts is that they can simplify the problems encountered in adjusting to varying national cultures by limiting the number of significantly different countries or regions. The results of several studies suggest groupings of the following countries, based on their cultural similarities:[18]

- *Anglo.* Australia, Canada, Ireland, New Zealand, South Africa, United Kingdom, United States.
- *Arab.* Abu-Dhabi, Bahrain, Kuwait, Oman, Saudi Arabia, United Arab Emirates.
- *Far Eastern.* Hong Kong, China, Indonesia, Malaysia, Philippines, Singapore, Vietnam, Taiwan, Thailand.
- *Germanic.* Austria, Germany, Switzerland.
- *Latin American.* Argentina, Chile, Colombia, Mexico, Peru, Venezuela.
- *Latin European.* Belgium, France, Italy, Portugal, Spain.
- *Near Eastern.* Greece, Iran, Turkey.
- *Nordic.* Denmark, Finland, Norway, Sweden.
- *Independent.* Brazil, India, Israel, Japan, South Korea.

People with extensive international experience will probably suggest that some of these groupings hide significant within-group (between countries that are in the same group) differences (such as would be experienced among the different countries in the Far Eastern cluster).[19] Nevertheless, the various research efforts to identify countries with similar cultural characteristics do suggest that the countries in each group indeed exhibit significant similarities in their cultural profiles.

These kinds of studies—even if they only confirm managers' assumptions about certain country characteristics—can provide some guidance to general managers and HR managers as they structure policies and practices in foreign operations and activities. At a minimum, these studies provide support for decentralizing many aspects of organizational structure and management and offer suggestions for creating regional divisions for managing at least some aspects of the highly complex global firm.

The Observations of an Experienced Practitioner

One interesting and practical approach to understanding cultural differences is based on the observations and experiences of Richard Gesteland over a 30-year career as expatriate manager and international negotiator in many countries.[20] Gesteland has observed that variances in four general patterns of cross-cultural business behavior provide critical help in understanding international marketing, negotiating, and managing. These four patterns include:

- *Deal focus versus relationship focus.* Gesteland states that this focus on "making or doing the deal" rather than "building relationships" provides the "Great Divide" between business cultures, with differences in this focus often proving to be exceedingly difficult to bridge.
- *Informal versus formal cultures.* Problems occur here when informal business travelers from relatively egalitarian cultures cross paths with more formal counterparts from hierarchical societies.
- *Rigid-time (monochronic) versus fluid-time (polychronic) cultures.* One group of the world's cultures worships the clock while another group is more relaxed about time and scheduling, focusing instead on relationships with the people around them.
- *Expressive versus reserved cultures.* Expressive people communicate—verbally, nonverbally, and in writing—in radically different ways from their more reserved counterparts, which often causes great confusion that can spoil the best efforts to market, sell, source, negotiate, or manage people across cultures.

These four patterns suggest some similarities to and additional verification of those published by researchers, such as Hofstede and Trompenaars. And they suggest some slight differences, with an emphasis on what has been crucial to the practice of international management and negotiation.

The Dangers of Oversimplification

The attempts to isolate country variances and then to group countries and regions with similar profiles and to minimize the variables with which we try to understand cultural differences can simplify the management (and IHR management) task of figuring out how to interact effectively in various countries. But this may oversimplify the understanding of cultural differences.[21] For example, Brannen expresses the concern that the focus on country differences falls short on two levels:

1   That it provides little explanation of within-group differences, that is, it treats countries or cultures as homogeneous wholes, with everyone within the country or culture being alike; and
2   It provides little understanding of how cultures change, that is, it tends to treat cultures as a given—impermeable and static.[22] Brannen suggests that experience shows that cultures are not nearly as homogeneous nor as static as these studies suggest. There are considerable differences within cultures and cultures do, in fact, change over time.

COUNTRY CULTURE VERSUS MNE CULTURE

Just as countries develop unique patterns of values, norms, beliefs, and acceptable behavior, so also do companies. Most MNEs take great pride in their "organizational cultures," which reflect, at least initially, the values of their founders and evolve to create corporate personalities that give employees a template for how to behave, including how to make decisions, the importance and acceptance of operational concerns such as continual improvement, safety, and ethics, and how to treat fellow employees and customers.

For many firms, these organizational values take precedence over country cultures, particularly when there is a conflict between the two. For example, many large MNEs that originate in Scandinavian countries may feel very strongly about the assignment of women to senior management positions and will do this even in cultures where it is rare (and not supported by cultural norms) for women to have these types of appointments. Or MNEs from Western countries may feel strongly in favor of egalitarian and participative management styles and compensation practices and may decide that these values are so important that they will pursue strategies to implement these practices in their foreign operations, even though local culture supports a very different set of values. In addition, Asian MNEs might emphasize strong group loyalty and discussion, with deference to senior employees, in the ways they operate and make decisions, even in their foreign subsidiaries, and even when this is not an accepted or understood way to operate by local employees and managers.

CULTURAL CONVERGENCE AND/OR DIVERGENCE

One major issue that affects the relationship between national culture and corporate culture has to do with the conflict between centralization/standardization and localization/customization, as has been discussed a number of times already. This dilemma may never be fully resolved, and it will come up again, as it affects various aspects of IHRM policy and practice. But this is one of the consequences of the major cultural differences as described in this chapter. Even a huge MNE, such as McDonald's, the fast-food restaurant chain, struggles with insistence throughout the world on corporate standards for customer service and quality of product, while also trying to adopt local ideas for menu that meet local tastes and practices.

One of the continuing controversies that surrounds any discussion of the role of culture in IB is whether or not, due to increasing globalization, there is a growing convergence of cultural values and characteristics across countries.[23] There is some evidence to support both the point of view that modern technology and the modernizing of industries around the world is influencing firms to adopt similar "best practices" (convergence)[24] as well as support for the view that countries' cultural values and practices continue to exert quite strong influences on their business and HR practices (divergence).[25] It is likely that reality is somewhere in between:

> Convergence and divergence perspectives may represent polar extremes. As most firms struggle to find the optimal trade-off between globalization and localization, that is, "glocalization," perhaps the reality is closer to a more balanced or middle-ground view called "cross-vergence," or the intermixing of cultural systems between different countries.[26]

This issue of convergence versus divergence in cultural variance around the world is discussed throughout this text as it applies to various HR practices, such as in Chapter 12 in the discussion of global performance management, and particularly in Chapter 14 on comparative HRM. In any case, as the global economy continues to grow, it is likely that cultural differences will influence IB and IHRM practices in multiple and complex ways. Management and HR practices are likely to be both influenced by the practices of large MNEs from the developed economies as well as by the values and practices from the largest emerging economies, referred to as the BRIC (Brazil, Russia, India, China) countries, and from smaller, yet successful economies, such as Austria, Switzerland, the Scandinavian countries, South Korea, Singapore, and Hong Kong, creating potentially many different, yet successful, hybrid management systems.

RESEARCH IN IHRM

One of the reasons for the apparent slow pace of development of IHRM stems from the problems inherent in researching international organizational issues. This is largely due to the significant and complex impact of culture on such research.

IB research began to develop in the 1970s (along with the expansion of IB).[27]

Cross-cultural management research, however, remained largely limited throughout the 1970s and 1980s and, even now, represents only a small percentage of published research on management and organizational topics.[28] In addition, at least until recently, much of the published research was from an Anglo perspective, much of it performed by American (or American-trained) or European researchers,[29] and mostly done in the top industrialized or developed countries.[30] Research published by non-Western scholars (or published in non-English language sources), such as in Western and Eastern Europe and Japan and in emerging economies, such as the BRIC countries, has gone largely unnoticed in the US, in particular, and in other major English-speaking countries.[31] And among the business disciplines, management, organization, and HRM have been among those topics receiving the least attention.[32] All of this has contributed to the lack of research related to IHRM.

The limited research published on international and comparative management and organization in general, and IHRM in particular, has also been criticized as lacking in analytical rigor, relying too heavily on description of organizational practices (as opposed to critically evaluating such practices), being expedient in research design and planning, and lacking the sustained effort needed to develop case material and other types of longitudinal studies.[33]

There are numerous reasons for this. Multinational—or cross-border or cross-cultural—research is expensive, takes more time, and typically involves more travel than domestic research, and often requires skills in multiple languages, sensitivity to multiple cultures, and cooperation among numerous individuals from different countries, companies, and, often, governments. All of this combines (and conspires) to make such research quite difficult, if not impossible for many researchers. Throw in problems with cultural differences among researchers and at research sites, translation problems (see the next few paragraphs), interpretation variances among multinational research teams, and difficulties with research designs such as the use of control groups and the creation of equivalent groups for comparison purposes, and one can see some of the reasons for the lack of rigorous research in international HRM in particular, and to a lesser extent, international management in general.[34]

The amount of research into topics of relevance to IHRM continues to grow, with the quantity and quality expanding.[35] However, as described above, and as with all research into topics related to international business (if not all areas of international research), there are a number of issues that make such research difficult to perform, difficult to describe, and difficult to get published.[36] The following is a short introduction to issues related to the conduct of research into IHRM, which should help those interested in both the conduct and the reporting of such research as well as help readers to evaluate the research that is reported, both of an empirical and of a more general, anecdotal nature.

General Frustrations

International management researchers have reported frustration with four particular problems:

- Inconsistent and vague definitions of terms like *culture* and *performance.*
- Inaccurate translation of key terminology (see the next few paragraphs).
- Difficulty in obtaining representative or equivalent samples of research subjects. It is very hard to isolate the variables of interest in different cultures.
- Difficulty in isolating cultural differences—versus identifying cultural characteristics that might be common across varying cultures—amid varying national economic and political realities (such as stages of development of the countries or cultures being studied and the nature of their political systems).

Forms of IHRM Research

IHRM research has basically taken one of three forms. These are:

- Cross-cultural, i.e., the study of issues or practices, comparing one country to another.
- Multicultural, i.e., the study of a practice or issue in a number of countries or cultures.
- HR practices in other countries, i.e., describing HR practices in one or more countries that are "foreign" to the researcher.

However, the majority of the published research has been of the first variety, primarily due to the many problems with conducting cross-border studies, as described earlier.

The Specific Case of Employee Surveys[37]

Although most IHRM research is conducted by academic researchers (with some done by consultants and practitioners), some is conducted by in-house scientists. One of the functions of IHRM research is to help firms evaluate their IHRM practices. One of the common methods used for such in-house research is employee surveys. Even though surveys may be relatively simple in terms of research design, they are still impacted by all of the issues described in this section. Every issue, from translation and item equivalence, to union or works council reviews, to length of time to administer, to varying privacy guidelines or attitudes, to methods for administration, to difficulties in working with multinational teams, to varying acceptance of such data gathering in different countries, can cause problems.

Basic Assumptions

The basic models and/or assumptions that underlie cross-cultural research have been described as falling into the following three "camps." The perspective of a particular researcher will obviously influence the approach taken, the types of questions examined, the type of data or information sought, and the interpretation and generalizability of the results.[38]

- *Universal.* A researcher with a universalist assumption has the attitude that there exist some universal cultural characteristics; his or her research task is to identify them and thus demonstrate that certain management and HR practices will work anywhere.
- *Situational.* A researcher with this perspective maintains that there are different managerial practices for different situations; thus his or her task is to identify the cultural situations in which HR or management practices differ or which practices differ based on which cultural variables.

■ *Convergent.* A researcher with this perspective begins with a view (and tries to verify) that countries with similar industrial and cultural backgrounds will converge to a common set of management practices as they approach similar levels of economic maturity.

Specific Difficulties

Some of the specific reasons for the difficulties in doing international/comparative management and IHR research and getting it published include the following.

The Particular Focus of the Researcher(s)

There are often the following two foci described:

■ *Emic.* Trying to identify culture-specific aspects of concepts/behavior, i.e., differences across cultures.
■ *Etic.* Trying to identify culture-common aspects, i.e., the same across all cultures.

These terms have been borrowed from linguistics: a phon*emic* system documents meaningful sounds specific to a given language, and a phon*etic* system organizes all sounds that have meaning in any language. Both approaches provide legitimate research orientations, but if a researcher uses an *etic* approach (i.e., assumes universality across cultures) when there is little or no support for doing so, or vice versa, it makes the results difficult to interpret—or leads to errors in research design and interpretation—and will cause problems with review and publishing.

These approaches obviously interact with the universalist versus situational perspectives. A universalist approach will look for evidence to suggest that there is really only "one best way" and that countries that have practices that diverge will eventually converge to the best way. Thus a longitudinal perspective becomes quite important. Most cultural research is pretty static—that is, it doesn't take into account a long-enough perspective to show that pressures even within a culture (or, broader, within the global environment) can lead to significant changes and adaptation. So, if the distinction between *emic* and *etic* approaches is ignored in research design, or if unwarranted universality assumptions are made, major methodological difficulties can arise.

Language Problems

Language problems are at the root of many of the problems encountered in conducting cross-national research (this is discussed in more detail later).

Measurement and/or Methodological Problems

Measurement and methodological problems can occur when conducting research in multiple cultures and/or languages (for example, attempting to get equivalence in the meaning of terms in various languages, particularly in questionnaire and interview research).[39] "Measurement error occurs when the measure or scale employed fails to reflect the correct extent to which the subject possesses the attribute being measured."[40] These errors can arise because of flaws in scale design or mathematical properties, problems with instrument validity, or because of incorrect application of the scale. These are general methodological problems and can occur in any type of research. However, the complexities of cross-national research add additional problems involving issues such as the reliability of the measures in terms of equivalence of language in different versions of the instrument and equivalence in various versions of the instruments, themselves.[41] In addition, the cross-cultural researcher needs to be aware of the need for equivalence of administration of research and of response to the research in different national or cultural locales.

Equivalence Problems in Cross-cultural Research

The three critical equivalence issues that arise in conducting cross-cultural and cross-national research include:[42]

- *Metric* (stimulus) equivalence. This deals with trying to ensure that the psychometric properties of various forms of the research instruments, such as questionnaire surveys or interviews, which have to be translated into languages different from the original form, are the same; this is usually accomplished through back translation, i.e., having translators convert the translated forms back into the original language, to see if the back-translated questionnaire is the same as the original. Most cross-cultural research focuses here, and this step is pretty much required of all such research, in order to get published. But, as is demonstrated in the next few paragraphs, more is needed.
- *Conceptual* equivalence. The concern here is to ensure that not only do the words translate the same, but that they have the same meaning in different cultures and produce the same level of consistency in results, i.e., the measurement results are similar. For example, in a cross-cultural survey administered in China, South Korea, Japan, and the US, researchers found significant effects attributable not only to country differences but also to the type of scale used, e.g., Likert or semantic differentials.[43] The authors' conclusion was that reactions to various attitude scales are culturally bound and, thus, the scales need to be matched to country situations.
- *Functional* equivalence. This form of equivalence is concerned with ensuring that the terms used and the translations developed are viewed in each culture in similar ways, which requires having "insider" knowledge about the culture, adequate to determine what various cultures value and what the concepts really mean in each culture so as to produce "functional" similarity. In addition, functional equivalence is concerned with ensuring that the concepts work the same way and are implemented the same way in each culture.

The point here is that the results achieved through cross-cultural research may be due to the nature of the research itself (the scales, the language, the wording, the translations, administration, etc.) rather than with any "real" differences in the variables being studied. In addition, there are two more issues that need to be considered:

- *Subjectivity of the topics themselves*. There can be differences between cultures in how they approach the very concept of doing research. The emphasis in Western research is on objectivity and specificity (at least, as viewed within Western cultural norms). But there are potentially a number of points at which people from non-Western (and even some from within Western) cultures would view research differently. For example, the choice of topics to research, that is, the topics that are seen as most important to research, are likely to vary from country to country. And topics, themselves, are likely to be viewed very differently and approached very differently in different cultures. For example, US business (males) have traditionally shown a bias for action but French business (males) prefer thought before action. Whether action or thought comes first could well be researched using objective measurement; but which is the "correct" managerial bias is subjective. And, indeed, women in either culture may view this issue differently yet.
- *Factors other than culture*. Lastly, there may also be factors other than culture that make interpreting the results of cross-cultural and cross-national research very problematic. For example, a review of research published in Arabic showed conflicting results over preferences for various leadership or management styles in Arab countries.[44] The author concluded that management styles used in these countries varied with situational factors other than culture.

Research Content in IHRM

Traditionally, the majority of published IHRM research and writing has been related to the selection and preparation of expatriates (now more commonly referred to as international assignees). Gradually more research interest has been focused on local foreign workforces and on other HRM practices in MNEs and in foreign operations. Clearly there are many practices of importance in IHRM that are gaining increased attention from researchers and writers. This is reflected in the chapters throughout the rest of this book.

IMPACT OF CULTURE ON IHRM

The discussion in this chapter has illustrated just how important culture is in the conduct of international business and international HRM. Indeed, every aspect of IB and IHRM is impacted by national and organizational culture. Every topic throughout the rest of this book is influenced by the realities of varying country and company cultures. This is true for the HR management of international assignees as well as for the HR management of local workforces in subsidiaries and joint ventures.

A study by the Society for Human Resource Management (SHRM) in the US suggests that the situations in which particular cultural influences on IHRM are important include:[45]

- recruiting and hiring practices;
- building business relationships;
- the role and use of multiple languages and communication;
- perceptions of organizational justice (such as fairness in treatment, quality of treatment, and fairness of outcomes);
- decision making;
- performance evaluations and feedback;
- management and leadership development;
- development of a global mindset; and
- varying perspectives on careers across cultures.

CONCLUSION

This chapter has described the concepts of national and MNE cultures and discussed their importance to the successful conduct of international business and international human resource management. It described the basic research findings of two of the best known researchers, Geert Hofstede and Fons Trompenaars, and the conclusions of one of the most-experienced international executives, Gesteland. The chapter also described the importance of culture to IHRM and the importance of culture to and its impact on the difficulties encountered in conducting IHRM research. Cultural differences impact international business and IHRM in ways that make both much more challenging and complex. MNEs and their managers need understanding and appreciation for these differences as well as cultural competencies in working within these varying cultural contexts.

This chapter has only provided an introduction and a frame of reference. The concepts and ideas are utilized throughout the rest of the text to help describe the complexities and challenges of IHR. The chapter has provided a framework within which the rest of IHRM and this book can be understood.

DISCUSSION QUESTIONS

1   How would you define or describe the concept of culture?
2   How is the research of Trompenaars and Charles Hampden-Turner similar to or different from that of Hofstede?

3 What do you consider to be the most important factors of culture in terms of their impact on business?

4 Are national cultures converging or diverging?

5 What are the most important difficulties in conducting research on IHRM that stem from differences in national cultures and languages?

CASE STUDY 5.1: Internationalization and Cross-cultural Expansion of a Local Manufacturer: Barden (US) and FAG (Germany)

The experiences of Barden, a precision ball-bearing manufacturer based in Danbury, Connecticut, illustrate how workforce planning has become a global activity even for a local firm. In the late 1980s, Barden had an opportunity to significantly increase its business. In order to achieve this, it needed to increase its hourly labor force by about 125 employees over the next year. However, the local Danbury labor market was experiencing unprecedented low unemployment. The human resource department thought they could find enough new employees, but indicated they would have to be very creative (for example, by using bonuses to current employees for successful referrals, open houses to recruit applicants, etc.) and, importantly, by recruiting recent immigrants whose English was likely to be very poor.

In the past, Barden had found that, for example, Portuguese immigrants became very reliable, long-term employees. Barden had used a "buddy" system to help new employees learn their jobs and to acquire an adequate "Barden" work vocabulary. But it was clear that this would be inadequate to prepare—in a short period of time—the large new group of potential employees that had been identified. It turned out that there were a significant number of bright recent immigrants from a large and diverse number of countries (e.g., Laos, Cambodia, Brazil, Colombia, the Dominican Republic, Guatemala, Chile, Lebanon, Pakistan, Thailand, and Yemen), but who spoke little or no English.

To become functioning, qualified Barden employees, newcomers would have to master the basic "Barden" vocabulary and be able to look up standard operating procedures as well as material safety data sheets, and master basic shop mathematics, measurement processes, and blueprint reading. This was a major challenge for the immigrants, even though many of them, it was discovered, had received surprisingly good educations back in their home countries. In order to teach these new employees enough English to pay their way, a language training firm, Berlitz, was retained to develop a special, intensive course in cooperation with Barden's training unit. In a fairly short period of time six groups of eight new employees were taught through this special program. All the students were put on the payroll while they met with a Berlitz instructor for four hours a day for 15 consecutive workdays during work hours.

The program had a number of effects, beyond enabling Barden to fill its employment needs to meet its new corporate growth strategy and to integrate this veritable United Nations group into its workforce. The confidence level of the students soared as they used their new language abilities. Barden's supervisors were impressed—and gained some new cross-cultural awareness and competence as well (which came in handy over the next decade as Barden became an international company). And the word spread to the community with the positive result of attracting new high-quality recruits.

In 1991, Barden became affiliated with FAG, a German company in Schweinfelt, Germany, and Stratford, Canada, and later developed subsidiaries in the UK, as well. Today, Barden/FAG is recognized as the industry leader in the manufacture of ball-bearings to super-precise/

super-critical tolerances, for machine tools and special machinery and equipment in the aerospace, automotive, and medical industries. And their success has been recognized as deriving, at least in a major way, from their diverse and multicultural workforce.

Sources: Schuler, R.S. and Walker, J.W. (1990). Human resource strategy: Focusing on issues and actions. *Organizational Dynamics*, summer, 4–20; updated 2014 at: www.bardenbearings.com.

Discussion Questions

1   Are immigrants a good source of workers to fill vacant positions? What are some of the barriers to employing immigrants? Are immigrants always welcomed by every country to fill job vacancies?
2   Do current global demographics accommodate or require the hiring of foreign immigrants? Should a consideration for foreign immigrants be part of every firm's workforce strategy? How do host-country and third-country hires relate to the hiring of immigrants?
3   What cultural barriers had to be crossed with the hiring of immigrants at Barden? What cultural challenges do you think were experienced with the affiliation of Barden with FAG of Schweinfelt, Germany, and Stratford, Canada?
4   How would you (as Barden HR manager) have dealt with the need for new employees and then global expansion?

NOTES

1   Source: a UAL billboard in the terminal at Germany's Frankfurt Airport.
2   Much of this chapter is based on Schneider, S., Barsoux, J-L., and Stahl, G. (2014). *Managing across Cultures*, 3rd rev. ed., Upper Saddle River, NJ: Pearson Education Limited; Steers, R., Nardon, L., and Sánchez-Runde, C. (2013). *Management Across Cultures: Developing Global Competencies*, New York: Cambridge University Press; Chanlat, J-F., Davel, E., and Dupuis, J-P. (2013). *Cross-Cultural Management: Culture and Management Across the World*, London/New York: Routledge; Primecz, H., Romani, L., and Sackman, S. (2012). *Cross-Cultural Management in Practice: Culture and Negotiated Meanings*, Cheltenham, UK/Northampton, MA: Edward Elgar.
3   Schell, M.S., and Solomon, C.M. (1997). *Capitalizing on the Global Workforce*, Chicago: Irwin, p. 9.
4   Adapted from F. Trompenaars and C. Hampden-Turner (2001). Cultural answers to global dilemmas. *Financial Times*, Jan. 15, p. 14.
5   See Vietnam gets a taste for the Big Mac: Country's first McDonald's serves 400,000 customers in first month, Daily Mail.com (24, March 2014) website: http://www.dailymail.co.uk/travel/article-2586011/Vietnams-McDonalds-serves-400–000-customers-month.html#ixzz3GtYlXJPy; Ives, M. (Feb 7, 2014). McDonald's opens in Vietnam, bringing Big Mac to fans of Banh Mi, *New York Times* website: http://www.nytimes.com/2014/02/08/business/international/mcdonalds-chooses-its-moment-in-vietnam.html?_r=2.
6   Maresca, T. (Feb 10, 2104). The first McDonald's in Vietnam opened Saturday in Ho Chi Minh City.", USA Today website: http://www.usatoday.com/story/money/business/2014/02/09/vietnam-mcdonalds-ho-chi-minh-city/5337103/.
7   Schell and Solomon (1997), p. 8.

8   See, for example, Hofstede, G., Hofstede, G. J., and Minkov, M. (2010). *Cultures and Organizations: Software of the Mind*, 3rd ed., New York: McGraw-Hill; Hofstede, G. (2001). *Culture's Consequences*, 2nd ed., London: Sage; Schneider, S., Barsoux, J-L., and Stahl, G. (2014). *Managing Across Cultures*, 3rd rev. ed., Upper Saddle River, NJ: Pearson Education Limited; Hooker, J. (2003). *Working Across Cultures*, Stanford, CA: Stanford Business Books; Moore, K. (2003). Great global managers, *Across the Board*, May–June, 40–44; Peterson, B. (2004). *Cultural Intelligence*, Yarmouth, ME: Intercultural Press; Stroh, L. K., Black, J. S., Mendenhall, M. E., and Gregersen, H. B. (2005). *International Assignments*, Mahwah, NJ/London: Lawrence Erlbaum Associates; Thomas, D.C., and Inkson, K. (2009). *Cultural Intelligence*, 2nd ed., San Francisco: Berrett-Koehler Publishers; Trompenaars, F. (1992/1993). *Riding the Waves of Culture: Understanding Diversity in Global Business*, Burr Ridge, IL: Irwin, chapter 1; and Trompenaars, F., and Hampden-Turner, C. (2004). *Managing People Across Cultures*, West Sussex, England: Capstone Publishing Ltd.

9   Schell and Solomon (1997); Hofstede (1991). *Cultures and organizations: Software of the mind*. London: McGraw-Hill; Trompenaars (1992/1993); Trompenaars and Hampden-Turner (2004).

10 McCall, M. W., Jr., and Hollenbeck, G. P. (2002). *Developing Global Executives: The Lessons of International Experience*, Boston, MA: Harvard Business School Press.

11 Levin, D. (2010). Helping to bridge a cultural divide in China, *International Herald Tribune*, Dec. 22, 4.

12 Hofstede, G. (2001); Hofstede (1991); Hofstede, G. (2001); Hofstede, G. (2002). Cultural constraints in management theories, *CRN News*, 7(4), 1–3, 12–13, 16, 19, 22–23.

13 Source: www.geert-hofstede.com (the Hofstede Center) 4/18/14; www.BusinessMate.org 4/18/14; www.andrews.edu/~tidwell/bsad560/hofstede.html 4/18/14; Hofstede, G. (2001).

14 See, for example, Hofstede, G. (1984). Clustering countries on attitudinal dimensions: A review and synthesis, *Academy of Management Review*, 9(3), 389–398; Hofstede, G. (1983). The cultural relativity of organizational theories, *Journal of International Business Studies*, 14(2), 75–90.

15 Saari, L., and Schneider, B. (2001). Global employee surveys: Practical considerations and insights, paper presented at Going global: Surveys and beyond, workshop at the annual conference, Society of Industrial/ Organizational Psychology, San Diego, April.

16 Hampden-Turner, C., and Trompenaars, F. (2012). *Riding the Waves of Culture: Understanding Diversity in Global Business*, 3rd ed., New York: McGraw-Hill; Hampden-Turner, C., and Trompenaars, F. (1993). *The Seven Cultures of Capitalism*, New York: Currency/Doubleday; Trompenaars, F. (1992/1993); and Trompenaars, F., and Hampden-Turner, C. (2004).

17 To learn more about GLOBE see Dorfman, P., Javidan, M., Hanges, P., Dastmalchian, A., and House, R. (2012). GLOBE: A twenty-year journey into the intriguing world of culture and leadership. *Journal of World Business*, (4), 504; Javidan, M., Dorfman, P. W., Mary Sully de, L., and House, R. J. (2006). In the eye of the beholder: Cross-cultural lessons in leadership from Project GLOBE. *Academy of Management Perspectives*, (1), 67; Javidan, M., and House, R. J. (2000). Cultural acumen for the global manager, *Organizational Dynamics*, 29(4), 289–305; Globe Research Team (2002). *Culture, Leadership, and Organizational Practices: The GLOBE Findings*, Thousand Oaks, CA: Sage; and Graen, G. B. (2006). In the eye of the beholder: Cross-cultural lessons in leadership from Project GLOBE, *Academy of Management Perspectives*, 20(4), 95–101; and the response to this analysis: House, R. J., Javidan, M., Dorfman, P. W., and de Luque, M. S. (2006). A failure of scholarship: Response to George Graen's critique of GLOBE, *Academy of Management Perspective*, 20(4), 102–114.

18 See Ronen, S., and Shenkar, O. (2013). Mapping world cultures: Cluster formation, sources and implications. *Journal of International Business Studies*, 44(9), 867–897; Ronen, S., and Shenkar, O. (1985). Clustering countries on attitudinal dimensions: A review and synthesis, *Academy of Management Review*, 10(3), 435–454; Ronen, S., and Shenkar, O. (1988). Using employee attitudes to establish MNC regional divisions, *Personnel*, August, 32–39.

19 See, for example, Earley, P. C., and Erez, M. (eds.) (1997). *New Perspectives on International Industrial/Organizational Psychology*, San Francisco: The New Lexington Press; Gesteland, R. R. (1999).

Cross-cultural Business Behavior: Marketing, Negotiating and Managing Across Cultures, Copenhagen, Denmark: Copenhagen Business School Press; Gundling, E. (2003). *Working Globesmart*, Palo Alto, CA: Davies-Black Publishing; Hodge, S. (2000). *Global Smarts: The Art of Communicating and Deal-making Anywhere in the World*, New York: Wiley; Moran, R.T., Harris, P.H., and Moran, S.V. (2007). *Managing Cultural Differences*, 7th ed., Burlington, MA: Butterworth-Heinemann; and Scherer, C.W. (2000). *The Internationalists*, Wilsonville, OR: Book Partners.

20 Gesteland (1999).

21 Brannen, M.Y. (1999). The many faces of cultural data, *AIB Newsletter*, first quarter, 6–7.

22 Ibid.

23 See, for example, Festing, M. (2012). Strategic human resource management in Germany: Evidence of convergence to the U.S. model, the European model, or a distinctive national model? *The Academy of Management Perspectives*, (2), 37; Lertxundi, A., and Landeta, J. (2012). The dilemma facing multinational enterprises: Transfer or adaptation of their human resource management systems. *International Journal of Human Resource Management*, 23(9), 1788–1807; Škerlavaj, M., Su, C., and Huang, M. (2013). The moderating effects of national culture on the development of organisational learning culture: A multilevel study across seven countries. *Journal for East European Management Studies*, 18(1), 97–134; Brewster, C. (2012). Comparing HRM policies and practices across geographical borders, in Stahl, G.K., Björkman, I., and Morris, S.S. (eds.), *Handbook of Research in International Human Resource Management*, 2nd ed., Cheltenham: Edward Elgar, pp. 76–96; Mayrhofer, W., and Brewster, C. (2012). *Handbook of Research on Comparative Human Resource Management*, Cheltenham: Edward Elgar; Peretz, H., and Fried, Y. (2012). National cultures, performance appraisal practices, and organizational absenteeism and turnover: A study across 21 countries. *Journal of Applied Psychology*, 97(2), 448–459; Mayrhofer, W., Brewster, C., Morley, M.J., and Ledolter, J. (2011). Hearing a different drummer? Convergence of human resource management in Europe—a longitudinal analysis. *Human Resource Management Review*, 21(1), 50–67; Sparrow, P., Schuler, R.S. and Jackson, S. (1994). Convergence or divergence: Human resource practice and policies for competitive advantage worldwide. *International Journal of Human Resource Management*, 5(2), 267–299.

24 Mayrhofer, W., Brewster, C., Morley, M.J., and Ledolter, J. (2011); Brewster, C. (2012); Huo, Y.P., Huang, H.J., and Napier, N.K. (2002). Divergence or convergence: A cross-national comparison of personnel selection practices, *Human Resource Management*, 41(1), 31–44; Von Glinow, M.A., Drost, E., and Teagarden, M. (2002). Converging on IHRM best practices: Lessons learned from a globally distributed consortium on the theory and practice, *Human Resource Management*, 41(1), 123–140.

25 Yongsun, P., Chow, I., and Vance, C.M. (2011). Interaction effects of globalization and institutional forces on international HRM practice: Illuminating the convergence-divergence debate. *Thunderbird International Business Review*, 53(5), 647–659; Drost, E., Frayne, C., Lowe, K., and Geringer, M. (2002). Benchmarking training and development practices: A multi-country comparative analysis, *Human Resource Management*, 41(1), 67–85; Gerhart, B., and Fang, M. (2005). National culture and human resource management: Assumptions and evidence, *International Journal of Human Resource Management*, 16(6), 971–986; Pucik, V. (1997). Human resources in the future: An obstacle or a champion of globalization? *Human Resource Management*, 36(1), 163–167.

26 Vance and Paik (2011). The concept of "crossvergence," originated in Ralston, D., Holt, D., Terpstra, R.H., and Yu, K.-C. (1997). The impact of national culture and economic ideology on managerial work values: A study of the United States, Russia, Japan, and China, *Journal of International Business Studies*, 28(1), 177–207. See also Shimoni, B., and Bergmann, H. (2006). Managing in a changing world: From multiculturalism to hybridization—The production of hybrid management cultures in Israel, Thailand, and Mexico, *Academy of Management Perspective*, August, 76–89.

27 Pierce, B., and Garvin, G. (1995). Publishing international business research: A survey of leading journals, *Journal of International Business Studies*, 26(1), 69–89.

28 Adler, N.J. (1983). Cross-cultural management research: The ostrich and the trend, *Academy of Management Review*, 8(2), 226–232; Pierce and Garvin (1995).

29 Boyacigillar, N., and Adler, N.J., (1991). The parochial dinosaur: Organizational science in a global context, *Academy of Management Review*, 16(2), 262–290.

30 Thomas, A.S., Shenkar, O., and Clarke, L. (1994). The globalization of our mental maps: Evaluating the geographic scope of JIBS coverage, *Journal of International Business Studies*, 25(4), 675–686.

31 Thomas, A.S., et al. (1994); Hickson, D.J. (1996). The ASQ years then and now through the eyes of a Euro-Brit, *Administrative Science Quarterly*, 41(2), 217–228.

32 Inkpen, A., and Beamish, P. (1994). An analysis of twenty-five years of research in the *Journal of International Business Studies, Journal of International Business Studies*, 25(4), 703–713; Melin, L. (1992). Internationalization as a strategy process, *Strategic Management Journal*, 13, 99–118; Parker, B. (1998). *Globalization and Business Practice: Managing Across Borders*, Thousand Oaks, CA: Sage; Thomas et al. (1994).

33 Dowling, P.J. (1988). International HRM, in Dyer, L. (ed.), *Human Resource Management: Evolving Roles and Responsibilities*, Washington, DC: Bureau of National Affairs; Earley, P.C., and Singh, S.H. (2000). Introduction: New approaches to international and cross-cultural management research, in Earley, P.C., and Singh, S.H. (eds.), *Innovations in International Cross-cultural Management*, Thousand Oaks, CA: Sage; McEvoy, G.M., and Buller, P.F. (1993). New directions in international human resource management research, paper presented at the Academy of International Business annual meeting, Maui, HI, October 21–24; Tayeb, M. (2001). Conducting research across cultures: Overcoming drawbacks and obstacles, *International Journal of Cross-cultural Management*, I(1), 91–108; Triandis, H.C. (1998). Vertical and horizontal individualism and collectivism: Theory and research implications for international comparative management, *Advances in International Comparative Management*, XII, Greenwich, CT: JAI Press, 7–35.

34 See, for example, Zhan, G. (2013). Statistical power in international business research: Study levels and data types. *International Business Review*, (4), 678; Peterson, M.F., Arregle, J., and Martin, X. (2012). Multilevel models in international business research. *Journal of International Business Studies*, (5), 451; Michailova, S. (2011). Contextualizing in international business research: Why do we need more of it and how can we be better at it?. *Scandinavian Journal of Management*, (1), 129; Geringer, J., and Pendergast, W. (2012). Firmly rooting international business research in the soil of relevance: Integration and recommendations. *Thunderbird International Business Review*, 54(2), 263–269; Aguinis, H. and Henley, C. (2003). The search for universals in cross-cultural organizational behavior, *Organizational Behavior: The State of the Science*, 2nd ed., Mahwah, NJ/London: Lawrence Erlbaum Associates; Baruch, Y. (2001). Global or North American? A geographical-based comparative analysis of publications in top management journals. *International Journal of Cross-cultural Management*, 1 (1), 109–125; Bond, M.H. (1997). Adding value to the cross-cultural study of organizational behavior: Reculer pour mieux sauter, in Earley, P.C., and Erez, M. (eds.) *New Perspectives on International Industrial/Organizational Psychology*, San Francisco: The New Lexington Press, pp. 256–275; Earley, P.C., and Mosakowski, E. (1995). Experimental international management research, in Punnett, B.J., and Shenkar, O. (eds.) *Handbook for International Management Research*, Cambridge, MA: Blackwell Publishers, pp. 83–114; Gelfand, M.J., Holcombe, K.M., and Raver, J.L. (2002). Methodological issues in cross-cultural organizational research, in Rogelberg, S.G. (ed.), *Handbook of Research Methods in Industrial and Organizational Psychology*, Malden, MA: Blackwell Publishers, pp. 216–241; GLOBE Research Team (2002). *Culture, Leadership, and Organizational Practices: The GLOBE Findings*, Thousand Oaks, CA: Sage; Graen, G.B., Hui, C., Wakabayashi, M., and Wang, Z.-M. (1997). Cross-cultural research alliances in organizational research, in Earley, P.C., and Erez, M. (eds.), *New Perspectives on International Industrial/Organizational Psychology*, San Francisco: The New Lexington Press, pp. 160–189; House, R.J., Hanges, P.J., Javidan, M., Dorfman, P.W., and Gupta, V. (2004). *Culture, Leadership, and Organizations. The GLOBE Study of 62 Societies*, Thousand Oaks, CA: Sage; Mattl, C. (1999). Qualitative research strategies in international HRM, in Brewster, C., and Harris, H. (eds.) *International HRM: Contemporary Issues in Europe*, London: Routledge; and Wright, L.L. (1995). Qualitative international management research, in Punnett, B.J., and Shenkar, O. (eds.), *Handbook for International Management Research*, Cambridge, MA: Blackwell Publishers, pp. 63–81.

35 See specific academic journals and trade publications dedicated to IHRM such as *The International Journal of Human Resource Management, Journal of Global Mobility, The Asia Pacific Journal of Human Resources*,

South Asian Journal of Global Business Research, South Asian Journal of Human Resources Management, International Journal of Manpower, The Journal of Chinese Human Resource Management, and *Human Resource Management International Digest* among others; for example, Aycan, Z., Kanungo, R. N., Mendonca, M., Yu, K., Deller, J., Stahl, G., and Kurshid, A. (2000). Impact of culture on human resource management practices: A ten-country comparison, *Applied Psychology: An International Review,* 49, 192–221; and (the most recent publication from this group) Sackett, P. R., Shen, W., Myors, B., Lievens, F., Schollaert, E., Van Hoye, G., Cronshaw, S. F., Onyura, B., Mladinic, A., Rodriguez, V., Steiner, D. D., Rolland, F., Schuler, H., Frintrup, A., Nikolaou, I., Tomprou, M., Subramony, S., Raj, S. B., Tzafrir, S., Bamberger, P., Bertolino, M., Mariana, M., Fraccaroli, F., Sekiguchi, T., Yang, H., Anderson, N. R., Evers, A., Chernyshenko, O., Englert, P., Kriek, H. J., Joubert, T., Salgado, J. F., König, C. J., Thommen, L. A., Chuang, A., Sinangil, H. K., Bayazit, M., Cook, M., and Aguinis, H., Perspectives from twenty-two countries on the legal environment for selection, in Farr, J. L., and Tippins, N. T. (eds.) (2010). *Handbook of Employee Selection,* Clifton, NJ: Psychology Press, pp. 651–656.

36 Caligiuri, P.M. (1999). The ranking of scholarly journals in the field of international human resource management, *International Journal of Human Resource Management,* 10 (3), 515–518; House, R. H., Hanges, P. J., Antonio Ruiz-Quintanilla, S., Dorfman, P. W., Javidan, M., Dickson, M., Gupta, V., and GLOBE Country Co-investigators (1999). Cultural influences on leadership and organizations: Project GLOBE, in Mobley, W. H., Gessner, M. J., and Arnold, V. (eds.), *Advances in Global Leadership,* Vol. I, Stamford, CT: JAI Press; House, R. J., Wright, N. S., and Aditya, R. N. (1997). Cross-cultural research on organizational leadership: A critical analysis and a proposed theory, in Earley, P. C., and Erez, M. (eds.), *New Perspectives on International Industrial/Organizational Psychology* San Francisco: The New Lexington Press.

37 Harzing, A., Brown, M., Koster, K., and Zhao, S. (2012). Response style differences in cross-national research: Dispositional and situational determinants. *Management International Review,* (3), 341; Harzing, A.W., Reiche, B.S., and Pudelko, M. (2013). Challenges in international survey research: A review with illustrations and suggested solutions for best practice. *European Journal of International Management,* vol. 7, no. 1, 112–134; Saari, L., and Schneider, B. (2001). Global employee surveys: Practical considerations and insights, paper presented at "Going Global: Surveys and Beyond," workshop at the annual conference of the Society for Industrial/Organizational Psychology, San Diego, CA, April.

38 Lubatkin, M. H., Ndiaye, M., and Vengroff, R. (1997). The nature of managerial work in developing countries: A limited test of the universalist hypothesis, *Journal of International Business Studies,* fourth quarter, 711–733; Punnett, B. J., and Shenkar, O. (eds.) (1996). *Handbook for International Management Research,* Cambridge, MA: Blackwell Publishers; Sparrow, P., Brewster, C., and Harris, H. (2004). *Globalizing Human Resource Management,* Routledge, London; and Vance and Paik (2011).

39 Mullen, M. R. (1995). Diagnosing measurement equivalence in cross-national research, *Journal of International Business Studies,* 15 (3), 573–596.

40 Cavusgil, S. T., and Das, A. (1997). Methodological issues in empirical cross-cultural research: A survey of the management literature and a framework, *Management International Review,* 37 (1), 81.

41 Cavusgil and Das (1997); Douglas, S. P., and Craig, S. (1983). *International Marketing Research,* Englewood Cliffs, NJ: Prentice Hall; Samiee, S., and Jeong, I. (1994). Cross-cultural research in advertising: An assessment of methodologies, *Journal of the Academy of Marketing Science,* 22 (3), 205–217.

42 Mullen (1995).

43 Yu, J. H., Keown, C. F., and Jacobs, L. W. (1993). Attitude scale methodology: Cross-cultural implications, *Journal of International Consumer Marketing,* 6 (2), 45–64.

44 Mattl (1999).

45 Lockwood, N. R., and Williams, S. (2008). *Selected Cross-Cultural Factors in Human Resource Management, SHRM Research Quarterly,* Third-Quarter, Alexandria, VA: the Society for Human Resource Management.

Chapter 6

International Employment Law, Labor Standards, and Ethics

Baker & McKenzie has been global since inception. Being global is part of our DNA.
Baker & McKenzie Corporation, the world's largest
global employment law firm[1]

Learning Objectives

This chapter will enable the reader to:

■ Describe the three major legal systems and their key differences.
■ Describe international labor law and standards and explain their impacts.
■ List and describe the goals of the various international trade agreements.
■ Describe how EU directives impact IHRM.
■ Identify the major issues impacting HR with regard to immigration/visas, personal data protection, anti-discrimination and harassment, termination and reduction in force, and intellectual property.
■ Integrate existing employment laws and regulations, ethical standards, CSR, and corporate governance into IHRM policies and practices.

One of the most important components of the global context for IHRM is employment law and regulation and their application. Thus, this chapter is about international employment law and labor standards and ethics in the global economy. All global firms must contend with varying employment laws in the countries in which they conduct business, as well as abide by whatever international standards also exist.[2] Typically, foreign laws and practices differ considerably from what MNEs are familiar with at home. So there can be considerable risk of making mistakes, pursuing risky strategies, and putting the enterprise at considerable legal liability from not understanding adequately what these laws, standards, and codes require.

When an employee is in Japan one day and Mexico the next, or an employee in the UK meets with a colleague from Sweden to finalize a project in Spain, or executives from anywhere are making strategic decisions about operations anywhere else, their organizations must make sure that any number of standards (based in legislation or country culture) are not violated. In addition to varying from country to country, statutes and regulations are also continually being revised and updated, making it difficult and exceedingly complex to stay current and legal.

International standards, national trade agreements, commercial diplomacy efforts with governments, and varying country laws and cultures all impact how MNEs must operate. National, supranational, and extra-territorial laws have varying legal and regulatory impacts on nation-states and their actors (firms, labor organizations, regulatory bodies, and individuals). In addition to legal compliance, a number of other IHR regulatory issues also have an impact on the activities of MNEs (such as immigration controls, cross-border data privacy protections, discrimination regulations, termination and reduction-in-force regulations, and intellectual property protections). Finally, moving beyond a pure concern with compliance with the law, there is growing legal and public concern with MNEs showing ethical conduct in their relationships with all of their stakeholders, being responsible corporate citizens, and establishing transparent corporate governance mechanisms. Failure to comply with local employment laws and any regional or international employment standards that apply can carry liabilities at many levels, including of course legal and financial liabilities, but also can include the potential consequences of negative employee and public opinion, stockholder unrest, consumer dissatisfaction, and hostile local governments.

Seven general areas are discussed in this chapter:

1   the general legal context in differing countries;
2   international employment law and enforcement;
3   comparative employment law;
4   extra-territorial application of national law;
5   enforcement of national law to local foreign-owned enterprises;
6   immigration law; and
7   international labor standards and ethics.

THE INSTITUTIONAL LEGAL CONTEXT OF INTERNATIONAL BUSINESS (IB)

The legal environment in which MNEs and their IHR managers operate is quite complex. At least three different major legal systems operate in the nations of the world.[3] In general, law establishes rules for behavior, usually enforced through a set of institutions. It shapes government, economics, and society in numerous ways and serves as a primary social mediator of relations between people, between people and organizations, and between organizations. As a consequence, each of these three legal systems has its own unique methodologies for creating laws, for developing the content of laws, and for enforcing laws. These three systems include the common law system as developed in England and its colonies, including the US, the civil code approach (often referred to as the Napoleonic code), as developed in France, and religious law, the most common form of which, today, is Islamic law, or Sharia, as practiced in a number of Islamic states, such as Saudi Arabia and Iran.

Common Law

Under common law, a constitution enunciates a few, long-standing, general principles to which everyone is subject. The law, then, is based on tradition as stated in the constitution, past practices, and legal precedents set by courts through interpretation of the constitution, legislative statutes, and past rulings. Under common law, legislation and statutes tend to be quite general, the specifics developing over time. Interpretation when there is a question or disagreement is done in court, typically before a jury, and typically for the purpose of deciding whether the general law applies to the situation. Under common law, legislation tends to establish basic principles, with precedence and practice determining what people can and cannot do.

Civil Code or Law

A civil law or code is based on an all-inclusive system of written rules, of which there are three types: commercial, civil, and criminal. Statutes tend to be very specific, defining people's basic rights and duties, in some cases even tracing these rights and duties back as far as to early Roman law. Enforcement and interpretation in civil law is a problem of determining whether or not a person did something that was not allowed under the code.

Religious Law

The third form of law is religious law, the most common of which is Islamic law, or Sharia, which refers to the "way" Muslims should live or the "path" they must follow. It is derived from the sacred text of Islam (the Qur'an) and Traditions (Hadith) gathered from the life of the Islamic prophet, Muhammad. Traditionally, Islamic jurisprudence interprets and refines Sharia (often by senior religious figures) by extending its principles to address new questions. Islamic judges apply the law; however, modern application varies from country to country. Sharia deals with many aspects of life, including crime, politics, economics, banking, business, contracts, family, sexuality, hygiene, and social issues, where personal standards for behavior, as interpreted from the Qur'an, take precedence in all aspects of life. Islamic law is now the most widely used religious law, and thus one of the three most common legal systems of the world.

Having to cope with three very different legal systems makes it necessary for firms to understand the differences in order to know what to expect and how to behave with regard to the law and regulatory systems, particularly as it relates to their management and human resource management policies and practices, such as standards proscribing discrimination for various groups (which will vary between countries) and determining holiday and termination standards (which, again, will vary between countries). These systems not only apply to firms in their operational and management decisions, but also to employees and their families in their everyday lives. If employees (and their managers), particularly those on international assignment, and their families are not briefed carefully on how the particular local set of laws, police authorities, and courts operate, they can (and often do) find themselves in major difficulties, often for reasons they don't understand.

In order for IHR managers from MNEs to develop policies and practices that stay within the laws and regulations of each country in which they operate, they need to be familiar with those laws, regulations, and enforcement mechanisms (or, as is often the alternative, to rely heavily on the expertise of local legal consultants).

ESTABLISHMENT OF LABOR STANDARDS BY INTERNATIONAL INSTITUTIONS

In addition to these general legal systems, a number of international institutions are also involved with establishing labor standards that apply to most (or many) countries and to their enterprises that conduct business across borders.[4] Gradually these institutions are developing a certain level of consensus on basic employment rights. These generalized standards are shown in Exhibit 6.1. The International Labour Organization's (ILO) Declaration on Fundamental Principles and Rights at Work are not only accepted by various international groups, but also by regional political affiliations and by national legislatures, which are gradually incorporating them into local law and jurisprudence.

EXHIBIT 6.1: ILO Declaration on Fundamental Principles and Rights at Work

- ■ freedom of association and the effective recognition of the right to collective bargaining;
- ■ elimination of all forms of forced or compulsory labor;
- ■ effective abolition of child labor;
- ■ elimination of discrimination in respect of employment and occupation.

Source: http://www.ilo.org/declaration/lang—en/index.htm.

International Organizations

A number of international organizations such as the United Nations (UN), the International Labour Organisation (ILO), the Organization for Economic Cooperation and Development (OECD), the World Bank, and the International Monetary Fund (IMF) have all promoted labor standards that impact employees and labor relations within MNEs. Some of these standards are voluntary while others are technically binding for member states of the international body. The following provides a short description of these bodies and the standards they have promulgated.

United Nations

The UN plays a relatively insignificant role in establishing employment laws or standards. Until recently, the UN only operated in this domain through agencies such as the International Labour Organisation (see below). Internally, the UN has primarily focused on the social dimensions of international trade through its Conference on Trade and Development (UNCTAD), with its focus on the transnational corporation,[5] and through regional economic commissions (such as the Economic and Social Commission for Asia and the Pacific). This has developed primarily through the convening of conferences and the commissioning of studies to focus on the social impacts of liberalized trade and the increased importance of transnational corporations.

In recent years, however, the UN has also tried to take on a more active role, particularly within the context of applying and giving visibility to its Statement of Universal Human Rights. In July 2000, the United Nations General Assembly adopted the Global Compact that calls on businesses around the world to embrace 10 universal principles in the areas of human rights, labor standards, and the environment.[6] Exhibit 6.2[7] lists the Compact principles that directly involve IHR. As is the case with most international standards, the Global Compact is not a regulatory instrument, but rather a voluntary initiative that relies on public accountability, transparency, and disclosure to complement regulation and to promote sustainable growth and good citizenship through committed and creative corporate leadership.

International Labour Organisation (ILO)[8]

Established in 1919, the ILO has as its primary goal the improvement of working conditions, living standards, and the fair and equitable treatment of workers in all countries. It is composed of member states with representatives from governments, employers, and workers. This tri-partite structure has remained as the mechanism through which the ILO carries on its work. The ILO currently has 185[9] member countries and is the only really global organization that deals with labor issues, such as stating generally accepted employment standards that apply to all members.

EXHIBIT 6.2: United Nations Global Compact Principles of Interest to IHRM

■ Human rights

❑ "Businesses should support and respect the protection of internationally proclaimed human rights"; and

❑ "Make sure that they are not complicit in human rights abuses."

■ Labor

❑ "Businesses should uphold the freedom of association and the effective recognition of the right to collective bargaining";

❑ "The elimination of all forms of forced and compulsory labour";

❑ "The effective abolition of child labour"; and

❑ "The elimination of discrimination in respect of employment and occupation."

Source: United Nations Global Compact: http://www.unglobalcompact.org/abouttheGc/TheTen-principles/index.htmʲ

The ILO sets two types of labor standards—conventions and recommendations—in industrial categories. Conventions are international treaties that are legally binding for the member states once they are ratified by them. Recommendations are non-binding guidelines that assist countries in the implementation of conventions. In 2000, the member nations of the ILO finally voted overwhelmingly to adopt the ILO Declaration of Fundamental Principles and Rights at Work (see Exhibit 6.1). An annual report examines trends toward compliance with each of the principles.

The Organization of Economic Cooperation and Development (OECD)

Established in 1960, the OECD evolved from the Organization for European Economic Cooperation (OEEC) that was formed by a number of European nations to administer the US Marshall plan to rebuild the war-ravaged economies of Europe at the end of World War II. Its focus is broader than that of the ILO as it coordinates economic policy among the industrialized countries and addresses globalization issues through the promotion of economic, environmental, and social policy among its members. OECD membership has gradually expanded to its current 34 members[10]—all industrialized countries that have developed to an agreed-upon threshold of per capita GDP and a demonstrated willingness to adhere to OECD standards and agreements. In addition OECD has cooperation with more than 70[11] non-member states that act as observers.

The OECD has many directorates dealing with many aspects of economic and social development, including a Directorate for Employment, Labour, and Social Affairs. Its main objective is to research issues related to these topics, such as changing employment patterns, the relationship of wages and working conditions to levels of employment, and the status of women in the workforce. The Directorate is not focused on the development of labor standards, per se.

However, one area of concern of the OECD has been the development of a set of Guidelines for MNEs. These guidelines aim to help businesses, labor unions, and NGOs by providing them with a global framework for responsible business conduct. In addition, the guidelines include strict standards for corporate behavior in areas including employment relations.

Since the OECD is a voluntary organization, it cannot set binding labor standards but only sets forth voluntary guidelines. These guidelines are issued under the umbrella of a "chapeau" agreement (i.e., a guiding framework for local laws and regulations) and provide recommendations on responsible business conduct for MNEs operating in or from adhering countries. Many OECD member states have used these guidelines as the basis for domestic laws concerning corporate behavior.

World Bank and International Monetary Fund (IMF)

Both the World Bank (founded in 1944)[12] and the IMF (founded in 1945)[13] have undertaken extensive research on the relation between trade policy reform and labor markets (wages, unemployment, etc.). Their primary interest has been in protecting "social safety nets" in the phasing and sequencing of their programs. For example, where structural reforms that they have introduced (such as privatization of government-owned sectors of the economy or reductions in protective tariffs) have led to significant retrenchment of jobs (such as in the public sector), they have introduced programs including severance payments and worker retraining schemes.

International Trade Organizations and Treaties

There are a number of international trade organizations and regional trade treaties that are pursuing, to greater or lesser extents, common labor standards throughout their areas of concern. The best known (and most fully developed) of the regional trade agreements is the European Union (EU), but they also include the North American Free Trade Agreement (NAFTA), Mercosur/Mercosul, and ASEAN, among other less-developed regional agreements. The following provides a short overview of key efforts in the arena of labor and employment standards.

World Trade Organization (WTO)

The WTO (established in 1995)[14] is the international body in which multilateral tariff reductions are negotiated, reductions in non-tariff trade barriers are negotiated, and international trade disputes are reviewed and adjudicated.[15] It replaced the earlier General Agreement on Trade and Tariffs (GATT). To this point in time, the WTO has not taken any direct action to define labor standards. But it is under constant pressure, primarily from the developed countries, and among them, primarily the US and the EU, to examine ways to link labor codes and human rights issues with tariff reductions.

Some industrial nations and labor advocates think the WTO should use trade sanctions as a means of pressuring countries that, in their opinion, are violating "core labor rights," a term that covers such matters as the use of child labor and forced labor and denial of the right to organize free trade unions. Advocates of such WTO sanctions argue that a country with lower standards for labor rights (which result in lower costs for labor) has an unfair cost advantage for its exports. Thus, they argue, it is an appropriate topic for consideration by the WTO. There has been considerable discussion within the WTO about ways to be involved with labor issues, such as linking with the ILO. But thus far, there is no consensus to do so nor on how to do it. Indeed, the general consensus appears, for now at least, to be for the WTO to defer to the ILO in the pursuit of global labor standards.

European Union (EU)

The European Union is the most highly developed economic trade treaty. It began as the European Economic Community (EEC—or just EC) under the Treaty of Rome in 1957 as an economic union (a "common market"), designed around reduced tariffs and freer trade. The EC originally included the six Western European countries of France, Germany, Italy, and the Benelux countries. Today the EEC has grown to an enlarged European Union (EU) of 28[16] member states (with another 6[17] countries on a "waiting" list) and has become a social and political union as well. As the number of countries has increased, so also has the size of the member population, with a population now estimated (2014) to be about 507.4[18] million people, and it has become the world's largest integrated trading bloc. The political structure of the EU consists of five distinct institutions (the European Parliament, the Council of the EU, the European Commission, the Court of Justice, and the Court of Auditors), each with specific responsibilities.[19]

Of particular interest to IHR is what is referred to within the EU as the social dimension.[20] The Social Charter of the EU, first adopted in 1989 and implemented in 1992, sets out 12 principles of fundamental rights of workers. Since the original adoption of these principles, the EU has been translating them into practice through directives, with the intent of defining a minimum set of basic rules to be observed in every member country. The intent is to raise the standards in the poorer countries, while encouraging countries that want to do so, to move to even higher levels of worker protections or to, at least, maintain their already higher standards. Of course, these principles and standards apply to all firms, locally owned or foreign owned, that operate within the EU.

Under the Maastricht Treaty of 1991, the following protocols with regard to the various areas of social policy were agreed for EU-wide adoption:

- Require unanimous agreement by all member states: social security, social protections, individual terminations, representation/collective defense including co-determination, third country national employment conditions, and financial aid for employment promotion.
- Require a qualified majority vote: issues related to the environment, safety and health, working conditions, information and consultation, equal opportunity—labor market opportunities/treatment at work, and integration of persons excluded from the labor market.
- Exempt (i.e., left to the discretion of individual states): levels of pay, right of association, and rights to strike or lockout.

Under the Treaty of Amsterdam in 1998, the EU included an Employment "chapter" in the basic treaty, with the purpose of promoting throughout all member states a high level of employment and social protection. Employment policy remains the responsibility of individual member states, but the new chapter on employment policy has the intention of providing a common and central focus on employment policy, including improving the employability of the labor force (particularly young workers and long-term unemployed), encouraging and facilitating entrepreneurship, encouraging greater adaptability of businesses and their employees (by modernizing work arrangements, such as flexible work arrangements and tax incentives for in-house training), and strengthening the policies for equal opportunity (tackling gender gaps in some economic sectors, reconciling conflicts between work and family life, facilitating reintegration into the labor market, and promoting integration of people with disabilities).

The EU has passed many directives (discussed later) that address specific areas of concern with the overall objectives of the Social Charter. It is necessary for IHR managers in any enterprise doing business within the EU to understand these regulations and to ensure that their firm's policies and practices abide by them. It is no longer possible to locate an MNE's operations in any specific country within the EU with the strategy of hoping to find "softer" employment standards and regulations. Now EU directives apply to all member states and as the number of member countries has increased to 28, the task of ensuring compliance within the EU has become even more extensive and complicated. The European Social Fund was established under the Social Charter with the purpose of promoting the geographical and occupational mobility of workers by focusing development funds on training and retraining schemes, particularly for younger workers and women, migrants, workers threatened with unemployment in restructuring industries, workers with disabilities, and workers in small- and medium-sized enterprises.

On December 1, 2009, the Lisbon Treaty went into force.[21] This most recent organizing document of the EU was negotiated to strengthen the role of the European Parliament and, in general, improve democracy throughout the institutions of the now 28-member EU. Included in the Lisbon Treaty were a number of steps of importance to the overall Social Charter. For example, it reinforced the Charter of Fundamental Rights, signed in 2000, including a number of social rights, such as personal data protection, the rights of asylum, equality before the law and non-discrimination, equality between men and women, the rights of children and elderly people, and important social rights such as protection against unfair dismissal and access to social security and social assistance.

North American Free Trade Agreement (NAFTA)

The North American Free Trade Agreement, between Canada, the United States, and Mexico, came into force in 1994,[22] aimed at promoting greater trade and closer economic ties between the three member countries. However, it provoked considerable protests from groups, such as labor unions, that were concerned about possible negative effects that such freer trade might have on employment, wages, and working conditions. As a response, the three member countries negotiated a supplemental (side) agreement on labor issues. This agreement (the North American Agreement on Labor Cooperation—NAALC) was included in NAFTA in 1993. Under this agreement, all three countries are committed to respect and enforce their own labor laws but, in addition, the NAALC provides mechanisms for problem-solving consultations when there are differences in policy and practice and provides ways to evaluate these varying patterns of practice by independent committees of experts.

For a number of recent years, largely out of the scrutiny of the public or the media, all countries in the Western Hemisphere (with the exception of Cuba) met to negotiate a free trade agreement for the Hemisphere (referred to as FTAA, or the Free Trade Area of the Americas).[23] One of the objectives of the FTAA was to include labor standards that would be even more inclusive than those enumerated in the Social Charter of the EU (refer to the previous section) or any other existing trade agreement. Originally, the plan was for the negotiations to be completed by 2005 and for the member countries to implement the agreement by 2006. But various countries expressed difficulties with parts of the agreement during the negotiations in late 2005 and now the final signing of this agreement has been postponed until the problems can be resolved. Some critics have suggested that it may be impossible (which may even be a good thing, they suggest) to resolve these difficulties.[24] In essence, the lesser-developed countries of the Americas have resisted the approach of the more developed countries. For example, the lesser-developed countries have wanted to retain protections for their agricultural industries while the more developed countries have wanted a reduction of these protections to provide open markets for their agricultural products. The result has been that the US has moved forward to negotiate bilateral trade agreements with single countries.

Latin American and Asian Trade Agreements

A number of trade treaties have been organized and signed among countries in both Latin America and Asia. Although some of them have mentioned concern over labor rights, none has incorporated specific language guaranteeing such rights within the treaty. Here is a short summary of the most significant of these treaties.

Mercosur/Mercosul is a "common market" agreement signed in 1991 for the free circulation of goods and services and the adoption of common trade and tariff policies between four Latin American countries (Argentina, Brazil, Paraguay, and Uruguay). Shortly after conclusion of the treaty, the Ministers of Labor of the four countries issued a declaration noting the need to take into account labor issues to ensure that the process of integration of the members' economies would be accompanied by real improvement and relative equality in the conditions of work in the four member countries. In 1994, the Presidents of the states issued a joint statement stressing the relevance, for the establishment of a common market, of issues related to employment, migration, workers' protection, and the harmonization of the labor legislation of the four countries. A tripartite (labor, management, and government) working sub-group was established in order to deal with labor relations, employment, and social security issues. In the final structure established in 1994, an Economic and Social Consultative Forum was established to make recommendations to the central commission about labor and social issues. Thus, labor and social issues form a part of the institutional structure of Mercosur, but it remains an advisory role.

The *Andean Community* was originally established as the Andean Pact in 1969, but has been known as the Andean Community since 1997. Member countries include Bolivia, Colombia, Ecuador, Peru, and Venezuela. The goal of the Andean Community is to achieve a balanced and harmonious development of the member countries under equitable conditions through integration and economic and social cooperation. As of now, there is no specific attention to labor issues.

The Association of Southeast Asian Nations (ASEAN) was founded in 1992 with the goal to accelerate economic growth, social progress, and cultural development and promote peace and stability in the south-east Asian region. The original ASEAN member states included Brunei, Indonesia, Malaysia, Philippines, Singapore, and Thailand, with additional countries joining since then (Vietnam, 1995; Laos and Myanmar, 1997; and Cambodia, 1999). ASEAN has undertaken a number of studies concerning the social dimensions and impacts of the liberalization of trade within the member states. So far, however, the members have not developed standards for member states, although it is expected that this will happen in the future.

Asia-Pacific Economic Cooperation (APEC) was founded in 1989 with the purpose to facilitate and enhance economic growth, trade, investment and cooperation among its 21 member economies in the Asia-Pacific region. Its membership represents about 40 percent of the world's population, about 54 percent of its GDP, and about 44 percent of world trade, thus it involves a significant portion of the world's economy. It operates in a cooperative manner with open dialogue based on non-binding commitments. However, it has not yet focused specifically on labor issues.

Commercial Diplomacy

As MNEs expand across the globe, learning to manage their relationships with the various governments and with the complex set of regulatory issues that affect their activities and business sectors has, of course, needed to be a major focus. Often this is referred to as commercial diplomacy, which is an emerging interdisciplinary field that refers to the processes of influencing foreign government policy and regulatory decisions that affect global trade. It is not just restricted to the efforts of commercial attaches and trade officials who negotiate tariffs and quotas on imports, but it also involves many other areas of IB, such as:

- Trade negotiations (tariff and non-tariff trade barriers; political interests; trade agreements; etc.).
- Impact of policy on decision making (business interests, macro-economic impact, public opinion).
- Government regulations (affecting banking, accounting, telecommunications, etc.).
- Legislation (anti-trust/competition law, EU directives, Sarbanes-Oxley in the US, etc.).
- Standards (health, safety, environment, data privacy, product safety, labeling, etc.).
- Industrial subsidies (agricultural, R&D, etc.).
- Corporate conduct (human rights, corruption and bribery, corporate governance, and corporate social responsibility—CSR).

While commercial diplomacy efforts are usually conducted by trade officials, they also include officials in various other governments and ministries, industry and professional associations, unions, non-governmental organizations (NGOs), and the international departments of MNEs. Because of IHR's concern with the international strategies of their firms, and their activities involved with establishing operations in foreign countries, they often are called upon to add value (provide information, analyze, consult, negotiate, etc.) to these commercial diplomacy activities.

THE GLOBAL LEGAL AND REGULATORY CONTEXT OF MNES

IHR managers need to understand international employee relations from all perspectives. For many IHR managers, their responsibilities allow them relative autonomy to develop

IHR policy and make decisions that can be applied in all countries. Since there is such a "patchwork" of varying legislative powers (at national, international, and extra-territorial levels), IHR must:

- Comply with the laws of the countries in which they operate, requiring knowledge of local laws and regulations.
- Comply with international standards and supra-national regulations, requiring knowledge of international labor standards and supra-national binding regulations.
- Comply with extra-territorial laws of their headquarters' country, requiring knowledge of extra-territorial laws.

National Laws and Regulations

As stated in the early part of this chapter, every country's employment laws vary significantly from every other country's employment laws, making this area of the IHRM environment very complex. In addition, as more and more firms operate in countries outside their original "home" borders, judicial systems within many countries are beginning to take into consideration laws from the parent countries of the MNEs that now operate within their jurisdictions, in addition to their own laws, making it increasingly difficult for MNEs to ignore either their own home-country laws in their foreign operations or the laws of their host countries.

One of the greatest mistakes IHR can make is to think that corporate HR at HQ can navigate alone the myriad of local laws and regulations. Because of this, most MNEs employ domestic HR practitioners (local HR generalists, HR country and regional managers) in the countries in which they operate. In addition, they use international employment lawyers as well as local attorneys to advise them with compliance. Even just understanding local laws is often not sufficient since the basis of the legal system can be radically different in different countries.

Supra-national Laws

International organizations, like the ILO and the OECD, and trade agreements and treaties, like the EU and NAFTA, have developed "binding" agreements, standards, and legal instruments for their affected member states. These institutions involve memberships of multiple countries. Thus their standards and laws apply to many countries and are referred to as "supra-national" laws. Note, however, that the notion of "binding" in many of these supra-national organizations implies that the laws and/or standards can be either "directly" or "indirectly" binding. Directly binding, at the member country level, requires "transposition" of the "standard" or "treaty" into the laws of the country. Typically, the member states must guarantee implementation via their national laws within a specific time frame. On the other hand, indirectly binding means that the stated rights and standards, though not directly passed into law, still infer obligations to individual employees and to their employers.

The EU has been the most prolific in passing laws that apply to its member states. The EU employs a variety of legal instruments, such as regulations, directives, decisions, opinions, and recommendations, with the first three being binding for member states.

EXHIBIT 6.3: The Scope of Selected European Union Directives Affecting the Labor and Social Policy of Businesses Operating in Member States

Acquired Rights

Protects and preserves the rights of workers when the undertaking, business, or part of a business in which they are engaged is transferred between employers as a result of a legal transfer or merger.

Transfer of Undertakings (TUPE) Regulations

Governs the transfer of undertakings and protects the rights of employees in a transfer situation. Employees enjoy the same terms and conditions, with continuity of employment, as they did with the previous employer (transposition of the acquired rights directive into the laws of the member states). Includes business transfers of a stable economic entity retaining its identity and service provision changes (outsourcing, insourcing, and subcontracting) for labor-intensive activities. TUPE regulates whether dismissals, as part of the transfer of operations, will be fair or unfair and affects information and consultation requirements and pension liabilities.

European Works Council

Regulates transnational information and consultation (I&C) on work matters as soon as there are two member states involved. It establishes the rights and procedures to I&C by requiring the establishment of Europe-wide works councils (EWCs) in undertakings of 1,000 employees in all member states combined, or at least 150 in each of at least two member states. If there is a pre-existing agreement on transnational I&C that covers the EU workforce, the directive does not apply but the agreement can be renewed when it expires; if not it falls under the directive. If there is no pre-existing agreement, the directive applies and central management is responsible for setting up EWC and I&C procedures.

Redundancies

Provides procedures (I&C phase) for making a defined number of employees redundant within a defined period of time.

Fixed-Term Work

Deals with the use of contract workers and protects fixed-term contract employees from comparable less favorable employment practices and benefits. Stipulates that a continuous fixed-term contract for four or more years is considered employment as a permanent employee.

Information and Consultation

Establishes a general framework and obligation of employers for I&C with employees. Applies to "undertakings" with a least 100 employees/establishments of at least 50 employees. The directive sets only a general framework for I&C and leaves the practical arrangements (such as works councils, trade unions, etc.) to be worked out by the member states.

Working Time

Provides a definition of working time and determines minimum rest periods, the maximum working week (48-hour average over 16 weeks), minimum annual leave, paid holidays, night and shift work.

Protection of Individuals with Regard to the Processing of Personal Data and the Free Movement of Such Data

Protects the right of privacy via strict limitations on the processing and transmission of personal data, wholly or partly, by automatic means. Affects HRIS, payroll systems, but also transmission of personal information via corporate Internet, email, fax, and voicemail to countries outside the EU that do not provide adequate data protection. The US is considered by the EU as a country that does not provide "adequate data protection" and has negotiated a special agreement with the EU (safe harbor).

Pregnancy and Maternity Leave; Parental Leave

Establishes measures to protect the health and safety of pregnant women, new mothers, female workers who are breastfeeding, including minimum leave time for pregnancy and childbirth and later to working parents.

Social Security

Avoids the loss of social security benefits when employees move within the EU for employment. Applies to employed and self-employed workers who reside in a member state and to whom legislation of a member state applies. The general principle is that the employee is subject to the social security legislation of the work state. Exceptions (subject to social security legislation of home country) include secondment and simultaneous employment in two or more member states.

Terms of Employment

Regulates the terms of the employment contract and requires a written statement of the main terms of employment. If no written contract has been drafted, one is implied.

EU Pension Funds

Aims to harmonize pension legislation across EU member states, protect pension funds and their beneficiaries, and reduce the cost of operating multiple pension funds. Allows the establishment of pan-European pension funds subject to detailed rules.

Fair Treatment and Non-Discrimination

Provides for equal treatment for men and women in working life; prohibits discrimination based on sex or marital or family status, race and ethnic origin, religion or belief, sexual orientation, disability, age; requires equal pay to women for equal work.

Sources: Birk, D. h.c. R. (2007). European Social Charter; Blanpain, R. (2010). European Labour Law, in Blanpain, R. (edit.), *International Encyclopedia for Labour Law and Industrial Relations*, The Hague, The Netherlands: Kluwer Law International; Keller, W. L., and Darby, T. J. (eds.) (2003, 2010, and annual updates). *International Labor and Employment Laws*, Washington, DC: Bureau of National Affairs; EU websites: http://ec.europa.eu/atoz_en.htm; http://ec.europa.eu/social/main.jsp?langId=en&catId=750.

Of the different EU legal instruments, the directives have the greatest impact on the practice of IHR as there are several EU directives that deal with employment issues. A summary of selected EU directives affecting labor and social policy is given in Exhibit 6.3. This list of EU directives clearly illustrates how encompassing is the Social Agenda within the EU.

The intention of EU directives is to harmonize legislation between the various member states by setting a common framework. Although member states must ensure a transposition into their national legislation that conforms to the general principles of a directive, the actual transposition details may vary substantially in the different member states. Overall, EU directives have been very effective (i.e., all member states have transposed the desired protective measures into their legislation). But, in spite of the EU's attempts to harmonize employment legislation, there is still an significant degree of diversity between the member states, and the differences in employment laws between even the three major European countries (United Kingdom, France, and Germany), and between the Old Europe and the New Europe (enlargement countries), remain considerable. The content of the Social Agenda components of the recently implemented Lisbon Treaty, as described earlier, illustrates just how serious the EU is with regard to employment rights). In addition, a lot more is expected from EU case law in the future (as existing directives and legislation are interpreted through the judicial systems of the EU). IHR practitioners must remain alert to these developments.

Extra-territorial Laws

In general, laws have the presumption of non-extraterritoriality, meaning that they only apply to the sovereign territory of the nation that enacted them. Unless a law explicitly states that it applies to a territory outside of that country, it is presumed to apply only within the country of jurisdiction. Some laws, however, have been designed with extra-territorial intent written into them. As a result, every MNE must consider the application of its parent-country laws to its overseas operations (referred to as the extra-territorial application of national law). In general, international jurisprudence holds that MNEs are accountable to the laws of the countries where they operate. However, there are some exceptions to this general rule. More than any other nation, the US has enacted a number of laws that it expects to be applied extra-territorially by its US-based MNEs. US laws with extra-territorial intent include most of its anti-discrimination legislation, its Foreign Corrupt Practices Act (FCPA), and the Sarbanes-Oxley Act (SOX). In particular, in terms of application to employment rights, US multinationals must comply with the extra-territorial application of three particular US anti-discrimination statutes, meaning these laws provide protection for US citizens working for US companies in their overseas operations. In 1991, the US Congress amended the Americans with Disabilities Act (ADA) and Title VII of the Civil Rights Act of 1964 to give extra-territorial effect to those laws. Earlier, in 1984, the Age Discrimination in Employment Act of 1967 (ADEA) was also given extra-territorial effect. Title VII prohibits discrimination and harassment on the basis of sex, race, national origin, color, and religion. The ADA prohibits discrimination against disabled individuals, and requires employers to make reasonable accommodation for those disabilities. And the ADEA prohibits discrimination on the basis of age against individuals age 40 and older and sets standards for retirement age.

The effect of these amendments was to grant American citizens working anywhere in the world, for a US-owned or controlled company, the right to sue in the US court for alleged violations of these acts, wherever they occur. For example, an employee of an American firm (who is a US citizen) who believes she has been subjected to any form of discrimination in a foreign assignment may bring a lawsuit in the United States to pursue these claims. Under any circumstance, the law of the foreign country in which a firm operates takes precedence, although in US courts, the viability of the defense of an act that is legal in the foreign jurisdiction but is illegal under US law is still unsettled. There is no doubt that, from a US perspective, US extra-territorial laws apply to US citizens when working for US companies worldwide. An as-yet unsettled legal question is whether the US extra-territorial laws also apply to non-US citizens working in foreign subsidiaries of a US company.

Potentially, this issue of extra-territoriality could extend from any country's legislation—and thus needs to be considered within any MNE, not just US-based MNEs. The problem for IHR becomes trying to determine which nation's laws govern a company's labor practices. Is it the extra-territorial law of the HQ/home country of the MNE or the local host country law? The fact that a law is extra-territorial (in this case usually from the US) does not necessarily mean that it applies universally (e.g., to all its employees everywhere). Which law applies (home or host) depends on the dynamics of control, location, and citizenship of the MNE. The standard that is used to resolve this question is what is referred to as the "integrated enterprise test": the more integrated the global operations of the MNE, the more likely the extra-territorial law will apply in the host country and extend to non-US citizens. Four factors determine the extent to which two operations are determined to be integrated:

1   the interrelation of their operations;
2   common management;
3   centralized control of labor relations, e.g., a common collective-bargaining agreement;
4   common ownership or financial control.

Application of National Law to Local Foreign-owned Enterprises

The general "rule" for MNEs is that they must abide by the laws of the countries in which they do business. Thus the issue of whose laws apply can also be viewed from the perspective of any country in terms of how it applies its laws to foreign-owned and operated firms within its national borders. Or it can be viewed from the perspective of the firm, as it tries to understand how it must operate its foreign subsidiaries and joint ventures. At a minimum, the MNE must understand that the local laws apply, not its home laws, although, as described above, MNEs from some countries, such as the US, may also find themselves subject to their home laws, at least in terms of treatment of their home-citizen employees (international assignees) in their foreign operations. So, for example, giving preference in job assignments or promotions to a firm's expatriates over qualified local employees may run afoul of local non-discrimination laws.

Treaty rights can also impact the operations of foreign companies within host jurisdictions. For example, since the end of World War II, the US has negotiated treaties with some 20 countries that are referred to as Friendship, Commerce, and Navigation (FCN) treaties. Among other things, these treaties provide that companies from each country can make employment decisions within the territories of the other party that give preferences to key personnel from their home countries.[25] Specifically, an FCN treaty gives foreign companies who establish themselves in the US the right to engage managerial, professional, and other specialized personnel "of their choice" in the US, even if giving such preferences might violate US anti-discrimination laws. (Of course, the opposite is also true: US firms can give precedence to their American employees in their operations in the foreign country with which the US has such a treaty.) For example, a Japanese company in the US can reserve its most senior executive positions for Japanese only. And US firms in Japan can give priority to American executives. A number of foreign companies that have been sued in US courts for national origin discrimination (i.e., giving preference in employment decisions in their local subsidiaries to their parent-country nationals) have used a defense that their FCN treaties give them the right to do that. US courts and legal experts have not developed a consensus as to whether or not such treaties provide that type of protection.

There are other complexities in US law that often require that each specific situation—particularly those involving treatment of US employees and parent-country nationals in foreign-owned subsidiaries in the US—needs to be interpreted separately. The bottom line is that IHR managers in MNEs need to make sure they understand the local legal landscape before establishing employment policy and practice in those foreign operations.

COMPARATIVE LAW

Employment laws vary from country to country. Important areas of concern to the MNE IHR director include immigration regulations, data privacy, anti-discrimination laws, termination laws, and intellectual property protection. Many of these areas overlap, making it important for IHR managers (and their firms' legal advisors) to know these connections and to consider them as firms make decisions that affect their workforces in the countries in which they operate.

Immigration/Visas

Every country exercises control over its definition of citizenship and the immigration that it allows into its territory. Some countries, such as Japan, allow very limited immigration. Others like the US, Canada, and Israel, even though they may exercise control over who is granted immigration rights, admit large numbers of immigrants every year. And still others, such as the UK and France, have generally allowed immigration from citizens of their former colonies. A country's attitudes about immigration vary according to its particular employment needs at any point in time (as well as according to other political and humanitarian concerns). And these change over time, as attitudes and needs change.

Virtually every country requires a work permit or visa whenever a "foreign" person is transferred to or takes on a job in its country for a period of six months or more. Of course, there are typically many other situations that can also trigger the requirement for a visa, even if the work will only last a couple of days. And, in recent years, due to the increased threats from various forms of terrorism, all visa requirements have become more difficult to meet in virtually every country. The activities that will trigger the need for such special visas and the amount of time required to process such visas vary from country to country and from situation to situation. Because of this, IHR managers must be sure, for example, when decisions are being made about sending employees on foreign assignments for anything from short-term business trips to longer-term relocations for a number of months or years, that the necessary visas are applied for and that an adequate amount of time is allowed to be able to gain the necessary approvals for such travel and transfers. Immigration law firms that specialize in helping firms acquire the necessary visas and work permits often provide the information needed to make such judgments.

Gaining approval of these various visas can be complicated and very time-consuming, expensive, and difficult, as countries tighten their procedures for even business-related and tourist visas. Firms that hire immigrants, move people around the globe, and seek talent all over the world must manage this complexity in order to effectively staff their global operations. HR's tactical role consists of anticipating roadblocks in the visa application process, being aware of application procedures to follow in different countries (or using the services of a specialized firm), and complying with the necessary record keeping and tracking of visas.

The EU creates a special case in terms of visas because of the treaty provisions for free movement of labor within its member countries. For transfers within the European region, there is no need to obtain visas. Having a valid identity card or passport is sufficient as EU nationals have the right of residence in any EU host country and the host country will issue a residence permit for any national of a member state. However, there are still some exceptions for some of the new EU members, where transition measures for free movement of labor are in place.

Personal Data Privacy/Protection

With the advent of the Internet and the ease of global communication, facilitating the sharing and distribution of information, concern over the protection of information about individuals (for example, employees and customers) has become of increasing concern in many countries.[26] Often, that concern is based in those countries' constitutional guarantees of protection of individual privacy. In other countries, such data protection is a function of cultural attitudes and values.

In Europe, these protections are particularly strong.[27] Because of this, in 1998 the EU issued a directive on the protection of employee privacy. Of particular interest to MNEs operating in Europe, under the terms of the directive (refer to Exhibit 6.3), personal data on European employees, including international assignees working in Europe, cannot be transferred out of the EU unless the country in which the data recipient resides has acceptable privacy protection standards in place. In any case, any firm transferring employee data from Europe to the US (or anywhere else outside Europe) must pay close attention to how such information is managed and shared with third parties. This has been of particular concern to American MNEs in Europe, since there has not been consensus in the US on how to provide adequate privacy protections, as of now wanting to rely more on self-regulation and laws applying to only particular sectors, such as health care and financial institutions. In late 2000, the EU agreed to a "safe harbor" principle from the US in which American firms that agree to abide by the basic European privacy standards will certify to the US Department of Commerce that they are in compliance, which will be reviewed by the EU. Such certified firms will be able to transfer data on European and international assignees from Europe to the US. The potential liability for American firms that do not certify compliance with basic European privacy laws through this "safe harbor" procedure is to lose their rights to do business anywhere in the EU.

Adding to these concerns are the widespread and increasing use of social media (such as Facebook, LinkedIn, Twitter, Google Plus+, Instagram, and YouTube) and search engines (such as Google, Yahoo!, Bing) on computers, cell phones, and e-tablets, that enable the global sharing of personal data with minimal controls. The technology (and acceptance) for such social networking is advancing faster than companies and governments can develop rules and regulations to control it. Plus there is increasing evidence that younger people that have grown up with the use of this technology have very different views (greater rejection) of the need to control content and sharing on social media. These realities make it ever clearer that IHRM must try to stay ahead of changes in technology and its use, as well as keeping abreast of various national jurisdictions in their attempts to regulate issues such as the protection of personal data.

Anti-discrimination

Around the world, countries are passing legislation to protect the rights of employees and job candidates to be free from discrimination and harassment based on their gender, race, color, religion, age, or disability. The laws in place in many countries, such as the US and now in the EU, are pretty well developed, although within the EU there has been a distinct lack of uniformity in many of these areas, with the possible exception of sex discrimination.[28] Until the turn of the millennium, many EU countries had not yet even moved beyond approval of protections as put forth by the ILO. However, in 2003, directives went into effect in the EU requiring all member states to pass legislation prohibiting discrimination on the basis of race, gender, disability, age, sexual orientation, family status, and religion or belief. And, as indicated earlier in this chapter, under the Lisbon Treaty, these rights have been finally institutionalized within the 34 member states of the EU.

Anti-discrimination laws are clearly an area of international labor standards to which every MNE must pay very close attention.[29] And because of national and regional cultures that in the past may have allowed practices that are now being prohibited, making sure that all managers and employees of the global firm abide by these new standards presents a major challenge to IHR. Although there is considerable convergence developing, there are still some significant variances. Since courts in some countries are beginning to refer to the laws of parent countries in cases involving MNEs within their jurisdictions, it certainly suggests that IHR and their MNEs must pay close attention to these differences.

Of particular interest is the issue and treatment of sexual harassment. The cultural interpretation around the world as to what constitutes such harassment and the legal framework protecting employees from harassment and bullying varies extensively between countries. The EU, UN, and ILO all address sexual harassment in the workplace. Several industrialized countries have specific sexual harassment prohibitions (e.g., Australia, Canada, France, New Zealand, Spain, Sweden, and the United States).[30] In these countries, sexual harassment in the workplace is protected by one of four different types of constraints (equal employment opportunity law, union contracts, tort/contract law, or criminal law). In the US, the sexual harassment prohibition is also applied extra-territorially. As this issue has received increased attention, an increasing number of countries have begun to consider prohibitions against sexual harassment in the workplace.[31] Indeed, a recent report of a global survey found that 10 percent of employees around the world report they have been harassed sexually or physically bullied at work.[32] The poll of approximately 12,000 people in 24 countries revealed considerable differences in reported levels of harassment between countries, with some large emerging market countries reporting the highest levels, but also showing that this is an issue that is gaining attention worldwide, irrespective of a country's basic cultural values.

Exhibit 6.4 provides a list of the anti-discrimination coverage of laws in 12 sample countries. This exhibit illustrates the high degree of variability among countries in this significant area of law. All multinational countries need to pay close attention to these laws as they conduct business around the globe. This also illustrates that most countries now include some sort of mention of legal coverage against sexual or moral harassment, as well.

Termination and Reduction in Force

In most countries, individual employment is protected by an employee contract that defines the terms and conditions of employment, including that it cannot be ended unilaterally or arbitrarily by the employer. The concept of "employment-at-will," as practiced in the United States (where the employer, with a few exceptions, has the right to terminate an

EXHIBIT 6.4: Protected Classes for Discrimination Prohibition in Select Countries

European Union	Sex, marital or family status, race and ethnic origin, religion or belief, sexual orientation, disability, age; equal pay for equal work
Brazil	Sex, age, color, family situation, pregnancy, union membership; equal pay for equal work; sexual harassment
Bulgaria	Age, caste, disability, language, nationality, race or ethnicity, region, religion, sex-gender-gender identity, sexual orientation, marital status, + EU
China	Nationality, race, sex, religion, disability, age, migrant workers, health status; equal pay for equal work; sexual harassment; protection of children and minors
Germany	Race or ethnic origin, sex or sexual orientation, religion or secular belief, disability, age; sexual harassment + EU
India	India lacks a comprehensive anti-discrimination law for the private sector. Nevertheless, the Constitution prohibits the state from discrimination on the basis of religion, race, caste, sex, and place of birth and allows positive discrimination (affirmative action) based on discrepancies in gender, social or financial background, or traditional caste-based disadvantage. Legislative acts address employee discrimination with respect to recruitment, wages, work-transfers, and promotion for men and women, people with disabilities, and socially and educationally backward classes of citizens.
Indonesia	Sex, ethnic group, race, religion, skin color, political alliance; special protection for women and child workers (<16); no sexual harassment law (but criminal code provides basis for filing sexual harassment complaint)
Mexico	Undeveloped, but constitutional protections against discrimination on basis of sex, race, religion, age, political views, nationality; discrimination law defines equal opportunity for persons based on ethnic or national origin, gender, age, disability, social or financial conditions, health condition, pregnancy, language, religion, opinion, sexual preference, marital status; limited protection for sexual and moral harassment, equal pay for equal work, child labor
Russia	Gender, race, nationality, language, social origin, property status, place of residence, religious beliefs, affiliations with social associations, pregnancy, and children; no special legislation on sexual or moral harassment

Continued overleaf

EXHIBIT 6.4 *Continued*

United Kingdom	Age, disability, gender, marriage and civil partnerships, pregnancy and maternity, race, religion or belief, sex and sexual orientation; sexual harassment
United States	Age (over 40), sex, national origin, race, color, religion, disability, veteran status, pregnancy and genetic information; sexual harassment

Source: Based on Baker & McKenzie (2012). *The Global Employer: Focus on Termination, Employment Discrimination, and Workplace Harassment Laws*, Baker & McKenzie International, a Swiss Verein with law firms around the world, US Headquarters, Chicago; plus individual country websites.

---

employee at will—and the employee has the right to quit at any time for any reason), does not exist in most countries. In most countries, employers' rights to terminate, layoff, reduce, restructure, move, outsource, or sub-contract work (and, therefore, workers) is highly constrained. In most countries, including the US, employees (or work) cannot be terminated on grounds of health and safety, pregnancy or maternity, asserting a statutory right, union activity, or the basis of one's gender, race, religion, or disability. In general, firms need to search for alternative employment (within the firm or externally, if nothing is available internally) and consult with their unions, works councils, and the individuals affected (typically at least 30 days prior to taking action if 20 to 100 people will be involved, and 90 days prior if 100 or more people are to be made redundant).[33] This includes any outsourcing, work transfers to other countries, and sub-contracting.

In terms of pure reductions in force, generally only three situations are seen as acceptable excuses:

1 business closure;
2 workplace closure; and
3 diminishing economic need for the work.

All of these situations involve requirements for notice and consultation with employees and/or their representatives.

In addition to notice of workforce redundancies, most countries also require payments to terminated employees. Indeed, in most countries it is very difficult to terminate any employee for any reason, even with notice and consultation. Particularly when the termination involves a number of employees (that is, it involves a downsizing, relocation, or significant layoff), notice and consultation are both necessary. However, even when terminations are possible and done, they usually still require significant severance payments to all individuals involved. Such payments are often required even when the termination is for disciplinary or poor performance. Separation practices differ between countries but still illustrate both the legal requirements for dismissals and the severance payment formula.[34] In most countries, the amount of severance pay is pro-rated by the employee's age, years of service, and last rate of pay or salary.

In some countries, employers will find it difficult to terminate employees at all. In Portugal, for example, all terminations are legal actions that must be defended in court, while in countries such as Germany, where there is a strong tradition of reliance on works councils, terminations are topics for mandatory consultation. Also, in many countries, all employer-paid benefits become what are referred to as acquired rights, that is, once offered, they cannot be taken away, even in the case of redundancies of any type, e.g., in acquisitions, employee transfers, work transfers, or closing of offices. Employers cannot move work or workers to new countries or locales and, in the process, create new compensation, benefits, or work designs that are less than in the previous location. In many countries, particularly in Europe, and in EU law, more specifically, the employee has "acquired rights" to his or her existing levels of compensation and benefits and to the nature of his or her work that cannot be reduced by either moving the employee or the work to another location. After notification and consultation, often MNEs "buy" their ways out of these liabilities by negotiating settlements with affected workers to compensate them for their acquired rights. But they cannot just unilaterally reduce the benefits. And the ultimate point is that redundancies of any type can be, at least in many countries, quite expensive and require close attention from IHR.

Intellectual Property

The concept of "intellectual property" includes forms of employee creation (sometimes, in the past, referred to as industrial property) such as patented inventions and/or discoveries, trademarks, geographic indications, and industrial and product designs as well as items that can be copyrighted such as literary and artistic works such as novels, poems, and plays, films, musical works, artistic works such as drawings, paintings, photographs, and sculptures, and architectural designs. Although it may not at first be obvious, there are several links between intellectual property and IHR. For example, inventions and intellectual contributions, which are a result of an individual's employment, are usually considered by the employer to be its property. As a consequence, employers take a number of steps to ensure that such "property"—referred to as trade secrets (such as client and customer lists), product and process technologies, and patents—are either filed for legal protection (patented) or are protected through non-disclosure agreements with their employees (meaning the employees do not have the right to share or give this information to anyone else, particularly, of course, competitors, or to use the information for their own personal gain). Also, publications such as the many training materials and product/service manuals that an employer develops for use by their employees and customers are copyrighted in order to protect them from use by outside people.

The situation of protection of intellectual and property rights is especially complicated when operating internationally because different countries have different conceptions of what constitutes property and vary in their practices related to its protection. In addition, there is no international institution that has the capability to extend intellectual and copyright protection to the MNE worldwide.[35]

With regard to industrial property, each country usually has an intellectual property office (IPO) or an administrative unit within the government that is in charge of administering the system of IP rights acquisition and maintenance. Depending on the country, these offices have varying ranges of resources. Poorer countries tend to have fewer resources for screening and approving pending applications for new patents and for maintaining databases of protected patents. The World Industrial Property Organization (WIPO) is a specialized agency of the UN responsible for the promotion of the protection of IP worldwide. WIPO administers the multiple international treaties and develops conventions for its member states. The Patent Cooperation Treaty (PCT) dramatically reduces the duplication of efforts with regard to patents (filing, researching, and execution) in different countries and allows for filing in a single national office. As an international procedural mechanism, if offers a trademark owner the possibility to have his trademark protected in several countries by simply filing one application directly with his own national or regional trademark office.

With regard to copyright, there is no single statute that extends copyright protection worldwide; rather, each country has its own copyright laws. There are, however, a number of bilateral agreements and international treaties among countries regarding copyright protection. Most countries abide by one of two international agreements: the Berne Convention (which provides national and automatic protection) and the Universal Copyright Convention (which provides only national protection). National treatment (minimal protection) means that local laws apply to all copyright infringements that take place within the country even if the original work was created elsewhere. Automatic protection means that local laws apply even to works that have not satisfied the country's required formalities (copyright notice and/or registration). To ensure full copyright protection, MNEs must investigate whether the country in question is a member of the Berne Convention or Universal Copyright Convention, and whether they have entered into any trade agreements with the country in which the original work was created. They must research the local laws of the countries that are NOT Berne Convention members as well as those for which any applicable trade agreements do not have an automatic protection provision and comply with any required formalities, such as registration with the national copyright office for these countries.

One additional consideration, particularly in firms with highly specialized technology or other forms of intellectual property that is critical to their ability to compete, involves different countries' attitudes about non-compete agreements. These agreements, signed by employees as part of their individual employment contracts, restrict their going to work within some particular time period for a competitor, setting up on their own a new competing business, or taking competitive-critical information with them to their new (former competitor) employer.[36] MNEs must take care to write these non-compete agreements in understandable language (not legal jargon) and translate these agreements into the local languages of the countries in which they operate (often required by local law).

THE INTERNATIONAL FRAMEWORK OF ETHICS AND LABOR STANDARDS

The conduct of international business increasingly involves concerns about the values and practices of MNEs when they conduct business outside their countries of origin.[37] International governing bodies, non-governmental organizations (NGOs), labor organizations, and special interest groups increasingly raise questions about the "ethical" nature of the business practices of many MNEs, often particularly as they relate to employment practices. Concerns over the impact of globalization, worker exploitation, and increasing inequities, particularly in less developed countries, are increasing, even though levels of poverty have declined and general population well-being has seemed to improve. Because of this, confusion about business rules, ethics, and HR policies and practices has intensified.[38]

This last section in this chapter provides an overview of concerns about international business ethics, particularly as they relate to IHRM. International ethics looks at what's right and wrong in business conduct across borders and the impact of cultural (country and company) variances on ethical conduct of MNEs. International ethics also deals with issues of corruption and bribery, and the various ethical dilemmas that MNEs face in the conduct of their international activities. Because MNE ethics, particularly issues that relate directly to employee relations, are often relegated to IHR, the primary focus here is the impact of ethics on global HR practices.

International Ethics and Culture

In the area of global ethics, even the best-informed, best-intentioned executives often have to rethink their assumptions. What works in an enterprise's home country may be viewed very differently in another country, which may have very different standards or perceptions of what is ethical conduct.[39] Evidence even suggests that not only is there variance among countries and cultures, but even among different industries.[40] Often one's national perspective clouds one's view of another country or culture's way of doing things. Even if there is relative agreement on basic human values (for example, refer to the United Nations Universal Declaration of Human Rights) and ethical principles around the world (a point with which some would disagree), clearly there is considerable variance in what might be referred to as the ethical climate in different countries.[41] That is, differing country cultures view various employment and business conduct issues, such as bribery, gifts or favors, tax evasion, or child labor, differently. Thomas Donaldson, one of the world's top experts on international ethics, tells the story of an expatriate manager of a large US company operating in China who fired an employee caught stealing and turned him over to local authorities, according to company policy.[42] Later, the manager was horrified to learn that the employee had been executed by local authorities for breaking an important law against stealing from one's employer. Obviously, the cultural context in which the company policy was formulated was vastly different from the cultural context in which the manager carried out the policy.

> *Ethical relativism* suggests that what is right is whatever a society defines as right. There are no absolute rights or wrongs.

In order to understand ethical variances such as this, ethicists describe possible approaches as being on a continuum, from ethical relativism to ethical absolutism. On one end of the continuum lies *ethical relativism*, which suggests that what is right is whatever a society defines as right. This definition may be at the individual (individual relativism) or at the societal (cultural relativism) level. In the relativistic view, there are no absolute rights or wrongs; rather the values of the individual or the society are sovereign in deciding what is right or wrong for that culture as long as no laws prohibit the behavior. In this perspective, if a society says that women shall not be paid the same as men for the same work or that child labor is all right, those rules would be seen as right for that society at that point in time. Under ethical relativism, there can be no external frame of reference for judging that one society's set of rules is better—or worse—than another's. So, under ethical relativism, IHR managers who try to impose their values on HR practices in a host country are guilty of what is often referred to as ethical imperialism, or ethical chauvinism. Under the philosophy of ethical relativism, it is entirely appropriate to follow local practices regarding the treatment of employees. Though appearing on the surface to be a liberal, open-minded approach, this view may result in actions that home-country constituencies (at least from the Western industrialized countries) would find entirely unacceptable, such as child labor or gross inequality. This view of "when in Rome, do as the Romans do," is challenged when one considers whether someone from an outside culture can really have a local understanding of what's right or wrong in that particular culture. Ethical relativism takes a particularistic view of the culture, namely that there are no universal standards, rather differing evaluation rules are based on the context or the situation.

> *Ethical absolutism* is the view that there is a single set of universal ethical standards or principles, which apply at all times, in all circumstances, in all cultures.

The opposite position is called *ethical absolutism*. This is the view that there is a single set of universal ethical standards or principles, which apply at all times, in all circumstances, in all cultures. This universalistic approach views moral values and principles as eternal and that they apply universally and equally in all places and times. This more standardized approach is often reflected in an MNE's global code of ethics (i.e., a set of universal principles that, under no circumstances, should ever be violated). This might be very useful to an IHR manager, as it would suggest which local practices—even though they may be quite different from those of the parent country—are morally acceptable because they do not violate universal principles and those which are not morally acceptable and must not be followed, because they do violate such universal principles. The problem with this view is specifying what the universal principles are and developing a logical case for why these, and only these, principles are truly universal. In adopting the values of a single culture or religion as universal one runs the risk of ethical imperialism. Thus both of these philosophies create potential problems for the IHR manager, for MNE employees around the world, and especially for international assignees who are posted to foreign subsidiaries. In order to deal with these extremes, some have suggested that situations often compel the MNE, through collaboration and/or imagination, to develop unique responses to cross-cultural ethical dilemmas, ones that try to find common ground among disparate moral views. This has been referred to as *cosmopolitanism*.[43] Such an approach calls for reconciling seemingly opposing differences in ethical choices and requires debate, effort, and compromise. But such solutions are far from easy for the diverse employees of the MNE and its international managers.

> *Cosmopolitanism* calls for reconciling seemingly opposing differences in ethical choices and requires debate, effort, and compromise. But such solutions are far from easy for the diverse employees of the MNE and its international managers.

Ethical Dilemmas in IHRM

One of the basic ethical dilemmas for IHR and MNEs involves what management should do when an employment practice that is illegal or viewed as wrong in the home country is legal or acceptable in the host country.[44] Examples might include sex or race discrimination in hiring, job placement, or compensation; use of child labor; or providing unsafe working conditions. Thomas Donaldson has tried to provide a framework for decision making in a multinational environment that tries to resolve these possible ethical dilemmas.[45] Donaldson states that the task is to "tolerate cultural diversity while drawing the line at moral recklessness."[46] In some ways, his approach is absolutist because it relies on a statement of 30 fundamental international rights (which have been recognized by international bodies, such as the United Nations, the ILO, and the OECD). Among these, maybe 10 or so apply directly to issues of concern to IHRM. These include the rights to freedom of physical movement; ownership of property; freedom from torture; a fair trial; non-discriminatory treatment; physical security; freedom of speech and association; a minimal education; political participation; freedom to work in fair and safe conditions, and to earn a decent standard of living. Organizations need to avoid depriving individuals of these rights wherever they do business (even though, in some countries, some of these "rights" are not very well recognized or agreed to).

The following IHRM in Action illustrates this point:[47]

IHRM in Action 6.1: Developing Global Labor Standards at Levi Strauss

Levi Strauss has global sourcing and operating guidelines that address workplace issues. The company uses these guidelines to select business partners who will manufacture its products. Established in 1992, its guidelines were [among] the first created by a multi-national company for its business partners. The terms of engagement detail everything from environmental requirements to health and safety issues. Among them: wages, discrimination, child labor, and forced- or prison-labor issues. To create these guidelines, the company used the Principled Reasoning Approach (a decision-making tool that Levi Strauss uses to teach its employees how to translate ethical principles into behavior). And to launch them, it conducted audits of contractors it was using worldwide.

Levi Strauss discovered that in Bangladesh, it had two contractors using workers in the factories who appeared to be underage. International standards have set a reasonable working age for factories at 14. When the company brought it to the attention of the factory owners, the owners asked the company what it wanted the factory to do. There were no birth certificates so there was no way to know exactly how old these children were. Also, even if the children were younger than 14, they would very likely be a significant contributor to the family income and probably would be forced into other ways for making a living that would be more inhumane than working in a factory—such as prostitution or begging.

"So, we were faced on the one hand with a set of principles that were very clear, but hard to implement, and on the other with the reality of underage workers and severely impacting their family incomes," says Richard Woo, senior manager for global communications for Levi Strauss. The solution? "The contractor agreed not to hire any more underage workers," he says. They also hired a physician to examine children who seemed to be less than 14 years old using growth charts identified by the World Health Organization. Although not hiring young workers may force them to find work elsewhere, Levi Strauss' position is to be ethically responsible for business issues it can control—such as responsible child labor conditions—as opposed to social conditions in a country that it has no control over.

Levi Strauss also negotiated for the contractors to remove the under-14 workers they already had from the production line and continue to pay them wages as if they were still working. In exchange, Levi Strauss covered the cost of the children's uniforms, tuition, and books so they could go to school. When the underage workers reach the age of 14, they are offered back their original factory jobs. The contractors complied with all this, "to maintain the contracts with us," says Woo.

However, the rights discussed above alone do not always provide sufficient practical guidelines for operating in an international environment. When IHR managers and the management of MNEs are trying to decide if their organizations can follow a practice that is legal and morally acceptable in the host country but not in the parent country, Donaldson suggests they ask themselves a series of questions in the ethical decision-making process.

First, ask *why* the practice is acceptable in the host country but not at home. Answers to this question fall into two categories:

1 because of the host country's relative level of economic development; or
2 for reasons unrelated to economic development.

If the answer is 1, the next question is whether the parent country would have accepted the practice when (or if) it was at that same level of economic development. If it would have (or did), the practice is permissible. An example might be the building of a fertilizer plant that provides a product necessary for the feeding of the population of the country, despite the fact that there is a risk of occupational disease for employees working in the plant. If the parent firm (or the parent country) were willing to accept this risk for itself under similar circumstances, then the building of such a plant would be all right within Donaldson's framework. The second answer, that the difference is not based on economic considerations, requires a more complicated decision process. The manager must ask two additional questions:

1 Is it possible to conduct business successfully in the host country without undertaking the practice?
2 Is the practice a clear violation of a fundamental right?[48]

The practice is permissible *only if* the answer to both questions is no. That is, the practice is acceptable if it is critical to doing business in the country *and* it does not violate a fundamental right. Otherwise, the organization should refuse to follow the local practice. For example, in the past, in Singapore, it has been common to see help-wanted ads seeking "Chinese women, age 21–28." This type of advertisement violates US (and other countries') laws and mores regarding age, gender, and ethnic discrimination. Would it be permissible from an ethical point of view for a US or EU subsidiary in Singapore to run an ad like that? (Note that legally, extra-territoriality of the US anti-discrimination legislation may apply to a US company operating in Singapore if the company meets the integrated enterprise test.) According to Donaldson, the answer is no because the discrimination is not tied to the level of economic development, is not necessary for doing business in Singapore, and violates fundamental international rights to nondiscriminatory treatment (a right that is codified in the resolutions of a number of international bodies, such as the United Nations and the International Labour Organisation, as well as in national laws in the EU and in the US).

There can be many difficulties when discussing issues of ethical attitudes and practices in various countries. Obviously, the gap between policy and practice can often be quite wide. Solutions to the problem of child labor, for example, are not necessarily easy to develop in a way that benefits the parties involved.[49]

Ethical issues have become a top concern to executives of MNEs as well as of governments and non-governmental organizations. There is a growing desire to find approaches to these issues that would both provide protection for the rights of employees worldwide as well as provide guidelines for organizations that enable them to conduct business in ways that benefit all of their constituencies: customers, employees, owners/shareholders, suppliers, and communities in which they conduct business. Many organizations and individuals have proposed guiding principles to balance the extremes.[50] IHR must proactively consider these global ethical issues, usually incorporated in a global code of business conduct, and entertain some of the solutions being suggested to these problems.

In the end, the assurance of ethical behavior and conduct of firms that conduct business outside their home borders depends on the attitudes and behaviors of their managers, at home and abroad. Accordingly, it is suggested that businesses can take three steps to help ensure that their employees (managers at home, expatriates abroad, and their parent and foreign employees) behave not only appropriately, but also ethically:[51]

1 Develop a clearly articulated set of core values as the basis for global policies and decision making.
2 Train international employees to ask questions that will help them make business decisions that are both culturally sensitive and flexible within the context of those core values.
3 Balance the need for policy with the need for flexibility or imagination.

Given these three points as general guidelines for an overall approach, Exhibit 6.5 illustrates a list of steps that provide some guidance on how an MNE might design a code of conduct and ensure an effective implementation of ethical standards for worldwide operations.[52]

The treatment of ethics in international context is very complex indeed. Yet, MNEs must confront the issue in their daily operations and resolve these difficult dilemmas. IHR, through education, training, and problem solving needs to play an integral role in raising the awareness of its firm's employees regarding ethical behavior.

Corporate Social Responsibility (CSR), Corporate Governance, and Sustainability

Many MNEs are beginning to pay attention to their roles as corporate citizens. CSR, corporate governance, and sustainability are taking on greater importance in the operation of MNEs, and IHR is increasingly playing an important role in implementing these activities in their global organizations.

CSR

CSR is the continuing commitment by businesses to not only behave ethically, but also contribute to the economic development of the communities in which they operate and to improve the quality of life of their workforces, their families, as well as society at large.

EXHIBIT 6.5: Guidance on How an MNE Might Design a Code of Conduct and Ensure an Effective Implementation of Ethical Standards for Worldwide Operations

Guideline	Description
Reasons for developing a global ethics program	Be clear about the reasons for developing a global ethics program—even if it is for compliance reasons (at home or abroad). Is it an opportunity to build bridges across varying cultures and constituencies or a way to instill a common set of corporate principles and values in order to unite the firm and its customers and suppliers around the world? Design and implement conditions of engagement for suppliers and customers that fit them into the ethics code.
Formalize standards	Treat corporate values and formal standards of conduct as absolutes, that is, once the program is developed, do not allow for local variations (except within the standards established in the program—see the rest of these guidelines).
Consult all stakeholders	Consult broadly with people who are affected, including international personnel who will need to implement the program and junior-level managers who may be the people implementing the program in the future. Allow foreign business units to help formulate ethical standards and interpret ethical issues.
Choose the words carefully	Many terms do not translate effectively into other languages. Even the term (or concept of) "ethics" does not translate well into many other languages and cultures. Alternatives, such as managerial responsibility, corporate integrity, or business practices are less culturally loaded and easier to translate.
Translation of codes	Translate the code carefully—when communicating the code to operations in foreign locales, the firm must be careful to translate the meanings and to screen for parent-country biases, language, and examples.
Translate the "ethics code" training materials	Translate the "ethics code" training materials (that is, don't leave it only in the parent-company home language). The training materials and activities need to be carefully translated and carefully presented.
Designate an ethics officer	Designate an ethics officer for overseas operations—for all regions where there are a large number of employees, a

Continued overleaf

EXHIBIT 6.5 *Continued*

Guideline	Description
	local ethics officer should be appointed, preferably a native who knows the language and customs of the region.
Highlight international law	Speak of international law, not just parent-country law. Acceptance is greater when the reference is to "the law in many countries," or the codes of the UN, or the ILO, or even the OECD.
Recognize the business case	In host countries, support efforts to decrease institutional corruption. And exercise moral imagination in dealing with cultural differences that conflict with your ethical standards. Be identified as the international firm with strong integrity but one that cares about local conditions. Companies with such reputations often gain a competitive edge both with consumers as well as with government agencies.
Recognize the common threads	While it is important to understand and be aware of the significant cultural differences that exist, fundamentally, people around the globe are more alike than they are different. They share many of the same priorities, interests, and basic ethical principles. Most of the time, the real challenge is how to communicate these principles effectively.

Source: Donaldson, T. (1996). Values in tension: Ethics away from home. *Harvard Business Review*, Sept.–Oct., 48–62.

CSR encourages MNEs to be aware that they produce both benefits and harm simply by the fact that they operate globally. Therefore, they should be as concerned about their global ecological footprints, or the impact of their actions (and inactions) on the natural environment, as they are about generating growth and profits.

The social responsibility of MNEs can be viewed on a continuum of providing value from stockholder to external stakeholder. While past thinking emphasized that organizations were expected only to meet the needs of their shareholders, customers, and employees, current thinking implies that organizations must also be explicit about the economic and social benefits that they bring to society.[53] Putting environmental concerns and people equity issues on an equal footing with shareholder return (also called the triple bottom line) is now considered a CSR responsibility of large MNEs. To take it even one step further, the social responsibility of businesses and business people is commensurate with their social power (such as size, financial resources, visibility). This is referred to as the iron law of social responsibility. Responsible MNEs are expected by their external stakeholders to focus on sustainability management and make sure that when they meet their present needs, they do so without compromising the ability of future generations to meet their needs.

CSR consists not only of a mindset but also of a set of deliberate actions that MNEs take to fulfill their social responsibilities. Many different types of activities fall under the umbrella as depicted in Figure 6.1.

There are several reasons why MNEs are increasingly paying attention to CSR. It enhances their reputations in the marketplace, may reduce business and legal risks, attracts customers and increases customer loyalty, averts pressure from investors and fund managers, and attracts and retains employees who desire to work for responsible companies. Many MNEs consult with other organizations (NGOs, consulting firms, etc.) to implement and improve their CSR programs. They also pay attention to social investment firms (who manage investment portfolios that only include companies considered to be socially and/or environmentally responsible), social entrepreneurs (who build business models around socially responsible or environmentally sustainable products that compete with them in the marketplace), and social-venture capitalists (who seek out promising social entrepreneurs in whom to invest).

IHR managers are increasingly becoming the implementers of CSR programs in MNEs. Recommendations for ensuring the success of CSR programs include the following:

■ Develop a global CSR policy—such a policy must be an integral part of the overall organizational strategy.

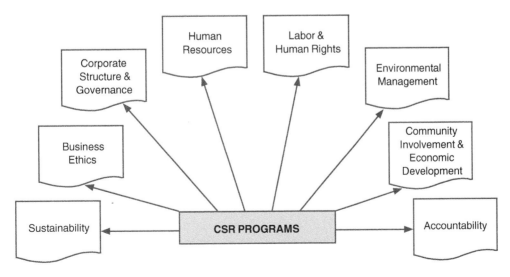

FIGURE 6.1 Umbrella of CSR Programs

Based on: Phillips. R., and Claus, L. (2002). Corporate social responsibility and global HR: Balancing the needs of the corporation and its stakeholders. *International Focus*, SHRM.

- Obtain a high level of support—CSR activities, such as any change activity, must clearly come with senior management support to enhance its implementation.
- Communicate—increase awareness of CSR activities and clearly communicate the CSR policy.
- Create a CSR culture—foster a culture that confronts difficult questions about ethics, the environment, and social responsibility.
- Provide adequate training—educate and train managers and employees on the MNE's code of conduct, the CSR activities, and the prescribed behaviors and activities.
- Install reporting and advice mechanisms—encourage employees to report questionable conduct and ask for help with their own ethical dilemmas (without retaliation).
- Include CSR in management's performance management—evaluate and reward employees for integrating company values in their daily work life.
- Communicate—use ongoing communication to keep the message alive and share stories and lessons learned.
- Lead by example—as with any managerial activity when actors are not leading by example, but are allowed to deviate from the principles without consequences, the CSR initiatives will not be taken seriously.

Corporate Governance

Corporate governance refers to the basis upon which decisions are made in organizations. It also involves the structure and relationships that determine how corporate objectives are first set and then met and regulated by the different performance-monitoring mechanisms (such as the management team, board of directors, investors, and shareholders). In light of many corporate scandals that have particularly plagued Western MNEs (for example, Anderson Consulting, Enron, WorldCom, Tyco International, Peregrine Systems, and Siemens), it is not surprising that this subject has received increased attention and is being regulated through legislation. The 2002 Sarbanes-Oxley Act in the US is an extra-territorial federal US law that requires compliance with enhanced standards for all US public company boards, management, and public accounting firms, and must be applied at home and abroad. It is a direct result of these corporate scandals.

Sustainability is the meeting of the needs of the present without compromising the ability of future generations to meet their own. Do management decisions meet these criteria?

- Is the decision *fair* to employees?
- Is the decision *sustainable* in the long run?
- Is the decision *green* in terms of pollution and the carbon footprint?
- Is the decision-making process *transparent* and open for scrutiny?

Sustainability

Sustainability is increasingly entering the attention of MNEs. The Bruntland Commission defined sustainability "as meeting the needs of the present without compromising the ability of future generations to meet their own."[54] Savitz and Weber in *The Triple Bottom Line* argue for the discovery of the sustainability sweet spot which they define as "the common ground shared by your business interests (those of your financial stakeholders) and the interests of the public (your non-financial stakeholders)."[55] For HR, the sustainability sweet spot is the place where the pursuit of organizational interests seamlessly blends with the pursuit of employee interests.

In the future, international HR practitioners will increasingly be called to defend management decisions made in MNEs in terms of the following factors:

1 Is the decision *fair* to employees?
2 Is the decision *sustainable* in the long run?
3 Is the decision *green* in terms of pollution and the carbon footprint?
4 Is the decision-making process *transparent* and open for scrutiny?

Development of a Strategic Global Code of Conduct Policy

The implication of this complexity in global employment law, regulation, standards, and ethics is that MNEs need to develop strategic policies that establish a code of conduct that defines acceptable behavior in terms of employment relations for their far-reaching managerial and employee workforces.[56] These codes of conduct should be defended as the "company culture," a culture that insists on and supports abiding by all national and international employee relations regulations and, further, defines what is seen as legal and ethical behavior when dealing with these regulations. Without this, the firms and their managers and employees can face any or all of the following: criminal liability, damaged individual careers, employee disengagement, damaged firm global reputations, lowered share prices, organizational and managerial confusion, misdirected workforce behavior, and even possible risk of total organizational disruption.

The point is, senior management must insist that this support for organizational ethics is the "way they want to run their business," that, for example, sexual or racial discrimination (or harassment) is not wanted because it limits the firm's ability to work as a team; such behavior is divisive, and it is just not wanted. Having such policy removes the possibility of managers disagreeing with certain practices because they perceive them to go against local or national cultural practices that vary from those in an MNE's parent country. In this way, the decision to abide by certain labor standards is based on the defined company culture and policies, not on any given individual's biases or preferences nor on reference to particular country's perceived cultural practices.

CONCLUSIONS

This chapter has examined the broad nature of international labor standards, global employment law and regulations, and international ethics and social responsibility. First, this chapter looked at the institutional context of international business. International organizations have promulgated labor standards for MNEs. Next this chapter looked at the global legal environment in which the MNE operates. It focused on compliance with national and supranational laws. Further, a number of comparative regulatory issues were discussed that affect the MNE such as immigration controls, data protection, anti-discrimination and harassment, termination and reduction in force, and intellectual property. Finally, this chapter looked at international ethics, its relation to culture, and how ethical dilemmas must be solved.

DISCUSSION QUESTIONS

1   Why are local employment laws important to IHRM? Are some laws more important than others? If so, which ones?
2   Why are international employment standards important to IHRM? Are some standards more important than others? If so, which ones?
3   Which employment laws and standards are most important for MNEs to pay attention to? Why?
4   Choose an employment-related HR ethical dilemma and analyze its ethical dimensions, including recommendations on how HR should deal with it.
5   What are sustainable HR practices and how do they affect employees?
6   How can HR discover the sustainability sweet spot(s) of an organization when it comes to employment relations?

CASE STUDY 6.1: Non-Compete Agreements and Intellectual Property: Value Partners SA (Italy) and Bain & Company (USA) Conflict in Brazil

Value Partners, headquartered in Milan, Italy, and recognized as one of the major European management consulting firms with clients in 40 countries and offices in 15 cities, was founded in 1993 by former partners of the Italian offices of McKinsey & Company. They opened their first overseas offices in São Paulo, Brazil, and Buenos Aires, Argentina, in 1994. By the end of 1997, its São Paulo office had 20 employees producing annual revenues of about US$5 million, assisting both Italian clients and local companies.

Rival Bain & Company, a major management consultancy, was founded in 1973 by seven former partners from the Boston Consulting Group, and is headquartered in Boston. Bain established its São Paulo office in October 1997 and by early November had hired away almost all of Value Partners' staff.

Value Partners filed criminal charges in Brazil and New York against Bain, alleging breach of trust and loyalty of its former employees (pirated away by Bain) and theft of confidential and proprietary information. The New York court ruled that the case would be more conveniently and efficiently dealt with in Brazil under the doctrine that New York was not the most convenient place to hear the case. Unfortunately for Value Partners, Brazilian law offered none of the US's significant compensatory and punitive damages for employee disloyalty and theft of intellectual property. However, the New York federal court also made it clear that Value Partners was permitted to re-file the lawsuit against Bain in a more convenient forum.

So Value Partners re-filed the case in Boston, the site of Bain headquarters. After a five-week trial, the jury found Bain & Company liable for unfair competition and tortuous interference and awarded Value Partners US$10 million in compensatory damages (the full award sought). The trial court, after awarding another US$2.5 million of interest, denied all Bain's post-trial motions.

As labor markets become global and firms develop new forms of relations with workers in foreign locales (such as IT workers or call centers in overseas locations), it becomes increasingly difficult to control the movement of workers from one employer to another and their taking of intellectual property (such as product or process technology or customer lists and preferences) from their current employer to their new one. Because the rules (and cultures) are so different from one country to another, it becomes very difficult to enforce any non-compete agreements in employment contracts.

This situation shows how difficult it can be to enforce covenants, like non-compete agreements, particularly in situations involving firms from outside countries. The more reasonable a restrictive covenant is, the more likely it is that courts worldwide will enforce it. But in some jurisdictions, such as in Latin America and the US state of California, non-compete clauses in employment contracts are considered illegal. Nevertheless, generally speaking, the shorter the time period of the restraint and the more narrowly defined the people covered, the more likely it is to be enforced across borders.

Sources: Hall, L. (2001). Protecting your vital assets. *Global HR*, July–August, 46–52; update (2014): http://en.wikipedia.org/wiki/Bain_&_Company; http://en.wikipedia.org/wiki/ Value_Partners.

Discussion Questions

1   Identify and compare the law(s) related to protection of intellectual property and non-compete agreements in three to five different countries.
2   Should employees be free to move at will from employer to employer? Should there be any constraints on this freedom of movement? Should employers be free to "pirate" employees from competitors?
3   What can HR do to minimize the impact of this sort of employee mobility?
4   Have the web and the Internet (and social media) changed the importance of intellectual property? Have they changed the way employers view IP? Have they changed the way employees view IP? How about the view of legal systems and cultures in various countries? How are they changing?

NOTES

1   Printed on literature of Baker and McKenzie, the world's largest global employment law firm.
2   See, for example, Florkowski, G. W. (2006). *Managing Global Legal Systems*, London/New York: Routledge, in the Global HRM series; and Baker and McKenzie (2012). *The Global Employer: Focus on Termination, Employment Discrimination, and Workplace Harassment Laws*, Baker & McKenzie International, a Swiss Verein.
3   See, for example, http://en.wikipedia.org/wiki/Law; Florkowski, 2006.
4   Much of the information in this section comes from documents of the International Labour Organisation, Geneva, Switzerland, such as the report on International Organizations by their Working Party of the Social Dimensions of the Liberalization of International Trade; and from Blanpain, R. (ed.) (original publication 1997, with frequent looseleaf updates), *International Encyclopedia for Labour Law and Industrial Relations*, The Hague, The Netherlands: Kluwer Law International; Bronstein, A. (2009). *International Comparative Labour Law: Current Challenges*, Geneva: ILO and Hampshire, England: Palgrave Macmillan;
      Keller, W. L. and Darby, T. J. (eds.) (2003 and 2010). *International Labor and Employment Laws*, Vols. I and II, Washington, DC: The Bureau of National Affairs, International Labor Law Committee, Section of Labor and Employment Law, American Bar Association.
5   See, for example, the *World Investment Report* (most recent edition, 2009), published by UNCTAD. Refer to the UNCTAD website at http://www.unctad.org for information on UNCTAD's work and access to extensive data about global foreign direct investment from and to various countries and the role of transnational corporations.
6   Berkowitz, P.M. (2003). Avoidance of risks and liabilities through effective corporate compliance, paper presented at the 4th Annual Program on International Labor and Employment Law, Center for American and International Law, Dallas, TX, 10 September; www.unglobalcompact.org; www.wikipedia.org/wiki/United_Nations_Global_Compact.
7   See United Nations Global Compact: http://www.unglobalcompact.org/abouttheGc/TheTenprinciples/index.html
8   Keller, W. L. and Darby, T. J. (eds.) (2003 and 2010); www.ilo.org.
9   Source: International Labour Organisation.
10   Source: Organisation for Economic Co-operation and Development (OECD): http://www.oecd.org/about/membersandpartners/list-oecd-member-countries.htm.
11   Source: Official website of the Organisation for Economic Co-operation and Development (OECD): http://www.oecd.org/about/membersandpartners/.

12 Source: Official website of the World Bank: http://www.worldbank.org/en/about/history.

13 Source: Official website of the International Monetary Fund: http://www.imf.org/external/about/hist coop.htm.

14 Source: Official website of the World Trade Organization: http://www.wto.org/english/thewto_e/ whatis_e/whatis_e.htm.

15 Florkowski, 2006; Murphy, E.E., Jr. (2001). The World Trade Organization, in Keller, W.L. (ed.). *International Labor and Employment Laws*, 2001 Cumulative Supplement to Volume 1, Washington, DC: Bureau of National Affairs and International Labor Law Committee Section of Labor and Employment Law of the American Bar Association, pp. 44–1 to 44–13.

16 Source: Official website of the European Union: http://europa.eu/about-eu/countries/index_en.htm.

17 Ibid.

18 Source: Demographics of the European Union, http://en.Wikipedia.org, 2014. Accessed July 7, 2014.

19 Source: Official website of the European Union: http://europa.eu/about-eu/institutions-bodies/index_en.htm.

20 Carby-Hall, J.R. (2006). The Charter of Fundamental Rights of the European Union—the social dimension, *Managerial Law*, 48 (4), 430–446; Federation of European Employers, The European social dimension (2014). available on their website: http://www.fedee.com/histsoc.html, accessed July 7, 2014; Nielsen, R. and Szyszczak, E. (1997) *The Social Dimension of the European Union*, 3rd ed., Copenhagen: Handelshøjskolens Forlag/Copenhagen Business School Press; Orbie, J. and Babarinde, O. (2008). The social dimension of globalization and EU development policy: Promoting core labour standards and corporate social responsibility. *Journal of European Integration/Revue d'Intégration Européenne*, 30 (3), 459–477; Orbie, J. and Tortell, L. (eds.) (2009). *The European Union and the Social Dimension of Globalization*, London: Routledge.

21 Official website of the European Union: http://europa.eu/lisbon_treaty/index_en.htm. Accessed July 8, 2014.

22 Source: Official website of the Office of the United States Trade Representative: http://www.ustr.gov/trade-agreements/free-trade-agreements/north-american-free-trade-agreement-nafta. Accessed Jan. 15, 2014.

23 Manley, T. and Lauredo, L. (2003). International labor standards in free trade agreements of the Americas, paper delivered at the 4th Annual Program on International Labor and Employment Law, Dallas, Texas, 30 September–1 October.

24 Official website of the FTAA: www.ftaa-alca.org.

25 Darby, T.J. (2001). Extraterritorial application of U.S. laws, in W.L. Keller (ed.) *International Labor and Employment Laws*, 2001 Cumulative Supplement to Volume 1, Washington, DC: The Bureau of National Affairs and the International Labor Law Committee Section of Labor and Employment Law of the American Bar Association, 50 (52), 50–74.

26 Hall, L. (2001b). Data dangers, *Global HR*, October, 24–28; Kremer-Jones, B. (2002). Think before you send. *Global HR*, July/August, 52–59; Liptak, A. (2010). When American and European ideas of privacy collide, *The New York Times*, Feb. 26, http://www.nytimes.com/2010/02/28/weekinreview/28liptak.html. Accessed Feb. 28, 2010; Society for Human Resource Management (SHRM) (2000). Protecting the privacy of employees based in Europe. *SHRM Global Perspectives* 1(1),1, 6–7 (originally published in HRWIRE, by the West Group); Wugmeister, M.H. and Lyon, C.E. (eds.) (2009). *Global Privacy and Data Security Law*, Arlington, VA: Bureau of National Affairs.

27 Society for Human Resource Management (2000). Are you EU privacy-compliant? *International Update* (newsletter of the SHRM Institute for International HRM, which later became the SHRM Global Forum), No. 3, 10; Martinez, M.N. (1999). European law aims to protect employee data. *International Update* (newsletter of the SHRM Institute for International HRM, now the SHRM Global Forum), No. 1, February, 1, 3; Minehan, M. (2001). Complying with the European privacy data directive. *SHRM Global Perspective*, No. 5, 1, 6–8; Minehan, M. and Overman, S. (2000). Companies to begin EU safe harbor registration. *HR News*, December, 19 (12), 1–2; Wellbery, B.S. and Warrington, J.P. (2001). EU data protection requirements and employee data: December 2001, International Focus White Paper of the SHRM Global Forum, Alexandria, VA: Society for Human Resource Management; and Wellbery, B.S., Warrington, J.P., and Howell, R. (2002). EU data protection requirements: An overview for employers. *Employment Law*, (Morrison and Foerster Newsletter), 14 (1), 1–12.

28 See, for example, It's a man's world, business study finds, report on World Bank study, *AOL News*, downloaded from http://www.aolnews.com/world-bank-study-shows-business-laws-in-most-countries-hold-. . . . Accessed Aug. 16, 2014.

29 See, for example, Baker & McKenzie (2000). *Worldwide Guide to Termination, Employment Discrimination, and Workplace Harassment Laws*, Chicago, IL: Commerce Clearing House; Conway, M. E. (1998). Sexual harassment abroad. *Global Workforce*, September, 8–9; Eurobarometer (2007). *Discrimination in the European Union*, Brussels: European Commission; Javaid, M. (2002). Race for knowledge. *Global HR*, November, 59–60; Keller, W. L. and Darby, T. J. (eds.) (2003 and 2010); and Mackay, R. and Cormican, D. (2002). The trouble with religion. *Global HR*, December/January, 26–30.

30 Webb, S. (1994) *Shockwaves: The Global Impact of Sexual Harassment*, London: MasterMedia, Ltd.; World Bank (2010). It's a man's world, business study finds, reported in *AOL News*, downloaded from http://www.aolnews.com/world/article/world-bank-study-shows-business-laws-in-most-countries-hold-. . . . Accessed Aug. 16, 2014.

31 www.de2.psu.edu/harassment/generalinfo/international.html. Accessed Feb. 11, 2007; ILO (2007). *ABC of Women Workers' Rights and Gender Equality*, 2nd ed., Geneva: ILO; Kaufmann, C. (2007). *Globalization and Labour Rights: The Conflict between Core Labour Rights and International Economic Law*, Oxford/Portland, OR: Hart Publishing.

32 Leonard, B. (2010). Report: 10 percent of employees report harassment at work, http://www.shrm.org/hrdisciplines/global/Articles/Pages/GlobalHarassment.aspx. Accessed Sept. 23, 2010.

33 Baker & McKenzie (2012). *The Global Employer: Focus on Termination, Employment Discrimination, and Workplace Harassment Laws*, a Swiss Verein, Baker & McKenzie; Berkowitz, P.M., Reitz, A. E. and Müller-Bonanni, T. (eds.) (2008). *International Labor and Employment Law*, 2nd ed., Vols. I and II, Chicago, IL: Section of International Law, American Bar Association; Blanpain, R. (2010); Keller, W. L. and Darby, T. J. (2003 and 2010).

34 Adapted from International Labour Organization (2000). *Termination of Employment Digest: A Legislative Review*, Geneva: International Labour Organization; and Shillingford, J. (1999). Goodbye, adios, sayonara. *HR World*, July/August, 27–31 (data on separation practices from Drake Beam Morin).

35 See, for example, Friedman, P. (2010). China's plagiarism problem, downloaded on 6/2/2010 from Forbes. com: http://www.forbes.com/2010/05/26/china-cheating-innovation-markets-economy-plagiarism . . . .

36 Hall, L. (2001a). Protecting your vital assets, *Global HR*, July/August, 46–52.

37 Briscoe, D.R. (2011). Globalization and international labor standards, codes of conduct, and ethics: An international HRM perspective, in Wankel, C. and Malleck, S. (eds.), *Globalization and Ethics*, Information Age Publishing, pp. 1–22.

38 Briscoe, D.R. (2000). *International Focus: Global Ethics, Labor Standards, and International HRM*, Alexandria, VA: Society for Human Resource Management White Paper, Winter; Digh, P. (1997). Shades of gray in the global marketplace. *HR Magazine*, April, 91–98; Florkowski, G., Schuler, R.S. and Briscoe, D.R. (2004). Global ethics and international HRM, in Berndt, R. (ed.). *Challenges in Management*, vol. 11: *Competitiveness and Ethics*, Berlin: Springer; Kumar, B.N. and Steinman, H. (eds.) (1998). *Ethics in International Management*, Berlin: de Gruyter; Gesteland, R.R. (1999) *Cross-Cultural Business Behavior*, Copenhagen, Denmark: Copenhagen Business School Press; and Morgan, E. (1998) *Navigating Cross-Cultural Ethics: What Global Managers Do Right to Keep from Going Wrong*, Burlington, MA: Butterworth-Heineman; Perkins, S.J. and Shortland, S.M. (2006). *Strategic International Human Resource Management*, 2nd ed., London/Philadelphia: Kogan Page; Tsogas, G. (2009). International Labour Regulation: What have we really learnt so far? *Relations Industrielles/Industrial Relations* (Université Laval). 64 (1), 75–94; Vickers, M.R. (2005). Business ethics and the HR Role: Past, present, and future. *Human Resource Planning*, 28, 26–32.

39 Donaldson, T. (1996). Values in tension: Ethics away from home. *Harvard Business Review*, September–October, 48–62; Singer, A.W. (1991). Ethics: Are standards lower overseas? *Across the Board*, September, 31–34.

40 Schlegelmilch, B.B. and Robertson, D.C. (1995). The influence of country and industry on ethical percep-tions of senior executives in the U.S. and Europe. *Journal of International Business Studies*, Fourth Quarter, 859–881.

41 Adler, N.J. with Gundersen, A. (2008). *International Dimensions of Organizational Behavior*, 5th ed., Mason, OH: Thomson South-Western; Armstrong, R.W. (1996). The relationship between culture and perception of ethical problems in international marketing. *Journal of Business Ethics*, 15 (11), 1199–1208; Fleming, J.E. (1997). Problems in teaching international ethics. *The Academy of Management News*, March, 17; McNett, J. and Søndergaard, M. (2004). Making ethical decisions, in Lane, H.W., Maznevski, M.L., Mendenhall, M.E., and McNett, J. (eds.). *Handbook of Global Management: A Guide to Manag-ing Complexity*, Malden, MA/Oxford: Blackwell Publishing; Moran, R.T., Harris, P.R. and Moran, S.V. (2007). *Managing Cultural Differences*, 7th ed., Burlington, MA/Oxford: Butterworth-Heinamann.

42 Donaldson, T. (1996). Values in tension: Ethics away from home, *Harvard Business Review*, Sept.–Oct., 48–62.

43 Buller, P.F. and McEvoy, G.M. (1999). Creating and sustaining ethical capability in the multinational cor-poration, *Journal of World Business*, 34 (4), 326–343.

44 This section is adapted from Fisher, C.D., Shoenfeldt, L.F., and Shaw, J.B. (1993). *Human Resource Man-agement*, 2nd ed., Boston, MA: Houghton Mifflin; Original sources: Stace, W.T. (1988). Ethical relativity and ethical absolutism, in Donaldson, T. and Werhane, P.H. (eds.) *Ethical Issues in Business*, Englewood Cliffs, NJ: Prentice Hall, pp. 27–34; Shaw, W. and Barry, V. (1989) *Moral Issues in Business*, Belmont, CA: Wadsworth, pp. 11–13; and Donaldson, T. (1989) *The Ethics of International Business*, New York: Oxford University Press.

45 See, for example, Donaldson, T. (1996).

46 Donaldson, T. (1989), p. 103.

47 Adapted from Solomon, C.M., Jan. 1996, Put your ethics to a global test, *Personnel Journal*, p. 239.

48 Donaldson, T. (1989), p. 104.

49 Cullen, H. (2007). *The Role of International Law in the Elimination of Child Labor*, Leiden/Boston: Martinus Nijhoff Publishers; Heppler, B. (2008). Is the eradication of child labour "within reach"? Achievements and challenges ahead, in Nesi, G., Nogler, L. and Pertile, M. (eds.), *Child Labour in a Globalized World: A Legal Analysis of ILO Action*, Hampshire, England/Burlington, VT: Ashgate Publishing, pp. 17–428.

50 Donaldson, T. (1996).

51 Digh, P. (1997).

52 Adapted from Tansey, L.A. (1996). Taking ethics abroad. *Across the Board*, June, 56, 58; Donaldson, T. (1996).

53 Phillips. R. and Claus, L. (2002). Corporate social responsibility and global HR. Balancing the needs of the corporation and its stakeholders. *International Focus*. SHRM, 1–7.

54 United Nations, Our Common Future: Report of the World Commission on Environment and Development, accessed at www.un-documents.net/ocf-02.htm#1. Accessed 7 July 7, 2014.

55 Savitz, A. and Weber, K. (2006). *The Triple Bottom Line*, San Francisco, CA: Jossey-Bass, p. 3.

56 Paskoff, S.M. (2003). Around the world without the daze: Communicating international codes of conduct, paper presented to the 4th Annual Program on International Labor and Employment Law, The Center for American and International Law, Dallas, Texas, 1 October.

Chapter 7

International Employee Relations

I would say this. We've had a great relationship with our workforce. I don't look at them as union and nonunion but as Ford workers. . . . We have a lot of second-, third-, fourth-, fifth- and even sixth-generation workers at Ford in our company. . . . Those employees helped pull the auto company (through the dark days).

William Clay Ford, Jr.
Executive Chairman, Ford Motor Company[1]

Learning Objectives

This chapter will enable the reader to:

- Describe the nature of union membership around the world.
- Describe the evolution and make-up of global industrial relations.
- Explain the relationship between unions and MNEs.
- Describe the various strategies with which MNEs approach global labor relations.
- Describe the various approaches taken to non-union worker representation.
- Explain the litigation risks in international labor relations.

This chapter is concerned with the international context of a topic that comes with many names, for example, employee relations, employment relations, labor relations, union relations, industrial relations. Here we will primarily use the term: employee relations. Since this text is concerned with the international context, we will use the term: international employee relations (IER). Normally this content deals primarily with the development of and current status of labor unions, primarily in manufacturing and extraction industries and the public sector. However, in recent years, many countries have developed alternatives to unions to represent the interests of employees, such as works councils, co-determination, and workers' cooperatives, and manufacturing has become a smaller component of most countries' labor forces, that is, the service and information technology sectors have become the largest sectors in most countries' economies. So this chapter uses the term employee relations to cover worker relations in its broadest context in all economic and government sectors as well as in an international sense, dealing with unions as well as other forms of employee representation.

Labor lawyers and HR practitioners are often unfamiliar with labor and employment policy laws, institutions, and practices in countries other than their own. Because the laws and customs of labor relations tend to be unique to each country, the employee and labor relations practices of MNEs need to vary as well. Indeed, MNEs are likely to face unfamiliar employee relations practices and unplanned-for restrictions in their foreign operations. As was emphasized in the last chapter, MNEs have to manage according to the employment laws of the countries in which they operate.

The most important point to understand about employee relations in the global context is that every country is different. Every country has developed its own particular set of values, practices, and regulations concerning the relationship between employees and employers. Thus businesses (and NGOs, charities, and governments) that operate internationally must develop understanding of and flexibility to deal with multiple approaches to unions and other forms of employee representation. The primary intent of this chapter, therefore, is to help readers understand this diversity of approaches in order to be able to manage their employment relations effectively. More specifically, this chapter provides an overview of labor or employment relations in the global arena and reviews a number of issues related to international employee relations, including international union membership, the evolution of international labor relations, alternative worker representative approaches, such as works councils and co-determination, and the policies and practices of MNEs in international employee relations.[2]

GLOBAL UNION MEMBERSHIP

Comparing union membership in different countries is as difficult as analyzing and comparing most other forms of international data. For example, accepting the integrity of data about union membership in different countries and being able to compare data with regard to union density (the percentage of the labor force in any given country that belongs to a union) is faced with problems like these: the sources of the basic information, definitions of terms, the nature of the statistical coverage of the reported data, reporting errors in the data, the quality of recording mechanisms for creating the data, the difficulties in keeping track of special groups who are outside the legal employment market, and the selection of the employment base for calculating union density. All of these issues vary considerably from country to country and thus make it difficult to compare and assess topics as simple as the actual union membership and density in various countries. Exhibit 7.1 displays union

EXHIBIT 7.1: Trade Union Membership, Selected Countries

Country	Trade union membership as a % of paid employment
Australia	18.2
Bermuda	23.0
Canada	31.4
Chile	14.6
China	41.2
Denmark	83.6
Ireland	29.5
Japan	17.9
Malaysia	9.3
Mauritius	25.4
New Zealand	20.5
Norway	71.8
Peru	1.8
Singapore	35.5
Sweden	80.9
Switzerland	19.8
United Kingdom	25.8
United States	11.3

Source: International Labor Organization (based on 2012 data), http://laborsta.ilo.org/xls_data_E.html

density for a number of countries. Data for Japan and the United States are provided for comparison. Even among this set of developed countries, the union densities are quite varied.

A second issue involves the *strength of trade unions*, which is usually measured by the size of union membership (relative to the number of people eligible to join a union). However, this measure does not really reflect what unions do nor how effective they are, but rather focuses on potential union bargaining pressure as based in the number of members.[3] The assumption often is that the more members a union has, the more influence it can exert in bargaining. Yet when a country's laws require employers to deal with all unions, no matter how small or when the unions represent all employees, no matter the size of the union's membership, these assumptions do not represent the reality "on the ground." In some countries, unions represent all workers even though only a small percentage are members, while in other countries unions only represent those who are actual members. In some countries, managers and professionals like engineers and scientists belong to unions while in other countries they don't, and in some countries, unions are seen as partners with management, while in other countries there is a long-standing antagonism between unions and firms (or between employees and their employers). In the former communist countries, unions used to be partners with management yet in most of these countries the communist party (and government) are now working to develop relationships similar to those found in non-communist countries. Thus, in some countries where unions are strong, their actual membership is small (e.g., Germany), while in other countries where unions may not be strong, their membership may actually be quite large (e.g., Mexico, Japan). Absolute union membership as a percentage of the workforce is largest in countries like Sweden while absolute membership is lowest in countries like the US. In countries such as China, unions are just beginning to develop traditional roles.

EVOLUTION OF INTERNATIONAL LABOR RELATIONS AND ORGANIZATIONS[4]

Although in the 19th century some aspects of the early union movement developed as a very international movement (after all, "l'Internationale" was the fight song of the union movement), fairly quickly unions became more nationalist and protectionist in nature, largely as a result of country variances in industrialization (which created much of the impetus for the development of unions) and the impact of two 20th-century world wars. However, at the end of World War II and partially due to the dividing of the world into a Western/capitalist sector and a Communist-dominated sector and the resulting Cold War between these two sectors, the international federations of labor divided into two factions: a Western-oriented group and a communist-supported group (and, as mentioned above, the roles of unions in these two very different economic and government systems were radically different as well). Then, with the end of the cold war in 1989–1991, and the rapid development of global trade, the traditional national focus of trade unions began to become once again more global.[5] Today, largely due to the uncontrolled growth of the power of MNEs, there is strong interest in the labor movement to cross borders and join together for the achievement of their common labor-related missions. The major institutions of the international trade union movements are now using the term "international" in their names. And over the last 50 years, or so, trade unions from different nations have combined in cross-border federations to create the beginnings of an international trade union structure in an attempt to develop some international focus and capabilities to deal more effectively with MNEs and their globalization. At the same time, employers have also created equivalent trade associations to provide a cross-border and cross-industry voice for global labor relations.

The following is a short summary of the international federations and labor union organizations.

World Federation of Trade Unions (WFTU)

The WFTU was established in 1945 to bring together trade unions around the world in a single organization modeled after the UN. After a split in 1949, when many Western trade unions formed the International Confederation of Free Trade Unions (ICFTU), the WFTU is now primarily a federation of state-run unions from communist countries. Despite the fall of communist regimes in the Soviet Union and Eastern Europe, and the defection of many of its national unions in several Central and Eastern European (CEE) countries, the WFTU has declined to join the ICFTU and subsequently formed the International Trade Union Confederation (ITUC).

The International Confederation of Free Trade Unions (ICFTU)

The ICFTU is an international confederation of national trade unions established in 1949 after a split with the WFTU. It grouped the major unions in the Western world. The ICFTU was dissolved in 2006 to join the ITUC.

The International Trade Union Confederation (ITUC)

The ITUC is an umbrella organization of national trade union federations (154 countries and 168 million workers) to defend workers' rights in the era of globalization. The ITUC's primary mission is the promotion and defense of workers' rights and interests, through international cooperation between trade unions and through global campaigning and advocacy within the major global institutions.[6]

European Trade Union Confederation (ETUC)

The ETUC was established in 1973 to promote the interests of working people at the European level and to represent them in EU institutions. Its prime objective is to promote the European Social Model by being actively involved in economic and social policy making at the highest level, working with all EU institutions.

World Confederation of Labour (WCL)

The WCL is an international trade union confederation inspired by the basic values of Christian humanism. It unites autonomous and democratic trade unions from countries all over the world, but mainly from Third World countries. In the last few years the WCL has adopted a critical attitude toward the neo-liberal model of economic globalization (where global free trade is promoted as the highest and best value) and questions its legitimacy.

Trade Union Advisory Committee (TUAC) to the OECD

The TUAC is an international trade union organization that has consultative status with the OECD. It is the interface for labor unions with the OECD and its various committees, particularly those that focus on worker and human rights (for more information about the OECD and its work on workers' rights, refer to Chapter 6 on International Employment Law, Labor Standards, and Ethics).

Global Union Federations (GUFs)

A GUF is an international federation of national and regional trade unions representing specific industrial sectors and occupational groups. Most major unions are members of one or more GUFs that represent the interests of their members. Currently there are 10 specific industry sectors or occupation groups with GUFs: education; building and wood-workers; journalists; metalworkers; textile, garment and leather workers; transport workers; food, agriculture, hotel, restaurant, catering, tobacco and allied workers; public services; chemical, energy, mine and general workers; and union network.

UNIONS AND MULTINATIONAL ENTERPRISES

In spite of the above-described developments in the labor movement, unions (and, therefore, labor relations) exist and operate mostly at the local and national level, even though a number of unions have the term *international* in their names and belong to international federations. The increase in global trade and in the number of MNEs has led to concern by trade unions about this primarily national and local focus by unions. Their major concern is that multinational firms can manipulate local unions (and, therefore, workers) in collective bargaining by having the ability to move work to areas of the world that either have no unions or where unions are weak or where, in general, wages and benefits are lower and working conditions are less protected (and, thus, the costs of labor are lower). And because unions are not organized on a global basis, and there are no international laws requiring bargaining on a cross-border basis, and because unions tend to be primarily focused on local and national concerns of their members (and thus sometimes find it difficult to work together with unions in other countries who often have different concerns), they perceive that the power balance between unions and MNEs is totally skewed toward business. MNEs operate in many countries and often in many industries. In contrast, unions almost always have membership in only one country and normally in only one industry. And thus unions can typically bring pressure to bear on only a small segment of an MNE—one industry (or even one firm within one industry) within one country.

What is currently happening in Australia illustrates the complexities for unions (local) and MNEs (international). A number of automobile companies have built manufacturing plants in Australia, e.g., Ford, General Motors, Holden, and Toyota.[7] By December 2013, two-thirds of the auto industry had announced it was pulling out, citing the excessive costs of producing cars in Australia with its limited market. Toyota was due (under an earlier contract) to pay two small pay increases in 2014, in spite of a likely decision to end production in Australia by 2016 or 2017. But the enterprise agreement with the union normally requires (upheld by the courts) a vote on "no extra claims" before it could call for a vote on the pay increases. Toyota had been expressing concerns over the Australian culture (and not just its arcane union practices, but also its attitudes about overtime, loose attitudes about attendance, and overall work performance). This new effort by the auto workers union to "punish" Toyota shows a labor relations "face" that Toyota is clearly unfamiliar with. But this is still a conflict between a local union and a large multinational.

In spite of what has been said above about the development of international confederations of unions, there has been very little cooperation between unions at the collective bargaining level across national borders, and there are no union structures similar to or parallel to that of MNEs, so that, for example, international unions have not been able to negotiate global agreements with MNEs that would apply to all of its operations around the world (although some recent collective bargaining agreements in the airline industry—which by its very nature is international—have moved in that direction).

In practical terms, what this means to labor relations is that unions view MNEs as being able to:

- Locate work in countries with lower social protections and lower wages and benefits (often this means countries with no unions or very weak unions), staying away from countries with stronger unions and stronger protections and higher wages and benefits.
- Force workers in one country, faced by competition from workers in other countries, to "bid down" their wages and benefits in order to keep their jobs.
- Take advantage of differences in legally mandated benefits for workers by restructuring the operations in countries where the costs of workforce adjustments are lowest and thus force excessive dislocation burdens on workers in these low-benefit countries.
- Outlast workers in the event of a labor dispute in one country because cash flows (and the ability to maintain business) are at least partially maintained by operations in countries where there are no disputes.

One result is that unions are beginning to look for ways to exercise influence over labor relations on a cross-border and multinational scale. National trade union federations and more recently established international federations and GUFs (as described above) are providing assistance to national unions in dealing with MNEs and have become closely involved with institutions like the ILO and the OECD, working with them to develop, enhance, and enforce their covenants and declarations on labor standards. Their ultimate goal is to develop transnational bargaining, although right now there are no laws or regulations that require such negotiations nor any international bodies that could enforce them. As described in the previous chapter, the ILO and OECD guidelines are trying to go beyond merely suggesting that MNEs abide by the industrial relations statutes in force in each of the countries in which they operate. And national courts are beginning to defer to or consider these international standards or a firm's parent-country laws when adjudicating labor disputes. This has been accomplished at least partially because of the pressures of these international union federations. Nevertheless, at this time these guidelines and standards are only as effective as individual firms and governments are willing to allow, as adherence to them is essentially voluntary.

Some interesting labor disputes in different parts of the world show the increasing pressure unions are putting on MNEs. When Renault (a French company) closed its Belgian plant in Vilvoorde, Belgium, and laid off 3,100 people (1997), the Belgian Labor Court ruled that Renault broke the rules on worker consultation, which require consultation ahead of layoffs. When Marks & Spencer (a British firm) (2001) announced that it was closing its 18 French stores (and laid off 1,500 employees), the French employees obtained a court ruling that M&S had violated French labor law. Rather than closing, the stores were eventually sold to French retailer Galeries Lafayette. At Siemens in Germany (2004), although workers accepted a workweek extension from 4 days to 40 hours without extra pay, it demonstrated the role of the union as protector of employment by avoiding outsourcing over 4,000 jobs. In the United Kingdom, the unofficial strike of British Airways baggage handlers in sympathy for Gate Gourmet (2005) forced the caterer to settle the dispute and offer enhanced redundancy deals to its employees. In Mexico, the National Mining Union took on Grupo Mexico (2006) after 65 miners were killed in a mining accident. Wildcat strikes at over 70 Mexican companies paralyzed the mining and steel industry after government action failed to support labor. These strikes demonstrated the political power of organized employees. An example of a recent labor dispute includes the dispute between Kimberly Clark (USA based) in Turkey (union group: Tümka-İş).[8]

There still remain a number of barriers to multinational bargaining. In addition to the global power of MNEs and the fractured nature of unions, and the unwillingness of nations to get involved under the existing lack of international governing covenants, other obstacles also will need to be overcome in order for progress to occur in movement toward multinational bargaining:[9]

- The widely varying industrial relations laws and practices among different countries.
- The lack of any central, international authority for labor relations or global labor law.

- Major economic and cultural differences among different countries.
- Employer opposition.
- Union reluctance at the national level, because the national leadership often fears that multinational bargaining will transfer power from them to an international leadership.
- Absence of a centralized decision-making authority for unions.
- Lack of coordination of activities by unions across national boundaries.
- Differing national priorities.
- Employee unwillingness to subordinate local concerns to concerns of workers in other countries.

As MNEs become more global and more connected across borders they must deal with these international labor organizations as well as the widely varying national and local unions. It is inevitable that multi-country, maybe even multi-employer and multi-union, negotiations involving employers and unions from multiple countries will develop. Business global issues are already part of the "relevant facts" for negotiations in many MNEs. And this will only increase in prevalence and importance. Before global labor relations evolve very far, however, the following types of questions will need to be addressed:

- What rules will apply to the resolution of disputes?
- What rules will apply to the process of negotiations?
- What law will cover the negotiations, e.g., between companies in two or more countries or between companies and their unions in multiple countries?

In spite of all of the above, unions have achieved a major impact on protection of individual worker rights, and union activities have resulted in the enactment of pro-labor and pro-employee legislation, especially in the EU and Japan. Many of the EU directives and agreements (e.g., parental leave directive, part-time work directive, fixed-term contracts directive, home working and teleworking framework agreement) are a result of union pressure and unions have often become strong social partners with government and management. In some EU countries, trade unions can invite the government to extend compulsory application of a collective agreement across geography and/or an entire industry sector.

In Japan, there is a different history of development of unions. Yet, even though the structure of unions in Japan is radically different than that present in Europe and the EU, Japanese unions can also claim major impact on employment relations and employee rights, such as lifetime employment practices and protection of seniority. Now the challenge being confronted by unions is to develop global mechanisms to accommodate and/or deal with the reality of global commerce.

MNES AND LABOR RELATIONS

MNEs must share decision-making power with unions (and/or other representatives of employees, such as works councils) and, often, agencies of government, to greater or lesser degrees throughout the world but almost always to some degree. For many businesses, what they confront in their foreign operations is often quite different than what they deal with at home. So, responsibility for labor relations is frequently left to those who are most likely to be familiar with local practice, that is, the HR (or labor relations) managers at the level of the local subsidiary or joint venture.

MNEs often develop worldwide approaches to issues such as executive compensation, but such a worldwide approach to labor and employee relations is quite rare. IHR departments within MNEs follow one of these seven approaches to labor/employee relations in the global context (see Exhibit 7.2).

US firms (and, sometimes, Asian) that have strong anti-union or at least very adversarial approaches to labor relations tend to operate at the levels of options 5, 6, or 7 (see

---

EXHIBIT 7.2: Seven Approaches to Labor/Employee Relations in the Global Context

1 Hands off (by headquarters of the parent firm)
In this approach, responsibility for labor/employee relations is left totally in the hands of local managers in the host countries.

2 Monitor
In this approach, headquarters IHR managers will try to forestall major problems for the parent company by asking intelligent and insightful questions about labor and employment responsibilities at each of their foreign locations. But primary responsibility still stays in the hands of local managers.

3 Guide and advise
This approach is a step beyond mere monitoring. Here IHR managers from headquarters will provide ongoing advice and guidance to subsidiary managers on how to conduct labor and employee relations, usually based on policies of headquarters. Of course, this requires a higher degree of knowledge about local labor relations regulations and practices. Still, overall control stays in the hands of local staff.

4 Strategic planning
At this level of involvement, international labor relations issues are fully incorporated into the MNE's strategic planning. Management of all aspects of the global firm, including labor and employee relations, is integrated into a centralized program, particularly for policy purposes. Local control may still exist, but all labor relations practices will follow this global strategy.

Continued overleaf

EXHIBIT 7.2 *Continued*

5	Set limits and approve exceptions	MNEs that follow this approach to their international labor/employee relations provide even more specific centralized control over local practices. Subsidiaries are allowed freedom of action only within quite narrowly defined limits, and any efforts to try different approaches must be approved by headquarters.
6	Manage from headquarters	In this scenario, local subsidiary staffs have no freedom of policy or practice in their labor/employee relations activities. Indeed, all labor relations actions are directed by staff from headquarters.
7	Integration of headquarters IHR and local management	In this final approach, labor and employee relations in the field, as managed by local (country) HR and management, are fully integrated with IHR assistance from headquarters, with common strategy and policy.

Exhibit 7.2). These firms try to ensure that their headquarters' approaches are followed as much as possible in their foreign operations. Of course, in many countries (e.g., where there are works councils and/or union negotiations are mandated), these firms must deal with third parties, whether they want to or not.

Still, much autonomy is often possible. And because each country is so different in its evolution of labor relations law and practice, leaving primary responsibility for labor and employee relations to the local level is often the only workable approach. Usually, this is achieved with certain overlying strategic objectives providing some guidance from headquarters.

It is not the intention of this book to provide in-depth coverage of union relations in various countries. Rather, a very limited sampling of the variations of the law and practice of labor relations is provided to inform students and IHR managers with a sense of the importance of understanding the impact of those variations on MNE operations around the globe. The case at the end of this chapter that describes the global labor relations scene for Ford Motor Company discusses a firm that has had global operations for almost 100 years.[10] Obviously, for an MNE like Ford, global labor relations are indeed quite complex.

One difficulty for IHR managers in assessing the power or importance of unions in various countries arises from the inconsistencies between countries in how they count membership and the differences in who is covered by union contracts. For example, even though a relatively low percentage of workers belong to unions in France (about 9 percent), the unions play a very important role in determining government policy and legislation concerning all workers and toward general industrial policy, and employers are required by law to negotiate with any union present (represented by as few as one employee) and to implement national policies on wage rates, and so on.[11] In fact, about 90–95 percent of all workers in France are covered by the contracts negotiated by unions, even though the actual membership of unions is quite low. In most Scandinavian countries, retired workers are still union members, although this is not usually the case elsewhere, and professionals such as teachers and members of professional associations, such as engineers, are sometimes included and sometimes not.

An additional problem is created by the rapid pace of change in employee relations so that data only a few years old can be out-of-date by significant amounts. Nevertheless, relative differences between countries remain quite obvious (refer to Exhibit 7.1).[12] As illustrated, some countries have quite low union membership (which doesn't necessarily indicate how many workers are covered by the contracts negotiated), while other countries have much higher union membership, such as Denmark and Sweden.

In terms of the patterns of labor relations practices themselves, some countries have developed industrial relations systems patterned after the laws and traditions of other countries. And yet others have pursued unique avenues to labor relations. Within this milieu, each country has developed a tradition and legal framework that reflects its own special history and political and social experiences. As a consequence, firms that conduct business on a multinational or transnational basis must understand and cope with a great deal of diversity in the performance of industrial relations around the world. This typically leads to decentralizing the labor relations function (much as is also true of the general HRM function), providing subsidiaries with considerable autonomy in managing employee relations.

EVOLUTION OF LABOR RELATIONS IN DIFFERENT COUNTRIES

The next few paragraphs provide a very short glimpse at the evolution of labor relations in a number of countries around the world. In some countries (e.g., Canada, the United States, Germany, and Japan), the focus of union activity is basically economic. That is, unions involve themselves primarily with economic issues of concern to their members, such as setting wage rates, determining hours of work, and ensuring job security. This is usually manifested through some form of union-management collective bargaining. This form of labor relations is often referred to as business unionism.

In other countries, particularly England, France, Italy, and those in Latin America, unions tend to be very political and generally achieve their objectives through political action rather than through direct collective bargaining. This is often referred to as political unionism. This is not to say that "business-focused" unions don't try to influence government to achieve legislation favorable to their members and that "politically focused" unions don't participate in collective bargaining. But the historical pattern for business unions has been the former forms of activity, rather than the latter. And the opposite has been true for political unions. In addition, in some countries, union activity is focused on industry-wide or even nationwide bargaining between federations of unions and associations of employers while in other countries union relations are very decentralized, taking place almost exclusively at the level of the local firm between a local union representing workers at a single firm with that firm.

Thus, even in industrialized (and usually heavily unionized) countries, major differences in labor relations can be found relative to issues such as (1) the level at which bargaining takes place (national, regional, industry, or single firm, even a single workplace); (2) the types of workers involved (craft, industrial, service, government, profession); (3) degree of centralization of union-management relations; (4) the scope of bargaining, that is, the topics that are usually included in negotiations and contracts; (5) the degree to which the government is involved or can intervene; (6) the degree to which employment issues, such as wage rates and benefits, are determined by legislative action versus collective bargaining; and (7) the degree of unionization. In order to be effective in labor relations throughout the operations of an MNE, IHR managers need to understand these issues and differences in each of the countries in which they conduct business.

And as a last general point, economic and political issues of concern to management and unions are not static. They are constantly changing. Globalization, technological and job changes, and changing demographics are heavily impacting the role and importance of unions (and companies, for that matter) in most countries, as well.[13]

Interestingly, US (and, often, Asian) MNEs often face even more difficult problems in understanding and coping with industrial relations around the world than is the case for many other MNEs, since their labor relations are quite different in many respects from those practiced in other countries. As an example from one important perspective, here is a quick summary of the primary features of the US labor relations scene:

- Only non-supervisory and non-managerial employees have the right to organize or join unions.
- Typically, professional and technical workers do not form or join unions.
- The only employees who belong to unions (and that can thus bargain with the employer) work for employers where a majority of those employees have voted in free but secret elections for union representation.
- Contracts between such unions and employers are negotiated primarily at the local level between a single union and a single employer.
- Such collectively bargained contracts are legally enforceable and typically last for three years.
- The only mandatory subjects for bargaining are wages, hours, and working conditions.
- Both unions and employers are restricted in their behaviors toward each other by a considerable amount of regulation.
- Disagreements over the meaning of contracts are handled through established grievance procedures (not by renegotiating the contract), settled by union and management acting together and settled in the case of impasse by a privately hired, neutral arbitrator.

This highly decentralized, "business" unionism (although extensively regulated) is significantly different from the form of unionism present in most other countries.[14] In most countries, labor relations practices are very different, even opposite, to these characteristics. Thus many US (and Asian) MNEs have difficulty coping with the diversity of labor relations practices, because their experiences and familiarity may well not provide adequate guidance for how to conduct labor relations in other countries.

There are also a number of issues concerning the local union environment that MNEs—no matter which country they come from—must consider. MNEs will need to seek answers to the specific types of questions regarding global labor relations practices wherever they operate (see Exhibit 7.3):

All of the questions in Exhibit 7.3 illustrate potentially significant differences between labor relations practices in different countries. This is just one of the many areas of complexity with which IHR managers and MNEs must learn to cope.

EXHIBIT 7.3: Local Union Environment Issues That MNEs Need to Consider

Existing trade unions	What is the nature of the unions in the particular country? Is recognition of a union an entitlement or not?
Level of organization	How are unions organized (by firm, region, industry, national, craft)? Are unions company-wide, regional, or national? Are there multiple unions within firms, so that the MNE must negotiate with multiple, often competing unions, within the same subsidiary or organization?
Scope of unions	Is the focus general or industry specific? Is most bargaining being conducted on a national and/or industry-wide level, applying to all or most employers and employees?
Affiliations	Are there political or religious affiliations? Are the unions associated with political parties and if so, which ones? Are they related to religious organizations; which ones?
Type of workers	Who belongs? Who is covered by the contracts? Is there white-collar unionization? Do managers belong to unions, such as the *dirigenti* in Italy? Are there closed-shop requirements or practices? That is, is the situation such that employees must belong to the union(s)?
Union density	What is the percentage of employees covered by collective bargaining agreements?
Vision of unions	Where does the focus of labor relations lie? Is it collective bargaining or individual representation or both? Is it economics or

Continued overleaf

EXHIBIT 7.3 *Continued*

	politics? What is the nature of the plant or site-level role of unions? Are there shop stewards? Are there works councils? And, if so, are they independent or essentially arms of the unions?
Negotiation partner	With whom does the firm have to negotiate? Who is the negotiation partner at company level? What is the role of government in bargaining? Employer's associations: What is the nature and role of the employers' associations in each country? Which associations exist? Should the MNE belong (why, why not)? What does membership entail, do most employers join, and can the firm avoid joining? Is there an obligation or recommendation to align with any of them?
Operation method	What is the procedure for labor relations in the workplace? Is there a legal obligation to install employee representative bodies in the company and comply with information and consultation procedures: What are the information and consultation requirements? Are ballots compulsory? Are there specific rights and protections for employee representatives?
Types of union agreement	What are the important issues typically covered by union agreements. What topics are contained in the contracts? Are they specific or general in nature?
Binding force of union agreements	Are agreements concluded at national, industry, and company level? What is the nature of the contracts or agreements with unions? Are the contracts enforceable? Are they breakable for any reason? When and under what circumstances are contracts renegotiated? If there are disagreements over the meaning or application of the terms of the contract, how are they determined? Is the contract renegotiated? Are work stoppages used? Is some form of mediation or arbitration used? Does the government play an active role in negotiations?
Strikes and industrial action	Under what circumstances can unions strike? For what reasons can and do unions go on strike? What forms of industrial action are common? If strikes occur are they legally regulated? Is 'secondary' industrial action common and/or legal? What sanctions are available to employers who find themselves the subject of industrial action?
Operating union-free	Is it possible to operate union-free? Can healthy employee relations be fostered in a union-free environment?

NON-UNION WORKER REPRESENTATION

In many countries, additional forms of worker representation have evolved. Three such alternative institutions are described here.

Works Councils

Works councils are a critical component of worker relations in many countries, particularly in Europe.[15] In many countries in Europe, particularly the Netherlands, Germany, France, Hungary, and Italy, there is a long tradition of worker rights to participate in decision making relevant to the operation of their employers. These rights are in addition to rights of organization and collective bargaining. Many other countries, such as the United States, Japan, China, Australia, Mexico, and the UK, do not have such histories and do not have built into their industrial relations systems the concept or practice of works councils. This makes it essential that IHR managers from such countries gain an understanding of what is involved in these works council requirements and/or retain professional legal advice.

Essentially, these works councils (which are made up of elected representatives of the firm's workforce) have the right to receive information and to provide consultation relative to many decisions a firm makes (particularly, to ease the social consequences of restructurings by companies and within industries). The extent to which the councils have authority to approve employment-related (or even more broadly, enterprise) decisions varies from country to country. For example, since many countries in Europe have long involvement with works councils, the European Union has gradually been passing directives that require employers with more than 50 employees in all member countries (or 20 in any single country) to inform and consult with their workforces—through works councils or other, equivalent forums—on employment-related matters such as job security, work organization, and terms and conditions of employment.[16] Under the most recent directive, member countries must pass legislation requiring works councils in every employer with more than 50 employees and establishing the obligation to inform and consult. Once the legislation is passed, employers—if they don't do it on their own—can be compelled to set up an "inform and consent" arrangement if workers request it.

IHRM in Action 7.1 describes the efforts of the first American firm (Hewlett Packard) to establish an IC framework in the UK.[17]

IHRM in Action 7.1: Cross-Border Worker Representation at Hewlett-Packard

The merger of Hewlett Packard and Compaq in May 2002 triggered extensive consultation with workers in Europe. Under EU requirements, such corporate mergers require companies with 1,000 or more employees in the EU, with at least 150 of those in each of two or more member states, to consult with their employee representatives (through their works councils) on any business decisions contemplated as a result of the merger, such as layoffs, restructuring, and changed work arrangements (all of which were triggered by the merger).

Because of that experience, Hewlett Packard took the initiative under the new EU Inform and Consult Directive and the pending UK enabling legislation to become the first US firm in the United Kingdom to announce an "Inform and Consult" framework that was approved by its workforce. At quarterly meetings, HP's management consulted with and informed their employee representatives on matters such as HP UK business strategies, financial and operational performance, investment plans, organizational changes, and anticipated critical employment decisions, such as layoffs, outsourcing, workforce agreements, and health and safety.

Key UK HP managers plus HP employee representatives elected to the HP Consultative Forum from each of the four UK business units meet on a quarterly basis. Wally Russell, HP's European employee relations director says, "My own preference is that we be the master of our own destiny. So let's work together now to [develop] a model that suits HP's culture. . . ."

In addition, an earlier EU directive required all employers with more than 1,000 employees throughout the EU and with at least 150 employees in each of two countries, to establish a European-wide works council to receive information and consultation on all decisions that cut across country boundaries. Under this directive, larger employers not only need to establish country-required works councils (which under the new directive, all countries must require), but must also establish a European-wide council. Firms that operate in Europe, but that come from countries where the concept of a works council does not exist, must learn to adapt to the EU requirements. This means that any decisions such as plant or office closings, work restructuring or transfer of work from one country to another—including outsourcing and sub-contracting, and employment downsizings—all require firms to inform and consult with their councils prior to implementation of such decisions. In some countries, such as Germany, the council must agree with the nature of the decision and its planned implementation; in other countries, such as the UK, extensive consultation about the impact and planned efforts to mitigate them, are required.

In October 2001, the EU adopted legislation giving companies operating in the EU the possibility of forming a central European company, also known as a "Societas Europeae" (SE), instead of having to form individual companies under the laws of each of the individual member countries. This way MNEs operating in Europe can form a single, centralized, entity to avoid the complexities of the different regulations in each of the countries in which they operate a business. The critical issue here is that, relative to employee involvement, the MNE does not need to establish an employee involvement mechanism where none already exists and this gives them, then, a way to establish a single, Europe-wide, employee-involvement procedure. While most works councils are found in continental European countries, other countries (e.g., Argentina, Bangladesh, Japan, Thailand, and South Africa) also have them. These works councils can be composed of both management and employee representatives (e.g., Denmark, Belgium); composed of employee representatives and overseen by a member of management (e.g., Japan, France); or composed of employee representatives without management oversight (e.g., Austria).

It should be noted that the minimum firm or location size for installation of works councils differs from country to country and the number of works council members varies with the number of local employees. Although works councils are core instruments of employee relations and representative bodies for information and consultation, the country-to-country variation is substantial. In some countries (e.g., Germany) they may even make joint decisions with management (co-determination) (see the next section).

Co-determination

Some countries, such as Germany, go a step further than informing and consultating with works councils. Germany has evolved a procedure referred to as "Mitbestimmung" or co-determination. Co-determination is a legal requirement in which employees are represented on supervisory boards or boards of directors and participate in major strategic decisions (that is, employees are not just consulted but management must obtain their agreement).

Co-determination differs from works councils in the sense that it includes a decision-making component. Most EU companies have some form of participation of employee representatives in the company's decision-making process. Only three countries have no national legislation regarding board-level representation (Belgium, Italy, and UK).

Employee involvement (in most EU countries) lies on a continuum, from operational issues to full strategic decision making, from simple informing and consultation to works councils and co-determination. Employee involvement may range from pure attendance with an advisory role (e.g., France, although employees there may take a more active role, insisting on power similar to full acceptance or agreement on decisions that affect them) to membership and co-decision powers (e.g., Germany).

There are three corresponding systems of co-decisions:

1   Dual system: where the supervisory board (on which employee representatives have 1/3 of the members) supervises the board of directors (e.g., Austria, Germany, Denmark);
2   Single-tier system: where there is only one board of directors and the employees have one or two representatives;
3   Mixed system: obligatory participation but only advisory role (e.g., France).

Worker Co-operatives [18]

A third form of employee relations involves worker co-operatives. Today, the best-known of these are the set of co-operatives based in the Basque country of northern Spain (head-quartered in the small town of Mondragon), called the Mondragon Co-operative Corpora-tion (MCC). This complex of worker-owned businesses and other institutions (e.g., schools, social security, and banks) was begun in the mid-1940s by a local priest to deal with local problems of poverty, lack of education, and lack of economic opportunity in the Basque provinces of northern Spain and southern France, with the work co-operatives founded in 1956 by the priest and five young local engineers. These co-operatives have expanded and evolved to now involve over 100,000 people, of which over 65,000 are worker-owners, with annual sales now larger than US$20 billion with US$1 billion in net profits, and with 225 companies (industrial, retail, and financial), including 150 co-operatives, in many countries.

The MCC has been very successful for many reasons. These include: being located in a Basque culture that has historically involved community co-operation and being founded and encouraged by a very activist Catholic priest who believed that Catholic social teach-ings about the dignity of people included work and the rights of workers, the importance of family, community, and participation in work. This priest believed that if this concept of participation could be applied to economic issues, it would mean workplaces owned and managed by workers themselves. Thus, an economic system open to everyone, democratic in operation, with worker-owner solidarity and equality has evolved with evident success. It is a model that many have studied, but few have been able to emulate. Even so, it does clearly provide an alternative approach to employee-employer relations.

LITIGATION RISKS IN GLOBAL EMPLOYEE RELATIONS

One of the most important pressures for IHRM and MNEs in international employment law and employee relations is the increased possibility of litigation. These risks involve errors in judgment and decisions in foreign jurisdictions, and mistakes when dealing with foreign employees and international assignees. In recent years there has been a significant upward trend toward holding MNEs accountable in various courts for their protections (or lack thereof) of employee and human rights in their foreign operations. Increasingly, MNEs are being sued in their home jurisdictions on the basis of allegations of breaches arising from the firm's activities in foreign jurisdictions. In the past, MNEs have been able to block such actions on the basis that the home courts were not the appropriate jurisdictions in which to litigate the disputes. However, recent cases are illustrating that this defense may not be sufficient as foreign courts are increasingly willing to hold parent firms accountable under both their parent-country laws and those of the foreign country in which such liti-gations are initiated.

CONCLUSIONS

This chapter has focused on the nature of employee-employer relations in the global context. This is the last chapter in this section of the text that deals with aspects of the context within which IHRM operates. Each aspect has been presented in the framework of importance in which it impacts IHRM policy and practice. As described in this chapter, the primary form in which employee relations has developed involves the form and activity of labor unions, although the chapter also summarizes three alternative forms of employee involvement and representation: works councils, co-determination, and co-operatives.

The chapter described and discussed the nature of unions, at local, national, and international levels, as well as the ways in which MNEs interact with those unions. Numerous examples were provided to illustrate the diversity of unions and employee relations in differing countries, showing how complex the employee relations environment is for MNEs, which have to cope with different forms of unions and local cultures and regulations related to employee relations in every country in which they do business.

Lastly, the chapter describes works councils (committees of elected employees with whom firms must inform and gain consent for business decisions that involve employees), co-determination (situations in which employees have the right to sit on boards of supervisors or directors, with varying powers to impact business decisions that impact employees), and co-operatives (a form of worker-ownership and management of business firms, the best example of which evolved in northern Spain but now has operations around the world).

DISCUSSION QUESTIONS

1 How do the various labor standards promulgated by international organizations affect the MNE? What is the nature of their impact?
2 How do European Union directives (such as those developed in the area of HR) impact member states and MNEs?
3 How is the labor movement evolving as a response to increased globalization?
4 What are non-union workers representations? Do you think we will see more of these types of representations in the future?

CASE STUDY 7.1: Global Industrial Relations at Ford Motor Company (USA/Global)

Ford Motor Company manufactures cars, trucks, and parts in 30 countries, with approximately 181,000 employees worldwide. It negotiates contracts with 56 different unions in every country where it manufactures except six (where there are no unions). In some countries, such as Italy, it must also negotiate with salaried staff and managers, who are also unionized.

Because of this great variety of unions and countries, bargaining takes on as many different forms as there are countries. For example, in Australia, all major issues are first discussed by sub-committees at the local level, which, after agreement is reached, are then taken to the full national bargaining committee for Ford Motor. In contrast, in Germany, negotiation is done for all auto companies and auto unions at the same time through the national employers' association and the national metalworkers' union, which represents workers at all automotive companies.

Even with this complicated bargaining reality, or maybe because of it, bargaining is handled almost exclusively at the local (country) level, with minimal coordination on a global level. As can be imagined, this not only causes coordination problems for the many unions involved, but also for Ford Motor Company itself. In spite of this, the office of the Director of International Labor Affairs Planning and Employee Relations (now consolidated in the office of Global Manufacturing and Labor Affairs) in Ford's headquarters in Dearborn, Michigan, is literally only one person. As the Director of International Labor Affairs said, "because I work in so many countries, one of my primary roles is to educate all the parts of the business in the US about what is going on around the world and how that affects the business."

Sources: Excerpted from a presentation by David Killinger, Director, International Labor Affairs, on Ford Motor Company's global labor relations, delivered at the Faculty Development Seminar on International HRM at the University of Colorado, Denver, June 8, 2000; Ford Annual Report 2013 (http://corporate.ford.com/our-company/investors/reports-financial-information/annual-reports).

Discussion Questions

1 Compare union relations in two major countries. How are the unions (and employers) organized? What is the nature and role of bargaining? What role does the government play? Are there additional forms of employee representation?

2 What problems do you see for MNEs that must bargain with unions in multiple countries? How would you advise those problems be resolved?

3 What do you predict for the future of unions and union relations in the global economy? Why?

NOTES

1 Source: Mentioned in Morganteen, Jeff (Thursday, 27 Mar 2014), Labor unions saved Ford in our "darkest" hour: Bill Ford. CNBC, http://www.cnbc.com/id/101529786. Accessed April 7, 2014.

2 For more detail, refer to the volume in this series on these topics: Morley, M.J., Gunnigle, P. and Collings, D.G. (2006). *Global Industrial Relations*, London/New York: Routledge.

3 Visser, J. (2006). Union membership statistics in 24 countries, *Monthly Labor Review*, January, 38–49.

4 This short summary is based on the following: Baker & McKenzie (2009). *Worldwide Guide to Trade Unions and Works Councils*, Chicago, IL: CCH Inc.; Bamber, G.J., Lansbury, R.D. and Wailes, N. (eds.) (2010). *International and Comparative Employment Relations*, 5th ed., Thousand Oaks, CA: Sage Publications; Ferner, A. and Hyman, R. (eds.) (1998). *Changing Industrial Relations in Europe*, 2nd ed., Oxford, UK/Malden, MA: Blackwell Publishers; Hansen, E.D. (2001). *European Economic History*, Copenhagen, DK: Copenhagen Business School Press; Hyman, R. (2001). *Understanding European Trade Unionism*, London/Thousand Oaks, CA: Sage Publications; Keller, W.L. and Darby, T.J. (eds.) (2009). *International Labor and Employment Laws*, 3rd ed., Washington, DC: The Bureau of National Affairs and the International Labor Law Committee Section of Labor and Employment Law, American Bar Association; Morley, M.J., Gunnigle, P. and Collings, D.G. (eds.) (2006).

5 Cf., ICTUR (2005). *Trade Unions of the World*, 6th ed., London: John Harper Publishing.

6 William, F. and Williamson, H. (2006). International unions form body to defend workers' rights in era of globalization. *Financial Times*, November 2.

7 Potter, B. (2014), Australian workplace culture partly to blame for Toyota's exit, *The Australian Financial Review*, Feb. 11, retrieved at http://www.smh.com.au/business/commment-and-analysis/australian-workplace-culture-partly-to-blame-for-toyotas-exit-20140211-32djv.html#ixzz2tXZ9MiGt. Accessed Feb. 15, 2014.

8 Kimberly Clark Workers in Turkey End 43-day Strike with Gains (2014). IndustriALL Global Union website: http://www.industriall-union.org/kimberly-clark-workers-in-turkey-end-43-day-strike-with-gains. Accessed March 1, 2014.

9 Rothman, M., Briscoe, D.R. and Nacamulli, R.C.D. (eds.) (1992). *Industrial Relations Around the World*, Berlin: Walter de Gruyter; Levinson, D.L., Jr. and Maddox, R.C. (1982). Multinational corporations and labor relations: Changes in the wind? *Personnel*, May–June, 70–77.

10 Excerpted from a presentation by David Killinger, Director, International Labor Affairs, on Ford Motor Company's global labor relations, delivered at the Faculty Development Seminar on International HRM at the University of Colorado, Denver, 8 June 2000.

11 Baker & McKenzie (2009); Goetschy, J. (1998). France: The limits of reform, in Ferner, A. and Hyman, R. (eds.) (1998). *Changing Industrial Relations in Europe*, 2nd ed.; Keller and Darby (eds.) (2009); Schneider, B. (2004), Global industrial relations, presentation to the Faculty Development Program in International Human Resource Management, June 7–11, Denver, CO.

12 Frege, C. (2006), International trends in unionization, in Morley, M.J., Gunnigle, P. and Collings, D.G. (eds.), pp. 221–238; and Gooderham, P., Morley, M., Brewster, C. and Mayrhofer, W. (2004). Human Resource Management: A universal concept? in Brewster, C., Mayrhofer, W. and Morley, M. (eds.), *Human Resource Management in Europe*, Oxford: Elsevier, pp. 1–25.

13 Refer to Part II: Contemporary developments in global industrial relations, in Morley, Gunnigle, and Collings (eds.) (2006).

14 Bamber, G.J., Lansbury, R.D., and Wailes, N. (eds.) (2010). *International and Comparative Employment Relations*, 5th ed.; and Rothman, M., Briscoe, D.R., and Nacamulli, R.C.D. (eds.) (1993) *Industrial Relations Around the World: Labor Relations for Multinational Companies*.

15 See, for example, Baker & McKenzie (2009); Gill, C. (2006), Industrial relations in Western Europe, in Morley, Gunnigle, and Collings (eds.) *Global Industrial Relations*, London/New York: Routledge, pp. 71–85; and Keller and Darby (eds.) (2009).

16 Fox, A. (2003). To consult and inform, *HR Magazine*, October, 87–92.

17 Adapted from Fox, A. (2003). To consult and inform, *HR Magazine*, October, 87–92.

18 This section deals primarily with Mondragon (Spain) workers' cooperatives. The information is drawn from Herrera, D. (2009). Mondragon Cooperative Corporation: The ten core principles and their foundations,

lecture to course on the Mondragon co-operatives, delivered in Mondragon, Spain, 7 July; Kasmir, S. (1996). *The Myth of Mondragon*, Albany, NY: State University of New York Press; MacLeod, G. (1997). *From Mondragon to America*, Sydney, Nova Scotia, Canada: University College of Cape Breton Press; MCC (2007). *Corporate Management Model*, Mondragon, Spain: Mondragon Corporacion Cooperativia; Ormaechea, J.M. (1993). *The Mondragon Cooperative Experience*, Mondragon, Spain: Mondragon Corporacion Cooperativa; and Whyte, W. F. and Whyte, K. K. (1991). *Making Mondragon: The Growth and Dynamics of the Worker Cooperative Complex*, Ithaca, NY: ILR Press.

SECTION 3

Global Talent Management

The third section of this book is titled "Global Talent Management" and has seven chapters:

- Chapter 8: International Workforce Planning and Staffing
- Chapter 9: International Recruitment, Selection, and Repatriation
- Chapter 10: International Training and Management Development
- Chapter 11: International Compensation, Benefits, and Taxes
- Chapter 12: International Employee Performance Management
- Chapter 13: Well-being of the International Workforce and International HRIS
- Chapter 14: Comparative IHRM: Operating in Other Regions and Countries

Taken together, the above chapters provide a comprehensive overview of the essential body of IHRM policies and practices. These IHRM policies and practices serve to attract, select, develop, evaluate, compensate, and retain employees, as well as provide for their safety and well-being. So this section of the book concentrates on specific IHRM policies and practice that MNEs can use in the context of the operation of an MNE from its home-country, headquarters perspective as well as from the perspective of IHRM at the local level, which is important to the operation of foreign-owned firms and subsidiaries and other forms of cross-border ventures and alliances. Chapters 8 and 9 focus on the attracting and selecting policies and practices. Chapter 8 discusses the nature of and problems associated with workforce planning and staffing for global enterprises including an overview of the many options that MNEs have available to them. Chapter 9 builds on the previous chapter and discusses the planning and staffing issues in the MNE with primary focus on the selection of international assignees (IAs). It also describes many of the issues confronted in the IA selection process and best practices in dealing with those issues including the all-important issue of repatriation. Chapter 10 focuses on training and development in the MNE, focusing on training and preparation issues for expatriates as well as local employees in foreign operations and on leadership and management development in MNEs. Chapter 11 discusses compensation and benefits issues in MNEs, again focusing primarily on these issues for expatriates, but also on describing MNE attempts to design and apply common compensation and benefits programs for their operations and employees around the world. Chapter 12 focuses on the many issues related to the management of employee performance in the international arena. And Chapter 13 describes the many issues surrounding health, safety, and security for global business travelers and international assignees and their families and the design of crisis management programs to deal with these issues. Chapter 14, the last chapter in Section 3, provides an overview of the wide variation in effective and appropriate IHRM policies and practices across regions of the world. MNEs have the necessity to understand local HR policies and practices so as to make informed and effective decisions as to the practical fit of headquarters' policies and practices with tradition and law across the many regions of the world.

Chapter 8

International Workforce Planning and Staffing

Our leaders search for the brightest talent from around the world and give them the resources they need to be the best at what they do.

Samsung Corporation[1]

Learning Objectives

This chapter will enable the reader to:

- Describe the process of international workforce forecasting and the challenges involved in planning the international workforce for an MNE.
- Explain the many options available to MNEs for staffing their operations in terms of the different types of international employees that MNEs can draw on to staff their operations in the global marketplace.
- Describe the implications of the different staffing options and the various types of employees for the MNE.

The quality of a firm's talent is central to its ability to learn, innovate, and perform. Having the right talent, at the right place, at the right time, and at the right price is an important global issue for every enterprise.[2] *International workforce planning and staffing* refers to the process of estimating employment needs, recruiting, selecting, and repatriating talent in organizations with operations in different countries (see Figure 8.1). The challenge of staffing the global enterprise is both complex and difficult. In addition to normal home-country hiring responsibilities, MNE staffing includes staffing in all foreign operations plus the highly challenging responsibilities connected to relocation of employees from one country to another. In today's talent shortage environment, staffing by MNEs has become the central problem of global talent management.

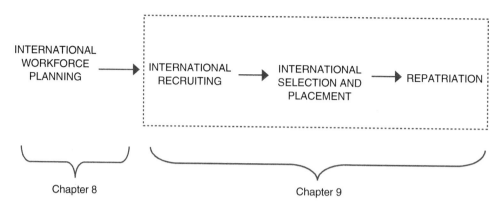

FIGURE 8.1 The International Workforce Planning and Staffing Process

Until quite recently, MNE staffing policies and practices were developed from the perspective of headquarters and the culture of the parent country, involving primarily concerns about employees sent on expatriate assignments to foreign subsidiaries and the staffing of local employees at home and in host country subsidiaries. But today, staffing policies and practices have become much more complex, involving a mobile, global workforce, located in acquired enterprises in foreign locales, plus those located in traditional subsidiaries, joint ventures, and partnerships, and involving local hires, hires from countries around the world, and employees from any operation on assignment to any other operation. Partially as a result of this globalizing of staffing, one of the recent trends has included a shift in the numbers of workers in MNEs from Western countries to a growing number from emerging markets. MNEs have even gone outside the boundaries of their organizations in their search for talent by using outsourcing, offshoring, insourcing, and, sometimes open source talent.[3]

This chapter introduces the nature of and problems associated with the planning for the staffing of MNEs' international operations. The chapter begins by describing the challenges involved in planning the international workforce for an MNE. And then it describes the many options now being reviewed by MNEs for staffing their operations around the world. Lastly, it presents some of the problems presented in trying to evaluate which approach works best when.

INTERNATIONAL WORKFORCE PLANNING

The objective of global workforce planning is to estimate employment needs of the MNE and to develop plans for meeting those needs. The term *workforce* applies to an enterprise's employees. The term *labor force* applies to the pool of potential employees, the labor market, from which a firm attracts and hires its workforce. The size—and location—of the potential labor force from which a firm recruits employees varies according to many factors, such as the participation rates of men and women in various locations, the overall unemployment rate, whether only local people would be expected to apply for particular jobs, whether people with the necessary education or skills are available locally, etc. As has been stated a number of times, one of the characteristics of today's global economy that adds complexity to HR management is the broad scope of enterprises' operations—likely to be spread all over the world, in dozens if not hundreds of locations, using an equally large number of languages, dealing with a like number of cultures, and subject to various employment laws. The labor pool from which MNEs recruit staff is therefore also located in all those places, speaking all those languages, expressing all that diversity of cultural values and behaviors, and regulated by widely varying employment laws.

As a consequence, enterprises with international operations must find staff in whatever location(s) they operate (or relocate the staff they need—if unavailable locally—to those locations), learn to recruit and hire in multiple locations and cultures, and deploy staff where it makes most sense for the enterprise. In the best of circumstances, HR professionals will be asked to provide information about the adequacy of local labor markets prior to their firms' decisions about where to locate their global operations and/or whether to participate in any cross-border acquisitions, joint ventures, or alliances. But, if not prior to such decisions, at least after such decisions are made, HR will be tasked with ensuring the timely staffing of the new or existing international operations. Because of the possible shortage of many skilled workers, the acquisition and deployment of talent is a key global HR imperative. In today's global environment, successful organizations of the future will be those who can attract the best global talent and nurture, develop, and retain it by having a compelling work environment and sophisticated succession management strategies.[4]

FACTORS THAT IMPACT INTERNATIONAL WORKFORCE PLANNING

There are several factors that can impact the process of international workforce planning, illustrated in Figure 8.2.

Availability of Data

One of the major obstacles to MNE workforce planning is the lack of accurate data about labor forces in many countries, particularly in less developed and emerging economies. Ideally, data about such labor force characteristics as participation rates (percentage of men and women of working age who work or look for work), levels and quality of education and literacy, availability of skill training, language skills, and unemployment rates, by country and metropolitan areas within countries, would be available to help IHR plan for their firms' local workforces. When available, these data are usually prepared by an agency of the government, or sometimes by international agencies, such as the International Labour

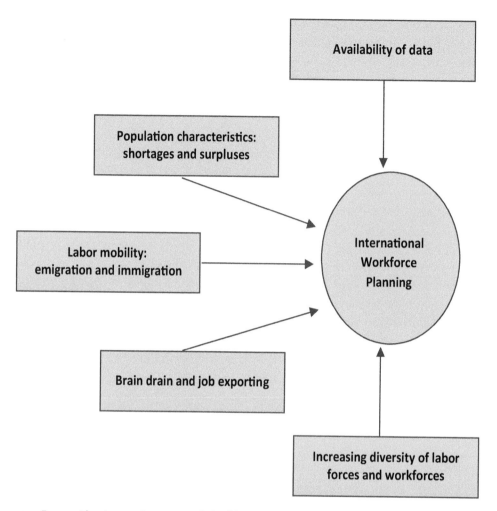

FIGURE 8.2 Factors That Impact International Workforce Planning

Organization (ILO) or the Organization for Economic Cooperation and Development (OECD). But in many emerging markets such government agencies don't always exist or the data they provide are inadequate, inaccurate, and/or politically motivated. In any case, they often do not provide data that are adequate for IHRM departments to be able to assess whether the people with the necessary skills and education are available or can be developed in any particular location in the numbers necessary to staff planned or acquired operations.

This usually implies that IHR professionals must develop such data from independent sources. Sometimes, such data is available from international or local consultancies. And, often, adequate information can be accessed from sources such as local chambers of commerce, embassies, firms that aid foreign companies in local employee sourcing, etc. In addition, IHR managers can often get some of the information they need from other firms that have prior experience in that particular foreign locale. The key point is that MNEs should not make the assumption that local labor forces will be adequate to provide the talent they need (although this is exactly what is typically done—leaving it up to HR to locate and hire the necessary workforce). This adequacy should be one component of the executive decision-making process for where and with whom to do business. In any case, it is IHR that is expected to provide such information.

Population Characteristics: Shortages and Surpluses[5]

Probably the most important labor force issue for developed economies is their aging populations and the resulting labor shortages, with more people retiring than entering the labor force to replace them, although the 2007 to 2009 global recession with its consequent high levels of unemployment may have forestalled the importance of this concern. In contrast, the labor force issue of concern in most developing and emerging economies is their large young labor forces who often lack the skill sets that jobs in MNEs require.

To a significant extent, these characteristics determine the nature of the labor pool in various countries, although other issues also contribute. Male and female labor force participation rates vary so much from country to country that this factor alone has a major impact on the size of any country's labor pool.[6] Of course, today, technology makes it possible to use workers from almost any location without them having to relocate to where the employer is. And where people want to live may also influence MNEs in their decisions as to where to locate their work.

In terms of aging, countries such as Japan, Germany, and the UK have a large percentage of their populations aged over 60 while countries such as India, Mexico, and South Africa have a small percentage of their populations aged over 60, with much higher percentages of their populations under the age of 25.[7] In some ways, these opposing profiles provide balance in the global labor force, with the surplus of young workers in the developing economies providing labor for the aging and shrinking labor forces in the developed countries. This happens in many ways, including the importing of workers and the exporting of jobs, through foreign direct investment, cross-border joint ventures and partnerships, outsourcing and subcontracting, and offshoring.

The following IHRM in Action[8] illustrates another example of how firms are coping with the labor shortage, in this case how the Dutch have dealt with it by hiring the retired. Indeed, all of these responses to labor shortages are intertwined, as countries seek new ways to deal with the shortages. Various countries and firms are discussing the preferences of using various hiring options, ranging from immigrants to retirees to working mothers to robots and computers. Not all options are equally desired in different cultures and countries. And these shortages suggest to MNEs that are pursuing strategies to extend their global operations into developed countries that they must take into consideration the possible lack of availability of the types of employees they may need to staff those operations.

IHRM in Action 8.1: Dealing with Labor Shortages in the Netherlands

Frans Tuijntjes, a former pilot who has flown all over the world, is now selling men's clothing and loving it. Recruiting the elderly—men and women who are either bored in retirement or need to supplement their pensions—is a new Dutch strategy to combat their labor shortage. In a program referred to as 65+, the Dutch created an employment agency designed specifically for recruiting the elderly.

Dutch companies find that their older employees are unusually motivated, experienced, and loyal. A short time ago, the Dutch welfare state was subsidizing retirement and encouraging people to retire early. Many people opted out. But now, with a labor shortage due to low birth rates over the last 40 years and fast economic growth in the Dutch economy, firms are finding the tight labor market is hampering growth because they can no longer fill vacancies.

Interestingly, the labor shortage is prompting a national debate [in the Netherlands as elsewhere] on some sensitive issues: How many more immigrants should be let into the country? Can the government force people to retrain? Should the government raise the retirement age and by how much?

At any rate, the retired Dutch who have gone back to work are finding it a rewarding experience. Frans Tuijntjes, the retired pilot, says, for example, "I've sold airplanes, so I figured I could sell a suit." He says his part-time job at Marks & Spencer is a lot of fun because he gets to meet a lot of people and he can use his many skills, such as practicing his multiple languages.

For firms that want to conduct business in emerging markets, IHRM's role in ensuring a qualified local workforce can be critical. For example, when the Edinburgh-based marine service firm BUE Marine moved into Azerbaijan's capital, Baku, to take advantage of its natural resources, it faced a large number of HR challenges, ranging from nepotism and theft to low skills and overstaffing and deceitful résumés. What they found was that when companies want a foothold in a developing country, they need to research labor costs, cultural differences, benefits, legal jurisdictions, and how to hire people locally, as well as the role that government plays in contracts and enforcement.[9] It falls upon IHRM to forestall labor problems and to provide information to senior executives on the costs of dealing with (or not) these kinds of such critical issues.

INCREASING DIVERSITY OF LABOR FORCES AND WORKFORCES

One of the results of increased globalization, modern technology, and global communications on the global labor market is that people with the education and skills needed in today's global economy are increasingly available everywhere, making potential employees available from all racial and ethnic origins and nationalities.[10] This has the effect of dramatically increasing the level of employee diversity with which global firms must cope. In addition, employees in the global firm come from many groups that in the past and in many countries did not participate much in the labor market, including the young and/or old, male and/or female, disabled, married or single, people from various religious affiliations, etc.

Labor Mobility: Emigration and Immigration

The world is experiencing migration (emigration and immigration) on an unprecedented scale. Some of it is voluntary and some of it is forced. Some of it is legal and some of it is considered illegal. Some of it is planned and purposeful and some of it is unplanned and without direct purpose. However, in all cases, it is creating mobility of workers in such large numbers that formal and informal emigration has to be taken into consideration as MNEs examine their options for developing their global workforces.

Millions of people work outside their home countries, either as traditional expatriates (on assignment by their employers) or hired to emigrate to fill vacant jobs in other countries. Some countries like the Philippines purposefully manage a percentage of their labor force to work in other countries every year. Others, such as Mexico, lose many workers with unofficial migration to their neighbors. And some, like Estonia, Romania, and Poland, lose many workers (legitimately) to other countries in their region, such as in this case to other countries in the European Union. In addition, millions are forced from their homes because of civil unrest or natural disasters and become permanent refugees. And some trade treaties such as the one that created the foundation for the European Union (1957 Treaty of Rome) include provisions to facilitate movement of workers between countries. This allows people to seek the best possible work opportunities, facilitates EU firms in creating high-quality workforces by drawing on talent from throughout the EU membership, and eventually levels the wage and benefits "playing field" across the member states, so that firms do not gain advantages or disadvantages because of differences in wages or in government practices between countries. Other treaties such as NAFTA, Mercosur, and ASEAN do not yet include such labor mobility provisions, but if the EU is developing the model for such regional trade treaties, it may only be a matter of time before other regions begin to look at ways to facilitate labor mobility as well (refer to the discussion of these treaties in Chapter 6 on employment law).

Brain Drain and Job Exporting

One of the major concerns created by the increasingly mobile labor force is what many countries, particularly emerging and developing countries, refer to as a brain drain, as their educated and skilled citizens leave for jobs with better pay in the developed countries.

From the point-of-view of developing countries, it is often wrong for firms from the rich countries to recruit and relocate their citizens after the major resources that they have expended on educating and training their citizens. They feel they need these human resources for the development of their own economies.

An alternative to this brain drain, and one that is increasingly pursued by many global firms and is encouraged by the governments of developing economies, is to export the work and jobs from the developed economies to developing countries, through subsidiaries, joint ventures, outsourcing, and offshoring. Both sides can benefit from this arrangement: the firm gets top talent from the foreign countries in a period and location of labor shortage in their home country and at a lower cost and the developing country gets to hold on to its top talent and gets jobs and income from the MNEs.

In summary, today's typical MNE, with operations in multiple countries (from dozens to over 100 countries), has a workforce that spans the globe. The task of IHR managers in these firms is to facilitate the hiring of competent, high-performing talent that enables sustainable, competitive advantage throughout the global marketplace. Planning for and hiring such a workforce is a complex activity. It involves determining what education and skills are needed and figuring out where to find that talent and how to recruit it and hire it. This is difficult enough for local hires for local operations. It is much more difficult for global operations. The first part of this chapter has described some of the complexities in that process.

The labor market is different in every country—and often also between regions within countries. The challenges for collecting or creating the information necessary for workforce planning and forecasting are often difficult to overcome. And yet the health of today's MNE is a function of IHRM's ability to match their firms' workforce forecasts with the supply of global talent. Indeed, "In a fast-changing global economy, world-class workforce planning is the key to success."[11] With global workforce forecasts and plans in place, MNEs' next moves are to fulfill those plans through recruiting and staffing, the subject of the rest of this chapter.

INTERNATIONAL STAFFING APPROACHES[12]

Staffing for the MNE involves hiring at the local level (in both the parent country and in all foreign locations where it does business or has operations of any kind) as well as management of the mobile workforce, that is, the employees who are hired in one locale and are relocated for varying times and purposes to other locales. In staffing the MNE, firms can use four approaches,[13] as illustrated in Exhibit 8.1. Three approaches are mostly used to staff important positions in subsidiaries such as managerial and executive positions.[14] Each approach has its own advantages and disadvantages.

It is important to note that as Exhibit 8.1 implies, IHR staffing practice is challenged by the problems associated with recruiting, hiring, training, compensating, managing performance and welfare, and retaining and deploying a global workforce, sourced from multiple locations and managed under the constraints of multiple national cultures and legal systems.

EXHIBIT 8.1: International Staffing Approaches

ETHNOCENTRIC STAFFING APPROACH	ADVANTAGES	DISADVANTAGES
MNEs tend to hire from the HQ country and send employees on international assignment to the subsidiaries This approach is used when: ■ There is a strong need for the HQ to control the subsidiaries. ■ The subsidiaries are in early stages of development. ■ There is a lack of local talent. ■ MNEs that have a global business strategy are most likely to use this approach.	■ Quickly fill key positions in subsidiaries when local talent is not available. ■ Allows HQ to control and coordinate subsidiary operations, and to maintain a common corporate culture across subsidiaries. ■ Allows parent-company nationals (PCNs) to acquire international experience.	■ Costly because PCNs are used. ■ Tension between PCNs and host-country nationals (HCNs) (e.g., because of compensation differences). ■ Prevents or slows the career development process of HCNs.

POLYCENTRIC STAFFING APPROACH	ADVANTAGES	DISADVANTAGES
MNEs prefer to use locals from the subsidiary country This approach is used when: ■ Need for localizing operations becomes important for competitive advantage. ■ Each subsidiary is relatively autonomous and adapts to its local conditions. ■ MNEs that have a multi-domestic business strategy are most likely to use this approach.	■ Access to local communities and markets. ■ Sends signal to the local community and government that subsidiary is committed to the local culture. ■ Relatively less costly than PCNs.	■ Locals may not be committed to the MNC. ■ Locals may not be able to acquire international experience. ■ For locals, career development and promotion opportunities may be limited.

Continued overleaf

EXHIBIT 8.1 *Continued*

REGIO-CENTRIC STAFFING APPROACH	ADVANTAGES	DISADVANTAGES
MNEs tend to favor using people from a specific region This approach is used when: ■ There is a strong need to organize subsidiaries into regions. ■ Each region works as a unique unit with considerable autonomy. ■ The MNE has several regional headquarters. ■ Key positions are filled by third-country nationals (TCNs) and HCNs.	■ Reduces costs by sharing resources within a region. ■ Managers can develop region-specific expertise. ■ Able to respond to specific needs of a region.	■ Lack of multicultural perspective. ■ Career opportunities limited to specific regions. ■ Not easy for region-based managers to move to company HQs.

GEOCENTRIC STAFFING APPROACH	ADVANTAGES	DISADVANTAGES
MNEs source talent from anywhere in the world, regardless of nationality This approach is used when: ■ MNE has a network of subsidiaries with various degrees of centralization and decentralization. ■ Highly integrated process across subsidiaries. ■ MNEs that have a transnational business strategy are most likely to use this approach.	■ Employees can develop a geocentric mindset. ■ Hires the best talent available. ■ Career opportunities for top performers are truly global. ■ Employees can work with other employees from different geographic, cultural, and regional backgrounds.	■ Managing a large number of international assignees can be costly (e.g., relocation and training costs). ■ Managing work authorizations in several countries is a complex process. ■ Requires a very high level of communication among employees from several countries.

Based on Scullion, H. and Collings, D. (2006). *Global Staffing*, London: Routledge; Collings, D. and Scullion, H. (2006). Global staffing, in Stahl, G.K. and Björkman, I. (eds.) *Handbook of Research in International Human Resource Management*, Cheltenham, UK, Edward Elgar; Harzing (2004); Borg, M. and Harzing, A.-W. (2004). Composing an international staff, in Harzing, A.-W. and Van Ruysseveldt, J. (eds.), *International Human Resource Management*, 2nd ed., Thousand Oaks, CA/London: Sage Publications, pp. 251–282.

Traditional International Assignees and Local Nationals

Until quite recently, staffing of MNEs was simplistically described as involving only three types of international employees: *parent-country nationals (PCNs), host-country nationals (HCNs),* and *third-country nationals (TCNs)*[15] (see Exhibit 8.2).

Most of the IHR literature has concerned itself with PCNs, When PCNs are transferred (posted/assigned/relocated) to another country, to work in a foreign subsidiary or other

EXHIBIT 8.2: Traditional International Assignees and Local Nationals

	Strengths	Weaknesses
Parent-country nationals *Employees of the MNE who are citizens of the country where the MNE's corporate headquarters is located*	■ Familiar with the MNE's corporate cultural values, goals, and objectives ■ International experience may lead to career opportunities ■ Provides control over the subsidiary's operations ■ Effective transfer of corporate values culture and knowledge from HQ to subsidiary and vice versa	■ Cross-cultural adjustment to the new culture can be difficult ■ Can clash with local government's policy of promoting local hires ■ Can be costly (e.g., relocation, compensation, possibility of failure) ■ Repatriation process can be challenging and difficult
Host-country nationals *Employees of the MNE who work in the foreign subsidiary and are citizens of the country where the foreign subsidiary is located*	■ Familiarity with the local cultural, economic, political and legal environment ■ Relatively less costly (e.g., limited or no relocation, local compensation levels) ■ Can respond effectively to the host country's requirements for localization of the subsidiary's operations ■ Accepted by the local colleagues, workers, employees, and government officials.	■ Lacks familiarity with parent-country culture ■ Lowers or reduces the ability to maintain control over the subsidiary operations ■ May not be the most qualified ■ Low loyalty to HQ

Continued overleaf

EXHIBIT 8.2 *Continued*

	Strengths	Weaknesses
Third-country nationals *Employees of the MNE who are citizens of a country other than the parent country or the country of the subsidiary to work in one of its foreign subsidiaries*	■ Generally viewed as a compromise between PCNs and HCNs ■ Less expensive to maintain than PCNs ■ Can add skills not available in country of the subsidiary ■ Can add diversity/multiculturalism to the work environment ■ Easier to relocate (e.g., move from subsidiary to subsidiary)	■ Lacks familiarity with parent-country culture and MNE corporate culture ■ Mobility may be limited due to travel restrictions in certain countries or locations ■ May not be accepted well by the local nationals

Based on Scullion, H. and Collings, D. (2006). *Global Staffing*, London: Routledge; Collings, D. and Scullion, H. (2006). Global Staffing, in Stahl, G.K. and Björkman, I. (eds.) *Handbook of Research in International Human Resource Management*, Cheltenham, UK, Edward Elgar; Harzing (2004); Borg, M. and Harzing, A.-W. (2004). Composing an international staff, in Harzing, A.-W. and Van Ruysseveldt, J. (eds.), *International Human Resource Management*, 2nd ed., Thousand Oaks, CA/London: Sage Publications, pp. 251–282.

type of operation (such as a joint venture or alliance) of the MNE for more than one year, they are generally referred to as expatriates or *international assignees*. Historically, the term "expatriate," as used by companies, referred to employees who were relocated from the parent company or headquarters to foreign subsidiaries or "overseas" operations. Today, the term "international assignee" is more generally used to describe the process of moving any employee from one country to another for a period of more than one year, while staying in the employment of the same firm.

When expatriates return home, they are referred to as repatriates. Administering the traditional expatriate has historically been the primary time-consuming responsibility of the IHR manager and staff (and the primary research focus of academics).

Most of the literature in IHRM that deals with expatriates or international assignees—individuals who are or have been on international assignments—has assumed that all employees who are on foreign assignments are traditional expatriates. Studies have invariably referred to "international assignment experience" or "expatriate" to simply refer to anyone who has been on an international assignment for more than one year. But, as with everything else in IHRM, international assignments have also become more complex. So, the next few paragraphs provide an introduction to the many different types of international assignees (IAs), before the chapter describes in more detail the many issues surrounding recruiting and staffing for international assignments.

It is important to point out that when host-country nationals (HCNs) are relocated to the headquarters of the parent firm, generally for assignments of one year or less, for the purpose of learning the organization and its products and culture, they are generally referred to as inpatriates (although they are probably viewed by themselves and their home-country families, colleagues, and friends as expatriates from their home countries). Inpatriation is discussed in the next chapter.

Purpose(s) of Assignments

There have been a number of approaches to describing the purposes for sending people on international assignments.[16] In general, these purposes can be combined into two broad categories: *demand-driven* and *learning-driven*. The demand-driven purposes include using IAs as general managers or directors, for subsidiary start-ups and to roll out new products, for technology transfer, to solve problems, to perform functional tasks such as accounting, sales, and manufacturing, and for organizational control. The learning-driven purposes include management development (of both international business skills and general management skills for both PCNs and HCNs), transfer of knowledge, and the socialization of locals into the corporate culture and values. Except for the need for general managers, increasingly all of these purposes are being pursued with shorter-term assignments (business travel, commuters, or transfer for less than a year, for sure less than three years), rather than the more common three- to five-year relocations found in years past.[17] Some of the demand-driven purposes are being converted to *permanent transfers* or what is often referred to as *localization*.

As more firms globalize and develop more operations in an ever-increasing number of locations, they have begun to create additional options for staffing foreign work assignments. One consequence of this has been an effort to find a better term to describe the many types of international employees, as a replacement for "expatriate." Thus terms such as "international assignee," "transpatriate," even "transnational" have been used by various companies in attempts to find a term that might describe anyone on a foreign assignment. None has been found, as will be shown in the next section, which covers all types of foreign employees. The term most often used today, "international assignee," is generally used as a "catch-all" term but mostly refers to the traditional PCN on a typical expatriate assignment as well as to the inpatriate and other HCNs and TCNs who are moved from subsidiary to subsidiary. Yet, even with a generally expressed dissatisfaction with the term "expatriate," observation at many recent IHRM conferences suggests it is difficult to break the habit of the use of this term.

Today's Diversity of International Employees

Even though the use of expatriates has seemed to be the logical choice for staffing international operations, at least for start-ups, technology transfer, and major managerial positions, such as director general and sales manager, several current problems with the use of expatriates has led MNEs to seek other options for achieving their objectives in their foreign operations. Some of these issues include making mistakes in the choice of employees for international assignments, the high cost of these assignments, difficulties in providing adequate training and support for employees and their families on international assignments and the resulting problems with their adjustment to the foreign situation, too-frequent failures of international assignees, local countries' desires for hiring local employees and managers, problems encountered in managing repatriates, and a growing suspicion that local hires may actually perform better.[18] One result of this is that many MNEs are finding that it no longer makes sense to give all attention and priority to expatriates.

Indeed, international managers can and do come from just about everywhere, not just the HQ of the traditional large MNE.[19] Exhibit 8.3 provides a summary of the many

EXHIBIT 8.3: Types of International Assignees

Local hires or nationals	Employees who are hired locally (a host-country national hired under a polycentric staffing approach).
Domestic internationalists	Employees who never leave home but conduct international business with customers, suppliers, and colleagues in other countries (via telephone, teleconference, email, fax, or even snail mail).
International commuters	Employees who live in one country (typically their home country) but who work in another (host) country and regularly commute across borders to perform aspects of their work. They may live at home in one country yet commute on a daily or weekly basis to another country to work.
Frequent business trips	Employees who, on a frequent basis, take international trips that last a few days, weeks, or months at a time. These international trips usually include travel to a variety of countries or continents to visit MNE sites or customers.
Short-term international assignees	Employees on assignments that last less than one year but more than a few weeks (increasingly being used to substitute for longer-term international assignments and typically do not include the relocation of the employee's family).

International assignees	This is an international assignment that lasts more than one year and includes full relocation. This is the traditional expatriate and the focus of most research and surveys about international employees. These international assignments may be intermediate-term assignments (12 to 24 months) or long-term assignments (24 to 36 months).
Localized employees	Often referred to as localization, this normally refers to the situation where an employee is sent to work in a foreign country but hired as a local employee (with some allowances for relocation). This may be because they really want to work in that country, often because they marry a local spouse or for some other reason want to spend the rest of their careers in that location. It may also involve an international assignee who is converted to permanent local status once the assignment period is over. Obviously, this option reduces the overall costs for the MNE.
Permanent cadre or globalists	These are employees who spend essentially their whole careers in international assignments, moving from one locale to another.
Stealth assignees	This is the term used to describe international assignees who are relocated by their managers without ever informing HR (that is, they "fly under the radar"), so that they do not show up in the records, benefits, and support systems used to manage such employees. Many short-term assignees fall under this category.
Immigrants (A)	This refers to traditional TCNs, employees who are hired to work in a foreign subsidiary but whose home of citizenship is another country, thus they become immigrants to the country of the subsidiary.
Immigrants (B)	These are people hired by the parent firm (either in country or as new immigrants and brought into the country) to work in the parent country. Making things even more complex, immigrants may be born in a foreign country and raised in the parent (of the firm) country; they may be born and raised in a foreign country and then later in life immigrate; or they may be born in the parent country of foreign immigrant parents and raised in either the parent country or their native (foreign) country. Any of these possibilities creates varying skills and cultural competencies.
Internships (temporary immigrants)	These are workers brought into a firm's home country to work for short (six months to two years) periods as interns or trainees, used especially to fill in for labor shortages.
Returnees	These are emigrants who are hired (or selected, if already employed by the firm) to return to their home countries to work for the firm there.

Continued overleaf

EXHIBIT 8.3 *Continued*

Boomerangs	These are individuals who have emigrated and are hired by firms in the firm's parent country to return to their original homes or are foreigners with experience in the firm's parent country, who have returned to their original homes and are now hired to work in the foreign (to the firm, but home to the individual) country
Second-generation expatriates	These are naturalized citizens (immigrants who have become citizens) and are sent on foreign assignments to countries other than their countries of birth. The assumption is that since they have lived through the "expatriate" experience once, they should be better able (than those without this experience) to handle it the second time.
Just-in-time expatriates	These are ad hoc or contract expatriates, who are hired from outside the firm just as they are needed and just for one assignment.
Reward or punishment assignees	These are employees who are late in their careers and who are either given a desirable foreign assignment to enjoy and to pad their pensions for when they retire in a couple of years (pay is higher on foreign assignments) or are sent to a difficult locale or undesirable assignment as a way to sideline them to finish out their careers, rather than have to discipline or terminate them because of marginal performance.
Outsourced employees	This is the situation that occurs when the MNE decides to pay someone else (in another country) for the services of an "employee" or group of employees. That is, the firm moves work to another country, subcontracting to a local firm to do the work. If the employees stay in the employ of the firm, yet are located in a foreign locale, this is generally referred to as offshoring. In recent years, global employment companies (GECs) have evolved, which provide a few employees or whole staffs for overseas locations. Some firms use their own GEC to house all of their globally mobile employees, simplifying pay and benefits, since everyone in the GEC gets the same pay and benefits, no matter where they work within the firm, possibly with cost-of-living adjustments. Other firms use independent GECs to staff overseas work.
Virtual IEs	This is the situation where all or most of the work is performed across borders via electronic media: tele conferences, email, telephone, video conferences, fax, etc. Virtual cross-border teams are discussed in more detail in Chapter 10, Training and Development.
Self-initiated foreign workers	This term refers to individuals who travel abroad (usually as tourists or students) but who seek work as they travel and are hired in the

> foreign location, often by firms from their home countries. They may also be individuals who travel to foreign countries seeking work in those countries. In either case, the initiative is taken by the individuals who are purposely seeking work in a foreign country. Or they are individuals who travel to another country for schooling or training and then stay to work.
>
> Retirees   This refers to the hiring of a firm's retirees for short-term foreign assignments.

different types of international employees that MNEs draw on to staff their operations in the global marketplace.[20] There are many different options available to MNEs, and there are probably even more examples that the authors have yet to come across.

INTERNATIONAL STAFFING CHOICES: IMPLICATIONS FOR MNES

IHRM professionals need to develop an appreciation for the fact that their responsibilities related to their international employees (IEs) vary according to the particular form of international employee and their countries of operation, the type of foreign operation (for example wholly owned subsidiary or international joint venture), or the firm's phase of globalization.[21]

This increased variety of employees presents all sorts of new challenges for the selection, preparation, deployment, and management of a global workforce. Not the least of these is the increased need by all managers—and for IHR managers in particular—to increase their cross-cultural awareness, knowledge, and skills, their foreign language abilities, and their overall management competencies within this new international setting.

For example, firms have much to learn about how to manage the performance of a global workforce. The performance management of traditional expatriates, themselves, is not always handled well (this is discussed in Chapter 12), even though many global enterprises have many years of experience dealing with them. But the cross-national interaction among all the many different types of international employees described in this chapter and between global managers and IEs creates many new performance management problems, which become even more difficult as the variety of employees expands. All of these become critical concerns: the impact of national culture on performance and how it is defined, on standards for performance, on the review-ability of reviewers, on who reviews (their cultural experience and savvy), etc.[22]

Pay and support services are also likely to be structured differently for a short-term business traveler sent on an assignment for six months to finalize the start-up of a new foreign subsidiary than for a manager sent for three to five years to run such a subsidiary. Differences would also be pretty important between the pay and support services of the immigrant or foreign student (and each of these would be different from each other) hired to return home to work in a foreign subsidiary in comparison to a person who makes a career out of moving from one foreign assignment to another. Compensation issues are discussed in more depth in Chapter 11.

Exhibit 8.4 highlights some of the types of questions that IHR and the global enterprise need to address in order to better manage their global workforces. These questions can help guide readers as they read the rest of the chapters in this section.

EXHIBIT 8.4: Questions to Better Manage a Global Workforce

1 What is the extent of the use of each type of IE?

2 How does the preparation and support for each type of IE vary? What form does the preparation and support take for each type of IE?

3 Does the international strategy or structure of the firm influence the type of IE employed? Or, stated from the other direction, which type of IE tends to be used under which strategy (international, multi-domestic, global, transnational) or structure (subsidiary, joint venture, alliance, sub-contract) or managerial orientation (ethnocentric, region-centric, geo-centric)?

4 Which international-business or cross-cultural competency is required by which type of international employee? For example, does every type of international employee require full cross-cultural preparation, training, and support? Does every type need full knowledge of how to conduct international business?

5 Which performance management problems arise for which type of international employee? And which solutions are most appropriate?

6 Are there specific management, organizational, and IHR outcomes that differ according to the type of international employee? For example, do difficulties with performance or retention vary with type of international assignment? Do the staffing, training, compensation, and management solutions also vary with the type of international assignment?

7 For which type of work and business purposes—management, sales, control, technology transfer, business development, product development, management development—are the various types of international employees used? Why? Which is most effective? Will the outsourcing and offshoring of this type of work continue? What will be the impact on the domestic workforces of MNEs that do this?

Purposes for these various employment or assignment situations will vary significantly. For example, these purposes could include any of the following: an ongoing assignment to perform manufacturing operations, a project team to install a new product, a short-term negotiation of a deal, intermediate-term transfer of technology, longer-term managerial and control assignments (managing director, comptroller), personal developmental assignments, or assignments to start new operations. Obviously the end result that is sought in each situation is different and the skills and competencies sought by the employing organization should also vary according to the purpose of the assignment. At the same time, the need for cross-cultural understanding and competency may be similar.

■ Which types of international employee are most cost-effective? Which provide the best business results? The extent of the cost variances and the ability of IHRM to measure and to manage these differences (and the extent to which IE choices are made based on these differences) needs to be examined. In the authors' experience, even though the costs of IE assignments are rarely measured, the benefits are almost never measured, making any assessment of ROI of foreign assignments almost always impossible. Since MNEs are under constant and strong cost pressures, it would seem that this should be an area for major attention (and for payoff from results of such attention).

■ What are the best practices among various types of international firms in terms of the utilization of various types of international employees?

■ Do varying types of IE experience result in differential amounts of stress or other forms of personal problems? Recently, researchers have begun to look at issues such as stress as associated with varying forms of international activity, seeking, for example, to identify the extent and nature of particular problems associated with different types of international assignments.[23]

The answers to the types of questions suggested here and the analyses of these problems can go a long way toward helping to fill the business need for ensuring the best (most effective, productive/profitable, and cost-efficient) utilization of employees in this increasingly complex global business environment. In order for IHR to adequately fulfill its mission in support of the MNE's staffing, it needs to clarify which type of international employee works best when and for which purpose.

Managing a global workforce creates many issues for IHRM.[24] This chapter has provided an introduction. The rest of this section provides detail of the many components of the whole process. Most of the section deals with the management of international assignees. But, as this chapter has pointed out, firms with a global workforce in multiple countries must also cope with local workforces as well as the mobility of employees from country to country.

CONCLUSION

This chapter provides an introduction to planning, forecasting, and staffing the global enterprise. It began by providing a description of the constantly changing labor markets around the world and discussed how MNEs plan for creating their workforces from those labor markets. The nature of those markets in various countries, in terms of their demographic characteristics, the skills and abilities of their individuals, and their accessibility and cost varies dramatically from country to country and region to region and can be a major determinant in the success of IB decisions such as where to locate operations. The chapter also provided an overview of the many options that MNEs have available to them for that staffing.

DISCUSSION QUESTIONS

1　Why is planning and forecasting a global workforce so difficult?
2　Why are so many countries bothered by their "brain drains"?
3　If you are given the opportunity in your next job to go on an extended foreign assignment, what types of support programs would you expect or ask for? If you are working in IHRM, what policy or practices would you create to deal with foreign assignments?
4　What are the trends over the next 10 years in global staffing for many MNEs?

CASE STUDY 8.1: Firms Woo Executives from "Third" Countries (Global)

In the new world of a global workforce and firms' foci on global talent management, multinational firms are tapping more "third-country" nationals for overseas posts. The increase in operations in emerging markets, the high costs of traditional international assignments, and shortages of needed skills in many markets has led to the search for employees from countries other than the parent country of headquarters or the host country of subsidiaries, employees who are referred to as "third-country" nationals (TCNs). These TCNs often win jobs because they speak several languages (particularly English and the host-country language) and know an industry and or foreign country well. The average number of third-country nationals continues to rise from year to year, according to consultants such as Organization Resources Counselors.

Pioneer Hi-Bred International employs 29 TCNs in key jobs abroad, triple the number five years earlier, partly because they accept difficult living conditions in Africa and the Middle East. Raychem has a dozen such foreigners in top European posts, up from eight a few years ago. "The numbers are going to increase" as Europe's falling trade barriers ease relocation, suggests Edward Keible, a senior vice-president. A Frenchman runs the company's Italian subsidiary, a Belgian is a sales manager in France, while a Cuban heads the unit in Spain.

Scott Paper, whose ranks of TCN managers has grown from two to 13 within a couple of years, says it will step up its recruitment of young foreigners "willing to move around Europe or around the Pacific," says Barbara Rice, their HR chief.

Sources: European Migration Network Focused Study 2013: *Attracting Highly Qualified and Qualified Third Country Nationals*, European Commission; Baker & McKenzie (2014). Mobilizing the work force globally. *The Global Employer*, (2), 1–3; Fouad, S., Hahm, W. and Leisy, B. (2010). *Managing Today's Global Workforce*, New York: Ernst & Young; Lubblin, J. S. (1991). Firms woo executives from "third countries," *Wall Street Journal*, September 16, B1

Discussion Questions:

1 What culture-related problems and issues do you see in these uses of third-country nationals?
2 How can those culture-related concerns be understood and dealt with?
3 What role does international HR need to take in coping with the cultural issues presented by the use of TCNs?
4 Are there other alternatives for finding enough talent to fill global needs?

NOTES

1 Source: Samsung corporate website (www.samsung.com). Values and pphilosophy. Retrieved from http://www.samsung.com/us/aboutsamsung/samsung_group/values_and_philosophy/. Accessed Nov. 24, 2014.

2 Sparrow, P., Scullion, H., and Tarique, I. (eds.) (2014). *Strategic Talent Management: Contemporary Issues in International Context*, Cambridge: Cambridge University Press; Collings, D. (2014). Integrating global mobility and global talent management: Exploring the challenges and strategic opportunities. *Journal of World Business*, 49, 253–261, Tarique, I., and Schuler, R.S. (2010). Global talent management: Literature review, integrative framework, and suggestions for further research. *Journal of World Business*, 45(2), 122–133.

3 This term refers to the ability of firms to use the input of non-employees for in-house projects, much like the development of "open source" software. Sometimes this is referred to as the "Wiki Workplace," which refers to the use of mass collaboration, which is taking root in the workplace connecting internal teams to external networks or individuals facilitated by the Web 2.0 platform for collaboration. As a result, the boundaries of the organization are extended in terms of the workforce that can be accessed by the firm. See, The wiki workplace, in Tapscott, D. and Williams, A.D. (2006). *Wikinomics: How Mass Collaboration Changes Everything*, New York: Portfolio Penguin Group, pp. 239–264.

4 Kelly, L.K. (Heidrick and Struggles) (2007). Mapping global talent. *Essays and Insights,,* Economist Intelligence Unit, London: *The Economist.*

5 There are many references on this subject—although there has been far less attention to it during the 2007–2010 global recession. Even so, many employers have expressed difficulties in finding employees with the high level of skills they need, even during a period of high unemployment. Here are only a few of the references to labor shortages: *2013 Talent Shortage Survey, Research Results*, Manpowergroup (www.manpowergroup.com); Spears, V.P. (2012). Global talent shortage worries multinationals more than revolution or recession. *Employee Benefit Plan Review*, 67(2), 27; Boardman, M. (1999). Worker "dearth" in the twenty-first century, *HR Magazine*, June, 304; Golzen, G. (1998). Skill shortages around the globe. *HR World*, November–December, 41–53; Herman, R., Olivo, T., and Gioia, J. (2003). *Impending Crisis: Too Many Jobs, Too Few People*, Winchester, VA: Oakhill Press; Johnston, W.B. (1991). Global work force 2000: The new world labor market. *Harvard Business Review*, March–April, 115–127; Leonard, S. (2000). The labor shortage, *Workplace Visions*, 4, 1–7; Patel, D. (2001). HR trends and analysis: The effect of changing demographics and globalization on HR. *Global HR*, July–August, 9–10.

6 Female labor force participation rates as % of active (employed plus unemployed) population between the ages of 15 and 60. Rates published by OECD, 2013. www.oecd.com, Accessed 15 Sept. 15, 2013.

7 Estimates from data provided by the World Bank, *World Development Indicators*. Available at www.worldbank.com/world-development-indicators. Accessed Oct. 13, 2014.

8 Adapted from, Amid shortage of workers, Dutch find reward in hiring the retired (2000). *San Diego Union-Tribune*, April 23, p. A–29.

9 Hall, L. (2001). Talent mapped out, *Global HR*, April, 30, quoting Alan Tsang, Managing Director for Asia of the search and selection firm Norman Broadbent.

10 Friedman, T.L. (2005). *The World Is Flat*, New York: Farrar, Straus and Giroux.

11 Sullivan, J. (2002). Plan of action, *Global HR*, October, 22.

12 See, for example, Caligiuri, P., Lepak, D., and Bonache, J. (2010). *Global Dimensions of Human Resources Management: Managing the Global Workforce*, New York: Wiley; and Dickman, M. and Baruch, Y. (2011). *Global Careers*, London/New York: Routledge.

13 Perlmutter, H.V. and Heenan, D.A. (1986). Cooperate to compete globally. *Harvard Business Review*, March/April, 135–152.

14 Harzing, A.-W. (2004). Composing an international staff, in Harzing, A.-W. and Van Ruysseveldt, J. (eds.), *International Human Resource Management*, 2nd ed., Thousand Oaks, CA/London: Sage Publications, pp. 251–282.

15 See, for example, Harzing (2004).; Caliguiri, Lepak, and Bonache 2010; Fernandez, F. (2005). *Globalization and Human Resource Management*, New York: HNB Publishing; Gross, A. and McDonald, R. (1998). Vast shortages in talent keep employers searching. *International HR Update*, July, 6; Melton, W.R. (2005). *The New American Expat*, Yarmouth, ME: Intercultural Press; Schell, M.S. and Solomon, C.M.

(1997). *Capitalizing on the Global Workforce*, Chicago: Irwin; Stroh, L. K., Black, J. S., Mendenhall, M. E., and Gregersen, H. B. (2005). *International Assignments: An Integration of Strategy, Research, and Practice*, Mahwah, NJ/London: Lawrence Erlbaum Associates; Vance, C. M. and Paik, Y. (2010). *Managing a Global Workforce*, 2nd ed., Armonk, NY/London: M. E. Sharpe. The terms PCN, TCN and HCN were first introduced into the IHRM literature by Patrick Morgan, at that time (1986) director of international HR at Bechtel: Morgan, P. (1986). International human resource management: Fact or Fiction? *Personnel Administrator*, 31 (9), 43–47.

16 See, for example, Edström, A. and Galbraith, J. R. (1977). Transfer of managers as a coordination and control strategy in multinational organizations. *Administrative Science Quarterly*, 22 (June), 248–263; Harzing, A.-W. (2001a). Of bears, bumble-bees, and spiders: The role of expatriates in controlling foreign subsidiaries. *Journal of World Business*, 36 (4), 366–379; Hays, R. (1974). Expatriate selection: Insuring success and avoiding failure. *Journal of International Business Studies*, 5 (1), 25–37; Roberts, K., Kossek, E. E. and Ozeki, C. (1998). Managing the global work force: Challenges and strategies, *Academy of Management Executive*, 12 (4), 6–16; Tahvanainen, M. (1998). *Expatriate Performance Management*, Helsinki: Helsinki School of Economics Press; and Tung, R. L. (1991). Selection and training of personnel for overseas assignments. *Columbia Journal of World Business*, 16 (1), 68–78.

17 Carpenter, M. A., Sanders, W. G. and Gregersen, H. B. (2001). Bundling human capital with organizational context: The impact of international assignment experience on multinational firm performance and CEO pay. *Academy of Management Journal*, 44 (3), 493–511; Harzing, A.-W. (2001a); Harzing, A.-W. (2001b). Who's in charge? An empirical study of executive staffing practices in foreign subsidiaries. *Human Resource Management*, 40 (2), 139–158; Stahl, G. T., Miller, E. L. and Tung, R. L. (2002). Toward the boundaryless career: A closer look at the expatriate career concept and the perceived implications of an international assignment. *Journal of World Business*, 37 (3), 216–227; and Tung, R. L. (1998). American expatriates abroad: From neophytes to cosmopolitans. *Journal of World Business*, 33 (2), 125–144.

18 Adler, N. J. with Gundersen, A. (2008). *International Dimensions of Organizational Behavior*, 5th ed., Mason, OH: Thomson/South-Western; Bachler, C. (1996). Global inpats: Don't let them surprise you. *Personnel Journal*, June, 54–56; Forster, N. (2000). The myth of the international manager, *International Journal of Human Resource Management*, 11, 126; Groh, K. and Allen, M. (1998). Global staffing: Are expatriates the only answer? Special report on expatriate management. *HR Focus*, March, 75–78; Minehan, M. (1996). Skills shortage in Asia, *HR Magazine*, 41, 152; Tung, R. (1987). Expatriate assignments: Enhancing success and minimizing failure, *Academy of Management Executive*, 1 (2), 117–126.

19 Black, J. S., Morrison, A. J. and Gregersen, H. B. (1999). *Global Explorers: The Next Generation of Leaders*, New York/London: Routledge; Fernandez, F. (2005). *Globalization and Human Resource Management*, New York: HNB Publishing; Ferraro, G. (2002). *Global Brains: Knowledge and Competencies for the Twenty-first Century*, Charlotte, NC: Intercultural Associates; Hodge, S. (2000). *Global Smarts: The Art of Communicating and Deal-making Anywhere in the World*, New York: Wiley; Keys, J. B. and Fulmer, R. M. (eds.) (1998). *Executive Development and Organizational Learning for Global Business*, New York/London: International Business Press; McCall, M. W., Jr. and Hollenbeck, G. P. (2002). *Developing Global Executives: The Lessons of International Experience*, Boston, MA: Harvard Business School Press; Moran, R. T., Harris, P. R. and Moran, S. V. (2007). *Managing Cultural Differences*, 7th ed., Burlington, MA/Oxford: Butterworth-Heinemann; Rosen, R., Digh, P., Singer, M. and Phillips, C. (2000). *Global Literacies: Lessons on Business Leadership and National Cultures*, New York: Simon & Schuster; Scherer, C. W. (2000). *The Internationalists: Business Strategies for Globalization*, Wilsonville, OR: Book Partners; Stroh et al. (2005); Vance, C. and Paik, Y. (2011), *Managing a Global Workforce*, 2nd ed., Armonk, NY/London: M. E. Sharpe.

20 This is just a summary. If the reader would like more information, more complete descriptions, and references to support these different types of international employees, please contact the lead author, Dr. Dennis Briscoe, at dbriscoe@sandiego.edu.

21 See, for example, Adler, N. and Ghadar, F. (1990). Strategic human resource management: A global perspective, in Pieper, R. (ed.), *Human Resource Management: An International Comparison*, Berlin: de

Gruyter, pp. 235–260; Black, J.S., Gregersen, H.B. and Mendenhall, M.E. (1992); Stroh, L.K., Black, J.S., Mendenhall, M.E., and Gregersen, H.B. (2005). *International Assignments: An Integration of Strategy, Research, & Practice*, Mahwah, NJ/London: Lawrence Erlbaum Associates; Evans, P., Pucik, V., and Björkman, I. (2011). *The Global Challenge: International Human Resource Management*, 2nd ed., New York: McGrawHill/Irwin; Luthans, F., Marsnik, P.A., and Luthans, K.W. (1997). A contingency matrix approach to IHRM, *Human Resource Management*, 36(2), 83–199; and Shenkar, O. (1995). Contingency factors in HRM in foreign affiliates, in Shenkar, O. (ed.), *Global Perspectives of Human Resource Management*, Englewood Cliffs, NJ: Prentice Hall, pp. 197–209.

22 Borkowski, S.C. (1999). International managerial performance evaluation: A five country comparison. *Journal of International Business Studies*, 30(3), 533–555; Briscoe, D.R. (1997). Assessment centers: Cross-cultural and cross-national issues, in Riggio, R.E. and Mayes, B.T. (eds.), Assessment centers: Research and applications [Special Issue], *Journal of Social Behavior and Personality*, 12(5), 261–270; Caligiuri, P.M. (1997). Assessing expatriate success: Beyond just "being there." *New Approaches to Employee Management*, vol. 4, 117–140; Gregersen, H.B., Hite, J.M., and Black, J.S. (1996). Expatriate performance appraisal in U.S. multinational firms, *Journal of International Business Studies*, 27(4), 711–738; Milliman, J., Nason, S., Gallagher, E., Huo, P., Von Glinow, M.A., and Lowe, K.B. (1998). The impact of national culture on human resource management practices: The case of performance appraisal. *Advances in International Comparative Management*, 12, 157–183; and Oddou, G., and Mendenhall, M. (2000). Expatriate performance appraisal: Problems and solutions, in Mendenhall, M. and Oddou, G. (eds.), *Readings and Cases in International Human Resource Management*, 3rd ed., South Western, pp. 213–223.

23 See, for example, DeFrank, R.S., Konopaske, R., and Ivancevich, J.M. (2000). Executive travel stress: Perils of the road warrior. *Academy of Management Executive*, 14(2), 58–71; and Harris, H. (2000). Alternative forms of international working, *Worldlink*, 10(4), 2–3.

24 This introduction to the rest of this section of the text is partially based on Boudreau, J.W. (2010). *IBM's Global Talent Management Strategy: The Vision of the Globally Integrated Enterprise*, Alexandria, VA: Society for Human Resource Management; CARTUS and National Foreign Trade Council (2010). *Navigating a Challenging Landscape*, Global Mobility Policy and Practice Survey, New York: Authors; Deloitte Development LLC (2010). *Smarter Moves: Executing and Integrating Global Mobility and Talent Programs*, New York: Deloitte Touche Tohmatsu; and Gerdes, D.R. and Kessler, J.H. (eds.) (2010). Mobilizing the work force globally—best practices to maintain compliance and manage staffing needs, in Baker & McKenzie, *The Global Employer*, XV (2). May issue.

Chapter 9

International Recruitment, International Selection, and Repatriation

People who work at BP as an expat often describe their position overseas as one of the most fulfilling and valuable experiences they've ever had.

BP Corporation[1]

Learning Objectives

This chapter will enable the reader to:

- Describe the broad issues involved in staffing subsidiaries with international assignees or expatriates.
- Describe the various issues involved in recruiting international assignees or expatriates.
- Describe the general process of selection of international assignees (IAs) for international assignments and the issue of failure in an IA assignment and reasons for it.
- Describe the characteristics of successful IA selection programs and exemplary practices.
- Explain the essential nature of repatriation.

The previous chapter introduced the complex responsibilities of international workforce planning and staffing for firms that operate in a multinational environment. In addition to normal domestic hiring responsibilities—which in today's global economy often involve the recruitment and selection of employees from numerous nationalities and cultures—the international staffing manager takes on a number of new responsibilities, including recruiting and staffing the traditional types of employees utilized by international businesses (e.g., PCNs, HCNs, and TCNs). This chapter focuses primarily on the issue of *recruiting, selecting*, and *repatriating* traditional PCNs, or expatriates, although some of the chapter discusses the selection of the other traditional types of international employees (HCNs and TCNs) as well.

- *Recruiting* involves searching for and attracting qualified applicants to create a pool of candidates for screening for possible hiring.
- *Selecting* focuses on gathering and analyzing information about applicants in order to select the most suitable person or persons for the job.
- *Repatriating* refers to the process of bringing international assignees (IAs) and their families back "home" from their foreign assignments.

STAFFING WITH EXPATRIATES OR INTERNATIONAL ASSIGNEES

Typical employment practices for managerial, marketing, and technical operations positions in foreign subsidiaries, particularly in the early stages of "going international," place heavy emphasis on the use of expatriates.[2] There are many reasons that MNEs transfer personnel from one country to another. But the key reasons still appear to be for their technical or functional expertise, for control, and to start new operations.[3] In addition, MNEs are increasingly recognizing the importance of international experience for higher-level managerial positions, making development through an international assignment an increasingly prominent focus, as well (although, as will be shown later in this chapter, the rhetoric may be stronger than the reality).[4]

Historically, the term "expatriate," as used by companies, referred to employees who were relocated from the parent company or headquarters to foreign subsidiaries or "overseas" operations. Today, the term "international assignee" is more generally used to describe any employee who is relocated from one country to another for a period of more than one year, while staying in the employment of the same firm. Both terms are used throughout this text.

Exhibit 9.1 illustrates the four common options used by MNEs to staff their foreign operations. The first option in Exhibit 9.1—*secondment,* while remaining an employee of the parent firm—is the most commonly used practice to relocate expatriates—either from headquarters out to subsidiaries or from subsidiaries to headquarters or to other subsidiaries. The other options—*transfer of employment, global employment company*, and *dual employment*—are used less frequently.

Even though global enterprises are using multiple ways and multiple types of employees to staff their international businesses, there is still major interest in and use of traditional international assignees (option 1 in Exhibit 9.1). Many large multinationals that have been international for a long time, such as Unilever, the large Anglo-Dutch consumer products firm, Royal Dutch Shell, an Anglo-Dutch oil company, and Ford Motor Company, move managers from subsidiary to subsidiary and country to country (as well as from HQs out to subsidiaries) to help build global relationships and to develop a common corporate identity

EXHIBIT 9.1: Employment Options for International Transfers

Who will be the employer? The typical options involve one of these four:

1 *Secondment*—the employee remains employed by the home country employer (normally headquarters but sometimes a subsidiary) and is "loaned" or seconded to work for an entity (normally a subsidiary or sometimes headquarters) in the host country. This is the typical expatriate or inpatriate.
2 *Transfer of Employment*—the employee is terminated by the home country employer and is rehired by a new employer in the host country.
3 *Global Employment Company*—the employee is terminated by the home country employer and transferred to the employment of a global employment company (GEC). The GEC in turn seconds the employee to work for an entity in a host country. Sometimes the GEC is owned by the home country employer and services all the subsidiaries of the parent firm.
4 *Dual Employment*—the employee maintains more than one employment relationship simultaneously during the course of the assignment (that is, works for two or more employers with split payroll).

Source: Baker & McKenzie (2014). *The Global Employer: Focus on Global Immigration and Mobility*, Baker & McKenzie International, a Swiss Verein with member law firms around the world.

and business culture among their management ranks, as well as to ensure they have the necessary talent in the right location at the right time.

Increasing use of international assignees. In the typical MNE of any size, there are divergent forces operating relative to the use of international assignees:

■ Larger MNEs use a greater number and percentage of local hires, but they also need international experience in their management team. So to develop this experience, they are increasingly likely to move managers from the parent company or regional HQs, as well as their foreign managers, to assignments in countries other than their countries of origin.
■ Firms that are newly developing their international businesses, of which there are a constantly increasing number, typically rely heavily on international assignees from the home office for the development of that business, both because they trust their existing managers more than unknown foreign managers and because they lack experience in working with foreign operations and it seems easier to establish their new foreign businesses with their existing managers.

- Sometimes there is simply a shortage of qualified skills in local nationals, although, with global communications and hundreds of thousands—if not millions—of students from the developing world getting higher education in developed countries and many developing or emerging economies providing world-class education to millions of their own citizens, this is rapidly becoming less of a concern. A more pressing concern is the lack of supervisory and managerial skills in these emerging markets.

Several studies show that the number of international assignees is increasing, and the prediction[5] is that the absolute numbers will continue to grow as global business opportunities are expanding, especially in large markets like China and India.

It is important to keep in mind that the number of international assignees can vary with the stages of international operations. The use of international assignees (especially from HQs) is high during the initial stages of foreign operations in order to implement operational and office start-up—and all that is involved with this in a new country, technology transfer—including production and management technologies, and product-knowledge transfer. The number of international assignees will then decline as the firm's local managers and technical and functional staff assimilate this knowledge. The number may later expand, again, as local operations become increasingly integrated into a global operational framework. In addition, as enterprises become more global, they develop a need for international managers with greater international experience as they develop their worldwide competitive advantages. However, at this stage, these global managers may well come from any country, not necessarily, or even primarily, from the country of the parent company.

Thus, the global movement of employees is essential to multinational organizations doing business in different countries. As stated by Baker & McKenzie, the world's largest global employment law firm: "Getting the right people to the right places at the right time with proper support in a lawful manner is critical to the success of global business."[6]

THE INTERNATIONAL RECRUITMENT FUNCTION

Recruitment is defined as the process that involves searching for and attracting qualified applicants to create an applicant pool for open positions. Recruitment is highly dependent on the workforce planning process discussed in the previous chapter. Recruiting begins after an organization's immediate and long-term labor needs are defined. For example, several questions[7] such as the following need to be addressed before the recruiting process can start:

- How many positions does the organization need to fill? Are these needs short term (less than a year) or long term (greater than a year)?
- Does the organization need applicants for short-term assignments or long-term assignments?
- What compensation strategy does the organization want to pursue? That is, does the organization intend to offer compensation packages that are below market average, at market average, or above market average?

- Does the organization seek applicants who differ from the company's current employees? How will this affect the recruiting process?
- What type of competencies does the organization seek in new applicants?

Once the number, types, and quality of employees being sought are specified, then organizations need to determine which labor markets—which are potentially widely geographically dispersed—are most likely to provide the employees desired. This process of finding candidates is referred to as *sourcing*, and there are two broad recruiting sources available to organizations: *internal recruiting sources* and *external recruiting sources*.

Internal recruiting sources focus on global candidates from within the organization and include:[8]

- *Global talent management inventories:* Electronic records of work-related information for employees from throughout the organization including their knowledge, skills and abilities, education, past performance, interests, etc.
- Attendees from *in-house global leadership programs:* Educational programs designed to provide global leadership competencies to high potential employees.
- *Former/current expatriates:* Individuals who have been on foreign assignments or are currently on an assignment.
- *Nominations:* Recommendations from current or potential supervisors and/or former or current expatriates.
- *Internal job posting/intranet:* Job advertisement that can only be viewed by current employees, usually posted on the company's intranet system. It is expected that employees with an interest in an international assignment will look for these postings and apply when they see a job for which they have an interest.
- *International succession planning programs:* Internal programs designed to prepare high potential employees for overseas positions such as "look-see visits" or "short-term developmental" foreign assignments.

Internal recruiting sources are often favored because they reduce labor costs, are valued by employers and employees, and can enhance the reputation of the company as an employer of choice. However, internal recruiting sources can also limit the size and to some extent the quality of the applicant pool, and may encourage infighting and inbreeding.

External recruiting sources locate candidates from outside the organization and include:[9]

- *Employee referrals:* Recommendations from current employees or expatriates.
- *Job fairs:* Organized events where employers and potential applicants can meet each other.
- *Company Internet sites:* Companies' dedicated career websites that allow potential applicants to learn about employment opportunities within the organization. Each country/region/subsidiary within the firm may have its own dedicated career website.
- *Executive search firms:* Recruiting firms that specialize in particular types of individuals, jobs, or industries. Particularly helpful here are search firms with global networks and contacts.

- *Professional associations or networks:* Members of professional associations and networks are potential applicants (e.g., LinkedIn) or may provide a platform or network for connection to possible international assignments.
- *Competing firms:* Current expatriates or former expatriates from competitor firms are potential applicants. Recruiting existing employees from other firms is referred to as *employee raiding,* which can be unethical or illegal in certain environments or countries.
- Generic *global leadership programs* for the public (offered by consulting firms or training companies) or offered in universities and colleges: Most of these programs typically prepare interested managers or senior-level students for global leadership positions.

Managers should always use multiple recruiting sources so as to increase diversity and to generate a larger pool of applicants.

Although all of the above recruiting sources may be used to find candidates for foreign assignments (PCNs or TCNs) or HCNs for local hires, attracting candidates to work internationally raises an important challenge for MNEs[10]—how to find individuals interested in a specific international assignment as well as those interested in permanent international careers.[11] MNEs need to use recruiting sources that find candidates with high *receptivity to international careers,*[12] which refers to an individual's attitude toward international careers and is one of the most frequently studied factors in assessing why people undertake careers in international work.[13]

Several factors influence an individual's receptivity to an international career or willingness to accept an international assignment (these factors are described in more detail in the selection section later in the chapter):[14]

- job suitability/technical ability;
- cultural adaptability;
- personality characteristics;
- desire for foreign assignment;
- the maturity of the candidate;
- ability to handle foreign language(s);
- possession of a favorable outlook on the international assignment.

In addition to the above factors, there are other factors that can influence receptivity to international careers:

- prior international experience;
- age;
- gender;
- family status;
- marital status;
- education;
- destination country;
- opportunities for career support;
- company culture;

■ career and repatriation planning;
■ length of the foreign assignment;
■ overseas health care plan;
■ income tax equalization policy;
■ host country housing assistance;
■ spouse job assistance;
■ spouse's willingness to travel overseas;
■ children's education allowance.

Another challenge for MNEs, especially if recruiting candidates from an external labor market, is to develop an *employer reputation*[15] that attracts candidates to the organization. Employer reputation—sometimes referred to as employer brand—refers to the evaluation by potential candidates of an organization as a desirable place of work and to seek international experience. An organization's employer reputation is strongly based on the signals or messages the organization sends to individuals outside the organization. These signals can come through the media (e.g., newspapers and business magazines), former employees, recruiting advertisements, customer reactions to company products and services, and company websites, and can include information about potential compensation, benefits, prestige, and career advancement. For potential candidates, employer reputation is critical since most candidates' understanding of an organization is limited to the employer's reputation in the marketplace rather than the organization's actual HR policies and practices.[16]

The final challenge for MNEs is to manage talent shortages that occur when employers cannot find workers with the needed competencies.[17] Talent shortages occur in countries during times of economic boom, as well as in times of economic uncertainty.[18] This is more serious in the service sector, especially when economic conditions improve.[19]

In the context of talent shortages, the challenge for MNEs to develop strategies to attract high performers and specialists. Location (where to find talent) becomes a critical issue.

The following IHRM in Action illustrates this point:

IHRM in Action 9.1: Locating Near the Talent with a Global Workforce

Today, it is still important to be located near your customers. But in the war for talent, it may be equally as important to be located in the best place to attract the high performers and specialists your business needs. Over the last few years, specific locations have arisen as preferred places to live and work. High talent employees can establish themselves in locales that enable them to create the life-work balance that meets their current needs.

So, where are such places?

As it turns out, people don't look so much at countries as they do at cities, and often it is small cities that provide the lifestyles they are looking for. For example, it includes Groningen, a small, obscure town in the north of the Netherlands, and Eindhoven, another small town—but major business location—in the Netherlands. Of course, the traditional, popular big cities continue to have appeal, but there are also new areas that are attracting the talent that today's MNEs need.

In Europe, this would include an area marked on a map by a gentle curve drawn from Barcelona, across southern France, northern Italy, Switzerland, and southern Germany, an area that already boasts the highest per capita income level in the world. The big cities of interest in Europe still include Amsterdam, Brussels, London, Paris, Nice, Berlin, Milan, Dublin, and Zurich. In Asia, these cities would include Sydney and Brisbane, Auckland, Singapore, Kuala Lumpur, Tokyo, Seoul, and Shanghai. If a global firm cannot find talent where its customers want them to locate, then maybe it needs to figure out where the talent is and go there.

THE INTERNATIONAL SELECTION FUNCTION

Selection refers to the process of gathering and analyzing information about applicants in order to select the most suitable person or persons for the job. The *selection decision* for international assignees is critically important. Errors in selection can have major negative impact on the success of overseas operations as well as on the careers of relocated managers.

Selection Decisions

A good selection decision will identify, and/or most likely predict, IAs who are likely to perform well on the assignment (in a different culture) and to remain in their foreign assignments until the end of their contracts.[20] In addition, a good selection decision will predict IA who are most likely to stay committed to their organizations while on the assignment and after returning from the assignment.[21]

Successful expatriate experience

From the perspective of HQs, an important consideration in making good selection decisions is to fully understand the process of a "successful expatriate experience" (see Figure 9.1).

As with all HRM activities, a thorough job analysis of the assignment (including an examination of the foreign work environment and culture) is necessary in order to make appropriate international assignment selections. Thus, the first step in understanding the process of a "successful expatriate experience" is to fully analyze the requirements in both technical and cultural terms of the jobs to which expatriates will be assigned (see Part A in Figure 9.1) as well as of the country of assignment (see Part B in Figure 9.1).[22] Based

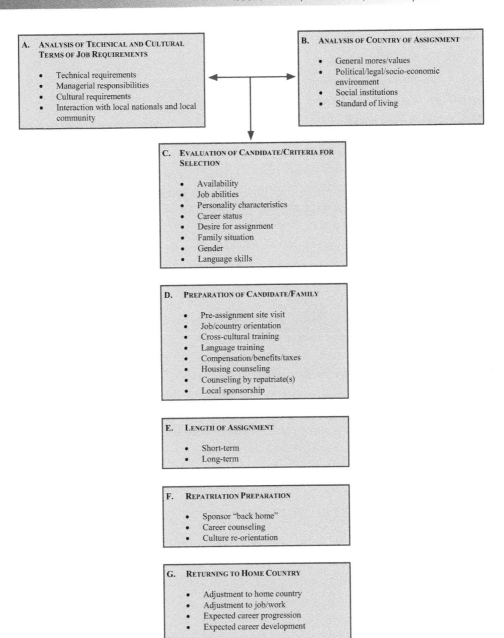

FIGURE 9.1 Successful Expatriate Experience

Source: Adapted from Briscoe, D.R. and Gazda, G.M. (1989). The successful expatriate, *Proceedings: Managing in Global Economy*, third biannual international conference, Eastern Academy of Management, Hong Kong, November.

on this information, the candidate is evaluated for his/her ability to successfully live and work overseas (Part C in Figure 9.1). If the candidate is selected, then he/she is prepared for the overseas assignment (Part D in Figure 9.1), and supported during the assignment depending on the length of the assignment (Part E in Figure 9.1). Then the IA is prepared to repatriate to the home country (Part F in Figure 9.1), and eventually returns to the home country (Part G in Figure 9.1).

Shortage of Potential IAs

Increasingly the problem of selection of international assignees involves finding employees with the necessary skills to function successfully in the new "global" environment and convincing them to take on the assignment. Because of dual career families, disruption of employees' lives, employee work-life balance concerns, and uncertainty about the impact of a foreign assignment on their careers, employees are becoming increasingly reluctant to take on international assignments.[23]

Competency Profile

The competency profile of an assignee is an important aspect of the selection decision-making process. Exhibit 9.2 lists the skills that are being cited as important for the twenty-first-century expatriate manager.[24] In the words of two MNE executives:[25]

"The top 21st-century manager should have multienvironment, multicountry, multifunctional, multicompany, multi-industry experience," according to Ed Dunn, corporate vice president of Whirlpool Corp. Michael Angus, chairman of Unilever PLC, adds, "Most people who rise toward the top of our business will have worked in at least two countries, probably three. They will probably speak another language and they most certainly will have worked in different product areas."

EXHIBIT 9.2: The 21st-century Expatriate Manager Profile

Core skills	Managerial implications
Multidimensional perspective	Extensive multi-product, multi-industry, multifunctional, multicompany, multicountry, and multienvironment experience.
Proficiency in line management	Track record in successfully operating overseas strategic business units and/or a series of major overseas projects.
Prudent decision-making skills	Competence and proven track record in making the right strategic decisions.
Resourcefulness	Skillful in getting him/herself known and accepted in the host country's political hierarchy.
Cultural adaptability	Quick and easy adaptability into the foreign culture—individual with as much cultural mix, diversity, and experience as possible.

Core skills	Managerial implications
Cultural sensitivity	Effective people skills in dealing with variety of cultures, races, nationalities, genders, religions. Sensitive to cultural difference.
Ability as a team builder	Adept in bringing a culturally diverse working group together to accomplish the major global mission and objectives of the enterprise.
Physical fitness and mental maturity	Endurance for the rigorous demands of overseas assignments.
Curiosity and learning	Constant interest in learning about all aspects of international cultures, foreign countries, and global business.

Augmented skills	Managerial implications
Computer literacy	Comfortable exchanging strategic information electronically.
Prudent negotiating skills	Proven track record in conducting successful strategic business negotiations in multicultural/multinational environments.
Ability as a change agent	Proven track record in successfully initiating and implementing strategic and global organizational changes.
Visionary skills	Quick to recognize and respond to strategic business opportunities and potential political and economic upheavals in the host country.
Effective delegatory skills	Proven track record in participative management style and ability to delegate in cross-cultural environments.
International business skills	Proven track record in conducting business in the global environment.

Sources: Black, J.S. (2006). The mindset of global leaders: Inquisitiveness and duality, in Mobley, W.H. and Weldon, E. (eds.), *Advances in Global Leadership*, vol. 4, pp. 181–200; Black, J.S., Morrison, A. and Gregersen, H. (1999). *Global Explorers: The Next Generation of Leaders*, New York: Routledge; Howard, C.G. (1992). Profile of the 21st-century expatriate manager, *HR Magazine*, June, 96; Marquardt, M.J. and Berger, N.O. (2000). *Global Leaders for the 21st Century*, New York: State University of New York Press; and Rosen, R., Digh, P., Singer, M. and Philips, C. (2000). *Global Literacies: Lessons on Business Leadership and National Cultures*, New York: Simon and Schuster.

Placing high importance on the alignment of selection decisions with corporate strategy and goals is also becoming more common.[26] Successful global firms link their global staffing decisions to their global business goals. The more important the international strategy and the more complex the structure developed to implement that strategy, the more critical are the international staffing decisions.

Selection decisions also need to consider the receiving (host country) managers and location. Successful international assignments make demands not only on the IA but also on both the receiving manager and company as well as the sending manager and company.[27] Often the sending manager has little (or no) international experience and, therefore, does not have a clear idea of what it takes to handle a foreign assignment—and may also downplay the importance of the difficulties of the foreign assignment. And receiving managers may have the same problems—they have not worked at headquarters or elsewhere outside their home countries and they do not know what strengths it takes for a successful expatriate assignment. Thus, the sending company can have a negative impact on the success of the IA by relying on domestic experience for guidance on how to manage and evaluate the IA and not understanding the pressures of the foreign environment. And the receiving firm may compound the problems by not understanding the perspective of the parent company.

From the viewpoint of persons being considered for international assignments, studies suggest that two specific factors—in addition to a strong personal interest in getting a foreign experience, usually based on having previously enjoyed living overseas—are primary in their decisions to take on such an assignment: increased pay and perceived improved career opportunities. This suggests the importance of paying close attention to the following factors when making selections for international assignments.

Criteria for Selection

The specific criteria an MNE uses to select its IAs play a major role in determining their future successes or failures in their international assignments. First this section takes a look at a number of criteria that are used by various global firms to select their IAs. Then the section examines the consequences of making mistakes in either choosing IAs or in preparing and supporting them in their assignments or in helping them make a successful return to home at the end of their international assignments. The most important selection criteria for international assignments include job suitability/technical ability, cultural adaptability, and desire for international assignment.

- *Job suitability/technical ability*. Most firms primarily base their choices for international assignments on candidates' technical expertise.[28] That is, the primary focus is on their ability to perform the target job requirements. Experience suggests, however, that all the other topics discussed in this text are at least as important as the individual's job competencies. Nevertheless, at least in smaller and medium-sized firms (and, regrettably, still too often in larger firms), the parent-company supervisor usually makes the choice of individual to be sent on an international assignment and that choice is usually based on the individual's perceived ability to fill a perceived (and usually immediate) functional or technical need in the foreign operation.
- *Cultural adaptability*. Experience in MNEs suggests that cultural adaptability is at least as important to the successful completion of an overseas assignment as is the

individual's technical ability.[29] Expatriates must be able to adjust to their new and often alien environments while effectively delivering their technical and managerial expertise. They must graciously accept their new cultures but not at the expense of not getting their jobs done. While technical expertise is usually important (and the primary reason most firms send a particular expatriate to a foreign assignment), the principal difficulty faced by most expatriates lies in the inabilities of the managers and their families to adapt to the foreign cultures. Maybe not surprisingly, American firms tend to be more likely to place the most emphasis on the individual's work experience and expertise than is the case for many MNEs from other countries, and as a consequence tend to experience more difficulties with expatriate adjustment.

One of the most important components of cultural adaptability is cross-cultural adjustment,[30] which refers to the extent to which individuals are psychologically comfortable living in a new culture and is conceptualized as an individual's reactions to and feelings about working in the host country (work adjustment), about interacting with host country nationals (interaction adjustment), and about the general non-work environment in the host country (general adjustment).[31]

■ ***Personality characteristics***.[32] Researchers have found that successful and well-adjusted international assignees tend to share certain personality traits. Certain personality characteristics enable international assignees to be open and receptive to learning the norms of new cultures, to initiate contact with host nationals, to gather cultural information, and to handle the higher amounts of stress associated with the ambiguity of their new environments. The Big Five personality traits[33] have been related to cross-cultural adjustment, work performance, and IAs' desires to terminate their assignments.[34] The Big Five personality traits include:

1 Extroversion (extent to which an individual is sociable, active, talkative, fun loving, and affectionate)[35]
2 Agreeableness (extent to which someone is cooperative, sociable, forgiving, tolerant, and argumentative)[36]
3 Conscientiousness (the degree to which an individual is purposeful, hardworking, organized, dependable, and self-disciplined)[37]
4 Emotional stability (describes individuals in terms of anxiety, calmness, self-confidence, worry, insecurity, and nervousness)[38]
5 Openness to experience (extent to which an individual is original, intellectual, curious, creative, imaginative, and conventional)[39]

■ One of the most important personality characteristics, with respect to predicting IA success is openness to experience.[40] IAs high on openness to experience are likely to:[41]

❏ correctly assess the social environment in the new culture;
❏ accurately perceive and interpret the new culture;
❏ have fewer rigid views of right and wrong, and what is appropriate and inappropriate in the new culture; and
❏ accept the values, norms, and accepted behaviors in the new culture.

■ ***Desire for foreign assignment (candidate and family)***. Since adaptation to the foreign culture is so important to an IA's performance, his or her desire for that foreign assignment is critical to their willingness to make the necessary efforts to adjust. This needs to be assessed in the early stages of candidate review.

In addition to the above criteria, selections for international transfer are also most successful when the following factors are also evaluated:[42]

■ The maturity of the candidate (i.e., being a self-starter, able to make independent decisions, having emotional stability, sensitive to others who are different, and having a well-rounded knowledge of on- and off-the-job subjects to facilitate discussion with foreign colleagues and contacts who are often quite knowledgeable and interested in such topics).
■ Ability to handle foreign language(s). Local language ability has shown to be positively related to international assignee success.[43]
■ Possession of a favorable outlook on the international assignment and locale by the expatriate and his or her family (i.e., s/he wants to go overseas).
■ And possession of appropriate personal characteristics, such as excellent health, this being an appropriate time in the individual's career and family life, individual resourcefulness, adaptability, and desire to learn and experience new things and new people; all are related to increasing the likelihood that a foreign assignment will be successful.

Testing for Successful IAs

Several companies and consultants have compiled profiles of successful IAs and, from these, developed IA selection tests.[44] These profiles are then used to screen potential IA candidates on the generally valid assumption that candidates with similar profiles are more likely to do well in international assignments. These profiles usually include factors such as experience, education, personal interests and activities, signs of flexibility, family situation, and desire for such assignment. Some of the tools are basically self-assessment tools for candidates for international assignments and their partners, to allow them and their employers to assess their readiness for such an assignment. And some of the tools provide information to help coach candidates on any necessary preparation they need for a successful assignment.

When an organization first begins to develop international business, it normally doesn't have the luxury of developing its own international managers in-house. And it may not have employees who already have the necessary knowledge and experience or cultural and language competencies. It will need to recruit such people from the outside or acquire the expertise from consulting firms. Of course, many firms pursue international opportunities with inexperienced managers and salespeople, but this inevitably leads to months, and often years, of frustration while these managers "learn the [international] business." Such expertise can also sometimes be recruited from the overseas countries themselves. And, over the long term, future foreign managers can often be recruited from local universities of either the country of the parent firm or the countries in which the firm is operating.

Selection Methods

Different organizations rely on differing procedures in their selection of individuals for international assignments. They rely on varying criteria, as summarized above. And they use one or more of the following in application of those criteria. This is just a short summary of selection methods and illustrates that methods used in selection for international assignments are probably not much different from the methods used in domestic staffing decisions. As with everything international, however, the differences lie in the impact of culture in how these procedures are applied and in the focus in each procedure.

- *Interviews (IA and spouse/partner)* may be best done with a representative of the home country (representing the technical requirements of the position), a represent-ative of the host country (possibly the host manager), and an interculturalist, i.e., someone with the ability to assess the candidate's and family's ability to adjust to the foreign culture.
- *Formal assessment*. There are a number of formal assessment instruments designed by industrial psychologists that primarily evaluate a candidate's personal traits and compe-tencies that have been found to be important to successful foreign culture adjustment, such as adaptability, flexibility, openness to new experiences, and good interpersonal skills.[45] Critical here is whether such instruments are reliable and valid for predicting expatriate success. IHR or other managers who seek to use such instruments need to make sure they get evidence of their reliability and validity from any consultant or manager that is requesting their use.
- *Committee decision*. In many large MNEs, the process of selecting individuals for inter-national assignments is a committee decision, a committee made up of someone from corporate HR, home country HR, host country manager, director of development, and the individual's functional manager with a decision based on the individual's prefer-ences, assessment of past performance and future potential, needs of the foreign assign-ment, and developmental needs of the individual candidate.
- *Career planning*. The choice of IA may be made as one step in the individual's career and succession plan with the MNE.
- *Self-selection*. Many MNEs use some combination of the above procedures but rely, in the end, on self-selection by the candidate (after being accepted through the above "screens"). In particular, the MNE is interested in candidates taking the time (and usu-ally using some type of formal self-assessment instrument) to look at the issues involved with relocation to a foreign country and culture and assessing whether they think they are ready or have the necessary skills, experience, or attitudes to be successful in the overseas assignment.[46] Such self-assessment may result in the individual realizing they

aren't ready now for such a move, but that they would like to take such an assignment at some later time in their career. So, rather than relocating now, they begin a process to gain the skills and experiences necessary to be chosen for such an assignment at a later date. This self-assessment process then is part of a larger career planning process. Candidates may also self-opt out when they realize the importance of their family members (and their lack of desire to relocate to another country) in making the international assignment successful.

- ■ *Internal job posting and individual bid*, usually then combined with interviews and/or other assessment actions.
- ■ *Recommendations* from senior executives or line managers with overseas human resource needs.
- ■ *Assessment centers*. A few organizations use assessment centers as a tool for evaluating candidates for suitability for foreign assignments.[47] But it is rare for MNEs to adequately think through the impact of culture on all the aspects of assessment centers, including everything from the nature of the exercises used to the cultural sensitivities of the evaluators used, in order to be able to use such a tool to assess IA candidates for international assignments.

The actual selection methods used are probably an extension of procedures used for domestic staffing decisions. Thus, there may be an *ad hoc* nature to this, using whatever technique seems easiest and quickest given the circumstances surrounding any particular need for an IA. Smaller firms are likely to use less formal and more *ad hoc* procedures, while larger, more experienced firms are likely to have developed more formal and standardized procedures. The primary outcome of the selection process is to choose individuals who will stay for the duration of their global assignments and who will accomplish the tasks for which they were sent abroad. Executives who make these choices should, therefore, consider both enterprise-based as well as individual- and family-based factors to enhance the probability that the international assignment will be successful.

MISTAKES AND FAILURES

MNEs want to select managers who, with their families, will be most able to adapt to another country and who also possess the necessary expertise to get the job done. Many firms that lack experience in international operations often overlook the importance of cultural adaptation. Indeed, even more experienced firms may do this as well. This attitude, combined with firms' inclinations to choose employees for foreign relocation because of their technical competencies, generally leads to individuals being sent on international assignments without the benefit of training or help in acculturation.[48] This may—and all too often does—lead to failures in foreign assignments with individuals returning home early, or even being dismissed in the foreign locale.

Success or failure is a more complex issue than simply not completing the assignment.[49] Success or failure for international assignees is usually defined in terms of three types of failure: drop out, finishing the assignment but without cultural adaptation or acceptance of the local experience, or turnover upon repatriation. An IA *drop-out* returns early from the assignment but usually stays with the company. Although this is considered a failure, in fact, it is better than not realizing at all that the assignment was a mistake. In a failure with assignment completion but without job or cultural adaptation, the IA does not return early but performs poorly and is ineffective in the assignment. As a result of this type of failure the IA may initiate projects that are costly and not effective, damage relationships with the local employees, or drive out high potential local nationals. A last type of failure is when the assignee leaves the company within a short period of time (usually thought of as within one year) after repatriation. This is the most costly type of failure for the company.

These three forms of assignment failure are the traditional forms of failure that MNEs have focused on. However, international assignment failure can also be defined in terms of personal dissatisfaction with the experience, lack of adjustment to local conditions, lack of acceptance by local nationals, or the inability to identify and train a local successor (see Exhibit 9.3). In addition, a number of factors seem to influence the severity of expatriate failure rates (and help to explain why Japanese and European firms don't experience the

---

EXHIBIT 9.3: Definition of Expatriate Failure

- usually defined in terms of *early return home* or *termination*;
- but could also be defined in terms of:

    - ❏ poor quality of performance in foreign assignment;
    - ❏ employee not fully utilized during assignment;
    - ❏ personal dissatisfaction with experience (by expatriate or family);
    - ❏ lack of adjustment to local conditions;
    - ❏ no acceptance by local nationals;
    - ❏ damage to overseas business relationships;
    - ❏ not recognizing or missing overseas business opportunities;
    - ❏ inability to identify and/or train a local successor;
    - ❏ leave soon after repatriation;
    - ❏ not use foreign experience in assignment after repatriation.

- *Compounding factors:*

    - ❏ length of assignment;
    - ❏ degree of concern about repatriation;
    - ❏ overemphasis in selection on technical competence to disregard of other necessary attributes;
    - ❏ degree of training for overseas assignment;
    - ❏ degree of support while on overseas assignment.

high rates of expatriate failure experienced by many American firms). These include length of assignment (longer assignments appear to be based on the employer's willingness to provide the IA with more time to adjust and to "get up to speed" in job performance, which is more common among Japanese and European firms), receipt of training and orientation (with training and orientation about the new country and culture being associated with more successful adaptation), the lack of participation by HR in the selection process, too much emphasis placed on expatriates' technical expertise to the exclusion of other attributes that might aid in adaptation, and lack of support provided by home office for IAs and their families while on foreign assignment.

A number of surveys and studies have found the most important factors in the early return of expatriates lie in the inability of their families (and/or themselves) to adjust to the foreign assignment.[50] To the extent that preparation is provided, often the parent company will provide that preparation only for the new transferee, not to his or her family. In addition, after arrival in the foreign locale, IAs have the advantage of personal contacts and involvement with their colleagues at work, while their spouses and families are often left on their own to "figure out" their new surroundings and to develop local relationships,

---

EXHIBIT 9.4: Reasons for Expatriate Failure

- inability of spouse/partner to adjust or spouse/partner dissatisfaction;
- inability of expatriate to adjust;
- other family-related problems;
- mistake in candidate/expatriate selection or just does not meet expectations;
- expatriate's personality or lack of emotional maturity;
- expatriate's inability to cope with larger responsibilities of overseas work;
- expatriate's lack of technical competence;
- expatriate's lack of motivation to work overseas;
- dissatisfaction with quality of life in foreign assignment;
- dissatisfaction with compensation and benefits;
- inadequate cultural and language preparation;
- inadequate support for IA and family while on overseas assignment.

Sources: Adapted from National Foreign Trade Council (NFTC), Society for Human Resource Management (SHRM), and GMAC Global Relocation Services (GMAC GRS)/Windham International *Global Relocation Trends Annual Survey* Reports, 2000–2014; Stroh, L.K., Black, J.S., Mendenhall, M.E. and Gregersen, H.B. (2005). *International Assignments: An Integration of Strategy, Research, & Practice*, Mahwah, NJ/London: Lawrence Erlbaum Associates; and Tung, R.L. (1987). Expatriate assignments: Enhancing success and minimizing failure. *Academy of Management Executive*, 1 (2), 117–126.

often with little understanding of the culture and an inability to speak or read the language. Thus the individual expatriate often finds adjustment easier and less "lonely" than does his or her spouse and family. Exhibit 9.4 lists the most common reasons for expatriate failure, when defined as early return or termination from the foreign assignment.[51]

Of course, the IA's inability to adjust and/or experience of difficulty in merging with the new culture can also be major handicaps.[52] Too often, expatriates bring stereotypes and prejudices against the foreign culture—as well as strongly felt biases in favor of their own culture's ways of doing things—that keep them from feeling comfortable in their new foreign assignments.[53]

MNE Mistakes in IA Selection

MNEs typically do a number of things that lead to problems with their international assignees.[54] These include:

- Decision to relocate people made with too little lead time.
- Assignees not provided with any or adequate pre-relocation cultural training and/or language training.
- Spouses or partners not included in the decision to relocate.
- Spouses/partners and kids not included on pre-assignment visits.
- Spouses/partners and kids not included in language lessons.
- Spouses/partners and kids not included in cultural training.
- Spouses/partners do not receive counseling on jobs and other opportunities.
- Spouses have no home office contact.
- Little or no support is provided for IA or family before or after arrival in the host country.

Challenges to Successful Staffing with IAs

All of this discussion points to the reality that there are many challenges to MNEs in their quests to ensure that the best employees are selected for international assignments. The following paragraphs summarize eight specific issues: spouses and partners, language, family, women expatriates, lifestyle, localization (or "going native"), career development, costs, and inpatriation.

Spouses or Partners

It is not just the business situation that determines expatriate success. There are also a number of personal and cultural issues that are also important. For example, research by ORC (Organization Resources Counselors) found that international HR managers believe that dual-career-couple overseas assignments are among the top five challenges they face.[55] According to a survey by Bennett Associates of accompanying career spouses, worldwide, active involvement in the career of the accompanying spouse is the type of assistance preferred by dual-career couples above all other possible interventions.[56]

According to surveys by Runzheimer International and ORC, nearly 50 percent of firms offer some form of spouse assistance for dual-career international assignees.[57] Of those firms, 87 percent provide ad hoc interventions (helping in ways that seem necessary) but only 13 percent have formal policies. Support programs for spouses fall into three broad categories: personal adjustment, career maintenance, and offset of loss of income. These surveys find that support services by employers for trailing spouses were critical to their satisfaction with their foreign relocations. The types of interventions found in these surveys to be desirable included the following:

- Pre-acceptance assessment sessions and site visits.
- Career and life planning counseling.
- Pre-departure and re-entry job hunting trips.
- Couple/family counseling.
- Specially adapted cross-cultural/language training.
- Relocation assistance to help spouse settle in and network quickly.
- Search firm retained to help spouse find employment.
- Company employment or consulting opportunities.
- Intra- and inter-company networking and job search assistance.
- Visa and work permit assistance.
- Shorter-term assignments for expatriate employee.
- Commuter marriage support.
- Tuition and/or training reimbursement.
- Paying for professional development trips.
- Arranging and paying for child care provisions.
- Partial compensation replacement for spouse.
- Increased employee compensation, bonus, and non-cash benefits.
- Re-entry outplacement services (to find job upon return to home country).
- Tax equalization for second income.
- Spouse "inconvenience" or incentive payment.
- Set allowance to be applied to a "cafeteria" selection of assistance programs.

Language

One of the continuing issues with both IAs and foreign workforces concerns the issue of language. As mentioned earlier the ability to speak and understand the local language has shown to be positively related to international assignee success.[58] Do IAs on foreign assignment need to learn the language of the country to which they are posted? And to what extent do local employees need to know or learn the language of the parent firm? Like concern with cultural differences, concern with language differences also impacts most of international business. And it certainly is an issue with the selection of IAs.

Even though English has become the international language of business, with most large MNEs using English among their top management around the world, it is just as important for international assignees to have a working knowledge of the language of the countries to which they are assigned as it is for the local management of subsidiaries to speak the language of the parent firm. IAs need to speak their customers' and colleagues' languages—if their business relationships are going to flourish.[59] MNEs approach the need to provide language training in a variety of ways, but they typically find the increased numbers of employees who can speak foreign languages an asset in the development of their global businesses.

Foreign language training provides employees with language skills that are needed to communicate with co-workers and individuals in other countries.[60] In surveys of expatriates, language is often mentioned as the most important personal or professional challenge in their assignments.[61] An expatriate living in Germany says, "Speaking only English during an assignment is a big mistake. You can be a friend and a colleague speaking English, but to be 'one of them,' you must speak their language."[62] An expatriate living in Brazil offers the advice: "Persevere with the language at all costs."[63] Often, one major factor in the inability of MNEs to fill key expatriate assignments is the lack of language expertise and preparation. And as is discussed in this section, many firms do not provide any opportunities for language training.

English has become the international language of business for a number of reasons.[64] Even so, not all interactions are likely to take place in English, particularly within the host country. As stated above, dealing with customers, suppliers, and employees is often best done in the local language. Still, transnational exchanges are more and more expected to take place in English. It is in fact now estimated that estimated that, after Chinese (Mandarin), English is the most commonly used language in the world.[65] One result of this may be that employing local nationals that are fluent in English may be as important as requiring expatriates to be fluent in the local language(s). Even so, it is clear that an ability to speak the local language is still quite important—for IAs to deal with local nationals and local customers and suppliers, as well as to adapt to the host culture (and be accepted into that culture), both of which are major keys to successful expatriate assignments.

Family

Many of the challenges presented by IAs involve their families. Increasingly, the types of managers and specialists that either seek foreign assignments or are asked by their employers to relocate have spouses (or partners) and/or children. Often the spouses or partners are involved in their own careers (as discussed in the first topic of this section on challenges). If the IA candidate has an unmarried partner, it is likely to be quite difficult for the MNE to acquire a visa for the partner. The IAs may have problems with their adolescent children, health problems with family members, dependent parents who they have responsibility for, marital conflicts, or mental health problems of their own, such as depression—or even something like a flying phobia, or special education requirements for their children (such as children with disabilities or learning problems or gifted children—or even children getting ready for college). In addition, candidates for expatriation (or members of their families) with medical problems like AIDS, substance or alcohol abuse, or problems like multiple sclerosis, can cause what may seem like insurmountable problems for IHRM and the firm in being able to get overseas work visas. These types of individual or family problems are both a problem in expatriate selection as well as posing problems for acceptance into and adaptation to foreign cultures. And yet firms, in order to find the numbers of expatriates they need and stay away from possible charges of illegal discrimination in staffing decisions, must accept and find ways to accommodate IA candidates with these types of problems.

Many of these concerns make a health screening of the international assignee and her or his spouse and family members advisable, both to determine if a health problem exists that might either preclude relocation or be aggravated by a relocation or need special support services. Often even minor health problems are not treatable in the foreign country because qualified health professionals or facilities are not available.

Probably the most important of the family challenges today revolve around the dual-career couple and problems with relocating non-married partners. In both cases, an IA candidate's partner can pose difficult-to-resolve challenges for IHR.

Women Expatriates

Most IAs are men. Gradually, over the last 25 years or so, the percentage of women on international assignments, as determined by surveys, has increased from about 5–6 percent to 20–22 percent today.[66] This low percentage may have as much to do with stereotypes about foreign acceptance of women in professional or managerial roles as to the realities in the host countries.[67] Early research showed that one of the key factors in women not receiving overseas assignments was that selecting executives generally assumed that women would not be accepted in the foreign culture.[68] Other barriers to women receiving international assignments include their dual-career marriages, domestic managers not choosing them, perceptions that women were not interested in such assignments, etc.[69] In recent years the number of women who have successfully taken on foreign assignments, even to countries such as Japan, Brazil, and China, has risen considerably, although it still is a relatively small proportion of the total IA population, except in some industries, such as banking.[70] Of course the assignment of women IAs, except in very specialized professional positions, is likely to remain limited to some countries such as Saudi Arabia.[71]

The evidence, though, suggests that the fact that there are only a comparatively few women working abroad for MNEs may be due more to bias and stereotyping in the home country and company than to prejudicial treatment or limitations in the host country or foreign subsidiary.[72] Women are not only as likely to welcome such opportunities as are their male colleagues (for the same reasons their male counterparts seek them), but they often perform better than their male colleagues, even in traditionally male-dominated cultures, such as in Asia and the Middle East.[73]

Typically, female expatriates are treated first as representatives of their firms or as professionals, and rarely experience the bias that the stereotypes from their home firms presume. This isn't meant to imply that women never experience stereotyping and treatment in line with cultural norms that may not accept women in the workplace, except in very menial tasks. This does happen.[74] But the evidence suggests that women are frequently quite successful in international assignments.[75]

In addition, women expatriates also have trailing spouses and unmarried partners and families to consider, and thus need to be given the same considerations received by their male counterparts. Women are clearly interested in international positions and have demonstrated that they can perform well in global assignments.[76] Increased global competition pressures MNEs to make the best use of all of their resources, including their women employees.[77]

Lifestyle

Increasingly MNEs are having to deal with employees who either seek foreign assignments or who are eligible for such postings who live what might be referred to as "alternative" lifestyles that may not be acceptable in target foreign locations. This might involve "gay" or unmarried couples or single parents or employees who live with their parents or who are taking care of elderly parents. Or it just might concern employees who are involved in outside-of-work activities that are very important to the individual and they may not be able to pursue them in the host location. All of these situations create challenges for IHR to overcome.

Localization or "Going Native"

One challenge that has been confronted by many MNEs involves expatriates that stay for an extended period (usually at the firm's request, but sometimes at the IA's request) in a foreign assignment (beyond their original assignments).[78] This becomes an issue because IAs in this situation continue to draw their expatriate allowances and incentives, even though they have learned to live "like locals." These particular IAs may be critical to the success of the foreign operations, which may make it difficult to change their status. Often they have married a local and are raising a family in the foreign locale. To deal with this issue, many firms have developed policies, such as requiring that all IAs convert to a local compensation package if they stay on their assignment for longer than the assignment contract period. Even with such a policy, it still creates problems for dealing with this particular situation. Without such a policy, this can be an especially challenging problem.

Career Development

Since it is often expected that an international assignment is highly developmental, and since many firms now expect managers above some level in the organization to have international experience, it is becoming more common to make a posting to a foreign assignment a critical part of an individual's career plan.[79] The challenge is to manage this process, both from the standpoint of the organization (where key managers may have their own ideas as to who they want to fill open foreign positions) and the individual, who may not see the career advantages. The firm may state the importance to one's career advancement, but observation suggests that IAs on return to the parent firm are not always given assignments that use or take advantage of the foreign experience.

Costs of International Assignments

From the firm's perspective, a major IA challenge is to contain costs. Moving employees from country to country is expensive, both in direct remuneration (compensation and benefits) and the administration of their relocation expenses. Consequently, many MNEs are searching for ways to reduce the costs.[80] For example, MNEs are dealing with these high costs by replacing IAs with more short-term assignments and extended business trips, outsourcing the administrative aspects of managing IAs, and looking for ways to reduce the compensation incentives and add-ons that make international assignments so expensive. And at least some MNEs are recognizing they can minimize the costs of failed assignments through developing better selection processes, better preparation and orientation, better destination support services for both IAs and their families, and improved repatriation processes. But even though firms say IAs are too expensive, some surveys find that many firms are not doing much to counter the high costs.[81]

Inpatriation

As mentioned in the previous chapter, the term "inpatriate" was developed to describe particular employees (HCNs or TCNs) who are relocated from a foreign subsidiary or joint venture to the parent company in the HQ country. This posting is usually for a relatively short period of time (from a few months to one or two years) and is for the purpose of teaching the "subsidiary" employee about the products and culture of the parent firm and to introduce the employee to the operations, ways of thinking, and corporate culture of the headquarters.[82] Increasingly, these assignees are also used to fill functional or technical needs in the parent company for a limited period of time or to serve on multinational teams for a specified period of time. The challenges of selecting and managing inpatriates are basically the same as those for expatriates. From the standpoint of the foreign subsidiary, the inpatriate is an "expatriate," going on a foreign assignment. From the standpoint of headquarters, the individual is an inpatriate. In this situation, the issues for IHRM are to consider the experiences of headquarters in receiving relocated employees—in addition to the "normal" issues related to the experiences of any relocated employees.

SUCCESSFUL EXPATRIATION AND "BEST PRACTICES"

Expatriation success is the flip side of the issue of expatriate failure. Typically, expatriate success is defined as:

1   completion of the foreign assignment (achieving the original goals and objectives);
2   cross-cultural adjustment while on assignment; and
3   good performance on the job while on the foreign assignment.[83]

Sometimes these factors are viewed as a unitary construct, that is, they are seen as a package of issues that go together to define a successful assignment. But research shows them to be separate constructs, meaning that each needs attention.[84] This demonstrates that the foreign environment (company and national culture and practices), local management, technical skills, and expatriate personal characteristics all ultimately play a role in expatriate success.

A number of IHR consulting practices, surveys, and research projects have identified what might be considered "exemplary practices" in the selection of IAs.[85] A summary of these findings can be found in Exhibit 9.5. Following these suggestions will go a long way toward helping IHR be successful in its management of international assignees.

Host-Country Nationals

In general, MNEs staff their subsidiaries—at least below the top management levels—with local nationals (AKA host-country nationals, HCNs). At times, these workers may be supplanted by TCNs, described in the next section, and international assignees from the home office or region. Of course, whether or not there are enough potential employees with adequate training, education, and technical, business, managerial, and language skills is always of utmost importance to an MNE strategy of staffing with HCNs. In the case where the decision is made to locate a subsidiary or business unit in a country where the local population lacks the necessary education or training (or there is a shortage of the types of workers the MNE needs, as is increasingly the case, for example, in China[86]), then IHR must find other ways to staff the necessary workforce, for example by training locals, hiring TCNs, or bringing in parent-company international assignees.

Relying on Local Managerial Talent

Expensive international assignees and their not-infrequent failures in assignments, combined with a general trend toward local staffing (using and developing local talent), regiocentrism (using regional talent), and geocentrism (a truly global approach to resources, markets, and staffing), has led in recent years to a greater reliance on local managers in foreign operations.[87] Foreign nationals already know the language and culture and do not require huge

EXHIBIT 9.5: Best Practice in IA Selection

- Involve HR in global strategic planning.
- Link each assignment to corporate strategies.
- Involve HR in assignment decisions and support services.
- Help assignees and their families make the smoothest transition into, during, and out of assignments.
- Utilize an assessment process that promotes the selection of the best employees for international positions.
- Administer consistent international assignments through comprehensive programs that cover each step from design of the assignment to return of the employee and family.

More specifically, these reports suggest:

- Periodically, review relocation policies and practices to ensure fit with the current business and strategic situation.
- Train home office staff in dealing with international assignees.
- Be honest about the job and location when recruiting candidates for foreign assignments.
- Provide adequate lead time for relocation.
- Involve spouse/partner/family at the outset of the expatriation process (i.e., at the beginning of the selection process).
- Provide language and cultural training for IA and family.
- Recognize the importance of dual-career and trailing spouse/partner issues, financially and otherwise (pre-departure job counseling, networking contacts, education and training, job hunting assistance, legal assistance for work permits, career assistance upon repatriation, etc.).
- Provide pre-assignment site visit for whole family.
- Don't neglect repatriation issues.

Sources: GMAC Global Relocation Services/Windham International, National Foreign Trade Council, and SHRM Global Forum (2014 and previous years). *Global Relocation Trends Annual Survey Report*, New York: GMAC GRS/Windham International; Lomax, S. (2001). *Best Practices for Managers and Expatriates*, New York: John Wiley & Sons; Stroh, L.K., Black, J.S., Mendenhall, M.E. and Gregersen, H.B. (2005). *International Assignments: An Integration of Strategy, Research, & Practice*, Mahwah, NJ/London: Lawrence Erlbaum Associates; Vance, C.M. and Paik, Y. (2006). *Managing a Global Workforce*, Armonk, NY: M.E. Sharpe.

relocation expenditures. In addition, host-country governments tend to look favorably on a greater degree of local control and the development and use of local personnel and may even have passed legislation that requires the use of local workers in foreign enterprises and JVs. Indeed, some countries require that most staff come from the local labor force. On the negative side, however, local managers may have an inadequate knowledge of home-office goals and procedures and may have difficulty with the parent-company language. Thus the staffing of foreign positions—particularly key managerial and technical ones—is necessarily decided on a case-by-case basis. Firms that are new to international business may feel more comfortable having parent-country managers in control in the firm's new foreign locales, while MNEs that have been global for many years and have operations around the world may find it easier to operate with fewer parent-country nationals on international assignments. It is also likely that these global MNEs will be more likely to move managers and functional specialists from country to country for developmental purposes as well as for control and coordination reasons, rather than using traditional expatriates. Lastly, the need for large numbers of highly qualified personnel has also made it increasingly necessary to use larger numbers of foreign (host-country/local) nationals.[88]

Most MNEs favor hiring local nationals for foreign subsidiaries, home-country nationals at headquarters, and, where a regional organization exists, a mix of foreign and home-country managers for regional positions. Within this general approach, however, the nationality mix will vary with the nature of the firm's business and its product strategy. Where area expertise plays a major role, as in the case of consumer goods and/or a limited product line, the use of home-country personnel for overseas assignments will be minimal. Where product expertise is highly important and/or industrial markets are being served, home-country personnel will be used more extensively for foreign assignments because they generally have quick access to the home-country sources of supply and technical information. Service industries also tend to have more home-country personnel in foreign posts, particularly where the firm is serving home-country multinationals in foreign areas, as has been the case in banking.[89]

Third-Country Nationals

TCNs tend to be used particularly in situations where there is either a shortage of people with the skills the firm needs or where there is a relatively free movement of people from one country to another. In recent years, with the global shortage of, for example, IT and computer specialists and engineers, many firms have relied on the hiring of people from third countries who have these skills to fill positions in their foreign subsidiaries, just as they do at home. And, increasingly, TCNs are being used if parent-company managers and technicians are not readily available or not available in the numbers needed, for example, to make major staffing commitments to new operations in China and India.[90]

While much of the world's skilled and unskilled human resources are being produced in the developing world, most of the well-paid jobs are being generated in the cities of the industrialized world (or their enterprises)—although this is changing as more developed country firms subcontract to firms in developing countries, hire employees offshore to work via telecommunications, invest directly in operations in the developing world, and entrepreneurs and business leaders in developing countries develop their own successful global enterprises. This increasing equality of jobs and talent between where the potential employees are and where the jobs are has several implications:

- It will trigger massive relocations of people, including immigrants, temporary workers, retirees, and visitors. The greatest relocations will involve young, well-educated workers flocking to jobs, wherever they are located.
- It will lead some industrialized nations to reconsider their protectionist immigration policies as they come to rely on and compete for foreign-born talent.
- It may boost the fortunes of nations with "surplus" human capital. Specifically, it could help well-educated but economically underdeveloped countries such as China, the Philippines, India, Egypt, Cuba, Poland, Hungary, Brazil, Argentina, South Africa, and, maybe, Mexico.
- It will compel labor-short, immigrant-poor nations like Japan to improve labor productivity dramatically to avoid slower economic growth. They will use more technology and transfer more work to labor-surplus and cheaper labor locales.
- It will lead to a gradual standardization of labor practices among industrialized countries. Within 50 years or so, European standards of vacation time (five to six weeks) will likely be common in the US. The 40-hour work week will have been accepted in Japan. And world standards governing workplace safety and employee rights will emerge.[91]

Much attention has focused on the current or looming labor shortages in the industrialized world, particularly in the US, Europe, and Japan, due to their aging populations.[92] Yet the overall world labor supply continues to grow (primarily in the developing world). In addition, the growth in the labor force in the developing world is magnified by the entrance of women into the labor force, a phenomenon that has pretty well worked itself out in most of the developed world (although not all of it, as participation rates for women are still quite low in some developed countries, such as Germany and Japan). When these demographic differences are combined with the different rates of economic growth between the developed and developing world, it becomes more likely that firms in the developed world will increasingly seek workers among the developing countries and will move jobs to those countries as well. Just as product and service markets have become or are becoming global, such is also happening to labor markets. In one sense, this may alleviate the pressures created by labor surpluses in developing countries; but in another sense it may also exacerbate the economic differences between the countries of the developing world and those of the developed world as MNEs hire the educated and trained citizens of developing countries, lessening those countries' available human resources for their own developmental needs.

An extension of the focus on local managers and technical specialists, as described at the end of the previous section on HCNs, involves the increasing willingness to look for management and technical expertise from all countries for assignment to any country. These TCNs are often the solution to overseas staffing problems.

Immigration Law

An important concern to IHRM staffing concerns the nature and application of immigration law. This topic was introduced in Chapter 4, but needs consideration here because it is central to staffing the global firm, as new immigrants are hired, visas are acquired for international assignees, and HR managers work with officials in other countries as they arrange work visas for the managers and technicians they send abroad as expatriates. It is beyond the scope of this book to examine the wide variety of immigration regulations found in varying countries. Suffice it to say that every country controls immigration quite closely and now, with increased concern over global terrorism, most countries are even more concerned about the level and nature of immigration into their countries. It is necessary for IHR managers to either manage all the forms of visas and immigration issues their firms confront or to know where to get the necessary expertise to ensure that the firm adheres to every nation's laws and policies.

REPATRIATION

At the end of the assignment, the IA either repatriates to the home country, is redeployed to another country, or becomes localized in the host country. As mentioned earlier, repatriation involves the move of the IA and family back "home" from the foreign assignment. For many expatriates and their families, the move "back home" is even more difficult than the original move abroad. Even so, it is often overlooked or minimized in the management of the total expatriation process.[93]

The international experience is generally challenging, exciting, highly developmental, and full of visibility and exposure for the assignee. The international assignee is the representative of the parent company, of headquarters, and is therefore looked to for perspective, help, and favors. In addition, because the compensation practices of most MNEs reward their international assignees quite well, the IA and family typically live quite well in the foreign location, often better than they did "at home." Thus expatriates usually return from such experiences quite "charged"—and with high expectations that their employers will use their new experiences and excitement in new and better positions and family and friends back home will share their enthusiasm.

But if an MNE is to reap the benefits of its IAs' learning while on foreign assignments, it is imperative that these valuable employees stay with the organization long enough to share their experiences. This should encourage MNEs to place a strong emphasis on the repatriation experiences of their IAs.

The kinds of practices that MNEs have used to ensure a successful expatriation and repatriation experience include assigning a "sponsor" back home to look after the expatriate while s/he is away (including keeping the expatriate informed about significant events and changes back home and looking after the expatriate's career interests, including putting the expatriate's name into consideration for key openings when the expatriate is ready to return home), providing career counseling to ensure job assignments upon return that meet the needs of the repatriate, orientation for the expatriate and his/her family for adjustment back into the home culture, use of the skills acquired overseas in special task forces and projects, and special support networks for the repatriate and her/his family both during the overseas assignment and upon return home.[94] These steps go a long way toward ensuring a successful readjustment. IHRM in Action 9.2 describes how Monsanto Corporation has redesigned its repatriation efforts in order to more effectively use its expatriates and their international experiences, integrating them with their domestic operations.[95]

IHRM in Action 9.2: Repatriation at Monsanto

Monsanto Corporation undertook a detailed change of its repatriation policy, concentrating on the logistical planning for returning its expatriates home, the kinds of skills and cultural development the company wanted its expatriates to learn, and the placing of its repatriates, after their return, in projects where their recent overseas experience was needed. The manager of international assignments in human resources at the time said there was growing concern about the firm gaining from the personal and cultural development that expatriates were assumed to experience while on their foreign assignments.

Amato says that the repatriation process now begins six to 18 months prior to return in both the host and the home countries. This primarily involves identifying a position for the expatriate to return to for which the operating unit is responsible. An extensive orientation program is also run for the employees and their families.

The repatriate orientation is exceptionally thorough: he or she is debriefed with peers and managers in the new job and is expected to provide recommendations about global development and to provide a view other than that of domestic Monsanto. Peers are expected to discuss the differences and changes in the organization that occurred while the expatriate was abroad. Managers are encouraged to free up repatriates for committees, work groups, and demonstrations where their new global knowledge is needed, over and above the employee's regular job. Repatriates are counseled to be aware of how much they and the organization have changed when they come back.

Challenges on Re-entry

But the reality is more likely to be: "out of sight, out of mind." Firms often fail to use the experience or knowledge gained internationally and most likely have not thought much about the career implications of this experience. Typically, the repatriate is reassigned to a position similar to the one he or she left two or three years before while their colleagues most likely have been promoted. Repatriates often find it difficult to relate the value of their global experience to managers with a domestic focus.[96] Domestic managers, themselves usually without any international experience, cannot relate (this is also likely to be true for the expatriate's friends and colleagues). For the repatriate, this makes re-entry and the job search within the company quite challenging. The global experience may be viewed as helpful to the specific foreign situation; but the domestic manager usually views domestic experience as more important. To many domestic line managers, developing international experience and a global mindset to operate internationally is the CEO's problem. Globalization is often not a concern to the line manager trying to achieve a specific set of local objectives.

Organizational Support for Repatriates

MNEs can provide several support practices to repatriates to address the above problems. These practices can be organized according to three phases: before the foreign assignment, during the foreign assignment, and after the completion of the foreign assignment. Figure 9.2 shows the various IHRM practices that support the repatriation process.

Before the Foreign Assignment

Career-related planning for expatriates needs to begin prior to an international assignment and be updated regularly during the assignment. The assignment needs to be part of a larger plan for the firm so that the repatriate returns to a specific position that uses the international learning and experience. One of the programs used by some firms is a

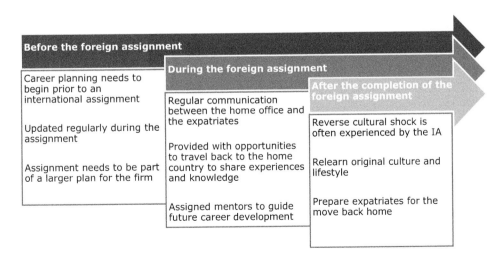

FIGURE 9.2 Organizational Support for Repatriates

back-home mentor or sponsor, who is both a contact in the home office for the expatriate who is at least partially responsible for looking after the interests and prospects of the expatriate while he or she is on assignment, but who also provides an avenue for keeping the IA informed about what is going on back home.

During the Foreign Assignment

Support activities during this period are critical in terms of ensuring a high retention rate.[97] There has to be clear, constant, and regular communication between the home office and the expatriates. The expatriates should be provided with opportunities to travel back to the home country to share experiences and knowledge with other members of the organization. This provides the expatriate with the opportunity to maintain high visibility with supervisors and peers. Expatriates should also be assigned mentors to guide future career development.[98] Intraoffice communications through emails and intranet should include the expatriate and the expatriate should be actively encouraged to communicate with colleagues and mentors back home.[99]

After the Completion of the Foreign Assignment

The readjustment is not only challenging for the international assignee but for the family members as well. Repatriates and their families often have trouble adjusting to the lifestyle back home. Reverse cultural shock (readjustment to the home culture) is often experienced by the IA (and accompanying family). Most people are changed by the foreign experience and not only must relearn their original culture and lifestyle, but probably view it quite differently than when they left. Indeed, time does not stand still while the expatriate is abroad. While changes at home may be all but invisible to those who experience them gradually (those at home), to the returnees, they can be overwhelming.[100] Just as MNEs need to provide their expatriates with cross-cultural training for the move abroad, so should they prepare their expatriates for the move back home and prepare themselves to use these individuals' overseas experiences in their home assignments. This preparation can make the difference between an overall favorable attitude by the repatriates about the whole experience and a failed expatriate experience. Ultimately, an unfavorable attitude will likely lead to the individual returnee's turnover. A dissatisfied repatriated employee is more likely to resign and seek a position with another employer that will utilize that individual's foreign experiences and skills.

Knowledge Transfer upon Repatriation[101]

The foreign assignment provides repatriates with the opportunity to gain international knowledge (e.g., knowledge about complexities of global operations, characteristics of national markets, business climate, cultural patterns). They have firsthand experience of how their organization is viewed in another country. As such, repatriates play an important role in accelerating the transfer of knowledge from host countries to headquarters, and vice versa. MNEs need to design the most appropriate mechanisms (e.g., mentoring programs, training sessions) for capturing, retaining, and integrating the knowledge and expertise gained by their repatriates.

CONCLUSION

This chapter focused on the IHRM responsibility for staffing. It explained issues related to recruiting, selecting, and repatriating in MNEs, but primarily it focused on expatriation and repatriation, the movement of employees from country to country, and the employment of host-country and third-country nationals. Because the use of parent-country nationals is so important to IHRM in MNEs, much of this chapter discussed the selection and management of PCNs, including their failures and adaptation to foreign assignments, and their repatriation at the end of their assignments. The chapter also examined the difficulties experienced in the selection and management of IAs and suggested some of the approaches successful MNEs use to ensure positive experiences with those expatriates and repatriates.

DISCUSSION QUESTIONS

1 If you are given the opportunity in your next job to go on an extended foreign assignment, what types of support programs would you expect or ask for?
2 If you ever have the responsibility to select an associate for a foreign assignment, how would you go about doing that and what characteristics would you look for to ensure success?
3 What do you think is the most significant challenge for IHRM in managing international assignees? Why?

CASE STUDY 9.1: A World Marketplace for Jobs in Project-Based Work Environment (Global)

It used to be necessary to bring workers to where the work was. But with the advent of the World Wide Web, the Internet, and mobile phones and the global communication they make possible, it is now possible to send work to wherever workers are by putting together multinational project teams, by using the Internet to recruit employees on a global scale, or by using open-source software to accommodate global collaboration. These new styles of work and employment are arising particularly in response to the capabilities of the computer and to the chronic needs for IT skills in growing numbers of industries.

For example, one firm from Bern, Switzerland, recruited from the web a group of doctorates in discrete mathematics and graph theory from as far away as Belarus, India, Israel, and Ireland, for a semiconductor design project. Team members never left their home countries and the team leader never left his home office. And the task group beat its deadline.

In industry after industry, as customers expect quicker service and competition forces shrinking product life cycles, employers are being driven to apply a "Hollywood model" to their tasks. They assemble the best talent available at the moment from anywhere in the world (which is the way teams are put together to film a movie). When the project is complete, the team breaks up and the members move on to new projects. The end result is a new and highly efficient global labor market unlike any seen before.

Even for small businesses: their new talent pool is the world. A new generation of online services is providing small businesses with opportunities to find specialized expertise and affordable labor. Main Street businesses can shop a virtual international bazaar of freelancers to recruit computer programmers in Russia, graphic designers in Italy, or data analysts in India. A small business of one can look to the world like a very large company and have access to all kinds of services. Technical advances have made remote work and virtual teams more feasible. And, increasingly, freelancers are taking on assignments like customer service, data entry, writing, accounting, human resources, marketing, payroll—virtually any "knowledge process" that can be performed remotely, even setting up and managing business profiles on social networking sites like Facebook and Twitter.

In some cases, the cost savings can be substantial: for example, the hourly rates of programmers in Russia, India, or Pakistan are a fraction of those in North America or Europe. And these freelance marketplaces also allow small businesses to assemble teams quickly, find specialized expertise, begin new initiatives, and then be able to drop everything when it's no longer needed.

When John Wilde, chief executive of Tailor Made Products, a small manufacturing firm in a small town in Wisconsin, in the US, wanted to build a website for a new line of children's kitchen gadgets called the Curious Chef, he turned to oDesk and hired a firm in India. He paid about US$20,000, which he estimates was roughly half what he would have paid in the US.

Sources: Travelling talent. (2014, Oct 10). *The Economist* (Online); www. https://www.odesk.com (2014); Pattison, K. (2009). Enlisting a global work force of freelancers. *The New York Times*, June 24, 2009, Small Business Guide; Norris, C.D. (2000). Already starting: A world marketplace for jobs. *International Herald Tribune*, August 8, 6.

Discussion Questions

1   Where are the best places in the world to live (and work)? Where do *you* want to live and work? Do you want to work from home? Are you interested in working on global teams? What skills and competencies will enable someone to live and work wherever he or she wants? Are you interested in creating or working on a micro-multinational?
2   What are the human resource implications of these new ways of working?

NOTES

1   Source: http://www.bp.com/en/global/corporate/careers/working-at-bp/expats.html. Accessed Jan. 25, 2014.
2   For more complete discussion of the management of expatriates, refer to the following sources:, Brewster, C. (1991). *The Management of Expatriates*, London: Kogan Page; Fernandez, F. (2005). *Globalization and Human Resource Management*, New York: HNB Publishing; Lomax, S. (2001). *Best Practices for Managers and Expatriates*, New York: Wiley; Melton, W.R. (2005). *The New American Expat*, Yarmouth, ME: Intercultural Press; Scullion, H. and Collings, D.G. (eds.) (2006). *Global Staffing*, London/New York: Routledge; Morgan, B.S. (ed.) (2014). *The Global Employer: Focus on Global Immigration and Mobility*, Chicago: Baker & McKenzie; Stroh et al. (2005); and Caligiuri, P.M. and Colakoglu, S. (2007). A strategic contingency approach to expatriate assignment management, *Human Resource Management Journal*, 17(4), 27–54
3   GMAC Global Relocation Services/Windham International, National Foreign Trade Council, and SHRM Global Forum (2014 and previous years). *Global Relocation Trends Annual Survey Report*, New York: GMAC GRS/Windham International; Morgan, B.S. (ed.) (2014).
4   For more information on international experiences see Takeuchi, R., Tesluk, P., Yun, S. and Lepak, D. (2005). An integrative view of international experiences: An empirical examination. *Academy of Management Journal*, 48, 85–100: Selmer, J. (2002). Practice makes perfect? International experience and expatriate adjustment. *Management International Review*, 42, 71–87.
5   For example, see Cartus (2014). Trends in global relocation. *Global Mobility Policy and Practices*, Danbury, CT: Cartus; Brookfield (2013). *Global Mobility Trends*, New York and Toronto: Brookfield Global Relocation Services.
6   Morgan, B.S. (ed.) (2014), p. 1.
7   Jackson, S., Schuler, R., and Werner, S. (2012). *Managing human resource*, Cengage Learning; Mason, OH; Heneman, H., and Judge, T. (2009). *Staffing Organizations*, Middleton, WI: McGraw-Hill Irwin; Phillips, J., and Gully, S. (2009). *Staffing Organizations*, Upper Saddle River, NJ: Pearson, Prentice Hall.
8   Based on Heneman, H., and Judge, T. (2009); Phillips, J., and Gully, S. (2009).
9   Heneman and Judge (2009); Phillips and Gully (2009).
10   Tarique, I., and Schuler, R. (2008). Emerging issues and challenges in global staffing: A North American perspective. *The International Journal of Human Resource Management*, 19 (8), 1397–1415.
11   Ibid.
12   Tharenou, P. (2002). Receptivity to Careers in International Work—Abroad and at Home, *Australian Journal of Management*, 27, 129–136 ; Tharenou, P. (2003). The initial development of receptivity to working abroad: Self-initiated international work opportunities in young graduate employees, *Journal of Occupational and Organizational Psychology*, 76, 489–515.
13   Tharenou (2002); Tharenou (2003). Also see the work on self-initiated expatriation: Cao, L., Hirschi, A., and Deller, J. (2014). Perceived organizational support and intention to stay in host countries among self-initiated expatriates: The role of career satisfaction and networks, *The International Journal of Human Resource*

Management, 25(14); Tharenou, P. (2013). Self-initiated expatriates: An alternative to company-assigned expatriates? *Journal of Global Mobility*, 1(3), 336–356; Doherty, N., Dickmann, M., and Mills, T. (2011). Exploring the motives of company-backed and self-initiated expatriates. *The International Journal of Human Resource Management*, 22(3), 595; Doherty, N., Richardson, J., and Thorn, K. (2013). Self-initiated expatriation and self-initiated expatriates. *Career Development International*, 18(1), 97–112; Nolan, E.M., and Morley, M.J. (2014). A test of the relationship between person-environment fit and cross-cultural adjustment among self-initiated expatriates, *The International Journal of Human Resource Management*, 25(11), 1631; Rodriguez, J.K., and Scurry, T. (2014). Career capital development of self-initiated expatriates in Qatar: Cosmopolitan globetrotters, experts and outsiders, *The International Journal of Human Resource Management*, 25(7), 104; Selmer, J., and Lauring, J. (2011). Acquired demographics and reasons to relocate among self-initiated expatriates, *The International Journal of Human Resource Management*, 22(10), 2055; Tharenou, P., and Caulfield, N. (2010). Will I stay or will I go? Explaining repatriation by self initiated expatriates, *Academy of Management Journal*, 53(5), 1009.

14   Another term used in the expatriate management field is "willingness to accept a foreign assignment." This list includes factors that influence both an individual's receptivity to an international career and his/her willingness to accept a foreign assignment. The list was derived from: Konopaske, R. and Werner. S. (2005). US managers' willingness to accept a global assignment: Do expatriate benefits and assignment length make a difference? *The International Journal of Human Resource Management*, 16(7), 1159–1175; and Tharenou (2002); Tharenou, P. (2003). For additional information see Benson, G., Pérez-Nordtvedt, L., and Datta, D. (2009). Managerial characteristics and willingness to send employees on expatriate assignments, *Human Resource Management*, 48(6), 849; Konopaske, R., Robie, C. and Ivancevich, J. (2005). A preliminary model of spouse influence on managerial global assignment willingness, *The International Journal of Human Resource Management*, 16(3), 405–426.

15   For more information see Friedman, B. (2009). Human resource management role implications for corporate reputation. *Corporate Reputation Review*, 12(3), 229–244; Baruch, Yehuda (1997). Evaluating quality and reputation of human resource management. *Personnel Review*, 26(5), 377–394; Hannon, John M, and Milkovich, George T. (1996). The effect of human resource reputation signals on share prices: An event study. *Human Resource Management*, 35(3), 405

16   Caligiuri, P., Colakoglu, S., Cerdin, J., and Kim, M. (2010). Examining cross-cultural and individual differences in predicting employer reputation as a driver of employer attraction. *International Journal of Cross Cultural Management: CCM*, 10(2), 137.

17   Sparrow, P., Scullion, H. and Tarique, I. (2014). *Strategic Talent Management: Contemporary Issues in International Context*, Cambridge University Press.

18   Tarique, I., and Schuler, R. (2010). Global talent management: Literature review, integrative framework, and suggestions for future research. *Journal of World Business*, 45, 122–133.

19   Tarique, I. (2014). *Seven Trends in Corporate Training and Development: Strategies to Align Goals with Employee Needs*, Upper Sadler River, NJ: Pearson.

20   Caligiuri, P., Tarique, I., and Jacobs, R. (2009). Selection for international assignments. *Human Resource Management Review*, 19, 251–262; Black, J.S., Mendenhall, M.E. and Oddou, G. (1991) Toward a comprehensive model of international adjustment: An integration of multiple theoretical perspectives. *Academy of Management Review*, 16(2), 291–317; Caligiuri, P.M. (2000a). Selecting expatriates for personality characteristics: A moderating effect of personality on the relationship between host national contact and cross-cultural adjustment. *Management International Review*, 40(1), 61–80; Doms, M., and zu Knyphausen-Aufseß, D. (2014). Structure and characteristics of top management teams as antecedents of outside executive appointments: a three-country study. *International Journal of Human Resource Management*, 25(22), 3060–3085; Bhatti, M.A., Kaur, S., and Battour, M.M. (2013). Effects of individual characteristics on expatriates' adjustment and job performance. *European Journal of Training & Development*, 37(6), 544–563; Downes, M., Varner, I.I., and Hemmasi, M. (2010). Individual profiles as predictors of expatriate effectiveness. *Competitiveness Review*, 20(3), 235–247.

21 Caligiuri, Tarique and Jacobs (2009); Florkowski, G., and Fogel, D. (1999). Expatriate adjustment and commitment: The role of host-unit treatment. *International Journal of Human Resource Management*, 10, 782–807.

22 Refer to the model.

23 Global mobility in the context of global talent management. World Bank Community Conference on Global Mobility, Washington DC, 2011.

24 Dragoni, L., Tesluk, P.E., VanKatwyk, P., In-Sue, O., Moore, O.A., and Hazucha, J. (2014). Developing leaders' strategic thinking through global work experience: The moderating role of cultural distance. *Journal of Applied Psychology*, 99(5), 867–882; Holt, K., and Kyoko, S. (2012). Global leadership begins with learning professionals. *T+D*, 66(5), 32–37; Caligiuri, P., and Tarique, I. (2014). Individual accelerators of global leadership development, in Osland, J., Li, L. and Wang, L. (eds.), *Advances in Global Leadership*, 8th ed., Bingley, UK: Emerald Publishing; Caligiuri, P. and Tarique, I. (2009). Developing managerial and organizational cross-cultural capabilities, in Cary Cooper and Ron Burke (eds.), *The Peak Performing Organization*, Abingdon, UK: Taylor & Francis; Caligiuri, P., and Tarique, I. (2009). Predicting effectiveness in global leadership activities. *Journal of World Business*, 44, 336–346; Black, J.S. (2006). The mindset of global leaders: Inquisitiveness and duality, in Mobley, W.H. and Weldon, E. (eds.), *Advances in Global Leadership*, vol. 4, pp. 181–200; Black, J.S., Morrison, A. and Gregersen, H. (1999). *Global Explorers: The Next Generation of Leaders*. New York: Routledge; McCall, M.W., Jr. and Hollenbeck, G.P. (2002). *Developing Global Executives: The Lessons of International Experience*, Boston, MA: Harvard Business School Press.

25 Quoted in Howard, C.G. (1992). Profile of the 21st-century expatriate manager. *HR Magazine*, June, 93–100.

26 See, for example, Caligiuri, P., Tarique, I. and Jacobs, R. (2009). Selecting international assignees. *Human Resource Management Review*, 19, 251–262: Donegan, J. (2002). Effective expatriate selection: The first step in avoiding assignment failure. *Expatriate Advisor*, spring, 14–16.

27 Hawley-Wildmoser, L. (1997). Selecting the right employee for assignments abroad. *Cultural Diversity at Work*, 9 (3), 1, 12–13.

28 See, for example, the discussions of this point in Collings, D.G. and Scullion, H. (2012). Global staffing, in G.K. Stahl, I. Björkman and S. Morris (eds.), *Handbook of Research in International Human Resource Management* (2nd ed.), Cheltenham, UK and Northampton, MA, USA: Edward Elgar Publishing, pp. 142–161; Lazarova, M.B. and Thomas, D.C. (2012). Expatriate adjustment and performance revisited, in Stahl, G.K., Björkman, I. and Morris, S. (eds), *Handbook of Research in International Human Resource Management*, 2nd ed., Cheltenham, UK and Northampton, MA, USA: Edward Elgar Publishing, pp. 271–292; and Stroh et al. (2005).

29 Cf endnote 16.

30 Black, J.S. (1990). The relationship of personal characteristics with the adjustment of Japanese expatriate managers. *Management International Review*, 30, 119–34; Black, J.S., and Gregersen, H.B. (1991). When Yankee comes home: Factors related to expatriate and spouse repatriation adjustment. *Journal of International Business Studies*, 22, 671–694.

31 Black, J.S. and Stephens, G.K. (1989). The influence of the spouse on American expatriate adjustment and intent to stay in Pacific Rim overseas assignments. *Journal of Management*, 15, 529–44; Caligiuri, P., Tarique, I., and Jacobs, R. (2009). Selection for international assignments. *Human Resource Management Review*, 19, 251–262.; and Stroh et al. (2005).

32 Caligiuri, P., and Tarique, I. (2012). International assignee selection and cross-cultural training and development, in Stahl, G.K., Björkman, I., and Morris, S. (eds.), *Handbook of Research in International Human Resource Management*, 2nd ed., Cheltenham, UK and Northampton, MA: Edward Elgar Publishing; Caligiuri, P., Tarique, I., and Jacobs, R. (2009). Selection for international assignments. *Human Resource Management Review*, 19, 251–262.; Stuart (2009).

33 Digman, J. (1990). Personality structure: The emergence of the five factor model. *Annual Review of Psychology*, 41, 417–440. McCrae, R., and John, O. (1992). An introduction to the five factor model and its applications. *Journal of Personality*, 60, 175–216.

34 Caligiuri, P. (2000b). The big five personality characteristics as predictors of expatriate success. *Personnel Psychology*, 53, 67–88; Caligiuri (2000a).

35 Costa, P., and McCrae, R. (1992). Normal personality assessment in clinical practice: The NEO Personality Inventory. *Psychological Assessment*, 4, 5–13; Caligiuri (2000b).

36 Barrick, R., and Mount, K. (1991). The big five personality dimensions and job performance: A meta-analyses. *Personnel Psychology*, 44, 1–26.; Costa, P., and McCrae, R. (1992). Normal personality assessment in clinical practice: The NEO Personality Inventory. *Psychological Assessment*, 4, 5–13.

37 Barrick, R., Mount, K., and Judge, T. (2001). Personality and performance at the beginning of the new millennium: What do we know and where do we go next? *International Journal of Selection and Assessment*, 9, 9–30; Barrick, R., and Mount, K. (1991). The big five personality dimensions and job performance: A meta-analyses. *Personnel Psychology*, 44, 1–26.

38 Barrick and Mount (1991); Costa and McCrae (1992).

39 Barrick and Mount (1991); Costa and McCrae (1992).

40 Caligiuri, P., and Tarique, I. (2012); Caligiuri, P., Tarique, I., and Jacobs, R. (2009). Selection for international assignments. *Human Resource Management Review*, 19, 251–262; Caligiuri, P. (2000b).

41 Caligiuri, P., and Tarique, I. (2012); Caligiuri (2000a).

42 See, for example, Kempen, R., Pangert, B., Hattrup, K., Mueller, K., and Joens, I. (2015). Beyond conflict: The role of life-domain enrichment for expatriates. *International Journal of Human Resource Management*, 26(1), 1–22; Mahajan, A., and Toh, S.M. (2014). Facilitating expatriate adjustment: The role of advice-seeking from host country nationals. *Journal of World Business*, 49(4), 476–48; van Erp, K.M., van der Zee, K.I., Giebels, E., and van Duijn, M.J. (2014). Lean on me: The importance of one's own and partner's intercultural personality for expatriate's and expatriate spouse's successful adjustment abroad. *European Journal of Work and Organizational Psychology*, 23(5), 706–728; Kawai, N., and Strange, R. (2014). Perceived organizational support and expatriate performance: Understanding a mediated model. *International Journal of Human Resource Management*, 25(17), 2438–2462; Hippler, T., Caligiuri, P., and Johnson, J. (2014). Revisiting the construct of expatriate adjustment. *International Studies of Management and Organization*, 44(3), 8–24; Black, J.S. and Mendenhall, M. (1990). Cross-cultural effectiveness: A review and a theoretical framework for future research. *Academy of Management Review*, 15, 113–136; Brocklyn, P. (1989). Developing the international executive. *Personnel*, March, 44–48; Callahan, M. (1989). Preparing the new global manager. *Training and Development Journal*, March, 29–31; Conway, M.E. (1998). Sexual harassment abroad. *Global Workforce*, Sept., 8–9; Hixon, A.L. (1986). Why corporations make haphazard overseas staffing decisions. *Personnel Administrator*, March, 91–94; Hogan, G.W. and Goodson, J.R. (1979). The key to expatriate success. *Training and Development Journal*, January, 50–52; Lanier, A.R. (1979). Selecting and preparing personnel for overseas transfers. *Personnel Journal*, March, 160–163; Stuart, K.D. (1992). Teens play a role in moves overseas. *Personnel Journal*, March, 71–78; Tung, R.L. (1987). Expatriate assignments: Enhancing success and minimizing failure. *Academy of Management Executive*, 1 (2), 117–126; Tung, R.L. (1988). Career issues in international assignments, *Academy of Management Executive*, 2 (3), 241–244.

43 Mol, S., Born, M., Willemsen, M., and Van der Molen, H. (2005). Predicting expatriate job performance for selection purposes—A quantitative review. *Journal of Cross-Cultural Psychology*, 36, 590–620; Bhaskar-Shrinivas, P., Harrison, D., Shaffer, M., and Luk, D. (2005). Input-based and time-based modes of international adjustment: Meta-analytic evidence and theoretical extensions. *Academy of Management Journal*, 8, 257–281.

44 This discussion is based on Frederick, M. (2011). Key considerations for a successful global assignment, Webinar, IOR Global Services, www.iorworld.com, Dec. 14; and Stuart, D.K. (2009). Assessment instruments for the global workforce, in M. Moodian (ed.) *Contemporary Leadership and Intercultural Competence: Exploring the Cross-cultural Dynamics Within Organizations*, Thousand Oaks, CA: Sage, 175–190. Also see assessment tools such as *Self Assessment for Global Endeavors* (http://rw-3.com/solutions/), *Global Competencies Inventory* (http://kozaigroup.com/inventories/the-global-competencies-inventory-gci/),

Intercultural Development Inventory (http://idiinventory.com/), and *Tucker Assessment Profile* (http://tuck erintl.com/).

45 Refer to endnotes 27 and 39.

46 Caligiuri and Tarique (2012).

47 Briscoe, D.R. (1997). Assessment centers: Cross-cultural and cross-national issues, in Riggio, R.E. and Mayes, B.T. (eds.), *Assessment Centers: Research and Application*, special issue of the *Journal of Social Behavior and Personality*, 12 (5), 261–270.

48 For overviews of these issues, look at Dowling, P.J., Festing, M., and Engle, A.D., Sr. (2013). *International Human Resource Management*, 6th ed., Andover, UK: Cengage; Stroh et al. (2005); Vance, C.M. and Paik, Y. (2011). *Managing a Global Workforce*, 2nd ed., Armonk, NY/London: M.E. Sharpe.

49 Nasif, E.G., Thibodeaux, M.S. and Ebrahimi, B. (1987). Variables associated with success as an expatriate manager. *Proceedings*, Academy of International Business, Southeast Region, annual meeting, New Orleans, November 4–7, 169–179.

50 Refer to sources in previous notes plus Black, J.S. and Gregersen, H.B. (1991). The other half of the picture; Antecedents of spouse cross-cultural adjustment, *Journal of International Business Studies*, second quarter, 225–247; Fuchsberg, G. (1990). As costs of overseas assignments climb, firms select expatriates more carefully, *Wall Street Journal*, April 5, B–1, B–5; Gomez-Mejia, L. and Balkin, D.B. (1987). The determinants of managerial satisfaction with the expatriation and repatriation process, *Journal of Management Development*, 6 (1), 7–18; Savich, R.S. and Rodgers, W. (1988). Assignment overseas: Easing the transition before and after, *Personnel*, August, 44–48; Tung (1988).

51 Adapted from National Foreign Trade Council (NFTC), Society for Human Resource Management (SHRM), and GMAC Global Relocation Services (GMAC GRS)/Windham International *Global Relocation Trends Annual Survey* Reports, 1993–2014; Stroh et al. (2005); and Tung (1987).

52 Sanchez. J.I., Spector, P.E., and Cary, C. (2000). Adapting to a boundaryless world: A developmental expatriate model. *The Academy of Management Executive*, 14, 96–107.

53 Black, Mendenhall, and Oddou (1991).

54 Based on Perraud, P. and Davis, A. (1997). Assignment success or failure: It's all in the family, presented to the annual conference of the Institute for International Human Resource Management, early division of the US Society for Human Resource Management, Los Angeles, CA, April 15–17; and *Global Mobility in the Context of Global Talent Management* (2011). World Bank Community Conference on Global Mobility, Washington, DC.

55 Perraud and Davis (1997).

56 Bennett, R. (1993). Solving the dual international career dilemma. *HR News*, January, C5.

57 Reported in *Expatriate Advisor*, autumn, 28–29; Punnett, B.J. (1997). Towards effective management of expatriate spouses, *Journal of World Business*, 32 (3), 243–257; Thaler-Carter, R.E. (1999). Vowing to go abroad, *HR Magazine*, November, 90–96.

58 Mol, S., Born, M., Willemsen, M., and Van der Molen, H. (2005). Predicting expatriate job performance for selection purposes—A quantitative review. *Journal of Cross-Cultural Psychology*, 36, 590–620; Bhaskar-Shrinivas, P., Harrison, D., Shaffer, M., and Luk, D. (2005). Input-based and time-based modes of international adjustment: Meta-analytic evidence and theoretical extensions. *Academy of Management Journal*, 8, 257–281.

59 Dolainski, S. (1997). Are expats getting lost in translation? *Workforce*, February, 32–39.

60 Caligiuri, P., Lazarova, M, and Tarique, I (2005). Training, learning, and development in multinational corporations, in H. Scullion and M. Linehan (eds.), *International Human Resource Management*, London/ New York: Palgrave Macmillan, pp. 71–90.

61 See, for example, Is there a problem, officer? Second time around expat describes benefits of language skills, *Global Voice*, Berlitz Newsletter of International Communication and Understanding (no date), 6 (1), 1; and *Reading across Boundaries* Newsletter of International Orientation Resources, July, 1994, 1–6.

62 *Reading across Boundaries* (1994), 1.

63 Ibid.

64 Solon, L. (2000). The language of global business, *SHRM Global*, December, 12–14.

65 The world's most widely spoken language, cited from a number of sources posted on the website of St. Ignatius High School website, www.ignatius.edu/. Accessed Mar. 13. 2015.

66 Refer to surveys by Mercer Human Resources Consulting (www.mercerhr.com) and GMAC Global Relocation Services/Windham International, Prudential Relocation, and Cendant International Assignment Services.

67 Adler, N.J. (1984a). Expecting international success: Female managers overseas, *Columbia Journal of World Business*, 19 (3), 79–85; Adler, N.J. (1987). Pacific Basin managers: A *gaijin*, not a woman. *Human Resource Management*, 26 (2), 169–191; Adler, N.J. (1984b). Women do not want international careers—and other myths about international management. *Organizational Dynamics*, 13 (2), 66–79. Adler, N.J. (1984c). Women in international management: Where are they? *California Management Review*, 26 (4), 78–89; Adler, N.J. and Izraeli, D. (eds.) (1988). *Women in Management Worldwide*, Armonk, NY: Sharpe; Adler, N.J. and Izraeli, D.N. (eds.) (1994). *Competitive Frontiers: Women Managers in a Global Economy*, Cambridge, MA and Oxford: Blackwell; Corporate women: A rush of recruits for overseas duty, *Business Week*, April 20, 1981, 120ff; Jelinek, M. and Adler, N.J. (1988). Women: World-class managers for global competition. *Academy of Management Executive*, 2 (1), 11–19; Kirk, W.Q. and Maddox, R.C. (1988). International management: The new frontier for women. *Personnel*, March, 46–49; Lockwood, N. (2004). *The Glass Ceiling: Domestic and International Perspectives*, Alexandria, VA: SHRM Research Quarterly.

68 Adler, N.J. (1984d). Managers perceive greater barriers for women in international versus, domestic management. *Columbia Journal of World Business*, 19 (1), 45–53.

69 Ibid.; Pomeroy, A. (2006). Outdated policies hinder female expats. *HR Magazine*, December, 16 (reporting on survey results from Mercer Human Resource Accounting); Mercer HR Consulting (2006). More females sent on international assignment than ever before, survey finds, retrieved from www.mercerhr.com, 12/30/2006.

70 See above, plus surveys by GMAC Global Relocation Services/Windham International/SHRM Global annual reports.

71 Abraham, Y. (1985). Personnel policies and practices in Saudi Arabia. *Personnel Administrator*, April, 102; Thal, N. and Caleora, P. (1979). Opportunities for women in international business, *Business Horizons*, December, 21–27.

72 Adler (1984b); Golesorkhi, B. (1991). Why not a woman in overseas assignments? *HR News: International HR*, March, C4; Kirk and Maddox (1988).

73 See above, plus Brown, L.K. (1989). *Women in Management Worldwide*, Armonk, NY: Sharpe; Catalyst (2000). *Passport to Opportunity: U.S. Women in Global Business*, New York: Catalyst; Maital, S. (1989). A long way to the top. *Across the Board*, December, 6–7.

74 Ibid., 41–44; Sappal, P. (1999). Sometimes it's hard to be a woman. *HR World*, January–February, 21–24.

75 Caligiuri, P.M. and Cascio, W.F. (1998). Can we send her there? Maximizing the success of Western women on global assignments. *Journal of World Business*, 33 (4), 394–416; Caligiuri, P.M. and Cascio, W.F. (2000). Sending women on global assignments, *World at Work Journal*, second quarter, 34–41; Caligiuri, P.M. and Tung, R.L. (1999). Comparing the success of male and female expatriates from a US-based multinational company. *International Journal of Human Resource Management*, 10, 763–782; Taylor, S. and Napier, N. (1996). Working in Japan: Lessons from Western expatriates. *Sloan Management Review*, 37, 76–84.

76 Varma, A., Stroh, L.K. and Schmitt, L.B. (2001). Women and international assignments: The impact of supervisor-subordinate relationships. *Journal of World Business*, 36 (4), 380–388.

77 Harris, H. (1999). Women in international management, in Brewster, C. and Harris, H. (eds.), *International Human Resource Management*, London: Routledge.

78 Joinson, C. (2002). No returns: "Localizing" expats saves companies big money and can be a smooth transition with a little due diligence by HR. *HR Magazine*, November, 70–77.

79 See, for example, Black, J.S., Gregersen, H.B., Mendenhall, M.E., and Stroh, L.K. (1999). *Globalizing People through International Assignments*, Reading, MA: Addison Wesley; Hauser, J. (1997). Leading practices in international assignment programs. *International HR Journal*, summer, 34–37; McCall, M.W., Jr. and Hollenbeck, G.P. (2002). *Developing Global Executives: The Lessons of International Experience*, Boston, MA: Harvard Business School Press; Stahl, G.K., Miller, E.L. and Tung, R.T. (2002). Toward the boundaryless career: A closer look at the expatriate career concept and the perceived implications of an international assignment. *Journal of World Business*, 37, 216–227; Stroh et al. (2005).

80 Gregson, K. (1997). Outsourcing international assignments. *International HR Journal*, fall, 38–40; Joinson, C. (2002). Save thousands per expatriate. *HR Magazine*, July, 73–77; Smith, J.J. (2006). Executives say HR needs to improve to attract top global talent, reporting on findings reported in the Economist Intelligence Unit's *CEO Briefing: Corporate Priorities for 2006 and Beyond*, retrieved from http://www.shrm.org/global/news_published/CMS_0117960.asp. Accessed June 15, 2007.

81 Smith, J.J. (2006). Firms say expats getting too costly; but few willing to act, reporting on findings of the KPMG *2006 Global Assignment Policies and Practices* survey, retrieved 9/11/2006 from http://www.shrm.org/global/news_published/CMS_018300.asp.

82 The term "inpatriates" is a little more than 10 years old. It is a term developed by MNEs to describe a particular type of international employee, as described in the text. Subsequently, most of the literature describing inpatriates has been written by practitioners, consultants, or journalists writing in magazines with a primarily practitioner readership. For example, refer to Bachler, C.J. (1996). Global inpats: Don't let them surprise you. *Personnel Journal*, June, 54–64; Cook, J. (1998). A whole new world. *Human Resource Executive*, March 19, 1–2; Copeland, A.P. (1995). Helping foreign nationals adapt to the U.S. *Personnel Journal*, February, 83–87; Finney, M. (2000). Culture shock in America? For foreign expatriates, absolutely. *Across the Board*, May, 28–33; Harvey, M.G. and Buckley, M.R. (1997). Managing inpatriates: Building a global core competency. *Journal of World Business*, 32 (1), 35–52; Harvey, M.G., Novicevic, M.M. and Speier, C. (2000). An innovative global management staffing system: A competency-based perspective. *Human Resource Management*, 39 (4), 381–394; Joinson, C. (1999). The impact of "inpats." *HR Magazine Focus*, April, 5–10; Kent, S. (2001). Welcome to our world. *Global HR*, February–March, 32–36; Lachnit, C. (2001). Low-cost tips for successful inpatrition. *Workforce*, August, 42–47; Ladika, S. (2005). Unwelcome changes. *HR Magazine*, February, 83–90; Solomon, C.M. (1995). HR's helping hand pulls global inpatriates on board. *Personnel Journal*, November, 40–49; Solomon, C.M. (2000). Foreign relations. *Workforce*, November, 50–56.

83 Caligiuri, P.M. (1997). Assessing expatriate success: Beyond just "being there," *New Approaches to Employee Management*, 4 (1), 17–40.

84 Ibid.

85 Many of the references in this chapter deal with various aspects of Best Practice in selection of IAs. In addition, refer to Berlitz International, PHH Relocation, and SHRM Institute for International HRM (1996–1997), executive summary, *International Assignee Research Project*, Berlitz, PHH, SHRM; Lomax, S. (2001). *Best Practices for Managers and Expatriates*, New York: Wiley; Black, J.S. and Gregersen, H.B. (1999). The right way to manage expats. *Harvard Business Review*, March–April, 52–63; Herring, L. and Greenwood, P. (2000). "Best practices" leverage international assignment success in the United States. *International HR Journal*, spring, 21–28; Institute of Personnel and Development (1999). *The IPD Guide on International Recruitment, Selection, and Assessment*, London: IPD; Melton (2005); Prudential Relocation Global Services (no date). *Leading Practices in International Assignment Programs*, Valhalla, NY: Prudential Relocation; Stroh et al. (2005); Toh, S.M. and DeNisi, A.S. (2005). A local perspective to expatriate success. *Academy of Management Executive*, 19 (1), 132–146; GMAC Global Relocation Services/Windham International, National Foreign Trade Council, and SHRM Global Forum (2007 and previous years), *Global Relocation Trends Annual Survey Report*, New York: GMAC GRS/Windham International; Lomax, S. (2001). *Best Practices for Managers & Expatriates*, New York: John Wiley and Sons; Stroh et al. (2005); Vance, C.M. and Paik, Y. (2006). *Managing a Global Workforce*, Armonk, NY: M.E. Sharpe.

86 Barboza, D. (2006). Sharp labor shortage in China may lead to world trade shift. *The New York Times*, April 3, A1, A10; Clouse, T. (2006). Firms in China faced with tight supply of skilled labor. *Workforce Management*, September 11, 37–38; Fox, A. (2007). China: Land of opportunity and challenge. *HR Magazine*, September, 38–44; Lee, D. (2006). Job hopping is rampant as China's economy chases skilled workers. *Los Angeles Times*, February 21, C1.

87 Kent, S. (1999). Cultivating home-grown talent. *HR World*, November–December, 24–28.

88 Halley, J. (1999). Localization as an ethical response to internationalization, in Brewster, C. and Harris, H. (eds.), *International Human Resource Management*, London: Routledge; Kent, S. (1999). Cultivating home-grown talent. *HR World*, November–December, 24–28; Solomon, C.M. (1995). Learning to manage host-country nations. *Personnel Journal*, March, 21–26.

89 Robock, S.H. and Simmonds, K. (1989). *International Business and Multinational Enterprises*, 4th ed., Homewood, IL: Irwin, p. 559.

90 Smith, J.J. (2006). More third-country nationals being used, retrieved from the SHRM Global HR Focus Area: http://www.shrm.org/global/news_published/CMS_017348.asp. Accessed June 15, 2006.

91 Friedman, T.L. (2005). *The World Is Flat: A Brief History of the Twenty-First Century*, New York: Farrar, Straus and Giroux; Johnston, W.B. (1991). Global work force 2000: The new world labor market. *Harvard Business Review*, March–April, 115–127.

92 For example, refer to Briscoe, D.R. (2008). Talent management in the global learning organization, in Vaiman, V. and Vance, C.M. (eds.), *Smart Talent Management: Building Knowledge Capital for Competitive Advantage*, Cheltenham, UK/Northhampton, MA: Edward Elgar Publishing, pp. 195–216; Herman, R., Olivo, T. and Gioia, J. (2003). *Impending Crisis: Too Many Jobs, Too Few People*, Winchester, VA: Oakhill Press; Johnston (1991); Leonard, B. (2006). Immigration rises sharply in most developed nations, retrieved from the SHRM Global HR Focus Area: http://www.shrm.org/global/news_published/CMS_017977.asp. Accessed Jan. 31, 2006; Richman, L.S. (1990). The coming world labor shortage. *Fortune*, April 9, 70–77; Schramm, J. (2006). *Global Labor Mobility*, Workplace Visions, No. 2, Alexandria, VA: Society for Human Resource Management; Templeman, J., Wise, D.C., Lask, E. and Evans, R. (1989). Grappling with the graying of Europe. *Business Week*, March 13, 54–56.

93 Adler, N.J. and Gundersen, A. (2008). *International Dimensions of Organizational Behavior*, 5th ed., Ohio: Thomson/Southwestern; Black, J.S. (1991). Returning expatriates feel foreign in their native land. *HR Focus*, August, 17; Brewster, C. (1991). *The Management of Expatriates*, London: Kogan Page; Harvey, M.G. (1989). Repatriation of corporate executives: An empirical study. *Journal of International Business Studies*, spring, 131–144; Howard, C.G. (1987). Out of sight—not out of mind. *Personnel Administrator*, June, 82–90; Stroh et al. (2005); Tyler, K. (2006). Retaining expatriates. *HR Magazine*, March, 92–102; Vance and Paik (2006); Welds, K. (1991). The return trip. *HR Magazine*, June, 113–114.

94 Brewster, C., Bonache, J., Cerdin, J.-L. and Suutari, V. (2014). Exploring expatriate outcomes. *The International Journal of Human Resource Management*, 25 (14), 1921–1937; Brewster, C. (1991). *The Management of Expatriates*, London: Kogan Page.

95 Adapted from Ettorre, B. (1993). A brave new world: Managing international careers. *Management Review*, April, 15.

96 Shumsky, N.J. (1999). Repatriation can be the most difficult part of a global assignment. *CRN News*, May, 21.

97 See Oddou, G., Szkudlarek, B., Osland, J.S., Deller, J., Blakeney, R., and Furuya, N. (2013). Repatriates as a source of competitive advantage: How to manage knowledge transfer. *Organizational Dynamics*, 42(4), 257–266; Bailey, C., and Dragoni, L. (2013). Repatriation after global assignments: Current HR practices and suggestions for ensuring successful repatriation. *People and Strategy*, 36(1), 48–57; Ren, H., Bolino, M.C., Shaffer, M.A., and Kraimer, M.L. (2013). The influence of job demands and resources on repatriate career satisfaction: A relative deprivation perspective. *Journal of World Business*, 48(1), 149–159; Oddou, G., Szkudlarek, B., Osland, J.S., Deller, J., Blakeney, R., and Furuya, N. (2013). Repatriates as a source of competitive advantage: How to manage knowledge transfer. *Organizational*

Dynamics, 42(4), 257–266; Kraimer, M. L., Shaffer, M. A., Harrison, D. A., and Ren, H. (2012). No place like home? An identity strain perspective on repatriate turnover. *Academy of Management Journal*, 55(2), 399–420. Lazarova, M and Caligiuri, P. (2001). Retaining repatriates: The role of organizational support practices. *Journal of World Business*, 36(4), 389–401; Kraimer, M., Shaffer, M., and Bolino, M. (2009). The influence of expatriate and repatriate experiences on career advancement and repatriate retention. *Human Resource Management*, 48(1), 27; Lazarova, M and Cerdin., J. (2007). Revisiting repatriation concerns: Organizational support versus career and contextual influences. *Journal of International Business Studies*, 38(3), 404–429.

98 Lazarova and Caligiuri (2001); Kraimer, Shaffer, and Bolino (2009); Lazarova and Cerdin (2007).

99 Lazarova and Caligiuri (2001).

100 Munkel, N. and Nghiem, L. (1999). Do multinationals face up to the challenges of repatriation? *KPMG Expatriate Administrator*, 4, 6–8.

101 Lazarova, M., and Tarique, I. (2005). Knowledge transfer upon repatriation. *Journal of World Business*, 40, 361–373.

Chapter 10

International Training and Management Development

It is part of our philosophy as an attractive employer to invest continuously in developing the skills of our employees. In the past seven years alone, we have invested approximately €1.5 billion in training.

Norbert Reithofer
Chairman of the Board of Management, BMW Corporation[1]

Learning Objectives

This chapter will enable the reader to:

- Advocate for training and development programs for the MNE's global managers and workforce.
- Identify the challenges of training an international workforce.
- Explain key learning objectives that drive training programs aimed at enabling a productive global workforce.
- Design cross-cultural training programs that enable international assignees to successfully complete their assignments and develop an effective global management team.
- Develop a global mindset, global competencies, and global leadership in the international organization.
- Improve the effectiveness of global and virtual teams.

MNEs confront a number of special problems related to the training and development (T&D) of their global workforces and managers. Responsibility for T&D is traditionally one of HR's core functions. So when an enterprise's international business reaches a significant level, when it is involved with multiple subsidiaries and partnerships in other countries, when it transfers its technology to other countries, when it develops and pursues a global strategy and markets its products and/or services on a global scale, and when it relocates a number of employees to international positions, the T&D function takes on a new and more complex nature.

In this chapter, T&D is examined from the perspective of MNEs. *Training* refers normally to activities designed to develop or improve employee job skills. *Development* is the term that refers primarily to the development of managers and executives (or the preparation of employees to become managers and/or executives, although less frequently it refers more broadly to career development of all employees). In this text, when the term "development" is used, the discussion is concerned primarily with *management, executive,* and *leadership development*. T&D is almost always imbedded in the HR department, and in this chapter the discussion will primarily be focused on the training and management development activities of MNEs, including needs assessment and instructional design issues that arise when T&D programs are developed and delivered for a global workforce. These design concerns include the sharing of knowledge and best practices across MNEs, the design and delivery of global management/leadership development programs, the development of global mindsets for managers and employees, the special training needs of people on international assignments, the importance of technology today in both the content of training and the delivery of that content, and the preparation of employees to work effectively in virtual and global teams.

In addition to the adoption of formal global training and management development programs, the increasingly complex nature of global firms also requires attention to the development of informal relationships and networks. These, too, may require training or access to learning opportunities to facilitate. IHR needs to be prepared to analyze the MNE's formal and informal global training and development needs, to design, develop, and implement T&D programs to meet those needs, and to evaluate whether these T&D initiatives ultimately help the MNE achieve a competitive advantage in its global operations. It is the objective of this chapter to provide the basics for this IHR responsibility.

THE TRAINING FUNCTION

Since an MNE's human capital may be its most important source of competitive advantage, a well-trained and educated global workforce is critical to success in the global marketplace.[2] Therefore, the following seven imperatives have been suggested as keys to global organizational learning and T&D.[3] Further, these imperatives provide a statement of the values that underlie this chapter's discussion of training and management development for successful MNEs.

- **Think and act globally.** That is, a global enterprise must think about and prepare for a presence in all the critical markets in the world, not just in its home region.
- **Become an equidistant global learning organization.** That is, learning must be facilitated from and in all cultures.[4] In Kenichi Ohmae's words: *"It may be unfamiliar and*

awkward, but the primary rule of equi-distance is to see—and to think—global [not local] first. Honda, for example, has manufacturing divisions in Japan, North America, and Europe—all three legs of the [major markets of the world]—but its managers do not think or act as if the company were divided between Japanese and overseas operations. In fact, the very word overseas has no place in Honda's vocabulary, because the corporation sees itself as equidistant from all its key customers."[5]

- **Focus on the global system, not its parts.** That is, T&D programs need to focus on breaking down the silos of departments and even the boundaries between countries and those that separate customers and suppliers. They should focus on the "big picture" global organizational system.

- **Develop global leadership skills.** That is, global leadership requires competencies different from those needed in the domestic marketplace. These should be one of the key foci of global training and development programs.

- **Empower teams to create a global future.** That is, cross-border and virtual teams should be increasingly used and empowered to perform critical organizational projects and problem-solving activities. In addition, these global teams can, themselves, be a major tool in the development of cross-cultural competencies.

- **Make learning a core competence for the global organization.** That is, the global organization needs to become a global learning organization, where learning and development permeates all that the organization does.[6] As Arie de Geus, former head of strategic planning at Royal/Dutch Shell, put it, *"Over the long term, the only sustainable competitive advantage may be an organization's ability to learn faster than its competitors."*[7]

- **Both the global organization and its individual members must constantly reinvent themselves.** That is, constant self-development must become the cornerstone of strategies for success for both individuals and organizations in today's highly competitive global economy.

The challenge of mastering the ever-and-rapidly-changing and expanding global needs of individuals and organizations may be overwhelming. But it is exactly this challenge for IHRM that is addressed in this chapter on global training and management development.

Issues Related to Global Training and Development

The instructional model, referred to by the acronym ADDIE[8] (analysis, design, development, implementation, evaluation), as commonly used by instructional designers, focuses on the various stages of T&D. Many of the decisions that are made during these stages are impacted by the fact that T&D programs in an MNE are developed and used in multiple locations, cultures, and languages. When enterprises operate subsidiaries and partnerships around the world, the training of the members of their global workforce takes on special importance and difficulty. The major issues related to global training and development center around the design, development, implementation, and communication of the training programs, including both technical and non-technical training.

It is risky to roll out global training programs without localizing the content and implementation, since such centralized approaches are likely to reduce both the acceptance and effectiveness of the training interventions. Localization of training programs requires "needs analysis" based at the local level and includes localized translation, adaptation to the local cultural practices, and compliance with local laws affecting training. Too often, corporate T&D simply tries to apply successful training programs from headquarters. But this often does not work. The types of problems confronting the MNE when it begins to discuss the need for training of its local workforces around the world include the following:[9]

- Who should deliver training in the foreign subsidiaries and joint ventures? Trainers from headquarters? Local trainers? Independent trainers?
- How should the training be delivered? Are there local cultural differences and learning preferences that need to be considered?
- What are the effects of language differences? Will there be translation problems (for both written and orally presented materials)? Are there differences in the meanings of words? Are there terms and phrases that don't exist in the "foreign" language(s)? Who should take responsibility (headquarters personnel, host-country specialists, or third-party vendors) for translation? Should training programs be exported from headquarters or should overseas employees be brought to centralized or regional training facilities? How effective is e-learning in the MNE? Can training programs be developed in various locations and made available to everyone? What are the effects of the various options?
- Should courses for management development be handled differently than training for host-country and third-country employees?
- To ensure respect for each host country's culture, should each subsidiary or joint venture develop its own training? Do they have the capability? Or are there strong reasons to insist on centrally developed training programs?
- How does an MNE adapt a training program (in terms of both the content and the process of the training) to different countries and cultures?
- And, last, the needs analysis must to assess the differing content (skills and knowledge) that each locale requires.

Of course, part of the challenge for MNE trainers and IHR is that there are no easy answers to these questions. Because of that, many firms develop international training practices to fit their particular needs and resources, and make assumptions about what should work best. The approaches taken by differing MNEs to training of local workforces in their foreign subsidiaries and joint ventures range from total localization, with all training designed and managed at the subsidiary level, to total integration, with all training directed from headquarters and with the goal of full integration with the culture and perspectives of the parent firm. These issues are discussed in more detail in the section on cross-cultural training and development and as modeled in Exhibit 10.3, later in the chapter.

Localized Approach to Global Training and Development

Cross-cultural differences play an important role in the design, development, and implementation of T&D in MNEs. In addition, the effectiveness of T&D is likely to be impacted by structural concerns such as legal obligations to train, labor force educational levels, and different approaches to education and educational systems. For example, an American MNE spent several million dollars on upgrading its IT systems in all of its plants around the world, as well as on training initiatives to make sure that everyone understood the new system.[10] Yet its HR director couldn't understand why months after the training had taken place, some subsidiaries were still using the old procedures. Although the Scandinavians and the British welcomed the new ideas, the French, Italians, and Latin Americans were reluctant to accept another dictate from US headquarters. And although the Asians didn't complain during the training sessions, they, too, failed to implement the new system. It's a common scenario, says Richard Harlow, senior development consultant at global training consultancy TMA in the UK.[11]

> Time and time again, I hear similar stories of global training initiatives not having the desired effect. And it boils down to a number of reasons. Sometimes badly interpreted material is to blame, other times internal politics may be at play, or perhaps employees in a particular location are just not accustomed to the way the briefing/training is delivered. And companies end up digging deeper in their pockets to retrain or troubleshoot.

Sometimes, firms face such disappointments because they simply transfer a program devised at HQ straight to another country, without taking cultural norms into account. The problems go much deeper than just translating the training material into another language; trainers have to work around the cultural nuances as well. In many cases, the "global" training falls flat because it is just completely inappropriate for the particular culture.

Although there is no general roadmap for adjusting T&D programs to local conditions and cultures, at a minimum, IHR professionals must make the effort to understand local laws, practice, level of employee skills and knowledge, and employer obligations in order to improve the probability of achieving the required learning and development objectives. The next sections deal with T&D localization issues in terms of culture, language, learning styles, education levels and forms, local T&D laws, and transfer of learning.

Culture

National (and even professional and organizational) culture influences training in a number of ways. Before they set up a training program in a foreign subsidiary, IHR professionals must understand how that culture views the educational process. For instance, in many

Asian cultures, education is considered to be a very authoritarian phenomenon—although this is changing with the increasing interaction and integration of enterprises around the world and the subsequent exposure to different training methods and approaches. The teacher is seen as the expert whom students should respect. Teachers impart knowledge through one-way conversation: the teacher lectures and students listen respectfully. In such a context, students do not ask questions, and teachers do not solicit students' opinions. In such high-power distance cultures, the atmosphere is formal and respectful toward authority. In contrast, for example, US educational techniques, which are less formal, and which focus on interactivity and encourage student participation, can be ineffective in such Asian environments.

The degree of deference to instructors influences the extent to which a participative style can be used and the extent to which participants will ask questions or offer opinions and become involved in open discussion. Culture will influence adherence to a hierarchy among students, such as deference to the most senior member of a training group in discussion and stating of opinions. Culture influences all forms of interactions with instructors, as well, and influences what a training group will accept in terms of behavior of instructors, e.g., degree of formality and appearance. Culture influences the roles of students, e.g., based on their gender and positions, in ways that may be different from that which is familiar to the trainer or to those who developed the training. Training that is delivered to employees from cultures that are foreign to that of the people who designed the training or delivered by people from different cultures must take into account these and other issues related to culture or the success of the training may be limited.

Exhibit 10.1 illustrates how the cultural characteristics of a number of countries might influence choice of training pedagogies.[12] As Exhibit 10.1 suggests, students from high-power distance cultures (acceptance of status differences between students and instructors) and strong uncertainty-avoidance cultures (unwillingness to take risks and to try new things) are likely to desire and perform better in training programs that rely more heavily on structured and passive learning techniques, such as reading assignments and lectures versus those who come from weak uncertainty-avoidance and low-power distance cultures, who will probably do better with experiential training techniques (class discussions, interactive activities, and team projects). Of course, individuals within a culture may vary from these guidelines and any particular country subsidiary may have developed a company culture that supports the use of training techniques that are different from the norm for the particular culture.

Learning Styles

Learning styles are also related to culture. It is clear that, in addition to differing personal learning styles, people from differing cultures and countries are used to differing training and teaching styles. And thus their most comfortable learning approach needs to be considered in the design and delivery of training.

EXHIBIT 10.1: The Match of Training Techniques to Country Culture

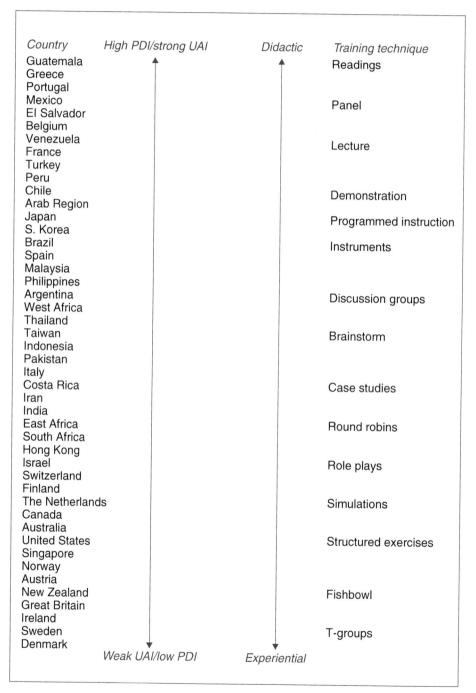

Country	High PDI/strong UAI	Didactic	Training technique
Guatemala			Readings
Greece			
Portugal			
Mexico			Panel
El Salvador			
Belgium			
Venezuela			Lecture
France			
Turkey			
Peru			
Chile			Demonstration
Arab Region			
Japan			Programmed instruction
S. Korea			
Brazil			Instruments
Spain			
Malaysia			
Philippines			
Argentina			Discussion groups
West Africa			
Thailand			
Taiwan			Brainstorm
Indonesia			
Pakistan			
Italy			
Costa Rica			Case studies
Iran			
India			
East Africa			Round robins
South Africa			
Hong Kong			
Israel			Role plays
Switzerland			
Finland			
The Netherlands			Simulations
Canada			
Australia			
United States			Structured exercises
Singapore			
Norway			
Austria			
New Zealand			Fishbowl
Great Britain			
Ireland			
Sweden			T-groups
Denmark	Weak UAI/low PDI	Experiential	

Source: Tyler, K. (1999). Offering English lessons at work, *HR Magazine*, December, 112–120.

Education Levels and Forms

One of the reasons that the provision of training and management development to multiple subsidiaries around the world is so complex is because the basic educational infrastructure varies so much from country to country. The basic level of literacy varies dramatically; the nature of the educational system and the type of education it provides varies significantly (e.g., whether theoretical or practical in orientation); the level, nature, and availability of higher education varies; the availability of vocational education varies considerably; and teaching and, therefore, learning styles used in any country's school system vary from country to country as well. Familiarity with various teaching techniques and media as well as relationships between students and instructors also vary so much that it is often impossible to transfer directly either the content or the method of instruction from one place to another. And increasingly, young people who have grown up with technology may expect different training styles as well.

Language

There are a number of issues in global T&D that involve language. One has to do with whether to provide training for the global workforce in a single, common language, or to translate training programs into varying languages for the global workforce. If the training is provided in a single language that language will likely be the language of the HQ or English. Another has to do with providing language classes, themselves, in order to enable employees to be able to interact more effectively both within the enterprise as well as to interact effectively with external constituencies, such as suppliers, sub-contractors, and customers (refer back to the Barden case in Chapter 8). In today's shrinking world, the ability to communicate accurately and effectively takes on increasing importance. Even though "business" English has become the primary language in which global business is conducted, it is clear that being able to sell, negotiate, discuss, and manage in the language of one's neighbors, customers, and employees can improve the probabilities of successful communication and, therefore, successful business transactions.

MNEs have learned how important foreign-language skills are. The ability to speak another language is seen as so important it has become a major plus when recruiting new employees. Language acquisition opens the door to deeper cultural understanding—speech patterns, thought patterns, and behavior patterns (for example, of customers) are interlinked. And, therefore, language study is a link to better understanding (and interaction with) the customer (as well as with employees). Increasingly within MNEs, internationalists having multilingual and multicultural capabilities are becoming the most sought-after type of employee. As a specific example, Chinese (particularly Mandarin) has become more popular for foreigners as firms send increasing numbers of employees on assignment to China. Making this issue more difficult, however, is the increasing use of short-term business travel to manage an MNE's foreign operations. It is relatively impractical to expect such traveling managers and executives to be able to speak the five to 10 languages they need for a typical trip to subsidiaries and/or customers/suppliers/sub-contractors, etc., to say nothing of the next five to 10 languages for the next trip. Many MNEs today operate in dozens of countries. Many large MNEs operate in well over 100 countries, with as many local languages in use. For these reasons, among others, using a single language for international interactions, such as training and development activities, makes much practical sense. Invariably, and for many reasons, English has become the language of choice for the conduct of most aspects of international business.

Therefore, teaching everyone to speak a common language, usually English, has become popular, at least in some firms. Such programs (usually referred to as ESL—English as a Second Language—or ESOL—English for Speakers of Other Languages) not only help new employees adapt (in the case of recent immigrants into an English-speaking country, for example) but also help others do their jobs better and increase worker loyalty and improve customer relations.[13] Again, for an example of this in a local manufacturer, refer to the Barden case described in Chapter 8. To the extent possible, language lessons should be presented in terms of workplace situations and required skills, which enhance the training's immediate usefulness. Even some countries, such as South Korea, have recognized the value of fluency in English for their citizens, such that they are developing a large multi-campus university facility (to have at least 12 branches from prestigious Western schools) where everyone will speak English and all programming will be in English.[14] The intent is to bolster opportunities for Koreans and to attract investment from abroad. For at least South Korea, widespread ability in English is seen as a competitive advantage in the global economy.

Another area of central concern relates to the language of the training itself. Global enterprises must make difficult decisions about whether to translate training materials into the languages of local (foreign) workforces and whether to provide the training, itself, in the language(s) of local workforces (either through the use of local trainers or through translators, if the trainers come from regional or corporate headquarters training groups and they don't speak the local language). If the decision is made to provide the training through translators, then the selection of interpreters and translators needs to be given special attention, since being good at interpretation and translation requires more than training in the original and the foreign language. It also requires close familiarity with the nature of the business and any technical and special managerial terminology that may not translate easily into the foreign language or back into the original language (refer back to the discussion of language and translation in Chapter 5 on culture, particularly the section on cross-cultural research).

In addition, of course, MNEs may be obligated by local law (or national pride) to provide the training in the language(s) of the country in which they operate. For example, even though Chinese employees may understand the training in English, they may want to receive the training in Mandarin as a matter of pride. In the state of California, in the US, all training, such as safety training, must be provided in any language of employees if the enterprise has more than 15 employees for whom a language other than English is their first language.

Training and Development Laws

MNEs must also take account of national laws and regulations. These laws may focus on the requirement to spend a certain percent of payroll expenses on training (or, alternatively, pay a percentage of payroll expenses in taxes to a government-sponsored training program), to train on certain subjects (i.e., safety, sexual harassment, cross-train, reduction in force, etc.), to translate material into the local language, to provide financial resources for employees to receive training, or to comply with labor contracts.

Transfer of Learning

Finally, transfer-of-learning issues are especially critical in cross-border T&D. This has to do with the extent to which people receiving training are able to (and/or actually do) apply what they learn to their jobs. Trainers have to consider not only the nature of cross-border training (as discussed above) but also must pay close attention to who needs to receive training. In the end, transfer-of-learning concerns (in the traditional sense of transfer from training program to job performance as well as in the sense of transfer from one country to another) arise in a number of special situations for the multinational enterprise, including in the merging of various company and national cultures in cross-border acquisitions and joint ventures, when coping with increased cross-national diversity due to the development of global workforces, and when dealing with the many problems of cross-cultural work teams.

Standardized Approach to International T&D

Even though there are many cultural reasons to localize training, MNEs also must think about how to integrate their T&D activities, not only to achieve economies of scale and scope, but to ensure that the same T&D is available for all of their worldwide employees on a timely basis. In a globally integrated enterprise there will always be a need to develop T&D interventions around common processes, practices, and organizational principles. This is especially the case in non-technical training (e.g., around management and leadership development issues). With the advance of communication and IT technologies, barriers to information and knowledge being readily accessible to everyone have been quasi-eliminated. MNEs are now taking advantage of the development opportunities provided through IT by making training programs on virtually every conceivable topic available through company-sponsored websites or from global online sites. MNEs are developing learning portals and making technical information and a wide array of T&D courses available to their employees online and accessible through personal computers, laptops, personal digital assistants (PDAs) and downloadable to handheld devices, such as cell phones, iPads, and other types of tablets. The once very expensive development of computer-based training (CBT) is being democratized and put at the fingertips of everyone through e-learning tools.

Problems with e-learning, however, remain and should not be overlooked. Although e-learning may be an efficient and cost-effective means of delivering training, there may still be implementation and cultural acceptance issues. These may include issues such as the following: Is the training standardized (reflecting parent-country management and regulations only) or is it localized to reflect local management practices and laws? Does everyone have access to the technology and is everyone familiar with its use? How acceptable is the type of training being offered and the form of communication in which it is delivered in different cultures? Have all or most of the online courses been developed only in the country of headquarters or only in Western, developed countries? Are there courses available in local languages and covering topics of importance to local subsidiaries? Even though there may be good reasons to pursue standardization of T&D programs, some localization is likely to always be necessary and desirable.

VIRTUAL AND GLOBAL TEAMS

The changing nature of organizations (and the type of work and the manner in which it is performed) requires that employees work increasingly on projects and in teams.[15] Global interconnectedness, especially as a result of delocalization, disassembly of work in manufacturing and services, and the development of new technologies, has made the use and nature of teams increasingly more global, virtual, and common. And, now, where a team was usually thought of as comprising 5 to 15 people, larger teams (as many as 100 or more) are increasingly becoming common in MNEs.[16] These teams, in turn, must now organize themselves in sub-teams to achieve their goals. This has made it increasingly necessary for MNEs to organize training programs and curricula around the formation and management of teams.

Teamwork and team effectiveness have been subjects of research in organizational behavior for many decades and are heavily influenced by culture.[17] For example, how does one build and earn trust in different societies; how do team members from different cultures manage conflict on their teams; and how do team members from different cultures deal with confrontation when there is a problem on a team? Friendships and personal networks that are formed with people inside and outside of the group, business-centered relationships that are developed with people in other parts of the organization, and relationships that extend into the social sphere (often referred to as social capital) have all been found to also be important to successful team operation.[18] Indeed, team members from cultures that are relationship- rather than task-oriented may be more effective in utilizing their networks to benefit the team than are people who come from cultures where the nature of the deal is most important. The point is that the cultural norms of the people who are members of a team have a lot to do with how—and how well—the team will function. And this makes training for team members quite important, to ensure smooth interaction between team members.

Individuals' preferred team roles impact the overall effectiveness of teams, but do not adequately take into account the global and cultural context in which teams now increasingly must operate, such as their increased size.[19] First, team members are increasingly geographically dispersed and work in different time zones. Second, cross-border teams are more likely than domestic teams to be very heterogeneous in terms of national cultural and ethnic backgrounds. Third, they tend to be larger than co-located teams because they often work on issues related to the global enterprise and must have geographic representation. Fourth, they most likely communicate in English, which is likely to not be the native language of many or most of the global team members. No matter how challenging effective teamwork may be in co-located teams, the problems are compounded in dispersed teams due largely to the fact that team members are (usually) not working face-to-face. Hence, virtual teams present some unique leadership and training challenges. IHR becomes the function responsible for making sure that global team members receive the necessary training to work effectively with one another.

Long before the current interest in virtual global and far-flung teams, researchers have been interested in assessing whether culturally homogenous teams are more or less effective than heterogeneous teams.[20] The results indicate that diverse teams that are well managed perform better than homogeneous teams, but poorly managed diverse teams do not perform with the same effectiveness as homogeneous teams. The reason for the increased performance of well-managed heterogeneous teams is due to the synergy that comes from their diversity. The reason for their ineffectiveness when poorly managed comes from their problems overcoming the complexity of their teams (see Figure 10.1). When heterogeneous

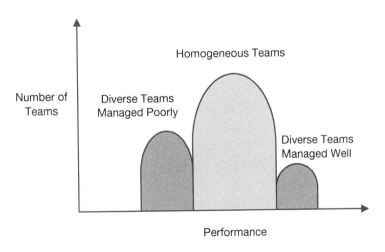

FIGURE 10.1 Effectiveness of Homogeneous and Heterogeneous Teams

Source: DiStefano, J. J. and Maznevski, M. L. (2000). Creating value with diverse teams in global management. *Organizational Dynamics, 29*(1), 45–63.

teams can overcome the difficulties of managing their diversity, they are able to capture the benefits of their synergy and be more effective than is the case with homogeneous teams. Thus, a major topic for team training becomes diversity training, whether the teams are co-located or dispersed, cross-border, and virtual.

Since MNEs are increasingly using these cross-border and virtual teams, their effectiveness has become of paramount importance. Creating training programs that help create such productivity then becomes a high priority for IHR. Several sets of best practices with regard to the effectiveness of virtual teams are currently being proposed. Tips for virtual teams include: start with a face-to-face meeting in order to develop personal relationships; keep the team as small as practical; have a code of practice for communicating; communicate regularly, but don't overdo it; ensure everyone understands everyone else's roles; have a supportive sponsor; keep strong links with the parent organization; and reward team results—not how individual people work.[21]

Best practices related to virtual team leadership include:

1   establishing and maintaining trust through the use of communication technology;
2   ensuring that distributed diversity is understood and appreciated;
3   managing virtual work-life cycle meetings;
4   monitoring team progress using technology;
5   using team building to enhance virtual team performance;
6   continuing periodic face-to-face meetings;
7   enhancing visibility of virtual members within the team and outside the organization; and
8   enabling individual members of the virtual team to benefit from the team.[22]

As more MNEs are using virtual and global teams, the knowledge of how to make these teams more effective and how to prepare employees for such team experiences can be expected to grow in the future. And one could predict that the need for and delivery of training programs (on a global basis) to improve team effectiveness can also be expected to grow.

GLOBAL LEADERSHIP DEVELOPMENT

T&D is also responsible for the development of managers and global leaders for the MNE. Here, too, the effect of globalization is being felt. Most early and contemporary management and leadership development theories originated in the Western world. At the turn of the 21st century, with its rapid globalization, a number of leadership books[23] questioned whether the characteristics that made Western leaders effective should be universally applied. If leadership theories are context-specific, then it became legitimate to question whether US- and Western-centric leadership concepts and practices are as effective in multicultural and international environments as they have been in Western contexts. Hence, a number of new "global leadership" theories and models emerged as a complement to the emerging "global company" model.

Global Leadership Theories

The GLOBE (acronym for Global Leadership and Organizational Behavior Effectiveness) research project is the largest academic study on leadership from a global perspective (based on data from 62 countries).[24] The primary objective of the research was to identify global leadership characteristics that are universally accepted and effective across cultures. The main finding of the GLOBE research has been that charismatic/transformational leadership styles are strongly endorsed across cultures. Transformational leadership is a leadership style in which leaders develop (transform) their followers into new leaders.[25] Transformational leaders focus themselves and their followers on achieving higher-level visions and missions (through the development of commitment, trust, loyalty, and performance). They take the time to get to know the people they work with, what these people need to know to perform at their best, and how far they can be stretched, challenged, and supported. They are respected for taking stands on important causes and concerns; for encouraging people to question and to use their intelligence; and for being able to tap into the full potential of those being led.

The identification of high-potential individuals, the development of their leadership skills through challenging job assignments, and the accelerated learning processes geared at key talent for succession planning in the global organization are considered crucial competitive advantages, especially in an era of increased war for talent. The following provides a short summary of these processes that are so critical to global management development.

Global Executives: Developing Managers in the Global Enterprise

There comes a time in the development of global enterprises when they examine the development of their managers from an international perspective. They begin to realize that not only is international experience necessary for their parent-country managers, but they also begin to realize the importance of developing managerial talent throughout their organizations. Indeed, probably the most formidable task in human resources facing global firms today is the development of a cadre of team members, managers, and executives who have a deep understanding of the global marketplace, have the capability to transfer this knowledge into resolute global action, and who expect to see their rewards and personal and professional growth linked to opportunities for global careers in which to exercise this understanding.[26] Global companies need executives (and probably other employees as well) who can easily switch from one culture to another, people who are fluent in several cultures and languages, and who can work effectively as part of an international team, keeping misunderstandings to a minimum.[27] Such executives are the keys to global business success. But it's not easy to build a cadre of such leaders. To date, too many companies have been slow to become truly culturally aware simply because their key decision-makers lack the necessary international experience and exposure, and, therefore, global vision.

Many global firms have invested well in the development of their local staffs (in both their parent-country and host-country operations) and can thus identify competent managers who are well qualified to handle local operations in most of their principal markets. At the same time, though, they are short of seasoned executives with broad international skills who are closely attuned to the firm's global strategy. Too much localization has often resulted in insufficient globalization of the managerial ranks. But reversing this reality is not easy, in terms of both the cost and complexity of developing a new breed of global executives and the challenge this creates for the established process of management development.

Often, the global business environments that international firms experience are radically different than what they are used to. In such situations, IHR must tailor its policies and practices to local conditions while at the same time modifying the mindset and technical skills of local managers and employees to accept and match world class standards. To facilitate and manage this globalization, it becomes critical for firms to identify and develop leaders who are capable of functioning effectively on a global scale and with a global perspective. In a global economy, this strategic preparation of global leaders has become a major component of IHR's contribution. In essence, IHR must design HR processes, including global training and management development programs, which encourage and facilitate the organization so as to ensure that its "global whole" is greater than the sum of its domestic parts.

The following IHRM in Action describes Colgate's global management development program.[28] It provides a good synthesis of many of the ideas presented here and it seems to have paid off well for Colgate, making it one of the most successful of global firms.

IHRM in Action 10.1: Global Management Development Program at Colgate Palmolive

Mary Beth Robles, a New York native, is director of marketing for Colgate-Palmolive in Brazil. Fluent in English, Spanish, and Portuguese, in addition to a little French, she is a product of Colgate's global management development program. Robles epitomizes their international cadre of employees, the people behind their global sales, almost 70 percent of which comes from outside the US. She's lived in Madrid and D.C. and her stints for the company include Mexico, Uruguay, and Atlanta, in addition to her current position in Sao Paolo.

Colgate-Palmolive has been operating internationally for more than 60 years. Its products, such as Colgate toothpaste, Palmolive soap, Fab clothes detergent, and Ajax cleanser, are household names in more than 170 countries.

Colgate understands global complexities, having been in the global arena for decades. It doesn't underestimate the importance of HR and staffing needs for bottom-line results. However, it wasn't until quite recently that Colgate looked to HR to design a strategy that would directly affect its global staffing.

As Colgate-Palmolive greatly expanded its overseas reach, it began to focus more clearly on its need for a global workforce. It became clear that HR's ability to identify and develop global talent to meet business goals would directly impact the bottom line. As HR addressed this issue, it became clear that certain decisions were going to have to be made, decisions that were complicated by the size and scope of the global business. For example, how were they going to staff their overseas operations? When was it most effective to rely on expatriates versus local nationals? Who is it best to send abroad? What personal and professional qualities lead to success? What about host-country employees? How could they develop a team of global managers?

Next, a global team of 25 Colgate HR leaders and senior line managers began a year-long quest to develop a global staffing plan. The group met to develop global criteria for selection, succession planning, coaching, and performance management. Brian Smith, director of global staffing and HR strategy, said:

> This global business strategy requires identifying a certain type of manager who understands not only the particular niche and communities in which we operate locally, but who also has that global perspective and understands the tremendous benefits of a global product line. It allows managers to move quicker and be more competitive internationally, while it demands that they wear a global hat and take the global perspective.

One direct result of this planning was the Global Marketing Program. It takes approximately 15 high-potential recent MBA graduates per year and rotates them through various departments for 18 to 24 months. Recruits learn about the sales process, experience the global-business development group, and get exposed to manufacturing and technology. After their stint at company headquarters, they're deployed overseas. The program is seen as such a powerful tool for creating the international cadre of global management that Colgate needs, that more than 15,000 people stand in line for the slots every year. Typically, participants have a master's degree, speak at least one foreign language, and either through past experiences or personal travels, demonstrate an interest in living abroad.

As Colgate moves these people up the global ladder, it looks for individuals who have developed functional competencies, who have developed sensitivity to diverse cultures, and who understand their own expectations of living abroad. The fact that Colgate rotates the individuals early in their careers helps people figure out early on if they can handle this kind of responsibility. If they can, it is common in this program for someone to move functionally from finance to marketing to human resources, and move from Ivory Coast to Panama to Thailand before returning to New York headquarters some dozen years later. And it isn't just about recruiting US nationals; it attracts people from around the world.

Building on the success of the Global Marketing Program, the company has replicated it in other functional areas as well, such as in finance and human resources. In addition to recent grads, other high-potential people early in their careers already in the company are also encouraged to apply. It gives them exposure and perspective.

As a part of these programs and for other business needs, Colgate offers an array of overseas assignments to its employees: long-term, short-term, and stop-gap for particular expertise needs. Because of the firm's reputation, it attracts people who want to become globalites—those who want global skills so that they can have international careers anywhere in the world. Colgate makes possible a diverse and fluid environment in which people frequently move in and out of US headquarters. The result is that fully 60 percent of the company's international assignees are from places other than the US, and since 1960, half its CEOs have not been US nationals. In addition, all of the top executives speak at least two languages. This is a global company for which management development on a global scale has certainly paid off.

Patterns of Global Management Development

As important as management development with an international focus is for today's MNEs, the reality is that there has not been much research into patterns or methods employed for such development by major firms. Nevertheless, the following few paragraphs summarize what has been identified.[29]

The most important of these common elements for MNEs is the priority placed on identifying and developing management talent. At firms such as IBM, Shell, Philips, and Unilever, responsibility for international executive development is so important that it is specifically a board concern and the executive in charge of this activity reports directly to the CEO. These firms have found that the lack of globally savvy management talent has been a major inhibitor in setting up overseas businesses or developing new global projects, even in some cases preventing them from staffing projects that have been technically feasible. Even smaller firms have come to understand the importance of having a cadre of global managers. In the words of Graham Corbett, who a few years ago was senior partner for KPMG's Continental European practice: "We are on a fast growth track, and our major task is to attract and develop enough professional talent to enable us to support the [global] growth rates we are experiencing."[30]

Firms from different countries appear to have evolved varying approaches to management development. Yet there are some common elements among them. These include practices such as:

1   the early identification of individuals with executive potential, either through early-in-career assessment procedures and close monitoring of job performance or

recruiting at only elite universities and "grand écoles" or the use of in-house apprenticeships that lead to increasing levels of management responsibility; and

2   the use of close monitoring and mentoring of those individuals who have been identified through whichever procedure(s) to be candidates for positions of executive leadership.[31]

The primary purpose of the close monitoring is to manage the careers and job assignments of these high-potential employees. The movement (or mobility) of these individuals is controlled so as to ensure that they experience job assignments, including overseas assignments, of adequate variety, challenge, and appropriate responsibility (to include multiple functional, product, and country experiences, and important developmental content, often away from the individual's area of proven expertise) and length, so as to ensure that individuals learn how to achieve results in new settings and through new associates, particularly colleagues from other countries and cultures. A number of observers have also noticed that this mobility among international locations creates informal networks that enable information and problem solving to be shared worldwide in a more effective way than the formal, traditional, hierarchical structures appear to provide.

Senior executives from Europe, Asia, and the US indicate that their firms have a shortage of managers with the necessary competencies to operate effectively in a global marketplace.[32] They indicate that this is a major constraint on their abilities to expand their operations and to compete well in the global marketplace. In this context, then, IHR managers must ask themselves the following questions: If global enterprises do indeed have such shortages, then what does a global executive "look like" (so that they can be developed)? That is, what are their characteristics? And how can an MNE develop them? Or is it possible to just copy in the international arena that which is done on the domestic front? This section of the chapter addresses these types of questions.

Identification of High-Potential Leaders

The way organizations identify their leaders is influenced by cultural practices and different leadership identification approaches that can be traced according to national culture.[33] The "elite cohort" approach is a model for identifying talent at the time of initial entry into the workforce when cohorts are recruited from top universities, carefully selected, screened, trained, and developed for a number of years. It is most typical of the Japanese model of leadership identification. The "elite political" approach is a model for identifying talent at the time of entry when individuals are recruited from elite schools (such as the "grandes écoles" in France). The top graduates are given managerial positions without a trial period. This model is most typical of Latin European countries, particularly France. In the "functional" approach, leaders are identified for their functional excellence. This is quite typical in German companies. In the "managed development" approach, the decentralized responsibility for functional development lies at the local level while the overall process of management development is centralized at the corporate level. This is most typically found in large multinational companies. Each of these culture-based models of leadership identification follows a somewhat different leadership development plan. By contrast, in many developing countries, where many large businesses are either family-owned or government-owned enterprises, top managers tend to come from family ties or political connections.

Development of Global Leadership Competencies

Some research has argued that leadership is not a function of position but of action.[34] Through in-depth interviews of 130 global executives from some 50 companies throughout North America, Europe, and Asia, Black, Morrison, and Gregersen concluded that two-thirds of the global leadership capabilities are driven by global dynamics and one-third by business-specific dynamics.[35] They found that global leaders require a certain set of unique skills and abilities that arise from country affiliation, and from industry, company, and functional dynamics. Global leadership was found to be a function of being interested and competent in global business. In their study, every global leader had a core set of global attributes and was consistently competent in four important areas:

- *Inquisitiveness* (curiosity)—the characteristic of inquisitiveness and curiosity was the glue that held the other characteristics together. Effective global leaders are unceasingly curious. Far from being overwhelmed by all the differences in language, culture, government regulations, and so on that exist from one country to another, they are invigorated by the diversity. They love to learn and are driven to understand and master the complexities of the global business environment.
- *Perspective* (how leaders look at the world)—global leaders also have a unique perspective on the world. While most managers have learned to avoid uncertainty and structure their environments to get rid of it, global leaders view uncertainty as an invigorating and natural aspect of international business.
- *Character* (emotional connection and unwavering integrity)—global leaders show the ability to connect emotionally with people of different backgrounds and cultures through the consistent demonstration of personal integrity. This is essential for engendering trust and goodwill in a global workforce and with a global firm's many customers and partners.
- *Savvy* (exceptional business and organizational savvy)—demonstrated by the ability to recognize global business opportunities and then to mobilize organizational global resources in order to capitalize on them. Global leaders are highly skilled at both identifying market opportunities and applying organizational resources to make the most of those opportunities.

MNEs are not only interested in developing leadership throughout their organizations, they also want their leaders to have global competencies and experiences. It is almost unheard of today that the CEO or senior leader of any large MNE could occupy such a position without prior international experience (although it is still too common in smaller and newer MNEs). Therefore, many MNEs are insisting on the development of a set of global competencies in the job descriptions of their key leaders and managers, including the ability to:[36]

■ Describe clearly the forces behind the globalization of business.
■ Recognize and connect global market trends, technological innovation, and business strategy.

EXHIBIT 10.2: Skills of the Transnationally Competent Manager versus Those of the Traditional International Manager

Transnational skills	Transnationally competent managers	Traditional international managers
Global perspective	Understand worldwide business environment from a global perspective	Focus on a single foreign country and on managing relationships between HQs and that country
Local responsiveness	Learn about many cultures	Become an expert on one culture
Synergistic learning	Work with and learn from people of many cultures simultaneously	Work with and coach people in each foreign culture separately or sequentially
	Create a culturally synergistic environment	Integrate foreigners into the organizational headquarters' national organizational culture
Transition and adaptation	Adapt to living in many foreign cultures	Adapt to living in a foreign culture
Cross-cultural interaction	Use cross-cultural interaction skills on a daily basis throughout assignments	Use cross-cultural interaction skills primarily on foreign assignments
Collaboration	Interact with foreign colleagues as equals	Interact within clearly defined hierarchies of structural and cultural dominance
Foreign experience	Transpatriation for career and organization development	Expatriation or inpatriation primarily to get the job done

Source: Adler, N.J. and Bartholomew, S. (1992). Managing globally competent people. *Academy of Management Executive*, 6(2), 52–65.

- Outline issues essential to effective strategic alliances.
- Frame day-to-day management issues, problems, and goals in a global context.
- Think and plan beyond historical, cultural, and political boundaries, structures, systems, and processes.
- Create and effectively lead worldwide business teams.
- Help one's company adopt an effective global organization structure.

The skills and competencies required by transnational firms have been further differentiated from those traditionally expected of managers in less-complex international firms.[37] First, transnational managers must understand the worldwide business environment from a global perspective, not just from a multi-domestic perspective. And they must develop a series of skills for working with businesses and people from multiple countries and cultures. Exhibit 10.2 summarizes the skills of a transnational manager and contrasts them to those required of the traditional international manager.

GLOBAL MINDSET: AN INTRODUCTION

People try to make sense out of the confusing effects of globalization with their existing *mindsets*. Essentially people's mindsets are the interpretive frameworks that come from their experiences and cultures and that guide how they classify and discriminate events and people in ways that help them to understand what they observe and perceive. These mindsets determine people's perceptions of and reactions to international experiences and observations of people from other countries and cultures. But their lack of international experience and exposure often limits their abilities to be successful in their international experiences (except maybe as travelers, although a domestic mindset can cause problems even while traveling). In the words of Catherine Scherer, who has studied those whom she calls *internationalists*, a global mindset is characterized by tolerance, flexibility, curiosity (inquisitiveness), and the ability to deal with ambiguity.[38] Everyone seems to agree that a global mindset is crucial to effective global management. Yet, because of the rather elusive nature of the concept of global mindset, the next few paragraphs first define what it is, identify its major characteristics, identify patterns of organizations with a global mindset, and discuss how people can develop a global mindset.

The development of a global mindset is at the core of global leadership development. First, this section takes a look at the concept of a global mindset.[39] One of the goals of many management development programs in the global arena is to develop a cadre of managers who have what is referred to as a global mindset.[40] As will be discussed, an international management development program alone may not achieve this objective, depending on its components. This global perspective includes sensitivity to multiple cultures and their differences, work experience in more than one country, and knowledge and willingness about how to seek customers, financial resources and supplies, technology, innovations, and employees throughout the world.

The internationalization of jobs, companies, technology, products, money, and neighborhoods has caught many people and firms off-guard. People's domestic thinking has not caught up with the global reality of a flat world: life and business is being globalized at a fast pace. Few people have much long-term experience working or living with people from other cultures. The result is that few people are familiar with the rules to follow when engaging in business across international borders. And most people assume that the rules they are familiar with and that work well "at home" should be adequate when they work abroad. But, as has been emphasized throughout this book, this is seldom the case. Thus, the opportunities for being embarrassed and making mistakes are ever present. Often, the reaction of managers and employees, in their interactions with colleagues, customers, and suppliers from other countries is: "Why can't they be like us?" But they aren't and their ways of behaving and conducting business too often seem strange and difficult. Because of this, businesses are increasingly concerned about how to develop managers and employees that exhibit a global mindset, that is, an ability to think and function effectively in a multiculture world.

Definition of a Global Mindset

Knowing how to live and work across cultures is the essential competency of people with a global mindset. For most people, developing this mindset is both an emotional education as well as an intellectual one. The lessons are professional—and yet often also profoundly personal.[41] It is the complexity of the professional lessons and the transformational quality of the personal lessons that leads to the broader perspective of those with a global mindset. It is in fact this unique perspective that underlies this quality called a *global mindset*. One author, with extensive international business experience and writing for the American Society for Training and Development, says this global mindset

> is a way of being rather than a set of skills. It is an orientation to the world that allows one to see certain things that others do not. A global mindset means the ability to scan the world from a broad perspective, always looking for unexpected trends and opportunities that may constitute a threat or an opportunity to achieve personal, professional, or organizational objectives.[42]

Another set of authors, who are European academics and consultants, define the global mindset in terms of both its psychological (personal) and its strategic (professional) perspectives.[43] That is, they see it as "the ability to accept and work with cultural diversity" as well as involving "a set of attitudes that predispose individuals to balance competing business, country, and functional priorities which emerge in international [situations] rather than to advocate any of these dimensions at the expense of the others."

Ultimately, the global manager must become the facilitator of personal and organizational change and development on a global scale. To achieve this, the global manager must not only be attentive to and a developer of organizational cultures, values, and beliefs that reach well beyond the manager's own cultural, technical, and managerial background, but s/he must also be a consummate reframer of the boundaries of the world in which s/he works.[44] This global mindset is about balancing perspectives, not just about being global. The global manager needs to continue to understand, appreciate, and accommodate local, cross-cultural differences and variations while at the same time maintaining a global view. As a precaution, however,

> . . . academics and others writing from a normative perspective sometimes have the tendency to see global or cosmopolitan as superior to local, calling for a "universal way that transcends the particular of places." What is "local" is seen as parochial and narrow-minded. However, in our view, global mindset requires an approach that may be seen as the opposite to such one-dimensional universalism—it calls for a dualistic perspective, an immersion in the local "particulars" while at the same time retaining a wider cross-border orientation.[45]

Characteristics of a Global Mindset

Learning a global mindset requires the developing of a new set of competencies. Even though there is much disagreement over exactly what are the characteristics of those who possess this global mindset, the following is a synthesis of the efforts to describe these characteristics.[46] Those with a global mindset exhibit the ability to:

- *Manage global competitiveness*—they have broader business skills, exhibiting the ability to conduct business on a global scale as well as to design and manage complex international structures and strategies.[47] They demonstrate awareness of national differences, global trends and options, and the global impact of their decisions and choices. These technical and business skills provide them with credibility in their various international assignments.
- *Work and communicate with multiple cultures*—they show the ability to interact with people (employees, customers, suppliers, colleagues) from many cultures with sensitivity to their cultural and language differences. They understand differing cultural contexts and incorporate that understanding in their work and communication styles. And they understand the impact of cultural factors on communication and work relationships and are willing to revise and expand their understanding as part of their personal and professional growth and development.
- *Manage global complexity, contradiction, and conflict*—they show the ability to manage the complexity, contradictions, and conflict that are experienced when dealing with multiple countries and cultures. They develop a sensitivity to different cultures and cultural values; they function effectively in different cultural environments;[48] and they show the ability to handle more complexity and uncertainty than is experienced by

their domestic counterparts.[49] They consider more variables when solving problems and are not discouraged by adversity.

- *Manage organizational adaptability*—they demonstrate the ability to manage organizational change in response to new situations (that is, they are able to manage the global corporate culture and adapt it to multiple cultural environments). They show the ability to reframe their fields of reference, to be flexible, changing the cultures in their organizations when necessary.[50] And they possess extensive curiosity and openness toward other ways of living and speaking, from which they draw ideas for organizational adaptation.

- *Manage multicultural teams*—they are able to effectively manage (and manage effective) cross-border and multicultural teams. They value the diversity present in such teams and are able to be a cross-border coach, coordinator, and mediator of conflict for such teams.[51] They relate well with diverse groups of people and are able to develop the necessary cross-border trust and teamwork that is important to the effective performance of such teams.[52]

- *Manage uncertainty and chaos*—they are comfortable with ambiguity and patient with evolving issues that are so characteristic of global experience. They can make decisions in the face of uncertainty and can see patterns and connections within the chaos of global events. They show extensive curiosity about other cultures and the people who live in them.

- *Manage personal and organizational global learning*—both for themselves and for others with whom they work.

The success of employees' and managers' interactions with global customers, suppliers, and colleagues often is dependent on their abilities to think and act with a global frame of mind and reference. Indeed, the ability to cope with the conflict between a global focus and a local/national focus is one of the critical competencies in today's business world.[53] Such a global mindset predisposes people to cope constructively with these competing priorities (global versus local), rather than advocating one set of cultural values (most likely to be the individual's home country values) at the expense of all others. This mindset involves being able to form and sustain a holistic global outlook; a completely different way of looking at the world, and being able to synthesize the many complex and conflicting forces.[54]

Characteristics of Organizations with a Global Mindset

An organization with a global mindset is often referred to as geocentric. That is, the ultimate goal of its leaders is to create an organization with a globally integrated business system that has a leadership team and workforce that have a worldwide perspective and approach. They recruit employees for their global and expatriate potential, because their perspective is that all employees must contribute to the global success of the firm. The whole workforce needs to be globally aware and to support the enterprise's global strategy.

As indicated by IBM's CEO Sam Palmisano,[55] a globally integrated enterprise, such as IBM, is a fundamentally new architecture where the firm is locating work and operations anywhere in the world based on the combination of best locations for economics, employee expertise, and the right business environment and then integrating their operations horizontally and globally. One of the key challenges of this model is that it needs to create a pool of truly global leaders. In Palmisano's words the challenge is, "How do we develop people who can lead truly global teams and operations and understand cultural and societal norms and expectations all around the world? Where will this new generation of leaders come from?"

Acquiring a Global Mindset

The four Ts (travel, training, team, and transfer)[56] have been described as effective ways to develop a global mindset. However, the bottom-line experience that is required for developing a global mindset is living in another culture and going through the culture shock that is necessary to learning how to accept and to enjoy living in the foreign culture.[57] Although frequent international business travel and short-term international assignments (defined as less than one year) help broaden a person's perspective, they do not develop the cultural and leadership skills that are required for acquiring a global mindset. Reasons given for this are that short-term travel and assignments do not require acculturation and assimilation into a foreign culture. Hence, they are not as effective at developing a global mindset because they do not really require the person to acquire the coping skills to overcome cultural shock.[58]

A number of people have argued that, in the end, employees who seem able to operate effectively in a global environment are not just described by a list of attributes that are largely extensions of the knowledge, skills, and abilities needed by those who are effective in a purely domestic environment. Indeed, the evidence is accumulating that at some point a fundamental transformation takes place for globally successful people—a transformation that can be described in shorthand as the acquisition of a global mindset.[59] Such transformed people become more cosmopolitan, they extend their perspectives, and they change their cognitive maps of the world. Out of this deep change, the individual develops a *new perspective or mindset.* This is not just a new view of oneself but also a new view of one's organizational and professional role. This change goes far beyond a change in the skill-set—it is a change in the *person.* It is known that these deep changes in personal identity occur as a result of being confronted with a higher level of complexity in the environment—and that is precisely what happens in an international assignment. Not only does the person develop new perspectives, but he or she also *develops skills in the taking of new perspectives, and developing and holding multiple perspectives.* This ability to acquire and hold multiple, perhaps competing, perspectives (i.e., the ability to see a situation through another person's eyes) is a quality of a more "evolved" identity.[60] As studies are now finding, the lessons of cultural adaptability are pretty much *only* learned with expatriation, that is, through living in another culture.[61]

As with most managers and executives, global executives also report learning from challenging assignments, significant other people, perspective-changing events, etc. But, when these experiences take place in different cultures, they take on a decidedly different tone; they are decidedly more complex—and more effective. Learning to function in a country significantly different than one's own is an experience for which there is no substitute. And then doing it a second time, in a yet substantially different culture, is transformational. However, people don't necessarily learn about others or develop this global mindset purely through being in close proximity or through osmosis. Proximity doesn't necessarily lead to better communication or understanding. Nor does common sense and goodwill take the place of deliberate education. That is, one must work at it, one must want to learn from their new cultural experiences and must let go of the attitude that what is familiar is necessarily best.[62] To develop cultural literacy or competency, one must take deliberate steps to learn about another country's or culture's practices and values. One must make a concerted effort to learn about the deep values that motivate people and provide the context for their actions. One must experience the culture shock of coping with a new culture in order to begin to fully understand it so as to function effectively within it. In addition, such learning is enhanced through the coaching and mentoring of someone who has previously undergone this type of experience. It is this type of experience and learning that IHRM and MNEs must facilitate and encourage.

Many MNEs, learning from their own and others' experiences, now make overseas experience a necessity for the career progression of executives.[63] These international assignments, of course, work best when the expectations of the organization and the individual are aligned. That is, the real (and psychological) contract between the firm and the individual assignee needs to be in agreement and both sides need to live up to their obligations and to the other sides' expectations.[64] And this requires constant vigilance by both sides as well as regular discussions about both expected consequences from the assignment and how the assignment is to unfold compared to how it actually does unfold. (For an example of the sorts of problems that can arise when these practices are not followed, refer to the integrative case at the end of the book on Fred Bailey.)

CROSS-CULTURAL PREPARATION AND INTERNATIONAL ASSIGNMENTS

The first international training responsibility for an HR manager usually involves the training and preparation of international assignees and their families. Indeed, for many enterprises that have recently "gone international," this may well be the only international training issue looked at for some time after the enterprise begins developing its international operations. Management development programs will typically not involve any international considerations and the training of local workforces stays primarily the concern of local-national HR managers. Yet, at some point, the global enterprise usually comes to recognize the importance of training and preparing its expatriates. That is the subject of this section of the chapter.

The preparation of international assignees prior to going abroad (and after arrival) is at least as important to their successful performance as selecting the right candidate and family in the first place. For example, recent surveys have found that a majority of organizations understand the importance of intercultural training or cross-cultural training;[65] cross-cultural training should be provided to both the family and IA, and cross-cultural training was important to assignment success.[66] And yet the inability to adjust or to perform the expected role—both of which can be improved through training and orientation—generally provide the major reasons for "failure" in an overseas assignment. When international executive relocations fail, they generally fail either because expatriates can't fathom the customs of the new country or because their families can't deal with the emotional stress that accompanies relocation.[67] In both cases, orientation to the "culture shock" they will experience in their new environments seems particularly important.

Cross-cultural Adjustment

Many international assignees and their families experience difficulties adjusting to their new, foreign situations.[68] Most of the time, the spouse or significant other (usually a woman, since most—about 80 percent—of IAs are men, although this is slowly changing) has to give up a job, house, friends, and family to accompany her spouse on his foreign assignment. The husband may also give up house, friends, and family, but he still has his job and relationships from work at the new assignment. Consequently, the wife typically has more difficulty adapting to the foreign environment. Some of the adjustment problems faced by people, men and women, as they move to a new, unfamiliar, foreign assignment relate to their changing routines, to the culture shock they experience as they try to figure out how to perform. Many of life's established routines have to change in a foreign locale. This includes everything from eating habits and favorite foods to initiating and developing relationships. This disruption takes significant energy and time to combat. And the greater the scope, magnitude, and criticality of the disruptions the more draining and, depending on one's success in dealing with them, the more depressing they can be. *Culture shock* is the set of psychological and emotional responses people experience when they are overwhelmed by their lack of knowledge and understanding of the new, foreign culture and the negative consequences that often accompany their inadequate and inexperienced behavior. The psychological and emotional symptoms of culture shock include frustration, anxiety, anger, and depression. Disruption of one's routines is usually the key cause of these consequences.

But culture shock often leads to reactions that go beyond even this. Most people don't experience culture shock at the beginning. There is usually a form of euphoria and excitement about the new experiences in the early stages of the assignment—what is often referred to as the "honeymoon" period. The IA and family usually don't even know enough at this stage to understand they are breaking local cultural taboos. But after a while, the IA and her/his family will begin to realize they don't know or understand many of the basic cultural ground rules, and this creates a major blow to their egos. The more significant the ground rules being broken, the more significant the blow to one's ego, and the greater the subsequent feelings of culture shock and depression. Some never recover from this culture shock and many of these return home early. Yet others stay and eventually work their way through culture shock, learn to understand and accept the local culture, and gradually adjust to living and working in—even integrating into and enjoying—the foreign locale. The pain of mistakes is the primary cause of culture shock but it is the learning to which these mistakes lead that shows the way out of it. Once a cultural mistake is made and, more importantly recognized, it is less likely to be repeated or to become an ongoing source of frustration, anger, or embarrassment. Gradually, by making mistakes, recognizing them, and observing how others in the culture behave (and putting forth the effort to understand the deeper values that underlie local cultural behavior), people learn what to do and say and what not to do and say.[69]

The Design and Delivery of Cross-cultural Training

Training for cross-cultural adjustment should focus on helping IAs and their families do three things: 1) become aware that behaviors vary across cultures, including being different than what they are used to, and provide practice at observing these differences; 2) build a mental map of the new culture so they can understand why the local people value certain behaviors and ideas and how they might appropriately integrate into those behaviors and ideas; and 3) practice the behaviors they will need to be effective in their new overseas assignments. Without training of this sort, most people are much less likely to be successful in learning how to adapt to their new cultures.[70]

Exhibit 10.3 provides an outline of the five phases of a process for designing an effective cross-cultural training (CCT) initiative.[71] The five phases are:

1 Identify the type of global assignment for which CCT is needed.
2 Determine the specific cross-cultural training needs (from the organization-level, assignment-level, and the individual-level).
3 Establish the goals and measures for determining training effectiveness.
4 Develop and deliver the CCT program.
5 Evaluate whether the CCT program was effective.

The more effort and time both trainers and trainees put into such training and preparation, that is, the more rigorous the training, the more likely the IA and family members will be to learn the behaviors and attitudes they will need for success in the foreign assignment and to remove the barriers based in lack of knowledge about the assignment and the new location.

Matching rigor to the needs of the IA and family and to the degree of "differentness" of the new country and culture is the key to the design of a valid cross-culture training and preparation program (Exhibit 10.3).

Preparation for the International Assignment

Experienced IHR managers think it is essential for success in international assignments to first provide international assignees (IAs) and their families enough information about the assignment and location for them to be able to make informed decisions about the desirability of such an assignment (beyond the self-assessment discussed in the prior chapter).[72] This needs to be more than a short familiarization trip to the proposed location, even though this is important and should be seen as a necessary part of the preparation and orientation process. Both the employee and spouse should be well briefed on the new assignment's responsibilities, as well as on the firm's policies regarding IA compensation, benefits, taxes, security procedures, and repatriation. In addition, the employee and family need to be provided with all the information, skills, and attitudes that they will need to be comfortable, effective, and productive in the overseas assignment. Much of this orientation and training must be focused on the cultural values and norms of the new country and their contrast with those of their home country. Exhibit 10.3 illustrates how many of these concerns might be sequenced and delivered in the preparation of an IA for an overseas assignment.[73] Given a number of different types of problems that IAs and their families might face plus a number of possible development objectives, the particular methods chosen for training and orientation should vary as well.

First, in the development of such an IA preparation and training program, IHR must recognize the various types of problems that exist for IAs. These range from difficulties with business relationships (either within or external to the firm or with headquarters), difficulties within the IA's family, or difficulties with either the host- or home-country governments. Each of these potential sources of difficulty has its own particular solutions with its own specific objectives that will help overcome the problems. For example, developing a working knowledge of the host-country language can lead to improvements in a number of the possible relationship concerns. And the particular development methods chosen should be matched to specific development needs. As the differences between the culture of the IA and his or her family become greater relative to that of the new foreign location, the length and rigor of the training should also become greater.[74] Ultimately, the objective is for the IA to be successful in his or her assignment, to remain in the foreign locale for the duration of that assignment, and to return to the parent firm to an assignment that effectively uses the IA's new skills and motivation.

In terms of design for training for international assignees, research and writing about training, in general, has suggested a number of guidelines that seem appropriate here.[75] For example, training needs to take into account the influence of the environment, which seems particularly relevant to cross-cultural training. And it ought to progress in terms of

EXHIBIT 10.3: Five-Phase Process for Designing Effective CCT Programs

Phase	Description
(PHASE ONE) Identifying the type of global assignment	This phase identifies the type of foreign assignment for which cross-cultural training is needed. There are various types of foreign assignments and cross-cultural training will differ based on the goals required for the successful completion of each assignment.
(PHASE TWO) Determining training needs	This phase determines the specific cross-cultural training needs from the three levels: 1 *Organization level:* How does cross-cultural training support the firm's business strategy? 2 *Assignment level:* What cross-cultural competencies are needed to successfully complete the foreign assignment? 3 *Individual level:* Are there any special needs that have to be addressed for the individuals receiving training?
(PHASE THREE) Establishing goals and measures	This phase involves establishing short-term goals and long-term goals for determining cross-cultural training effectiveness: *Short-term cross-cultural training goals* focus on cognitive, affective, and behavioral changes. *Long-term cross-cultural training goals* focus on improving the rate of cross-cultural adjustment
(PHASE FOUR) Developing and delivering the program	This phase develops and delivers the cross-cultural training program. 1 Determining the specific instructional content (culture general vs. cultural specific). 2 Determining the methods to deliver the instructional content (didactic vs. experiential). 3 Timing of delivery (pre-departure vs. post-arrival). 4 Mode of delivery (face to face vs. technology based, such as web based).
(PHASE FIVE) Evaluating the program	This phase evaluates whether the cross-cultural training program was successful in meeting short- and long-term goals (established in phase three).

Source: Adapted from Tarique, I. and Caliguiri, P. (2004), Training and development of international staff, in Harzing, A.-W. and Van Ruysseveldt, J. (eds.), *International Human Resource Management*, 2nd ed., London: Sage Publications.

content and pedagogy in relation to the knowledge, experience, and competencies of the trainees. Lastly, it has been suggested that IA training should focus on developing the acquisition of knowledge and facts about other cultures; the ability to adapt to diverse conditions, to communicate in other cultures, to scan the country environment capably, to show skill at human relations in another culture, learn the appropriate etiquette and protocol, and to manage stress effectively in a foreign environment; as well as the ability to perform well in the assigned business or organizational tasks in another culture.[76]

In the broader picture, many firms divide their preparation of IAs into two categories: counseling and training. The counseling component deals primarily with the mechanics of a move abroad while the training tries to develop skills and sensitivities to national and cultural issues that will better enable the IA and family to adapt to and enjoy their new situation. Increasingly, firms are realizing how important such preparation is to the international business success of their IAs.

Such an extensive program of preparation can minimize the high level of premature returns and bad experiences due to maladjustment to foreign assignments by IAs and their families and the consequent inadequate levels of performance in the foreign assignment.

Even though there is much controversy as to the ability of people to learn about other cultures through training programs (some authors suggest one must experience a culture firsthand in order to gain a real understanding and/or adaptation to it—this is discussed in more detail in the section on developing global executives), at least some evidence suggests that these sorts of training programs do help.[77] Indeed, the experience of the American University-based Business Council for International Understanding in its work with Shell Oil Company in the United States shows that pre-departure training can reduce dramatically the IA failure rate).[78] For example, prior to providing any training to its employees being sent to Saudi Arabia, Shell was experiencing a 60 percent early return rate. With three days of training, that rate dropped to 5 percent. With a six-day pre-departure program, the figure dropped to 1.5 percent! It is estimated that without any pre-departure cross-cultural training, only about 20 percent of Americans sent overseas do well.[79]

As stated in the discussion of culture shock, IAs and their families must learn to cope with—depending on the country—a varying number, importance, and criticality of disruptions to their normal routines and ways of living. Accordingly, effective pre-departure training must vary its content and intensity according to the distance between what is normal and familiar and what will be experienced in the new assignment. The greater the distance between the home culture and the host culture (i.e., cultural distance), the more extensive and lengthy the training should be. And, whenever possible, both pre-departure and post-arrival training should be provided, with the post-arrival training focusing on the more complicated aspects of the new culture, since the typical IA and family is not ready for the more detailed cultural training until they have experienced the culture firsthand.[80]

The paragraphs in this section have primarily focused on the training and preparation of international assignees and their families. But some form of training and/or orientation would also seem appropriate for other employees of an MNE, especially those working on the international side of the business and/or managing diverse workforces. This would include domestic internationalists, international commuters, business travelers, and virtual internationalists, as well as traditional short-term and long-term international assignees. If the global enterprise really wants to expand its workforce's global business capabilities, then it seems essential that it provides cross-cultural training and orientation to everyone.

KNOWLEDGE MANAGEMENT AND MNES

A true transnational company is globally integrated through standardization of business processes, responsiveness to local pressures in order to adapt to local cultural and legal practices, and the sharing of knowledge across the enterprise.[81] Although the benefits of knowledge management are well known, effectively sharing knowledge and best practice across the MNE is much harder to achieve. Many barriers to knowledge sharing in domestic environments become exaggerated when the firm gets larger, more complex, and global. Common barriers to knowledge management and sharing include:

- ignorance and lack of relationships;
- lack of a system for sharing;
- belief that knowledge is power (so one doesn't want to share it);
- insecurity about the value of one's knowledge;
- lack of trust;
- fear of negative consequences related to sharing what one knows;
- the belief that best practices do not move across borders and cultures;
- language and translation issues;
- superiority and/or condescending attitudes; and
- intra-organizational competition.

As discussed throughout this chapter and text, IHRM must work to minimize these types of barriers and to facilitate the sharing of knowledge and learning throughout the multinational enterprise. Only through the types of programs and practices discussed in this chapter can MNEs develop the human capital necessary for successful global operations.

CONCLUSION

This chapter on T&D in the MNE has focused on one of the key assets of successful MNEs, namely the development of competent workforces, employees that are capable of operating in global teams and with the most recent technologies equipped with global mindsets, and are able to provide leadership in the global arena. It also has emphasized the importance of cross-cultural preparation, especially for international assignees. While many of these elements are considered to be the "soft" part of global management, an

MNE's ability to build these competencies in its workforce is considered a key global competitive advantage.

DISCUSSION QUESTIONS

1 What are the major issues related to international T&D?
2 How can the effectiveness of global virtual teams be improved?
3 How can global leadership be developed?
4 How does one acquire a global mindset?
5 What is the role of cross-cultural preparation in international assignment management?
6 How can MNEs overcome barriers for knowledge sharing across borders?

CASE STUDY 10.1: Management Training in Africa (Malawi)

Malawi was once a British colony—but is now a relatively small (population about 17.4 million) but independent country in Central Africa. Thus, it inherited a British administrative tradition, which is very Western and very bureaucratic. And thus it also benefits from significant investment from Western MNEs, with many local subsidiaries. However, traditional Malawi cultural values, which emphasize family membership and attention to status, are also superimposed onto local and multinational business administrative systems, mostly imported from Europe and the US. In the Malawian culture, workers view employers as an extension of their families. They expect to be provided with a broad array of benefits from their employers, such as housing and transportation. Malawi society also places great importance on status differences. The relationship between managers and subordinates is viewed as authoritative; workers give deference and expect managers to act paternally. Malawians view proper protocol as very important. Managers often resist accepting individual blame for their mistakes and do not directly criticize their subordinates. Malawian managers rarely delegate authority because the culture believes that delegation strips managers of their authority and thus lowers their status in the eyes of their subordinates. How do these cultural practices influence the development of T&D programs by MNEs in Malawi? MNEs setting up local operations in Malawi must consider the following three realities when developing training programs:

- Western models of innovation, motivation, leadership, etc. will not work well in Malawi. For example, most Western (European and Anglo) management experts believe that proper leader behavior depends on the situation: there is no one right way to lead. However, the Malawian culture believes that leaders should always be authoritative. Consequently, HR professionals must first learn how these issues apply in a Malawian culture and then train Malawian workers accordingly.
- Status-conscious Malawian managers will resent being told to attend a training program. They will interpret this gesture as an indication that they are considered "below-average" performers—and will assume that their subordinates will make the same assumption. A company must thus carefully prepare a strategy to solicit trainee attendance in a way that will not cause managers to "lose face" with their peers or subordinates.
- Training methods must be congruent with employee learning styles. Malawians learn best in "process-oriented" education settings. Consequently, training methods that use experiential and small-group techniques and other "supportive learning" techniques should be used in lieu of those that focus on lectures and rote learning.

Source: Adapted from Jones, M.L. (1989). Management development: An African focus. *International Studies of Management and Organization*, *19*(1), 74–90; and updated (2014) from the following: http://www.afribiz.info/content/2014/foreign-transnational-corporations-in-malawi; and 2014 CIA World Factbook. Available at https://www.cia.gov/library/publications/the-world-factbook/.

Discussion Questions

1 Are there any training techniques that are culture free? Why or why not?

2 How would you design a training program (e.g., to use a new software for tracking sales) for Malawi? What would it look like? Who should deliver it? How should it be delivered? What language and cultural variables would you take into consideration?

NOTES

1 Norbert Reithofer, Chairman of the Board of Management, BMW (from 2013 annual report).

2 See, for example, Stephan, M., Vahdat, H., Walkinshaw, H., and Walsh, B. (2014). *Global Human Capital Trends 2014: Engaging the 21st Century*, a Report by Deloitte Consulting LLP and Bersin, Westlake, TX: Deloitte University Press; *Lionbridge 2104 Global Training and Development Survey. Survey Results.* Published by Lionbridge Lionbridge Technologies (www.lionbridge.com), Waltham, Massachusetts; The very BEST learning organizations of 2013 (2013). *T+D*, 67 (10), 34–82; Training Top 125. (2012). *Training*, 49 (1), 66–107; Beliveau-Dunn, J. (2013). Developing talent amid rapid change. *HR Magazine*, 58 (1), 36–38; Cleghorn, L. (2014). Addressing the challenges of growing mobility: International. *Benefits and Compensation International*, 44 (3), 25; Ruiz, G. (2006). Kimberly-Clark: Developing talent in developing world. *Workforce Management*, 85 (7), 34; the chapter on "Growing people" in Sirkin, H. L., Hemerling, J. W., and Bhattacharya, A. K. (2008). *Globality: Competing with Everyone from Everywhere for Everything*, New York: Business Plus.

3 Keys, J. B. and Fulmer, R. M. (1998). Introduction: Seven imperatives for executive education and organizational learning in the global world, in Keys, J. B. and Fulmer, R. M. (eds.), *Executive Development and Organizational Learning for Global Business*, New York: International Business Press, pp. 1–10. Also see the entire special issue of *Human Resource Management*, Summer/Fall 2000, nos. 2 and 3; Oddou, G. R. and Mendenhall, M. R. (2013). Global leadership development, in Mendenhall, M. E., Osland, J. S., Bird, A., Oddou, G. R., Maznevski, M. L., Stevens, M., and Stahl, G. (eds.), *Global Leadership*, 2nd ed., London/New York: Routledge, pp. 160–174; and Sparrow, P., Brewster, C. and Harris, H. (2004) *Globalizing Human Resource Management*, London/New York: Routledge.

4 Slocum, J., Jr., McGill, M. and Lei, D. T. (1994). The new learning strategy: Anytime, anything, anywhere. *Organizational Dynamics*, 23 (2), 33–47.

5 Ohmae, K. (1990). *The Borderless World*, New York: Harper Collins, 18.

6 See, for example, Jamrozy, K. (2013). The current state of research on culture of learning organization. *Organization and Management*, (157), 77–88; Argote, L. (2012). *Organizational Learning: Creating, Retaining and Transferring Knowledge*, New York: Springer; Kearney, J., and Zuber-Skerritt, O. (2012). From learning organization to learning community. *The Learning Organization*, 19 (5), 400–413; Watkins, K. E., and Dirani, K. M. (2013). A meta-analysis of the dimensions of a learning organization questionnaire: Looking across cultures, ranks, and industries. *Advances in Developing Human Resources*, 15 (2), 148; Wen, H. (2014). The nature, characteristics and ten strategies of learning organization. *The International Journal of Educational Management*, 28 (3), 289–298; Ahmed, P. K., Kok, L. K. and Loh, A. Y E (2002). *Learning Through Knowledge Management*, Oxford, England and Woburn, MA: Butterworth-Heinemann; Argyris, C. (1999). *On Organizational Learning*, 2nd ed., Oxford, England and Malden, MA: Blackwell Publishers; Chawla, S. and Renesch, J., (eds.) (1995). *Learning Organizations: Developing Cultures for Tomorrow's Workplace*, Portland, OR: Productivity Press; Davenport, T. O. (1999). *Human Capital: What It Is and Why People Invest It*, San Francisco: Jossey-Bass; DiBella, A.J. and Nevis, E. C. (1998). *How*

Organizations Learn, San Francisco: Jossey-Bass; Dotlich, D. L. and Noel, J. L. (1998). *Action Learning: How the World's Top Companies Are Re-Creating Their Leaders and Themselves*, San Francisco: Jossey-Bass.

7   de Geus, A. (1980). Planning is learning. *Harvard Business Review*, March–April, 71; and de Geus, A. (1997). *The Living Company*, Boston: Harvard Business School Press; Sparrow, Brewster and Harris (2004).

8   For an explanation of the ADDIE model see Mayfield, M. (2011). Creating training and development programs: Using the ADDIE method. *Development and Learning in Organizations*, 25 (3), 19–22; Rothwell, W. J. and Kazanas, H. C. (2004). *Mastering the Instructional Design Process*, 3rd ed., San Francisco: CA: John Wiley & Son.

9   Adapted from Geber, B. (1989). A global approach to training. *Training*, September, 42–47. See also Schuler, R. S., Tarique, I. and Jackson, S. E. (2004). Managing human resources in cross-border alliances, in Cooper, C. and Finkelstein (eds.), *Advances in Mergers and Acquisitions*, New York: SAI Press, pp. 103–129; Odenwald, S. B. (1993). *Global Training: How to Design a Program for the Multinational Corporation*, Homewood, IL: Business One Irwin and Alexandria, VA: The American Society for Training and Development; Reynolds, A. and Nadler, L. (1993). *Globalization: The International HRD Consultant and Practitioner*, Amherst, MA: Human Resource Development Press; and Miller, V. A. (1994). *Guidebook for Global Trainers*, Amherst, MA: Human Resource Development Press.

10 Sappal, P. (2000). ¿Entiendes? Capiche? Comprenez-vous? *HR World*, September/October, 28–32.

11 Quoted in Sappal (2000).

12 Skerlavaj, M., Su, C., and Huang, M. (2013). The moderating effects of national culture on the development of organisational learning culture: A multilevel study across seven countries. *Journal for East European Management Studies*, 18 (1), 97–134; Hassi, A., and Storti, G. (2011). Organizational training across cultures: Variations in practices and attitudes. *Journal of European Industrial Training*, 35 (1), 45–70; Coget, J. (2011). Does national culture affect firm investment in training and development? *The Academy of Management Perspectives*, 25 (4), 85; Burke, M. J., Chan-Serafin, S., Salvador, R., Smith, A., and Sarpy, S. A. (2008). The role of national culture and organizational climate in safety training effectiveness. *European Journal of Work and Organizational Psychology*, 17 (1), 133; Flynn, D., Eddy, E. R., PhD., and Tannenbaum, S. I., PhD. (2006). The impact of national culture on the continuous learning environment: Exploratory findings from multiple countries. *Journal of East–West Business*, 12 (2), 85–107; Francis, J. L. (1995). Training across cultures. *Human Resource Development Quarterly*, 6 (1), Spring, reprinted in Albrecht, M. H. (ed.) (2001). *International HRM*, Oxford, England and Malden, MA: Blackwell Publishers, pp. 190–195, adapted from Hofstede, G. (1991). *Cultures and Organizations: Software of the Mind*, New York: McGraw-Hill; and Pfeiffer, J. W. and Jones, J. E. (1983). *Reference Guide to Handbooks and Annuals*, San Diego: University Associates. Similar efforts are reported in Keys, J. B. and Bleicken, L. M. (1998). Selecting training methodology for international managers, in Keys, J. B. and Fulmer, R. M. (eds.) (1998).

13 Tyler, K. (1999). Offering English lessons at work. *HR Magazine*, December, 112–120.

14 Sang-hun, C. (2010). English-language schools sprout in South Korea, downloaded 8/23/2010 from *The New York Times*, http://www.nytimes.com/2010/08/23/world/asia/23schools.html.

15 Lockwood, N. (2010). Successfully transitioning to a virtual organization: Challenges, impact and technology, *Society for Human Resource Management Research Quarterly*, first quarter; O'Neill, T. A., Lewis, R. J., and Hamley, L. A. (2008). Leading virtual teams—Potential problems and simple solutions, in Nemiro, J., Beyerlein, M., Bradley, L., and Beyerlein, S. (eds.), *The Handbook of High-Performance Virtual Teams: A Toolkit for Collaborating Across Boundaries*, San Francisco: Jossey-Bass; Right Management Consultants (2005). *Understanding the HR Dimensions of Virtual Team Building*, Executive Research Summary, Philadelphia: Right Management Consultants.

16 Gratton, L. and Erickson, T. J. (2007). Eight ways to build collaborative teams. *Harvard Business Review*, November, 100–109.

17 Katzenback, J. R. and Smith, D. K. (2003). *The Wisdom of Teams*, New York: Harper Business Essentials.

18 See Oh, H., Labianca, G., and Chung, M-H. (2006). A multilevel model of group social capital. *Academy of Management Review*, 3, 569–582; and Labianca, G. (2004). The ties that bind. *Harvard Business Review*, October, 19.

19 Belbin, R.M. (1996). *Management Teams: Why they Succeed or Fail*, London: Butterworth-Heinemann. See also www.belbin.com.

20 DiStefano, J.J. and Maznevski, M.L. (2000). Creating value with diverse teams in global management. *Organizational Dynamics*, 29 (1), 45–63.

21 Maitland, A. (2004). Virtual teams' endeavors to build trust. *Financial Times*, 8 September; Right Management Consultants (2005). Virtual teaming study: High-tech global teaming still needs human touch. *Communique*, downloaded 5/10/2005 from http://www.envoynews.com/philadelphia/e_article00039803.cfm?x=b4Syd43,b1p6cFKh.

22 Malhotra, A., Majchrzak, A. and Rosen, B. (2007). Leading virtual teams. *Academy of Management Perspective*, 21 (1), 60–70.

23 Some of the leadership books that take a global perspective and question the Western-centric view of leadership include: Trompenaars, F. and Hampden-Turner, C.M. (2000). *21 Leaders for the 21st Century*, Oxford: Capstone; Evans, P., Pucik, V., and Barsoux, I. (2011), *The Global Challenge: International Human Resource Management*, New York: McGrawHill/Irwin; Lipman-Blumen, J.C. (2000). *Connective Leadership: Managing in a Changing World*, Oxford, UK: Oxford University Press; Black, J.S., Morrison, A.J. and Gregersen, H.B. (1999). *Global Explorers: The Next Generation of Leaders*, New York/London: Routledge; Kets de Vries, M.F.R. (2006). *The Leadership Mystique; Leading Behavior in the Human Enterprise*, London: FT Prentice Hall.

24 House, R.J., Hanges, P.J., Javidan, M., Dorfman, P., and Gupta, V. (eds.) (2004). *Leadership, Culture, and Organizations: The GLOBE Study of 62 societies*, Thousand Oaks, CA: Sage Publications; House, R.J., Hanges, P.J., Ruiz-Quinanilla, S.A., Dorfman, P.W., Javidan, M., Dickson, M.W., Gupta, V., et al. (1999). Cultural influences on leadership and organizations: Project GLOBE, in Mobley, W.H., Gessner, M.J. and Arnold, V. (eds.), *Advances in Global Leadership*, Stamford, CT: pp. JAI, 171–233; and Javidan, M., Stahl, G.K., Brodbeck, F. and Wilderom, C.P.M. (2005). Cross-border transfer of knowledge: Cultural lessons from Project GLOBE. *Academy of Management Executive*, 19 (2), 59–80.

25 Avolio, B. (1999). *Full Leadership Development: Building the Vital Forces in Organizations*, Thousand Oaks, CA: Sage Publications.

26 Black, Morrison and Gregersen (1999); McCall, M.W., Jr. and Hollenbeck, G.P. (2002). *Developing Global Executives: The Lessons of International Experience*, Boston, MA: Harvard Business School Press; Pucik, V. (1992). Globalization and human resource management, in Pucik, V., Tichy, N.M. and Barnett, C.K. (eds.), *Globalizing Management: Creating and Leading the Competitive Organization*, New York: John Wiley; Scherer, C.W. (2000). *The Internationalists: Business Strategies for Globalization*, Wilsonville, OR: Book Partners, Inc.; and Steers, R.M., Nardon, L., and Sanchez-Runde, C.J. (2013). *Management across Cultures: Developing Global Competencies*, 2nd ed., Cambridge, UK: Cambridge University Press.

27 See, for example, *Competing in a Global Economy* (1998). Executive Summary of the Watson Wyatt Study of Senior Executives across the Globe, Bethesda, MD and Reigate, England: Watson Wyatt Worldwide.

28 Solomon, C.M. (1994). Staff selection impacts global success. *Personnel Journal*, January, 89–95.

29 Caliguiri, P.M., Lepak, D., and Bonache, J. (2010). *Managing the Global Workforce*, Chichester, UK: John Wiley and Sons; Evans, P.A.L. (1992). Human resource management and globalization, keynote address presented to the Third Bi-Annual Conference on International Personnel and Human Resource Management, Ashridge Management College, Berkhamsted, Hertfordshire, UK, July 2–4; Evans, P., Lank, E. and Farquhar, A. (1989). Managing human resources in the international firm: Lessons from practice, in Evans, P., Doz, Y. and Laurent, A. (eds.), *Human Resource Management in International Firms*, London: Macmillan Press Ltd; Evans, P., Pucik, V. and Barsoux, J-L. (2002); and McCall, M.W., Jr. and Hollenbeck, G.P. (2002). For a broader look at executive development programs, particularly looking at executive training programs, refer to Keys, J.B. and Fulmer, R.M. (eds.) (1998).

30 Quoted in Evans, P., Lank, E. and Farquhar, A. (1989), pp. 33–114.

31 In addition to the other references on global management development, most of which make reference to the importance of early identification of candidates for global development, see Spreitzer, G.M., McCall, M.W., Jr. and Mahoney, J.D. (1997). Early identification of international executive potential, *Journal of Applied Psychology*, 82 (1), 6–29.

32 See, for example, Adler, N.J. and Bartholomew, S. (1992). Managing globally competent people, *Academy of Management Executive*, 6 (2). 52–65; Black, J.S., Morrison, A.J. and Gregersen, H.B. (1999); Cascio, W. and Bailey, E. (1995). International human resource management, in Shenkar, O., Ed., *Global Perspectives of Human Resource Management*, Engelwood Cliffs, NJ: Prentice-Hall; McCall, M.W., Jr. and Hollenbeck, G.P. (2002); Minehan, M.E. (1996). The shortage of global managers [reports on 2 major studies, one from 30 countries and one from Europe], *Issues in HR*, Alexandria, VA: Society for Human Resource Management, March/April, 2–3; Rosen, R. (2000). *Global Literacies: Lessons on Business Leadership and National Cultures*, New York: Simon and Schuster; and Thaler-Carter, R.E. (2000). Whither global leaders? *HR Magazine*, May, 82–88.

33 Evans, Pucik and Barsoux (2002).

34 Black, J.S., Morrison, A.J. and Gregersen, H.B. (1999).

35 Black, Morrison, and Gregersen (1999).

36 Marquardt has published extensively on the subject of organizational learning and the learning organization, including in the global context. This particular information is adapted from Marquardt, M.J. (1999). *Action Learning in Action*, Palo Alto, CA: Davies-Black Publishing.

37 Adler, N.J. and Bartholomew, S. (1992). Managing globally competent people, *Academy of Management Executive*, 6 (3), 52–65.

38 Scherer, C.W. (2000). *The Internationalists: Business Strategies for Globalization*, Wilsonville, OR: Book Partners.

39 See, for example, Briscoe, D.R. (2007). Developing a global mind-set: Its role in global careers, *Proceedings*, 9th Bi-annual Conference, International Human Resource Management, 12–15 June, Tallinn, Estonia; Gupta, A.K. and Govindarajan, V. (2002). Cultivating a global mindset, *Academy of Management Executive*, 16 (1). 116–126; and Morrison, A, J. (2000). Developing a global leadership model, *Human Resource Management*, Summer/Fall, 39 (2 and 3). 117–131.

40 Evans, Pucik, and Barsoux (2002); and Mendenhall, M.E. and Stahl, G.K. (2000).

41 McCall and Hollenbeck (2002).

42 Rhinesmith, S.H. (1993). *A Manager's Guide to Globalization: Six Keys to Success In a Changing World*, Homewood, IL: Business One Irwin and Alexandria, VA: The American Society for Training and Development, 24.

43 Evans, Pucik, and Barsoux (2002), 385–387.

44 Rhinesmith, S.H. (1992). Global mindsets for global managers, *Training and Development Journal*, 46 (10), 63–68; and Rhinesmith (1993).

45 Evans, Pucik, and Barsoux (2002), 396–397.

46 See, for example, Javidan, M., and Walker, J. (2013). *Developing Your Global Mindset: The Handbook for Successful Global Leaders*, Edina: Beaver's Pond Press; Cseh, M., Davis, E.B., and Khilji, S.E. (2013). Developing a global mindset: Learning of global leaders. *European Journal of Training and Development*, 37(5), 489–499; Javidan, M., and Walker, J.L. (2012). A whole new global mindset for leadership. *People and Strategy*, 35(2), 36–41; Smith, M.C., and Victorson, J. (2012). Developing a global mindset: Cross-cultural challenges and best practices for assessing and grooming high potentials for global leadership. *People and Strategy*, 35(2), 42–51; Story, J.S.P., Barbuto, John E., Jr, Luthans, F., and Bovaird, J.A. (2014). Meeting the challenges of effective international HRM: Analysis of the antecedents of global mindset. *Human Resource Management*, 53(1), 131; Stroh, L.K., Black, J.S., Mendenhall, M.E., and Gregersen, H.B. (2005). *International Assignments: An Integration of Strategy, Research, & Practice*, Mahwah, NJ/London: Lawrence Erlbaum Associates; Black, Morrison, and Gregersen (1999); Claus, L. (1999).

Globalization and HR professional competencies, paper presented at the 22nd Annual Forum, the Institute for International Human Resources (later called the Global Forum). Society for Human Resource Management, Orlando, FL, April 13; Dalton, Ernst, Deal, and Leslie (2002);

47 Adler, N.J. and Bartholomew, S. (1992). Managing globally competent people, *Academy of Management Executive*, 6 (3). 52–65; Evans, P., Pucik, V. and Barsoux, J-L. (2002).

48 Kets de Vries, M.F.R. and Mead, C. (1992). The development of the global leader within the multinational corporation, in Pucik, V., Tichy, N.M. and Bartlett, C.K. (eds.). *Globalizing Management: Creating and Leading the Competitive Organization*, New York: John Wiley and Sons, 187–205.

49 Lancaster, H. (1998). Managing your career, *Wall Street Journal*, June 2, C1.

50 Lobel, S.A. (1990). Global leadership competencies, *Human Resource Management*, 29 (1). 39–47.

51 Barham, K. and Wills, S. (1992). *Management Across Frontiers*, Ashridge, England: Ashridge Management Research Group.

52 Lancaster, H. (1998).

53 See, for example, Bartlett, C.A. and Ghoshal, S. (2002) *Managing Across Border*, (2nd ed.). Boston: Harvard Business School Press; Dalton, M., Ernst, C., Deal, J. and Leslie, J. (2002). *Success for the New Global Manager: How to Work Across Distances, Countries, and Cultures*, San Francisco: Jossey-Bass; Evans, P., Pucik, V. and Barsoux, J-L. (2002); Ferraro, G. (2002). *Global Brains: Knowledge and Competencies for the 21st Century*, Charlotte, NC: Intercultural Associates, Inc.; Hodge, S. (2000). *Global Smarts*, New York: John Wiley and Sons; and McCall and Hollenbeck (2002); Rosen, R. (2000). *Global Literacies: Lessons on Business Leadership and National Cultures*, New York: Simon and Schuster.

54 Kedia, B.L. and Mukherji, A. (1999). Global managers: Developing a mindset for global competitiveness. *Journal of World Business*, 34 (3), 230–251.

55 Palmisano, S. (2007). The globally integrated enterprise, Address to the Forum on Global Leadership, Washington DC, July 25 (also in Foreign Affairs, 2006).

56 Black, Morrison, and Gregersen (1999).

57 McCall and Hollenbeck (2002).

58 Claus, L. et al. (2004). *Worldwide Benchmark Study. Trends in Global Mobility: the Assignee Perspective Research Report*. Cendant Mobility.

59 McCall and Hollenbeck (2002).

60 Hall, D.T., Zhu, G. and Yan, A. (2001). Developing global leaders: To hold on to them, let them go! In Mobley, W. and McCall, M.W., Jr. (eds.), *Advances in Global Leadership*, vol. 2, Stamford, CT: JAI Press.

61 McCall and Hollenbeck (2002).

62 Bennett, J.M. and Bennett, M.J. (2003). Developing intercultural sensitivity: An integrative approach to global and domestic diversity, in Landis, D., Bennett, J.M. and Bennett, M.J. (eds.), *The Handbook of Intercultural Training*, Thousand Oaks, CA: Sage; and Hodge (2000).

63 See, for example, Seibert, K.W., Hall, D.T. and Kram, K.E. (1995). Strengthening the weak link in strategic executive development: Integrating individual development and global business strategy. *Human Resource Management*, 34, 549–567; and Yan, A., Zhu, G. and Hall, D.T. (2002). International assignments for career building: A model of agency relationships and psychological contracts. *Academy of Management Review*, 27 (3), 373–391.

64 Yan, Zhu and Hall (2002).

65 Global Monility Trends Survey (2014). Brookfield Global Relocation Services, Brookfield Global Relocation Services (www. brookfieldgrs.com).

66 Global Mobility Policy and Practices, 2014 Survey Executive Summary Report, Cartus (www.cartus.com)

67 Quoted in Blocklyn, P.L. (1989). Developing the international executive, *Personnel*, March, 44–45.

68 Stroh, L.K., Black, J.S., Mendenhall, M.E. and Gregersen, H.B. (2005) *International Assignments: An Integration of Strategy, Research, and Practice*, Mahwah, NJ: Lawrence Erlbaum Associates; Sparrow, Brewster and Harris (2004).

69 Stroh, Black, Mendenhall and Gregersen (2005); and Ward, C. and Kennedy, A. (1993). Where's the "culture" in cross-cultural transition? *Journal of Cross-Cultural Psychology*, 24, 221–249.

70 Stroh, Black, Mendenhall and Gregersen (2005); Black, J. S. and Mendenhall, M. E. (1990). Cross-cultural training effectiveness: A review and a theoretical framework for future research, *Academy of Management Review*, 15 (1), 113–136; and Keys and Bleicken (1998).

71 Caligiuri, P., Lazarova, M., and Tarique, I., (2005). Training, learning, and development in multinational corporations, in H. Scullion and M. Linehan (eds.), *International Human Resource Management*, Palgrave Macmillan; and Tarique, I. and Caliguiri, P.M. (2004). Training and development of international staff, in Harzing, A.-W. and Van Ruysseveldt, J. (eds.), *International Human Resource Management*, Thousand Oaks, CA: Sage Publications.

72 Bennett, R., Aston, A. and Colquhoun (2000). Cross-cultural training: A critical step in ensuring the success of international assignments. *Human Resource Management*, summer/fall, 39 (2 and 3), 239–250.

73 Based on Rahim, A. (1983). A model for developing key expatriate executives. *Personnel Journal*, April, 23–28.

74 Stroh, Black, Mendenhall, and Gregersen (2005); Francis (1995); Keys, J.B. and Bleicken, L.M. (1998); and Ronen, S. (1989). Training the international assignee, in I.L. Goldstein and Associates (eds.), *Training and Development in Organizations*, San Francisco: Jossey-Bass.

75 A good summary of this research and application to training programs for IAs is found in Keys and Bleicken (1998); also see Stroh, Black, Mendenhall, and Gregersen (2005); and Mendenhall, M.E. and Stahl, G.K. (2000). Expatriate training and development: Where do we go from here? *Human Resource Management*, summer/fall, 39 (2 and 3), 251–265.

76 Keys and Bleicken (1998).

77 Black, J.S., Gregersen, H.B. and Mendenhall, M.E. (1992). *Global Assignments*, San Francisco: Jossey-Bass; Black, Gregersen, Mendenhall and Stroh (2005); Black, J.S. and Mendenhall, M.E. (1989). Selecting cross-cultural training methods: A practical yet theory-based approach. *Human Resource Management*, 28 (4), 511–540; Black and Mendenhall (1990); Caudron, S. (1991). Training ensures success overseas. *Personnel Journal*, December, 27–30; Earley, P.C. (1987). Intercultural training for managers: A comparison of documentary and interpersonal methods. *Academy of Management Journal*, 30 (4), 685–698; and Stroh, Black, Mendenhall, and Gregersen (2005).

78 Kohls, L.R. (1993). Preparing yourself for work overseas, in Reynolds, A. and Nadler, L. (eds.), *Globalization: The International HRD Consultant and Practitioner*, Amherst, MA: Human Resource Development Press; and Budhwar, P.S. and Baruch, Y. (2003) Career Management practices in India: An empirical study. *International Journal of Manpower*, 24(6), 69–719.

79 Kohls (1993).

80 Stroh, Black, Mendenhall and Gregersen (2005); and Mendenhall and Stahl (2000).

81 Bartlett, C.A., Ghoshal, S. and Birkinshaw, J. (2003). *Transnational Management: Text, Cases and Readings in Cross Border Management*, 4th ed., Burr Ridge, IL: McGraw-Hill.

Chapter 11

International Compensation, Benefits, and Taxes

The field of global compensation and benefits is complex and its scope is huge. No one in the world is an expert on every aspect of the subject. Today's mantra of "think globally, act locally," while descriptive, is not sufficient to guide the IHR professional.

Calvin Reynolds (Consultant in international compensation)[1]

Learning Objectives

This chapter will enable the reader to:

- Outline the basic objectives of global compensation and benefits (C&B).
- Distinguish between global remuneration and international assignment C&B.
- Identify critical issues in C&B of the global workforce of the MNE.
- Describe the types of compensation systems available for international assignees.
- Explain the balance sheet approach, as well as other approaches, of designing international assignment C&B packages.
- Identify the challenges of dealing with various tax structures and methods affecting international assignment C&B.

The design and maintenance of an enterprise's total reward system is always a critical responsibility for HR managers. International business makes this responsibility more difficult and requires additional HR competencies in global remuneration and international assignment (IA) compensation and even closer collaboration with business partners in the accounting, finance, tax, and legal divisions, as well as with the line managers of the MNE. The determination of compensation and benefits (C&B) on an international basis requires new considerations, including for subsidiary workforces in multiple countries, employees from many different countries (such as inpatriates, host-country nationals, and third-country nationals), varying country approaches to and levels of pay and benefits, international assignees who move across borders for differing periods of time, and problems such as dealing with differing standards and costs of living, multiple currencies, exchange rates, inflation rates, tax systems, and tax rates. One of the most time-consuming aspects of these new responsibilities for international HR managers includes creating and managing compensation, benefit, and tax packages for expatriates.[2] When development of compensation systems for subsidiaries and determining pay and benefits for a global workforce is added to these IHRM responsibilities, it is easy to see why this area of concern is so important.[3]

In global C&B, a distinction is made between global remuneration and IA compensation. *Global remuneration* deals with the compensation and benefit structure for employees of the MNE in various locations/subsidiaries around the world. Global remuneration is more complex than domestic compensation because salary levels and benefit provisions invariably differ significantly among the various countries in which an MNE operates.[4] Employees performing essentially similar jobs in different countries may have different titles and will receive differing amounts and forms of compensation. This is due to differing costs of living and pay levels throughout these economies and varying traditions and values for particular jobs. *International assignment compensation* deals with the compensation and benefits of globally mobile employees—or those who cross borders as part of their employment with the MNE, either as short-term international assignees or as long-term expatriates. IA compensation is also complex because it deals with people relocating to different countries and are, thus, subject to special incentives, different laws and regulations, cost-of-living adjustments, varying taxation systems, exchange rate fluctuations, and varying inflation/deflation rates. In addition, the cost of attracting and maintaining expatriates and an international cadre of managers and technicians in traditional ways has become so expensive that MNEs are now looking for new ways to handle international compensation.[5]

The effective design of a global C&B philosophy is absolutely necessary. How an MNE copes with these C&B issues tends to, at least partially, be a function of the company's overall rewards strategy, its level of international development, its corporate culture, and the other talent management elements in HR (such as competency management, performance management, training and development, and deployment). A well-designed global C&B system will balance the costs and benefits for the company while ensuring that the total reward system retains attractiveness for the recruitment and retention of employees. Therefore, the main objectives for the typical MNE global C&B program include:

- Attraction and retention of the best qualified talent to staff the MNE, in all of its locations.
- Attraction and retention of employees who are qualified for international assignments.
- Facilitation of transfers between the various employment locations within the MNE.
- Establishment and maintenance of a consistent and reasonable relationship between the compensation of employees at home and abroad.
- Maintenance of compensation that is reasonable in relation to the practices of competitors yet minimizes costs to the extent possible.

If these objectives are achieved, the MNE will be able to attract the best talent, design a compensation system that will be externally competitive and internally equitable, and remove financial obstacles to the geographic mobility of its employees. To address the issues related to the design of a global C&B system, this chapter first looks at the design of the system and examines the problems associated with the design of worldwide C&B programs and policies. Second, this chapter looks at the problems associated with C&B for international assignees and reviews the different expatriate compensation approaches used by MNEs. Because of the extreme complexity of this subject (MNEs usually contract with specialists to design and administer the details of compensation, benefits, and taxes of international assignees), this chapter can only provide an introduction to the many issues related to global C&B.

The following IHRM in Action summarizes the approach taken by a major consumer-products firm to develop its global compensation programs.[6] Colgate-Palmolive has found ways to globalize its compensation programs and, thus, to attract and retain the best talent available throughout the world.

IHRM in Action 11.1: Developing a Global Compensation Program at Colgate Palmolive

Colgate-Palmolive is a US$9 billion global company with operations in over 80 countries and 50 percent of its executives are US nationals stationed in other countries. They use global expatriates for many of their key management positions around the world. Because of this, Colgate-Palmolive has developed a global compensation program in order to attract and retain the best talent to help the firm achieve its vision of becoming "the best truly global consumer products company." Colgate benchmarks its salaries and benefits against the best in its industry and then tries to improve on them.

Its global compensation plan consists of three parts: a base salary program that varies significantly from country to country; annual incentives that cover all key managers worldwide, based on sales and profit targets, adjusted for local conditions; and a long-term incentive plan for all global senior executives and managers, made up of global stock options and bonuses based on achievement of significant global business objectives.

Colgate struggles with the willingness of employees to accept overseas assignments, even though it is clearly identified and communicated that such experience is an integral part of the career track for all employees. There are many reasons for the resistance, but this global compensation plan often provides the necessary response to those concerns. The firm has clearly found that the role of the expatriate has proven invaluable for the success of the company as a global player in the consumer products industry.

INTERNATIONAL REMUNERATION AND THE MNE

Global remuneration involves two components. First it involves developing an overall philosophy of how an MNE pays its employees (a common set of principles on which the organization bases its reward system). And second it involves taking consideration of the external constraints placed by the various countries in which the MNE operates (i.e., cultural and company practices, laws, and tax systems). Because the strategic dilemma of whether to centralize or localize HR practices also impacts C&B, generally the rewards strategy in MNEs opts for standardization (in order to be aligned with overall strategic objectives) while the specific C&B practices tend to be localized (to fit the cultural, legal, and taxation context of each specific country). The firm's compensation approach can be to lead, lag, or be at market equivalency compared with the competition in the same industry and/or geographic location. This decision will mainly depend on its corporate culture and values regarding employee rewards. Yet, the specific national context in which the employee works will determine a number of compensation issues such as comparability, cultural factors, salary-benefit ratio, tax laws, sunshine rules, and salary expression, to name a few. In best HR practice, a compensation approach starts with a job analysis (job description and job specification) and job evaluation. This determines what the job entails (job description), what kind of people to hire for the job (job specifications), and how much the job is worth (job evaluation).

International Remuneration Issues and Challenges

C&B specialists encounter a number of new challenges when developing a total reward system for the MNE. Especially important in global remuneration is the issue of *comparability* or determining who is a peer for a job in the various countries and subsidiaries. For example, the term "manager" may have different meanings and connotations in different countries. In one country the job of "manager" may be a job exempt from overtime compensation (such as is usually the case in the US), while in another country it may be a unionized job (such as is sometimes the case in certain Western European countries). In some countries, a car and fuel credit card may be a standard benefit for a manager, while in others a car may only be provided if needed as part of the job requirement.

Obviously, national and organizational *cultures* also influence how people perceive the value of the various rewards available in the compensation system. For example, the culture may be performance-driven (and pay for performance is a well-established norm) or it may be entitlement-oriented (with longevity of service rewarded). In some cultures people are more willing to accept risk in their compensation while in others people are quite risk-averse. In addition, the level of uncertainty avoidance in a culture may determine the amount of fixed versus variable pay that people will accept.

The *salary-benefit ratio*, or the amount of compensation that is salary versus benefit, may also differ by country as a result of cultural practices, laws, or regulations. In addition, *tax laws* have a major impact on how MNEs structure their C&B systems. Not only are people taxed differently on their incomes and their benefits are treated in differing ways across national tax systems, but C&B expenses of companies are treated differently in different countries in terms of corporate tax expense deductions. Therefore, a benefit that, in principle, may seem to have general appeal from headquarters' perspective, may very well be viewed as unacceptable, depending on how it is taxed locally. Countries also differ in terms of *sunshine rules* and how they *express salaries*. Whether or not employees' salary information is confidential or disclosed is generally dictated by local cultural practice and law. In some countries and some occupations, everybody knows what everyone else makes (openly disclosing salary information to the public is called a sunshine rule); in others, salary information is strictly confidential. In some countries salaries are quoted in net amounts while in others they are stated in gross amounts, or in weekly, monthly, or annual terms. In some countries, 13th and 14th month payments (usually end-of-year and vacation/holiday stipends) are part of the annual compensation package, no matter the performance of employees, while in other countries they are part of a bonus plan for only certain groups of employees. So, knowing how base salary is expressed (net or gross, weekly, monthly, or annual) and what is included in the amount is important to reduce misperceptions and errors in judgment about appropriate levels of compensation and benefits based purely on home practices. Understanding these issues is highly important for IHRM as it attempts to design C&B programs and practices for the global operations of the MNE. IHR practitioners should never assume, especially with regard to C&B, that things are done in other parts of the world the same way as they know it at home or at headquarters.

In addition to these challenges, other factors such as economics, labor relations, laws and regulations, and the level of government-provided and -mandated benefits play a critical role. A global staffing approach within the MNE implies that the right people are hired, with the right skills, and are located at the right place, at the right time, at the right cost. Yet the *global law of economics* with regard to staffing must be considered, with work needing to be located where the quality and cost of the production of goods and services are optimized. Important variables in determining the best locations for MNE operations include employee C&B expenses, operational logistics, and proximity to raw materials and the customer base. Labor costs differ considerably around the world. Exhibit 11.1 presents international comparisons of hourly compensation costs for production workers in manufacturing industries in select countries. Hourly compensation costs include:

1   hourly direct pay; and
2   employer social insurance expenditures and other labor taxes.

They are appropriate measures for comparing levels of employer labor costs. Using the US as the index (=100), labor costs are higher in Scandinavia, Western Europe, and Australia and lower in Southern Europe, Central and Eastern Europe, Latin America, and much of Asia. Considering $ equivalency, hourly labor costs in manufacturing range from $2.01 in Philippines to $64.15 in Norway.

EXHIBIT 11.1: Hourly Compensation Costs for Production Workers in Manufacturing, 2011 (most recent data available: can change significantly from year to year largely due to fluctuating exchange rates)

Country	Index (US = 100)	Hourly $US
Argentina	45	15.91
Australia	130	46.29
Austria	121	43.16
Belgium	154	54.77
Brazil	33	11.65
Canada	103	36.56
Czech Republic	37	13.13
Denmark	145	51.67
Estonia	29	10.39
Finland	124	44.14
France	119	42.12
Germany	133	47.38
Greece	61	21.78
Hungary	26	9.17
Ireland	112	39.83
Israel	60	21.42
Italy	102	36.17
Japan	101	35.71
Korea, Republic of	53	18.91
Mexico	18	6.48
Netherlands	119	42.26
New Zealand	66	23.38
Norway	181	64.15
Philippines	6	2.01
Poland	25	8.83
Portugal	36	12.91
Singapore	64	22.60
Slovakia	33	11.77
Spain	80	28.44
Sweden	138	49.12
Switzerland	170	60.40
Taiwan	26	9.34
United Kingdom	87	30.77
United States	100	35.53

Source: US Bureau of Labor Statistics: http://www.bls.gov/web/ichcc.supp.toc.htm

International HR practitioners—in order to make effective decisions about the best locations for MNE operations—must develop metrics of the fully loaded cost of labor and productivity by employee groups in different parts of the MNE so as to be able to balance staffing decisions based on the strategic priorities of their organizations.

Labor relations, collective bargaining, and employee representation also differ greatly from country to country. Job security, compensation, benefits, and worker entitlements tend to be the major concerns of labor unions. Therefore, relations with unions are bound to impact the MNE's local C&B plans.

In addition, countries around the world have passed various extensive *laws and regulations* impacting remuneration of employees such as minimum wage, overtime, compulsory bonuses and other entitlements, severance payments, employee contract requirements, and taxation of employee and corporate incomes. This includes great variance from country to country in *government-provided and mandated benefits*. HR must know which benefits are government-provided and mandated in each country in which they operate, especially in terms of the severance-related entitlements, paid time off, social welfare benefits (such as health care and retirement), and various leave requirements.

Finally, the global C&B specialist plays a critical role in the due diligence and post-merger integration phases of a merger/acquisition. Critical in the due diligence phase (prior to an acquisition) are reviews of C&B practices, funding regarding future pension obligations, potential severance liabilities, equity and stock option plans, vacation accruals, and any other unwritten but established reward practices. In the post-merger integration phase, the redesign of the new global C&B system is critical.

IHR C&B specialists must examine the MNE's C&B programs for their employees at each and all of its subsidiaries and foreign operations. The greater the number of foreign subsidiaries and joint ventures and the greater the number of countries within which the MNE operates, the greater will be the problems associated with establishing, monitoring, and controlling C&B programs on a worldwide basis. The stage of the MNE's evolution or development (as described in Chapters 2 and 3) makes a big difference in how it handles C&B for all of its global employees as well. If it is still in stage one (export) or two (sales subsidiaries), it will differentiate between parent-country (PCN), host-country (HCN), and third-country (TCN) employees and most IHRM attention from headquarters will be given to C&B packages for expatriates (PCNs). Later, when in stages three (international), four (multinational), five (global), six (transnational), or seven (born global), i.e., becoming more global in emphasis and attention, the C&B package will be more likely to be designed for all employees worldwide based on the same reward strategy, yet with local implementation tactics. Global remuneration must achieve a delicate balance between standardization and adaptation. Advanced MNEs usually have a consistent strategic approach to compensation of their employees in different locations around the world emanating from their corporate culture, HQ mandate, and overall strategy. Yet, they also develop local C&B tactics for each country in which they operate because of differing cultural practices, legal requirements, and tax systems. A critical step in this is for global C&B specialists to determine the specific compensation model in each country in which they operate so they can appropriately localize their C&B packages.

A last major challenge of global remuneration is the issue of equity versus comparability: are comparable employees in different parts of the organization treated equitably—or fairly? When dealing with a global company, this perceived equity is of the utmost importance to maintain employee engagement. Fairness is a culturally laden concept: what is considered fair in one culture may not be so in another and a seemingly universally fair procedure may even appear unfair in some cultures solely because of the fact that it is standardized.[7] The MNE's efforts to design a global C&B program, therefore, have to address these types of questions:[8]

- Under which country's C&B programs should employees be covered—parent country, host country, or some specially designed program for everyone?
- How should potential gaps or inequities in pension and health care coverage be bridged? Can employees be covered under a single plan throughout their careers, particularly if they move around during those careers?
- Is benefits coverage adequate for all employees? What's more, is the benefits package equitable when compared with benefits of peers in other countries, both within and without the parent firm? Should employees be covered under the provisions of selected home *and* foreign programs?
- How can the cost of providing social benefits be minimized? Can coverage under employees' home country social programs be maintained, even as they move around? Should there be a global umbrella program to provide equitable coverage for everyone?
- What are the tax effects to employers and employees of special benefit arrangements for all global employees?

To better understand the complexity of global remuneration, the next two sections examine issues that apply specifically to global compensation and to global benefits.

International Compensation

A number of different options (for establishing a worldwide compensation system) have been used by various MNEs. One option is the use of a HQ scale. In this approach, worldwide salary levels are established at HQ with differentials for each subsidiary according to their differing costs of living. This option is usually reserved for managerial and executive-level positions. A second option is to base the salary scale on local geography (i.e., the country where the work is performed). In this option, employees are basically paid on a local scale (i.e., Indian employees working in India are paid according to Indian norms and Brazilian employees working in Brazil are paid according to Brazilian norms). This option tends to be used for the broader employee base (usually excluding executives and globally mobile employees). Another option is to determine a global base per position for everyone, possibly with affiliate differentials. This, then, becomes a form of equal pay for equal work on a worldwide basis. The global approach is usually followed when there is a global labor market for the type of talent sought (e.g., software engineers, nurses, designers, etc.) and therefore is of high value because of specific competencies and shortages. This approach also tends to be reserved for employees above a particular job or salary classification.

MNEs often create two classifications—local and international with regard to compensation. All local nationals above a certain level are placed on the headquarters scale, with salaries that are at least partially performance-based. The rest of the employees are paid on a local scale. Practices can vary enough so as to make this strategy difficult to implement and may lead to two common problems for host-country nationals in the subsidiaries.[9] The first problem relates to a possible in-country gap in compensation between the highest and lowest paid employee. In most Western countries, there is typically a fairly constant differential between job classifications (e.g., there is typically about a 15 percent increase in salary from job class to job class, and this tends to be the case across all job classifications. In many developing countries and emerging markets, where there tends to be more unskilled labor, it is common to have low pay at all of the lower job classifications, with very little differential between them and then a major jump in compensation only at the upper few classifications. This creates a situation where there can be a much greater ratio between top management and lower level employees than would be the case for the typical Western, or other developed-country, MNE workforce. The second problem relates to the gap in executive compensation of the senior managers of the MNE between countries. Comparing the total compensation of CEOs in 12 different OECD countries, US executive compensation is the highest, followed by the UK. Japan has the lowest executive compensation and continental Europe is somewhere in between. In addition, the proportions of base (+ bonus) compensation, long-term compensation, and all benefits/perquisites of executives are also wide ranging, indicating that executive compensation practices are contextual in terms of practices and taxation.[10]

Not only is there great disparity between wage rates and salary levels in different countries, but it is also difficult to get reliable data on what those rates and levels are, so that MNEs can establish competitive pay scales for themselves. Nevertheless, there are a few organizations that publish comparative wage rate data for at least some common locations for MNEs, such as international banks (e.g., the Union Bank of Switzerland[11]), consulting firms (e.g., Hay International and Mercer[12]), and the International Labor Comparisons by the US Department of Labor.[13]

However, even the best global compensation program will not eliminate future claims by employees of perceived continued inequity. That is because variations in local labor laws, tax systems, and the cost of living will ensure that dissimilar programs and varying gross pay levels will continue to be a fact of life in a global organization. The goal, therefore, of a global compensation system, is not to eliminate employees' questions about compensation (they do talk to each other across national borders), but rather to remove the de-motivational impact of inexplicable variations in compensation across borders.

Designing a global compensation program in this way can enable IHR to create a working environment that hopefully will attract and retain good employees and keep them focused on performance.

International Benefits

However, salary is only one aspect of total remuneration. A second critical component involves the benefits package that employees receive as part of their employment relationship. The design of a comprehensive C&B program for all worldwide employees must, of course, include these non-salary benefits. The development of benefit programs from a global perspective has its own challenges.

The major concern that MNEs face in designing their benefit packages is the widely varying approaches to employee benefits in each country.[14] These include differences in government-provided and -mandated benefits and taxation of these benefits (at the individual and corporate level). In addition, benefits make up a significant (yet varying) portion of the cost of payroll (for example, averaging about 33 percent of payroll expenses in the US, 43 percent of payroll in Germany, 53 percent of payroll in Belgium, and 14 percent of payroll in New Zealand).[15] The problems this creates cannot be overstated. Many benefits that are provided as a voluntary payment by the employer in one country may be provided or mandated by the government (and paid for through employer social taxes) in another, or not offered at all. Benefits include such offerings as health care, retirement programs/pensions, vacations, and holidays. If they are provided by the government in a particular country, then there is no need for a firm to offer them on a private and voluntary basis. A prime example involves the handling of health care. In some countries, such as the US, health care is basically a private system paid for either by individuals and/or their employers. In most other developed countries, though, health care is provided by a tax-supported system of government-subsidized and/or managed medicine. In yet other countries, such as Great Britain and Mexico, in addition to the government-sponsored, tax-supported system of health care, there is also a competing private medical system, mostly paid for by insurance, with premiums paid by some employers, particularly for higher-level managers and professionals. This makes the provision of many benefits, such as health care, by necessity very localized to the particular country of operation.

In every area of benefits, the variance from country to country in terms of what is normally provided, what is paid by the government from tax revenues, and what employees expect of their employers, is quite wide. The global benefits manager in the MNE is faced with such tremendous complexity that it is very difficult for any such manager to be knowledgeable about benefits administration in more than a few countries. As with taxes, the MNE must typically seek advice and assistance from specialized, international accounting and HR consulting firms. The following illustrates this country-by-country variation for a number of common benefits and incentives such as holidays and vacations, pension plans, insurance, leaves, flexible benefits, and equity-based compensation.

EXHIBIT 11.2: Average Annual Hours Per Year Per Person in Employment (most recent data as of 2013)

Country	2003	2013	Δ Decade
Australia	1743.30	1675.5	–67.8
Austria	1786	1623	–163
Belgium	1581.10	1570.17	–10.93
Canada	1739	1706	–33
Chile	2235	2015.11	–219.89
Czech Republic	1815	1771.78	–43.22
Denmark	1462.14	1411.39	–50.75
Estonia	1985	1868	–117
Finland	1719	1666	–53
France	1484.38	1489.19	4.81
Germany	1435.90	1387.90	–48
Greece	2112	2037	–75
Hungary	1978.17	1883	–95.17
Iceland	1811.09	1703.97	–107.12
Ireland	1887	1815	–72
Israel	1974	1867	–107
Italy	1826	1752	–74
Japan	1799	1735	–64
Korea	2424	NA	
Luxembourg	1651	1643	–8
Mexico	2276.53	2236.62	–39.91
Netherlands	1401	1380	–21
New Zealand	1820	1760	–60
Norway	1400.69	1408.09	7.4
Poland	1984	1918	–66
Portugal	1768	1712	–56
Slovak Republic	1698	1770	72
Slovenia	1724	1547	–177
Spain	1719	1664.90	–54.1
Sweden	1582	1607	25
Switzerland	1626.81	1584.77	–42.04
Turkey	1943	1832	–111
United Kingdom	1674	1669	–5
West Germany	1419	NA	
United States	1800	1788	–12
Russian Federation	1993	1980	–13

Based on data from average annual hours actually worked per worker, http://stats.oecd.org/index.aspx?DataSetCode=ANHRS in OECD.StatExtracts http://stats.oecd.org. Accessed Oct. 28, 2014.

Working Hours

The number of hours worked per year varies considerably from country to country (see Exhibit 11.2). In general, there has been a decline in the number of working hours per year around the world. Annual working hours are much higher in the Central and Eastern European countries as compared to Western Europe.

Holiday and Vacation Benefits

There are wide variances among countries in holiday and vacation entitlements. National (e.g., a country's founding-day holiday) and religious holidays (the religious observances of the major faith groups) are part of the cultural fabric of most societies. While in most Western Christian societies, no one would consider calling an important company meeting on Christmas Day, yet, they often seem ignorant or oblivious to major religious holidays celebrated by other faiths of their non-Christian employees and religious observances in their foreign subsidiaries.

Exhibit 11.3 illustrates how vacation and holiday benefits are mandated in some countries and voluntarily provided in others. It shows the paid vacations days and legally mandated paid holidays in a number of different countries.[16] Among the countries listed, vacation provisions range from 6 days for employees with one year of service in Mexico to 30 days for such employees in Austria and Denmark. A US worker must often stay at a job for 30 years to match (and most never reach that level, even in 30 years) the level of paid vacation time that is commonly provided to beginning workers in many European countries. The US, Canada, New Zealand, and Japan are the developed countries that provide the shortest paid vacation time for employees—each granting an average of only 10 to 15 days a year. In the US, paid vacation time is left to the discretion of each company, a situation that is true for most benefits. Most firms base the amount of time provided to employees on the employee's length of service. The average received by American employees in their first years at a firm is 11 days. After five years of service, they earn 15 days, on average. Ten years of service results in 17 days, and 30 years earns employees 24 days of paid vacation. In contrast, most European countries (and others as well), mandate more-extensive paid vacation for workers, e.g., Denmark mandates 31 days of paid vacation while Austria requires companies to give their employees 30 days of vacation; France requires 5 weeks; and Germany mandates 24 days. In addition, most European employers actually extend employee vacation time to six weeks. In the UK, employees average 22 days off with pay.

Pension Plans

Retirement benefits create their own special set of complexities for MNEs.[17] Some countries have defined-benefit plans (pays a fixed periodic benefit upon retirement) while others have defined-contribution plans (distributes retirement benefit based on contributions to

EXHIBIT 11.3: Paid Vacation Days and Legally Mandated Paid Holidays

Country	Legally mandated paid vacation days	Legally mandated paid holidays
France	30	1
UK	28	0
Austria	25	13
Norway	25	2
Denmark	25	0
Finland	25	0
Sweden	25	0
Portugal	22	13
Spain	22	12
Italy	20	11
Belgium	20	10
Germany	20	10
New Zealand	20	10
Ireland	20	9
Australia	20	8
Greece	20	6
Netherlands	20	0
Switzerland	20	0
Canada	10	9
Japan	10	0
USA	0	0

Adapted from Ray, R., Sanes, M., and Schmitt, J. (2013). *No-Vacation Nation Revisited*, Center for Economic and Policy Research, Washington, DC.

the plan); some have government social security systems (albeit with varying retirement pay-outs) while others have different (e.g., Providence Funds in some Asian countries) or no retirement plans at all. This makes it difficult for an MNE to streamline the pension plan benefits. For example, when Johnson & Johnson examined its pension system a few years ago, it "discovered" that it not only had a US defined-benefit pension plan covering some 20,000 participants with $1.2 billion in assets, but that it also had another 15 plans with 15,000 participants worldwide and another $700 million in assets.[18] And this is only one of the many benefit programs with which MNEs must concern themselves.

Insurance

Another area of benefits that can add complexity to the design of benefits programs, especially for international assignees, is insurance benefits (such as life, disability, and long-term care insurance). Most large MNEs provide their managers and senior technicians with different insurances as part of their employee benefit package. But many insurance policies have territorial and null and void clauses (for example in case of declared or undeclared war). As a result, the firm may need to purchase special coverage while international assignees and their families are in foreign locations. Depending on the location, the firm may also have to provide special "work risk" insurance, for more dangerous or remote locations and, possibly, other forms of special insurance, e.g., kidnapping insurance.

Leaves

An area of employee benefits that has been receiving increasing attention involves the provision of leaves for a variety of reasons (e.g., maternity, paternity, parental, family, sabbatical, military, etc.) with or without pay, often with a guarantee of getting one's job back at the end of the leave. This is a benefit provided by most Western countries. Even so, most Western countries tend to be further advanced on the provision of family leave benefits than, say, the US. Approximately two-thirds of all nations, including most industrialized countries, have provisions for paid and job-protected maternity leaves of four to 12 months prenatal and three to 29 months postnatal.[19] Many countries have parity in terms of maternal and paternal leave. The leaves may be paid for by the employer, by the government, or both. Leave of absence management differs greatly among countries. Even though the EU is trying to develop common practices on these types of social policies, there exists diversity even within these close-proximity countries. The IHR practitioner will often need to rely on country-based leaves of absence specialists to comply with national regulations within the MNE.

Flexible Benefits

Flexible benefits are offered by an increasing number of US domestic and multinational companies. In essence, employees are typically given choices, up to a certain dollar limit, among a series of options for their benefits (including such things as pension contributions, health insurance options, dental insurance, life insurance, etc.). They may choose not to get certain benefits because they are provided to them by other means (e.g., through a spouse or partner) or are not attractive to them in their particular family situation (e.g., childcare assistance when an employee has no children). MNEs are beginning to examine flex benefits for their global operations, designing global flex-benefit plans similar to what has been tried within the US.[20] This is happening because:

- Flex benefits have been successful in the US, so employers in other countries are beginning to take a look at the idea.
- MNEs have a need to attract and retain more diversified work forces (in terms of age, marital status, family situation), thus they are looking at flex benefits as a way to attract workers with diverse benefit needs.
- Foreign firms are investing in American health care companies and are thus being exposed to how important flex benefits are in the US for controlling rising health care costs.
- The increased aging of the labor force around the world is leading MNEs to look at flex benefits as a way to provide diverse benefits to all workers with a single benefits program.

Issues such as tax treatment of benefits, private versus state health care, employee expectations and culture, non-standardized social benefits from country to country, and varying company structures all need to be addressed in order to design flexible benefit packages that might be used throughout an MNE. Nevertheless, such an approach may help simplify worldwide comprehensive compensation systems for multinational firms.

Equity Compensation

In recent years there has been a trend in global firms to look for ways to internationalize their employee equity participation schemes.[21] In particular, this has included experimenting with ways to grant stock options and restricted stock to their overseas employees.[22] Equity compensation programs are being used by MNEs (especially in young, growth-oriented companies and firms in high-tech/telecommunication industries) to attract, motivate, reward, and retain key employees. When employees have a stake in the business by which they are employed, it creates an ownership culture that better aligns individual employee objectives with organizational objectives. Equity compensation programs are generally seen as powerful and competitive talent management tools for attracting and retaining talent, providing an incentive for higher productivity, and reducing turnover.

Major types of equity programs used by MNEs to reward talent on an international scale include employee stock ownership plans (ESOP), employee stock purchase plans (ESPP), stock option plans, stock appreciation rights (SAR), and phantom stock (note that phantom stock is not really equity-based).[23] An overview of these different types of equity compensation plans is presented in Exhibit 11.4. Note that these different plans affect performance and retention in differing ways.

These equity-based compensation plans are treated in various ways in terms of their taxation status. Equity-based compensation gives young companies an effective way to attract talent, at little cost, and the opportunity to share prospective wealth created by the growth of the company with critical employees. This is often viewed by employees as a very desirable incentive. Yet using equity-based, long-term incentive compensation has ramifications for the MNE. Varying national accounting tax rules, exchange and currency

EXHIBIT 11.4: Types of Equity Compensation

ESOP   Gives employees shares of company stock (in a bonus or profit-sharing plan) for individual and overall company performance. The benefit is usually redeemable by employees when they leave the company. Awarding employees with stocks is a practice known as "non-restrictive" stock bonus.

ESPP   Gives employees an opportunity to purchase company stock, usually through payroll deduction and at discounted price, during a certain period.

Stock or call options   Grants certain employees the right to receive or purchase company shares at a specific price called a "strike" or "exercise" price. In other words, it gives employees an options or the right to buy stock in the future at today's price. These grants may be offered "at the money" (the exercise price matches the stock price at the time of the grant), "out of the money" (the exercise price is higher than the stock price at the time of the grant—premium option), or "in the money" (the exercise price is lower than the stock price—discount option). The MNE may choose to grant stock options only to executives or to many employees to create broad-based ownership by its workforce. Stock options may be restricted or non-restricted. Common restrictions are that the stock cannot be sold to a third party, that it must be vested (usually after one to five years after they are granted), that it must be exercised before a defined maturity date (usually 10 years), and that it does not qualify for dividends.

SAR   Awards a grant to the employee, subject to a vesting schedule, but he/she receives no benefit unless the underlying stock value appreciates. This gives the holder an incentive to improve the financial performance of the company and subsequent stock value appreciation. Obviously, this type of grant is only an incentive for the employee if the stock value increases.

Phantom stock   Is a simulated equity plan that grants the employees a number of fictitious (pretend) stock units whose value corresponds to the price fluctuations of a given number of shares. On maturity, the employee is paid a cash bonus based on how much the stock grew by vesting time. Phantom stocks, if structured properly, have certain advantages for the employee and the company. There are no tax consequences to either the company or employee when a phantom stock unit is granted. It merely gives employees the economic benefits of owning stock without any actual transfer of stock and it doesn't dilute the ownership rights of existing shareholders. Phantom stocks, although not actual equity, are tied to the value of the company's stock.

controls, and tax-withholding requirements make managing equity-based compensation at a global level quite complex.

In terms of stock options, for example (see Exhibit 11.4), accounting rules in the US used to allow firms to treat these offerings to employees as an expense (i.e., companies were able to deduct the value of these stock options—because they are taxable to the employee—from their own taxable corporate income, even though they didn't really have to spend actual money to provide the options with the exception of administrative expenses). However, the Securities and Exchange Commission (SEC) in the US has added new requirements for the disclosure to shareholders of option grants and the reporting of income from options. Stock options have an impact on shareholder value, primarily in terms of earnings dilution. Corporate-fraud scandals, especially backdating of stock options (i.e., pretending that options had been issued earlier than they really were at more favorable prices) are being investigated in several MNEs.

Because of the various country tax rules and currency exchange restrictions, an MNE must adapt its stock options offerings to employees in its subsidiaries to deal with the complexity of operating in different countries.[24] Different countries treat stock options differently in terms of employee taxation. In some countries, employees pay tax when they exercise their stock options (even if they may not get any future value for them). This highly reduces the incentive of the award. In other countries, employees pay taxes on the capital gains when they redeem their options. Still, other countries tax their employees both at the issuance and redemption of stock options. When giving stock options to employees worldwide, MNEs must consider the often-detrimental effect of local tax implications, foreign exchange controls, and the overall after-tax income effect. They must also comply with the different payroll withholding requirements that are in effect in different countries. Rules become even more complex when dealing with international assignees and the cross-border tax implications of stock option taxation and currency exchange. For example, the tax code of the host country (where the employee is located) may have a considerable impact as the stock options may be seen as compensation for employment services performed outside their home countries—even for shares that were granted to them prior to their departures from their home countries.

Adaptation of global stock option plans must focus on ensuring local compliance and reducing the negative consequences of taxation. Therefore, MNEs must give out options judiciously and hire compensation specialists (global stock plan administrators) who have specific competencies to manage equity-based compensation plans in terms of compliance and effectiveness. MNEs must evaluate the local and cross-border implications of their global stock option plans and make appropriate adjustments country-by-country while trying to maintain internal equity among employees. Changing market conditions and expected changes in national tax regulations and international accounting rules will continue to increase the complexity and cost of effectively using and managing stock option plans.

Global firms with equity compensation plans for their worldwide employees are also affected by the accepted accounting and tax rules that govern the MNE's balance sheet and its employee and corporate tax treatments. Today, stock options for employees throughout the company are a quite popular form of incentive compensation, particularly in the US and in the information technology industry. More and more, non-US multinational companies are adopting widespread stock option programs as well. For example, Canon, a Japanese MNE, has adopted decidedly non-Japanese incentive schemes to support its global competitiveness.[25] And, even though this strategy does not fit well with Japanese values, Canon has been able to use these programs to its advantage. Yet, some American MNEs, where these programs have been created, have experienced difficulties as they have tried to extend their employee stock ownership plans overseas.[26] IHR needs to work collaboratively with the global stock plan administrator (who usually resides in the accounting and finance department or is outsourced to an accounting or consulting firm with this specialization) to structure effective global compensation plans, customize these plans to local operations, communicate them to managers and employees, and respond to equity-based compensation inquiries. Ultimately, equity-based compensation must remain cost-effective for the company and motivational for employees to be used as a competitive talent management tool for attracting, motivating, and retaining key employees.

International Benefits in Practice

Because of these widely varying benefit practices in different countries, corporate policy on establishing and changing benefits must be monitored in such a way as to minimize unnecessary differences among subsidiaries while maintaining parent-company concern for costs, competitiveness, and comparability from locale to locale.[27] Since a foreign subsidiary's benefits program may be more difficult to monitor or control than the parent-company's domestic counterpart, it often makes sense to appoint an effective local manager in each country to act as that country's benefits coordinator, responsible for coordination and liaison with headquarters. And yet there must also be global, or at least regional, co-ordination as well. When managers transfer from one country to another, they will expect to at least retain benefits, such as vacation time comparable to that from their home country, or comparable to the most liberal available in any subsidiary in the firm's global operations. For international assignees moving from countries with relatively low levels of such benefits, this will not create a problem. But for managers moving in the other direction, this can be the source of significant concerns.

MNEs should develop both qualitative parity and quantitative parity in terms of benefits.[28] Qualitative parity is a commitment to offer something from each core category of benefit to every employee worldwide. This would include:

- *core benefits*—basic items that the company commits to making available to all employees worldwide, such as a certain level of health care;
- *required benefits*—compensation items or non-cash benefits required by local law;
- *recommended benefits*—less essential compensation or benefit programs to be made available wherever cost considerations permit, such as life insurance; and
- *optional benefits*—non-essential compensation items to be made available if it is a competitive practice in the local marketplace, such as local transportation or meal support.

The use of qualitative parity is one component of a firm's global compensation approach that provides a way to make a commitment to the entire workforce while still preserving local variations in pay for the less skilled and less mobile employees.

INTERNATIONAL ASSIGNEES AND COMPENSATION AND BENEFITS

Determining the C&B package of international assignees (or employees who are relocated as part of their employment for a certain period of time to another country) is a major component of the IHRM practitioner's job.[29] While, in general, MNEs favor hiring locally in the countries in which they operate (for cost, cultural, and social responsibility reasons), they still often need to relocate some employees, for short or long-term durations, across borders because of the need for home-country managers in operation start-ups, management control, and talent development in specific locations of the MNE. Thus this chapter reviews the evolution of expatriate compensation, its specific purposes, the different types of international assignees who may require different packages, the various approaches to IA C&B (with a major focus on the balance sheet approach), and some special issues inherent to IA C&B, such as payment methods, inflation, exchange rate fluctuations and taxation.

The Evolution of Expatriate Compensation

In the early stages of internationalization, a firm's primary international involvement consists of supporting a limited number of international assignees sent abroad to market its products, transfer its technology, and manage relatively small operations. At this stage of development, remuneration concerns are largely limited to providing adequate compensation and incentives for these expatriates. But as firms' international involvement developed further, concerns about C&B packages for employees from multiple countries moving around the world as well as equity among workforces in many different global locations present many new challenges.

One of the most important considerations for MNEs in the design of their IA C&B programs is the problem of comparability (although cost is probably a very close additional and critical consideration). Indeed, in at least one survey, 77 percent of the expatriates surveyed were dissatisfied with their salaries and benefits and their international compensation packages in general.[30] (Not all surveys show this level of dissatisfaction, but these results suggest that at least some samples of expatriates are unhappy with their compensation.) And a significant portion of this dissatisfaction was due to feelings of inequity in their salaries and benefits. This problem of comparability has at least two significant components:

1   maintaining comparability in salaries and benefits to similar employees in other firms and to peers within the firm for employees who transfer from one country to another

(either from the parent company to foreign subsidiaries or from one subsidiary to another or to headquarters);

2   maintaining competitive and equitable salaries and benefits among the various operations of the organization.

Until recently, most MNEs felt it was necessary for expatriates to receive a salary and benefit package at least comparable to what they were receiving in their countries of origin.[31] Because of the high cost of expatriates and because of changing attitudes about and approaches to international assignments—such as the use of alternative assignments (short-term assignments, frequent business trips, international commuting) and localized transfers—this view about expatriate compensation is being questioned.[32] But comparisons between local nationals and expatriates (and between local nationals in different locales of the MNE) are inevitably made.

In a globally competitive economy (or, even, a regionally competitive one, such as within Europe or Asia), attracting and retaining the best employees and motivating them to take on international assignments requires developing a compensation strategy and policy that will minimize problems associated with such comparisons.

IA C&B Strategy and Policy

Determining a cross-border compensation philosophy and establishing an overall IA policy should be the starting point for firms that are newly developing their international presence. The compensation component of the IA policy (note that there are other components to an IA policy dealing with the multiple aspects of the IA process) usually describes whether something is paid for by the company or can be considered for payment. The purpose of developing an IA policy is to ensure greater consistency and equity among international assignees and reduce barriers to global mobility. In other words, C&B differences should not be an obstacle nor primary incentive to refuse or take on an IA. The IA policy educates employees on the important issue in the international assignment and sets realistic expectations in terms of what the company will and will not provide as part of the IA package. With the IA policy (and its exceptions) companies determine the extent to which they want to set precedent for their future presence in the international arena; whether they want any particular practice or policy to be its program for all future situations; or whether they want to customize compensation packages for each international assignee and subsidiary. In general, a well-thoughtout policy should not be subject to many exceptions. It is one of the IHR roles to educate managers and employees on the content of the IA policy and the importance of policy adherence.

The compensation package for IAs must meet certain objectives in order to be effective. These include:

1   providing an incentive to leave the home country for a foreign assignment;
2   maintaining a given standard of living;

3 taking into consideration career and family needs; and
4 facilitating reentry into the home country at the end of the foreign assignment.[33]

To achieve these objectives, MNEs typically pay a high premium over and beyond base salaries to induce potential international assignees to accept IAs. The costs to firms often range from 2 to 2.5 times to 4 to 4.5 times the cost of maintaining the manager in a comparable position at home.[34]

Determinants of IA Compensation Approach

When determining the most suitable approach to IA compensation, IHR must consider a number of questions.

1 *What is the type of employee population being relocated abroad?* Is the IA an executive who needs an international posting for additional global leadership experience, an experienced employee relocated for technical or managerial skills, or a young and relatively inexperienced employee? Is the IA part of an international cadre of expatriates who move from one foreign assignment to another or is the IA someone who seeks to become established abroad permanently? Each of these types of IAs has different needs with regard to their compensation.

2 *What is the purpose or reason for the international assignment?* Is the assignment demand-driven (i.e., the international assignee is sent because the MNE wants control and consistency in the foreign operations or the employee has the necessary competencies to solve a particular problem for the company) or learning-driven (the international assignment is for the purpose of employee competency development and career enhancement)? Demand-driven assignments may require a better compensation package than learning-driven assignments as the IA will derive developmental benefits from the latter and should not be provided as many additional incentives to do so.

3 *What is the anticipated duration of the international assignment?* Is it a short-term assignment (usually less than one year and probably within the same calendar/tax year) or long-term expatriation (usually one to three years)? Duration (and especially the number of days out of the home country in a particular tax year) usually has important tax ramifications for the employee (and for the employer, if it is taking responsibility for part of the tax obligation).

4 *What happens with the IA at the end of the assignment?* What are the repatriation plans for the IA upon completion of the assignment? Is the employee returning to the home country, continuing in the same country with an extended contract, or moving on to a third country?

5 *Where is the IA leaving from and going to?* Which are the home and host countries of the IA and what is the context of these countries with regard to C&B (especially taxation) laws, regulations, and practices?

6 *Who is the peer of the IA?* What typical employee will the IA compare him/herself to in terms of equity with regard to this assignment? The IHR manager should know who the peer group is of the particular employee considered for assignment so that they can justify the elements of the C&B package.

7 *What is the overall cost of the international assignment?* Based on the answers to the above questions, what is the overall cost of the assignment and will the various decision-makers (management and IA) consider that the benefits derived from the assignment will balance the costs?

MNEs are realizing that not all international assignees or locations are alike. Therefore, they should not be treated as though they were the same. Rather, varying compensation approaches may provide better solutions. This has led to the development of a number of different IA C&B approaches and even greater administrative complexity (although computer programs have made administration less cumbersome than it used to be in the earlier pre-personal computer IHR days) for different groups of employees within the MNE. Many MNEs are beginning to recognize these options and are looking for more flexible and cost-effective IA compensation systems. The next section describes the most common approaches now being used by MNEs.

Approaches to IA Compensation

There are a number of basic approaches followed by MNEs to compensate their IAs. These include ad hoc negotiation, balance sheet, localization, lump sum, cafeteria, regional, and global plans. Although these approaches will be discussed separately, MNEs often use multiple compensation systems to suit their types of international assignee and global/local contextual needs. Thus this discussion revolves around what each compensation approach entails and when it is most appropriate to use each approach.

Negotiation/Ad Hoc

When firms first start sending employees on international assignments and while their number of IAs is still relatively few, the common approach to determining pay and benefits is referred to as ad hoc, or the C&B package for each individual being considered for a foreign posting is negotiated separately. At the early stages of "going international" the firm sends its best expert abroad and pays the price it must to make it happen. There usually isn't much of a search; and the firm does whatever it takes to get the person relocated and pays whatever costs arise. Because the person and the assignment are so important, the firm tends to take care of all of their concerns. This approach may appear quite simple initially, and, given the inexperience of HR managers at this stage, the limited amount of information available about how to design a C&B system for IAs, and the many complexities in such a package compared to domestic C&B, it is easy to see why IHR managers follow this approach.[35] Yet, according to IA compensation experts, this approach is fraught with complications and, therefore, not recommended. In negotiation, the best negotiator (whether it is the IHR practitioner, the manager, or the employee) wins and the bar gets set high for what future IAs will want in their international C&B packages. Such an approach is also difficult for systematic tracking of IA C&B packages and complicates effective tax planning. It is recommended that, even when a company only has a few IAs, IHR put an IA policy together to set a standard framework for what the company is willing to provide.

Balance Sheet

This approach is followed by most MNEs in the US (and to a lesser extent in other countries) when their international business expands to the point where the firm has a larger number of international assignees (a dozen or so). At this stage, the negotiation, or ad hoc, approach will have led to too many inconsistencies between the compensation packages of its many IAs and the firm will realize it needs to develop policy and practice that will apply to all expatriates. In addition, the ad hoc approach will now be viewed as taking too much time—and cost—to negotiate, develop, and manage such a unique package for each IA. The firm will seek a more standardized approach and will begin to make policy about what will and what will not be covered in the expatriate C&B package.

In essence, the balance sheet approach involves an effort by the MNE to ensure that it is easier for the IA to leave for an assignment and more likely to return home from a successful assignment.[36] The "old" balance sheet terminology emphasized keeping the employee "whole." That is, at a minimum, the IA should be no worse off in terms of compensation, benefits, and lifestyle for accepting an international assignment. It was common to assume that the C&B package not only should make the expatriate "whole" but also should provide incentives to take the foreign assignment, remove any worry about compensation issues while on that assignment, and ensure that the individual and his or her family felt good about having been on the assignment. Today, in an environment that increasingly asks IHRM to control all employment costs, including the costs of expatriation, the balance sheet approach is being used to minimize total compensation losses or gains as a result of the assignment and the terminology used no longer implies that the employee will be kept "whole" and that the "home" lifestyle will be replicated in the "host" environment. To the contrary, IAs are counseled to be flexible and urged to make some adaptation to the local culture as part of their own acculturation and assimilation process.

The use of the balance sheet approach is particularly favored in the US for experienced senior- and mid-level assignees who will return home at the end of their assignments. However, the balance sheet (referred to as the buildup system in the UK) is rather complex to explain to all parties involved. Some IAs have complained that this approach to determining their compensation (especially determining normalized spending patterns to calculate the differentials) is much more intrusive into their personal lives than is true for the traditional domestic compensation package. Theoretically, the balance sheet approach "balances" out the differences between costs in the home and host countries. It ensures that the IA can maintain purchasing power parity while on assignment. As a result, taking on the international assignment should result in only minimal changes to the IA's lifestyle. However, nowadays, the IA (and family) are often asked to make some adjustments.

The next few pages will explain the details of the balance sheet approach. Figure 11.1 illustrates how this strategy is described visually. As this explanation continues, you will realize how complex this approach can be. But hopefully, this illustration will help you to understand this approach.

The balance sheet approach standardizes the C&B approach for each international assignee by starting with the employee's home compensation (salary, benefits, and any other forms of monetary or non-monetary remuneration). To this is added two other components: a series of equalization components that ensure the international assignee does not suffer from foreign-country differences in salary or benefits and a series of incentives to accept (and enjoy) the foreign posting. Interestingly, today, even with pressure to reduce the high cost of IA compensation, most MNEs still find it necessary to provide significant incentives to encourage potential assignees to accept foreign postings. This is often because there are many more pressures today for employees to turn down an international assignment because of the disruption of family, concerns over spouses' careers, impact on lifestyle choices, concerns over negative impact on the employees' careers, and a general reluctance to live abroad.

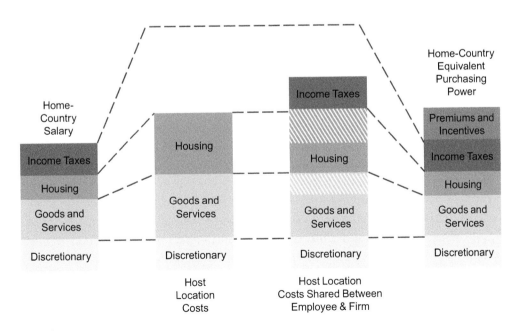

FIGURE 11.1 The Balance Sheet

Source: Understanding the balance sheet approach to expatriate compensation (2004), ORC Worldwide, International Compensation Services.

One of the key complications in this balance sheet approach is how to determine the base upon which to add adjustments and incentives.[37] A number of possibilities exist, including basing the IA's salary on:

- home-country salaries (this is the primary base for the home-country-based balance sheet approach);
- HQ salaries (an international standard based on HQ levels of compensation);
- regional salary standard (e.g., regions such as "old" and "new" European Union countries, US and Canada, Latin America, and Southeast Asia);
- host-country salaries (this uses destination salaries in the host location); and
- better of home or host approach.

The choice of base to use may be best related to the nature of the firm and its international business strategy.[38] It can also be based on the salary rates of the particular home and host countries (is the assignee going from a developed country to an emerging market, or vice versa), and the length of the assignment. If the assignment is long (two to three years or longer) and assignees are likely to transfer from one foreign country assignment to another, then an international standard (HQ-based balance sheet) is probably most appropriate (but it will still probably be based on the parent-country/company base, particularly if the MNE is from a high-wage, developed country). If IAs go to foreign postings for relatively short assignments and then return to the parent country, then a home-country base makes more sense. For some truly global firms or firms that operate within a specific region of the world, it may make sense to use regional bases.

To date, most companies base their IA compensation on either a home- or host-country philosophy (or some combination).[39] The home-based, balance sheet approach is used by most firms, particularly in situations where the IA is opening new markets and new operations, transferring technology, and training local staff.[40] These are clearly not jobs similar to those performed by locals. Thus the need to maintain equity is greatly lessened. But where the operations are ongoing and in developed countries, the IA is likely to be alongside locals performing similar jobs and the need for equity is high and a host-country base makes more sense. In addition, an MNE with operations in many foreign countries may opt for a home-country or headquarters (international) approach because of the sheer size of the administrative complexity involved handling multiple IA packages. On the other hand, if the firm only operates in one or two countries, a host-country approach may be necessary because of local legal or cultural differences.

An approach sometimes used is to offer compensation based on the better of home or host remuneration (also called net-to-net). It compares the net pay under the home country compensation system to a local (location of IA) net salary. The IA then receives the higher of the two. The philosophy underlying this system is that an international assignee will never have to live at a lower standard than a local counterpart, but that the IA will also be protected when the home-country package requires a higher standard than the local counterpart receives.

With all the attention given to designing IA C&B compensation packages, surveys show that even when expatriates are satisfied with their financial packages they still tend to be dissatisfied with the limited career planning, lifestyle support, and cultural training that is provided.[41] This suggests that more attention ought to be paid to these non-compensation factors. There are, however, two issues in the balance sheet approach that MNEs need to decide, namely:

1   What type of adjustment (differential) will they need to pay to make up for the differences in home- and host-country costs of living?

2   What additional incentives and premiums will be required to motivate the employee to take on the international assignment?

Determining the Type and Amount of Adjustments

Because of home-host country differences, MNEs must provide a number of equalization adjustments. These are payments whose purpose is to adjust for differences (generally in a higher direction), hence the name differentials, in mandated payments that the IAs have no control over—some of which are paid by the IA and some of which are paid to the IA. These have included adjustments for differences in (higher) costs of living; fluctuations in exchange rates between the IA's parent-country currency and that of the foreign assignment location; all locally mandated payments, such as payment of salary for additional days or weeks per year (in many countries, firms must pay employees for 13 or 14 months every year, or as in Saudi Arabia, must pay for seven days' work per week, i.e., must pay for rest days as well as work days); an agreement to adjust for decreases in the value of the expatriate's compensation due to high inflation in the foreign country; similarly, reimbursement for any mandatory payments into the host country's welfare plans, such as health insurance or social security; and ensuring that the IA will not have to pay more in income taxes while on the foreign assignment than he or she would have to pay while at home.

To understand how adjustments are calculated under the balance sheet approach, an understanding of the different balance sheet components is necessary. The balance sheet is made up of different components: reserves or savings, goods and services, housing, and income taxes (refer to Figure 11.1: The Balance Sheet). These will be different in the home versus host countries. To understand how these will vary, some additional terminology (such as housing norm, home- and host-country spendables) is useful. Note that these definitions all assume a certain level of income and family size of the international assignee.

The *housing norm* is an average expense for housing in the home country (i.e., what an employee with a certain income and family size is likely to pay for housing in the home country). Note that this is *not* the actual housing expense but a normative amount that IAs—on the average—are likely to spend in the home country based on his/her situation. Depending on the firm, these housing norms may be the average in the home country or the average in specific regions or cities of the home country. The employee will be expected to contribute that portion as a share in the housing expenses while on assignment since they would have paid for it at home if they had not relocated on assignment.

The *home-country spendable* is the normal dollar amount spent for goods and services or the portion of salary spent on goods and services in the home country according to salary and family size of the IA. The *host-country spendable* is the amount for goods and services that the IA is assumed to spend in the host country or the amount needed for the spend-ables in the assignment location. The *differential* is the difference between the home and host country spending for the IA and accounts for the cost-of-living adjustment (COLA) between home and host countries. It is usually calculated as a goods and services index. A number of international consulting firms provide data to help companies determine local costs-of-living around the world. Such data are available for most countries as base countries to most other countries as receiving countries. Most companies use average coun-try data and do not differentiate by area within the country. The purpose of the COLA is to enable IAs to maintain as closely as possible the same standard of living in the foreign assignment as they would have had at home (or better, if coming from a low-cost-of-living city or country). Since the typical IA resides in a major city in the host country where costs of living tend to be quite high (particularly the costs of transportation and housing, which may not be available—except at very high cost—in forms comparable to what the expa-triate family experienced at home), COLAs of 50 percent or more are relatively common. The ratios vary according to family size and income, and the consulting firms that provide this type of data will alter the estimates based on these factors. These adjustments also vary according to the technology that the consulting firm uses to determine the cost of living in various foreign locations.[42] An example of variations in costs of living is reflected in Exhibit 11.5, ranking the 10 most expensive cities in the world. Obviously, different approaches to determining city costs-of-living create very different results. For example, using the US dollar to determine costs around the world will favor high costs in cities where the US dol-lar is valued low against local currency. IHR managers need to be careful when they assess which rankings to use for determining IA cost-of-living adjustments. In addition, there are other factors that can influence the decision where to assign expats. The third column in Exhibit 11.5 lists countries to multiple criteria.

There are at least two common techniques used to determine costs of living. One of these uses staff of the consulting firm that are located in the particular foreign cities to estimate the cost of living in those locations based on their surveys of costs in a standard-ized (typical expenditures from the home location) market-basket of goods and services. A second technique involves the surveying of existing and former expatriates of the clients of the particular consulting firm for their typical spending in the particular foreign locale. Often this second technique—which arguably assesses the actual items that IAs typically buy, as opposed to a theoretical market-basket of goods and services—results in a lower cost-of-living than that arrived at by the first technique. This second technique implies the concept of the IA becoming a more efficient purchaser in the host country as times goes by. The *Efficient Purchaser Index (EPI)* implies that the assignee, after some accommodation to the host country, has learned to purchase better because of increased familiarity with

EXHIBIT 11.5: The 10 Most Expensive Countries/cities in the World

Rank* (most expensive)	EIU survey*	Mercer survey**	HSBC survey (overall experience)***
1	Tokyo, Japan	Luanda, Angola	Switzerland
2	Osaka, Japan	N'Djamena, Chad	Singapore
3	Sydney, Australia	Hong Kong	China
4	Oslo, Norway	Singapore	Germany
5	Melbourne, Australia	Zurich, Switzerland	Bahrain
6	Singapore, Singapore	Geneva, Switzerland	New Zealand
7	Zurich, Switzerland	Tokyo, Japan	Thailand
8	Paris, France	Bern, Switzerland	India
9	Caracas, Venezuela	Moscow, Russia	Hong Kong
10	Geneva, Switzerland	Shanghai, China	Canada

*Source: Economist Intelligence Unit: Worldwide cost of living 2013 (least expensive cities mostly in Asia). (Website: http://www.worldwidecostofliving.com.)

**Source: 2014 Mercer Consulting's Annual Cost of Living Survey, 10 most expensive designations. (Website: http://www.imercer.com/content/cost-of-living.aspx.)

***Source: 2014 study done by HSBC ranking countries according to criteria including economics, experience, and raising children.
(Website: http://www.expatexplorer.hsbc.com/#/countries.)

the location. Nowadays, the EPI is usually built into the differential calculations at the very beginning of assignment planning, since phasing in lower host spendables (declining over time that the international assignee lives in the foreign location) is much more difficult and may be demotivational.

In addition, companies often offer *destination services*, which help the IA and family to be more efficient from the start. Obviously, MNEs have an interest in trying to minimize the level of the differential, which as shown above can often involve a significant amount of money.

Due to the complexity of costing out an international assignment, IHRM will usually rely on an international C&B tax consultant to develop an IA compensation worksheet. Based on the balance sheet approach, Exhibit 11.6 shows the different components and estimated costs associated with a relocation from the US (average city in the US) to

EXHIBIT 11.6: Balance Sheet Example

MERCER

Assignment Balance Sheet		

Base Salary :	$220,000	
Bonus	$260,000	
Family Size Home:	3	
Family Size at Post:	3	
Location:	United States to Hong Kong	

ORC Goods & Services Index:	*Expatriate - Standard Index*	146.1788
Foreign Exchange Rate:		7.8074
Effective Date:		27-Aug-07

	US$
COMPENSATION SUMMARY	
Base Salary	$220,000
Bonus	260,000
Hypothetical Federal Tax [1]	(116,726)
Hypothetical State Tax [1]	(24,515)
Social Security [1]	(13,005)
Net Income Home Country	***325,754***
plus:	
Goods and Services Differential [2]	36,344
Home Housing Norm [2]	(31,046)
Foreign Housing Cost [3]	149,358
Incremental Assignment Allowances	***154,656***
Net Income on Assignment	***$480,410***

RECOMMENDED METHOD OF PAY:		
Portion paid in Assignment Location	US$	HK$
Goods and Services Spendable Income [2]	$78,702	614,458
Goods and Services Differential	36,344	283,749
Host Spendable	$115,046	898,207
Foreign Housing Cost	149,358	1,166,100
ASSIGNMENT LOCATION TOTAL	$264,404	2,064,307
Portion paid in the Home Country		
Base Salary	$220,000	
Bonus	260,000	
Goods and Services Spendable Income	(78,702)	
Home Housing Norm	(31,046)	
Hypothetical Income Tax	(141,241)	
Social Security Tax	(13,005)	
HOME COUNTRY TOTAL	$216,006	
NET COMPENSATION	$480,410	

Notes:

(1) Tax calculated on base plus bonus, totaling US$480,000 for a family size of 3 in the US. Any other income would be subject to additional hypothetical tax.

(2) G&S differential, G&S spendable, and housing norm are based on base salary only.

(3) Average monthly rent (HK$95,000) + utility (HK$ 2,175) cost for an unfurnished 2 bedroom apartment in an expensive expatriate appropriate neighborhood in Hong Kong. [Deep Water Bay, May Rd., Repulse Bay, South Bay, Tai Tam, The Peak]
~~~~~~~~~~~~~~~~~~~~~~~~~~~~~~~~~~All figures are annual~~~~~~

Source: Prepared for this text by Rebecca Rosenzweig, Director, International Compensation Services, Mercer/ORC Worldwide.

Hong Kong. While this worksheet will usually be prepared by an external IA C&B consultant, IHR will need to be able to explain the worksheet to a potential international assignee and his or her manager and respond to inquiries. Note that a number of elements contained in the worksheet, such as taxes and exchange rate fluctuations, will be discussed right upfront with the potential assignee.

Determining the Type and Amount of Allowances and Incentives

Once the base salary has been determined, and the needed adjustments calculated, the firm must decide which incentives it feels are necessary to convince its employees that it will be to their financial advantage (or, at least as is being increasingly maintained, not to their disadvantage),[43] to take the foreign assignment. In the past (and still normally for less-developed multinational firms), many incentives were offered, often with sizable monetary benefit to the expatriate. One of the current issues, however, is the high cost of expatriation (at least for more experienced MNEs) and the subsequent need to contain costs.

One of the most common incentives has been an additional *foreign premium*, used to compensate the international assignee and her/his family for the "dislocation" of having to move to an unfamiliar country and to live in what might be seen as an uncomfortable (i.e., different) environment; provide an incentive to take the foreign assignment; and keep up with the practices of other MNEs. These premiums used to average about 25 percent of the expatriate's base pay. Today, it is more common for this premium to be about 15 percent of base pay. Increasingly, firms are questioning whether it is necessary to pay this premium for an IA (or, at least, for most foreign assignments).[44] Critics argue that in a truly global economy with improved communication and transportation, general availability of global consumer products, and accepted international business norms, there is no longer as much trauma and dislocation associated with an overseas transfer. Still, a large number (although declining) of MNEs continue to pay such premiums.[45] And MNEs are now finding that assignments to emerging market economies and cities may involve lower standards of living that require higher premiums.

Additional forms of incentive include premiums for "hardship" postings and dangerous postings, which could include many assignments to developing countries, locations where the threat of kidnapping or terrorist activity is high, or to remote locations (such as the outback in Indonesia or on an ocean oil drilling platform) or locations with less modern or more restrictive living or environmental conditions. The three broad areas typically considered in evaluating the extent of hardship include physical threat, level of discomfort, and inconvenience.[46] The physical threat category includes potential or actual violence, hostility to foreigners from the local population, prevalence of disease, and the adequacy of local medical facilities and services. The discomfort category evaluates the physical environment, climate, and pollution as well as geographical, cultural, and psychological isolation. And the inconvenience category rates the local education system, the availability and quality of local housing, access to recreational and community facilities, and the availability, quality, and variety of consumer goods and services. Hardship allowances typically range from 5 to 25 percent of base pay with danger pay maybe adding another 15 to 20 percent to base pay. Depending on the location, hardship and danger-pay incentives could add as much as 30 percent to an expatriate's income.

Additional incentives usually (or may) include *housing allowances*, either to ensure the expatriate lives as well as her/his foreign peers or to make her/his housing comparable to what s/he had "back at home"—and to take care of her/his home in the parent country and the storage of household goods; settling-in allowances; *education allowances* for the expatriate (e.g., for language courses), her/his spouse, and any other dependents (e.g., for private schools for the expatriate's school-age children); all travel and *relocation expenses* necessary to go to and return from the foreign assignment; local *transportation* in the foreign locale; any *language and cultural training* expenses prior to leaving for the assignment; and special *perquisites*, such as club memberships in the foreign assignment and special R&R (rest and relaxation) and home leaves, for the expatriate and her/his family. Depending on the location, these incentives and adjustments typically cost the MNE more than $150,000 annually per expatriate relocation. Indeed for some locations, where the cost of living and cost of housing are particularly high, this figure can reach $500,000 or more annually. This is in addition to base salary and benefits. For example, in Tokyo, the rent for an expatriate family often exceeds $300,000 per year.[47] It is no wonder that the cost of expatriate failure is so high (often figured to be in the neighborhood of US$1 million for a two-to-three year assignment). And it is no wonder that large MNEs are beginning to reconsider their approaches to IA compensation.

One of the consequences of these increasing costs, is that firms are increasingly looking to provide the higher IA salaries through various forms of incentive pay based on performance (either individual or organizational) for at least part of the pay package, just as they are using such programs in their domestic operations.[48] In order to minimize costs, firms are designing bonus deferrals (paid at the end of the assignment), in-kind benefits, and equity-based plans for international assignee (as well as HCN and TCN executives) tied to achievement of long-term strategic objectives in the subsidiaries (such as growth in subsidiary revenues and profits or return on capital employed at the subsidiary level). Another way to remedy the high cost of long-term expatriation is to use more alternative types of international assignments (usually shorter-term assignments that do not require families to accompany the assignee).[49]

Exhibit 11.7 provides a cost estimate based on balance-sheet planning (illustrating many of the allowances, adjustments, incentives, and tax consequences of a typical three-year assignment for an assignee relocating from New York to Beijing, a quite-common relocation in recent years. This particular example documents a US$2.6 million cost for such a three-year relocation—and illustrates why many MNEs today are seeking ways to reduce such costs while still meeting the challenges of effectively managing their far-flung foreign operations.

EXHIBIT 11.7: Cost Estimate for Three-Year Assignment

MERCER

Cost Estimate
New York Metro to Beijing, China

Base Salary : 433,000 US$
Total Family Size: 3
Effective Date: 4/27/2010
Assignment Period: June 1, 2010 - May 31, 2012

	2010	2011	2012	2013	Total
Base Compensation					
Base Salary	$253,900	$446,000	$190,800	$ -	$890,700
Incentive Bonus	80,800	142,700	61,300	-	284,800
Hypothetical Tax Deducted	(120,400)	(214,500)	(90,800)	-	(425,700)
	214,300	374,200	161,300	-	749,800
Assignment Allowances					
Goods and Services Differential	35,200	61,800	26,500	-	123,500
Host Housing Allowance	45,100	79,200	33,900	-	158,200
Housing Norm Contribution	(43,300)	(76,000)	(32,500)	-	(151,800)
Transportation Allowance	12,000	21,100	9,100	-	42,200
Appliance Allowance	5,000	-	-	-	5,000
Home Property Management	2,900	5,000	2,100	-	10,000
Storage Fees	3,300	5,600	2,300	-	11,200
Foreign Service Premium (Mobility Premium)	-	-	-	-	-
Relocation Allowance	10,000	-	10,000	-	20,000
Location (Hardship) Premium	-	-	-	-	-
Tuition	12,500	24,400	11,900	-	48,800
Spousal Allowance	5,000	-	-	-	5,000
Home Leave	-	17,800	-	-	17,800
Language Lessons	8,000	-	-	-	8,000
Tax Preparation Fees	5,000	5,000	5,000	-	15,000
	100,700	143,900	68,300	-	312,900
Relocation Costs - Taxable					
Destination Services	5,500	-	-	-	5,500
Temp Living/lodging - initial move	14,100	-	-	-	14,100
Temp Living/lodging - repatriation move	-	-	17,100	-	17,100
Loss on sale of private car	5,000	-	-	-	5,000
Pre-Assignment Visit	13,700	-	-	-	13,700
	32,800	-	17,100	-	49,900
Relocation Costs - Non-Taxable					
Household Goods Shipment	28,000	-	28,000	-	56,000
Cultural Training	4,000	-	-	-	4,000
Immigration	6,000	-	-	-	6,000
Relocation Airfare	15,300	-	21,500	-	36,800
	53,300	-	49,500	-	102,800
Home Residual Tax (Employer paid)					
Federal Tax	-	77,400	-	79,100	156,500
Medical/Social Tax	-	19,100	21,900	19,300	60,300
State Tax	-	65,500	85,800	67,400	218,700
Tax Settlement (after yr-end reconciliation)	-	(64,400)	-	(96,700)	(161,100)
	-	97,600	107,700	69,100	274,400
Tax Reimbursement (Host Tax Costs)					
Federal/National Tax	260,200	447,600	260,200	-	968,000
Medical/Social Tax	-	-	-	-	-
State/ Canton Tax	-	-	-	-	-
Home Gross-Up (final reconciliation upon repatriation)	-	-	-	45,400	45,400
	260,200	447,600	260,200	45,400	1,013,400
Employer Benefits Costs - Home					
Medical Insurance	12,400	15,300	12,700	-	40,400
Social Security Tax	6,600	6,600	6,600	-	19,800
	19,000	21,900	19,300	-	60,200
Employer Benefits Costs - Host					
Disability and Medical Insurance	-	-	-	-	-
Nursing Insurance	-	-	-	-	-
Pension Insurance	-	-	-	-	-
Unemployment Tax	-	-	-	-	-
	-	-	-	-	-
Tax Credit Carryback/ Carryforward	-	-	-	-	-
Total Assignment Costs	$680,300	$1,085,200	$683,400	$114,500	$2,563,400

Source: Prepared for this text by Rebecca Rosenzweig, Director, International Compensation Services, Mercer/ORC Worldwide.

Localization

A relatively new approach to IA compensation is referred to as localization. This approach is being used to address many problems of high cost and perceived inequity among staff in foreign subsidiaries. Under localization, international assignees are paid comparably to local nationals and no equalizers are provided except for some additional allowances. These employees usually are early in their careers eager for learning-driven international assignments, they are seeking employment abroad for a relatively long-term or indefinite period of time, they will not be repatriated after their assignment is over or desire to stay in the host location, or they are TCNs or returnees (people who have studied/worked abroad and return to their home country). Localization tends to be relatively simple to communicate and administer (if done locally). Yet localization is seldom pure, especially when it involves moving from developed to developing country, and medical benefits, taxes, and comparable (or adequate) housing may also be an issue. Since these international assignees may come from different standards of living than that experienced by local nationals, special supplements are usually provided (referred to as local +).

In the past, localization was also used to convert IAs who were relocated on traditional expat arrangements and who then overstayed their original contracts, for business reasons (they became important for the business, such as maintaining relations with local customers) or for personal reasons (e.g., they learned to enjoy the local environment and decided to stay or may even have married a local partner and now have family locally). In all these cases, there are no longer valid reasons for the expat to continue on expat incentives, allowances, and premiums. Thus the decision to localize such IAs.

Lump Sum

Another approach that some MNEs are trying, particularly in response to concern over the perception that the balance sheet intrudes too heavily into expatriates' lifestyle decisions, is the lump sum approach.[50] In this approach the firm determines a lump sum to cover all the major incentives and adjustments, and then lets the IA determine how to spend it (for example, on housing, transportation, travel, home visits, education, lifestyle, and so forth). In essence, the lump sum is more of a payment method than a compensation approach as the amount of the lump sum is usually calculated the same way as the balance sheet (housing and goods and services) but allowances are not paid out for each component. This lump sum allowance is a single payment, made at the start of the relocation process, to the transferring IA to cover all of the above, or only the costs associated with the relocation, itself. Or, sometimes, the lump sum payment is split between payment at the outset of the assignment and the remainder paid upon successful completion of the assignment (as an incentive to perform successfully and to stay with the firm until the end of the assignment and to avoid tax hits). It should be noted that how the lump sum allowance is paid has an impact on taxes whether in the host or home country. Also, according to IA C&B experts, the lump sum should be avoided for items that are currency sensitive.

Cafeteria

An approach that is increasingly being used for very high salaried executives is to provide a set of choices of benefits—as in a cafeteria, up to a pre-determined monetary limit in value. The advantages accrue to both the firm and to the individual and are primarily related to the tax coverage of benefits and perquisites as compared to cash income (paycheck). Since the individual doesn't need as much cash (since most expenses are paid for by the firm), this approach enables the IA to gain benefits such as a company car, insurance, company-provided housing, and the like that may not increase the assignee's income for tax purposes. The cafeteria approach is usually not used for things that are fundamental to the assignment (such as goods and services), but the company gives choices on things that are not really critical to the success of the assignment (for example, loss on the sale of an automobile). It should be noted that IHR and management usually decide whether an item is essential or not and a cafeteria item, not the international assignee.

Regional Systems

For international assignees who make a commitment to job assignments within a particular region of the world, some firms are developing a regional C&B system to maintain equity within that region. This is usually seen as a complement to the other approaches. And if such individuals are later moved to another region, their pay will be transferred to one of the other regional systems, depending on what is used there, such as the balance sheet approach.

Global Systems

A final approach being followed, at least for international assignees above a certain pay level (i.e., therefore, for professional/technical/managerial employees), is to implement a common global pay and benefits package for each covered job classification applied to everyone in that classification, worldwide. This is often done in recognition of the fact that for many specialized occupations (such as, for example, software engineers and programmers) and for executives there is in fact a global labor market, with qualified specialists from anywhere and everywhere in the world all applying for the same jobs. In this approach, MNEs will have two general pay classifications: local employees below a defined level and international. The international level will almost always include a performance-based variable pay component. The standard used is usually the level paid for those occupations at the firm's headquarters.

MNEs that have employees from many different countries will usually have multiple IA C&B systems at work. While they may have a global philosophy and IA policy, the need for multiple systems is often dictated by the type of assignee, the intricacies of the country/region of operation (and the corresponding tax systems), and the cultural practice of providing certain C&B components. Not using multiple systems, or making adjustments, may result in failure to meet the needs of the international assignee and increased cost due to taxation.

Current methods for determining the C&B package of international assignees are being criticized for many different reasons. There is concern that all of these approaches don't adequately take into account the nature of the IA or the country of assignment and often actually discourage expatriates from assimilating into the local culture.[51] The housing differentials, for example, frequently serve to provide host-country housing that is likely to be better than that enjoyed by their host-country counterparts, although, as mentioned above, whether or not that is appropriate will depend on the nature of the international assignee's assignment. Even the continuation of home-based consumption patterns for goods and services does not encourage the cultural awareness so critical to the international assignee's success in the host country. In addition, critics argue, it seems as though IA C&B systems ought to pay more attention to the differences in perceptions by international assignees and by host-country nationals about issues like the value of money compensation versus other types of perquisites or forms of motivation.[52] A flexible menu of perquisites, traditional incentives and adjustments, and tax reimbursement schedules might well meet some of the criticisms while actually reducing overall costs to the firm. Such an approach might even enable an MNE to replace the traditional cost-of-living concerns with a quality of life or a quality of career opportunity focus.

Additional Important IA Compensation Issues

A number of additional compensation issues, such as payment method, inflation, exchange rate fluctuations, and social security are inherent to any IA C&B approach.

Method of Payment

Once the amount of the international assignee's compensation and benefits package has been determined, the firm must decide whether the expatriate will be paid in the local host country currency, in the home-country currency, or a split pay combination. Where there is limited convertibility between the home-country currency and that of the foreign host locale, or there is rapid inflation, it is probably better for the firm to take care of providing the international assignee's salary in the local currency (of course, with more frequent re-evaluation that guarantees against loss of purchasing power if there is rampant inflation).

However, when the international assignee maintains home-country financial obligations while on assignment, there will be a need for partial payment in the home country currency to meet these obligations. It is typical for many MNEs to pay the IA's base salary and differential partly in local currency (with the amount in local currency pegged to ordinary living expenses) and the remaining amount in the home currency. Bonuses tend to also be paid in the home currency and typically left in home accounts as well. This is referred to as a split-payroll or split-currency approach. This payment method helps the IA cover daily living expenses and maintains purchasing power in the host country while covering remaining financial obligations in the home country. It also, partially, protects against currency exchange rate fluctuations and the impact of differential inflation.

Impact of Exchange Rate Fluctuations

While the differential home and host calculations in the balance sheet approach are made at the beginning of the international assignment, there are bound to be fluctuations in the home and host currencies during the course of the international assignment. Fluctuating exchange rates (Fx) will alter the figures in the balance sheet for the IA. As exchange rates fluctuate up and down, they impact the index and the differential (between the host and home country spendables) as the comparative prices in the host and home locations change.

The general rule is that as the exchange rate goes up, the differential the company pays to the IA goes down. Similarly, as the exchange rate goes down, the differential goes up. In other words, the exchange rate and differential are indirectly related. The IHR C&B specialist will have to be able to explain to the IA why the differential that the firm pays changed as a result of the currency fluctuation and how an adjustment to the differential is in reality balanced out. If the international assignee is paid in both currencies (split pay), there is not really a concern for exchange rate fluctuations as they may cancel each other out. MNEs will usually adjust for currency fluctuations when they reach a certain percentage and indicate this in the assignment letter of the international assignee.

Impact of Inflation

Inflation/deflation can occur in either the home or host country or in both (if occurring in both, they could possibly cancel each other out). What happens with the balance sheet differential when there is inflation? When net inflation goes up (compared to prices in the home country on which cost comparisons are based), host country spendables increase. As a result, the differential goes up. In case of deflation, host country spendables are less and the differential goes down.

As a general rule, net inflation is directly related to the differential (goes up when inflation goes up, and goes down when inflation goes down). Obviously, in reality the differential is impacted simultaneously by both currency fluctuation and inflation.

Social Security

An additional factor involves the varying country-specific practices related to social security taxes and government-provided or -mandated social services, ranging from health care to retirement programs. These can add considerably to the foreign taxation burden. Countries that have established social security systems have negotiated bilateral social security treaties with each other in order to eliminate double taxation—referred to as *totalization agreements*. For example, since the 1970s, the US has negotiated totalization agreements for social security taxes with 21 countries (Australia, Austria, Belgium, Canada, Chile, Finland, France, Germany, Greece, Republic of Ireland, Italy, Japan, Luxembourg, Netherlands, Norway, Portugal, South Korea, Spain, Sweden, Switzerland, and United Kingdom).[53] The purpose of these agreements is to eliminate dual social security taxation (when a worker from one country works in another country and is required to pay social security taxes to both countries on the same earnings) and to help fill gaps in benefit protection for workers who have divided their careers between the United States and another country. These treaties generally provide tax exemption to residents of one treaty country on short-term assignment—typically 183 days' presence in a year—to the other country. Under the "territoriality" rule, an employee remains subject exclusively to the coverage laws of the country in which he or she is working. Under the "detached-worker" rule, an employee who is temporarily transferred to work for the same employer in another country remains covered only by the country from which he or she has been sent. Under these totalization agreements, the IHR department files for a *certificate of coverage* in the home country (i.e., for the international assignee to remain in the home social security system and be exempt from host social security taxes) prior to departure. Note that these totalization agreements are bilateral between countries and may differ in their stipulations. Some countries that do not have social security systems may have funds (e.g., Provident Retirement Fund in Singapore, Australia, and Hong Kong) that require payment by the IA into the fund. Sometimes, these retirement contributions may be recovered when the IA leaves the host country. The IHR department must be knowledgeable of these terms in the different countries where they deploy IAs so that they can file on behalf of the employee.

Taxes on Expatriate Income

A major determinant of an IA's lifestyle abroad can be the amount of money the expatriate must pay in personal income taxes. Employees who move from one country to another are confronted with widely disparate tax systems, philosophies, and rates and may be required to pay taxes in both home and host countries, depending on the tax policies of the two countries. To make things even more difficult, tax systems and rates are constantly changing, often every year. Thus, taxes not only create one of the most complicated compensation issues for IHRM, it is also potentially the largest expense for an IA. This includes both income taxes and social security taxes (for those countries that have social security systems).

Exhibit 11.8 shows the widely varying average tax wedge (the combination of income and social security taxes, as a percentage of average wages) for a number of countries.

Of course, social insurance rates and benefits also vary dramatically from country to country, even more than income tax rates. International assignees (or their firms) may be responsible for taxes on the international assignee's income independently of where it is earned (this can mean in both their home countries and their host countries). Typically MNE policies will protect incremental cost as a result of dual and increased taxation. The firm will cover these differential costs for their international assignees, i.e., over the tax amount the assignee would pay if he or she had stayed in the home country. This is called *hypothetical tax* or the tax that the international assignee would have paid if he/she had remained in the home country. The MNE must determine a strategy for dealing with these

EXHIBIT 11.8: Average Tax Wedge

Average Taxation of Individual Wage Income (2003 and 2013) (unit = %)

Country	2003	2013
Australia	28.25	27.41
Austria	47.38	49.12
Belgium	55.74	55.8
Canada	31.68	31.06
Chile	7	7
Czech Republic	43.21	42.38
Denmark	42.36	38.24
Estonia	42.32	39.9
Finland	44.77	43.12
France	50.11	48.92
Germany	53.2	49.33
Greece	39.91	41.56
Hungary	50.76	49.03
Iceland	31.52	33.45
Ireland	24.39	26.6
Israel	27.66	20.66
Italy	45.97	47.78
Japan	27.36	31.64
Korea	16.4	21.41
Luxembourg	33.47	37.01

Continued overleaf

EXHIBIT 11.8 Continued

Country	2003	2013
Mexico	16.72	19.22
Netherlands	37.17	36.94
New Zealand	19.46	16.89
Norway	38.09	37.34
Poland	38.24	35.56
Portugal	37.37	41.15
Slovak Republic	42.51	41.13
Slovenia	46.16	42.34
Spain	38.58	40.66
Sweden	48.23	42.93
Switzerland	22.43	21.99
Turkey	42.2	38.64
United Kingdom	33.8	31.48
United States	29.89	31.33

Based on data from Taxing Wages – Comparative Tables http://stats.oecd.org/index.aspx?Data SetCode=AWCOMP in OECD.StatExtracts http://stats.oecd.org/, accessed on Oct 28, 2014.

variances and potentially heavy costs. In general, MNEs follow one of four alternative tax strategies: laissez-faire, tax equalization, tax protection, or an ad hoc policy.[54]

Laissez Faire

This approach is uncommon, but smaller employers and those employers just beginning to conduct international business may follow this approach with their taxation policies. In essence, under this approach the IA is expected to take care of his or her own taxation, even if it means tax obligations in both home and host countries. One of the dangers is that the employee may not be in compliance with tax payments owed to the home and host countries, either intentionally and/or due to lack of knowledge.

Tax Equalization

This is the most common approach, since it supports the home-country system of the balance sheet approach. Because tax rates and obligations vary so much from country to country, tax equalization provides equitable treatment for all international assignees regardless of IA location. Under this strategy, the firm withholds a hypothetical tax from the IA's income (the tax obligation in the home country that they would otherwise have to pay anyway) and then pays all actual taxes in the home and host counties. In essence, the taxes that the international assignee must pay are equalized between home and host countries. This can, obviously, be quite expensive if the international assignee is posted to a high-tax country, such as many European countries. However, tax equalization facilitates tax planning for the MNE and reduces non-compliance. The company usually provides these tax services to the IA.

Tax Protection

Under the tax protection strategy, the international assignee pays both the home and host taxes, but the hypothetical tax is compared to the actual taxes. If the actual taxes are greater than the hypothetical tax, the employer pays the difference to the IA. If the tax rate is less in the foreign assignment, then the employee receives the difference as a windfall. In essence, the employer protects the IA against higher taxes. Although this method used to be more popular, it is becoming less commonly used today. Rather than giving the tax windfall to the IA, MNEs use tax equalization to reduce their costs and control tax compliance. Note that when an IA is out of compliance when working abroad, it may have repercussions for the MNE as well as to the employee.

Ad Hoc

Under this strategy, each international assignee is handled differently depending on the individual package she or he received or negotiated with her or his employer. The ad hoc method usually goes hand in hand with the negotiation approach. In addition, the typical allowances paid to international assignees are often viewed as taxable income in certain countries. So the resulting tax bill—in both the home and host country—can negate the financial incentives provided the international assignee.

To compensate, companies usually reimburse their IAs for the global tax costs in excess of the tax they would have been responsible for if they had remained at home. The purpose is—as with other components in the IA compensation package—to not penalize the employee for taking on the IA. Indeed, surveys find that at least 75 percent of responding firms provide the following benefits tax-free to their employees on foreign assignment (usually by adding to the paycheck the costs of the taxes for these items—referred to as "grossing up" the salary):[55]

- tax reimbursement payments;
- international premium;
- cost-of-living adjustment;
- housing allowances;
- automobile reimbursements (for business use);

- emergency leave;
- moving expenses;
- dependent education.

In addition, many firms provide tax-free (if deductible in the host country) a car for personal use (48.3 percent) or club memberships (62 percent). MNEs that operate in many countries are subject to widely disparate tax rates. Because of this and the complex systems of taxation, with differing attitudes toward what is and what is not taxed in various countries (i.e., what is counted as income), MNEs must use international accounting firms for advice and for preparation of the international assignee's tax returns.

Tax experts also provide practical advice to MNEs for saving money in their complicated global tax obligations.[56] Some of these ideas will work in some countries. But, there are really no approaches that will work uniformly everywhere. Nevertheless, the following precautions and advice make good general sense:[57]

- Get professional tax advice for all international assignees.
- Don't leave tax affairs to the responsibility of international assignee. Mistakes can impact an organization's corporate reputation and relations with the host government (and potentially create legal liabilities).
- Tax agreements between most developed nations mean that with openness and good planning, employees should not lose.
- Tax havens are a great way to avoid paying tax only so long as that is where the firm or the individual is doing business and nowhere else. In other words, it is best to stay away from suggested ways to dodge taxes.

INTERNATIONAL COMPENSATION AND BENEFITS MANAGEMENT

It should be obvious by now that global C&B management is more complex than its domestic counterpart. This is at least partially due to the following problem areas not confronted in domestic HRM. First, the collection of data about pay rates, benefit packages, government practices, and taxation systems in different countries, and in different languages and cultures, from unfamiliar sources, makes it very difficult to design comparable pay packages for international assignees or for consistency among various overseas operations. Second, pay systems (particularly for international assignees) must contend with government currency controls (for instance limiting amounts that can be taken out of the country) and constantly changing exchange and inflation rates, making it necessary to constantly adjust the incomes of international assignees in local currencies. A third issue that adds to the complexity are the varying rates of inflation encountered in foreign locations, which may also require frequent adjustment of international assignees' pay rates to counteract the effects of sometimes high inflation rates. Add to this the desire to export Western compensation concepts such as incentive pay, pay for performance, equity compensation, and the desire to create a common global database to keep track of all the variances, global C&B gets complicated indeed. When all of this combines with variances in legal systems and in country practices in C&B, it may be a miracle that MNEs ever satisfy either international assignees or local workforces with their reward structures. Additionally, there are practical C&B problems related to global C&B that just add to IHR's stress, such as getting valid salary data, payroll maintenance, data privacy, cost concerns, and benchmarking.

Salary Data

It is often very difficult for MNEs to get country-specific compensation data that has much reliability. Very few governments (at least in developing countries) collect or publish adequate data. And there exists in only a few locations local trade associations that collect and publish such information (as is available in most developed countries). Therefore, MNEs must rely on the information provided by accounting firms with international practices, consulting firms that specialize in developing such data (as may be available from local governments and international organizations), specialized consulting firms, or even develop their own data through local MNE "compensation clubs" that share such information). None of these options provide necessarily reliable data, particularly in less developed countries, illustrating the difficulties encountered by IHR managers as they try to develop cost- and managerially effective compensation packages for their international assignees and equitable compensation programs for their employees in subsidiaries around the world.

Payroll Maintenance

An additional problem with global C&B programs involves the maintenance of payroll files on international personnel (international HRIS—for detail see Chapter 13) and the development of global systems for handling payroll and benefits.[58] Domestic HRIS is usually not designed to handle all the additional pieces of information that are common to multiple locations and multiple currencies. In particular for international assignees, C&B items such as premiums, language training expenses, education allowances for dependents, storage of household goods, currency conversion, etc. are usually not available in standard payroll systems. Compounding the problems associated with maintaining these files is that typically MNEs use multiple IA C&B approaches. And, of course, tax and withholding requirements are different in every country as well. Therefore, consulting firms have developed separate IA tracking systems for their customers. But even these systems do not always allow the tracking of short-term and alternative types of assignees.

Data Privacy

Keeping these files up-to-date and using the information in them for employee decision making, such as pay increases or adjustments or career and job-assignment decisions, gets even more difficult as many countries maintain laws against the transfer of "private" employee information out of country or region (e.g., EU Data Protection Directive—refer back to Chapter 6 for more information about this topic). There are no easy answers to these problems, short of designing a computer program specifically to handle the problems of your international employees or hiring a firm to handle them for you, but for sure they must be considered when tackling the issue of creating and managing a compensation program for an international workforce.[59]

Cost Concerns

Another concern for the development of global C&B systems involves efforts by MNEs to include IHR issues in the strategic management of the enterprise. Global C&B systems are affected at a number of points, including the following: decisions to downsize often include expatriates because of their high expense, but then it becomes more difficult to convince new people to accept foreign postings; pressuring IHRM to control costs; fitting IHR compensation systems into the firm's efforts to localize while globalizing; merging compensation systems in cross-border acquisitions; designing or negotiating new compensation systems in international joint ventures and cross-border partnerships and alliances; trying to simplify the design and administration of the international compensation system; coping with the new types of international assignees, including dual-career couples; and figuring out how to apply US extra-territorial anti-discrimination laws in the global context to compensation issues, such as those that "protect" the disabled, employees over 40 years of age, and employees on the basis of their religion, gender, race, or national origin.

Benchmarking

Many firms are now trying to determine what successful MNEs are doing in terms of design and implementation of their international compensation systems.[60] Often this attempt to benchmark the best practices seems like an exercise in "codification of ignorance," since there is so little research to identify what works best when.[61] Surveys of practices of MNEs may be doing nothing more than identifying what is currently being done. But as the above discussion indicates, many practices have evolved over time, without much knowledge or research to indicate which practices are best and under which circumstances. Over time this may result in many firms following what are totally wrong, costly, or inappropriate practices. There is clearly a need for more and better research on international C&B practices.

CONCLUSION

This chapter has presented IHRM practices related to the development of C&B plans in MNEs and discussed the many problems that firms confront as they try to design and implement C&B programs throughout their global operations. The discussion followed a dual focus; first we discussed global remuneration in the MNE among the various locations of their workforces, and then we focused on C&B programs for international assignees.

Country differences in laws (especially tax laws) and cultural practices complicate the design of effective C&B programs and make a global standardized approach ineffective. But pressures for equity and ease of administration provide the motivation to IHR to work on development of such globally integrated programs. For MNEs that operate in multiple countries with local subsidiary workforces, having an understanding of these country-specific variances becomes critical to designing rational HRM practices for the total firm.

The chapter also described the special case of C&B for international assignees and reviewed several alternative approaches to IA compensation, with extensive discussion of the balance sheet approach. This method of IA compensation adds numerous allowances and incentives to a parent-country base and is the most commonly used method for paying US international assignees. But the complexity of the balance sheet approach and the necessity for firms to get deeply involved in the personal lives of their international assignees when using this approach (as well as the high cost of IA compensation and administration of the balance sheet) has led many firms to begin experimenting with one of the other possible approaches. The issue that adds most of the complexity to the compensation of international assignees involves taxation practices and taxation rates in different countries. In an effort to ensure that their international assignees don't need to pay double taxation (for both their countries of origin and their countries of residence while on foreign assignment), MNEs use one of four methods: laissez-faire, tax equalization, tax protection, or ad hoc method. In all cases, the purpose is to limit the tax liabilities of the international assignee. Finally, we reviewed other C&B concerns of a more practical nature that result from the global operations of a MNE.

The design and management global remuneration programs around the world and IA compensation packages is indeed a complex and difficult function. This chapter has made it clear why it absorbs the bulk of the typical international HR manager's time and energy. To deal with these complex issues, the C&B specialists working in this global environment have acquired additional global C&B competencies.

DISCUSSION QUESTIONS

1   What is the difference between global remuneration and international assignm compensation?

2   What are the major issues related to the effectiveness of global remuneration plan

3 How are equity compensation plans affected when used as incentive compensation with employees from different countries in an MNE?

4 What are common international assignment management compensation systems, what are advantages and disadvantages of each system, and when are they used most appropriately?

5 What different tax approaches can be used by MNEs for international assignment compensation?

CASE STUDY 11.1: Compensation Problems with a Global Workforce (Global, Thailand, Philippines, Japan, Bolivia)

Expanding the international workforce to include non-parent-country employees has brought increased capabilities and decreased costs—along with a new set of compensation problems. For example, the director of international HR for a large multinational IT company faced just such a dilemma:

> It seems as though our international compensation program has gotten out of hand. I have parent-country expatriates, third-country nationals, and inpatriates yelling at me about their allowances. [In addition] headquarters is yelling at me because the costs are too high. Quite frankly, I can't seem to get any answers from our consultant about how to handle compensation for such a global workforce, and no one else in the industry seems to know how to approach the problem, either.

This IT multinational has 40 highly paid US expatriates working as field engineers and marketing managers in 14 countries. But it also has foreign national employees from the Philippines, Japan, and Bolivia working alongside the US employees in eight locations worldwide. And, finally, it has foreign nationals from Thailand and the Philippines working with US nationals at the organization's headquarters. In all cases, it is the firm's policy to send such employees out on foreign assignments for less than five years and then return them to their home countries. An example of the types of complaints that were being received from the expats involves the following problem concerning inpatriate employees working at headquarters.

The firm has a field engineer from the Philippines who's earning the equivalent of US$35,000 in Manila. It has another field engineer from Thailand who's earning the equivalent of US$40,000 in Bangkok. And they've both been relocated to headquarters and are working side by side with American field engineers who earn $80,000 for the same job. Not only do they work side by side, but they live near each other, shop at the same stores, and eat at the same restaurants. The problem that IHR has is that it's spending a lot of money on cost-of-living adjustment data for expats from two different home countries, both going to headquarters, and yet their current standard of living is the same, and the same as that of their local peers. They're angry because their allowances don't reflect how they live in the headquarters' country. Their allowances also don't reflect how they lived in their home countries, either.

So what we have are two employees, one earning $35,000 and the other earning $40,000 (plus cost-of-living adjustments), working and living side by side with headquarters' counterparts who are earning $80,000. The solution that most companies have tried is to simply raise the foreign nationals' salaries to the $80,000 level, thereby creating a host-country pay system for a home-country employee.

Unfortunately, there's nothing more pathetic than the tears of your foreign nationals when it's time to return home, and you have to tell them you're cutting their salary to the pre-headquarters' assignment level. What you are looking for is a pay system that will compensate your foreign nationals either by pay or by provided benefits [including, e.g., housing and local transportation], in a consistent, fair and equitable manner, and will allow you to repatriate them with minimal trauma.

Source: adapted and updated (2014) from Crandall, L. P. and Phelps, M. I. (1991). Pay for a global work force. *Personnel Journal*, February, 28, 30.

Discussion Questions

1   What would you do if you were the IHR manager?
2   What kind of global compensation policy would deal effectively with this sort of problem?

NOTES

1   Source: Reynolds, C. (2000). *2000 Guide to Global Compensation and Benefits*, San Diego, CA: Harcourt Professional Publishing.
2   Gomez-Mejia, L.R. and Werner, S. (eds.) (2008). *Global Compensation: Foundations and Perspectives*, London/New York: Routledge; Herod, R. (2009). *Expatriate Compensation Strategies*, Alexandria, VA: Society for Human Resource Management; Reynolds (2000); Reynolds, C. (1992). Are you ready to make IHR a global function? *HR News: International HR*, February, C1–C3; Reynolds, C. (1997). Expatriate compensation in historical perspective. *Journal of World Business*, 32 (2), 118–132; Senko, J. (2008). Objectives in expatriate compensation. *Essentials of International Assignment Management*, 2008 Webinar Series hosted by IOR Global Services, Nov. 5; Senko, J. and Hicks, J. (2010). Challenges in global mobility, *Essentials of International Assignment Management*, 2010 Webinar Series hosted by IOR Global Services, Sept. 22.
3   Herod, R. (2008). *Global Compensation and Benefits: Developing Policies for Local Nationals*, Alexandria, VA: Society for Human Resource Management.
4   See, for example, Crandall, L.P. and Phelps, M.I. (1991). Pay for a global work force. *Personnel Journal*, February, 28–33; Czinkota, R.M., Rivoli, P. and Ronkainen, I.A. (1989). International human resource management. *International Business*, Chicago: The Dryden Press; Green, W.E. and Walls, G.D. (1984). Human resources: Hiring internationally. *Personnel Administrator*, July, 61–64, 66; Gross, R.E. and Kujawa, D. (1995). Personnel management. *International Business: Theory and Managerial Applications*, 3rd ed., Homewood, IL: Irwin; *Fortune* (1984). Are you underpaid? 19 March, 20–25; Stuart, P. (1991). Global payroll — A taxing problem. *Personnel Journal*, October, 80–90.
5   See, for example, Overman, S. (1992). The right package. *HR Magazine*, July, 71–74; Senko (1991).
6   Adapted from Murphy, E. (1998). Payday around the world. *IBIS Review*, July, 17–20
7   Traavik, L.E. and Lunnan, R. (2005). Is standardization of performance appraisal perceived as fair across cultures? Paper presented at the Academy of Management in Honolulu, HI, August.
8   Adapted from Hait, A.G. (1992). Employee benefits in the global economy. *Benefits Quarterly*, Fourth Quarter, reprint, pp. 21–27.
9   Latta, G.W. (1995). Innovative ideas in international compensation. *Benefits and Compensation International*, July/August, 3–7; Luebbers, L.A. (1999). Laying the foundation for global compensation. *Workforce Supplement*, September, 1–4; Minehan, M. (2000). The new face of global compensation. *SHRM Global*, December, 4–7; Murphy (1998); Ritchie, A.J. and Seltz, S.P. (2000). Globalizations of the compensation and benefits function, in Reynolds, C. (ed.) *Guide to Global Compensation and Benefits*, San Diego: Harcourt Professional Publishing; Sutro, P.J. (1999). Thinking about a global share plan? Think smart.

Compensation and Benefits Review, reprint (no pages); and Townley, G. (1999a). Leveling the global paying field. *HR World*, March/April, 75–80.

10 Abowd, J.M. and Kaplan, S.D. (1998). Executive compensation: Six questions that need answering. US Department of Labor, Bureau of Labor Statistics, Working Paper 319.

11 See www.ubs.com. An example study includes the 2012 edition of the Prices and Earnings report from UBS.

12 See www.imercer.com. An example study includes Mercer's 2014 Cost of Living City Rankings, Nov. 5, 2014.

13 See US Bureau of Labor Statistics (International Labor Comparisons), http://www.bls.gov/bls/international.htm.

14 Bernstein, Z.S. and Kaplan, C.Y. (2000). Benefits: Introduction and retirement programs, in Reynolds, C. (ed.), *2000 Guide to Global Compensation and Benefits*, San Diego: Harcourt Professional Publishing, pp. 263–294; Kaplan, C.Y. and Bernstein, Z.S. (2000). Other benefits, in Reynolds, C. (ed.), *2000 Guide to Global Compensation and Benefits*, San Diego: Harcourt Professional Publishing; Hempel, P.S. (1998). Designing multinational benefits programs: The role of national culture. *Journal of World Business*, 33 (3), 277–294; and Outram, R. (2000). Cherry pickings. *HR World*, March/April, 30–34.

15 Source: International Comparisons of Hourly Compensation Costs in Manufacturing, 2012, Bureau of Labor Statistics. Website: http://www.bls.gov/fls/ichccindustry.htm, Oct. 12, 2014.

16 Adapted from report by Ray, R., Sanes, M., and Schmitt, J. (2013). No-Vacation Nation Revisited, Center for Economic and Policy Research, Washington, DC.

17 Bernstein and Kaplan (2000); Spencer, B.F. (1998). Governments continue to hinder development of centralized approach to funding pensions. *IBIS Review*, July, 10–12; and Townley, G. (1999b). In the twilight zone. *HR World*, January/February, 76–79.

18 Di Leonardi, F.A. (1991). Money makes the world go "round," interview with Eugene Barron, assistant treasurer of Johnson & Johnson, *The Wyatt Communicator*, Spring, 15–19.

19 Reported in Kaplan, C.Y. and Bernstein, Z.S. (2000). Other benefits, in C. Reynolds, (ed.). *op. cit.*; Most nations require employers to provide maternity leave, meeting told (1990) *BNA's Employee Relations Weekly*, April 2, 433. For current information on maternity and related leaves, refer to Keller, W.L. (ed.) (vol. 1–1997, vol. 2–2001, and annual updates). *International Labor and Employment Laws*, International Labor Law Committee Section of Labor and Employment Law, American Bar Association, Washington, DC: The Bureau of National Affairs.

20 Johnson, R.E. (1991). Flexible benefit programs: International Style. *Employee Benefits Journal*, 16 (3), 22–25.

21 Freedman, R. (1997). Incentive programs go global. *Worldwide Pay and Benefits Headlines* (Towers Perrin Newsletter) February, 1; Gross, A. and Lepage, S. (2001). Stock options in Asia, *SHRM Global Perspective*, 3 (1), 8–9; Andersen, A. (2001). New global share plan survey data released. *International Mobility Management Newsletter*, 4th quarter, 7; Pacific Bridge (2001). Stock options in Asia: Legal and regulatory roadblocks. *Asian HR eNewsletter*, May 10, 1–2 ; Perkins, S.J. (1998). The search for global incentives. *HR World*, Nov./Dec., 62–65; William M. Mercer International and Arthur Andersen and Co. (1990). *Globalizing compensation: extending stock option and equity participation plans abroad*, New York, NY: Anderson & Co.; Solomon, C.M. (1999). Incentives that go the distance. *HR World*, May/June, 40–44; Rodrick, S.S. (ed.) (2002). *Equity-Based Compensation for Multinational Corporations*, Oakland, CA: The National Center for Employee Ownership (NCEO); Thompson, R.W. (1999). U.S. subsidiaries of foreign parents favor pay incentives. *HR Magazine*, April,10; US-based long-term incentive plans go global (2000). *International Update* (reporting on a Towers Perrin report: *The Globalization of Long-Term Incentive Plans by US-Based Companies*) 3, 8; US version stock plans filter into Europe (1999). *International Update*, February, 9; and Veloitis, S. (2000). Offshore equity compensation plans: Focus of audit activity in many countries. *KPMG eNewsletter, The Expatriate Administrator*, August 28, 1–4.

22 Hewitt Associates (1993). *Granting Stock Options and Restricted Stock to Overseas Employees*, New York, NY: Hewitt Associates.

23 Hall, B.J. (2000). What you need to know about stock options. *Harvard Business Review*, 78 (2),121–129; *Rosen*, C., Case, J. and Staubus, M. (2005). Every employee an owner. *Harvard Business Review*,

83 (6), 122–130; Corporate Secretary Guide, *Global stock plan management*, www.fidelity.com/stock plans (2006).

24 Gibson, V.L., Doyle, J.F. and Tanner, C.P. (2002). Tax and legal issues for global equity compensation plans, in Rodrick, S. (ed.), *Equity-Based Compensation for Multinational Corporations*, 4th ed., Oakland, California: The National Center for Employee Ownership (NCEO), pp. 133–141; Schneider, C. (2001). Implementing a global stock plan, in Rodrick, S. (ed.), *Equity-Based Compensation for Multinational Corporations*, 4th edition, Oakland, California: The National Center for Employee Ownership (NCEO), pp. 133–141.

25 *Fortune* (2002). Canon loves to compete. 22 July 22, S5.

26 Lublin, J.S. (1991). Employee stock plans run into foreign snags. *The Wall Street Journal*, Sept. 16, B1.

27 Krupp, N.B. (1986). Managing benefits in multinational organizations. *Personnel*, September, 76–78; Murdock, B.A. and Ramamurthy, B. (1986). Containing benefits costs for multinational corporations. *Personnel Journal*, May, 80–85.

28 Towards a global compensation model: Two key concepts (2001). *International Mobility Management Newsletter* (Arthur Andersen), 2nd quarter, 2–3.

29 Harris, A.A. (ed.) (2013). *Workforce Strategies: Expatriate Compensation: Structuring Pay and Benefits for International Assignments*, vol. 31, no. 7, Arlington, VA: Bloomberg BNA.

30 Black, J.S. (1991). Returning expatriates feel foreign in their native land. *Personnel*, August, 17.

31 Clague, L. (1999). Expatriate compensation: Whence we came, where we are, whither we go. *Corporate Relocation News*, April, 24, 25, 31; Reynolds, C. (1994). *Compensation Basics for North American Expatriates*, Scottsdale, AZ: American Compensation Association; Reynolds (1997); Reynolds (2000a) Global compensation and benefits in transition. *Compensation and Benefits Review*, January/February, 28–38; Reynolds, C. (1996). What goes around comes around. *International HR* (Organization Resources Counselors, Inc.), spring, 1–10; and Ritchie, and Seltz (2000).

32 See, for example, Deloitte (2010). *Smarter Moves: Executing and Integrating Global Mobility and Talent Programs*, New York: Deloitte Development LLC (www.deloitte.com); US National Foreign Trade Council and Cartus Corporation (2010). *Navigating a Challenging Landscape: Global Mobility Policy and Practices Survey*, New York: NFTC and Cartus Corporation; Senko (2008); and Senko, J. and Hicks, J. (2010). *Global Mobility: A Changing Landscape*, Session 3 of 2010 IOR Global Services "Essentials of International Assignment Management" webinar (based on Airinc's 2010 Mobility Outlook Survey).

33 Stone, R.J. (1986). Compensation: Pay and perks for overseas executives, *Personnel Journal*, January, 64–69.

34 Czinkota, M.R., Rivoli, P., and Ronkainen, I.A. (1989). International human resource management. *International Business*, Chicago: The Dryden Press, p. 580; Stone (1986).

35 Herod (2009).

36 Ibid.

37 Black, J.S., Gregersen, H.B., Mendenhall, M.E. and Stroh, L.K. (1999). *Globalizing People Through International Assignments*, Reading, MA: Addison-Wesley; Chesters, A. (1995). The balance sheet approach: Problem or solution? *International HR Journal*, fall, 9–15; Frazee, V. (1998). Is the balance sheet right for your expats? *Global Workforce*, September, 19–26; Infante, V.D. (2001). Three ways to design international pay: Headquarters, home country, host country. *Workforce*, January, 22–24; Organization Resources Counselors, Inc. (1998). *Understanding the Balance Sheet Approach to Expatriate Compensation* (pamphlet) New York: Organization Resources Counselors.

38 O'Reilly, M. (1995). Reinventing the expatriate package. *International HR Journal*, fall, 58–59; Reynolds, C. (2000). Global compensation and benefits in transition. *Compensation & Benefits Review*, January/February, 28–38; and Sheridan, W.R. and Hansen, P.T. (1996). Linking international business and expatriate compensation strategies. *ACA Journal*, spring, 66–79.

39 Crandall and Phelps (1991).

40 For discussions of these issues, see Gould, C. (1995). Expatriate Compensation. *International Insight*, winter, 6–10; Gould, C. (1998). Expatriate policy development, in C. Gould, and B. Schmidt-Kemp (eds.)

International Human Resources Guide, Boston, MA: Warren, Gorham and Lamont; Infante (2001); Kearley, T. (1996). An effective blueprint for international compensation. *Benefits and Compensation Solutions*, November, reprint; Overman, S. (1992); Pollard, J. (2000). Chapter 7: Expatriate practices, in Reynolds, C. (Ed.). op. cit; Reynolds (1996); Reynolds (2000); and Solomon (1999).

41 *Global Relocation Trends Annual Survey Report*, New York: GMAC Global Relocation Services/Windham International, New York: National Foreign Trade Council, Inc., and Alexandria, VA: Society for Human Resource Management (SHRM) Global Forum; and Society for Human Resource Management/ Commerce Clearing House, *1992 SHRM/CCH Survey on International HR Practices*, Chicago: Commerce Clearinghouse.

42 Pollard (2000).

43 Overman (1992).

44 Senko, J.P. (1990). The foreign service premium and hardship differential. *Mobility*, May, 10–12.

45 Ibid.; and *The 2005 Global Relocation Trends Annual Survey Report*, New York: GMAC GRS/Windham International, New York: National Foreign Trade Council, and Society for Human Resource Management (SHRM) Global Forum.

46 Senko (1990).

47 Senko (1991).

48 See, for example, Bishko, M.J. (1990). Compensating your overseas executives, Part 1: Strategies for the 1990s. *Compensation and Benefits Review*, May–June, 33–43; Brooks, B.J. (1988). Long-term incentives: International executives. *Personnel*, August, 40–42; Brooks, B.J. (1987). Trends in international executive compensation. *Personnel*, May, 67–70.

49 Global Relocation Trends 2005 Survey Report, *op. cit.* Global Relocation Trends 2005 Survey Report, GMAC Global Relocation Services. Produced in association with National Foreign Trade Council (NFTC) and the SHRM Global Forum, Woodridge IL.

50 Gould (1998), Chapter 7; Littlewood, M. (1995). Total compensation: A new way of doing things. *International HR Journal*, fall, 17–21; Reynolds, C. (2000). Chapter 5, *op. cit.* and Runzheimer International (2000). Lump-sum allowances: The efficient approach to handling relocation expenses. Pamphlet published by Runzheimer International, Rochester, WI.

51 Gregsen, K.J. (1996). Flexpatriate remuneration: An alternative method for compensating foreign assignees. *International HR Journal*, winter, 24–28; Reynolds, C. (2000). Chapter 5: Expatriate compensation strategies, in C. Reynolds (ed.) op. cit. pp. 73–96.

52 Milliman, J., Nason, S., Von Glinow, M.A., Huo, P., Lowe, K., and Kim, N. (1995). In search of "best" strategic pay practices: An exploratory study of Japan, Korea, Taiwan, and the United States. *Advances in International Comparative Management*, 10, 227–252; Schuler, R.S. (1998). Understanding compensation practice variations across firms: The impact of national culture. *Journal of International Business Studies*, 29 (1), 159–177; and Toh, S.M. and Denisi, A.S. (2003). Host country national reactions to expatriate pay policies: A model and implications. *Academy of Management Review*, 28 (4), 606–621.

53 International Programs, US International Social Security Agreements, http://www.ssa.gov/international/agreements_overview.html. Accessed Oct. 6, 2014.

54 See, for example, Russo, S.M. and Orchant, D. (2000). Chapter 8: Expatriate taxation, in Reynolds, C. (ed.) op. cit.; Stuart (1991).

55 Presented in Stuart (1991), p. 81. See also surveys such as the Global Relocation Trends Annual Report from GMAC Global Relocation Services/Windham, National Foreign Trade Council, and SHRM Global Forum, op. cit.

56 Adapted from Stuart (1991), pp. 84.

57 Adapted from Outram, R. (2001). The taxman cometh. *Global HR*, February/March, 22–25.

Chapter 12

International Employee Performance Management

A high performance culture supported by differentiated rewards and development is key to the delivery of individual and business objectives. This is driven by the alignment of clear and challenging responsibilities and priorities and ensuring that employees are aware of how their work impacts Nestlé.

Nestlé Corporation[1]

Learning Objectives

This chapter will enable the reader to:

- Describe the importance of developing an international performance management system.
- Explain the characteristics of a successful international performance management system.
- Identify and overcome the major challenges to international performance management.
- Describe the role of cultural value dimensions in the design, implementation, and evaluation of an international performance management system.
- Formulate evaluation criteria and practices that meet parent-company requirements while addressing the host-culture's norms and expectations.
- Identify and overcome the major challenges related to the performance management of international assignees.

High performance organizations—such as MNEs—care a great deal about the performance of their employees, teams, projects, business units, as well as of the overall organization. They work hard to align job expectations with the strategic intent of the organization and rely on highly competent and engaged employees and teams to achieve their objectives. Measuring the performance of individuals and teams becomes an important tool to ensure organizational performance and identify possible gaps to be closed. Hence, the establishment of an employee performance management (PM) system is an integral component of managing the talent of an MNE. In addition, an employee PM is linked to other HR activities such as job analysis, total rewards, learning and development, and talent deployment. It is the design and management of this employee PM system as practiced in MNEs around the world that is the focus of this chapter.

As with everything in the global arena, managing employee performance in an international enterprise is a lot more complex than is the case with solely domestic operations. There are a number of reasons for the complexity of an international PM system. First, culture heavily impacts management practice in terms of issues such as the meaning of performance management, employee acceptance of the review process, and the cultural value dimensions that affect performance appraisal (PA). Second, designers of PM systems in MNEs face a major dilemma in terms of reconciling whether PM should be a single, standardized practice throughout the organization or whether divergent systems can be used to reflect local culture and local management practices. And third, the PM of international assignees presents particular challenges for managers and employees alike.

THE PERFORMANCE MANAGEMENT FUNCTION

There is a widely accepted body of knowledge within HR related to PM.[2] Yet, in the international context, issues arise for MNEs because most of the knowledge base has been developed from a purely Western perspective and in a largely domestic context. A number of particular characteristics are associated in the Western context with the concept of PM. For example, it is seen as a human resource activity or process that includes a number of necessary steps: setting employee performance expectations that are aligned with organizational objectives; regularly monitoring performance; providing ongoing feedback to employees; conducting periodic (annual or semi-annual) face-to-face performance appraisals (PA); giving employees a chance to provide input; providing developmental and career guidance opportunities based on the results of the PA; and linking the reward system with individual and group appraisal results. This PM process is commonly described by practitioners in Western enterprises as the "performance wheel."

Yet, in recent years, a notable shift has occurred related to the practice of PM in these predominantly large, Western companies. The trend is toward greater accountability of employee performance, use of more objective measures and metrics, involvement of multiple raters, and ongoing coaching and development of employees as critical components of the PM system (see Exhibit 12.1, which summarizes these changes).

In this chapter, we review especially the challenges that confront international PM as opposed to the practice of domestic PM. We start by looking at employee PM for MNEs and review the purposes of international PM systems, the impact of culture on the PM

EXHIBIT 12.1: Shifts in Western PM

From	To
Focus on past performance	Focus on future performance
Subjective judgmental measures	Objective behavioral measures
Periodic (annual or semi-annual) PA interviews	Ongoing evaluation and coaching
Defensive and control oriented	Development oriented
Single rater	Multiple raters
Linked to negative employment decisions	Linked to positive employee development and rewards
Individual performance	Individual and multilevel organizational performance
Distinct (PM) HR activity	PM activity aligned with other elements in HR portfolio (talent management)
Complex to administer	Simple to administer
Individual results	Organizational metrics
Service and entitlement culture (experience, equality)	High performance culture (accountability, equity, output measurement)
Hard paper process documentation	Use of software tools for process documentation and interactive employee communication
Domestic focus	International and global focus

process, and the design choices (standardization versus adaptation) that MNEs must make to integrate their PM systems into their global operations. Then, we focus on the PM of a group of employees of special interest to this book, namely international assignees, who are on short-term or long-term assignments to foreign locales of the MNE.

PERFORMANCE MEASUREMENT AND THE MNE

When discussing PM in the MNE, the term "international PM (IPM) system" is used to distinguish this process from the practice of PM in the domestic operations of the firm. In our view, an international employee PM system is a designed, implemented, and evaluated intervention of an MNE for the purpose of managing the performance of its global workforce so that performance (at the individual, team, and organizational level) contributes to the attainment of strategic global objectives and results in overall MNE desired performance.

A firm's performance appraisal system can greatly impact the performance of its workers. Yet conducting valid performance appraisals, even in the domestic environment, is quite a difficult task. PA is just one activity of the global PM system, the one that refers to the periodic formal evaluation of employees' performance, usually by supervisors. Appraising performance and conducting effective performance appraisals is even more challenging in the international arena.[3] It is this international context of PM that is described in this chapter.

Purposes of International Performance Management

Organizations develop PM systems for a number of reasons, but primarily for evaluation and development.[4] As the purposes of PM intervention differ, they are likely to impact the satisfaction of employees with the system. These purposes, however, are much the same for domestic and international operations. The major difference is, as mentioned before, that the implementation of these goals is much more complex in the global arena. Typically, most attention is paid specifically to the purposes of the performance appraisal process. The following describes these two broad purposes for PA: evaluation and development.

Evaluation goals for performance appraisals in the international environment include:

- Provide feedback to employees so they will know where they stand.
- Develop valid data for pay, promotion, and job assignment decisions, and provide a means of communicating these decisions.
- Identify high-potential employees and manage their talent for optimal performance and retention.
- Help management in making discharge and retention decisions, and provide a means of warning employees about unsatisfactory performance.

Development goals for performance appraisals in the international environment include:

- Help managers improve their performance and develop future potential.
- Develop commitment to the company through discussion of career opportunities and career planning with the manager.
- Motivate employees via recognition of their efforts.
- Diagnose individual and organizational problems.
- Identify individual training and development needs.

Of course, the national cultures of the countries where the MNE operates, the design choices the MNE makes with regard to its international PM system, and the nature of international assignments all impact the ability of any global organization to achieve these objectives.[5]

Culture and Performance Management

With increased globalization, particularly by developed-country MNEs, Western HR practices (such as PM) are being applied around the world, even in non-Western cultural contexts. Thus, an important question is raised as to the robustness of these practices in different national and cultural environments. Although the PM body of knowledge is highly US-centric, a number of researchers are increasingly turning their attention to the application of the concept to other countries and situations.[6]

As discussed in Chapter 3, the application of culture to management practices has focused largely on differences in *value dimensions* reflective of national cultures.[7] Using these dimensions, a number of empirical studies have identified cultural differences in several aspects of PA implementation. Many of these comparisons have involved Western and Asian cultures and have focused on the need to adapt PM practices to the cultural environment. Cultural value dimensions such as power distance, collectivism, harmony, and face have been shown to influence the way in which performance is evaluated.[8] For example, in collectivistic, high-power distance cultures, which is common among most Asian cultures, PM is culturally more compatible with a focus on broad performance targets rather than specific performance criteria, group-oriented appraisal accountability rather than individual accountability, maintaining harmonious relationships, saving face (*mianzi*) and connections (*guanxi*) rather than using direct confrontation, greater acceptance of ambiguity in feedback versus direct constructive feedback, avoiding conflict versus direct confrontation, focus on personal obligations of loyalty to the organization versus the self, and reliance on hierarchical judgments versus employee involvement. Considering these differences in cultural value dimensions, the PM process has to be adapted to align with the cultural characteristics of host countries in order to be effective.

Researchers have also looked at whether PM practices are becoming more convergent and easily transferred from the West or if they remain divergent and require cultural localization. As mentioned in Chapter 3, this line of thinking within cultural management theory is referred to as the convergence-divergence hypothesis. Similar to other areas of management research, the empirical evidence is divided. Proponents of *convergence* have shown that there are only small differences between, for example, American and Japanese managers of MNEs in terms of control processes like responsibility, rewards, and monitoring.[9] They have also shown, for example in Ghana and Nigeria in Africa, that there are more similarities than dissimilarities in PA practices than reported in the US literature, even in these very different cultures.[10] In spite of cultural differences in HRM practices, some empirical studies suggest that there are considerable signs of convergence in PM practices toward accepted best practices,[11] that differences in PA practices are gradually declining, and that Western and non-Western management approaches are moving closer together.[12]

Proponents of *divergence* have received somewhat greater support in the PM literature. This literature suggests that differences in cultural practices remain important,[13] that observed differences in PA link directly to known cultural differences,[14] that the assumptions of convergence should be rejected even in countries belonging to the same culture cluster and region,[15] that a one-size-fits-all approach without making allowance for local adjustment is not likely to produce desired results,[16] and that there is a high need to localize the methods used in performance appraisal to fit local cultural values and norms.[17] It is generally accepted that best PA practices do not exist independently of cultural context.[18] And it is also generally accepted that the notion of *crossvergence* in PM, namely applying a relatively similar appraisal concept but adapting the process to align with cultural characteristics is more likely to produce favorable results.[19] The argument supports the notion that while many of the PA practices in the West are easily transferred to another country with a different culture, tradition, and economic, legal, and political system, some of the local uniqueness must be maintained. Practices are more likely to transfer when the HR department enjoys a high status and can successfully promote convergence of HRM practices at the firm level.[20] For a very practical view of how these issues "play out" in a specific situation, read the case of Richard Evans at the end of this chapter, which describes a European manager's struggle with PA in a firm in Thailand.

The theoretical framework of *cultural fit* focuses on the influence of the socio-cultural context on HRM practices and the transferability of the Western practice of PM to another culture with a fundamentally different socio-cultural environment.[21] The impact of culture is particularly evident in three areas of PA, namely performance criteria, method of appraisal, and performance feedback. With regard to performance criteria, it is suggested that a focus on narrowly defined, task-related competencies, and a result orientation fit cultures with higher performance orientation, universalism, and lower power distance, while broadly defined, interpersonal competencies, and a process orientation fit high power distance, high collectivism, low performance orientation, and fatalism-oriented cultures. With regard to methods of performance appraisal, multiple assessors, formal, systematic, objective, and periodic assessments are characteristics of low power distance and high performance orientation cultures while single assessor, top-down, informal and subjective assessment are characteristics of low performance orientation, high power distance and high collectivism cultures. With regard to performance feedback, individual or group-based, explicit and direct confrontational feedback are characteristic of specific, low context, and high performance oriented cultures while individual- or group-based, subtle, indirect and non-confrontational feedback are characteristic of diffuse, high context and high collectivism cultures.[22]

In addition to the external context of national cultural, the cultural fit theory also explores how the fit can be mediated by internal *organizational culture*. Organizations with strong performance cultures and socialization mechanisms offer somewhat of a buffer for the impact of local national culture. Companies with strong corporate cultures and centralized decision making may be inclined to favor a more standardized PM system aligned with their organizational goals and other management practices than those organizations that are highly decentralized. Yet, the challenge for MNEs remains to design and implement PM systems that fit the global as well as the local context of their operations.[23]

Standardization versus Localization of International Performance Management (IPM) Systems

As an HR management activity, PM can be expected to be time and place specific. MNEs, because of their predominantly Western country-of-origin headquarters, are likely to use a Western and standardized approach to PM across their subsidiaries. MNEs often use an "exportative" approach to PM.[24] In other words, the Western concept of PM is transferred from headquarters to the subsidiaries and applied, in a standardized manner, across the worldwide operations of the MNE.[25] Yet many managers and academics express concern with the implementation of a management process developed and tested in the West and applied to a different context—largely because of differences in national cultures, laws, and emerging market practices. For example, there is concern about the implications this might have for the operating Western paradigm of PM. Further, there are questions about whether or not a well-established Western practice, such as PM, can be transferred to another external context and retain its intended value. Such questions have not yet been answered and pose challenges for both researchers and practitioners. Again, for a specific examination of this situation, look at the case study of Richard Evans's experience in Thailand.

There are some valid reasons that suggest such a standardized approach may be warranted for the sake of global integration, uniformity, organizational culture cohesiveness, fairness, mobility of global employees, and as a control mechanism. An important question, however, becomes how this Western concept of PM is impacted when used throughout the international operations of MNEs, particularly in non-Western cultures and emerging economies with different external contexts. In addition, MNEs are likely to have globally mobile employees and international assignees requiring expatriate PM. MNEs are also often involved in international mergers, acquisitions, joint ventures, and alliances where varying PM practices may have to be modified or integrated.

Companies basically have a choice of three different strategic options when it comes to international PM: an "exportive" strategy that develops the PM system in the home country and transfers it to foreign units, an "adaptive" strategy that develops unique PM practices in each foreign unit, and an "integrative" strategy that combines local PM practices with those within the region and around the world. Each of these strategies has obvious advantages and disadvantage for the MNE.[26] The key strategic decision that MNEs must make with regard to the design of their PM is whether to standardize or localize their system, that is, whether to truly incorporate both global integration (GI) and local responsiveness (LR) in the design, implementation, and evaluation of their PM system and achieve a truly "glocal" system. PM resides at the focal point of the global/local dilemma because it represents the enactment of upstream company strategy at the downstream local individual level. Upstream refers to company-wide strategy-type decision making at the HQ level favoring convergence and standardization. Downstream refers to the flow of these decisions to the local level and favors divergence and localization. There are major upstream and downstream considerations with regard to global performance management.[27] Upstream considerations include strategic integration and coordination workforce alignment and organizational learning and knowledge management. Downstream considerations include responsiveness to local conditions sensitivity to cross-cultural differences establishment of performance management relationship, and comprehensive training.

A Model of IPM in MNEs

In practical terms, the MNE can look at its IPM system in terms of three distinct phases: design, implementation, and evaluation. The major issues affecting international PM and its three phases are described in Figure 12.1 (a model of employee PM for the MNE).[28]

The *design* phase deals with the choices that management of an MNE must make with regard to its PM system. These decisions relate to identifying the purpose(s) of PM (why), performance criteria (what), method of evaluation and instrumentation (how), frequency of evaluation (how often), rater identification (who), and whether a standardized or localized approach will be used. The outcome of these decisions will depend on a host of factors including the internal organizational environment (i.e., corporate culture) and the external global context (or the socio-cultural environment). The *implementation* phase relates

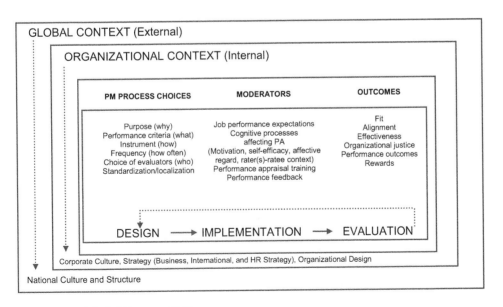

FIGURE 12.1 A Model of IPM in an MNE

Source: Claus, L. and Briscoe, D. R. (2006). What we know and don't know about performance management from an international/global perspective: A review and analysis of empirical research. Paper presented at the annual conference of the Academy of Management, 11–16 August, Atlanta, GA.

to communicating job-position performance expectations, identifying cognitive processes that affect the PA, frame-of-reference training for the PM process, and performance feedback to evaluated employees. In the implementation phase, cognitive processes related to the conduct of PA (such as ratee self-efficacy, affective regard, and motivation, and rater(s)-ratee relationship) play a dominant role. Many of these factors are impacted by cultural practices. Finally, the *evaluation* phase consists of identifying and evaluating outcomes of the PM process. Fit, alignment, effectiveness, fairness, and performance outcomes play a dominant role in the evaluation phase. Again, many of these factors are subject to cultural interpretations.

The above discussion indicates that such an international PM system is complex for an MNE due to cultural differences associated with a global enterprise and the dilemma of reconciling standardization versus local adaptation. Therefore, an international PM system should be carefully designed, implemented, and evaluated in the MNE, in order to achieve its stated objectives.

Guidelines for International Performance Management in an MNE

MNEs can do a number of things to ensure that valid performance evaluations are made in their global operations, or at least, to increase the likelihood of good results from the PM system. The most important concern for the MNE with regard to an effective IPM system is to find the right balance between standardization (for control, administrative ease, and employee global mobility purposes) and localization (for cultural fit purposes). How to achieve such a "glocal" strategy and reconcile such seeming opposing dimensions is not an easy task. The research evidence on PM in an international perspective, although limited, permits us only to provide a number of preliminary, yet practical, recommendations for the design, implementation, and evaluation of a "glocal" employee PM system in an MNE. These recommendations (summarized in Exhibit 12.2) focus on reconciling the standardization-adaptation dilemma within each of the phases of the PM system.[29]

There are a number of additional things that can be done to improve the effectiveness of an MNE's IPM system. These include the following:

Relevance—IHR needs to ensure that the criteria and process for evaluation are relevant to the content and requirements of the job. This involves IHR and reviewers having a clear understanding of the unique situation of the job requirements in different locations of the MNE.

Acceptability—the criteria and processes used need to be acceptable to those using it, i.e., both evaluators and ratees. One aspect of this is that the criteria being rated need to be in control of the ratee. The rater needs to objectify the evaluation as much as possible, while considering the "contextual" realities, using input from as many sources as possible, including from the employees themselves. In addition, the rater needs to follow standard procedures and the appraisal results need to be seen, particularly by the ratee, as fair and

EXHIBIT 12.2: Globalization of Key Elements in the Design, Implementation, and Evaluation of the PM System of an MNE

Design	*Standardization (global)/adaptation (local) reconciliation recommendations*
Purpose of PM (why)	■ Determine multiple purposes of the PM system so that they meet global and local needs. ■ Explicitly state and communicate throughout the organization the global and local intended purposes to be achieved.
Performance criteria (what)	■ Analyze performance dimensions and criteria in terms of their cultural neutrality and/or bias ■ Analyze performance dimensions and criteria in terms of perceived importance by diverse groups of employees, business units, and the company overall. ■ Use a combination of soft and hard performance criteria and weigh them accordingly.
Method of evaluation and instrument (how)	■ Use a combination of quantitative and qualitative measurements in the instrument and weigh them accordingly.
Frequency of evaluation (how often)	■ Have ongoing informal feedback for developmental purposes. ■ Have discreet (annual) feedback session for reward purposes.
Rater identification (who)	■ Determine the cultural acceptability of different types of raters. ■ Use multiple raters to reduce rater bias.

Implementation	*Standardization (global)/adaptation (local) reconciliation recommendations*
Job/position performance expectations	■ Clarify the global and local performance expectations for each job (some jobs may have only global or local expectations, others may have both).
Cognitive processes that affect PA: Motivation	■ Assess the manager's motivation in conducting PA and providing feedback to subordinates. ■ Reinforce the importance of the manager in PM training.

Continued overleaf

EXHIBIT 12.2 *Continued*

Implementation	*Standardization (global)/adaptation (local) reconciliation recommendations*
Self-efficacy	■ Focus the PM training at the individual/collective level based on the individual/collective cultural background of supervisor/subordinate.
Affective regard	■ Provide means for managers/subordinates to maintain trust relationships when conducting PAs and adapt those means to the cultural background.
Rater(s)-ratee context	■ Understand the importance of the nationality of rater/ratee (in self-rating, upward and downward evaluations). ■ Use multiple raters.
Frame-of-reference training	■ Provide training on the PM process. ■ Provide FOR training on how to rate performance from both local and global perspectives. ■ Emphasize the impact of culture and the cognitive processes that may affect the PM process. ■ Customize the training to reflect individual/collective value dimensions of participants.
Performance feedback	■ Distinguish between ongoing and discreet (annual) feedback. ■ Identify different culturally appropriate ways to provide ongoing and discreet performance feedback. ■ Increase the frequency of the ongoing feedback.

Evaluation	*Standardization (global)/adaptation (local) reconciliation recommendations*
Fairness	■ Determine the different levels of organizational justice for the organization's PM system in terms of cultural differences and expectations. ❏ procedural justice: fairness of the methods used in organizations; ❏ interactional justice: the quality of the treatment; ❏ distributive justice: the perception of due process and fairness of the outcomes.
Performance outcomes	■ Use a combination of individual and collective performance outcomes and weigh them accordingly.

Evaluation	Standardization (global)/adaptation (local) reconciliation recommendations
Rewards	■ Use of combination of individual and collective rewards and weigh them accordingly.

Source: Claus, L. (2008). Employee performance management in MNCs: Reconciling the need for global integration and local responsiveness. *European Journal of International Management, 2*(2), 132–152.

accurate. The appraisal form itself needs to accommodate special or unique circumstances; the ratee needs to receive timely feedback, the rater should suggest how the ratee can improve, and the ratee should get the necessary resources to improve, such as training programs. All of this is to say that the process needs to be seen as having "face" validity, i.e., it needs to be seen as fair, reasonable, and accurate.

Sensitivity—an effective IPM system takes into consideration cultural and international business realities. It will include input from people with experience in the particular foreign setting (such as local employees and former expatriates). It needs to take into account issues like the operational language of the foreign organization, the cultural distance between the foreign firm and the parent, and the importance of contextual issues (such as, for example, the power of local unions, exchange rate fluctuations, local circumstances). IHR can build into the evaluation process a numerical factor based on the unique difficulty of the foreign location, freeing the home evaluator from having to directly assess this himself or herself.

Practicality—and, finally, the performance evaluation system needs to be easy to use. If it is either too complex or too difficult to administer, managers will not use it. Or they will only give it surface attention, shortcutting a serious evaluation and thus abrogating any potential value from the assessment process and making it impossible to achieve the objectives set out for an effective IPM system.

All of these characteristics illustrate how important it is for evaluators (usually managers) to be trained in the use of international evaluation systems. The effectiveness of an IPM system can be improved, but it requires IHR to get involved and to work on implementing the types of characteristics described here. As stated by Cascio,

> Performance appraisal has many facets. It is an exercise in observation and judgment, it is a feedback process, it is an organizational intervention. It is a measurement process as well as an intensely emotional process. Above all, it is an inexact, human process.[30]

And when an organization has to add cultural and international dimensions to the process, it is even more difficult on every one of these characteristics. It is up to IHRM in the MNE to ensure that the IPM process makes the important contribution that it can and should.

PERFORMANCE MANAGEMENT AND INTERNATIONAL ASSIGNEES

An additional complexity in international PM is the PA of international assignees. The remainder of this chapter focuses on the special case of expatriate PM. The performance of international assignees, whether on short- or long-term expatriate assignments, is critical to the success of the MNE. PA of international assignees is especially important because expatriates are very expensive (in terms of total international compensation) and many international assignments are not successful due to premature repatriation of expatriates, stress-induced performance problems while on assignment, or higher than average turnover of repatriated assignees upon their return from assignment. However, one of the most serious stumbling blocks to the effective management and development of these assignees is the frequent lack of recognition of the value of their foreign experience and expatriation, in general, and the informality with which firms often evaluate the performance of these employees. Indeed, studies of large MNEs with many international assignees and many foreign subsidiaries report that most (83 percent) do not use PM to measure the success of their international assignees. And many (35 percent) don't use any type of measurement at all.[31]

Appraising performance and conducting effective PAs of international assignees presents major challenges.

The following IHRM in Action illustrates how Nokia has developed an effective performance appraisal system for its expatriates that utilizes many of the approaches described in this chapter.[32] This system uses multiple raters, multiple criteria for evaluation, and multiple ratings in terms of types of ratings, forms for ratings, and frequency of ratings.

IHRM in Action 12.1: Expatriate Performance Management at Nokia

Nokia, the Finnish-based former world leader in the telecommunications industry, recently acquired by Microsoft in the US, had extensive experience with sending and receiving people on foreign assignments, with about 1,200 expatriates on foreign assignment at any one time. Because of this, Nokia had to learn how to manage the performance of this large group of employees who were so key to the success of the firm's global business. Nokia developed a comprehensive performance management program that included goal setting, performance appraisal and feedback, continuous training and development, and performance-related compensation. One thing that Nokia learned was that the performance of its various types of expatriates, who were in varying types of assignments and situations, should be managed dissimilarly, even within the context of trying to apply a standard approach throughout their global operations.

Nokia put in place what looks, on the surface, like a global, standardized performance management system, with the objective that all employees' performance was managed (to a great extent) the same. In terms of expatriates, however, in Nokia's terminology it turned out that there were at least five different types of expatriates, including:

- top managers;
- middle managers;
- business establishers;
- customer project employees;
- R&D project personnel.

For each of these groups, there were some common practices. For example, all expatriates knew what was expected of them, how well they were performing, and what the opportunities were for them to develop new competencies in order to meet present and future job requirements.

However, the various expatriate groups also experienced some differences in how their performance was managed. These differences revolved around the following:

- Whether and how performance goals were set, who set them, and what types of goals were set.
- How performance was evaluated and who conducted the evaluation.
- Whether training and development plans were agreed upon with the expatriate.
- Whether expatriates had the opportunity to attend training while on their foreign assignments.
- What type and how clear the linkage was between expatriate performance and pay.

For example, as might be expected, the higher the expatriate's level, the more independent was their position and the more distant was their performance management. In addition, they and their bosses were more likely to have a longer-term focus, both for their present international position and in terms of their careers and developmental concerns.

Middle manager expatriates reported typically to a local manager and had local, relatively short-term, goals and focus. Feedback was given by the local manager and the local manager determined financial incentive rewards. Performance goals for business-establisher expatriates and for customer-project expatriates were tied to the nature of their assignments, more so than the earlier two categories with start-up objectives for the former and deadlines for network operation common in the latter. Indeed, in all four areas tracked (goal setting, performance evaluation, training and development, and performance-related pay), performance management criteria were implemented differently for the five different groups of expatriates, even though all expatriates were managed in some form or another in all four areas. This major global firm illustrated the high degree of importance that contingency factors play when managing expatriate performance. Even though Nokia put in place a standard performance management system intended for global use, the reality was that expatriate performance was managed differently in the five categories of expatriate assignments. Evidently, off-the-shelf solutions did not produce the desired improvements in expatriate and company performance.

As the Nokia case illustrates, regardless of the effectiveness or availability of performance management (PM) tools, expatriate PM success depends largely on the manager and expatriate in question: how well they both understand, internalize, and accept PM, and how skillful they are in its implementation. To this end, appropriate PM training should be available for all expatriates, including their superiors.

One of these challenges for global organizations is that the types of skills developed and used in an international job are different from those developed and used in the domestic environment. The international assignee (as well as other foreign managers) must, of course, develop and use the competencies necessary for any managerial assignment. But, in addition to these capabilities, they must also develop the following abilities:[33]

- to manage an international business and all the complexities that entails;
- to manage a workforce with cultural and sub-cultural differences;
- to conceptualize, and plan for, the dynamics of a complex, multinational environment;
- to be open-minded about alternative methods for solving problems;
- to be flexible in dealing with people and systems;
- to understand and manage the interdependences among the firm's domestic and foreign operations.

These skills are a natural outgrowth of the increased autonomy that international assignees and their foreign manager colleagues experience in the international environment. In addition, this autonomy results in a greater impact on the subsidiary's performance than would be possible at that same level in the home-country situation. With increased decision-making responsibilities in the foreign environment, international assignees are typically subjected to a more intense working environment to which they have to adjust fairly completely and quickly. But the often distant evaluators seldom understand these difficulties and tend to not take them into consideration when evaluating the international assignee's performance. In order for the individual contributor and his/her organization to benefit, however, from this enhanced learning and performance, the organization must have a way to track and evaluate it. The reality usually is, though—as stated above—that this doesn't happen, either very well or not at all. There are many reasons that the international performance evaluation system doesn't work very well for international assignees, including:

- Problems with the choice of evaluator (e.g., whether from the local subsidiary or from the parent company).
- Inadequate contact between home-country rater and subsidiary ratee.
- Difficulties with long-distance and virtual communication with home or headquarters management.
- Differences in parent- and host-country management's perceptions of what is valued in terms of performance and in terms of perceptions of the actual behavior.[34]
- Inadequate establishment of performance objectives for the foreign operations (unclear and/or contradictory) and means for recording levels of individual and organizational performance.
- Home-country ethnocentrism and lack of understanding of the foreign environment and culture.
- Frequent indifference to the foreign experience of the expatriate and to the importance of the international business in general.

Given these major differences between the domestic and international PM environments and because the job context of an international assignee is different from that encountered in the traditional, domestic, assignment, experts agree that the PA system requires modifications for expatriates[35] and inpatriates.[36]

The central themes in the expatriate PM literature relate mainly to the tactical issues (what? who? when? how?) inherent in managing the performance of an employee who is sent abroad on assignment. That is, they focus on what criteria are appraised, who does the PA, when (and how often) an appraisal is done, and how the appraisal is carried out (i.e., what format is used). In addition, they focus on the cultural and structural contexts of managing the performance of international assignees as well as the repercussions for failing to do so effectively.[37]

What Should be Evaluated?

The answer to this question, that is, what criteria should be used to evaluate the performance of IAs, is indeed complex. They need to meet parent-company standards and they need to do it within the international and local-cultural contexts. So the evaluation system needs to take both sets of standards into account. The problem is, criteria, roles, and performance expectations are typically defined in the home country but performed in the host country and the cultural norms that define performance in the parent country may not be the same as those considered appropriate in the foreign locale. This can cause significant role conflict for the international assignee.[38] If the international assignee adapts his or her behavior according to the role behavior expected in the host environment, it may well conflict with that predetermined by and expected at headquarters. This type of role conflict is likely to result in situations where the assignee has an understanding of the host-country culture and realizes that the use of headquarters procedures or actions may lead to ineffective management. Evidently, the higher the degree of intercultural interaction and cultural distance, the more problems the IA is likely to have with role conflict. Such role conflict is also compounded by the lack of autonomy sometimes experienced in foreign assignments (where headquarters may impose more structure and defined protocols), allowing less space to deal with the conflicting expectations.[39] And this concern over conflicting role expectations is even more pronounced for third-country nationals than it is for host-country nationals or parent-country nationals.[40]

Each performance criterion is composed of a number of sub-categories. One attempt to suggest a set of criteria and sub-categories for international appraisals is found in Exhibit 12.3.[41] The first category refers to *qualifications*, meaning the criteria used to select the IA for the foreign assignment. These are included under the understanding that performance of the international assignees should be a function of the original assessment of their qualifications for the assignments and their ongoing evaluations should continue to assess whether the original qualifications were accurate. The other categories take into account the variety and complexity of criteria that have been suggested as being so necessary in this environment. Normally, a variety of factors are applied, depending on the international assignee's job descriptions and local circumstances. However, observation of common IPM practices of international assignees suggests that use of detailed criteria (such as listed in Exhibit 12.3) may not really be so common but that the broader standards and more general evaluations are probably more the norm.

Obviously, business strategy largely dictates the overall expectations for an IA's performance in any specific country. For example, it might not make sense to focus heavily on profits as a standard for success for a global manager in the early years of a subsidiary in the People's Republic of China. Efforts in the early years are most likely to be concentrated on development of relationships and on building a base of customers. To expect the international assignee to produce profits equal to those generated in a similar kind of operation at home is unrealistic and will cause heavy frustration and possibly lead to wrongly destroying a manager's career. There needs to be alignment between parent-company strategy and the realities of the local situation. In order to ensure this type of alignment, the home office will have to spend adequate time and attention to understand the local/foreign situation. Executives must travel to the foreign locale to observe and ask a lot of questions in order to

EXHIBIT 12.3: Criteria for Appraisal of International Assignees

Qualifications
Training
Experience
Technical skills
Social and language skills
Education

Targets
Directly derived from the parent company's objectives
Directly derived from the subsidiary's objectives
Directly derived from local objectives
Individually dictated, e.g., developmental goals

Attitude for
Flexibility
Interpersonal understanding and communication skills
Ability to cope with the stress (culture shock) of the assignment
Openness to change

Job performance
Result areas
Development of local team
Communication and decision making
Personal growth and development
Application of (newly gained) expertise

gain understanding and insight into the local culture and operating situation. At the home office, outside experts from universities and consulting firms, as well as former expatriates (i.e., repatriates) from that country, should be brought in to help provide the information upon which executives can best judge the factors for success in the foreign locations in question. Interestingly, research finds that transnational corporations are more likely to use the same basic performance criteria throughout their operations, with some variance in criteria importance depending on country situations.[42]

Ideally, a manager who has returned to the home office from an overseas site should be a permanent part of the team that updates performance criteria for overseas assignments. Reevaluating the criteria and their prioritization periodically will ensure that the performance criteria will remain current with the reality of the overseas situation.[43] One way to deal with this important performance evaluation issue is to include both soft and hard criteria in the performance review of international assignees.

Who Should do the Evaluation of the IA?

Given all the problems in implementing an effective IPM, the issue of who should conduct performance appraisals of expatriates also becomes quite complex. How can the MNE and IHRM compensate for the many problems described above? The answer developed by most MNEs is found in the use of multiple reviewers.[44] These additional reviewers may not all be as directly familiar with the work of the international assignee (although some may actually be more familiar, given the problems of time and distance), but they may be able to add necessary perspective: peers, subordinates, customers or clients. This is an application of what is referred to as the 360-degree review process, i.e., using reviews from above, below, and beside the candidate reviewee, and even using self-review. In the domestic context, the 360-degree review process is relatively complex (certainly more complex and messy, at least, than the traditional superior-only review process). In the international context, it is even messier. In the case of an international assignment, the different raters of the performance of the international assignee may be located many miles and time zones away from the ratee. They may not come into contact with the work of the international assignee so that it is difficult for them to render a valuable evaluation of the individual's performance. In their expatriate jobs, most international assignees have some type of direct supervision from someone in the home country plus usually a direct supervisor in the host country as well. In addition, the international assignee will entertain regular visits from home-country staff and line employees, people on missions to check in on the foreign operation and will also have frequent direct contacts in the foreign location with local customers, suppliers, banks, and government and community officials. The nature and complexity of all the international assignee's job activities will be much more difficult to assess from the home country. Exhibit 12.4 illustrates the results of a survey of MNEs in terms of the percentages of usage of various types of potential evaluators.[45] Clearly home-country and host-country supervisors are the most common, although other home-country and host-country and regional executives also get involved frequently. Interestingly, a high percentage of firms also use self-evaluation. But some typical raters in 360-degree evaluation systems, such as customers and peers, turned out to not be used much at all.

Conducting 360 reviews for an international assignee is also logistically complicated. Let's take, for example, a list of potential reviewers for an international assignee, in this case a sales and marketing manager sent from The Hague (Netherlands) to Bucharest (Romania) for an American firm headquartered in Philadephia, PA (USA):

- Her immediate manager (home country) sending her on assignment, located in The Hague, Netherlands.
- The director of sales and marketing, located at product headquarters in Chicago, Illinois, USA.
- The country manager in Romania.

EXHIBIT 12.4: Raters of International Assignee Performance

Inside host country		Outside host country	
Rater	%	Rater	%
Customers	1	Sponsor	7
Subordinates	7	Corporate HR professional	17
Peers	10	Regional executive	23
HR professionals	12	Supervisor	41
Self	39		
Supervisor	75		

Note: Percentages refer to average percentage in which each type of rater is involved in evaluations across sample MNEs.

- The regional HR director in the shared service center for Central and Eastern Europe (CEE), located in Budapest, Hungary.
- The marketing director, European region, located in the European regional headquarters in Brussels.
- The corporate head of marketing, located at corporate headquarters in Philadelphia, Pennsylvania, USA.
- Her expatriate and CEE sales and marketing peers, including the manager of sales of Romania, located in Romania and various other CEE capitals (Warsaw, Poland; Zagreb, Croatia; Bratislava, Slovenia; Prague, Czech Republic).
- The entire team of subordinates in the Bucharest operation working for her.
- Selected clients and customers in the CEE market.

Granted, the use of such multiple ratings is complicated; but the many difficulties involved with PA of international assignees in international operations indicates the need to collect multiple perspectives to enhance the accuracy and validity of an expatriate's performance evaluation.

Multinational firms, participating in a survey by a large global consulting firm (see Exhibit 12.5), gave the following responses to their use of various types of raters in the PAs of their international assignees.[46]

EXHIBIT 12.5: Use of Different Types of Rater in PAs of Expatriates

Type of review	%
Performance review in host country	71
Performance review in home country	56
Regular expatriate visits to home office	44
Regular manager visits to host office	39
Annual expatriate surveys (self-reports)	19

Obviously, as was suggested earlier, often the expatriate evaluation process is a pretty informal process. The survey also found that companies with fewer than 100 expatriates favored home-country reviews, while companies with more than 100 expatriates favored host-country appraisals. Apparently, once the foreign operations reach a certain size, the preference is to delegate the appraisal process to the local level where, presumably, managers with a more direct contact with the international assignee are able to provide more accurate and complete evaluations, although there is no direct research to verify that local managers do any better job at the PA of international assignees than do home-country or regional-office managers. Indeed, given the many perceptual issues stemming from differences in cultural values and norms and from problems with cultural adaptation, there is some reason to question the assumption that local managers are better equipped to perform these evaluations than are home-country managers (provided, of course, that these distant home-country managers have been able to observe the performance of the international assignee and understand the context under which they perform their jobs). One additional result of the previous survey that relates to who does the assessments is that firms reported that international assignees are, on the average, evaluated by three individuals, while the same firms reported an average of six raters for their home-country positions.[47] So even here in the admittedly more complex and difficult situation, international assignees do not receive the same level of management attention and involvement as occurs in the purely domestic environment.

Here are some of the advantages and disadvantages of using home- versus host-country managers as raters:

Home-country managers. In many cases, the final appraisal is done in the parent country, where the appraisers typically have little knowledge of local circumstances or of local culture and their impacts on the overall unit performance or on the expatriate or local manager's performance. Achieving results equivalent to a comparable unit or manager in the home country may well require larger efforts in terms of flexibility and creativity, to say nothing of interpersonal and managerial skills, all of which are difficult to quantify or measure, and therefore aren't taken into consideration.

Host-country Managers

In view of the geographical, communicative, and cultural distance between the foreign subsidiary or joint venture and the home-country appraiser, local management is often called in to give an opinion. In the case of the international assignee, the immediate supervisor responsible for the evaluation is probably a local manager. The assumption is that they are familiar with the international assignee's performance and are, therefore, in the best position to evaluate and explain it within the local situation and environmental factors. However, their perceptions and, therefore, their evaluations will be governed by their own cultural backgrounds and biases. Thus, for example, a parent-company manager who is used to guiding and managing with a high degree of involvement and participation might at least initially find resistance from local team members, who expect strong leadership and ideas and initiative from their bosses, and thus not get the desired level of team performance, resulting in a negative (or lower than expected) evaluation.[48]

How Should the Evaluation of the IA be Done?

There are a number of issues presented in answering the question of how international performance evaluations should be done. These include concerns about the specific form of the appraisal, the frequency of the appraisal, and the nature of feedback provided to the IA/FM as a part of the evaluation process.

Form

There continues to be much controversy over the specific form or instrument to be used in any performance review process, although this is not an area that has received any attention specifically focused on the international setting. So, presumably, all of the concerns over evaluation based on achievement of objectives versus trait-based reviews, or other approaches, such as critical-incident methods, that have been researched in the domestic context would also apply to the international context. In addition, however, the international context must also take into account issues over language and translation or interpretation of terms and phrasing as well as the cultural context, such as the nature of relationships between subordinates and superiors, etc. (For example, refer to the case at the end of this chapter.)

It is typical for firms to develop standard forms for their appraisal processes.[49] And there are valid reasons to retain such forms, including the importance of experience, comparative data for extended usage, costs, etc. These reasons remain valid, as long as the context of the performance doesn't change. However, for international assignees, the context most obviously does change. Thus, using standard forms, developed for the domestic situation, can be problematic. Despite this, surveys find that US firms, at least, tend to use the same standardized forms developed for the home-country environment for their expatratiates, and, presumably, their foreign manager populations.[50] This makes the problems associated with consideration of cultural context in the actual assessment of performance that much more important, but probably results in even less attention being paid to these contextual issues.

Frequency

This is one area where, at least in terms of general performance appraisals, some basic guidelines can be established. According to Wayne Cascio, a major contributor to knowledge about the Western PA process:

> Research over the past twenty years has indicated that once or twice a year is too infrequent. Considerable difficulties face a rater who is asked to remember what several employees did over the previous six to twelve months. . . . People often forget the details of what they have observed and they reconstruct the details on the basis of their existing mental categories.[51]

Supervisors tend to evaluate what they remember from the last few weeks or days, rather than over the six-to-twelve-month period. Even if they have maintained good records of events and performance, they are likely to be most persuaded and influenced by recent events (called recency bias). Ultimately, of course, to the extent the purpose of the evaluation is to provide feedback to the ratee for development purposes, the more frequent the evaluation and feedback, the better.

The frequency of evaluation should also vary according to the role of the evaluator.[52] On-site superiors should rate their subordinate international assignee after the completion of significant projects, tasks, or milestones. This helps the superior to focus clearly on the specific context of the particular performance being assessed. These can then be reviewed at the time of the annual or semi-annual official reviews. It is probably best to ask other reviewers, such as peers, subordinates, and customers, for reviews that fit the schedule of the formal review.

Feedback

Usually, an important component of any effective IPM system would include the provision of timely feedback of the results of the evaluation. This may, however, may prove to be problematic in many cultural settings. And, in addition, given time and distance issues separating many raters and their ratees, provision of this feedback is also likely to not take place in a timely manner, if at all. And evaluation by a distant manager probably only has face validity.

Guidelines for Performance Management of International Assignees

These recommendations for the PM of IAs, based on the limited research related to the PM of international assignees, are preliminary, but consistent with what has been reported:

- Put the specifics of the PA into the expatriate's international assignment plan and discuss the process prior to departure.
- Set clear performance expectations for the international assignee and the home- and host-country managers.
- Specify what successful performance in the host country entails.
- Use soft and hard performance criteria.
- Conduct frame-of-reference training for both the raters and the ratee.
- Modify the frequency of evaluations in terms of giving the international assignee more frequent evaluations yet also more time to obtain results.

As Oddou and Mendenhall indicate:

> Regardless of the effectiveness or availability of performance management tools, expatriate performance management success depends largely on the manager and expatriate in question: how well they both understand, internalize, and accept performance management, and how skillful they are in its implementation. To this end, appropriate PM training should be available for all expatriates, including their superiors.[53]

The case at the end of this chapter, Cross-Cultural Performance Evaluation in Thailand, takes a look at most of these issues that MNEs confront in the use of performance evaluations in cross-border situations. The challenges that Richard Evans has to deal with should help the reader to more thoroughly understand why MNEs and their expatriates and local employees have so many difficulties in managing the performance of a global workforce.

CONCLUSIONS

This chapter has addressed the crucial issue of performance evaluation and performance management for MNEs and their employees (whether local, global, or mobile international assignees) and managers. It has described the many difficulties encountered in trying to implement an effective IPM system in the international arena, not the least of which is figuring out how to accommodate in the evaluation process factors stemming from the nature of the local cultural environment. It is clear that it is inadequate to simply apply a PM process designed at the home-country level for domestic use to the international setting. It is necessary to make some accommodations for problems with cultural adaptation and associated with the complexities of conducting international business. The chapter also focused on the design, implementation, and evaluation of effective IPM systems for employees of MNEs and then looked at the special issues related to the PA of international assignees. Each section ended with a discussion of a number of suggestions and guidelines for improving the process of implementing an effective IPM system.

Appropriately assessing employee performance is a question of fairness to the employee; but it is also a question of ensuring that the MNE receives full value from its managers, employees, and international assignees and the best subsidiary or joint venture performance possible. Ultimately, an MNE's objectives relative to a workable IPM system are to effectively manage employee talent to the benefits of the employee, the manager, and the overall organization. An effective talent management strategy not only focuses on attracting (recruiting and selecting) the best employees but also on evaluating and developing them and positioning them within the organization so that the firm's global business strategy will be increasingly guided by those who have experienced and understand the firm's worldwide operations and markets.

DISCUSSION QUESTIONS

1 What are the tensions between standardization and localization of the performance management system of the MNE?
2 How does the international character of the MNE impact the *design* of the performance management system?
3 How does the international character of the MNE impact the *implementation* of the performance management system?
4 How does the international character of the MNE impact the *evaluation* of the performance management system?
5 What are the major issues involved in performance management of international assignees?

CASE STUDY 12.1: Cross-Cultural Performance Evaluation in Thailand: The Case of Richard Evans, Expatriate Managing Director (Switzerland/Thailand/UK)

Richard Evans, managing director of Siam Chemicals Company (SCC) in Thailand, a division of Chimique Helvétique Ltd (CHL), a Swiss chemicals group headquartered in Basle, had only been in his position for 18 months. But dealing with the evaluation of Mr. Somsak, one of his local mainstays, was about ready to drive him back to Switzerland or to England, from where he had originally come. This was Richard's first assignment outside Europe, and he had not found it an easy adjustment. Between the long commutes from home to the plant, due to the terrible traffic, the lack of sidewalks for taking his young son out in his pram, and the incredibly strong attitude of deference the Thai employees exhibited toward him, most of his first 18 months had been spent trying to get used to the locale and the culture. It was his first time in Asia and the culture shock for himself and his family (wife and three young children) had been harsh.

To move from international schools and skiing in clean, dry air in Switzerland to hot, humid, dirty, and polluted Thailand, where they spoke not a word of the local language and had no idea of the local customs, was indeed quite a shock.

It was shortly after arrival that he had had his first encounter with Mr. Somsak, considered one of the senior and longer-established employees after only three years on the job. Somsak worked both for Mr. Evans and for James Brown, the regional marketing manager, in the firm's regional offices in Singapore. Somsak had resigned right after a meeting that Richard had had with him to try to counsel him on how to function better within the matrix organizational structure of CHL. Somsak had explained to Mr. Evans that Thai people found the concept of two bosses impossible to reconcile with their strong sense of hierarchy. They preferred to know exactly who was their senior boss so they would know whose approval to seek. Richard had seized on the opportunity to counsel Somsak in a style that had always worked with his European managers. He had been stunned when Somsak had reacted with these words: "I realize from what you have said that I am not doing a good job. I am not suitable for my post and so the only thing I can do is to resign." Only through the strenuous efforts of Somsak's other boss, James Brown, to whom Somsak owed a strong sense of allegiance, had he been persuaded to stay.

But now, 18 months later, Richard was trying to figure out how to reconcile a major dilemma in how to complete the corporate evaluation form on Mr. Somsak. During the past 18 months, Mr. Somsak had maintained a very polite and correct but by no means warm attitude toward his managing director. For his part, Richard had come to appreciate that Somsak was a very hard-working and meticulous manager. He was willing to work every hour of the day, was highly intelligent, and spoke excellent English, since he had been dealing with European firms for many years. Richard had made every effort to convey his appreciation of Somsak's efforts and had recently been heartened by signs of a more trusting, comfortable relationship. Now the evaluation problem threatened all the gains Richard felt he had so carefully made. Richard knew that corporate headquarters (both his own direct supervisor and the corporate HR director) wanted all subsidiaries to adopt a more consistent form. The annual evaluation process was imposed on all CHL's subsidiaries and had been in use in Thailand ever since the company's foundation seven years ago. The same format was used company-wide for all management grades. The basis of the form was a set of six to seven key objectives to be achieved by a certain point in time during the coming year. The actual process involved two one-on-one meetings between the supervisor and the subordinate managers. The first meeting was to go over that year's performance and the second was to set objectives for the next year.

Richard realized that his local managers found the very idea of sitting down with their bosses to discuss their performance a threatening and alien concept. Even the most senior, who had a good command of English and had been with the company for some time, found it difficult both to meet with Richard for their own evaluations, and also to carry out the process with their own staffs. It was not for them to make any judgment about their performances, that was the job of the boss.

The most difficult part of the process involved the assigning of a letter grade. The chemical group used a standard A–E grading in which a normal distribution was to be applied, with an A grade being applied to the top 3–4 percent of really outstanding managers and the C category, into which 60–70 percent of managers usually fell, implying a good, standard performance with all requirements fulfilled. Looking through the records, Richard found that his predecessors had decided it was best not to disturb the relationships with local staff and had been awarding A grades to over 90 percent of the local managers.

Richard thought it was part of his obligation, as managing director and as representative of the parent company, to move the local evaluation system to reflect the international standards. In addition, the corporate HR director was championing the idea of developing an international cadre of managers who could help to staff the rapidly growing expansion of CHL's global operations. He had indicated how important a role the performance evaluation system was in that effort to identify the best managers within the local subsidiaries to begin developing them for other assignments.

In terms of achievement of objectives for the regional office, Somsak had done an A job. But in terms of meeting other objectives that Richard had set for him, such as dealing with better integrating his team with the broader firm, Richard felt that he had not done what was expected. He had built up his team but had only succeeded in forming an isolated clique. The team acted like a family centered on Somsak. In his own mind, Richard thought an overall C grade was totally appropriate. But the reality was that Somsak (and probably James Brown) would not understand and would again resign, and Richard would lose a very important contributor. And it was entirely possible in this culture that he would lose the whole team.

He had no idea how to proceed.

Source: Adapted from Butler, C. and de Bettignies, H.-C. (2001). Case: The evaluation, in Albrecht, M. H. (ed.), *International HRM: Managing Diversity in the Workplace*, Oxford and Malden, MA: Blackwell.

Discussion Questions

1 If you were Richard Evans, how would you proceed? Explain your approach.
2 Are there—or can there ever be—universal approaches to performance appraisal?
3 If you were the local HR manager, how would you counsel Richard (or Mr. Somsak)?

NOTES

1 Source: Nestlé Corporate Website: http://www.nestle.com/jobs/your-career-at-nestle/performance-culture. Accessed Nov. 18, 2014.

2 See Aguinis, H. (2013). *Performance management*, 3rd ed., Upper Saddle River: Prentice Hall; Cascio, W.F. (2012). Global performance management systems, in G. Stahl, I. Björkman and S. Morris (eds.), *Handbook of Research in International Human Resource Management*, 2nd ed., Cheltenham, UK: Edward Elgar, pp. 176–198; Boselie, P., Farndale, E., and Paauwe, J. (2012). Performance management, in Brewster, C. and Mayrhofer, W. (eds.), *Handbook of Research on Comparative Human Resource Management*, Cheltenham, UK: Edward Elgar, pp. 369–392; Biron, M., Farndale, E., and Paauwe, J. (2011). Performance management effectiveness: Lessons from world-leading firms. *International Journal of Human Resource Management*, 22(6), 1294–1311; Claus, L., and Briscoe, D. (2009). Employee performance management across borders: A review of relevant academic literature. *International Journal of Management Reviews*, 11(2), 175–196; Björkman, I., Barner-Rasmussen, W., Ehrnrooth, M., and Mäkelä, K. (2009). Performance management across borders, in Sparrow, P. (ed.), *Handbook of International Human Resource Management: Integrating People, Process, and Context*, Chichester, UK: John Wiley and Sons, pp. 229–250.

3 See, for example, Festing, M., Knappert, L., Dowling, P.J., and Engle, A.D. (2012). Global performance management in MNEs—conceptualization and profiles of country-specific characteristics in China, Germany, and the United States. *Thunderbird International Business Review*, 54(6), 825–843; Biron, Farndale, and Paauwe (2011); Bailey, C., and Fletcher, C. (2008). International performance management and appraisal: Research perspectives, in Harris, M.M. (ed.), *Handbook of Research in International Human Resource Management*, New York: Lawrence Erlbaum, pp. 127–143; Caligiuri, P. (2006). Performance measurement in a cross-cultural context, in Bennett, W., Jr., Lance, C.E. and Woehr, D.J. (eds.), *Performance Management: Current Perspectives and Future Challenges*, New York: Lawrence Erlbaum, pp. 277–244; Evans, P., Pucik, V., and Björkman, I. (2011). Global performance management, in Evans, P. Pucik, V. and Björkman, I. (eds.), *The Global Challenge: International Human Resource Management*, New York, NY: McGraw-Hill, vol. 2, pp. 346–390.

4 See Cascio (2012); Varma, A., Budhwar, P.S., and DeNisi, A. (eds.) (2008). *Performance Management Systems: A Global Perspective*, London, New York: Routledge; Lee, C.D. (2005). Rethinking the goals of your performance-management system. *Employment Relations Today*, 32(3), 53–60; Pudelko, M. (2006). A comparison of HRM systems in the USA, Japan and Germany in their socioeconomic context. *Human Resource Management Journal*, 16(2), 123–153.

5 Varma, Budhwar, and DeNisi (2008).

6 Claus and Briscoe (2009).

7 See Hofstede, G., Hofstede, G., and Minkov, M. (2010). *Cultures and Organizations Software of the Mind*, New York, NY: McGraw Hill; Hall, E.T., and Hall, M.R. (1990). *Understanding Cultural Differences*, London, UK: Intercultural Press, Inc.; Trompenaars, F., and Hampden-Turner, C. (2012). *Riding the Waves of Culture: Understanding Diversity in Global Business*, New York: McGraw Hill; Kluckhohn, F., and Strodtbeck, F. (1961). *Variations in Value Orientations*, Westport, CT: Greenwood Press.

8 See, for example, Festing, Knappert, Dowling and Engle (2012); Biron, Farndale, and Paauwe (2011); Haines III,V. and St-Onge, S. (2012). Performance management effectiveness: Practices or context? *The International Journal of Human Resource Management*, 23(6), 1158–1175; Bai, X., and Bennington, L. (2005), Performance appraisal in the Chinese state-owned coal industry. *International Journal of Business Performance Management*, 7, 275–287.

9 Sullivan, J., Suzuki, T., and Kondo, Y. (1985). Managerial theories and the performance control process in Japanese and American work groups. *Academy of Management Proceedings*, pp. 98–102.

10 Kamoche, K. (2011). Contemporary developments in the management of human Resources in Africa. *Journal of World Business*, 46, 1, 1–4; Arthur, Jr. W., Woehr, A., Adebowale D.J., and Strong, M. (1995). Human resource management in West Africa: Practices and perspectives. *International Journal of Human Resource Management*, 6, 347–66.

11 See The Cranfield Network on International Human Resource Management (Cranet) (Website: http://www.cranet.org/home/Pages/Default.aspx); Sparrow, P., Farndale, E., and Scullion, H. (2014). Globalizing the HR architecture: The challenges facing corporate HQ and international mobility functions, in P. R. Sparrow, H. Scullion, and I. Tarique (eds.), *Strategic Talent Management: Contemporary Issues in International Context*, Cambridge: Cambridge University Press, pp. 254–271; Budhwar, P. S., Schuler, R., and Sparrow, P. (2009). Preface: Cross national comparative HRM, in P. S. Budhwar, R. S. Schuler, and P. R. Sparrow (eds.), *International Human Resource Management*, London, UK: Sage, vol. 4, pp. vii–xiii; Brewster, C., Mayrhofer, W., and Reichel, A. (2011). Riding the tiger? Going along with Cranet for two decades — A relational perspective. *Human Resource Management Review*, 21(1), 5; Faulkner, D., Pitkethly, R. and Child, J. (2002). International mergers and acquisitions in the UK 1985–1994: A comparison of national HRM practices. *International Journal of Human Resource Management*, 13, 106–122.

12 Shadur, M.A., Rodwell, J., and Bamber, G.J. (1995). The adoption of international best practices in a Western culture: East meets West. *International Journal of Human Resource Management*, 6, 735–757.

13 Bai and Bennington (2005).

14 Easterby-Smith, M., Malina, D., and Yuan, L. (1995). How culture sensitive is HRM? A comparative analysis of practice in Chinese and UK companies. *International Journal of Human Resource Management*, 6, 31–59.

15 Paik, Y., Vance, C., and Stage, H.D. (2000). A test of assumed cluster homogeneity for performance appraisal in four Southeast Asian countries, *International Journal of Human Resource Management*, 11, 736–750; Vance, C.M., McClaine, S., Boje, D.M., and Stage, H.D. (1992). An examination of the transferability of traditional performance appraisal principles across cultural boundaries. *Management International Review*, 32, 313–326.

16 Paik, Y. and Choi, D.Y. (2005). The shortcomings of a standardized global knowledge management system: The case study of Accenture. *Academy of Management Executive*, 19, 81–84.

17 Björkman, I., and Lu, Y. (1999). The management of human resources in Chinese-Western ventures. *Journal of World Business*, 34, 306–324.

18 Von Glinow, M.A., Drost, E., and Teagarden, M. (2002). Convergence of IHRM practices: Lessons learned from a globally distributed consortium of theory and practice. *Human Resource Management*, 41, 123–141.

19 Entrekin, L., and Chung, Y. (2001). Attitudes towards different sources of executive appraisal: A comparison of Hong Kong Chinese and American managers in Hong Kong. *International Journal of Human Resource Management*, 12, 965–987.

20 Galang, M.C. (2004). The transferability question: Comparing HRM practices in the Philippines with the US and Canada. *International Journal of Human Resource Management*, 15, 1207–1233.

21 Mendonca, M., and Kanungo, R.N. (1996). Impact of culture on performance. *International Journal of Manpower*, 17, 65–69; Aycan, Z. (2005). The interplay between cultural and institutional contingencies in human resource management practices. *International Journal of Human Resource Management*, 16, 1083–1119.

22 Aycan (2005).

23 Vance, C.M. (2006). Strategic upstream and downstream considerations for effective global performance management. *International Journal of Cross Cultural Management*, 6, 37–56.

24 Davis, D.D. (1998). International performance measurement and management, in Smither, J.W. (ed.), *Performance Appraisal: State of the Art in Practice*, San Francisco, CA: Jossey-Bass, pp. 95–131.

25 Suutari, V., and Tahvanainen, M. (2002). The antecedents of performance management among Finnish expatriates. *International Journal of Human Resource Management*, 13, 55–75.

26 Davis (1998); Stroh, L.K., Black, J.S., Mendenhall, M.E. and Gregersen, H.B. (2005). *International Assignments: An Integration of Strategy, Research, and Practice*, Mahwah, NJ/London: Lawrence Erlbaum Associates; other studies show a similar range of findings, e.g., Woods, P. (2003). Performance management of Australian and Singaporean expatriates. *International Journal of Manpower*, 24, 517–534.

27 Vance (2006).

28 Briscoe, D. and Claus, L. (2008). Employee performance management: Policies and practices in multinational enterprises, in Varma, A., Budhwar, P.S. and DeNisi, A. (eds.) *Performance Management Systems: A Global Perspective*, London/New York: Routledge, pp. 15–39.

29 Claus, L. (2008). Employee performance management in MNCs: Reconciling the need for global integration and local responsiveness. *European Journal of Management*, 2 (2), 132–153.

30 Cascio, W.F. (2002). *Managing Human Resources: Productivity, Quality of Work Life, Profits*, 6th ed., New York: McGraw-Hill Irwin.

31 Figures from a survey by the former Arthur Andersen's Human Capital Services Practice, reported in Juday, H. (1999). Employee development during international assignments. *Corporate Relocation News*, August, 18, 35.

32 Tahvanainen, M. (2000). Expatriate performance management: The case of Nokia Telecommunications. *Human Resource Management*, summer/fall, 39 (2 and 3), 267–275.

33 See, for example, Oddou and Mendenhall (2006).

34 See, for example, Trompenaars, F. (1994). *Riding the Waves of Culture: Understanding Diversity in Global Business*, New York: Irwin. Dr. Trompenaars found that managers from various countries ranked qualities for evaluation in significantly different orders.

35 Oddou, G., and Mendenhall, M. (2000), Expatriate performance appraisal: Problems and solutions, in Mendenhall, M., and Oddou, G. (eds), *Readings and Cases in International Human Resource Management*, Cincinnati, OH: Southwestern College Publishing; Harvey, M.G. (1997). Focusing on the international personnel performance appraisal process. *Human Resource Development Journal*, 8 (1), 41–62.

36 Harvey, M.G. and Buckley, M.R. (1997). Managing inpatriates: Building a global core competency. *Journal of World Business*, 32 (1), 35–52.

37 See, for example: Biron, M., Farndale, E., and Paauwe, J. (2011). Performance management effectiveness: Lessons from world-leading firms. *International Journal of Human Resource Management*, 22 (6), 1294–1311; Haines,V. Y., I.,II, and St-Onge, S. (2012). Performance management effectiveness: Practices or context? *The International Journal of Human Resource Management*, 23 (6), 1158; Black, J.S., Gregersen, H.B., Mendenhall, M.E. and Stroh, L.K. (1999). Chapter 7: Appraising: Determining if people are doing the right things, *Globalizing People Through International Assignments*, Reading, MA: Addison-Wesley; Caligiuri, P.M. (1997). Assessing expatriate success: Beyond just "being there," in Aycan, Z. (ed.), *New Approaches to Employee Management*, 4 (JAI Press), 117–140; Gregersen, H.B., Black, J.S. and Hite, J.M. (1995). Expatriate performance appraisal: Principles, practice, and challenges, in Selmer, J. (ed.), *Expatriate Management: New Ideas for International Business*, Westport, CT: Quorum; Oddou, G. and Mendenhall, M. (2000). Expatriate performance appraisal: Problems and solutions, in Mendenhall, M. and Oddou, G. (eds.), *Readings and Cases in International Human Resource Management*, Cincinnati, OH: South-Western College Publishing; Schuler, R.S., Fulkerson, J.R. and Dowling, P.J. (1991). Strategic performance measurement and management in multinational corporations. *Human Resource Management*, 30 (3), 365–392; Bonache, J., and Noethen, D. (2014). The impact of individual performance on organizational success and its implications for the management of expatriates. *The International Journal of Human Resource Management*, 25 (14), 1960.

38 Dowling, P.J., Festing, M., and Engle, A.D. (2013). *International Human Resource Management*, 6th ed., London: Cengage Learning; Janssens, M. (1994), Evaluating international manager's performance: Parent

company standards as control mechanisms, *The International Journal of Human Resource Management*, 5 (4), 853–873.

39 Birdseye, M.G., and Hill, J.S., (1995). Individual, organization/work and environmental influences on expatriate turnover tendencies: An empirical study. *Journal of International Business Studies*, 26 (4), 795–809; Feldman, D.C., and Thompson, H.B., (1993). Expatriation, repatriation, and domestic geographic relocation: An empirical investigation of adjustment to new job assignments. *Journal of International Business Studies*, 24 (3), 507–529.

40 Torbiörn, I. (1985). The structure of managerial roles in cross-cultural settings. *International Studies of Management and Organization*, 15 (1), 52–74.

41 Adapted from Logger, E., and Vinke, R. (1995). Compensation and appraisals of international staff, in Harzing, A.-W., and Van Ruysseveldt, J. (eds), *International Human Resource Management*, London: Sage in association with the Open University of the Netherlands, pp. 144–155.

42 Borkowski, S.C. (1999). International managerial performance evaluation: A five-country comparison. *Journal of International Business Studies*, 30 (3), 533–555.

43 Stroh, Black, Mendenhall, and Gregersen (2005).

44 Most of the references in note 2 made this point. In addition, see Lomax, S. (2001), *Best Practices for Managers and Expatriates: A Guide on Selecting, Hiring, and Compensation*, New York: Wiley.

45 Based on Stroh, Black, Mendenhall and Gregersen (2005).

46 *Global Relocation Trends*, 1998 and 1998 Survey Reports, New York: Windham International and National Foreign Trade Council, and Alexandria, VA: Society for Human Resource Management. For most current surveys see 2013 Brookfield Global Relocation Trends Survey, 2014 Global Mobility Policy and Practices survey – Cartus; Global Mobility Effectiveness Survey 2013 by EY.

47 Stroh et al. (2005).

48 Logger and Vinke (1995).

49 Gregersen, H.B., Hite, J.M. and Black, J.S. (1996). Expatriate performance appraisal in U.S. multinational firms. *Journal of International Business Studies*, 4th Quarter, 711–738.

50 Ibid.

51 Cascio (2002), pp. 302–303.

52 Stroh et al. (2005).

53 Oddou, G. and Mendenhall, M. (2006). Expatriate performance appraisal: Problems and solutions, in Mendenhall, M., Oddou, G., and Stahl, G.K. (eds.), *Readings and Cases in International Human Resource Management*, 4th ed., London/New York: Routledge, pp. 208–218.

Chapter 13

Well-being of the International Workforce and International HRIS

Our approach to promoting work–life balance varies from country to country. But it is always based on a common straightforward principle: we want to help our employees perform to their full potential.

Roche's Pharmaceutical Corporation[1]

Learning Objectives

This chapter will enable the reader to:

- Explain the importance of global health and safety.
- Describe IHRM's role in managing a global health, well-being, safety, and security program.
- Describe an effective crisis management program.
- Describe the various support services delivered by IHR.
- Explain IHRM's role in global HR research.
- Describe the problems associated with implementing an effective global HR information system.

This chapter deals with two critical yet seldom reported aspects of IHRM policy and practice: concern for the well-being of the MNE's global workforce and the development and maintenance of the global HR information system. Both of these areas of concern are central to IHRM's ability to deliver on its vision of making a major contribution to the MNE's competitive advantage in the global marketplace. And taken together, they provide an important conclusion for the themes of this section of the text, with a look at both the practical side of IHRM and a focus on how MNEs are struggling to find ways to deliver strategic support while delivering necessary IHRM services within acceptable metrics.

WELL-BEING OF THE GLOBAL WORKFORCE

This continues to be one of the more challenging (yet important) topics to write about in IHRM. Periodically, events occur that put certain aspects of the topic on the front page, such as the overseas kidnapping of a well-known executive, an exposé about worker exploitation at a foreign subcontractor, a workplace accident that kills and/or injures scores of employees in a foreign plant, or the total lack of concern for the work-life balance of employees around the world, especially in rapidly developing emerging markets. Thank goodness catastrophes are fairly rare. Even so, employee health, well-being, and safety are increasingly important topics for MNEs for the following reasons:

- Increasing attention to employee well-being around the world.
- Increasing numbers of employees at potential risk because of increased global trade such as increasing number of workers in a growing number of locales in "at risk" jobs like manufacturing, and increasing number of people on short- and longer-term international assignments to an increasing number of countries, often with their families.

All of these factors create increasing concerns for the health, well-being, and safety of an MNE's global workforce—and potentially for the safe and continuing operation of the global business—as well as for the need to consider the employer's duty-of-care for its employees around the world.[2] Although it is not always the case, in most countries health and safety of workers is one of the responsibilities of HR and, therefore, in the global enterprise, of IHR.

There are a number of specific aspects that can be identified and discussed. These include:

1 Coping with health and safety practices and regulations that vary from country to country.
2 The establishment of health and safety policies on a global basis for all employees of the MNE.
3 Dealing with specific health and safety concerns of business travelers and international assignees and their families as they travel on business trips around the world or are posted to foreign assignments.
4 The very specific threat of issues like kidnapping and/or terrorist acts against foreign operations and international assignees and their families.
5 Dealing with real and potential, natural and man-made, threats and disasters.
6 The work-life balance of workers in markets with differing levels of economic development.

The following provides an introduction to at least some of the factors that an IHR manager might need to consider when dealing with international health, well-being, and safety issues. First, general issues for the MNE at the country or regional level are discussed. Then issues related to business travelers and international assignees are addressed. This section ends with a discussion of how MNEs might develop crisis management programs for preparing for and dealing with various health and safety contingencies.

Employee Health and Safety Around the World

In most large firms, headquarters-located HR managers responsible for international HR do not often deal with health and safety issues among their firms' foreign subsidiaries or joint ventures. Responsibility for these issues is normally left to local managers and their HR staffs to manage within the constraints of local custom, culture, and regulation. Clearly, attention to these concerns varies dramatically from country to country.[3]

Health and Safety Statistics

From a strategic point-of-view, it would be helpful if firms (and their IHR staffs) could compare occupational health and safety regulations and experience between countries, for example, to help assess the problems and potential costs that might be associated with locating operations in any given country. Yet, this remains quite difficult to do. Different countries follow differing reporting standards regarding what constitutes an injury and whether it must be reported. Even for workplace fatalities, variation in methods makes cross-national comparisons difficult. For example, some countries (but not all) include deaths that occur when an employee is traveling to or from work, whereas others exclude deaths that result from occupational diseases. It is also the case that developing countries, in general, report significantly higher occupational accident and fatality rates than do more developed countries.[4]

For IHR planning and decision-making purposes, the most important point is that accident and fatality rates vary widely for a number or reasons, only some of which are related to variances in record-keeping standards and practices. What may be more significant are factors such as the mix of industries present in each country, the percentage of service jobs, and the level of education and training among the general labor force. Some industries and jobs are inherently more dangerous than others. For instance, logging, mining, and quarrying tend to have the highest fatality rates in most countries, while construction, transportation, utilities, and agriculture have moderately high rates. World Health Organization data suggest that, worldwide, approximately half the world's workers are employed in hazardous jobs, both from risk of injury or illness and from death.[5] Retail trade, banking, and social service industries generally have many fewer injuries and illnesses, and fewer fatalities. Thus those countries that have a mix of industries that favor those with lower fatalities will have more favorable country-wide occupational health and safety statistics. Yet they still may have extra-dangerous working conditions even within their normally-high-risk industries.

Health and Safety Laws and Standards

In countries with strong industrial democracy, such as most of those within the European Union, Switzerland, and Australia, MNEs are more likely to find regulations empowering employees or their representatives in unions and works councils in the monitoring and enforcing of workplace safety than is the case elsewhere. Indeed, the European Union has adopted a common strategic framework for occupational health and safety.[6] The strategic framework identifies three major health and safety at work challenges: "1) to improve implementation of existing health and safety rules; 2) to improve the prevention of work-related diseases by tackling new and emerging risks without neglecting existing risks; 3) to take account of the ageing of the EU's workforce."[7]

At the opposite end of the spectrum, the setting and enforcement of occupational safety (and, even more so, health) standards in developing countries often leaves much to be desired. Most developing countries have only rudimentary employment safety laws and very limited funds for enforcing such laws. Often the efforts by developing countries to attract foreign investment are enhanced by offering a business environment relatively free of government regulation. Typically, unions are weak or are primarily focused only on issues such as politics, wages, and fair treatment of employees, not on workplace safety concerns. In addition, the tendency to rely on labor-intensive enterprises and dated equipment, the pressure to create and preserve jobs, and the lack of safety training for specialists as well as for workers, themselves, all contribute to the poor safety records in many developing countries.[8]

An additional area of concern for MNEs (and IHR) involves the differences in the nature and quality of medical systems in different countries, the coverage of the health care system, who pays for health care, and the form and level of support systems for various forms of disabilities.

All of these issues impact employment practices for both IAs and for local nationals. Attention to fitness and employee stress, use of drugs, awareness of problems with major health issues, problems with inadequate nutrition, and excessive pressures to perform are all issues that can influence IHR planning and practices in global operations.

Family-friendly Policies and Work-life Balance[9]

Family-friendly policies and work-life balance raise a whole new set of issues and opportunities for IHR, issues and opportunities that need to be taken into account when planning the nature of and locale for foreign operations. They have become central issues over the last decade, particularly in the European Union and in other developed countries, reflecting a growing concern over quality of work life, lengthening work hours and stress, growing support by governments for the health of families, and the growing concern by enterprises over meeting the needs and interests of today's complex and demanding workforce. The changing roles of men and women—both at home and at work—the changing make-up of families with increasing numbers of single parents, and the aging of the populations in many countries and the subsequent rise in eldercare, all have led firms (and governments) to look for ways to make work more attractive while allowing more balance between the demands of work and home. At a time when there is worldwide a growing shortage of critical talent, firms are finding they must do everything possible to make their workplaces desirable. And, even though these concepts originated in developed countries, MNE leadership and IHR must decide how to apply them to operations in emerging markets and in developing economies, where not everyone necessarily views the issues in the same way.

For more information about this issue, refer to Case 13.1, Global Health and Safety Concerns, at the end of this chapter.

The European Union has pioneered the legal framework for family-friendly policies (such as paid time off for maternity and paternity responsibilities, for eldercare and family illness needs, time limits on work hours, restrictions on night and shift work, provision of significant paid annual leave, and equal rights for part-time workers). There are many pressures (from governments and firms) for the development of family-friendly laws and policies, including the increased numbers of women in the workforce, low birthrates and the resultant labor shortages, variances between countries in such policies creating cost differentials for firms, female participation in various industries, etc. The result is that MNEs need to both become familiar with the legal and cultural constraints in the countries in which they operate or are considering operating as well as incorporating in their global strategic planning knowledge about these concerns around the world.

The current conversations on talent management and employee engagement within HR have pushed the topic of work-life balance (WLB) to the forefront. HR is increasingly being asked to play a role in balancing the needs for work performance in companies with the demands from many employees for greater balance in their lives—which, as Case 13.1 illustrates, can be confounded by new career and performance ambitions in some emerging economies.[10] WLB issues can be looked at from different perspectives—starting from a broad societal view, then moving to the view of an employing organization, and finally to the perspective of an individual employee. The issues under consideration at each level vary considerably.

- At the "macro" societal level, issues of WLB deal with different cultural, political, economic, demographic, and legal contexts that affect the WLB debate, often resulting in legislation that supports family obligations.
- The "meso" organizational level focuses on the new world of work that has created pressures for workers and the responses companies are proposing in terms of WLB-friendly policies and benefits.
- At the "micro" individual level, the WLB focus is on coping mechanisms of the individual (or groups of individuals) in their particular situations. Although WLB initiatives are often in the forefront in developed economies, the issue is also impacting people in emerging markets, although sometimes in unexpected ways.

HEALTH AND SAFETY AND INTERNATIONAL ASSIGNEES

Many of the above issues overlap with concerns for the health and safety of business travelers (BTs) and IAs and their families. Some are standard concerns for employees while traveling and some involve employees after arrival at their new assignments. These concerns involve many types of situations (for both BTs and IAs and their families), including concerns about kidnapping; having disabling accidents (for example, car accidents, which may be the most significant risk) while on foreign assignment; encounters with local law enforcement; coping with major natural disasters such as earthquakes, volcanoes, floods, and hurricanes/monsoons which affect all employees and operations; getting ill and having inadequate local health care; being mugged and losing passports and money, which have to be replaced; dying while on foreign assignment; and being hit by terrorist acts or civil unrest or just being traumatized by them or their possibilities.

In addition, being involved with any of these situations can be made worse because of inability to speak the local language, lack of familiarity with and/or distrust of local legal and medical or emergency services, inability to use the local phone systems (including inadequate phone systems); and being in distant time zones when needing help from headquarters. The issue of language is a particularly important one when confronting emergencies. The simple act of calling for help in the location of the problem can pose a major obstacle, e.g., not speaking the local language (or not speaking it well enough to describe the emergency), not knowing whom to call for help, problems with the local phone system, and problems with the competency of local police and emergency workers and hospitals/clinics.

In response to the importance of these issues, international BTs and IAs and their families need to be briefed on and prepared for dealing with problems of safety and health while traveling and in their new countries. They should be given an orientation to the different medical systems in the new countries, how to take care of prescriptions and any special medical conditions, the identification of doctors and hospitals to provide for health care in their new locations, and usually the acquisition of emergency medical and evacuation insurance to cover possible contingencies. IHR should also be prepared to provide assistance in case of crises in the firm's foreign operations as well as to aid in times of need for business travelers.

The following IHRM in Action provides a glimpse at the types of services that one of these companies (MEDEX Assistance Corporation—which provides for clients' prompt access to medical and related services anywhere in the world) can provide when a traveler (or expatriate) faces a medical problem.[11] Such assistance would be of most help to travelers and expatriates when in remote locations and/or developing countries.

IHRM in Action 13.1: The Need for Emergency Medical on Travel in Niger

On December 22, MEDEX was informed that a man had been hospitalized in a tiny clinic in the small village of Zinder in the Niger Republic in West Africa. The man—a Dr. Shaw—had suffered a serious leg injury when the vehicle in which he was riding overturned during a Young Europe for Africa expedition. Because the clinic lacked the necessary facilities and personnel to treat Dr. Shaw, MEDEX personnel immediately arranged a light aircraft to transport him to Naimey, some 1,000 kilometers away.

After assessing Dr. Shaw's injuries—torn leg tendons and a fractured left radius—the treating physician in Niamey stated that he could not perform the operation. He added, however, that if an operation was not performed within a very few days, the tendons and nerves may retract to the point that a successful operation could not be performed.

When it became evident that the first available seat on a scheduled flight would not be available for about five days, MEDEX arranged for Dr. Shaw to be flown—in the early hours of Christmas morning—to University College Hospital in London. The following day, the broken radium was corrected, the severed tendons were reconnected, and a knee wound was cleaned and closed. Dr. Shaw was released from the hospital on January 4.

In a lengthy letter of praise to MEDEX, Dr. Shaw wrote:

> I owe a huge debt of gratitude to your organization. I could have been trapped in Zinder for days, with a septic arthritis and in danger of losing my leg. It was a situation where each delay made the risks greater. Your ability to get me out within four days of the accident was remarkable. The French doctors and diplomats were very impressed. I am very thankful.
>
> On a more personal level, I and my family were touched by the care you took to keep us informed of developments. . . . My parents were delighted to be told in separate phone calls that the plane had left, that it was ahead of schedule, and that it had arrived safely.

Specific Health and Safety Concerns for BTs and IAs

Even though potential problems related to terrorism, crime, kidnapping, civil unrest and riots, natural disasters, and other traumatic events can seem overwhelming, it is often more likely that MNEs and IHR will have to deal with a number of specific health problems unrelated to these sorts of traumas. BTs and IAs and their families frequently (if not usually) suffer from less serious health complaints ranging from intestinal disorders due to exposure to new bacteria to major exotic illnesses, to which their systems have built no immunities.

Under all circumstances, business travelers and expatriates need to be briefed as to what to expect, how to prepare for conditions in the country or countries to which they are going, and how to react when confronted with health or safety problems. There can be several situations in which the lack of attention to health issues when an individual was sent on foreign assignment caused major problems for both the individual involved and the organization.

Death While on Assignment

Once in a while (thank goodness it doesn't happen very often), someone dies while on business travel or while on an international posting—given that millions of people work outside their countries of origin (for governments, NGOs, private firms—not counting military assignments), the number of deaths to accidents and natural causes is relatively small.[12] As bad as these events are, however, someone has to deal with them, and that someone in most organizations is HR. Coping with such situations includes dealing with the situation in the foreign locale as well as helping the family to cope. Death can occur from natural causes (illness, heart attack, stroke) or from some other event, such as an auto accident, a terrorist act, or a natural disaster. Whatever the cause, it usually catches everyone by surprise. Thus having thought about the possibility before it happens can make timely and adequate response more likely. Since there are so many aspects to dealing well with what can be a quite traumatic event for firms and families, IHR needs to be prepared for issues that are probably not normally considered, such as, for example, IHR (and employees and their families) needing to be aware that typical emergency medical insurance and programs do not take care of people after death.[13] The contracts end when death occurs. In addition, treatment of deceased people varies from country to country, culture to culture, and among differing religions, so IHR needs to get involved quickly to make sure that the wishes and traditions of the family are accommodated.

CRISIS MANAGEMENT

One important way for IHR to add to the value of their services, is to design and implement crisis management programs for dealing with the many forms of trauma and health and safety problems that individual employees and their employing organizations confront in today's global environment. Exhibit 13.1 highlights issues that may be considered when developing Expatriate Crises Management Programs.

EXHIBIT 13.1: Issues to Consider When Designing Expatriate Crisis Management Programs

Assess the risk	The first area of focus for IHR crisis planning is to assess the risks. This involves examining three issues:

- *Size of the risk.* Helping IAs and BTs to understand the nature of the risks is a first step in planning ways to prepare for the risks that do exist.
- *Types of potential problems for each locale.* IHR needs to assess (or get assistance from consultants that provide this information) the specific risks that do exist in a particular location. Not every overseas location poses the same level or type of risk.

■ *Relative risk for each situation.* Not all travelers and IAs face the same risks. (Well-known or prominent executives working in high-profile jobs or industries face greater risks than the typical BT or IA and thus require greater protection and attention.)

Prepare a crisis management plan

The second thing IHR needs to do to address global health, safety, and security issues is to prepare a plan for dealing with the issues identified.[1] Getting a plan prepared (even quickly) may be more important than thoroughness. Sensitivity (particularly when dealing with family members and with media) may be more important than any other consideration. And when a crisis is handled poorly, the firm is likely to lose personnel. So the benefits in employee morale and productivity are likely to outweigh the costs of the resources needed to prepare a crisis management plan. Responding to an employer's duty-of-care and potential liabilities, satisfying employee needs when in difficulty, and handling crises well all can contribute to an employer's employment brand and bottom line. Part of this action would involve tracking employees who are traveling or on foreign assignments and the status of their official documents, such as visas, exit permits, etc., so that the firm has a fairly clear idea of who is located in any particular place, so that when a crisis arises, IHR knows who and what part of the business is at risk and what is the nature of that risk.

Orientation and training

The third component of any plan to deal with global health, safety, and security issues is to develop a program for preparing BTs and IAs and their families for international travel and living. This orientation and training could include insurance for issues such as emergency medical and kidnapping ransom, information about potential risks in the areas of the world involved, pre-departure orientation, and post-departure follow-up—and, of course, explaining these to the travelers and assignees and their families. This preparation should also involve preparing security for IA homes and foreign facilities, plans for dealing with civil emergencies (such as plans for evacuation of foreign personnel), plans for dealing with media and family "back home," and developing lists of sources of information and help in case of real crises.

[1] See, for example, Arnold, J. T. (2008), Tracking Business Travelers, *HR Magazine*, November, Society for Human Resource Management reprint (www.shrm.org); Davidson, C. and Busch, E. (1996), How to cope with international emergency situations, *KPMG Expatriate Administrator*, April, 6–10; Gazica, E. (2010), Multinationals face an unhealthy contradiction, downloaded 5/11/2010 from http://www.hreonline.com/HRE/printstory.jsp?storyId=402063013; Kroll Associates (2000), *Secure Travel Guide and Guide to Personal Security*, New York: Kroll Associates.

Overall, planning can lessen the risks and the fears. It is important to keep in mind that plan design is important. Plan execution is key. IHR must take a leading role. If they don't, it is likely that no one else will—and it is IHR that deals most directly with travel and relocation/living issues for BTs and IAs and is usually in the forefront of media and family contacts when crises occur.

GLOBAL HR SUPPORT SERVICES AND INFORMATION SYSTEMS

In the typical domestic HR department, a number of activities are performed that are referred to as *support services for the core HR responsibilities*. These include:

- *the HR information system* (including maintaining records on employees and employee programs, such as hiring and job history, education and training and development, health insurance and other benefits, and providing HR reports);
- *HR planning* (including employee forecasts, career plans for managers, and succession planning for executives);
- *job analysis and the writing of job descriptions* (for recruiting and training purposes and the setting of performance expectations);
- *job evaluations and wage surveys* (for the development of job classification and wage rates).

IHR Information Systems

As firms internationalize their business operations they eventually reach the point where they need to internationalize their information systems (or, it could be a strategic policy initiative—to have only one information database and system). This includes their human resource information systems (HRIS). But, because the formats and purposes of the HRIS were established to service only HR in firms' home-country operations, internationalizing the HRIS can be a very complex and challenging activity, including integrating any existing foreign HRISs from developed or acquired subsidiaries or joint ventures.

Special Problems

Global HR information systems (HRIS) create special problems for HR. Global HRISs need to cope with all (and more) of the following special issues, all of which can create major problems: Keeping track of workforces in each country of operation, local employees, long-term IAs, short-term IAs, IA compensation and benefits:

- foreign currency conversions for payroll, which can vary daily;
- budgeting and tracking payroll given various currencies and currency fluctuations;

- government versus private health and pension benefits in various countries;
- major variances in leave of absences and paid time off from country to country;
- employment contracts (with their major variances from country to country);
- number of hours worked, vacation days, termination liabilities;
- tracking family information for IAs, including educational support;
- data privacy laws that protect personal information residing in HRIS and the back-up systems (often in another country)
- laws regarding the transfer of personal data from one country to another.

Management Considerations

There are a number of policy decisions that IHR must take to develop a global HRIS, including these types of concerns: Developing separate (for each location or region, for example) or integrated information systems, which would involve questions about treatment of wholly owned subsidiaries versus joint ventures and partnerships and comparability of computer hardware and software, language(s) to be used, form of HR data to be maintained, etc.; centralization or localization of the system; authority over and control of access to the information and movement of the data between locations (which may be regulated by country law); centralized or localized privacy protection rules; control and maintenance of data, accessibility, updating, and flow; and decisions about what data to maintain in the global HRIS, given the thousands of potential elements from various countries that might be included. Of course, there are additional issues that have to be resolved, such as dealing with country cultural differences in the creation and use of employee data, training in the use of the system, choices of vendors and technology, integration of new and old systems, etc. And then there are basic issues related to the actual design of the system and its capture of items like employee names (with the incredible variance in forms, lengths, languages), desirability of standardization of names of local firms (e.g., Inc., PLC, Gmbh, FrOres, SLA, Oy, etc.), differences in postal addresses (or lack of such), even variances in calendars, which must also be resolved. Maintenance and accessibility of all of this data and information becomes particularly important for IHRM if it is going to make decisions (such as compensation, promotions, performance evaluations, job assignments, training opportunities) about the firm's global workforce.

Special Capabilities: IHR Websites

In addition to the development of a global HRIS, HR has its own uses for technology, which can greatly enhance its ability to perform its responsibilities. For example, HR can develop an intranet within its own operations that can both help HR to deliver services, such as benefits information, as well as knowledge transfer among various HR business centers around the world. Such intranet portals and HR websites can promote and facilitate the sharing of ideas and resources across borders, allowing firms to benefit from pooled and archived IHR experience and expertise, relying less on outside consultants for routine information (and databases for finding the best consultants for the specialist help that is not available in-house). Technology such as this also allows for ever-increasing capabilities, such as language translation software and multilingual programming for conducting global employee surveys and benefits management. And with new technology, such as social networks, blogging, tweeting, mobile phones, e-tablets, etc., IHR can now enhance many of its projects and systems, such as global recruiting and staffing, communication with employees and potential employees worldwide, and enhancing the firm's employment brand.[14]

Relocation and Orientation

This area of service has traditionally been one of the most time consuming for IHR. Increasingly, however, at least in larger MNEs, these services are being outsourced to external firms or relegated to internal, central shared-service centers that specialize in transactional services such as relocations. To ensure that employees being assigned to foreign posts receive the best possible attention to the very personal concerns that accompany relocation to another country, most of these related services are sourced from firms that specialize in the delivery of these services directly to IAs and their families. These services typically involve helping relocating employees with problems such as the selling or renting of houses, the shipment of household goods internationally, the location of temporary living quarters in their new location, the purchase or rental of a new house or apartment (or provision of a company-owned or -leased residence), managing the international move itself, the control of family in-transit time, and the control of overall relocation costs. These concerns can often be quite intense for IAs and families relocating internationally (as well as for IHR staff that manage these processes). So ensuring the quality of these services (within reasonable costs), whether provided directly through the firm or through outsourced specialists, is a critical IHR responsibility.

Other than the issues involved with the physical relocation, as stated above, there are a number of other critical concerns that IHR needs to make sure are met. These include providing tax and financial advice; arranging visas and work permits; arranging medical exams and counseling related to medical services in the foreign locale; providing training and orientation (about financial issues, the travel arrangements and experience, the country and its history, culture, and language) for IAs and their families; and arranging education and schooling for IAs and their families while on assignment in another country.

Administrative Services

Many of the following support services could be provided elsewhere in the firm, but they are generally delegated to IHR staff. All of them are, at least initially, established to ease the process of transferring employees from one country to another. Then because IHR finds ways to resolve these challenges, they often find other responsibilities being sent their way. These services can include:

- Making travel arrangements (for international assignees and their families and also for all employees who travel internationally). These services can involve travel arrangements, travel visas, and travel insurance.
- Arranging housing in foreign locales. This can involve finding quality housing (hotel rooms, apartments), making reservations, negotiating contracts, and signing rental agreements.
- Determining the availability and operation of local transportation, including rental cars, chauffeurs, metro maps, bus schedules, and rail systems.
- Office services, such as translation and translators, printing documents such as contracts, housing and rental agreements, business letters, and business negotiations and locations.
- Currency conversion. IAs and international business travelers may, initially, need assistance with issues related to conversion of their home-country currency into that of host countries. IHR is often tasked with ensuring that these people understand whatever complications might arise as pay arrangements are worked out to accommodate different currencies and their varying exchange rates and varying local inflation rates.
- Local bank accounts. Since banking systems vary from country to country and access to familiar banking operations may be limited in availability, IAs may need assistance in establishing local bank accounts.
- Government relations. This will initially involve familiarity with the proper offices to get visas and work permits (or the consultancies that provide these services).

CONCLUSIONS

This chapter has discussed two topics of great importance to the IHRM professional: employee well-being and IHRM support services. Both these areas of responsibility play major roles in defining IHRM's ability to achieve a strategic contribution to MNEs' global success. First, the chapter described why MNEs must understand and cope with local and international health, safety, and security regulations and needs, and develop programs and policies that protect their global workforces in their many locations. Then the chapter described four particular support services that IHR provides for the international enterprise. These included IHR research, global HR information systems, relocation services, and special administrative services, such as providing translation and office services and developing information about local banking and transportation services for business travelers and international assignees.

DISCUSSION QUESTIONS

1 What makes managing employee health and safety programs around the world so difficult?

2 Why have family-friendly and work-life balance programs become so important?

3 Describe the kinds of health, safety, and security problems that international employees encounter and design a crisis management program to deal with them.

4 Why is designing and implementing a global human resource information system so difficult? What kinds of problems need to be overcome?

CASE STUDY 13.1: Global Health and Safety Concerns (Global, Romania, UK, Ghana)

Increasingly, MNEs are recognizing a duty to take care of their global workforces. In this case, we take a short look at two situations in which global firms have been confronted with crises due to unexpected health and safety problems among their global employees and the potential consequences of not taking seriously enough their duties of care.

Work–Life Balance (WLB) for Overworked Professionals in Emerging Markets

Sometimes, in emerging markets, the eagerness to succeed can lead to employees working lots of overtime and neglecting their private lives and personal health in stark contrast to the WLB notions of their multinational employers. Thus, even though it was never the intention of 31-year-old Raluca Stroescu of Romania, an audit manager for Ernst & Young, to work herself to death, that is essentially what happened in May 2007. Her friends and family relate that she had been working every day and her local management had not accepted her missing even one day. Within the three weeks prior to her death, she had been working on an important audit project and had lost a lot of weight, reaching less than 40 kilos (88 pounds). Her case was widely discussed in Eastern Europe and according to local public opinion it was considered the first case of a death due to overwork.

The central debate in these discussions was whether young professionals in emerging markets really do want work–life balance or would really rather trade WLB for advancement, fame, and fortune. Many (maybe most?) young professionals in emerging markets work very hard because exciting developmental opportunities are opening in their countries and there always seem to be new and interesting projects in which to become engaged. They do it because they receive recognition for their achievements, better annual reviews, and better chances for advancement. They also do it because they do not want to fail. They fear that if they slow down or take a break someone else will take their place.

In many emerging markets, there is the feeling that WLB is a concept that is valued only in the West; it is of no concern or interest in their own countries. MNEs may have the long-term well-being of their employees in mind, but young professionals in the emerging market subsidiaries must overcome the "we have to catch up with the rest of the world" mentality.

Potential Consequences of Sending an Expatriate on a Foreign Assignment with Inadequate Preparation

Kate Cawthorn, a young British trainee solicitor (attorney), was sent on a traineeship assignment to Ghana on very short notice (three days). Because of the short notice, she was unable to get the necessary vaccinations (her law firm did not provide any advice as to what preparations she should make and gave her no time to prepare) and they provided no support after arrival. On her first day in the country she contracted a severe dose of shigella dysentery. She continued to try to do her job for five weeks, with no medical tests or treatment, but finally needed to fly home for medical care. Her symptoms got worse, which left her unable to complete her internship and thus unable to complete her qualifications to become a solicitor. She never recovered well enough to go back to work. Eventually Kate sued her employer for a high six-figure sum. Not only did her firm not provide adequate preparation and advice, but they also showed too little concern about the implications of the locale of the assignment and its consequences for her career.

Sources: Claus, L. (2010). Duty of Care of Employers for Protecting International Assignees, their Dependants, and International Business Travelers, International SOS White Paper, Trevose, PA: International SOS; Claus, L. and Bucur, S. (2007). Work life balance (WLB) for young professionals in emerging markets, vignette published in Briscoe, D.R., Schuler, R.S., and Claus, L. (2009), *International Human Resource Management*, 3rd ed., London/New York: Routledge, accessible at www.willamette.edu/agsm/global_hr; and Dawood, R. (1998). Bills of health. *HR World*, winter, 57.

Discussion Questions

1 Are WLB issues different in newly developing countries from what is experienced in developed countries? Why or why not? Is there a trade-off between WLB and career ambition?
2 What is an employer's duty to prepare its employees for foreign assignments?
3 What is the employer's responsibility if something happens to its employees while on foreign assignment?
4 What is the responsibility of IHR in both of these circumstances? How could IHR have prevented these situations from occurring and having such dire consequences?

NOTES

1 Source: Roche Corporate Website (www.roche, 2014): http://www.roche.com/sustainability/for_employees/safety_health_wellbeing.htm.
2 Claus, L. (2009). *Duty of Care of employers for Protecting International Assignees, their Dependents, and International Business Travelers*, International SOS White Paper, providing extensive description and analysis of the legal duty of care in a number of countries, Trevose, PA: International SOS; Claus, L. (2010). International assignees at risk. *HR Magazine*, February, 73–75; Ferguson, M.B. and Carlson, M. (2010). *What Every Business Needs to Know about Employment Claims and EPL Insurance*, seminar sponsored by Ireland Stapleton and T. Charles Wilson, March 16, Denver, CO; Lockwood, N.R. (2005). Crisis management in today's business environment: HR's strategic role. *SHRM Research Quarterly*, Fourth Quarter, 1–10; Mair, D. (2008). Global security challenges for travelers and goods, Session 4, Webinar series *Essentials of International Assignment Management*, Oct. 22, IOR Global Services; McLean, D. (2010). *Mitigating Travel Risk for the Enterprise: Innovations to Manage the Duty of Care*, Webinar 10/13/10, presented

by Zurich, www.hr.com; Pomeroy, A. (2007). Protecting employees in harm's way. *HR Magazine*, June, 113–122; Wright, A.D. (2010). Experts: Be prepared when sending employees to disaster areas, downloaded 3/19/2020 from http://www.shrm.org/hrdisciplines/global/Articles/Pages/AidingDisasterVictims.aspx.

3 The most important reference on country health and safety practices is the International Labour Organization's four-volume *Encyclopeadia of Occupational Health and Safety*, by Jeanne Mager and Ed Stellman. The most recent edition is the 4th edition, published in 1998, in Geneva, Switzerland, by the ILO. Current databases, publications on specific aspects of health and safety issues, linkages to other organizations and national health and safety agencies, and other services related to global health and safety, are available at the International Occupational Safety and Health Information Center (CIS) at the ILO. The CIS is a network of health and safety centers from over 100 countries. The CIS's website can be found at: http://www.ilo. org/public/english/protection/safework/cis.

4 Locke, R.M., Fei Qin, Brause, A. (2007). Does monitoring improve labor standards? Lessons from Nike. *Industrial and Labor Relations Review*, 61 (1), 3–31; Roggero, P., Mangiaterra, V., Bustreo, F. and Rosati, F. (2007). The health impact of child labor in developing countries: Evidence from cross-country data. *American Journal of Public Health*, 97 (2), 271–275; Takala, J. (1999). *Introductory Report of the International Labour Office, Occupational Safety and Health Branch*, May, Geneva, CH: International Labour Organization; Wilson, D. (2007). The ratification status of ILO conventions related to occupational safety and health and its relationship with reported occupational fatality rates. *Journal of Occupational Health*, 49 (1), 72–79.

5 Reported in Half of the world's workers employed in risky jobs (1996). *Manpower Argus*, February, 5.

6 See Health and Safety at Work: new EU Strategic Framework 2014–2020. See http://europa.eu/rapid/ press-release_MEMO-14-400_en.htm.

7 See http://europa.eu/rapid/press-release_IP-14-641_en.htm.

8 Morse, T. (2002). International occupational health and safety, on-line lecture, retrieved 7 November 2007 from http://iier.isciii.es/supercourse/lecture/lec8271/001.

9 This section is adapted from Ackers, P. and El-Sawad, A. (2006). Family-friendly policies and work-life balance, chapter 13 in Redman, T. and Wilkinson, A. (eds.), *Contemporary Human Resource Management*, 2nd ed., Essex, England: Prentice-Hall/Financial Times, pp. 331–355; Bardoel, E.A., De Cieri, H. and Tepe, S. (2006). A framework for developing a work/life strategy in a multinational enterprise (MNE), Working Paper 1/06, Monash University, Australia; Daniels, G. and French, S. (2007). The growth of work-life balance and family-friendly policies and the implications for employee relations, in White, G. (ed.), *Family-friendly Employment Policies and Practices: An East-West Perspective on Work-life Balance*, Conference Proceedings, vol. 1, 14th International Employment Relations Association, 19–23 June, Hong Kong; Heinen, B.A. and Mulvaney, R.R.H. (2008), Global factors influencing work-life policies and practices: Description and implications for multinational companies. *World at Work Journal*, First Quarter, 34–43.

10 Claus, L. *An HR Framework for Work/Life Balance: An Exploratory Survey of the CEE Country HR Managers of MNCs*. Paper accepted at the International Human Resource Conference, Tallinn, Estonia, June, 2007.

11 Adapted from MEDEX Assistance Case History (1992), contained in MEDEX Assistance Corporation brochure, Baltimore, MD.

12 American is killed in Mexico City cab holdup (1997). *San Diego Union Tribune*, September 17, A–21; Evans, G. (2001). Last rites, *Global HR*, June, 36–40; Evans, G. (1999). Victim support. *HR World*, May–June, 46–52; Preston, A. (2002). The international assignment taboo: Expatriate death. *KPMG Expatriate Administrator*, summer, 1–3; Tragedy on a Turkish roadway (1998). *USAA Magazine*, March–April, 20–22; York, G. (1996). American's murder sows fear: Moscow a sinister business partner. *Rocky Mountain News*, November 14, 2A, 58A.

13 Evans (2001).

14 Cappelli, P. (2010). The promise and limitations of social media, downloaded 6/3/2010 from http://www. hreonline.com/HRE/printstory.jsp?storyId=432216581; Ciccarelli, M.C. (2010). It's personal: Online

social networking allows HR to identify and build relationships with potential recruits like never before, downloaded 9/27/2010 from http://www.hreonline.com/HRE/printstory.jsp?storyId=532780565; Fraunheim, E. (2006). Bumps in the road to going global: The state of HR technology. *Workforce Management*, Special Report, Oct. 9, 29–32; Freedman, A. (2010). Social media and HR, downloaded 9/27/2010 from http://www.hreonline.com/HRE/printstory.jsp?storyId=511617131; Gray, K.-A.G. (2010). Searching for candidate information, downloaded 1/28/2010 from http://www.hreonline.com/HRE/printstory.jsp?storyId=327202146; iVantage (2010), Go global with iVantage, downloaded 10/27/2010 from http://www.spectrumhr.com/Datasheet_PDFs/Int_article.pdf (description of capabilities for global HRIS through a particular approach offered by Spectrum); Shewmake, A. (2010). Social media recruiting, seminar at Colorado Human Resources Association, March 17, Westminster, CO; Taleo (2010). *Social Network Recruiting: Managing Compliance Issues*, Taleo Business Edition Summary Report, San Francisco: Taleo Corporation.

Chapter 14

Comparative IHRM: Operating in Other Regions and Countries

DHL is present in over 220 countries and territories across the globe, making it the most international company in the world. With a workforce exceeding 315,000 employees . . .

DHL Corporation[1]

Learning Objectives

This chapter will enable the reader to:

- Understand the field of comparative IHRM.
- Understand different types of regions in the world.
- Describe the institutional, economic, and cultural context for IHRM in different regions.
- Describe important features of IHRM in Europe, North America, Asia-Pacific, and Latin America.
- Explain the current debate over the convergence of IHRM across countries and regions.

As discussed in Section 2, there are a variety of environmental conditions that influence the approaches organizations use to manage their human resources. These conditions include exogenous factors such as national cultures, legal environments, institutional pressures, and economic and political conditions. These exogenous factors shape how human resources are managed across geographic boundaries. This chapter introduces the topic and challenges of *comparative IHRM*, which focuses on differences that exist between countries and regions and examines how these differences create similarities and differences in IHRM policies and practices.

Comparative IHRM is a developing field of inquiry—with several scholars, practitioners, and consultants exploring numerous new areas of investigation.[2] The field has grown considerably over the last decade. For example, there is now a dedicated *Handbook of Research on Comparative Human Resource Management*.[3] Several region-specific books by Routledge's Global Series in HRM focus on HRM issues in several area, including Europe, Eastern and Central Europe, Asia-Pacific, Middle East, North America, Latin America, and Africa.[4] There is also a four-volume set in International Human Resource Management that covers a variety of topics in this area,[5] as well as other texts that now focus on comparative HR.[6] It is beyond the scope of this chapter to cover all of the topics in comparative IHRM. Here we briefly introduce some of the issues in specific regions that shape their IHRM policies and practices.

COMPARATIVE IHRM

As the global economy continues to grow, *cultural* and *institutional* differences will continue to influence IHRM policies and practices in multiple and complex ways. As briefly discussed in Chapter 5, the diversity of IHRM policies and practices across nations are often examined using the *convergence* and *divergence* framework.[7] This framework examines how and why certain IHRM policies and practices differ across countries (divergence perspective) or whether or not there is a growing similarity of specific IHRM practice and polices across countries (convergence perspective). Convergence and divergence perspectives represent polar extremes. The convergence perspective suggests that over time organizational structures and business practices and values in differing countries and regions will become similar. The argument is that as institutions (e.g., business organizations) respond to the similar pressures, challenges, and features across countries and regions, they will create a pattern of common usage of HR policies and practices, with the role that MNEs play in creating this convergence being seen as critical. The convergence concept accepts the fact that policies and practices are "in the beginning" quite different—but argues that these differences are being or will be decreased.[8] In contrast, the divergence perspective suggests that institutional, national, and business values are deeply integrated and embedded in a society and resist change to accommodate policies and practices introduced from the outside, e.g., by foreign MNEs. Since most countries have unique institutions and national and business values, these will create and sustain unique national differences.[9]

This issue of convergence versus divergence in IHRM practices and policies around the world is discussed throughout this text as it applies to various IHRM practices and policies.

A Focus on Regionalization

As discussed in Section 1, an important challenge facing IHRM professionals today is to develop a global approach to managing HR within their firms that embraces a few universal principles that give their firms' entire global systems consistency while also allowing local autonomy. Achieving the right balance between centralized consistency and de-centralized autonomy requires continual evaluation and discussion about which policies and practices can be global and which can or should be local. It appears, however, that in order to minimize the complexity of international business, many international firms are seeing the importance of strategically organizing around specific clusters of countries (or geographic regions), such as Latin America, as one market and then to also customize their IHRM policies and practices in order to best serve the employee needs of a particular region. For some organizations it can be difficult to develop IHRM policies and practices that demonstrate consistency throughout the entire global organization—and sometimes even within regions. This results in part from the reality that local conditions relevant to IHRM policies and practices vary so greatly. Thus, as local units align their practices with local conditions, they invariably find themselves having different IHRM practices even across local units within regions.

Specific Regions[10]

A "region" can be described by various attributes such as geography, economic system, institutional structure, governmental jurisdiction, or by social or cultural characteristics.

Regions can be classified according to many criteria.

Micro-regions

A micro-region is usually an area bigger than a municipality but smaller than the state which it is in. The concept of a micro-region is utilized in *The Assembly of European Regions*,[11] which was formed in 1985 and includes regions developed from 35 countries and 15 interregional organizations.[12] Another example of the use of the concept of micro-region includes the "megacities," which include the world's largest cities (each with population of greater than 10 million).[13] Exhibit 14.1 lists the 30 megacities.

Overall, these cities account for more than 1.47 billion people, growing to an estimated 2 billion by 2025, and exhibit a significant portion of the world's economic activity plus a significant portion of the world's wealth.[14]

When a micro-region spreads across two or more countries, it is called a *cross-border region*.[15] Examples include Cascadia (between Canada and the United States), the Lake Constance region (parts of Germany, Switzerland, and Austria), the San Diego–Tijuana region (between the US and Mexico), Bothnian Arc (between Finland and Sweden), Hedmark-Dalarna (between Norway and Sweden), and Helsinki-Tallinn (between Finland and Estonia).[16]

Macro-regions

These regions or clusters include independent countries that share certain attributes such as social, economic, political, geographic, cultural, and historical characteristics. The most

EXHIBIT 14.1: World's 30 Largest Cities (2015 and 2025)

2015 Rank	2015 City	2015 Country	Population (million)	2025 Rank	2025 City	2025 Country	Population (million)
1	Tokyo	Japan	38.20	1	Tokyo	Japan	38.66
2	Delhi	India	25.63	2	Delhi	India	32.94
3	Shanghai	China	22.96	3	Shanghai	China	28.40
4	Ciudad de México (Mexico City)	Mexico	21.71	4	Mumbai (Bombay)	India	26.56
5	New York-Newark	USA	21.33	5	Ciudad de México (Mexico City)	Mexico	24.58
6	Mumbai (Bombay)	India	21.21	6	New York-Newark	USA	23.57
7	São Paulo	Brazil	21.03	7	São Paulo	Brazil	23.17
8	Beijing	China	18.08	8	Dhaka	Bangladesh	22.91
9	Dhaka	Bangladesh	17.38	9	Beijing	China	22.63
10	Karachi	Pakistan	15.50	10	Karachi	Pakistan	20.19
11	Kolkata (Calcutta)	India	15.08	11	Lagos	Nigeria	18.86
12	Buenos Aires	Argentina	14.15	12	Kolkata (Calcutta)	India	18.71
13	Los Angeles-Long Beach-Santa Ana	USA	14.08	13	Manila	Philippines	16.28
14	Lagos	Nigeria	13.12	14	Los Angeles-Long Beach-Santa Ana	USA	15.69
15	Manila	Philippines	12.86	15	Shenzhen	China	15.54
16	Istanbul	Turkey	12.46	16	Buenos Aires	Argentina	15.52
17	Guangzhou, Guangdong	China	12.39	17	Guangzhou, Guangdong	China	15.47
18	Rio de Janeiro	Brazil	12.38	18	Istanbul	Turkey	14.90
19	Shenzhen	China	12.34	19	Al-Qahirah (Cairo)	Egypt	14.74

EXHIBIT 14.1: Continued

2015 Rank	2015 City	2015 Country	Population (million)	2025 Rank	2025 City	2025 Country	Population (million)
20	Moskva (Moscow)	Russian Federation	12.14	20	Kinshasa	Democratic Republic of the Congo	14.54
21	Al-Qahirah (Cairo)	Egypt	11.94	21	Chongqing	China	13.63
22	Osaka-Kobe	Japan	11.78	22	Rio de Janeiro	Brazil	13.62
23	Paris	France	11.10	23	Bangalore	India	13.19
24	Chongqing	China	11.05	24	Jakarta	Indonesia	12.82
25	Jakarta	Indonesia	10.47	25	Chennai (Madras)	India	12.81
26	Kinshasa	Democratic Republic of the Congo	10.31	26	Wuhan	China	12.73
27	Wuhan	China	10.26	27	Moskva (Moscow)	Russian Federation	12.58
28	Chicago	USA	10.20	28	Paris	France	12.16
29	Bangalore	India	10.02	29	Osaka-Kobe	Japan	12.03
30	Chennai (Madras)	India	9.89	30	Tianjin	China	11.93

Source: United Nations, Department of Economic and Social Affairs, Population Division, World Urbanization Prospects: The 2011 Revision, The 30 Largest Urban Agglomerations Ranked by Population Size at each point in time, 2015.

important of these characteristics for the purposes of defining a macro-region include the geographic, economic, and cultural perspectives. Based on the major regions recognized by the United Nations, these macro-regions can be broken down into[17] Africa, Asia, Europe, Latin America and the Caribbean, Northern America, Oceania, and Sub-Saharan Africa. Within each macro-region, countries can be grouped into specific *sub-regions* such as the Middle East, Southeast Asia, and the Far East.

It is beyond the scope of this chapter to discuss IHRM issues in all regions but we do discuss selected IHRM issues in Europe, North America, Middle East, Latin America, Asia, and Africa.

HRM ISSUES IN EUROPE[18]

Europe includes 48 countries with a population of 741 million (2014).[19] Population growth is comparatively slow, and predicted to become negative over the next decades.[20] Exhibit 14.2 provides a snapshot of population and labor force characteristics in Europe. In addition, Exhibit 14.2 provides a labor market analysis in the five most populated countries within Europe.

In general, European countries tend to have low national birth rates with resulting older populations overall.[21] Twenty three percent of Europe's population is over 60 years of age. (For comparative purposes, Asia has 11 percent of the total population over 60 years of age.) It is assumed by demographers that this trend will continue into the future, based on current birth rates: in the year 2050, 34 percent of the total population of Europe will be greater than 60 years old and only 10 percent of the total European population will be between 15 and 24 years old.[22] The median age in the EU is relatively high in relation to the world's other regions (with the 2013 median age in Europe of 40.9 years).[23] Life expectancy at birth is 78, which is predicted to rise to be around 81.3 years by 2045–2050.[24]

An important economic (and increasingly political) region within Europe is the *European Union* formed in 1993 and which today includes 28 countries, with plans to grow to 35 or more countries. These countries are economically and politically linked and operate with a *single market* that allows the free movement of goods, capital, services, and labor within its member countries (with a current population of approximately 507 million).[25] The European Union has 24 official and working languages.[26] These languages include Bulgarian, French, Maltese, Croatian, German, Polish, Czech, Greek, Portuguese, Danish, Hungarian, Romanian, Dutch, Irish, Slovak, English, Italian, Slovene, Estonian, Latvian, Spanish, Finnish, Lithuanian, and Swedish.[27]

Europe (as defined geographically) is a relatively large continent with strong institutional, national, and regional differences. There are a number of regional clusters within Europe and hence the presence of major differences in HRM practices within Europe.[28] From a geographical perspective, Europe can be broadly split into the *North* (e.g., Channel Islands, Denmark, Estonia, Faeroe Islands, Finland, Iceland, Ireland, Isle of Man, Latvia, Lithuania, Norway, Sweden, United Kingdom, and Ireland); *East* (e.g., Belarus, Bulgaria, Czech Republic, Hungary, Poland, Republic of Moldova, Romania, Russian Federation,

EXHIBIT 14.2: Population and Labor Force Characteristics (Europe)

	2014	2030 (Estimated)	2050 (Estimated)
Population[1] (millions)	742	746	726

Age group	2013					2050 (Estimated)				
	0–14	15–24	25–59	60+	80+	0–14	15–24	25–59	60+	80+
Distribution of population (millions)[2]	116	87	370	170	33	109	73	289	238	67

	2013	2050 (Estimated)
Median age[3]	40.9	45.7

	Males (2013)	Females (2013)	Both (2013)
Life expectancy at birth[4]	74	81	78

	2010–2020	2020–2030	2030–2040	2040–2050
Average net number of migrants (thousands)[5]	1119	935	916	905

Labor Market Analysis in the Five Most Populated Countries in Europe

	Population[6] (2014, millions)	Labor force (2012, millions)[7]	Labor force participation rate % (2012)[8]	Net number of migrants (thousands) (2012)[9]	Percentage of workforce aged 25 years and older with upper secondary education[10]
Russia	143.7	76.9	Male (71%), Female (57%)	1,100	16.5% (2010)
Germany	80.9	41.8	Male (66%), Female (54%)	550	50.2% (2012)
France	64.1	30.1	Male (62%), Female (51%)	650	37.7% (2012)
United Kingdom	64.5	32.6	Male (69%), Female (56%)	900	53% (2011)
Italy	61.3	25.1	Male (59%), Female (39%)	900	33.7% (2012)

Classification of countries is based on United Nations categories: *World Population Prospects, The 2012 Revision, Highlights and Advance Tables*, New York, 2013.

Slovakia, and Ukraine); *West* (e.g., Austria, Belgium, France, Germany, Liechtenstein, Luxembourg, Monaco, Netherlands, and Switzerland); and *South* (e.g., Albania, Andorra, Bosnia and Herzegovina, Croatia, Gibraltar, Greece, Holy See, Italy, Malta, Montenegro, Portugal, San Marino, Serbia, Slovenia, Spain, and Macedonia).[29] It is beyond the scope of this chapter to discuss each cluster or country, therefore some generalizations are necessary to discuss HRM issues in Europe.[30]

Three HRM issues are discussed here:

1   government regulations;
2   influence of labor unions; and
3   the flexibility-security nexus.

Government Regulations

European countries in general have *extensive government regulations* in terms of labor standards and legislation. There is a strong tradition of pervasive government regulations that guide labor markets in terms of employee rights, social security provisions, health care/benefits, union negotiating rights, collective agreements, and other industrial relations services.[31] More specifically, when compared to other regions around the world, governments in Europe have more legislative control over employment relationships.[32] For instance, there is considerable focus on laws and regulations that protect employees' rights at work, contract of employment, working time, and health and safety.[33] The influential and extensive labor laws and regulations limit the HRM function's ability to staff, train, and terminate employees. The specific scope and extent of these laws and regulations differ within the various countries of Europe—yet remain extensive throughout. Even so, there is relatively more government and state intervention in Southern Europe while in the North there is relatively more liberalism and a relatively high level of management involvement in HR issues and decision making.[34]

Influence of Labor Unions

In general, European governments provide extensive oversight in governing labor unions, and there is a general sense of responsibility toward various types of employee representation and protection.[35] Labor unions focus on collective bargaining, dialogue between workers and management, and in general on good wages and benefits and good working conditions for employees. Several union confederations belong to *The European Trade Union Confederation* (ETUC), which attempts to "promote the interests of working people at European level and to represent them in the EU institutions."[36] It is important to keep in mind that as laws regulating labor markets differ from country to country, the resulting role and the function of unions will also vary from country to country.[37]

In addition to labor union regulation and empowerment, many European countries as well as the EU itself provide an additional form of employee representation known as *works councils*, which in general include both employer and elected representatives of employees and focus on issues of common interest (see Chapter 7 for a discussion of works councils). These councils concentrate on protecting employee rights, improving communication channels between workers and top management, and have legal powers, in general, to allow the interests of the employees to feature in all major operational decisions.[38] Both labor unions and works councils focus on providing a relatively high degree of job security and protection.[39]

The Flexibility-security Nexus[40]

The flexibility-security nexus refers to the balance needed under the free-trade rules of the EU as well as under global free-market competition to provide the increased flexibility within European labor markets that is necessary to enable global competitiveness—but which may require deregulating the legislative protections for employees.[41] There is evidence in recent years of the development of some increased flexibility. Some countries such as Germany, France, and Spain have made moves toward a more flexible employment contract by relaxing hiring and firing rules, and have facilitated employer recruiting of staff on a part-time or temporary basis.[42] Obviously, the HR function has an important role here to maintain this balance but often the strong government regulations restrict the HRM function's ability to manage this flexibility-security nexus. The role that the HRM function plays here is mostly of a broker between a company's management and the workforce. HRM develops, implements, and maintains policies and processes that reconcile the flexibility and security needs of both management and workers.[43] Here the HRM function can be seen as satisfying the needs of multiple stakeholders while achieving an appropriate balance among three key stakeholders: governments, employers, and employees, as represented by labor unions and works councils.[44]

Balancing the need of multiple stakeholders, however, is an enormous challenge for the HRM function. This is particularly true in Central and Eastern European companies, which usually have less-developed HRM functions and face the many challenges that companies in transition economies face, in general.[45]

HRM ISSUES IN NORTH AMERICA[46]

The North American region generally includes the countries of Bermuda, Canada, Greenland, Saint-Pierre-et-Miquelon, and United States of America, with a total population of about 355 million.[47] Exhibit 14.3 provides a snapshot of population and labor force characteristics in North America. Furthermore, Exhibit 14.3 also provides a labor market analysis for the United States and Canada.

EXHIBIT 14.3: Population and Labor Force Characteristics (North America)

	2014	2030 (Estimated)	2050 (Estimated)
Population[11] (millions)	355	396	444

Age group	2014					2050 (Estimated)				
	0–14	15–24	25–59	60+	80+	0–14	15–24	25–59	60+	80+
Distribution of population (millions) [12]	68	49	168	71	13	80	55	189	122	36

	2013	2050 (Estimated)
Median age[13]	37.7	40.9

	Males (2013)	Females (2013)	Both (2013)
Life expectancy at birth[14]	77	81	79

	2010–2020	2020–2030	2030–2040	2040–2050
Average net number of migrants (thousands)[15]	1220	1200	1200	1200

Labor Market Analysis in the Two Most Populated Countries in North America

	Population[16] (2014, millions)	Labor force (2012, millions)[17]	Labor force participation rate % (2013)[18]	Net number of migrants (thousands) (2012)[19]	Percentage of workforce aged 25 years and older with upper secondary education[20]
USA	317.7	147.1	Male (69%), Female (57%)	5000	47% (2012)
Canada	35.5	19.3	Male (71%), Female (62%)	1100	23% (2011)

Classification of countries is based on United Nations categories (World Population Prospects, The 2012 Revision, New York, 2013).

Some firms now also include Mexico in their internal organizational definition of North America because of the North American Free Trade Agreement (NAFTA), which includes Canada, US, and Mexico (even though, in terms of culture, Mexico would normally be included in the Latin America region). USA has a total population of 317.7 million and Canada has a total population of 35.5 million.[48] For these reasons, many MNEs, for HR planning purposes, view the region of North America in terms of the US and Canada.

Similar to Europe, the population growth in North America is relatively slow, and predicted to stay limited into the future. A substantial percentage (20 percent) of the total population is greater than 60 years old and this percentage is predicted to continue to increase into the future with 27 percent of the total population predicted to be over 60 years old by 2050, and only 12 percent of the total population will be between 15 and 24 years old by 2050.[49] The current median age is 37.7 years of age and predicted to reach 40.9 years of age by 2050.[50] Life expectancy at birth is 79 years of age, which is predicted to rise to be around 83.7 years by 2045–2050.[51]

Four HRM issues are discussed here:

1 intrusiveness of labor laws;
2 levels of unionization;
3 characteristic labor force values; and
4 the view of the HRM function as a strategic business partner.

Perceived Intrusiveness of Labor Laws

In the US, the government is less of a regulator of labor markets than is the case in other regions, particularly when compared to Europe. There are strong labor laws, but relative to European countries, labor laws in the US are less intrusive. Government laws promote and encourage free market forces to resolve many of the labor issues. In addition, the government laws give management great latitude in HR decision making. However, despite the non-interventionist nature of the US legal system there still are strong federal and state laws that provide a variety of rights and protections to workers against unfair, unsafe, and discriminatory employment practices—as well as strong perceptions among many managers that US restrictions are still too onerous. For example, an important force is the anti-discrimination and affirmative action legislation, protecting the rights of a number of "classifications" of workers. In this context the HRM function has a critical role of monitoring the legal and regulatory environment particularly, adherence to the anti-discrimination and affirmative action legislation.

Low Levels of Unionization

Compared to most European countries, the US has relatively *low levels of unionization*. In most industries and firms employers have a minimal influence from trade unions with respect to designing HRM policies and practices to maximize shareholder value.[52] Union membership trends in general show that during the last several years, union membership has declined considerably for a variety of reasons including:[53]

1 a shift from manufacturing to services sectors, with service jobs less likely to be unionized;
2 increase in white collar jobs, which are less likely to be unionized;
3 greater interaction between management and workers due to the general belief by management that treating people better will improve performance and thus there is less interest in the possible protections provided by unions; and
4 federal and state laws that provide legislation and agencies that provide considerable protection to employees such as the Family Medical Leave Act (FMLA) and Occupational Safety and Health Administration (OSHA).

Individualistic and Merit-based Labor Force

The US has a more individualistic and merit-based approach to its labor force than is the case in most other countries.[54] There is considerable focus on the individual's contribution to the organization's success. In the absence of contracts or some type of agreements or understanding that states otherwise, staffing policies and practices are significantly influenced by the *employment-at-will* doctrine, which allows either the employer or the employee to terminate employment without advance notice. Hiring and employee engagement and retention practices are largely influenced by emphasis on employee individual merit. Most employers depend on external labor markets to acquire talent and there is intense competition for acquiring top talent. Many organizations view training and development as a source of competitive advantage and, thus, invest considerable resources in developing individual competencies. Because of this, training of job-related competencies through "on the job training" is an important priority for many organizations. Several organizations have developmental programs that focus on leadership competencies, and again, considerable resources and management time is spent on development activities and responsibilities. As an additional factor in this individualistic and merit-based focus, for many workers, compensation is based on the pay-for-performance model. Employers have considerable freedom to formulate compensation strategies that reflect the current labor market conditions. In this overall employment situation in the US, the nature of employment itself is evolving. There is increased job stress, reduced employee commitment, and changes in employee benefit needs. More employees are focusing on work-life balance issues, with increased childcare and/or elder care responsibilities and increased interest in off-the-job activities.[55] Organizations are recognizing this trend and are focusing on HRM practices and policies that emphasize work-life balance.

HRM Function as a Strategic Partner

In recent years organizations have come to recognize the *HRM function as a strategic partner* that should be involved in the decision-making processes that affect the strategic direction of the organization. There is increasing focus on *HRM systems* rather than on individual HRM policies and practices. Managers are expected to focus on how HRM policies and practices support each other in a system and how HRM systems support an organization's business strategy. There is considerable interest in determining which HRM systems are better than others in terms of improving organizational effectiveness.[56] Along these lines, the HRM function faces considerable pressures to show (in the short term) the financial impact of these systems. HR professionals are expected to design metrics or measures to capture the impact of HRM systems on financial measures and demonstrate the ROI (return on investment) of HR policies.[57]

HRM ISSUES IN ASIA[58]

Asia is a large continent with a total population today of around 4 billion—and predicted to reach over 5 billion by 2050.[59] Exhibit 14.4 illustrates a snapshot of population and labor force characteristics in Asia. Additionally, Exhibit 14.4 provides a labor market analysis in the five most populated countries in Asia: China, India, Indonesia, Pakistan, and Bangladesh.

Currently, 17 percent of the total population is between 15 and 24 years of age and only 11 percent of the total population is greater than 60 years old. By 2050, 12 percent of the total population is predicted to be between 15 and 24 years old and 24 percent of the total population will be greater than 60 years old.[60] The current median age is 29.7 years of age and is predicted to reach 39.8 years of age by 2050.[61] Life expectancy at birth is 71 years old, which is relatively lower than Europe and North America and is predicted to reach around 76.9 by 2045–2050.[62]

There are various regional clusters in Asia. The *East Asian region* includes China, Hong Kong, North Korea, South Korea, Japan, and Mongolia. The *South-central Asian region* includes Afghanistan, Bangladesh, Bhutan, India, Iran, Kazakhstan, Kyrgyzstan, Maldives, Nepal, Pakistan, Sri Lanka, Tajikistan, Turkmenistan, and Uzbekistan. The *Southeast Asian region* includes Brunei Darussalam, Cambodia, Indonesia, Lao People's Democratic Republic, Malaysia, Myanmar, Philippines, Singapore, Thailand, Timor-Leste, and Vietnam. And the *West Asian region* (also referred to as the Middle East) includes Armenia, Azerbaijan, Bahrain, Cyprus, Georgia, Iraq, Israel, Jordan, Kuwait, Lebanon, Palestinian Territory, Oman, Qatar, Saudi Arabia, Syria, Turkey, United Arab Emirates, and Yemen. As a result of these regional clusters, it is important to understand that there are substantial differences in HRM within Asia—within regions and within countries within regions.

EXHIBIT 14.4: Population and Labor Force Characteristics (Asia)

	2014	2030 (Estimated)	2050 (Estimated)
Population[21] (millions)	4351	4907	5252

Age group	2013					2050 (Estimated)				
	0–14	15–24	25–59	60+	80+	0–14	15–24	25–59	60+	80+
Distribution of population (millions) [22]	1065	738	2027	469	58	925	642	2357	1239	220

	2013	2050 (Estimated)
Median age[23]	29.7	39.8

	Males (2013)	Females (2013)	Both (2013)
Life expectancy at birth[24]	69	73	71

	2010–2020	2020–2030	2030–2040	2040–2050
Average annual net number of migrants (thousands)[25]	–1397	–1256	–1245	–1233

Labor Market Analysis in the Five Most Populated Countries in Asia

	Population[26] (2014, millions)	Labor force (2012, millions)[27]	Labor force participation rate % (2013)[28]	Net number of migrants (thousands) (2012)[29]	Percentage of workforce aged 25 years and older with upper secondary education[30]
China	1364.1	787.6	Male (78%), Female (64%)	–1,500	13.5% (2010)
India	1296.2	484.3	Male (81%), Female (29%)	–2,294	na
Indonesia	251.5	118.4	Male (84%), Female (51%)	–700	21.1% (2011)
Pakistan	194	63.8	Male (83%), Female (24%)	–1,634	16.8% (2011)
Bangladesh	158.5	76	Male (84%), Female (57%)	–2,041	na

Classification of countries is based on United Nations categories (World Population Prospects, The 2012 Revision, New York, 2013).

Each region described above differs from the other regions in many ways. Each possesses its own set of environmental factors such as historic, economic, societal, and political components that impact HRM policies and practices.[63] Countries within each sub-region are also at different stages of industrial development, economic growth, and political development.[64] It is beyond the scope of this chapter to focus on each sub-region or countries within each sub-region. We examine one sub-region, the *Asia Pacific region*, which has, over the last two decades, seen an enormous level of economic growth and development.[65] Asia Pacific generally includes China, South Korea, Japan, Hong Kong, Taiwan, India, Thailand, Vietnam, Malaysia, Singapore, and Australia.[66] This sub-region produces more goods and services than North America and Europe, has several countries that appear on the emerging markets lists every year,[67] and attracts a large amount of foreign direct investment.[68]

Five HRM issues are discussed in this section:

1 shift to free-market policies;
2 transition from collectivist to individualist cultural values;
3 influence of labor unions;
4 changes in the traditional employment contract; and
5 challenges associated with talent flow.

Shift to Free-Market Policies

Relative to other regions (e.g., Europe and North America), HRM in Asian Pacific countries has been strongly shaped by globalization, technology, and the communication revolution. During the last few decades, both public and private sectors in countries like South Korea, Hong Kong, Singapore, Taiwan, Thailand, China, and India have witnessed enormous changes in HRM, employee relations, industrial relations, and labor legislation as a result of these macro-level pressures. In response to these pressures as well as to the recent economic and financial recession, in most Asian Pacific countries there seems to be a gradual *shift to free-market policies*. The burden of retirement planning and other employee benefits is moving from employers to individuals. In addition, there is the privatizing of many government-owned enterprises, the downsizing of organizations, and relatively greater job insecurity for workers in general.[69]

Transition from Collectivist to Individualist Cultural Values

The transition from collectivism to individualism in HRM policies and practices, especially in countries such as Japan, India, China, and Vietnam, is an important issue. The HRM function plays a significant role in developing a culture that focuses on individual contributions rather than group efforts. This has major implications for HR practices such as compensation, promotions, and other employee benefits. In countries such as China, a hybrid HRM system appears to be emerging.[70] There seems to be a simultaneous development of government initiated and controlled labor regulations and free-market-based HRM policies and practices.[71]

As a result of the low growth, globalization, international competitiveness, and the recent economic and financial recession, several organizations in countries such as Japan are finding it necessary to adjust to the new reality, which has led to the redesign of many of their traditional HRM practices such as lifetime employment and promotion based on tenure and seniority.[72] Organizations are finding that it is no longer feasible or cost-effective to afford these traditional HRM practices.[73] There are clear pressures to move toward merit-based and performance-oriented management processes. From an employee's perspective, however, this movement away from the traditional collectivist-oriented employment contract constitutes a violation of the *psychological contract*,[74] which is defined as a set of expectations employees have from employers. This trend can negatively affect the motivation, loyalty, productivity, morale, and expectations of employees. Interestingly, this shift is also taking place in several European countries. This is an enormous challenge for the HR function, in both Asian countries and European countries. The HRM function, for example, has to manage employee reactions and behaviors with respect to perceived violations of the psychological contract.[75]

Varied Influence of Labor Unions

Similar to Europe, the structure and *influence of labor unions* varies from country to country in the Asia-Pacific region.[76] For example, labor unions are relatively stronger in Japan, Singapore, and Australia than in Malaysia and Korea. But overall, the influence of labor unions is declining over time (except maybe in former socialist states where free-market unions are evolving to replace the form of unions that existed under socialism). There are several reasons for this trend:[77]

1   restrictive labor legislation;
2   anti-union government policies that discourage workers' representation;
3   lack of effective union leadership;
4   close alignment with political and religious parties leading to rivalries between unions and political leaders; and
5   lack of representation from all age groups, both genders, and from people from all socio-economic backgrounds.

Challenges Associated with Talent Flow

Another important HRM issue in the Asia Pacific region is the management of the *challenges associated with talent flow*, which refers to the migration of talented individuals between countries for a variety of reasons, such as to undertake advanced studies abroad and/or acquire foreign work experience, and then subsequently return to their country of origin to take advantage of economic opportunities and development.[78] Most of the Asian Pacific countries are witnessing the emergence of knowledge incentive sectors, and the notion of talent flow can be seen in this sector. In countries such as India, China, Taiwan, Singapore, and South Korea, high-tech industries are developing that are trying to attract back natives trained overseas.[79] An important challenge for the HRM function in this situation is the training and development of individuals moving back home and from country to country. Another challenge is the retention of individuals: what policies and practices can prevent individuals from leaving organizations? Countries such as Singapore and Hong Kong are concentrating on national strategies that will support and enhance talent development and life-long learning.[80]

HRM ISSUES IN LATIN AMERICA AND THE CARIBBEAN[81]

Latin America and the Caribbean have a total population of 618 million. Exhibit 14.5 displays the population and labor force characteristics in Latin America and the Caribbean. Additionally, Exhibit 14.5 provides a labor market analysis in the five most populated countries in Latin America: Brazil, Mexico, Colombia, Argentina, and Peru.

In this region 18 percent of the total population is between the ages of 15 and 24 years old and 11 percent of the population over 60 years old.[82] Similar to the trends in Asia, the predictions indicate that by 2050, 12 percent of the total population will be between 15 and 24 years old and 27 percent of the total population will be over 60 years of age.[83] Similar to Asia, life expectancy at birth is 75 years old and predicted to be 81.8 years old by 2045–2050.[84] The current median age is considerably lower than Europe, North America, and Asia, due to high birth rates and very young populations, standing at 28.3 years of age and predicted to only reach 40.6 years of age by 2050.[85]

There are various regional clusters in Latin America and the Caribbean. The *Caribbean region* includes many small island nations and territories, including Anguilla, Antigua and Barbuda, Aruba, Bahamas, Barbados, British Virgin Islands, Cayman Islands, Cuba, Dominica, Dominican Republic, Grenada, Guadeloupe, Haiti, Jamaica, Martinique, Montserrat, Netherlands Antilles, Puerto Rico, Saint Kitts and Nevis, Saint Lucia, Saint Vincent and the Grenadines, Trinidad and Tobago, Turks and Caicos Islands, and the United States Virgin Islands. The *Central American region* includes Belize, Costa Rica, El Salvador, Guatemala, Honduras, Mexico, Nicaragua, and Panama. The *South American region* includes Argentina, Bolivia, Brazil, Chile, Colombia, Ecuador, Falkland Islands, French Guiana, Guyana, Paraguay, Peru, Suriname, Uruguay, and Venezuela. Of course, there are other sub-regions within these regions as well.

Four HRM issues are discussed here:

1   the transitional role of labor unions;
2   family-oriented work values;
3   a person-centered view of HRM; and
4   emergence of an informal economy.

EXHIBIT 14.5: Population and Labor Force Characteristics (Latin America and Caribbean)

	2014	2030 (Estimated)	2050 (Estimated)
Population[31] (millions)	618	710	773

Age group	2013					2050 (Estimated)				
	0–14	15–24	25–59	60+	80+	0–14	15–24	25–59	60+	80+
Distribution of population (millions)[32]	166	109	276	65	10	137	97	351	196	44

	2013	2050 (Estimated)
Median age[33]	28.3	40.6

	Males (2013)	Females (2013)	Both (2013)
Life expectancy at birth[34]	71	78	75

	2010–2020	2020–2030	2030–2040	2040–2050
Average annual net number of migrants (thousands)[35]	–609	–533	–525	–526

Labor Market Analysis in the Five Most Populated Countries in Latin America and Caribbean

	Population[36] (2014, millions)	Labor force (2012, millions)[37]	Labor force participation rate % (2013)[38]	Net number of migrants (thousands) (2012)[39]	Percentage of workforce aged 25 years and older with upper secondary education[40]
Brazil	202.8	104.7	Male (81%), Female (60%)	–190	27.9%
Mexico	119.7	52.8	Male (80%), Female (45%)	–1200	17.5% (2012)
Colombia	47.7	23.1	Male (80%), Female (56%)	–120	22.1% (2011)
Argentina	42.7	18.9	Male (75%), Female (47%)	–100	na
Peru	30.8	16.2	Male (84%), Female (68%)	–300	33.8% (2012)

Classification of countries is based on United Nations categories (World Population Prospects, The 2012 Revision, New York, 2013).

Labor Unions' Transitional Role

Latin American countries in general have interventionist and authoritarian governments that strongly regulate the economy, labor markets, and organizational relationships in general.[86] Similar to trends in other regions (e.g., Europe and Asia Pacific), the role of labor unions in Latin America differs from country to country.[87] In general, labor unions are usually organized by type of firm or industry sector.[88] Historically labor unions have focused on creating jobs and job security for their members.[89] In terms of their influence on management, there is a clear public sector/private sector divide. Labor unions are much stronger in the public sector and have built a stronghold in government-owned companies. In the private sector, labor unions are much weaker. There are three important reasons:

1 private sector organizations are more active in their labor relations activities;[90]
2 private sector organizations are more likely to use effective union avoidance tactics;[91] and
3 because of employment security concerns in the private sector, labor unions have been careful with the collective bargaining process by focusing more on maintaining employment security and less on maintaining certain benefits for their members.[92]

Unions' influence on management, particularly in the private sector, has been threatened by alternative movements such as the *solidarismo movement* (anti-union forces) in Central America.[93] Workers can become members of solidarismo associations that provide workers with certain benefits, and in exchange, workers agree not to engage in any strike or interruption of work.[94]

Family-oriented Work Values

There is a strong collectivistic and a paternalistic attitude toward work values in Latin American countries. Organizations focus more on paternalistic leadership than on individuals' autonomy. The role of the Latin American manager/supervisor is that of a "father" to protect his/her subordinates, and the role of the organization is that of a "family" where employees trust each other and depend on each other for support.[95] At the same time, however, Latin American workers also value hierarchy as an important work value, which to them defines status and social distance between a manager and his/her subordinates; confrontation with superiors is discouraged and considered as an act of disobedience by management.[96] There is also considerable emphasis on symbolic attributes such as job titles, level of positions, and additional benefits, as these reflect the social status of an individual.[97]

HRM practices and policies[98] reflect collectivism as well as the strong family orientation. Staffing practices and decisions are generally based on individual traits such as personality traits and physical characteristics. Personal relationships and ties with wealthy families greatly influence promotion and career progression decisions. Internal recruiting is preferred with a focus on recruiting employees from elsewhere in the organization. Hiring family members or close relatives is a norm and this preserves the family traditions in the workplace. Similarly, social relationships influence the selection processes and decisions. The training and development function is less developed than in other regions. With respect to rewards and recognition, group and seniority recognitions are preferred over performance appraisals of individual accomplishments. Benefits include health care, food bonds, children's scholarships, discounts for school material and clothes, and mortgage credit. There is strong concern for a good quality of life for employees.

Person-Centered View of HR[99]

Work plays an important and a pivotal role in Latin American life. But the direction of the relationship is from work to life. As noted earlier, the meaning of work is to create a good quality of life. As the saying goes, people work to live (not live to work, as is the case in some countries in other regions of the world). This creates an implicit social contract between employers and their employees. The employment contract in Latin America reflects the involvement of firms in their workers' lives and highlights the fact that employers must provide for both social and economic needs. The HRM function acts as an advocate of the employee and its practices center around the employee.[100] The HRM policies and practices focus on values important to the employee, such as the welfare of individuals and their families, and on the creation of an organizational climate that promotes cohesion, teamwork, and a strong sense of community.

Similar to numerous other organizations worldwide, Latin American organizations also face serious macro-level pressures (e.g., recession, downsizing, privatization, de-regulation, globalization, etc.), which threaten the work values of this paternalistic system that has nurtured employment or job security, low unemployment levels, and protection of workers by unions and other regulations. Preserving this person-centered view of the role of HRM is a serious challenge for the HRM function and is being seriously threatened. The transition from paternalism and person-centered HRM to a performance-driven approach requires a delicate balance between employee interests and employee performance. Otherwise, moving away from a paternalistic system will be seen as a violation of workers' implicit social contract, which can result in low levels of commitment, loyalty, motivation, and productivity.[101]

Emergence of an Informal Economy

Throughout Latin America, an informal economy—defined as an economic sector that is not monitored or regulated by the government—has emerged. Some workers prefer this form of labor market. In some countries, the minimum wage is more likely to be paid to informal labor than to workers in the regular labor market. Self-employed workers can earn more money through the informal sector than in the regular labor market. The informal economy is a serious issue and not a temporary phenomenon.[102] Economists predict that it may continue to grow if economic growth in Latin American countries is not accompanied by improvements in employment levels and income distribution. The situation is therefore that the informal economy is continuously increasing in most developing countries, even in rural areas.[103] Estimates show that the informal workforce, as a share of nonagricultural employment, is 78 percent in Africa, 57 percent in Latin America and the Caribbean, and 45–85 percent in Asia.[104] For the HRM function, informal labor markets have serious implications to how organizations attract and recruit employees.

HRM ISSUES IN AFRICA[105]

The one region of the world that has received the least attention from a business perspective—and from an HRM perspective—is Africa. The African "region" is generally described in terms of five independent regions: North Africa, East Africa, Middle Africa, West Africa, and Southern Africa,[106] with a total population as of 2012 of about 1,136 million.[107] For many reasons, some of which will be discussed in this chapter, the continent of Africa has, at least until quite recently, received less attention in the globalization of commerce, than has been the case for most of the rest of the world. However, this is beginning to change. In this section we will describe the changing Africa and discuss the major challenges being faced there today by MNEs and HRM.

First, we will provide a description of the characteristics of the population of Africa. Exhibit 14.6 shows the population and labor force characteristics, and provides a labor market analysis of the five countries with the highest populations: Nigeria, Ethiopia, Egypt, Democratic Republic of Congo, and South Africa.

In terms of age, 20 percent of the population in Africa is between the ages of 15 and 24 years old, 34 percent of the population is between 25 and 59 years old, and only 5.4 percent of the population is over 60 years old.[108] Thus approximately one-third of the African population falls in the traditional main working age group. It is predicted that by 2050, 18 percent of the total population will be between 15 and 24 years old, 41 percent of the population will be between 25 and 59 years old, and 8.9 percent of the population will be over 60 years old.[109] Life expectancy at birth is 59 years old and predicted to be 68.9 years old by 2045–2050.[110] The current median age is considerably lower than that in Europe, North America, and Asia, standing at 19.4 years of age and predicted to only reach 24.7 years of age by 2050,[111] which indicates a quite young population.

A number of core issues have emerged over the years that are related to IHRM. Here we briefly discuss four HRM issues:

1   a growing workforce;
2   tribal work values;
3   Asia-Africa alliances and partnerships; and
4   human resource development.

EXHIBIT 14.6: Population and Labor Force Characteristics (Africa)

	2014	2030 (Estimated)	2050 (Estimated)
Population[41] (millions)	1,136	1,637	2,428

Age group	2014					2050 (Estimated)				
	0–14	15–24	25–59	60+	80+	0–14	15–24	25–59	60+	80+
Distribution of population (millions) [42]	454	217	380	60	5	771	437	973	212	20

	2013	2050 (Estimated)
Median age[43]	19.4	24.7

	Males (2013)	Females (2013)	Both (2013)
Life expectancy at birth[44]	58	60	59

	2010–2020	2020–2030	2030–2040	2040–2050
Average annual net number of migrants (thousands)[45]	–484	–497	–499	–498

Labor Market Analysis in the Five Most Populated Countries in Africa

	Population[46] (2014, millions)	Labor force (2012, millions)[47]	Labor force participation rate% (2013)[48]	Net number of migrants (thousands) (2012)[49]	Percentage of workforce aged 25 years and older with upper secondary education[50]
Nigeria	177.5	52.6	56.1	–300	na
Ethiopia	95.9	43.6	83.7	–60	2.9 (2011)
Egypt	87.9	27.2	49.1	–216	na
Democratic Republic of the Congo	71.2	25.9	71.9	–75	na
South Africa	53.7	19.1	52.1	–100	47.2 (2012)

Classification of countries is based on United Nations categories (World Population Prospects, The 2012 Revision, New York, 2013).

A Growing Workforce

Economic growth in Africa is accelerating. Several African countries are witnessing significant economic growth and progress (e.g., 54 African countries with an annual GDP growth of greater than 6 percent).[112] In fact, Africa has grown considerably during the last decade in terms of economic growth, sub-Saharan Africa has grown from US$344 billion (2000) to US$1,334 billion (2012), and it is predicted that output will reach US$1,877 billion by the year 2017.[113] Similarly, the population of Africa is continuing to grow quite rapidly with estimation of a workforce of one billion Africans by 2050.[114] Moreover, there is ongoing and increasing urbanization—the African content has 52 cities with one million or more people.[115] One consequence of this growth and rapid urbanization is an extremely large non-agricultural workforce in this decade and during the next several decades. With a large workforce and urban population comes the need for *increased infrastructure, education, health care, consumer goods, and retail—and because of the economic growth created by providing for these needs, the hope is that the resources will be created to pay for it.*[116] In addition, a large workforce faces several challenges such as a rapidly changing work environment, the rise of technology, and the need for new skills.[117]

One example of the development of the infrastructure needed to support the improving economies and workforces is the level of new connection being provided by technology:

> There were 778 million mobile subscriptions in Africa at end-June 2013 and the continent's mobile-subscription count will reach one billion during 2015 and 1.2 billion by end-2018, according to forecasts by Informa Telecoms & Media.
> (Africa Telecoms Outlook, 2014, p. 8)[118]

For MNEs, the availability of a large workforce that is mobile and technologically savvy allows for the potential to decrease costs and expenses, and to increase productivity.

Tribal Values

Africa is a continent of not only many countries (54) but it is also a continent with many cultures.[119] Therefore, it is incorrect to assume *homogeneity between countries, as well as within countries—many African countries differ from each other and have diverse groups values within them.*[120] For example, the cultures of the countries of northern Africa (Chad, Gambia, Mali, Niger, Senegal, Mauritania, Morocco, Algeria, Tunisia, Libya, Egypt, and northern Sudan) are closer to the Middle Eastern cultures (Muslim, Arab) than to the cultures of sub-Saharan (West, Middle, East, and Southern) Africa. In this section we primarily focus on the cultures of sub-Saharan Africa. Because of this diversity, it is necessary to be careful about generalizations.

The basic unit of sub-Saharan African society is the family, which includes the nuclear family and the extended family or tribe. The tribe is similar to a nation but does not have physical boundaries, like countries.[121] Tribes have collective solidarity, a strong network of interrelationships, and mutual obligations.[122] In traditional African society, the tribe is the most important community—obviously and typically more important than their country of citizenship.[123]

Despite the increasing urbanization (e.g., people moving from villages to cities), most people still try to maintain their family and tribal ties. There is a sense of responsibility to support family members who are still "back home" in the villages. It also affects Africans' attitudes about their business relationships with customers as well as their managers from abroad in terms of marketing and hiring practices.[124]

Asia-Africa Alliances and Partnerships

From an investment and trade perspective, countries in Asia have shown considerable interest in Africa, most specifically India and China.[125] China in particular has significant investments in Africa with the volume of trade between countries in Africa and China showing an exponential growth over the last several years (particularly in the commodities that China's growing economy so desperately needs).[126]

Trade ties between African countries present significant new opportunities. Yet much of the economic growth in Africa is coming from trade with countries and MNEs outside Africa. In particular, ties with Asian countries are producing much of this growth. Because of the nature of this trade, African firms and foreign MNE subsidiaries are having to develop human resource practices that bring modern workforce practices to Africa.

Even though Africa has benefited from significant investments by companies in India, Malaysia, and Singapore, Chinese organizations have had the most significant investments in Africa.[127] Initially, the Chinese methods of engaging in African markets were met with some level of resentment from local communities due to the culturally insensitive procedures employed by Chinese investors, including the heavy use of imported Chinese workers, particularly in infrastructure investments in North Africa. However, in recent years a more sophisticated approach has emerged in Chinese FDI practices—with more reliance on local hires, particularly in sub-Saharan investments, which have been welcomed by most African peoples. The investment strategies of Chinese MNEs have shifted in focus and are geared towards developing an infrastructure that goes beyond commodity extraction but instead involves the development of a production and service sector in the host African countries.

Human Resource Development

As multinational firms from South Africa and outside Africa expand their operations across the African continent, their needs for effective human resource management practices, including employee and talent development, are becoming increasingly apparent and important in order for their businesses to succeed.[128] There is an urgent need to improve talent management and for executives and human resource professionals to foster the creation and retention of capable African talent.[129] However, there are challenges:

- Only 62 percent of African adults (15 + years of age) are literate (female = 58 percent, male = 70 percent[130]).
- Literacy rates range from 90.70 percent (Zimbabwe) to 21.80 percent (Burkina Faso). Approximately 15 countries have adult literacy rates that are below 50 percent[131]
- Africa is also ranked lowest in the regional rankings of the 2011 and 2015 "global talent index." However, within Africa there is considerable disparity between countries.[132] For example, in a comparison between two major African countries: South Africa and Nigeria

> A sizeable disparity separates the two African nations. . . . South Africa's relatively high spending on education as a proportion of its GDP reveals the intention to develop its talent potential, whereas Nigeria finds itself at or near the bottom of the index in both 2011 and 2015, despite rapid population growth.
> (The Global Talent Index report: The Outlook to 2015, p. 9)[133]

Nevertheless, there is optimism. Public spending on education in Africa has increased over the last decade and is increasing each year. For example, public spending on education (total percentage of government expenditure) in South Africa has gone from 18 percent (2008) to 21 percent (2012).[134] In addition, there is much discussion among professionals, government officials, and academics about the need for talent development.[135] Some of the themes that have emerged include:

- Developing competencies such as entrepreneurial and leadership capabilities among the younger workers should be a priority at the national level (e.g., governments should allocate resources to human capital development).[136]
- The advantages of skills retention and talent development is appreciated and understood by African multinational corporations.
- In general people should be aware of the importance of skills and knowledge.
- Develop strategies to accelerate the learning of important competencies.
- Start developing leadership capability at a young age.
- Realization that there is a shortage of talent, and it is expensive to acquire and retain talent.[137]
- Focus on action learning as a strategy to develop talent.
- Encourage expatriates to return home and transfer the acquired skills.
- Acquire talent from outside Africa.
- Emphasize learning from skills transfer.
- Focus on region-specific competencies that are becoming increasingly important for success. Regions include China, India, and Singapore, for example.

Major Environmental Challenges[138]

Africa is considered a challenging continent in which to conduct business.[139] Despite the growth in population, workforce, and GDP, there are major challenges facing Africa.[140] These include political, trade, and social issues.

Political

Over the last several years African countries in general have become more politically stable. Governments across Africa are now widely aligned with market economics. The number of political coups has declined considerably since 1990.[141] In addition, there is considerable effort in several African countries to improve their democratic structures and procedures, which has resulted in more stable political conditions. For example, Kenya created a new constitution in 2010, which includes an overhaul of the judiciary system and an explicit code of ethics for political and business leaders. Elections are held more regularly in many countries, establishing governments for five-year periods, increasing predictability and stability.[142] Similarly, Tunisia passed a new constitution in 2014,[143] and Zimbabwe's new constitution was passed in 2013.[144]

Trade

Trading with Africa is challenging. Africa deals with a number of economic challenges in the development of its national and international markets. First, there is lack of predictability in the economic and market developments, which creates business environments that are highly risky, especially for MNEs seeking to invest in Africa. Second, the judicial systems are less reliable in many African nations, making contractual negotiations more complicated for MNEs. Third, most sub-Saharan African nations are ranked outside the top 100 for the ease of doing business by the World Bank (2014).[145]

Social

The social problems in Africa are staggering. Even though the majority of the African population is rural, migration to the cities is increasing, creating both challenges and opportunities.[146] Most African nations lack adequate, developed, and sufficient infrastructure[147] to accommodate and support MNEs in their efforts to expand into local markets.[148] For instance, the availability of and access to clean water, education (elementary, secondary, and post-secondary), adequate road systems, a reliable power supply and communication system, financial and banking institutions, and health services (for example, Africa has the highest risk of death from non-communicable diseases, such as HIV and Ebola)[149] are limited in many areas of the continent, and modern legal systems to uphold and enforce investments are only now being developed in many countries.

There are also issues related to a growing population, especially a younger workforce that requires access to education, jobs, and higher levels of skill and competencies.[150] Most importantly, lack of jobs and work opportunity—particularly for young people—can lead to social unrest.[151]

CONSIDERATIONS WHEN DESIGNING IHR POLICIES AND PRACTICES

As mentioned earlier, one needs to be careful about generalizations in Africa. Below is a list of general African values that can be helpfully taken into consideration when designing IHRM policies and practices:[152]

- employee tribal loyalties;
- adherence to social obligations;
- primary trust as a tribe;
- deference to seniority;
- reciprocity is sacred;
- good social and personal relations;
- cultural ethnocentric mindset;
- importance of diversity;
- preferences for particular ethnic groups or family members of an ethnic group;
- Africanization—that is, localization;
- high collectivism and group solidarity tendencies.

From a talent planning perspective, three employee groups emerge:[153] *local employees* (these include local nationals), *local-plus employees* (these include returning nationals who studied or worked overseas—can also be referred to as "returning diaspora"),[154] *international or global assignees* (these include individuals from any nationality).

It is important to remember that there is increasing political pressure on global companies to localize so focusing on local employees and/or local plus employees is preferred.[155] In addition, it is critical to facilitate the transfer of skills from international or global assignees to local employees.[156]

IHRM AND THE CONVERGENCE/DIVERGENCE DEBATE AMONG REGIONS[157]

As the above discussion suggests, there are certain HRM issues that are converging across regions and countries, such as the shift to a more performance-driven HRM function and certain HRM issues that are diverging across regions and countries such as the influence of labor unions. But the convergence/divergence debate is still ongoing and the answer to the question of the prominence of convergence depends on what data and results one looks at and who one asks.

With respect to HRM policies and practices, it is possible that there is more convergence in HRM polices than in HRM practices. It seems that HRM practices diverge considerably across regions and countries. An example would include an HRM policy of providing mandatory safety training across business units and subsidiaries. Under such a policy, there would be a convergence of safety training policy across regions and countries. How that safety training is administered and how much training is provided diverges across regions and countries.

There is also the issue of divergence between regions and within a region. There are two possibilities: there is more divergence between regions than within a region or there is less divergence between regions than within a region. Which is the case depends on the type of HRM practice. Some HRM practices will diverge more than others.

CONCLUSIONS

International enterprises have the necessity to understand local HR policies and practices so as to make intelligent decisions as to the practical fit of headquarters' policies with tradition and law in local jurisdictions. *Comparative IHRM* focuses on differences that exist between countries/regions and examines how these differences create the similarities and difference in IHRM policies and practices across countries and regions. This chapter provided an overview of the wide variances in HR practices from country to country and region to region. First the chapter described the meaning of the term "region" and explained the differences between macro- and micro-regions. Then the chapter focused on five specific regions: Europe, North America, Asia, Latin America, and Africa. Within each region, key HRM issues were examined with implications for HRM policies and practices.

DISCUSSION QUESTIONS

1   What are the major differences between macro- and micro-regions?
2   Moving to a performance-based HRM system seems to be an issue in many regions and countries such as Asia Pacific and Europe. What are some of the barriers organizations can face when trying to move to a performance-based HRM system?
3   It seems that some countries like China may be developing "hybrid HRM systems." What are some of the advantages and disadvantages of the hybrid HRM system?
4   In many regions and countries governments face pressures to increase the age when a person can retire. What are major implications for raising the retirement age from: a) a MNE's perspective? and b) the HRM manager's perspective?

CASE STUDY 14.1: The Impact of HR on Innovation: A Six-Country Comparison (Global)

Innovation is increasingly seen as a central need for economic growth and vitality for countries as well as for businesses and it now seems as though everyone wants to contribute. Continuous improvement in technology and business processes is vital to economic prosperity as well as to the ability to be competitive. The ability of governments, businesses, and individuals to identify, respond to, and especially to introduce change is the bedrock of competitive ability. And now we are seeing such abilities developing in new places, making global competition increasingly strong. For example, in the words of *The Economist*, "the emerging world, long a source of cheap labor, now rivals the rich countries for business innovation."[158] In the 2010 *Bloomberg Business Week* annual rankings of Most Innovative Companies, 15 of the Top 50 are Asian. For the first time, the majority of corporations in the Top 25 are based outside the US. Just as countries vary in their values and infrastructure for nurturing innovation, so also do firms. And, presumably, HR managers and their practices have a lot to do with the ability of firms to sustain innovation so as to achieve strategic competitive advantage in the global marketplace.

From a country's point of view, best practices in innovation include:

- Investment in the quality of human resources for innovation:

    - ❏ Enhance the capabilities of people:
        - – Training, education, internships, knowledge sharing and transfer, investment in knowledge
        - – Benefits for ambitious and talented students; employees
        - – Lifelong learning.

- Efforts to increase the number of young people entering science, engineering, and technology (SET) careers and those who work in SET.
- National plans for job creation and retention, reducing unemployment; cooperation between enterprises and universities, between government and enterprises, providing benefits for small enterprises (e.g., easier business development, reduced taxes for job creation).
- Investments in productivity improvements:

    - ❏ research and development; seed grants for new technology
    - ❏ focus on knowledge creation, intellectual property, patents, human capital
    - ❏ national talent management strategies
    - ❏ support for entrepreneurship/intrapreneurship; easier access to resources;
    - ❏ freedom of trial and error.

Countries differ considerably in their support of these practices and, thus, in their overall levels of innovation and the resulting competitive abilities. Nevertheless, many countries are quite aware of the necessity for actions to improve their national capacities for innovation. Here is a summary of some of the various practices supported in a few (six) select countries:

1   Poland: limited SET initiatives but increased focus on business training and business intern-ships in SET, with scholarships for PhD programs in strategically defined SET fields. No major efforts to support training to reduce unemployment. Level of tertiary education well below the European norm.

2   Germany: new efforts to open the German labor market to more foreign experts (Green Card program); initiatives to attract young people to enter SET fields; many efforts to improve overall education programs at all levels, structural reforms to ease labor mobility. National focus on internship programs for skill building is very effective for existing skills but not so good for new technologies and innovations.

3   Sweden: emphasis on new forms of cooperation between small enterprises and universi-ties in an effort to increase number of students in SET; seed financing for job creation and stimuli for R&D in small and medium-sized firms. However, job creation is a problem.

4   Spain: entrepreneurship program to diminish levels of school dropouts, increased quality of higher education, provide lifelong education and training for everyone (but invests only 52 percent of European average on these efforts). Lifelong learning efforts below European norms.

5   Canada: efforts to increase numbers of SET graduates (by 5 percent a year) and to reduce amount of talent leaving the country; strong efforts to support academic research.

6   Netherlands: increase the number of SET graduates and to hold on to SET workers through increased possibilities for mobility and offer of greater benefits for students entering SET. High labor productivity yet lower productivity growth in recent years.

From a management point of view, all of these country initiatives also have organizational and managerial counterparts. And, primarily, the managerial and organizational counterparts fall into the areas of responsibility of HRM.

Company best practices for encouraging innovation include:[159]

■   creating the space to innovate;
■   allowing a broad variety of viewpoints;
■   creating a conversation between senior management and employees about innovation;
■   participants should be pulled to join through incentives and engagement, not pushed;
■   tapping unused talent and energy keeps product development costs low;
■   collateral benefits in organizational engagement can be as important as the innovations themselves;
■   major emphasis on internal and external training opportunities in order to develop and retain talent;
■   total strategic and systemic focus on talent and knowledge management;
■   measurement of process and results is key.

From an HRM point of view, the linking of HRM policies and practices with a firm's strategic goals and objectives in order to improve business performance and develop an organizational culture that fosters innovation and flexibility is fundamental to a firm's competitive advantages and the resulting effects on the bottom line.

Sources: Arndt, M. and Einhorn, B. (2010), The 50 most innovative companies, *Bloomberg Businessweek*, April 25, 34–40; Nasierowski, W. (2009), Human Resources within national innovation systems: Some observations from six countries, in Odrakiewicz, P. (ed.), *Innovations in Management: Cooperating Globally*, Poznan University College of Business and Foreign Languages, Poznan, Poland: PWSBiJo Publications; Sirkin, H. L., Hemerling, J. W., and Bhattacharya, A. K. (2008), *Globality: Competing with Everyone from Everywhere for Everything*, New York: Business Plus; Spender, J. C. and Strong, B. (2010), Who has innovative ideas? Employees, *The Wall Street Journal*, August 23, R5; and Wooldridge, A. (2010), The world turned upside down: A special report on innovation in emerging markets, *The Economist*, April 17, 3–18.

Discussion Questions

1 Are there aspects of a country's culture that parallel its national efforts (or lack thereof) to support innovation?
2 Which of these country efforts to support innovation are most likely to lead to country competitive advantages? Why? Support your point of view.
3 What is the link between country efforts to support innovation and company efforts?
4 Are there regional variations in country and company efforts to support innovation? Which efforts do you think might be related to which regions of the world? Why? How might these stem from country and regional cultures?
5 How does HRM relate to efforts to increase innovation?

NOTES

1 Source: DHL company website, http://www.dhl.com/en/about_us/company_portrait.html. Accessed Dec. 8, 2014.
2 Brewster, C. (2012). Comparing HRM policies and practices across geographical borders, in Stahl, G.K., Björkman, I., and Morris, S. (eds.), *Handbook of Research in International Human Resource*, 2nd ed., Elgar original reference. Cheltenham, UK: Edward Elgar, pp. 76–96; Mayrhofer, W., Brewster, C., Morley, M.J., and Ledolter, J. (2011). Hearing a different drummer? Convergence of human resource management in Europe—A longitudinal analysis. *Human Resource Management Review*, 21 (1), 50; McDonnell, A., Lavelle, J., and Gunnigle, P. (2014). Human resource management in multinational enterprises: Evidence from a late industrializing economy. *Management International Review*, 54 (3), 361–380. Doi: http://dx.doi.org/10.1007/s11575-014-0202-y; Almond, P., and Menendez, M.C.G. (2014). Cross-national comparative human resource management and the ideational sphere: A critical review. *The International Journal of Human Resource Management*, 25 (18), 2591.
3 Brewster, C. and Mayrhofer, W. (eds.) (2012). *Handbook of Research on Comparative Human Resource Management*, Cheltenham, UK: Edward Elgar; Stavrou, E., Brewster, C., and Charalambous, C. (2010). Human resource management and firm performance in Europe through the lens of business systems: Best fit, best practice or both? *The International Journal of Human Resource Management*, 21 (7), 933; Brewster, C., Croucher, R., Wood, G. and Brookes, M. (2007). Collective and individual voice: Convergence in Europe? *The International Journal of Human Resource Management*, 18 (7), 1246.
4 See Routledge Global HRM Series, http://www.routledge.com/books/series/global_hrm_SE0692/.
5 See Sage website for the four-volume set: http://www.uk.sagepub.com/booksProdDesc.nav?prodId=Book232954&.

6 Rickard, C., Baker, J., and Crew, Y. (2010). *Going Global: Managing the HR Function Across Countries and Cultures*, Williston, VT: Gower Publishing.

7 For more information on examples of studies that have examined the convergence/divergence framework see Reiche, B.S. Lee, Y., Quintanilla Alboreca, J. (2012). Cultural perspectives on comparative HRM, in Brewster, C., Mayrhofer, W., *Handbook of Research on Comparative Human Resource Management*, Cheltenham, UK: Edward Elgar, pp. 51–68; Pudelko, M. (2005). Cross-national learning from best practice and the convergence-divergence debate in HRM. *The International Journal of Human Resource Management*, 16 (11), 2045–2074; Brewster, Croucher, Wood and Brookes (2007); Carr, C. and Pudelko, M. (2006). Convergence of management practices in strategy, finance and HRM between the USA, Japan and Germany. *International Journal of Cross Cultural Management*, 6 (1), 75–100; Rowley, C. and Benson, J. (2002). Convergence and divergence in Asian human resource management. *California Management Review*, 44 (2), 90–109.

8 Brewster, C. (2007). Comparative HRM: European views and perspectives. *The International Journal of Human Resource Management*, 18 (5), 769.

9 Ibid.

10 This section is based on content from United Nations University. See, A typology of regions. Retrieved Oct. 6, 2010, from the UN University OCW website: http://ocw.unu.edu/programme-for-comparative-regional-integration-studies/introducing-regional-integration/a-typology-of-regions or http://www.aughty.org/pdf/regions_defined.pdf.

11 For more information see The Assembly of European Regions website: http://www.aer.eu/.

12 Ibid.

13 State of the World's Cities 2012/2013 — Prosperity of Cities. Report by the UN Habitat for a Better Urban Future (website: http://www.unhabitat.org/); State of the World's Cities 2008/2009 — Harmonious Cities. Report by the UN Habitat for a Better Urban Future (website: http://www.unhabitat.org/); Demographia World Urban Areas (Built-Up Urban Areas or World Agglomerations), 10th annual ed., May 2014 rev. Report by Demographia (website: http://www.demographia.com/).

14 State of the World's Cities 2012/2013 — Prosperity of Cities. Report by the UN Habitat for a Better Urban Future (website: http://www.unhabitat.org/); State of the World's Cities 2008/2009 — Harmonious Cities. Report by the UN Habitat for a Better Urban Future (website: http://www.unhabitat.org/); this is an emerging area. For sample research see Goerzen, A., Asmussen, C.G., and Nielsen, B.B. (2013). Global cities and multinational enterprise location strategy. *Journal of International Business Studies*, (5), 427; Joseph, C., and Lundström, C. (2013). Gender, culture and work in global cities: Researching 'transnational' women. *Women's Studies International Forum*, 36, 1–4.

15 A typology of regions. Retrieved Oct. 6, 2010, from UN University OCW website: http://ocw.unu.edu/programme-for-comparative-regional-integration-studies/introducing-regional-integration/a-typology-of-regions or http://www.aughty.org/pdf/regions_defined.pdf.

16 For more information see A Typology of Regions, United Nations; Regions and Innovations. Collaborating Across Borders. Report by the OECD Reviews of Regional Innovation (2013); Blatter, J. (2000). Emerging cross-border regions as a step towards sustainable development. *International Journal of Economic Development*, 2, 402–439.

17 *World Population Prospects: The 2012 Revision*, Population Division, Department of Economic and Social Affairs, United Nations, New York (2013). http://esa.un.org/wpp/. Accessed July 9, 2014.

18 For more information on HRM in Europe see Ehnert, I., Harry, W. and Brewster, C.J. (2013). Sustainable HRM in Europe: Diverse contexts and multiple bottom lines, in Ehnert, I., Harry, W. and Zink, K.J. (eds.), *Sustainability and Human Resource Management: Developing Sustainable Business Organizations*, Springer, Heidelberg, pp. 339–358; Brewster, C. (2013). European model of human resource management, in Kessler, E.H. (ed.), *Encyclopedia of Management Theory*, London: Sage, Mayrhofer, W., Sparrow, P., and

Brewster, C. (2012). European human resource management: A contextualised stakeholder perspective, in C. Brewster, and W. Mayrhofer (eds.), *Handbook of Research on Comparative Human Resource Management*, Cheltenham: Edward Elgar, pp. 528–549.

19   *World Population Prospects: The 2012 Revision*. Population Division, Department of Economic and Social Affairs, United Nations, New York (2013). http://esa.un.org/wpp/. Accessed Aug. 8, 2014; Population Reference Bureau (2014) World Population Data Sheet. Mid 2014 data.www.prb.org. Accessed Aug. 8, 2014.

20   United Nations, Department of Economic and Social Affairs, Population Division (2013). *World Population Prospects: The 2012 Revision, Highlights and Advance Tables*. Working Paper No. ESA/P/WP.228.

21   Ibid.

22   United Nations, Department of Economic and Social Affairs, Population Division (2013). *World Population Prospects: The 2012 Revision, Highlights and Advance Tables (Table I.4)*. Working Paper No. ESA/P/WP.228.

23   United Nations, Department of Economic and Social Affairs, Population Division (2013). *World Population Prospects: The 2012 Revision, Highlights and Advance Tables (Table I.5)*. Working Paper No. ESA/P/WP.228.

24   *2014 World Population Data Sheet*, Population Reference Bureau. Available at www. prb.org. Accessed Oct. 15, 2014; United Nations, Department of Economic and Social Affairs, Population Division (2013). *World Population Prospects: The 2012 Revision, Highlights and Advance Tables (Table III.1)*. Working Paper No. ESA/P/WP.228.

25   The European Commission. http://epp.eurostat.ec.europa.eu/portal/page/portal/eurostat/home/. Accessed Sept. 27, 2014.

26   The European Commission. http://epp.eurostat.ec.europa.eu/portal/page/portal/eurostat/home/. Accessed Sept. 27, 2014.

27   Ibid.

28   United Nations, Department of Economic and Social Affairs, Population Division (2013). *World Population Prospects: The 2012 Revision, Highlights and Advance Tables*. Working Paper No. ESA/P/WP.228; http://esa.un.org/wpp/. Accessed Oct. 2, 2014.

29   Ibid.

30   Brewster (2007); Stavrou, Brewster, and Charalambous (2010).

31   Ibid.

32   Caliguiri, P., Leepak, D., and Bonache, J. (2010). *Managing the Global Workforce*, Chichester, UK: John Wiley and Sons, Ltd.

33   Uysal, G. (2009). Human resource management in the US, Europe and Asia: Differences and characteristics. *Journal of American Academy of Business*, Cambridge, 14 (2), 112–117.

34   Mayrhofer, Sparrow and Brewster (2012); Ehnert, Harry, and Brewster (2013); Brewster, C. (1995). Towards a "European" model of human resource management. *Journal of International Business Studies*, 26 (1), 1; Mayrhofer, W. and Brewster, C. (2005). European human resource management: Researching developments over time. *Management Revue*, 16 (1), 36–62.

35   Mayrhofer, Sparrow, and Brewster (2012); Communal, C., and Brewster, C. (2004). HRM in Europe, in Harzing, A. and Van Ruysseveldt, J. (eds.), *International Human Resource Management*, London: Sage, pp. 167–194; Caliguiri, Leepak and Bonache (2010).

36   The European Trade Union Confederation (website: http://www.etuc.org/claudia-menne-confederal-secretary). Accessed Nov. 14, 2014.

37   See Blanpain, R. (2014). Comparative labour law and industrial relations in industrialized market economies, 11th ed., The Netherlands: Wolters Kluwer Law and Business; Siles-Brèugge, G. *Constructing European Union trade policy: a global idea of Europe*. International Political Economy Series, Palgrave Macmillan; http://en.wikipedia.org/wiki/Trade_union. Accessed Nov. 14, 2014.

38 Mayrhofer, Sparrow and Brewster (2012); Brewster (2007).

39 Mayrhofer, Sparrow and Brewster (2012); Brewster, C. (2004), European perspectives on human resource management. *Human Resource Management Review*, 14, 365–382.

40 For more information on *The flexibility-security nexus* see Dewettinck, K., Buyens, D., Auger, C., Dany, F. and Wilthagen, T. (2006). Deregulation: HRM and the flexibility-security nexus, in Holt Larsen, H. and Mayrhofer, W. (eds.), *Managing Human Resources in Europe—A Thematic Approach*, New York: Routledge, pp. 45–62.

41 Ibid.

42 Sparrow, P.R. and Hiltrop, J. (1994). *European Human Resource Management in Transition*, London: Prentice-Hall; see also Dickmann, M., Sparrow, P. and Brewster, C. (2008). *International Human Resource Management: A European Perspective*, 2nd ed., New York: Routledge.

43 Dewettinck, Buyens, Auger, Dany and Wilthagen (2006).

44 Mayrhofer, Sparrow and Brewster (2012); Brewster (2004).

45 Morley, M., Herarty, N., and Michailova, S. (2009). *Managing Human Resources in Central and Eastern Europe*, New York: Routledge.

46 For more information on this topic see Ananthram, S., and Chan, C. (2013). Challenges and strategies for global human resource executives: Perspectives from Canada and the United States. *European Management Journal*, 31 (3), 223; Jackson, S.E., Schuler, R.S., and Jiang, K. (2014). An aspirational framework for strategic human resource management. *The Academy of Management Annals*, 8 (1), 1; Kaufman, B.E. (2012). Strategic human resource management research in the United States: A failing grade after 30 years? *The Academy of Management Perspectives*, 26 (2), 12; Lepak, D.P., and Shaw, J.D. (2008). Strategic HRM in North America: Looking to the future. *The International Journal of Human Resource Management*, 19 (8), 1486; Nkomo, S., and Hoobler, J.M. (2014). A historical perspective on diversity ideologies in the United States: Reflections on human resource management research and practice. *Human Resource Management Review*, 24 (3), 245; Jackson, S., Schuler, R.S., Lepak, D., and Tarique, I. (2011). Human resource management practice and scholarship: A North American perspective, in C. Brewster and W. Mayrhofer (eds.), *Handbook of Research in Comparative Human Resource Management*, Cheltenham, UK: Edward Elgar, pp. 451–477.

47 United Nations, Department of Economic and Social Affairs, Population Division (2013). *World Population Prospects: The 2012 Revision, Highlights and Advance Tables (Table I.4)*. Working Paper No. ESA/P/WP.228; Population Reference Bureau (2014). World Population Data Sheet. Mid 2014 data. Available at www.prb.org. Accessed Aug. 8, 2014.

48 United Nations, Department of Economic and Social Affairs, Population Division (2013). *World Population Prospects: The 2012 Revision, Highlights and Advance Tables*. Working Paper No. ESA/P/WP.228.

49 United Nations, Department of Economic and Social Affairs, Population Division (2013). *World Population Prospects: The 2012 Revision, Highlights and Advance Tables (Table I.4)*. Working Paper No. ESA/P/WP.228.

50 United Nations, Department of Economic and Social Affairs, Population Division (2013). *World Population Prospects: The 2012 Revision, Highlights and Advance Tables (Table I.5)*. Working Paper No. ESA/P/WP.228.

51 United Nations, Department of Economic and Social Affairs, Population Division (2013). *World Population Prospects: The 2012 Revision, Highlights and Advance Tables (Table III.I)*. Working Paper No. ESA/P/WP.228; Population Reference Bureau (2014) World Population Data Sheet. Mid 2014 data. Available at www.prb.org. Accessed Aug. 8, 2014.

52 Brewster (2007).

53 Jackson, S.E., Schuler, R.S., and Werner, S. (2010). *Managing Human Resources*, 10th ed., Mason, OH: Cengage/Southwestern Publishers.

54 Caliguiri, Leepak and Bonache (2010); Communal and Brewster (2004).

55 Werner, S. (2008). Managing human resources in North America: Current issues and new directions for research. *International Journal of Human Resource Management*, 19(8), 1395–1396; Werner, S. (ed.) (2007). *Managing Human Resources in North America: Current Issues and Perspectives*. London, UK: Routledge.

56 Lepak and Shaw (2008).

57 Huselid, M., Beatty, D. and Becker, B. (2009). *The Differentiated Workforce: Transforming Talent into Strategic Impact*, Boston, MA: Harvard Business Press; Becker, B. and Huselid, M. A. (2006). Strategic human resource management: Where do we go from here. *Journal of Management*, 32, 898–925.

58 For more information on HRM in Asia see Varma, A. and Budhwar, P. (2013). *Managing Human Resources in Asia Pacific*, 2nd ed. New York: Routledge; West, J. P., Beh, L., and Sabharwal, M. (2013). Charting ethics in Asia-Pacific HRM: Does East meet West, ethically? [Article]. *Review of Public Personnel Administration*, 33 (2), 185–204. Doi: 10.1177/0734371x13484826; Budhwar, P., and Debrah, Y. (2009). Future research on human resource management systems in Asia. *Asia Pacific Journal of Management*, 26 (2), 197–218; Rowley, C., and Warner, M. (2007). The management of human resources in the Asia Pacific: Into the 21st century. *Management Revue*, 18 (4), 374–391; Umeh, O. (2008). The role of human resource management in successful national development and governance strategies in Africa and Asia. *Public Administration Review*, 68 (5), 948–950; Uysal (2009); Zhu, Y., Warner, M. and Rowley, C. (2007). Human resource management with "Asian" characteristics: A hybrid people-management system in East Asia. *The International Journal of Human Resource Management*, 18 (5), 745.

59 United Nations, Department of Economic and Social Affairs, Population Division (2013). *World Population Prospects: The 2012 Revision, Highlights and Advance Tables (Table I.4)*. Working Paper No. ESA/P/WP.228.

60 Ibid.

61 United Nations, Department of Economic and Social Affairs, Population Division (2013). *World Population Prospects: The 2012 Revision, Highlights and Advance Tables (Table I.5)*. Working Paper No. ESA/P/WP.228.

62 United Nations, Department of Economic and Social Affairs, Population Division (2013). *World Population Prospects: The 2012 Revision, Highlights and Advance Tables (Table III.I)*. Working Paper No. ESA/P/WP.228; Population Reference Bureau (2014) World Population Data Sheet. Mid 2014 data. Available at www.prb.org. Accessed Aug. 8, 2014.

63 See Budhwar and Debrah (2009); Budhwar, P. and Mellahi, K. (eds.) (2006). *Managing Human Resources in the Middle East*, London: Routledge.

64 Ibid.

65 Budhwar, P. (2004). Introduction: HRM in the Asia-Pacific context, in P. Budwar, *Managing Human Resources in Asia-Pacific*, London: Routledge. Also see http://www.apec.org/apec/about_apec.html.

66 Varma, A. and Budwar, P. (2014). *Managing Human Resources in Asia-Pacific*, New York: Routledge.

67 An example of emerging market list can be seen on *globalEdge* (Michigan State University), http://globaledge.msu.edu/resourcedesk/mpi/. Accessed Dec. 11, 2014.

68 For more information see the FDI database at UNCTAD (United Nations Conference on Trade and Development): http://unctad.org/en/Pages/DIAE/FDI%20Statistics/FDI-Statistics.aspx. Accessed Dec. 11, 2014.

69 Varma, A. and Budwar, P. (2014). *Managing Human Resources in Asia-Pacific*, New York: Routledge; Budhwar, P. (2004). *Managing Human Resources in Asia-Pacific*, Routledge: London.

70 Cooke, F. (2004). HRM in China, in Budwar, P. (ed). *Managing Human Resources in Asia-Pacific*, London: Routledge, pp. 17–34.

71 Ibid.

72 For an example of how this change is taking place in Japan see Fackler, M. (2010). Japan goes from dynamic to disheartened. *New York Times*, Oct. 17, retrieved on Oct. 10, 2010, from http://www.nytimes.com/2010/10/17/.

73 Debra, Y., and Budhwar, P. (2004). HRM challenges in the Asia Pacific, in Budwar, P. (ed), *Managing Human Resources in Asia Pacific*, London: Routledge.

74 Ibid.

75 Ibid.

76 For more information see *Trade Unions, Employers and Labour Ministers Initiated a Sectoral Social Dialogue at ASEAN Level. Brochure about the Work of the ASEAN Services Employees Trade Union Council Including the Executive Summary of the Assessment Study "ASEAN Economic Integration and its Impact on Workers and Trade Unions,"* 3rd ed. (2012). Published by ASEAN Services Employees Trade Union Council (ASETUC) and Friedrich-Ebert-Stiftung (FES) Office for Regional Cooperation in Asia. Also see Varma, A. and Budwar, P. (2014). *Managing Human Resources in Asia-Pacific*, New York: Routledge; Budhwar (2004).

77 See http://www.fes-asia.org/pages/regional-programs/regional-trade-union-program-asia-pacific.

78 Carra, S., Inkson, K., and Thorn, K. (2005). From global careers to talent flow: Reinterpreting "brain drain." *Journal of World Business*, 40, 386–398; Tung, R. (2008). Human capital or talent flows: Implications for future directions in research on Asia Pacific. *Asia Pacific Business Review*, 14, 469–472.

79 Debra and Budhwar (2004).

80 Ibid.

81 For more information on HRM in Latin America, see Andreassi, J.K., Lawter, L., Brockerhoff, M., and Rutigliano, P.J. (2014). Cultural impact of human resource practices on job satisfaction. A global study across 48 countries. *Cross Cultural Management*, 21(1), 55–77; Dabos, G.E., and Rousseau, D.M. (2013). Psychological contracts and informal networks in organizations: The effects of social status and local ties. *Human Resource Management*, 52 (4), 485–510; Perez Arrau, G., Eades, E., and Wilson, J. (2012). Managing human resources in the Latin American context: the case of Chile. *International Journal of Human Resource Management*, 23 (15), 3133–3150; Carlier, S.I., Llorente, C.L., and Grau, M.G. (2012). Comparing work-life balance in Spanish and Latin American countries. *European Journal of Training and Development*, 36(2/3), 286–307; Bonache, J., Trullen, J., and Sanchez, J.I. (2012). Managing cross-cultural differences: Testing human resource models in Latin America. *Journal of Business Research*, (12), 1773; Davila, A. and Elvira, M. (2009). *Best Human Resource Management Practices in Latin America*. London: Routledge; Elvira, M., and Davila, A. (2005a). *Managing Human Resources in Latin America*, Routledge, UK; Osland, A. and Osland, J. (2006). Contextualization and Strategic International Human Resource Management Approaches—The Case of Central America and Panama. *The International Journal of Human Resource Management*, 16 (12). 2218–2236; Davila, A., and Elvira, M.M. (2012a). Humanistic leadership: Lessons from Latin America. *Journal of World Business*, 47 (4), 548; Davila, A. and Elvira, M. (2012b). Latin American HRM model, in Brewster, C. and Mayrhofer, W. (eds.), *Handbook of Research on Comparative Human Resource Management*, Northhampton, MA: Edward Elgan Publishing, pp. 478–493.

82 Table I.4 in Population Division of the Department of Economic and Social Affairs of the United Nations Secretariat (2013). *World Population Prospects: The 2012 Revision.* New York: United Nations.

83 Ibid.

84 2014 World Population Data Sheet, Population Reference Bureau (website: www.prb.org); Table III.1 in Population Division of the Department of Economic and Social Affairs of the United Nations Secretariat (2013). *World Population Prospects: The 2012 Revision.* New York: United Nations.

85 Table I.5 in Population Division of the Department of Economic and Social Affairs of the United Nations Secretariat (2013). *World Population Prospects: The 2012 Revision.* New York: United Nations.

86 Davila, and Elvira, (2012b); Elvira, M. and Davila, A. (2005b). Emergent directions for human resource management research in Latin America. In N. Ekvura and A. Davila, *Managing Human Resources in Latin America*, Oxford, Routledge UK:

87 Osland, A. and Osland, J. (2005). HRM in Central America and Panama, in Elvira, M.M. and Davila, A. (eds.), *Managing Human Resources in Latin America: An Agenda for International Leaders*. Oxford, UK: Routledge, pp. 129–147.

88 For more information on labor unions in Latin American countries, see Murillo, M.V. (2001). *Labor Unions, Partisan Coalitions and Market Reforms in Latin America*, Cambridge: Cambridge University Press; Murillo,

M. V. (2005). Partisanship amidst convergence: The politics of labor reform in Latin America. *Comparative Politics*, 37 (4), 441–458; Scartascini, C., Stein, E., and Tommasi, M. (2010). *How Democracy Works. Political Institutions, Actors, and Arenas in Latin American Policymaking.* Inter-American Development Bank and David Rockefeller Center for Latin American Studies, Cambridge, MA: Harvard University.

89 Davila and Elvira (2012b); Elvira and Davilla (2005b).

90 Ibid.

91 Ronconi, L. (2012). Globalization, domestic institutions and enforcement of labor law: Evidence from Latin America. *Industrial Relations: A Journal of Economy and Society*, 51 (1), 89–105.

92 Davila and Elvira (2012b); Elivira and Davilla (2005b).

93 Ibid.

94 For more information on the solidarismo movement, see http://www.solidarismo.com, cited in Elivira and Davilla (2005a).

95 Davila and Elvira (2012b); Davila and Elvira (2005a).

96 Ibid.

97 See How Culture Affects Work Practices in Latin America. Knowledge@Wharton, http://knowledge.wharton.upenn.edu/article/how-culture-affects-work-practices-in-latin-america/. Accessed May 4, 2014.

98 This paragraph is heavily based on Elvira and Davila (2005a).

99 Davila and Elvira (2012b); Elvira and Davila (2005b).

100 Ibid.

101 Ibid.

102 See Otis, J. (2012). Informal economy swallows Latin American workers. GlobalPost, www.globalpost.com. Accessed June 8, 2014; *Statistical Update on Employment in the Informal Economy*, International Labour Organization, Department of Statistics, June 2012. This document available at http://laborsta.ilo.org/informal_economy_E.htm. Accessed April 8, 2014; Tuesta, D. (2014). The informal economy and the constraints that it imposes on pension contributions in Latin America. BBVA Research, Working Paper: 14/19; Mexico economy: Quick view–six out of ten Mexicans work in the informals. (2012). *The Economist Intelligence Unit*, Dec. 18, 2012; Andrews, D., Sánchez, A.C., and Johansson, Å. (2011). Towards a better understanding of the informal economy, OECD Economics Department Working Papers, Organization for Economic Cooperation and Development (OECD). Doi: 10.1787/5kgb1mf88x28-en; Arbex, M., Freguglia, R., and Chein, F. (2013). Informal economy and spatial mobility: Are informal workers economic refugees? *Journal of Economic Studies*, 40 (5), 671–685; Williams, C.C., and Lansky, M.A. (2013). Informal employment in developed and developing economies: Perspectives and policy responses. *International Labour Review*, 152 (3), 355–380; Vuletin, G. (2008). Measuring the informal economy in Latin America and the Caribbean, IMF Working Paper WP/08/102.

103 Ibid.

104 Ibid.

105 This is a developing area of research. For example, see Horwitz, F., Human resources management in multinational companies in Africa: A systematic literature review. *International Journal of Human Resource Management*, published online July. Doi: 10.1080/09585192.2014.934899; Newenham-Kahindi, A., Kamoche, K., Chizema, A. and Mellahi, K. (2013). *Effective People Management in Africa*, New York: Palgrave Macmillan; Kamoche, K., Debrah, Y., Horwitz, F.M. and Muuka, G.N. (eds.) (2003). *Managing Human Resources in Africa*, London: Routledge.

106 Population Division of the Department of Economic and Social Affairs of the United Nations Secretariat (2013). World Population Prospects: The 2012 Revision. New York: United Nations.

107 Table I.1 in Population Division of the Department of Economic and Social Affairs of the United Nations Secretariat (2013). *World Population Prospects: The 2012 Revision*. New York: United Nations; 2014 World Population Data Sheet, Population Reference Bureau, www.prb.org.

108 Table I.4 in Population Division of the Department of Economic and Social Affairs of the United Nations Secretariat (2013). *World Population Prospects: The 2012 Revision*. New York: United Nations.

109 Ibid.

110 2014 World Population Data Sheet, Population Reference Bureau (website: www.prb.org); Table III.1 in Population Division of the Department of Economic and Social Affairs of the United Nations Secretariat (2013). *World Population Prospects: The 2012 Revision.* New York: United Nations; 2014 World Population Data Sheet, Population Reference Bureau, www.prb.org.

111 Table I.5 in Population Division of the Department of Economic and Social Affairs of the United Nations Secretariat (2013). *World Population Prospects: The 2012 Revision.* New York: United Nations.

112 Berman, J. (2013, 10). Vision statement: Seven reasons why Africa's time is now. *Harvard Business Review,* 91, 34–35.

113 Storey, D. (2014). Realising potential, EY 2013/1014 Sub-Saharan Africa talent trends and practice survey. Ernst and Young Advisory Services.

114 The Sun Shines Bright, *The Economist,* Dec. 2011.

115 Ibid.

116 Berman (2013, 10).

117 The Sun Shines Bright, *The Economist,* Dec. 2011.

118 *Africa Telecoms Outlook 2014.* Maximizing digital service opportunities. Available at www.informatandm.com. Accessed Nov. 17, 2014.

119 Kupka, B., Briscoe, D., and Everett, A. (2013). Paper presented at the Academy of Management Africa Conference, Johannesburg, South Africa, January 7–10, 2013.

120 Kamoche, Debrah, Horwitz, and Muuka (eds.) (2004).

121 Kupka, Briscoe and Everett (2013).

122 Horwitz F. (2014). Human resources management in multinational companies in Africa: A systematic literature review. *International Journal of Human Resource Management,* published online July. DOI: 10.1080/09585192.2014.934899; Horwitz, F. (2012). Evolving human resource management in Southern African multinational firms: Towards an Afro-Asian nexus. *International Journal of Human Resource Management,* 23 (14), 2938–2958.

123 Kupka, Briscoe and Everett (2013).

124 Ibid.

125 The Sun Shines Bright, *The Economist,* Dec. 2011.

126 See Cooke, F.L. (2014). Chinese multinational firms in Asia and Africa: Relationships with institutional actors and patterns of HRM practices. *Human Resource Management,* 53 (6), 877; Jackson, T., Louw, L., and Zhao, S. (2013). China in sub-Saharan Africa: Implications for HRM policy and practice at organizational level. *International Journal of Human Resource Management,* 24 (13), 2512.

127 Newenham-Kahindi, Kamoche, Chizema and Mellahi (2013).

128 *Developing Talent for Africa Rising.* Conference hosted by Frontier Advisory Consulting/Business Services. (http://www.frontier-advisory.com/), Sandton, Johannesburg, South Africa, April 15, 2014.

129 Mavuso, Z. (June 20, 2014). Talent development critical to sustaining 'Africa Rising' narrative, Creamer Media. www http://www.creamermedia.co.za. Accessed Nov. 29, 2014.

130 UNESCO Institute for Statistics (UIS).

131 Ranking of African countries by literacy rate: Zimbabwe No. 1 (July 6, 2013). *The African Economist.*

132 *The Global Talent Index Report: The Outlook to 2015,* published by Heidrick and Struggles and The Economist Intelligence Unit.

133 Ibid.

134 The World Bank, Data on public spending on education. Latest year available is 2012. http://data.world bank.org/. Accessed Oct. 6, 2014.

135 *Developing Talent for Africa Rising.* Conference hosted by Frontier Advisory Consulting/Business Services (http://www.frontier-advisory.com/), Sandton, Johannesburg South Africa, April 15, 2014.

136 The five issues are from Mavuso, Z. (June 20, 2014). Talent development critical to sustaining 'Africa Rising' narrative, Creamer Media. www http://www.creamermedia.co.za. Accessed Sept. 23, 2014.

137 These four issues are from Weidemann, R. (Aug. 25, 2014). Africa's talent conundrum, African Trader, Promoting Business in Africa. http://www.africantrader.co. Accessed Sept. 15, 2014.

138 See World Economic Forum reports on Regional Challenges: Sub-Saharan Africa, and Regional Challenges: Middle East and North Africa 2015. Available at http://reports.weforum.org/.

139 *Africa by Numbers. Assessing market attractiveness in Africa.* Report by Ernst and Young in collaboration with Oxford Economics (www.ey.com/za), 2012.

140 Ernst and Young Attractiveness Survey, Africa 2013 Getting Down to Business. www.ey.com/attractiveness. Accessed Nov. 14, 2014.

141 Berman (2013, 10).

142 Kupka, B., Briscoe, D., and Everett, A. (2013). Paper presented at the Academy of Management Africa Conference, Johannesburg, South Africa, January 7–10, 2013.

143 *Tunisia assembly passes new constitution.* Reported by News Africa, British Broadcasting Corporation (BBC) online, 27 January, 2014.

144 Constitution of Zimbabwe. http://www.zim.gov.zw/. Accessed Oct. 17, 2014.

145 Doing Business Ranking Data by the World Bank Group (http://www.doingbusiness.org/rankings). Accessed Nov. 2, 2014.

146 Kupka, Briscoe and Everett (2013).

147 Ramor, M. (2014). What's the biggest challenge for Africa in 2015? World Economic Forum; World Economic Forum reports on Regional Challenges: Sub-Saharan Africa, and Regional Challenges: Middle East and North Africa 2015. Available at https://agenda.weforum.org/2014/11/whats-biggest-challenge-africa-2015/. Accessed Dec. 6, 2014.

148 Ibid.

149 *Population ageing and the non-communicable diseases.* Department of Economic and Social Affairs, Population Division, United Nations, April 2012.

150 The Sun Shines Bright, *The Economist*, Dec. 2011.

151 2014 African Youth Forum: Equipping and inspiring the next generation for productive Jobs, World Bank Headquarters, Washington, DC, July 31, 2014.

152 Based on Horwitz (2014); Kamoche, K., Chizema, A., Mellahi, K., and Newenham-Kahindi, A. (2012). New directions in the management of human resources in Africa. *International Journal of Human Resource Management*, 23 (14), 2825–2834; Bernd, K., Briscoe, D., Andre E. (2013). Paper presented at the Academy of Management Africa Conference Johannesburg, South Africa, Jan. 7–10, 2013; Kamoche, K., Debrah, Y., Horwitz, F.M. and Muuka, G.N. (eds.) (2003). *Managing Human Resources in Africa*, London: Routledge.

153 Talent Mobility 2012 and beyond, PWC, http://www.pwc.com/hrs. Accessed Oct. 7, 2014.

154 *Realising Potential, EY 2013/1014 Sub-Saharan Africa talent trends and practice survey.* Report by Ernst and Young Advisory Services, South Africa, 2014.

155 Ibid.

156 Ibid

157 See the The Cranfield Network on International Human Resource Management (Cranet); website: http://www.cranet.org/home/Pages/Default.aspx. Accessed Oct.9, 2014; Sparrow, P., Farndale, E., and Scullion, H. (2014). Globalizing the HR architecture: The challenges facing corporate HQ and international mobility functions, in P.R. Sparrow, H. Scullion, and I. Tarique (eds.), *Strategic Talent Management: Contemporary Issues in International Context.* Cambridge: Cambridge University Press, pp. 254–227; Budhwar, P.S., Schuler, R., and Sparrow, P. (2009). Preface: Cross national comparative HRM, in Budhwar, P.S., Schuler, R.S. and Sparrow, P.R. (eds.), *International Human Resource Management*, Vol. 4, London, UK: Sage, pp. vii–xiii; Brewster, C., Mayrhofer, W., and Reichel, A. (2011). Riding the tiger? Going along with Cranet for two decades—A relational perspective. *Human Resource Management Review*, 21 (1), 5; Festing, M. (2012). Strategic human resource management in Germany: Evidence of convergence to the U.S. model, the European model, or a distinctive national model? *The Academy of Management Perspectives*, 26 (2), 37; Mayrhofer, Brewster, Morley and Ledolter (2011); Stavrou, Brewster and Charalambous (2010).

158 Wooldridge, A. (2010), The world turned upside down: A special report on innovation in emerging markets, *The Economist*, April 17, 3–18.

159 Spender, J. C. and Strong, B. (2010), Who has innovative ideas? Employees, *The Wall Street Journal*, August 23, R5.

NOTES TO EXHIBITS

1   2014 World Population Data Sheet, Population Reference Bureau, www.prb.org.

2   United Nations, Department of Economic and Social Affairs, Population Division (2013). *World Population Prospects: The 2012 Revision, Highlights and Advance Tables*. Working Paper No. ESA/P/WP.228

3   Ibid.

4   2014 World Population Data Sheet, Population Reference Bureau, www.prb.org.

5   United Nations, Department of Economic and Social Affairs, Population Division (2013). *World Population Prospects: The 2012 Revision, Highlights and Advance Tables*. Working Paper No. ESA/P/WP.228. Please note: As per the CIA World Fact book, Net migration rate compares the difference between the number of persons entering and leaving a country during the year per 1,000 persons (based on midyear population).

6   2014 World Population Data Sheet, Population Reference Bureau, www.prb.org.

7   Labor force is defined as individuals 15 years of age and older. Source: World Development Indicators, Labor Force Structure, World Bank (Website: http://wdi.worldbank.org/table/2.2). "Total labor force comprises people ages 15 and older who meet the International Labour Organization definition of the economically active population: all people who supply labor for the production of goods and services during a specified period. It includes both the employed and the unemployed" (World Bank).

8   Defined as % of individuals 15 years of age and older who are part "of a country's working-age population that engages actively in the labour market, either by working or looking for work. It provides an indication of the relative size of the supply of labour available to engage in the production of goods and services" (ILO).

9   World Development Indicators (Table 6.13): *Movement of People Across Borders*, World Bank, 2014.

10 `UNESCO, Global Education Digest 2011 and 2012 Percentage of the population aged 25 years and older with secondary education qualifications. The level of educational attainment is based on International Standard Classification of Education (ISCED) Level 3.

11 2014 World Population Data Sheet, Population Reference Bureau, www.prb.org; Table I.4 in Population Division of the Department of Economic and Social Affairs of the United Nations Secretariat (2013). World Population Prospects: The 2012 Revision. New York: United Nations.
    World Population Prospects, The 2012 revision, Highlights and Advance Tables, UN, 2013.

12 Ibid.

13 Based on UNESCO Institute for Statistics. Educational attainment of the population aged 25 years and older/latest year available. Percentage of the population aged 25 years and older with secondary education qualifications. The level of educational attainment is based on International Standard Classification of Education (ISCED) Level 3.

14 2014 World Population Data Sheet, Population Reference Bureau, www.prb.org.

15 World Population Prospects, The 2012 revision, Highlights and Advance Tables, UN, 2013.

16 2014 World Population Data Sheet, Population Reference Bureau, www.prb.org.

17 2014 World Development Indicators, Labor Force Structure, World Bank (Website: http://wdi.worldbank.org/table/2.2). "Total labor force comprises people ages 15 and older who meet the International Labour Organization definition of the economically active population: all people who supply labor for the production of goods and services during a specified period. It includes both the employed and the unemployed" (World Bank).

18 Based on The World Bank Word Development Indicators: http://data.worldbank.org/data-catalog/world-development-indicators and *Key Indicators of the Labour Market database*, eighth edition (2014), The International Labour Organization, Geneva. "The labour force participation rate is a measure of the proportion of a country's working-age population that engages actively in the labour market, either by working or looking for work. It provides an indication of the relative size of the supply of labour available to engage in the production of goods and services" (ILO. p. 29, *Key Indicators of the Labour Market database*, eighth edition (2014),)]

19 World Bank World Development Indicators: Movement of people across borders, 2014.

20 Based on UNESCO Institute for Statistics. Educational Attainment of the Population aged 25 years and older/latest year available. Percentage of the population aged 25 years and older with secondary education qualifications. The level of educational attainment is based on International Standard Classification of Education (ISCED) Level 3.

21 2014 World Population Data Sheet, Population Reference Bureau, www.prb.org.

22 United Nations, Department of Economic and Social Affairs, Population Division (2013). *World Population Prospects: The 2012 Revision, Highlights and Advance Tables.* Working Paper No. ESA/P/WP.228. Please note: As per the CIA World Fact book, Net migration rate compares the difference between the number of persons entering and leaving a country during the year per 1,000 persons (based on midyear population)

23 Ibid.

24 2014 World Population Data Sheet, Population Reference Bureau, www.prb.org.

25 Ibid (Net migration rate compares the difference between the number of persons entering and leaving a country during the year per 1,000 persons (based on midyear population).From the CIA World Fact Book

26 2014 World Population Data Sheet, Population Reference Bureau, www.prb.org.

27 2014 World Development Indicators, Labor Force Structure, World Bank (Website: http://wdi.worldbank.org/table/2.2). "Total labor force comprises people ages 15 and older who meet the International Labour Organization definition of the economically active population: all people who supply labor for the production of goods and services during a specified period. It includes both the employed and the unemployed" (World Bank).

28 Based on The World Bank Word Development Indicators: http://data.worldbank.org/data-catalog/world-development-indicators and *Key Indicators of the Labour Market database*, eighth edition (2014), The International Labour Organization, Geneva. "The labour force participation rate is a measure of the proportion of a country's working-age population that engages actively in the labour market, either by working or looking for work. It provides an indication of the relative size of the supply of labour available to engage in the production of goods and services" (ILO. p 29, *Key Indicators of the Labour Market database*, eighth edition (2014),)

29 World Bank World Development Indicators: Movement of people across borders, 2014

30 Based on UNESCO Institute for Statistics. Educational Attainment of the Population aged 25 years and older/latest year available. Percentage of the population aged 25 years and older with secondary education qualifications. The level of educational attainment is based on International Standard Classification of Education (ISCED) Level 3.

31 2014 World Population Data Sheet, Population Reference Bureau, www.prb.org.

32 United Nations, Department of Economic and Social Affairs, Population Division (2013). *World Population Prospects: The 2012 Revision, Highlights and Advance Tables.* Working Paper No. ESA/P/WP.228. Please note: As per the CIA World Fact book, Net migration rate compares the difference between the number of persons entering and leaving a country during the year per 1,000 persons (based on midyear population).

33 Ibid.

34 2014 World Population Data Sheet, Population Reference Bureau, www.prb.org.

35 Ibid (Net migration rate compares the difference between the number of persons entering and leaving a country during the year per 1,000 persons (based on midyear population). From the CIA World Fact Book.

36 2014 World Population Data Sheet, Population Reference Bureau, www.prb.org.

37 2014 World Development Indicators, Labor Force Structure, World Bank (Website: http://wdi.worldbank.org/table/2.2). "Total labor force comprises people ages 15 and older who meet the International Labour Organization definition of the economically active population: all people who supply labor for the production of goods and services during a specified period. It includes both the employed and the unemployed" (World Bank).

38 Based on The World Bank Word Development Indicators: http://data.worldbank.org/data-catalog/world-development-indicators and *Key Indicators of the Labour Market database*, eighth edition (2014), The International Labour Organization, Geneva. "The labour force participation rate is a measure of the proportion of a country's working-age population that engages actively in the labour market, either by working or looking for work. It provides an indication of the relative size of the supply of labour available to engage in the production of goods and services" (ILO. p 29, *Key Indicators of the Labour Market database*, eighth edition (2014)).

39 World Bank World Development Indicators: Movement of people across borders, 2014.

40 Based on UNESCO Institute for Statistics. Educational Attainment of the Population aged 25 years and older/latest year available. Percentage of the population aged 25 years and older with secondary education qualifications. The level of educational attainment is based on International Standard Classification of Education (ISCED) Level 3.

41 2014 World Population Data Sheet, Population Reference Bureau, www.prb.org.

42 World Population Prospects, The 2012 revision, Highlights and Advance Tables, UN, 2013.

43 Ibid.

44 2014 World Population Data Sheet, Population Reference Bureau, www.prb.org.

45 Ibid (Net migration rate compares the difference between the number of persons entering and leaving a country during the year per 1,000 persons (based on midyear population). From the CIA World Fact Book.

46 2014 World Population Data Sheet, Population Reference Bureau, www.prb.org.

47 2014 World Development Indicators, Labor Force Structure, World Bank (Website: http://wdi.worldbank.org/table/2.2). "Total labor force comprises people ages 15 and older who meet the International Labour Organization definition of the economically active population: all people who supply labor for the production of goods and services during a specified period. It includes both the employed and the unemployed" (World Bank).

48 Based on The World Bank Word Development Indicators: http://data.worldbank.org/data-catalog/world-development-indicators and *Key Indicators of the Labour Market database*, eighth edition (2014), The International Labour Organization, Geneva. "The labour force participation rate is a measure of the proportion of a country's working-age population that engages actively in the labour market, either by working or looking for work. It provides an indication of the relative size of the supply of labour available to engage in the production of goods and services" (ILO. p. 29, *Key Indicators of the Labour Market Database*, eighth edition (2014),)

49 World Bank World Development Indicators: Movement of people across borders, 2014.

50 Based on UNESCO Institute for Statistics. Educational Attainment of the Population aged 25 years and older/latest year available. Percentage of the population aged 25 years and older with secondary education qualifications. The level of educational attainment is based on International Standard Classification of Education (ISCED) Level 3.

SECTION 4

Role and Future of IHRM

The fourth section of the book, "Role and Future of IHRM," has one chapter:

■ Chapter 15: The IHRM Department, Professionalism, and Future Trends

Section 4 of the book is a single chapter. It takes a look at the IHRM department, its professionals, and future trends in IHRM. Chapter 15 examines the role of the IHRM department, including international support services that IHR departments are expected to develop and provide, the continuing internationalization (globalization) of HRM as it parallels the continuing internationalization (globalization) of business, the increasing professionalization of IHRM (including issues such as the codification of the "body of knowledge" of IHR, the development of IHR competencies and certification, the increase in training and experience in IHR, and the inclusion of IHR in career development plans of HR managers), and possible scenarios for the development of what some firms are calling "global HRM."

The IHRM Department, Professionalism, and Future Trends

HR will transform to adapt to a more global world, including adopting new talent sourcing strategies to match talent with task all over the globe, and adopting new management methods, such as supporting mobile workforces across geographic barriers.

Accenture Institute for High Performance[1]

Learning Objectives

This chapter will enable the reader to:

- Describe the ways the IHRM department will obtain more involvement in the MNE.
- Explain the current role and increasing professionalization of the IHRM manager.
- Explain the increasing complexities and challenges faced by IHRM.
- Describe the likely future of the IHRM department and profession.

The first 14 chapters of this book focused on the history and current development of IHRM. Now the description comes full circle. This last chapter focuses on the likely future of this new management discipline.

Previous editions of this book have emphasized that there are some aspects of IHRM that have achieved more attention than others—particularly the management of international assignees, including IA selection, preparation, compensation, and repatriation. There are other issues that have received less attention—although they, too, are covered in this book, such as performance management, employee well-being, labor relations, and the development of the profession. This last chapter, then, primarily provides a professional speculation about what the issues are that are likely to confront IHR managers in the future, as this discipline further develops in its role of becoming a major participant in the strategic management of at least the human resource aspects of the ever-increasing activity of international business.

For purposes of description, this chapter is divided into three major sections:

1   the role and nature of the IHR department;
2   the role and nature of IHRM as a profession; and
3   the future of IHRM.

As will be seen, there are linkages among these topics, and all are connected by the increasing competency and professionalization of IHRM.

THE IHRM DEPARTMENT

The first section of this chapter describes the role of the IHR department itself. This section discusses the department within which these activities take place and the role that is evolving for that department. It also discusses some of the support activities that IHR departments are generally called on to provide.

Organizational Advancement of IHRM

Achieving desirable results from ever-more-complex global business activities requires MNEs to pay increasing attention to more than the development of international operations, research and development, sales forces, and accounting systems. Increasingly, top-level attention must also be paid to the human aspects of cross-border business, to the merger of global workforces and cultures in acquisitions, joint ventures, and alliances, and to the development of the individual employees who represent multiple corporate and national cultures, speak multiple languages, and who have widely varying perspectives on customer, product, and business issues. It is IHR that is expected to provide and coordinate these capabilities and advise the rest of the enterprise on how to ensure performance in this cross-border complexity. It is IHR within MNEs that must focus on the difficulties encountered in the development of global human resource problems, such as global pension and health care systems, management development throughout the global enterprise, global employee and management recruiting, global compensation systems, etc.

In the end, the global and cultural aspects of international business boil down to finding ways for individuals with varying backgrounds and perspectives to work together; that is, finding ways to develop a corporate "glue" that will hold the organization effectively together. This type of organizational glue can be developed through the use of effective cross-national task forces and work teams, or the use of shared service centers and centers of excellence located throughout the global enterprise, and can thus be used to pull together employees from disparate country and corporate cultures. It will be IHR that will be looked upon to provide the global enterprise with the expertise to help design and implement such strategies and the knowledge to measure the return on investment of such practices.

Involvement of the IHRM Department

Given the many human resource problems that MNEs encounter in conducting business on a global scale, in the future they will need to encourage the following *agenda* for their IHRM departments.[2] Most of these have been discussed in one or more places earlier in the text. So this provides a way to pull them together and to focus them on the role of the IHRM department:

- *Lead*. Take the lead in developing processes and concepts for top management as they develop the global strategy.
- *Contribute*. Ensure IHR contribution as an integral partner in formulating the global strategy for the firm.
- *Competencies*. Develop the necessary competence among the senior IHR staff so that they can contribute as partners in the strategic management of the global firm.
- *Develop*. Build a framework to help top management fully understand the (increasingly complex) organizational structure and people implications of globalization.
- *Implement*. Facilitate the implementation of the global strategy by identifying the key skills that will be required by management and employees, assessing current global competencies in IHRM and in the rest of the management team, and developing strategies for locating outside talent that may be required.
- *Evaluate*. Develop the abilities to determine the value and return of the contribution of IHR practices and to explain these to senior management.
- *Share*. Distribute and share the responsibilities for IHRM. Increasingly, IHR will become a shared responsibility. Line management, IHRM managers, and work teams all will share in the objective of ensuring the effective hiring, development, deployment, and retention of the global firm's human resources.[3]

Operation of the Department

A world-class IHR department requires broad-range guidelines for an efficient and effective operation. These guidelines include the follow:

1   IHRM will be linked to the management of the business at strategic, as well as at operational, levels.
2   IHRM will shift from being primarily an operational activity (managing issues such as IA staffing, training, compensation, benefits administration, and legal compliance) to more of a strategic role in the management of the global firm (such as focusing on the broad importance of global talent management).

3 IHRM will shift from being primarily responsive to decisions made by top management to being proactive in the design and application of IHR programs and in the strategic management of the firm—this means they will seek out line managers to get to know their business needs and will try to help solve them.

4 IHRM will shift from doing IHR for line executives to assisting and counseling them on IHR matters.

5 IHRM will shift from operating primarily with a focus on individual employees to a focus on work teams.

6 IHRM will shift from focusing primarily on internal problems to focusing on issues external to the firm, even to a societal focus—responding to all stakeholders. This will be where senior IHR executives will make their most important contributions to the strategic management of the global enterprise.

Staffing the Department

The IHR department itself, in order to pursue this new role, will find it has a need for fewer specialists and more generalists; that it will need to be even more business-focused (this means IHR managers will need more line experience—particularly of a global nature—and training, and more line managers will need experience in IHR); that individual IHR managers will need to have more experience working in global teams themselves and more training in how to make teams work effectively together across borders; and that IHR managers will need to develop internal counseling and coaching skills (with line managers, helping them to solve their people problems) and become information specialists (creating, maintaining, and using/interpreting IHR data for themselves and for the rest of the firm).[4]

Linking the Department with the Business and Its Strategy

In the global firms of the future, IHR departments will need to be more closely linked to the actual management of the business, through development of IHR philosophies (values, culture, vision), policies (guidelines for action), and programs, practices, and processes (involving line managers at every step) that fit the vision and strategy of the firm.

Demonstrating the Contributions of the IHRM Department

The IHRM department of the future will need to learn how to demonstrate that the right things (needed by the organization to be successful) are being done right (as efficiently and effectively as possible, with a positive effect on the corporate bottom line).[5] One aspect of this will be research to determine what the best IHR practices are around the world and to use them to both judge the quality of a firm's IHR activities as well as to develop better IHR practices.

Indicators of Being World Class

The following provides a short list of possible criteria and metrics (for use in a "balanced" scorecard)[6] to use to determine whether the IHRM practices in any particular firm are indeed among the best in the world.

- inclusion of IHRM in key business issues—including both their formulation and their implementation;
- IHR and organization issues being seen as critical in strategy implementation;
- ability of IHRM to deal with events proactively;
- alignment of IHRM policies, procedures, and practices in all businesses, including a clear and shared statement of IHR vision and responsibilities;
- the number of individuals wanting to receive an IHR assignment;
- IHRM meeting its plans and objectives;
- IHRM having a structure, organization, and operation that services the strategic needs and interests of the business;
- IHRM having satisfied customers within the organization;
- IHRM activities being shared and understood by all employees;
- IHRM being flexible and adaptable to new conditions;
- IHRM measuring the effectiveness of its activities;
- IHRM measuring the efficiency of its activities;
- IHRM facilitating, or being capable of facilitating, major organizational change; and
- IHRM having competent, adaptive, and flexible staff.

Support Services

In the typical domestic HR department in a large firm, a number of activities are performed that generally support the core HR responsibilities. These include the HR information system (including maintaining records on employees and providing HR reports—discussed in Chapter 13), human resource planning (including employee forecasts, career plans for managers, and succession planning for executives), job analysis and the writing of job descriptions (for recruiting and training purposes and the setting of performance expectations), job evaluations and wage surveys and the development of job classifications and wage rates, labor market analyses to determine the availability and abilities of potential employees, the development of performance appraisal systems, domestic relocation services, and personnel/HR research.

The following discusses two of these support services that have not yet been covered and that will play an increasingly important role in IHRM: international relocation and orientation and global administrative services.

Relocation and Orientation

This area of service can consume much time from IHR managers. To ensure that employees being assigned to foreign posts receive the best possible attention to the very personal concerns of relocation to another country, most of these services are usually sourced from firms that specialize in the delivery of these services directly to IAs and their families.[7] Alternatively, some large MNEs are starting to combine their domestic and international relocation responsibilities. The relocation function evolved out of firms' needs, beginning in the 1950s and 1960s, when they began to move a large number of employees from one business location to another, for business and career purposes, to help their relocating employees with problems such as the selling of houses, the shipment of household goods, the identification of temporary living quarters in their new location, the purchase of a new house, the control of family during in-transit time, and the control of overall relocation costs.[8] These essential relocation activities turn out to be essentially the same for international relocations as for domestic ones (although the international transfer tends to be much more intense, particularly for spouses and families, and more complicated and expensive).

Exhibit 15.1 shows the six primary areas of service that are generally related to an international relocation.

Administrative Services

Most of these services could potentially be provided elsewhere in the firm, but they generally are delegated to the IHR department. All of them are, at least initially, established to ease the process of transferring employees from one country to another. Then because

---

EXHIBIT 15.1: International Relocation Services

International relocation services	Description
1 Tax and financial advice	*This is one of the first services provided by the IHR department to employees going overseas. Personal income tax preparation becomes quite complicated. And the overall handling of finances, in circumstances in which income is likely to increase dramatically as well as to involve multiple currencies, new banking systems, varying exchange rates, and so on, is likely to require assistance for the new IA and his or her family. This is generally coordinated by the IHR department.*

International relocation services	Description
2 Visas and work permits	It usually falls on the IHRM department to obtain the necessary visas for the expatriate (and his or her family) as well as to arrange for whatever work permits are required. Normally, this involves maintaining the personal relations with foreign government officials that are necessary to get these documents in a timely manner, since individual IAs often have limited time to make such preparations after the firm makes the decision to send them abroad (or IHR must maintain relations with consultants or vendors who provide this service, such as local law firms that specialize in visas and work permits). This can be quite complex if the firm tries to also find employment for the trailing spouse or other family members.
3 International moving	There are many complexities in arranging and managing successful international moves for IAs and their families. Needless to say, this is also typically one of the most stressful aspects of moving abroad for most employees and their families. Again, the IHRM department usually has responsibility to assure that the employee's move takes place in a smooth, problem-free way.
4 Medical exams for particular foreign locations	Where medical services may not be up to the parent-country standards, the firm will want to ensure that it isn't going to face any unnecessary health complications.
5 Training and orientation	Training and orientation (about the country, culture, and language of the country of the new assignment for the IA and family). This is discussed in Chapter 10.
6 Education and schooling for the IA and family while in the foreign assignment	Sometimes adequate schools for the IA and/or his or her family are not available locally, and the firm must pay for the children to be schooled elsewhere (e.g., in boarding schools), which will also entail extra expense for children to return home periodically or for parents to visit them. The IHR department will be expected to assist the IA family to locate acceptable schooling.

the IHRM department has found ways to resolve the availability of these services, they are often extended to other needs of the firm and stay within the responsibilities of the IHR department.

- *Travel arrangements* (as discussed above—and for everyone in the firm that travels internationally). This can involve acquiring necessary visas, making all necessary travel arrangements (airplane and hotel reservations, etc.), and buying travel insurance.
- *Housing in the foreign locale* (for all international travelers for the firm). This can involve negotiating contracts, signing rental agreements, finding hotel rooms, apartments, and so forth.
- Determining the availability and operation of *local transportation* in the foreign locale, including rental cars, chauffeurs, metro maps, bus schedules, and rail systems.
- *Office services*, such as translation and translators, for business contracts, housing and rental agreements, business letters, and business negotiations.
- *Currency conversion.* New IAs (and international business travelers) may not have experience with or an understanding of living in another country and having to deal with conversion of their home-country currency into that of the host country.
- *Local bank accounts.* Since banking systems vary dramatically from country to country, the IA often needs assistance in establishing a local bank account (if indeed that is possible) as well as an understanding of how the banking system operates in his or her new country of residence.
- *Government relations.* This will initially include familiarity with the proper offices to get visas and work permits but may eventually extend also to local government offices for business services such as telephones and business licenses.

IHRM in Action 15.1[9] shows the involvement of the IHRM function in Rio Tinto as it manages a major global workforce reduction.

IHRM in Action 15.1: IHRM in a Global Mining Company

Rio Tinto is a US$54 billion, 140-year-old international mining company, headquartered in London. It was originally formed by English investors in 1873 to mine ancient copper workings in Spain. It was incorporated in 1905, with today's company formed in 1962 with basic UK and Australian businesses, which were merged in 1997 to form today's Rio Tinto Group, with operations in more than 50 countries.

When the global recession hit in late 2008, greatly impacting the mining sector, the group announced a global workforce reduction of 14,000 employees and contractors out of 100,000 employees and thousands of contractors. Global HR was challenged to accomplish this incredibly difficult task with speed and sensitivity.

Three teams were established to coordinate HR efforts across the globe: the Americas, Europe, Middle East; Africa; and Australasia. Of course, the downsizing had to take place while HR continued to support the business—and while reducing its own staffs. The leaders of HR were prepared to meet these challenges largely because they had been involved in the initial business discussions and understood the necessity for the downsizing.

In the words of Andrew Slentz, vice-president of People and Organization Support for Rio Tinto Group, Americas:

> Equipped with a common global approach, regional severance policies, a comprehensive database, measurement tools to track the full impact of reductions, and global providers for outplacement, we completed most of the reductions in the first quarter of 2009. Early identification of high-potential leaders and workers with critical skills allowed us to move staff around internally to retain as much talent as possible. We also trained managers to help remaining employees stay focused. As a result, our chief executive was able to report on our progress to the market with confidence.

What enabled this reduction-in-force to take place with such little disruption? According to Slentz, it all began in 2004 with headquarters' launching of strategies throughout the global operations to increase efficiency and effectiveness to regain their competitive edge. In HR, this took the form of bringing every HR function on the global journey and building a model for delivering quality services worldwide at the lowest possible cost. Searching best practices in and beyond the mining industry led to the adoption of a consistent and standardized model for the major support functions. This was labeled a "3D" model—design, determine, and deliver. It detailed levels of people, structure, process, and systems:

- HR people: the need for HR professionals capable of operating within and across the 3D spectrum. Today, HR managers are provided opportunities that span product groups, locations, and HR specialization assignments.
- Structure: HR now performs a much more strategic role. Global practice leaders design corporate policies, programs, and strategies in five areas: leadership and people development, total rewards, recruitment and talent, organizational effectiveness, and HR information technology.
- Process: HR now tries to think globally first, then regionally, and then locally to ensure alignment from the mines' rock faces to corporate headquarters in London. Globally consistent HR philosophy is supported by policies and standards with the flexibility to accommodate country variables such as regulatory requirements, legislation, and collective bargaining agreements.

■ Systems: efficiencies can be obtained by digitizing processes and self-service tools. Rio Tinto is now most of the way through grafting critical global functions—such as talent and performance management, merit and incentive management, and recruitment—on the backbone of an enterprise resource planning (ERP) system.

Unifying disparate HR departments across multiple business units with harmonized plan designs and administration has increased HR's speed and lowered costs. HR's investment in end-to-end global HR functions with metrics and milestones continues to pay off, while resiliency in the model enables the pursuit of continuing inefficiencies. The company continues, of course, to invest in mining and processing technology, yet it now recognizes that leveraging its human capital, organizing effective teams, continuing to develop of talent, and fostering creativity and innovation remain the group's greatest source of potential competitive advantage. Rio Tinto's HR professionals have become astute strategic business partners, shared services experts, and global practice leaders of the business from now and into the future.

PROFESSIONALIZATION OF IHRM

This next to last section of this chapter (and of this text) deals with one of the most important topics: the role of the IHRM manager himself or herself. This section examines the ongoing professionalization of IHR, the competencies of IHR managers, and the global leadership that can and should be provided by today's IHR manager.

In order to achieve the above agenda and responsibilities, IHR as a management function will need to continue professionalizing. Organizations that operate in the increasingly competitive global economy of the future will need and expect their IHR managers to develop the professional competencies needed to help them successfully steer their organizations (at least the human side of them) through the chaos of global competition.

Importance of the Function

IHRM will need to be recognized by top executives, strategic planners, and line managers in general, as critical to the success of the global enterprise. Research supports that a focus on progressive IHR programs is related to gaining global competitive advantage.[10] Thus IHRM programs and departments must receive high-priority attention and resources. It will be critical for global managers to have experience in the IHR department, and it will be just as important for IHR managers to have experience in line management, and in global assignments as well.[11]

Development of IHRM Managers

Since the IHR function has evolved primarily from the management of expatriates, and is now developing into many other areas of responsibility, a major issue for IHR in the future will be the need to develop a broader perspective on and experience with the global enterprise. MNEs will need IHR executives who can do more than handle the selection, training, relocation, and compensation of expatriates. MNEs will need and expect their IHR executives to assist in the strategic management of their global businesses, to develop IHR policies for operations located around the globe, and hire and develop highly productive workforces in multiple countries. The development of this type of strategic IHR manager is becoming a central focus of the IHR profession.

The typical firm's management and executive development programs are designed and managed by HR, so it should make sense that HR would focus some of that attention on its own development, even though this is often not done. Indeed, if such a focus were aimed at IHR itself, the strengthening of IHR departments and development of more competency in IHR could be accomplished in a number of ways:[12]

- By assigning upwardly mobile domestic HR generalists to overseas regional staffs for two- to three-year periods. For example, Pepsi-Cola has done this successfully, assigning US HR managers to its regional offices in Europe, Asia, and Latin America. However, this is not yet a widespread practice.
- By considering assignments of one or more repatriated IAs from any function to IHR in either an operating division or the headquarters staff. Their overseas experiences will add credibility to the IHR function as well as a critical international perspective. In addition, experience in HR should be beneficial to their careers. (Assignment of non-performers, i.e., individuals who had difficulty in their international assignments, should be avoided. Such a move would weaken the IHR function.)
- By assigning several entry-level university graduates with degrees in human resources to overseas subsidiaries and regional positions. Instead of giving them typical expatriate compensation packages, pay them as locals. Indeed, these individuals might even be from the country of assignment, having attended university in the country of the parent firm.

Education

There are still only limited opportunities to gain an education in IHR, yet this is something that anyone interested in the discipline needs to pursue and is a major component of the professionalization of IHR. There are only a handful of master's degree programs in IHR. However, many universities now offer at least a survey course in IHR, often as part of a master's degree program in HR or as an elective course within a program on international business or in a general MBA curriculum. But this should only be the beginning of gaining an education in IHR.

Many IHR consulting firms and providers of IHR services offer short seminars and a few host annual conferences on IHR, with topics on various aspects of IHR typically presented by practitioners and consultants. Attendance at these seminars and conferences is one of the available ways to stay current on issues being addressed by MNEs and on MNE best practices in IHR. The American Society for Human Resource Management (as well as a few universities around the US) now offers a training program for preparation to take the Certificate in Global HR, described in the next section. In addition, there are a number of both university-level curricula and practitioner seminars on cross-cultural management, an area in which IHR practitioners need extensive training. Of course, one of the most important areas for learning for IHR managers should be the experience of living and working (hopefully, practicing HR) in another country and culture (or more than one other country and culture). And self-education must also become (and remain) a cornerstone of any effort to gain knowledge about IHR. This would involve reading the growing number of books and magazines on the subject of IHR as well as networking with other practitioners, including joining one of the growing number of local IHR discussion groups that are being created in many population centers.

The website that accompanies this book contains many of the references that are mentioned in this section and can be used to locate opportunities for further education in IHRM. And the Routledge website for the series on global HRM of which this text is a part showcases numerous books that focus on specific topic areas within IHRM as well as on IHRM as practiced in the many disparate regions of the world.

Certification: Testing and the Body of Knowledge

The Society for Human Resource Management (SHRM: the United States' largest professional society for HR professionals),[13] and the Human Resource Certification Institute (HRCI)[14] have identified and codified the "body of knowledge" in IHR (the body of knowledge is described in the first chapter) and designed testing procedures for certifying professional skill and knowledge in IHRM.[15] (For discussion of the certification process in England and elsewhere see the book in this series by Sparrow, Brewster, Budhwar, and De Cieri titled *Globalizing Human Resource Management*, 2nd ed.).[16] The work on identifying the IHR body of knowledge was completed in 2003 and the first certification test was administered in 2004. Possessing this certificate in IHR (GPHR credential) has signaled to employers that the holder has demonstrated a high level of knowledge in this relatively new discipline. There are now (2014) thousands of managers from around the world that have passed the exam and now have the Global Professional in HR certification. This is one additional step in the continuing process of professionalization of the IHR practitioner.

Competencies (General)[17]

The success of IHRM in the future will depend on the ability of companies to develop IHR executives with broad global perspectives (a global mindset, as discussed in Chapter 10), international experience, and strong technical and strategic business skills. This will include developing the following general competencies for IHR professionals:

- cross-cultural interpersonal skills;
- ability to learn about multiple cultures;
- local responsiveness (develop and maintain relationships with local colleagues and officials, know and understand local markets, regulations, and current affairs);
- cross-national adaptation;
- change and diversity management and international team skills; and
- coaching and development of global literacy (in themselves and others);
- ability to manage global risks, such as those presented by "accidental expatriates," global compliance, and global benefits and tax regulations;
- identifying procedures and measures for demonstrating the ROI, triple bottom-line, and balanced scorecard metrics for IHRM initiatives; and
- global strategic leadership for the whole organization and its many HR departments and HR managers.

In keeping with SHRM's mission of serving and advancing the HR profession, SHRM developed a model to identify what it means to be a successful HR professional—across the performance continuum, around the globe, from early to executive career levels. The competency model and the resources developed based on the model provide the foundation for talent management throughout the HR lifecycle. This competency model is now forming the framework for a new level of certification.

Competencies (Specific)[18]

In addition to general competencies, the competent IHR manager of the future will demonstrate a number of skills more specifically related to IHR. He or she will be able to:

- Implement effective recruiting and staffing to attract and retain the best talent for a global workforce;
- Implement formal systems to improve worldwide communications;
- Implement an International Human Resource Information System (IHRIS);
- Foster a global mindset in all employees through training and development;
- Develop global leadership through design of a program of developmental cross-cultural assignments;

- Position the HR function as a strategic business partner in the organization's global business (once considered a bonus for HR managers, business literacy—on a global scale—is now a prerequisite);
- Demonstrate the worth of IHR programs in terms of their global bottom-line contributions and their being a major source of worldwide strategic advantage; and
- Design and implement global HR systems, such as training, compensation, performance management, employee relations, and health and safety.

As described above, development of these competencies within IHR can be partially achieved by including one or more overseas assignments in the career paths of highly skilled HR managers, introducing some of the best foreign-affiliate HR talent into parent-company regional offices and headquarters, assigning repatriating parent-company managers from non-HR functions to IHR, and providing high-potential HR practitioners with international assignments early in their careers. Such experience is certainly just as important for HR as it is for managers in other functions. And yet MNEs rarely give such international development of HR managers any attention at all.

FUTURE OF IHRM[19]

This section of this last chapter describes the challenges that the IHRM function is facing in today's chaotic and hyper-competitive global marketplace and how it is dealing with them. In some ways, what is described here is a look at the future. And in some ways and for many MNEs the future is here now. In both cases, MNEs must confront these issues, now and into the future. As was discussed in Chapter 2, the emerging model for the 21st century is not the multinational enterprise (as it has come to be known and which is at the core of the IHR practices described throughout this text), but rather a globally integrated enterprise that is very different in structure and operation.

Challenges Faced by IHRM

Almost every chapter in this text has included some discussion of the challenges that IHR faces in each relevant area of responsibility. In addition, a number of issues that present strategic challenges to the IHR function as a whole are beginning to arise. These include the following:

- There is a growing realization, particularly in large MNEs, that there is a lack of HR talent around the world. There are too few opportunities for university education in HR and IHR; firms do too little to develop IHR talent internally, including the use of expatriates in HR assignments; and the new structures for delivering IHR services—such as outsourcing, shared services, and centers of excellence—are not being incorporated into HR development yet, either internally or externally.

- There are an increased number of employee relations issues—for example, comparisons between the rights and benefits of workers in various countries—making IHR programming and service delivery increasingly complex and difficult.

- Globalization and freer trade are leading many countries to change their legal frameworks (e.g., China joining WTO, India), which impacts IHR practices and local country management.

- There is too little consistency in HR infrastructures for effective delivery of IHR programs around the world.

- And what employees want in various locations around the world is constantly changing and often creates new and difficult challenges:

   ❏ Global workforces want top-level leadership from within their own countries, not just from headquarters.

   ❏ Local workforces and local HR staffs want their local office dynamics to be respected by corporate HQs.

   ❏ Local subsidiary and joint venture managements want expatriates to take ownership of becoming part of the country they are assigned to.

   ❏ Local employees want defined career paths for themselves and want to be included in corporate career planning as well. They expect the parent firm to initiate development opportunities for local employees.

   ❏ Local offices often feel left out of corporate planning. They want and expect to be included, particularly in communication on upcoming organizational changes.

   ❏ Local business units expect to be included in executive visits from headquarters, that is, to not be taken for granted.

   ❏ Increasingly, employees in foreign subsidiaries around the globe want variable compensation schemes to include them. And they also expect to be included in parent-company total rewards planning and bonus schemes.

The New MNE HR organization

These employee interests, combined with the types of social changes described in the first two chapters of this book, are leading to the need for major organizational changes, as well. Many executives were trained and developed during an era with very different demands than what is required today. Thus, a major disconnect is occurring between what executives know and understand and what the global business environment needs.

The demands of this "new world" impact HR (and IHR) even more so than many other areas of organizational leadership. Shifts from personnel administration (primarily transactional) to strategic HR, from mostly domestic to largely global HR, from traditional (paper and pencil) HR to delivery of services via electronic interfaces (e-HR), and from soft-sell (do it because it makes people feel good) to hard-sell (measuring the results of HR programs and showing they make positive impacts on a firm's profitability and its resultant market capitalization), all have changed the nature of HR services and competencies.[20] Of course, the traditional HR transactions haven't disappeared. Rather they are automated and/or outsourced, with domestic HR practices now being multiplied in the many different countries in which the firm operates. And tasks related to HR administration and legal compliance are now scrutinized and measured in terms of value-added contribution to the global business. As a result, HR practitioners are now challenged to develop new mindsets and distinct new professional HR competencies, such as global mindsets and skills in computers and HR process outcomes measurement.

In terms of traditional HR transactions, such as signing up new employees for payroll and benefits services and updating such services when changes are made, technology has made it possible to deliver these transactions through in-sourcing (i.e., shared services) and outsourcing (initially involving only specific individual HR business processes and now involving the entire HR function). So now HR professionals must focus on the integration of HR processes and managing HR projects across organizational and national boundaries.

One of the most significant challenges for IHR is that the HR function is, for many reasons, and in many (if not most) companies not a highly globalized function.[21] Within international business, HR is the most likely function to be localized. And, yet, many forces are driving firms to globalize even their HR (IHR) functions. As Brewster, Sparrow, and Harris have put it,

> Initiatives aimed at improving [global] temporal, functional, or financial flexibility are being introduced side by side with integrated programmes intended to link work practices to the need to deliver radical cost improvements [around the world]. In increasing flexibility, firms also want to change the nature of employee identification and their sense of involvement, and this changed identity knows few national borders.[22]

To meet these pressures, MNEs are pursuing several different models of IHR organization, with their IHR functions facing a number of challenges:[23]

- Consequences of global business process redesign, the pursuit of a global centre of excellence strategy and the global redistribution and relocation of work that this often entails.
- Absorption of acquired businesses, merging of existing operations on a global scale, the staffing of strategic integration teams, and attempts to develop and harmonize core HR processes within these merged businesses.
- Rapid start-up of international operations and organization development as they mature through different stages of the business cycle.
- Changing capabilities of international operations with increased needs for up-skilling of local operations and greater complexity.
- Need to capitalize on the potential that technology affords the delivery of HR through shared services, on a global basis, while ensuring that social and cultural insights are duly considered when it is imperative to do so.

- Changes being wrought in the HR service supply chain as the need for several intermediary service providers is being reduced, and as web-based HR provision increases.
- Articulation of appropriate pledges about the levels of performance that can be delivered to the business by the IHR function, and the requirement to meet these pledges under conditions of tight cost control.
- Learning about operating through formal or informal global HR networks, acting as knowledge brokers across international operations, and avoiding a "one best way" HR philosophy.
- Offering a compelling value proposition to the employees of the firm, and understanding and then marketing the brand that the firm represents across global labor markets that in practice have different values and different perceptions.
- And identity problems faced by HR professionals as they experience changes in the level of decentralization/centralization across constituent international businesses. As knowledge and ideas about best practice flow from both the center to the operations and vice versa, it is not uncommon for HR professionals at all levels of the firm to feel that their ideas are being overridden by those of other nationalities or business systems.

In pursuing these developments, IHR has to cope with five underlying challenges: managing the shift from domestic HRM to international/global HRM, enabling IHR capability development on a global basis, ensuring effective knowledge management across national and business unit boundaries, providing HR services cost-effectively, and moving the information system from a focus on the delivery of metrics about HR practices to a program of workforce analytics. In order to deliver on these realities and challenges, then, today, many global companies are evolving their IHR into a three-tiered organizational structure.[24] At the top of these MNEs is an HR headquarters organization made up of a small team of senior HR executives who deal with strategic organizational and HR issues. They work very closely on the organizational side with senior management providing HR insight on global strategy and on the HR side with two groups: a team of very specialized experts in the traditional functional areas of HR and a global team of country/regional HR managers who act as local business partners, dispersed throughout the MNE's global operations. At the bottom of this IHR organization are the traditional HR staff who administer the HR programs and functions at the level of the business unit. These services may be delivered internally through shared (by multiple business units) service centers or externally through outsourced vendors who deal on a day-to-day basis with the purely transactional issues—and which are largely delivered through an internal intranet, not face-to-face.

What makes this structure work are the HR business partners in the middle, implementing at the local level the strategy designed at the top and designing and overseeing the transactional services at the bottom. These HR business partners play a critical role, whether it is figuring out how to engage employees and manage and retain talent across the many business units, customizing employment deals, building sustainable HR practices, or creating and measuring HR value. Each of these three levels requires different competencies. Thus therein lies the challenges for IHR today and into the future.[25]

EXHIBIT 15.2: The Datafication of HR

Graduating from HR metrics to workforce analytics

Metrics	Analytics
Provide a standard system of measurement	Provide systematic computational analysis of data or statistics
Measure single data points	Connect multiple data points
Provide information	Provide insights
Guide tactics and operations	Drive strategy
State the past and present	State the past, present, and predict the future
Provide tabular outputs of counts and rates	Provide visual outputs of patterns and trends

Source: Adapted from Visier (2014), The Datafication of HR, White Paper, Vancouver, BC/San Jose, CA: Visier, Inc.

As IHRM increases its ability to better use the data it generates to show the benefits of its various programs (refer to Exhibit 15.2 for suggestions about the kinds of changes in its reporting and analysis that new data analytics allow), IHRM will become better able to get support and approval for those programs.[26]

Opportunities for Strengthening IHR

These shifts from the traditional MNE model with mostly self-contained HR offices at the country level, with oversight from headquarters, to this three-tiered model have led to debate over the quality of the contribution of IHR to the new global organizational strategy. Although most executives do not deny the important role that IHR can (and should) play in the global firm, critics claim that IHR is not doing an adequate job of playing that role, that HR is not being a true business partner, that it doesn't have the IHR competencies necessary to meet all the needs of the new three-tiered model and to meet the global organizational needs of human capital, innovation, and flexibility.

The IHRM Job of the Future

This last subsection provides a summary and conclusion to the chapter. A few years ago, IBM sponsored studies by Towers Perrin to identify the skills that would be necessary for

IHR in the future.[27] These capabilities were also identified as the ones for which the widest gaps exist between current IHR abilities and those that were perceived as needed in world-class organizations of the future. They included:

- The ability to educate and influence line managers on IHR policies, practices, and importance.
- Being computer- and technology-literate, so as to be able to create and use global databases and social networks for delivery of IHR advice and decision making and for delivery worldwide of IHR transactional services.
- Being able to anticipate internal and external changes, particularly of importance to the availability and qualification of human resource talent around the world.
- Exhibiting leadership for the IHR function and within the corporation, at headquarters level and at the business unit level.
- Focusing on the quality of IHR services within the enterprise.
- Defining an IHR vision of the future and communicating that to the IHR department and to the organization.
- Developing broad knowledge of many IHR functions.
- Being willing to take appropriate risks in the development and implementation of innovative IHR policies and practices.
- Being able to demonstrate the financial impact of IHR policies and practices.

So given the need for these capabilities, what must IHR of the future do? The following points summarize the suggestions and ideas made in this chapter (and throughout the text):

- *Hire for international experience.* IHR must convince managers of the MNE of the importance to global competitiveness of having a workforce that knows and understands international business. Thus, the firm needs to appreciate the importance of including international knowledge and experience as criteria in the recruiting and hiring process.
- *Disperse people with international experience throughout the firm* (including in HR). One way to improve the firm's overall IB competency is to disperse the people who have global knowledge and experience throughout the enterprise.
- *Learn how to recruit and assign on a global basis.* IHR must develop the ability to recruit talent from around the world and to assign such global hires throughout the firm's global operations.
- *Increase the firm's international information diet.* IHR should take a proactive role in providing all locations of the enterprise with information (e.g., general international magazines and newspapers) about not just the firm's global operations, but about global affairs in general, including actions of governments and competitors in countries where the firm operates.
- *Train everyone in cross-cultural communication, etiquette, protocol, negotiation styles, and ethics.* This is one additional, but specific, aspect of providing information to the

workforce about global business. These are areas of concern that greatly increase a global firm's competency in the conduct of international business.

■ *Ensure international developmental assignments.* IHR must make sure the global enterprise understands and supports the necessary system for ensuring that international assignments are kept as a major component in all executive development programs.

■ *Pursue GPHR certification.* HR practitioners who want to work in the global arena should acquire the basic global HR body of knowledge.

■ And, most important, IHR managers need to understand and appreciate the importance of developing themselves to better carry out their global mandates. This would include thoroughly understanding how the enterprise makes money globally and being able to articulate an IHR point of view using the language of business on all global strategy discussions, knowing how to measure global ROI on IHR programs, developing and using a global HR balanced scorecard to measure the overall contribution of IHR to the firm's global success, developing relationships and networks throughout the global enterprise, and creating a global HR learning organization, to constantly improve and better meet its changing global challenges.

To conclude, this final statement: though the exact nature of the IHR role of the future is still evolving (and will continue to evolve), the following roles will likely be among the critical roles being performed by the global HR manager of the future:

■ The CFO for global HR, that is, thoroughly knowledgeable about the financial impact of IHR programs.

■ The global IHR vendor manager, that is, effectively managing the vendors to whom IHR has outsourced its administrative and transactional functions.

■ The internal consultant to the global business on issues related to the enterprise's human capital knowledge management.

■ The global leader for HR.

CONCLUSION

This chapter examined the role of the IHRM department, including international support services that IHR departments are expected to develop and provide, the continuing internationalization (globalization) of HRM as it parallels the continuing internationalization (globalization) of business, the increasing professionalization of IHRM (including issues such as the codification of the "body of knowledge" of IHR, the development of IHR competencies and certification, the increase in training and experience in IHR; and the inclusion of IHR in career development plans of HR managers), and possible scenarios for the development of what some firms are calling "global HRM."

DISCUSSION QUESTIONS

1 Which challenges to IHRM do you think are the most important? Why?
2 How can HR managers develop the high level of competency in IHRM needed to meet these challenges?
3 In what ways can an MNE improve or change its approach to IHRM?
4 What actions would you suggest to HR managers in order to increase their professionalism and competency in handling global HR issues?

CASE STUDY 15.1: Becoming an HR Transnational at Germany's OBI (Germany)

Lisbeth Claus and Dennis Briscoe (written for this text)

OBI, the second largest DIY retailer in Europe and fourth largest in the world, operates about 540 stores in 13 European countries (as of late 2014), was founded in Germany in 1970 and expanded rapidly into other European markets in the 1990s and 2000s. As happens with internationalization in most retail businesses, new stores in new countries (in OBI's case, largely in Central and Eastern Europe) typically develop largely stand-alone operations and procedures. In OBI's case, as the firm grew very rapidly, independent and local HR practices began to present major problems.

While most of OBI's stores are owned and operated by the company, some operate under franchise agreements. And, in some countries, such as Russia and Ukraine, OBI entered into joint ventures with local partners as a way to expand its business while maintaining full operational control. In most of these new countries and new stores, coordination with parent-company headquarters depended more on an individual manager's willingness to network within the informal structure than on any requirement of formal corporate policies. This was especially true for human resource management practices, e.g., recruiting and staffing procedures and employee performance evaluations. To a large degree, each store developed its own way of doing things. There were several differing competency models, rating scales, and performance evaluation processes being used. And staffing activities were even more disparate.

So by 2008, corporate headquarters began to be concerned about the use of differing practices and the variances in approaches and, sometimes, in quality. It realized that in order to achieve economies of scale and to be able to draw upon global expertise and resources while still localizing its business practices in the different national markets, it would have to change its multi-domestic approach. The company needed to create a more centralized mode of operations and become a more transnational firm.

The challenge—supported by management—was to develop standardized systems to be used in all countries, no small feat considering that OBI operated in so many different countries: Germany, Italy, Austria, Hungary, the Czech Republic, Poland, Slovenia, Switzerland, Bosnia, Russia, Croatia, Ukraine, and Romania.

Thomas Belker, managing director of HR, remembers,

When I started my job in 2006, many line managers came and asked for support. [For example:] The international business was growing so fast that we were in dire need for expatriates to build up new country headquarters and to support the development of new stores. As a result, one of our most daring endeavors, the expansion in Russia, was at risk. The recruiting activities for the 2,000 employees OBI needed to hire that year came almost to a standstill because we couldn't find a sufficient number of expats for the management team.

And each country was pursuing its own approach to meeting its needs, which made it extremely difficult for HQs to provide assistance and make sure the firm would reach its expansion goals.

No standardized HR management practices existed, and in those countries where formal policies had been developed, they were rarely followed. As a result, in some cases line managers would request individualized guidance from headquarters as needed, and would then tailor the suggested solutions to their specific situations. In other cases, managers would formulate their own solutions, as headquarters did not always provide the necessary support. Once faced with a potentially huge shortage of qualified employees to support its international expansion, however, OBI realized that it needed standardized recruitment procedures. "I knew that my first meeting with all the country managers would be crucial if I wanted to convince everyone to understand multi-domestic [with all stores and countries independent of each other] as a deadlock," recalls Thomas Belker. "But how could I take away the fear of the dreaded centralization of processes that would cut off individual solutions by the country managers and local HR managers?"

As it turned out, this problem applied to all HR practices, including the performance evaluation system as well as the staffing practices. Local managers were concerned that a standardized model would give them less control over local hiring and evaluation decisions. OBI HQs had previously developed several models for various HR practices, although none of them had been uniformly applied. While creating a standardized policy would have the advantage of providing clear guidance, OBI headquarters was concerned that managers might not comply if the model could not address local concerns.

First and foremost, OBI headquarters realized that standardizing all of its HR practices would not necessarily lead to a well-integrated organization, and that there was considerable resistance in some countries to adopting centralized HR management. Therefore, for example, it forbade the use of the term "centralization" and instead encouraged each country's managers to help develop the core processes. The hope was that while the standards would eventually become company-wide, they could be initially formulated at any level of the organization. Second, recognizing that each local operation had been developing its own unique solutions to problems facing that country's operations, headquarters sought to determine which country addressed which problem the most effectively.

This whole process was begun with a core project group, established to represent the firm's organizational units: headquarters HR, country HR managers, and the sales division of the largest country—Germany. First, the group collected and analyzed data about the various practices being used in each country. During several workshops and meetings, various proposals were examined to focus more closely on overall business needs. Certain countries were identified as "Centers of Competency" for specific core HR processes. In this way, the guidelines for recruiting, training, performance management, etc. were established independently in one country and then later applied to other countries' operations.

However, implementation of these guidelines turned out to present its own difficulties. Monthly conference calls were implemented between headquarters and the local HR departments abroad. But, because of cultural differences, communication between people of Eastern and Western Europe often ran into difficulties. The main problems occurred when trying to get people to meet deadlines and in getting active participation and feedback during conference calls.

So, in order to meet deadlines, communication with all countries was doubled. In addition to sending emails about the deadlines and reminders about the necessity of the projects, colleagues were reminded during day-to-day business operations about the importance of the various projects.

Keeping participation levels and open discussions high proved far more difficult even than keeping deadlines and keeping projects alive. A two-day meeting involving all HR colleagues from abroad was scheduled. During this meeting the need to be creative was addressed and experiences and ideas were exchanged—however small, redundant, or silly. Demonstrating the core group ideas and unveiling the many wrong turns the group had taken helped create trust among most of the participants. Being an example for others helped achieve the frankness needed.

This had the added benefit of increasing interaction among HR managers and developing an international mindset throughout the organization. In the end, patience and gratitude helped. Intercultural cooperation always requires much more time than communication just within one's own organizational culture or structure. So by assigning each country's operations a key function in developing various HR policies, OBI HR was able to transform itself from a multi-domestic style of operating into a transnational organization.

Sources: Based on the vignette, Internationalization of HR at OBI: Integrated recruitment strategy in action, written by Dr. Lisbeth Claus and published in Briscoe, D., Schuler, R. S., and Claus, L. (2009), International Human Resource Management, 3rd ed., London/New York: Routledge; and available at www.willamette. edu/agsm/global_hr; Belker, T. (2010). Team effort helps make worldwide performance evaluations consistent, downloaded 2/18/2010 from www. shrmn.org/hrdisciplines/global/Articles/Pages/PerformanceEvaluations.aspx; and the firm's website at www.obi.com/de/company.

Discussion Questions

1   How did OBI capitalize on the strengths of its multi-domestic strategy when shifting its structure to a transnational organization?
2   Why did OBI create "Centers of Excellence"?
3   How does shifting from a multi-domestic to a transnational model affect an organization's culture?
4   How did it affect HR?
5   Does this case provide an example of the future for IHRM?

NOTES

1   The Future of HR: Research Overview (2013). Accenture (a global management consulting, technology services and outsourcing company). Available at http://www.accenture.com/SiteCollectionDocuments/ PDF/Accenture-Future-of-HR-Overview.pdf.

2   Adapted from Reynolds, C. (2000). Chapter 28: The future of global compensation and benefits, in Reynolds, C. (ed.), *2000 Guide to Global Compensation and Benefits*, San Diego: Harcourt Professional Publishing, pp. 559–570; and Tichy, N.M. (1988). Setting the global human resource management agenda for the 1990s. *Human Resource Management*, 27, 1–18. Also see Sheehan, C., De Cieri, H., Cooper, B., and Brooks, R. (2014). Exploring the power dimensions of the human resource function. *Human Resource Management Journal*, 24 (2), 193; Powers, R., and Chamberlain, D. (2014). The many moving elements of global mobility planning. *Benefits and Compensation International*, 43 (10), 13; McNulty, Y. and De Cieri, H. (2011). Global mobility in the 21st century. *Management International Review*, 51 (6), 897–919; Keegan, A., Huemann, M., and Turner, J.R. (2012). Beyond the line: Exploring the HRM responsibilities of line managers, project managers and the HRM department in four project-oriented companies in the Netherlands, Austria, the UK and the USA. *The International Journal of Human Resource Management*, 23 (15), 3085; Brandl, J., and Pohler, D. (2010). The human resource department's role and conditions that affect its development: Explanations from Austrian CEOs. *Human Resource Management*, 49 (6), 1025; De Wang, Y., and Niu, H.J. (2010). Multiple roles of human resource department in building organizational competitiveness—perspective of role theory. *International Management Review*, 6 (2), 13–19, 106.

3   Jackson, S.E., Schuler, R.S., and Werner, S. (2012). *Managing Human Resources*, 11th ed., Mason, Ohio: Cengage.

4   Frase-Blunt, M. (2003). Raising the bar. *HR Magazine*, March, 74–78; Grossman, R.J. (2003). Putting HR in rotation. *HR Magazine*, March, 50–57. Also see Schramm, J. (2014). The pulse of the HR profession. *HR Magazine*, 59 (2), 64; Minton-Eversole, T. (2014). How to find a good outplacement provider. *HR Magazine*, 59(9), 14; Labedz, C.S., and Lee, J. (2011). The mental models of HR professionals as strategic partners. *Journal of Management and Organization*, 17 (1), 56–76; Jackson, H.G. (2014). The evolution of HR continues. *HR Magazine*, 59 (10), 8; Glover, L., and Butler, P. (2012). High-performance work systems, partnership and the working lives of HR professionals. *Human Resource Management Journal*, 22 (2), 199.

5   Becker, B.E., Huselid, M.A. and Ulrich, D. (2001). *The HR Scorecard: Linking People, Strategy, and Performance*, Boston: Harvard Business School Press; Fitz-enz, J. (2000). *The ROI of Human Capital: Measuring the Economic Value of Employee Performance*, New York: American Management Association (AMACOM); Philips, J.J., Stone, R.D. and Phillips, P.P. (2001). *The Human Resources Scorecard: Measuring the Return on Investment*, Boston: Butterworth-Heinemann; Csoka, L., and Hackett, B. (1998). *Transforming the IHR Function for Global Business Success* (1998) New York: The Conference Board. Also see Douthitt, S., and Mondore, S. (2013). Creating a business-focused HR function with analytics and integrated talent management. *People and Strategy*, 36(4), 16–21; Falletta, S. (2013). In search of HR intelligence: Evidence-based HR analytics practices in high performing companies. *People & Strategy*, 36 (4), 28–37; Risher, H. (2013). Investing in managers to improve performance. *Compensation & Benefits Review*, 45 (6), 324–328; Arrowsmith, J. (2014). The prize and peril of HR analytics. *Human Resources Magazine*, 18 (6), 30; Becker, B.E., Huselid, M.A., and Beatty, R.W. (2005). *The Workforce Scorecard: Managing Human Capital to Execute Strategy*, Harvard Business School Press Books, 1; Levensor, A. (2011). Using targeted analytics to improve talent decisions. *People & Strategy*, 34 (2), 34–43.

6   Jackson, S.E., Schuler, R.S., and Jiang, K. (2014). An aspirational framework for strategic human resource management. *Academy of Management Annals*, 8 (1), 1–56; Schuler, R. (1991). *The HR Function in Effective Firms in Highly Competitive Environments in the 21st Century*. Special Report for the IBM Corporation that served as the basis for the global HR survey entitled, "A 21st Century Vision: A Worldwide Human Resource Study," conducted by TPF&C; Schuler, R. (1994). World Class HR Departments: Six Critical Issues, *The Singapore Accounting and Business Review*, January, 43–72. Refer to references in endnote 7.

7   This subject is a frequent topic for presentations at industry and IHR practitioner conferences. Here is a sample of some of the articles that have appeared in various sources over the last few years: *Trends Global Relocation. Global Mobility Policy and Practices*. 2014 Survey Executive Summary Report by Cartus Corporation; 2014 *Global Mobility Trends Survey* by Brookfield Global Relocation Services (Brookfield GRS);

Rafter, M. (2012). Global relocation rebounds. *Workforce Management*, 91 (7), 10; Cleghorn, L. (2014). Insights into employee relocation activity in 2013. *Global. Benefits & Compensation International*, 43 (7), 23; Leahman, K., Haroun, M., Abbot, E., and Meyer, E. (2014). Navigating the cultural minefield: Interaction. *Harvard Business Review*, 92 (7/8), 20; Gleeson, M. (2013). Planning for an overseas move. *Money Management*, 27 (44), 24–26.

8   Loewe, G.M. (1994). Evolution of the relocation function. *Journal of International Compensation & Benefits*, January/February, 43–46.

9   Sources: www.riotinto. com. (2014); Slentz, A. (2009). Going global to last. *HR Magazine*, August, 36–38.

10 Ulrich, D., Younger, J., Brockbank, W. and Ulrich, M. (2012). *HR from the Outside in: Six Competencies for the Future of Human Resources*, New York: McGraw-Hill; Buyens, D. and de Vos, A. (1999). Chapter 2: The added value of the HR department, in Brewster, C. and Harris, H. (eds.), *International Human Resource Management*, London: Routledge; Lawler, E.E., III (1992). *The Ultimate Advantage: Creating the High-Involvement Organization*, San Francisco: Jossey-Bass; Pfeffer, J. (1994). *Competitive Advantage Through People*, Boston: Harvard Business School Press; Pfeffer, J. (1998). *The Human Equation: Building Profits By Putting People First*, Boston: Harvard Business School Press; Stroh, L.K. and Calligiuri, P.M. (1998a), Increasing global competitiveness through effective people management. *Journal of World Business*, 33 (1), 1–16; and Stroh, L.K. and Caligiuri, P.M. (1998b). Strategic human resources: A new source for competitive advantage in the global arena. *The International Journal of Human Resource Management*, 9 (1), 1–17.

11 Grossman (2003); and Poe, A.C. (2000). Destination everywhere. *HR Magazine*, October, 67–75.

12 Frase-Blunt (2003); Grossman (2003); and Reynolds, C. (1992). Are you ready to make IHR a global function? *HR News: International HR*, February, 1–3.

13 See http://www.shrm.org/certification/pages/default.aspx.

14 See http://www.hrci.org/.

15 Latham, G. (2012, December). What we know and what we would like to know about human resource management certification. *Human Resource Management Review*, December, pp. 269–270; Lengnick-Hall, M.L., and Aguinis, H. (2012). What is the value of human resource certification? A multilevel framework for research. *Human Resource Management Review*, 22 (4), 246–257; Lester, S.W., and Dwyer, D.J. (2012). Motivations and benefits for attaining HR certifications. *Career Development International*, 17 (7), 584–605; Garza, A.S., and Morgeson, F.P. (2012, December). Exploring the link between organizational values and human resource certification. *Human Resource Management Review*, pp. 271–278; Hempel, G. (2008). What is HR certification? *Expatriate Advisor*, summer, 2–3; McConnell, B. (2003). HRCI to offer global HR certification in 2004. *HR Magazine*, March, 115, 117; also refer to the HRCI website: www. hrci.org/about/Intl.html.

16 Sparrow, P., Brewster, C., Budhwar, P., and De Cieri (2011). *Globalizing Human Resource Management*, London/New York: Routledge.

17 Claus, L. (1998). The role of international human resource in leading a company from a domestic to a global corporate culture. *Human Resource Development International*, 1 (3), 309–326; Claus, L. (1999). Globalization and HR professional competencies, paper presented at the 22nd Annual Global HR Forum (The Institute for International HR—now the Global Forum, a division of the Society for Human Resource Management), Orlando, FL, April 13; Sparrow, P., Brewster, C., and Harris, H. (2012). *Globalizing Human Resource Management*, 2nd ed., London/New York: Routledge; also see Strobel, K. (2014). Competency proficiency predicts better job performance. *HR Magazine*, 59 (10), 67; Ulrich, D., Younger, J., and Brockbank, W. (2012). HR competency. *Leadership Excellence*, 29 (8), 17; Brockbank, W., Ulrich, D., Younger, J., and Ulrich, M. (2012). Recent study shows impact of HR competencies on business performance. *Employment Relations Today*, 39 (1), 1–7; Johnson, C. (2012). So you want to be a strategic HR person?. *Human Resources Magazine*, 17 (3), 8–9; Long, C.S., Wan Ismail, W.K., and Amin, S.M. (2013). The role of change agent as mediator in the relationship between HR competencies and organizational performance.

International Journal of Human Resource Management, 24 (10), 2019–2033; Tyler, K. (2011). What are global cultural competencies? *HR Magazine*, 56 (5), 44–46.

18   Based partially on: Kochan, T. A. (2007). Social legitimacy of the human resource management profession: A US perspective, in Boxall, P., Purcell, J., and Wright, P. (eds.), *Oxford Handbook of Human Resource Management*, Oxford/New York: Oxford University Press; Odell, C. and Spielman, C. (2009). Global positioning: Managing the far-reaching risks of an international assignment program. *Benefits Quarterly*, Fourth Quarter, 25 (4), 23–29; Society for Human Resource Management (2010), *What Senior HR Leaders Need to Know*, Alexandria, VA: SHRM; Stroh and Caligiuri (1998b).

19   Jackson, Schuler and Jiang (2014); Kramar, R. (2014). Beyond strategic human resource management: Is sustainable human resource management the next approach? *International Journal of Human Resource Management*, 25 (8), 1069–1089; Conference Report 13th IHRM Conference (2014). Uncertainty in a flattening world: Challenges for IHRM June 24–27 (2014), Cracow, Poland; Zheng, C. (2013). Critiques and extension of strategic international human resource management framework for dragon multinationals. *Asia Pacific Business Review*, 19 (1), 1–15; Schuler, R. S., Jackson, S. E., and Tarique, I. (2011). Global talent management and global talent challenges: Strategic opportunities for IHRM. *Journal of World Business*, 46 (4), 506–516; Sheehan, M., and Sparrow, P. (2012). Introduction: Global human resource management and economic change: a multiple level of analysis research agenda. *International Journal of Human Resource Management*, 23 (12), 2393–2403; Ehnert, I., and Harry, W. (2012). Recent developments and future prospects on sustainable human resource management: Introduction to the special issue. *Management Revue*, 23 (3), 221–238; Boxall, P. (2014). The future of employment relations from the perspective of human resource management. *Journal of Industrial Relations*, 56(4), 578–593.

20   Baron, A. and Armstrong, M. (2007). *Human Capital Management: Achieving Added Value through People*, London/Philadelphia: Kogan Page; Fitz-enz, J. (2009). *The ROI of Human Capital*, New York: AMACOM; Fitz-enz, J. (2010), *The New HR Analytics*, New York: AMACOM; Huselid, M. A., Becker, B. E., and Beatty, R. W. (2005). *The Workforce Scorecard*, Boston: Harvard Business School Publishing Corporation; Lawler, E. E., III (2008). *Talent: Making People Your Competitive Advantage*, San Francisco: John Wiley and Sons; and Lawler, E. E., III and Boudreau, J. (2009). *Achieving Excellence in Human Resource Management: An Assessment of Human Resource Functions*, Stanford, CA: Stanford University Press.

21   Brewster, C., and Sparrow, P. R. (2007). *Globalising HR: Roles and Challenges for the International HRM Function*. Lancaster University: Centre for Performance-Led Human Resources.

22   Brewster, C., Sparrow, P. R. and Harris, H. (2005). Towards a new model of globalizing human resource management. *International Journal of Human Resource Management*, 16 (6): 957.

23   Brewster and Sparrow (2007); and Sparrow, Brewster, and Harris (2012).

24   Buyens, D. (2009). Strategic HRM: The three pillar model: A blueprint for future HR, keynote to the 9th bi-annual Conference on International HRM, June 14, Santa Fe, NM: Claus, L. (2007). Building global HR competencies, Master Class presentation at the CIPD Annual Conference and Exhibition, Harrogate, UK; and Claus, L. (2009), Operating in an uncertain world: New opportunities for Global HR, paper presented to the 9th bi-annual Conference on International HRM, June 14, Santa Fe, NM.

25   Claus. L. (2001). The future of HR. *Workplace Visions*, No. 6, 2–3.

26   Ahalt, S. and Kelly, K. (2013). The big data talent gap. *UNC Executive Development*, 32–40; McIlvaine, A. R. (2012). Rise of the quants. *HR Executive*, March, 4–8; Visier (2014). *The Datafication of HR*, White Paper, Vancouver, BC/San Jose, CA: Visier, Inc.

27   Towers Perrin (studies conducted for IBM) (1990). *A Twenty-first Century Vision: A Worldwide Human Resources Study* and (1992). *Priorities for Competitive Advantage*, New York: Authors.

Integrative Cases

CASE 1: Fred Bailey: An Innocent Abroad
A Case Study in Cross-Cultural Management (US/Japan)
Stewart Black

Fred gazed out the window of his 24th-floor office at the tranquil beauty of the Imperial Palace amidst the hustle and bustle of downtown Tokyo. It had been only six months since Fred Bailey had arrived with his wife and two children for this three-year assignment as the director of Kline & Associates' Tokyo office. Kline & Associates was a large multinational consulting firm with offices in 19 countries worldwide. Fred was now trying to decide if he should simply pack up and tell the home office that he was coming home or if he should try to somehow convince his wife and himself that they should stay and finish the assignment. Given how excited they all were about the assignment to begin with, it was a mystery to Fred how things had gotten to this point. As he watched the swans glide across the water in the moat that surrounds the Imperial Palace, Fred reflected on the past seven months.

Seven months ago, Dave Steiner, the managing partner of the main office in Boston, asked Fred to lunch to discuss business. To Fred's surprise, the business they discussed was not about the major project that he and his team had just finished, instead, it was about a very big promotion and career move. Fred was offered the position of managing director of the firm's relatively new Tokyo office, which had a staff of 40, including seven Americans. Most of the Americans in the Tokyo office were either associate consultants or research analysts. Fred would be in charge of the whole office and would report to a senior partner. Steiner implied to Fred that if this assignment went as well as his past projects, it would be the last step before becoming a partner in the firm.

When Fred told his wife about the unbelievable opportunity, he was shocked at her less-than-enthusiastic response. His wife, Jennifer (or Jenny as Fred called her), thought that it would be rather difficult to have the children live and go to school in a foreign country for three years, especially when Christine, the oldest, would be starting middle school next year. Besides, now that the kids were in school, Jenny was thinking about going back to work, at least part-time. Jenny had a degree in fashion merchandising from a well-known private university and had worked as an assistant buyer for a large women's clothing store before having the two girls.

Fred explained that the career opportunity was just too good to pass up and that the company's overseas package would make living overseas terrific. The company would pay all the expenses to move whatever the Baileys wanted to take with them, the company owned a very nice house in an expensive district of Tokyo that would be provided rent free, and the company would rent their house in Boston during their absence. Moreover, the firm would provide a car and driver, education expenses for the children to attend private schools, and a cost-of-living adjustment and overseas compensation that would nearly triple Fred's gross annual salary. After two days of consideration and discussion, Fred told Mr. Steiner he would accept the assignment.

The current Tokyo office managing director was a partner in the firm but had been in the new Tokyo office for less than a year when he was transferred to head up a long-established office in England. Because the transfer to England was taking place right away, Fred and his family had about three weeks to prepare for the move. Between transferring things at the office to Bob Newcome, who was being promoted to Fred's position, and getting furniture and the like ready to be moved, neither Fred nor his family had time to really find out much about Japan, other than what was in Wikipedia.

When the Baileys arrived in Japan, they were greeted at the airport by one of the young Japanese associate consultants and the senior American expatriate. Fred and his family were quite tired from the long trip, and the two-hour ride to Tokyo was a rather quiet one. After a few days of just settling in, Fred spent his first full day at the office.

Fred's first order of business was to have a general meeting with all the employees of associate consultant rank and higher. Although Fred didn't notice it at the time, all the Japanese staff sat together and all the Americans sat together. After Fred introduced himself and his general ideas about the potential and future directions of the Tokyo office, he called on a few individuals to get their ideas about how the things for which they were responsible would likely fit into his overall plan. From the Americans, Fred got a mixture of opinions with specific reasons about why certain things might or might not fit well. From the Japanese, he got very vague answers. When Fred pushed to get more specific information, he was surprised to find that a couple of the Japanese simply made a sucking sound as they breathed and said that it was "difficult to say." Fred sensed the meeting was not achieving his objectives, so he thanked everyone for coming and said he looked forward to their all working together to make the Tokyo office the fastest growing office in the company.

After they had been in Japan for about a month, Fred's wife complained to him about the difficulty she had getting certain everyday products like maple syrup, peanut butter, and good-quality beef. She said that when she could get it at one of the specialty stores it cost three and four times what it would cost in the States. She also complained that since the washer and dryer were much too small, she had to spend extra money sending things out to be dry-cleaned. On top of all that, unless she went to the American Club in downtown Tokyo, she never had anyone to talk to. After all, Fred was gone 10 to 16 hours a day. Unfortunately, at the time, Fred was preoccupied, thinking about a big upcoming meeting between his firm and a significant prospective client, a top 100 Japanese multinational company.

The next day, Fred, along with the lead American consultant for the potential contract, Ralph Webster, and one of the Japanese associate consultants, Kenichi Kurokawa, who spoke perfect English, met with a team from the Japanese firm. The Japanese team consisted of four members: the VP of administration, the director of international personnel, and two staff specialists. After shaking hands and a few awkward bows, Fred said that he knew the Japanese gentlemen were busy and he didn't want to waste their time so he would get right to the point. Fred then had the other American lay out their firm's proposal for the project and what the project would cost. After the presentation, Fred asked the Japanese for their reaction to the proposal. The Japanese did not respond immediately, so Fred launched into his summary version of the proposal, thinking that the translation might have been insufficient. But again the Japanese gave only the vaguest of responses to his direct questions.

The recollection of the frustration of that meeting was enough to shake Fred back to reality. The reality was that in the five months since that first meeting little progress had been made and the contract between the firms was yet to be signed. "I can never seem to get a direct response from the Japanese," he thought to himself. This feeling of frustration led him to remember a related incident that happened about a month after this first meeting with this client.

Fred had decided that the reason not much progress was being made with the client was that Fred and his group just didn't know enough about the client to package the proposal in a way that was appealing to the client. Consequently, he called in the senior American associated with the proposal, Ralph Webster, and asked him to develop a report on the client so that the proposal could be re-evaluated and changed where necessary. Jointly, they decided that one of the more promising Japanese research associates, Tashiro Watanabe, would be the best person to take the lead on this report. To impress upon Tashiro the importance of this task and the great potential they saw in him, they decided to have the young Japanese associate meet with both Fred and Ralph. In the meeting, Fred had Ralph lay out the nature and importance of the task, at which point Fred leaned forward in his chair and said to Tashiro, "You can see that this is an important assignment and that we are placing a lot of confidence in you by giving it to you. We need the report by this time next week so that we can revise and re-present our proposal. Can you do it?" After a somewhat pregnant pause, the Japanese responded hesitantly, "I'm not sure what to say." At that point, Fred smiled, got up from his chair and walked over to the young Japanese associate, extended his hand, and said, "Hey, there's nothing to say. We're just giving you the opportunity you deserve."

The day before the report was due, Fred asked Ralph how the report was coming along. Ralph said that since he had heard nothing from Tashiro everything was under control, but that he would double-check. Ralph later ran into one of the American research associates, John Maynard. Ralph knew that John was hired for Japan because of his language ability in Japanese and that, unlike any of the other Americans, John often went out after work with some of the Japanese research associates, including Tashiro. So, Ralph asked John if he knew how Tashiro was coming along with the report. John then recounted that last night at the office Tashiro had asked if Americans sometimes fired employees for being late with reports. John had sensed that this was more than a hypothetical question and asked Tashiro why he wanted to know. Tashiro did not respond immediately, and since it was 8:30 in the evening, John suggested they go out for a drink. At first Tashiro resisted, but then John assured him that they would grab a drink at a nearby bar and come right back. At the bar, John got Tashiro to open up.

Tashiro explained the nature of the report that he had been requested to produce. Tashiro continued to explain that even though he had worked long into the night every night to complete the report it was just impossible and that he had doubted from the beginning whether he could complete the report in a week.

At this point, Ralph asked John, "Why didn't he say something in the first place?" Ralph didn't wait to hear whether or not John had an answer to his question. He headed straight to Tashiro's desk.

Ralph chewed Tashiro out and then went to Fred, explaining that the report would not be ready and that Tashiro, from the start, didn't think it could be. "Then why didn't he say something?" Fred asked. No one had any answers, and the whole thing just left everyone more suspect and uncomfortable with one another.

There were other incidents, big and small, that had made the last two months especially frustrating, but Fred was too tired to remember them all. To Fred it seemed that working with Japanese both inside and outside the firm was like working with people from another planet. Fred felt he just couldn't communicate with them, and he could never figure out what they were thinking. It drove him crazy.

Then on top of all this, Jennifer laid a bombshell on him. She wanted to go home, and yesterday was not soon enough. Even though the kids seemed to be doing all right, Jennifer was tired of Japan—tired of being stared at, of not understanding anybody or being understood, of not being able to find what she wanted at the store, of not being able to drive and read the road signs, of not having anything to watch on television, of not being involved in anything. She wanted to go home and could not think of any reason why they shouldn't. After all, she reasoned, they owed nothing to the company because the company had led them to believe this was just another assignment, like the two years they spent in San Francisco, and it was anything but that!

Fred looked out the window once more, wishing that somehow everything could be fixed, or turned back, or something. Down below the traffic was backed up. Though the traffic lights changed, the cars and trucks didn't seem to be moving. Fortunately, beneath the ground, one of the world's most advanced, efficient, and clean subway systems moved hundreds of thousands of people about the city and to their homes.

Source: J. Stewart Black, Fred Bailey: An innocent abroad—a case study in cross-cultural management. Reprinted by permission of the author.

DISCUSSION QUESTIONS

1 Who has responsibility for this situation? What is the nature of various stakeholders' responsibilities? Headquarters HR? Japan HR? Fred Bailey? Jennifer Bailey? Dave Steiner, company managing partner? Management development?
2 What does the situation say about the firm's human resource department?
3 What are the root causes of the problems that Fred Bailey experienced?
4 What should Fred Bailey do now? What are his options and what are the pros and cons of his various options?

CASE 2: Bavarian Auto Works in Indonesia (Germany/Indonesia)

Dennis R. Briscoe, PhD, University of San Diego

The organizations involved:
Bavarian Auto Werks GMBH (BAW) Jakarta Electro-Assembly Ltd (JEA)
The IJV: Jakarta-Bavarian Auto Works Ltd (JBAW)

It has been one month since management at Bavarian Auto Werks in Germany had increased its stake in the Indonesian firm, Jakarta Electro-Assembly Ltd, to just over 50 percent. The initial negotiations for this joint venture had been lengthy and difficult, but finally there had been an agreement to move ahead with joint manufacturing on a limited scale, with BAW providing limited equity, technology and equipment, and managerial expertise. The initial collaboration seemed to work out, so now BAW was increasing its ownership. At the conclusion of the original negotiations, BAW had sent a team of managers and engineers to Jakarta to provide some management assistance to the ailing Indonesian firm. The head of that team, Stephan Ritter, had been a member of the original team that performed the due diligence to analyze the condition of Jakarta Electro-Assembly (JEA) and had headed the team that had negotiated the joint venture agreement. This was the first joint venture that either BAW or JEA had entered into, so both were inexperienced in this process of international negotiations. The joint venture was named Jakarta-Bavarian Auto Works Ltd (JBAW). Stephan and his wife, Nicole, were the first Germans to arrive in Indonesia. The pace of change had been incredibly rapid and now Stephan was wondering what could be done to ensure the success of the new restructuring, based on BAW's new majority ownership (now at 52 percent).

With the exception of a few of the most senior managers, employees at JEA (now JBAW) had no direct way to receive information about the negotiations or its results. Initially, JEA employees were quite supportive of a deal with BAW. But soon after the

deal was completed, and the new team of additional Germans had arrived (six specialists: an accountant and five manufacturing engineers), the high expectations were gradually replaced with fear of the actions the Germans were likely to take as they assumed
their management and operational roles. The existing senior Indonesian managers were
afraid that they would be replaced by younger managers who spoke English. And the other
Indonesian employees were afraid they would be laid off as the Germans sought higher
productivity and lower costs. Rumors, supported by inaccurate reports in local newspapers, ran rampant. One newspaper even reported that many Germans would be imported
to Indonesia from BAW in Germany. Anxiety mounted as speculation increased about
the magnitude of downsizing that BAW would implement as it restructured the Jakarta
Electro-Assembly business, now that they were majority owners of the joint venture operation. In general, since the Indonesians did not have much experience with Germans, they
expected them to take the same sorts of actions that other foreign firms had taken, such as
the American firms in Indonesia, with heavy layoffs and replacement of top management
with expatriates.

However, since only a few managers from BAW had been involved in the due diligence
and negotiations, the Germans were also well aware that they had gained only limited
knowledge and insight into the Indonesian culture. As a result, Stephan and Nicole had
spent a month prior to relocating to Jakarta in intensive study of Indonesian culture and in
language training, trying to pick up some fluency in Bahasa Indonesian, the official language,
influenced by Dutch, from the Netherlands, which was the governing colonial power for a
long time. The team of six Germans who has recently arrived expects to also spend at least
one month learning about the Indonesian culture and Indonesia itself before they begin
to make changes in the manufacturing equipment and processes. They recognize that this
process of adapting to the local culture will be an ongoing one that will not end at the end
of the first month. Even though most high-level communication in the new company is
expected to take place in English (a common language for the Germans and for at least
some of the Indonesian managers, as well as for most prospective customers), the Germans
realize the importance of gaining some ability to communicate with their counterparts and
other employees in their own language.

The Situation

Indonesia is the fourth most populous country (over 253 million people as of mid-2014)
and the most populous Islamic country, with a per person annual GDP (Purchasing Power
Parity) of about US $5,200 (2013 estimate).[1] The JEA is located on the outskirts of Jakarta,
the capital and largest city, located on the island of Java.

---

1   Data derived from the 2014 CIA World Factbook.

The IJV agreement is based on the continuation of JEA's business of making auto parts for the Indonesian after-market (for sale in auto parts stores and garages) and to add to this as soon as possible the manufacturing as a sub-contractor original equipment (OEM) auto parts for four German auto firms, Volkswagen, BMW, Opel (General Motors in Europe), and Ford Europe, who are all customers of BAW in Germany. The hope is that the IJV can eventually expand to other OEM business, such as for American and Japanese automobile manufacturers.

One of the issues that Stephan and BAW are concerned about is the type of organizational culture that will evolve in the new joint venture. In essence, as of now, there are three different possibilities, and it is not clear which would be best:

- The culture that is already present, from JEA (which was founded originally as a government-owned enterprise, but was sold to a group of Indonesian businessmen four years ago). This culture is that of a typical Indonesian business.
- A second possibility would be to implement a more traditional German culture, as exists in BAW.
- Or, as a third alternative, the new combined joint venture could work to create a new culture, a hybrid of some kind, using characteristics of both the Indonesian culture and the German culture. The joint venture is still in formation and is as yet largely undefined.

The primary objectives that BAW initially wants to achieve include the following:

- Develop an organization focused on the customer.
- Improve the productivity and efficiency of all operations and activities.
- Improve the firm's profitability.
- Improve the integrity and accuracy of the financial information.

Other issues that need to be addressed include managerial control issues (sharing of top management positions between BAW and JEA managers); schedule for transfer of technology from Germany to Indonesia; protection of intellectual property; sharing of revenues and distribution of costs; downsizing (amount and scheduling); performance management (use of performance appraisals, setting work goals and performance standards); health and safety concerns; and hiring standards. Stephan realizes that there are a number of communication challenges for the Germans. These include the overriding importance in Indonesia of family and friends and the nature of interpersonal relations and respect for "face" in all dealings. Since only a couple of the Indonesians in JEA speak German while a number of the managers (and a few of the lower-level employees) speak some English, it was decided that English would be the language for managerial meetings, including the ongoing negotiations to determine the nature of the new joint venture and to address the above objectives and concerns. However, it was also clear that there would be a need to use a translator for these meetings. Indeed,

Stephan thought it would be best to use two translators, one for the Indonesians and one for the Germans.

In the end, Stephan wanted to establish a culture within JBAW that would achieve and sustain world-class quality and world-class productivity in all operations and in all interactions with current and potential customers. So, Stephan now had to prepare for the negotiations and he needed to develop a plan for the ongoing operations of the joint venture that would move them toward his and BAW's hopes for JBAW. The question he needed to address was: how do I proceed?

Indonesian Negotiation Style

Indonesians do business typically only with persons they know and like. Establishing this personal relationship takes time and is vital for success. Establishing a successful business relationship hinges on establishing a social relationship as well, and this may take some time. The pace of business negotiations is quite slow, such that one needs to be quite patient and not rush or push for quick decisions. Foreigners should expect few decisions from Indonesians at the negotiation table. Indonesians expect to examine copious amounts of information, so negotiators in Indonesia need to always provide as much information and detail as possible, in response to their questions and in anticipation of their needs. Presentations should be well prepared and simply presented. Details are best left to questions and backup material, which should be translated into Bahasa Indonesian and left behind. Ideally, foreign negotiators should present their material to the Indonesians for study, along with a proposed agenda, prior to the meeting. Extra copies of the agenda should be made available, as it is likely that more people are likely to be present than are expected. Foreigners should negotiate with a well-organized team, whose roles have been clearly thought out and defined. Members of this team should never disagree with each other in front of the Indonesians, or appear uncertain, unsure, not authorized to make a decision, or out of control in any way.

Indonesians generally do not like to bargain, but when they do, they approach it as a win/win possibility (something should be in the agreement for both sides). In general, negotiations are viewed as time to build relationships. Although any negotiated contract must be legal down to the dotted i's, to the Indonesians it is a piece of paper that merely signifies that an agreement has been reached and which will be followed because of the trust and commitment that has been built between the parties.

The deal should be finalized with a celebratory meal or round of drinks, and the actual signing might be delayed until an auspicious or lucky day: this is likely to affect the schedule. Communications need to be kept open, especially when at a distance, and foreigners need to stay in touch often with their Indonesian associates: foreign negotiators should share more information than they normally would, not less; and because business is so intimately connected with the government and because the political situation is so fluid, foreign negotiators should try to have a source of information "on the ground" in Indonesia who can always keep them informed about what is really going on, if at all possible. All communications should be very formal and respectful of rank and hierarchy. Indonesians show great deference to superiors (even protective) and they expect other people to do the same. Thus, disagreeing with high-ranking Indonesians just is not done, and this can make negotiating with them quite difficult (as well as understanding or interpreting words like "no" or "yes, but"). Politeness is one of the most important attributes for successful relationships in Indonesia. But this politeness in no way hinders the determination of Indonesian businesspeople to get their own way. Always, decision making in Indonesia is a group process, so don't expect individuals in negotiation to make decisions quickly. Decisions will have to be discussed in private before agreement can be reached.

German Negotiation Style

Germans respect people who come to negotiations with established knowledge and experience. No detail is unimportant, and a carefully planned, logically organized proposal is key. Even from the beginning, Germans are very matter-of-fact. It would not be uncommon for Germans to get right down to business, without any socializing first (after introductions and greetings). Time is very important and is expected to be managed carefully, with meetings planned well in advance and a detailed agenda circulated prior to the scheduled date of the meeting. However, the pace of German decision-making can be quite slow. This is often because German companies have a parallel "hidden" series of advisors and decision-makers who must give their approval of any decisions.

Germans dislike exaggeration, and they expect people in negotiations to be able to back up their claims with lots of data and examples—and studies, if possible. German firms have a well-deserved reputation for superior quality, which is based in part on slow, methodical planning. Every aspect of a deal will be pored over by many executives and specialists, which can slow down negotiations. Germans believe that it takes time to do a job properly and well. Germans consider the contract to be sacred; once it is decided it determines the nature of the business relationship. If either party wants to change anything in a contract (or circumstances require the need for a change), it would be expected that there be a formal renegotiation of the contract. Contracts are considered enforceable in law, so Germans pay very close attention to the exact wording and punctuation of their contracts.

Germans can take a long time to establish close business relationships. Their apparent coldness at the beginning will vanish over time. Once they get to know you, they are quite gregarious.

DISCUSSION QUESTIONS

1   What role should HR play in the development of this IJV? In the negotiations? BAW HR? JEA HR? JBAW HR? Of the HR issues mentioned in the case, what kinds of

policies and practices should be developed? What should take precedence? Why? What other HR programs and policies should have been considered? Which of these policies and practices are likely to be areas of concern in the successful merger of these two firms?

2   What cultural problems do you foresee in the relationships between the Germans and the Indonesians? In negotiations? In day-to-day operations?

Source: derived from Bosrock, M.M. (1994/1995), *Put Your Best Foot Forward: Asia/Europe*, St. Paul, MN: International Education Systems; Foster, D. (2000). *The Global Etiquette Guide to Asia/Europe*, New York: John Wiley & Sons; Morrison, T. and Conaway, W.A. (2006). *Kiss, Bow, or Shake Hands: Asia*, Avon, MA: Adams Media, Inc.

Index

Note: Page numbers followed by "f" refer to figures. Page numbers in bold refer to tables.